FLIGHT INTO EGYPT

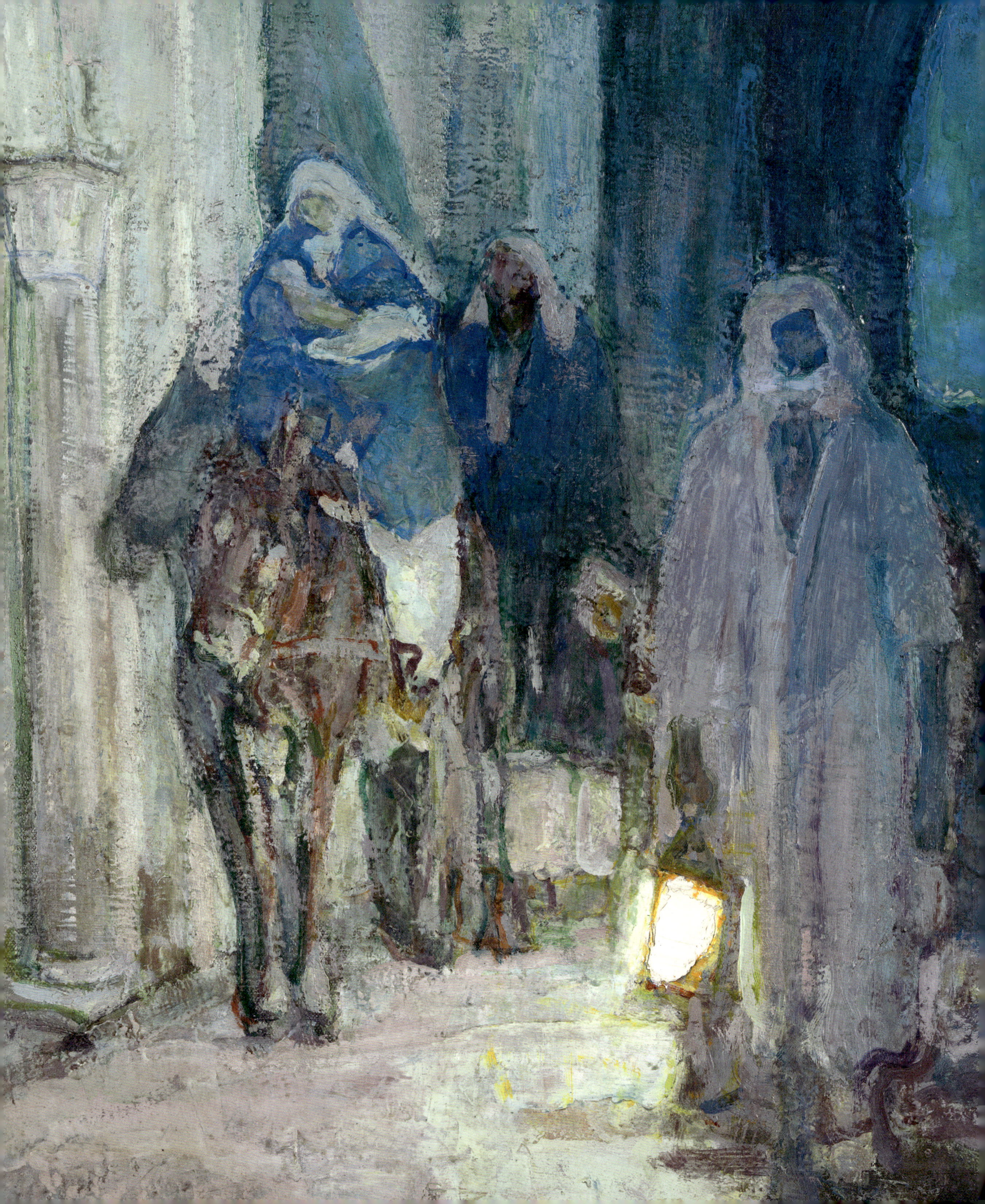

FLIGHT INTO EGYPT

Black Artists
and Ancient Egypt, 1876–Now

Akili
Tommasino

with contributions by

Andrea Myers Achi

Erykah Badu

Makeda Best

Barbara Chase-Riboud

Awol Erizku

Lauren Halsey

Iman Issa

Solange Knowles

Mia Matthias

Julie Mehretu

Kai Mora

Jennifer Newsom

Matthew Shenoda

Fred Wilson

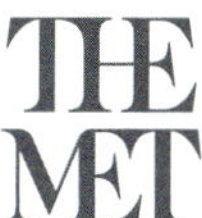

The Metropolitan Museum of Art, New York

Distributed by Yale University Press, New Haven and London

Contents

Director's Foreword   7

Acknowledgments   8

Lenders to the Exhibition   12

Contributors   13

Flight into Egypt: Black Artists and Ancient Egypt, 1876–Now   16
Akili Tommasino

The Problem of the Color Line: Black Americans and the Field of Egyptology   34
Andrea Myers Achi

"We Are Both Myths": Ancient Egypt and Opacity   40
Mia Matthias

Compressive of Ideas: Black Photography and Ancient Egypt   52
Makeda Best

63   **Plates and Artist Statements**
Matthew Shenoda
Barbara Chase-Riboud
Fred Wilson
Iman Issa
Solange Knowles
Erykah Badu
Awol Erizku
Julie Mehretu
Jennifer Newsom
Lauren Halsey

240   **Artist Biographies**
Kai Mora

244   Notes
249   Works in the Exhibition
258   Selected Bibliography
260   Index
267   Photography Credits

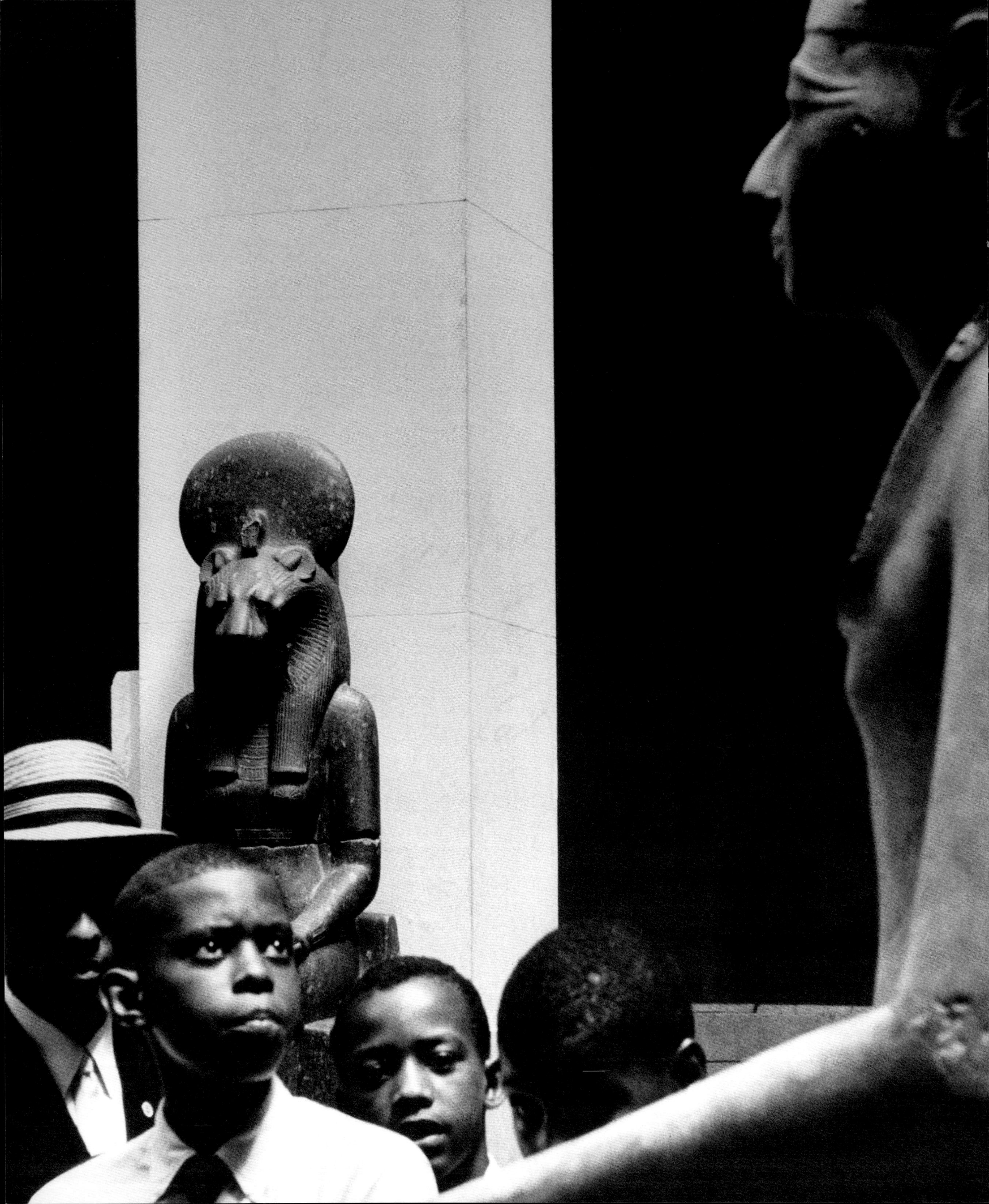

Director's Foreword

Max Hollein

Ancient Egypt is a symbolic source for people of the African diaspora that continues to inspire. *Flight into Egypt: Black Artists and Ancient Egypt, 1876–Now* is the first exhibition to examine the sustained engagement of Black cultural figures with ancient Egypt, connecting African diasporic history and contemporary experience to ancient African civilization. The exhibition and its catalogue, as well as related programming, present scholarship on nearly 150 years of remarkable cultural production. Featuring paintings, sculptures, drawings, prints, photographs, illustrated publications, video, audio, and interactive installations by artists active from the nineteenth century to the present day, *Flight into Egypt* follows three major threads: art history, the historiography of Egyptology, and the presence of ancient Egypt in African American popular culture, including music, film, fashion, and performance.

The artists and cultural figures included in *Flight into Egypt* represent a diverse range of artistic practices, intellectual formations, and identities. Although the exhibition primarily features the work of Black Americans, it also focuses on work by artists of African descent working in the Caribbean, United Kingdom, Europe, and United States, as well as the art of modern and contemporary Egyptian artists. The exhibition moreover brings to light overlooked contributions by Black archeologists and scholars to the study of ancient Egypt. From Henry Ossawa Tanner's painting *Flight into Egypt* (1923) to Barbara Chase-Riboud's majestic bronze *Cleopatra's Chair* (1994) to Madeleine Hunt-Ehrlich's new film *Cleopatra at the Mall* (2024) about Edmonia Lewis's sculpture *The Death of Cleopatra* (1876), the enduring influence of ancient Egypt on modern and contemporary artists of African descent is evident. Recent transhistorical exhibitions at The Met include *Before Yesterday We Could Fly: An Afrofuturist Period Room*, *The African Origin of Civilization*, and *Afterlives: Contemporary Art in the Byzantine Crypt*. Building on the strengths of these projects, *Flight into Egypt* is a historical survey that makes revelatory connections between art of the distant past and modern and contemporary art and culture.

I am tremendously grateful to the many colleagues at The Met who made *Flight into Egypt* possible. I wish to thank Akili Tommasino, Curator, Department of Modern and Contemporary Art, for spearheading this groundbreaking project and addressing its potentially contentious aspects with sensitivity. David Breslin, Leonard A. Lauder Curator in Charge of the Department of Modern and Contemporary Art, played an essential role in its success. I also salute the unprecedented curatorial collaboration with Limor Tomer, Lulu C. and Anthony W. Wang General Manager of Live Arts, to make performance an integral facet of this project. I offer my gratitude to the many contemporary artists participating in the exhibition both by lending and performing their work, and to the many institutions and individuals who have generously lent their works.

We would like to express our appreciation to the Gail and Parker Gilbert Fund, the Jane and Robert Carroll Fund, the Ford Foundation, and the Hobson/Lucas Family Foundation, which made the exhibition possible, and to The Hayden Family Foundation, Allison and Larry Berg, The Holly Peterson Foundation, The Andy Warhol Foundation for the Visual Arts, the National Endowment for the Arts, and DeWayne N. Phillips and Caroline A. Wamsler, PhD, for their own generous gifts. The catalogue benefits from lead support from Mellon Foundation and Denise Littlefield Sobel, as well as significant contributions directed by The Witten Family Foundation, Lonti Ebers, the Jeffrey and Leslie Fischer Family Foundation, and Kent Kelley, all of whom have our deep gratitude for their belief in this project. Last, though certainly not least, we thank Cynthia Hazen Polsky and Leon B. Polsky, and the Adrienne Arsht Fund for Resilience through Art for making possible programming in the Performance Pyramid throughout the exhibition's run.

Max Hollein
Marina Kellen French Director and CEO
The Metropolitan Museum of Art

Acknowledgments

Akili Tommasino

Now when I look back, I can see the things
You've done,
And I want to thank You, for my Savior and
your Son,
And I must give You praise.

> —Larry Heard, "Praise" (2001)

Although this project was formally conceived in 2018—during a conversation with Chet Gold about Fred Wilson's installation *Re:Claiming Egypt* (1993), in a staff stairwell at the Museum of Modern Art—*Flight into Egypt: Black Artists and Ancient Egypt, 1876–Now* is the product of a lifetime. I have compiled the checklist for the exhibition since my childhood, cultivated it during my tenure at The Met, and refined it up until the last minute. I am grateful, foremost, to God for the breadth of experiences that brought the heterogeneous works of art, scholarship, and documentation in this project to my attention, and for the opportunity to present them on a platform as august and visible as The Metropolitan Museum of Art—an institution that has moreover been fundamental to my own personal and professional formation as a first-generation New Yorker, born in Brooklyn and raised there by parents from St. Vincent and the Grenadines. Whereas any deficiencies of a project so personal must be attributed to my own shortcomings, any success is to the credit of the community that has endorsed, nurtured, and sustained it from its inception. Several of the individuals thanked below have made multifaceted contributions to *Flight into Egypt* and could be listed in more than one category. This project is made possible by donors and lenders who are also trusted advisors, colleagues who are also mentors, and artists who are also my friends.

I owe a debt of gratitude to my intellectual forebears, the thinkers of various professional manifestations who have modeled prioritizing African perspectives on Kemet and the art historians and curators who first promoted the work of the artists in this exhibition.

I would like to thank the informal advisors who have encouraged and guided me through crucial points in the development of this project, from facilitating contacts during the research phase before the Covid-19 pandemic to offering advice and troubleshooting logistical and philosophical quandaries throughout, as well as reviewing written materials; although sometimes intangible, their assistance has been substantial. I am indebted to Famiglia Andreotti / Nuti; Solange Ashby; Bryan C. Barnhill II; Thomas Batchelder; Nairy Baghramian; Naomi Beckwith, Deputy Director and Jennifer and David Stockman Chief Curator, Solomon R. Guggenheim Museum, New York; Anita K. Blanchard; Benjamin Bowling; Frank Bowling; Robin Buchholz; Benjamin H. D. Buchloh; Vaughn Caldon; Kevin Carter; Jordan Casteel; Kimberly Drew; Elizabeth Easton, Director and Co-Founder, Center for Curatorial Leadership, and her colleagues Christa Clarke, Emma Payne, Caitlin Palmer, and Grace Oller, as well as my CCL XVII cohort, Charles Aubin, Makeda Best, Katherine Larson, Nora Lawrence, Aimé Iglesias Lukin, Victoria Lyall, Oluremi C. Onabanjo, Caroline Shields, Megan Steinman, Susanna V. Temkin, and Michael Wellen; Samuel Ellison; Russell Franklin; Nathan Ford; Christian Greco, Director, Museo Egizio, Turin; Runako Gulstone; Chase Hall; Neal Hutchinson; Sandra Jackson-Dumont, Director and CEO, Lucas Museum of Narrative Art; Shayna Jeffers; Ute Klose, Neues Museum, Berlin; Edward Lamouth; Mark Luxama; Nora Mendis; Bonaventure Soh Bejeng Ndikung, Director and Chief Curator, Haus der Kulturen der Welt, Berlin, and his team; Rowan Ricardo Phillips; Adrian Piper; Lois Plehn; Frederick Schouler; Franklin Sirmans, Director, Pérez Art Museum Miami; James Snyder, Helen Goldsmith Menschel Director, the Jewish Museum; Mahrukh Tarapor; Julie and David Tobey; Eugenie Tsai; and Marvin Walker.

Contemporary artists are at the center of this project. I am grateful for the participation of all the artists whose work is included here, and especially to those who wrote statements for this volume or made work specifically for *Flight into Egypt*: Ghada Amer, Erykah Badu, Sidra Bell, Greg Broussard, LaKela Brown, Rashida Bumbray, Barbara Chase-Riboud, John Coney, Renee Cox, Shani Crowe, Jamal Cyrus, Damien Davis, Karon Davis, C. Daniel Dawson, Emory Douglas, Dream The Combine (Jennifer Newsom and Tom Carruthers, who received fabrication support from the Graham Foundation for Advanced Studies in the Fine Arts), Oasa DuVerney, Zekkereya El-magharbel, Tremaine Emory, Awol Erizku, Fred Eversley, Derek Fordjour, Genevieve Gaignard, Ellen Gallagher, Chet Gold, Lauren Halsey, David Hammons, Maren Hassinger, Chester Higgins, EJ Hill, Lonnie Holley, Madeleine Hunt-Ehrlich, Gregston Hurdle, Iman Issa, Steffani Jemison, Rashid Johnson, Greg Kadel, Armia Malak Khalil, Jas Knight, Beyoncé Knowles-Carter, Solange Knowles,

M. Lamar, Simone Leigh, Glenn Ligon, Maha Maamoun, Eric Mack, Julie Mehretu, Senga Nengudi, Lorraine O'Grady, Clifford Owens, Kamau Amu Patton, Robert Pruitt, Baaba Heru Ankh Ra Semahj Se Ptah, Betye Saar, Kaneza Schaal, Ahmed Shehaby, Lorna Simpson, Ming Smith, Luke Stewart, Tavares Strachan, Henry Taylor, Kara Walker, William T. Williams, and Fred Wilson.

I am also grateful to the artists no longer on this plane whose living legacies are essential to this project and to their estates: Slim Aarons, Terry Adkins, Eve Arnold, Ayé Aton, John Thomas Biggers, Barbara Higgins Bond, Janet Braun-Reinitz, René Burri, Ed Clark, Irene Clark, Robert Colescott, Houston Conwill, Noah Davis, Charles Clarence Dawson, Artin DerBalian, Jeff Donaldson, Aaron Douglas, Louis H. Draper, Meta Vaux Warrick Fuller, Sam Gilliam, Malvin Gray Johnson, Loïs Mailou Jones, Barbara Jones-Hogu, Freda Leinwand, Mahmoud Mokhtar, Ronald Moody, John W. Mosley, Gordon Parks, Mahmoud Saïd, Addison N. Scurlock, Henry Ossawa Tanner, Mildred Thompson, and Laura Wheeler Waring.

I offer my deepest gratitude to the scholars who have contributed essays to this volume: Andrea Myers Achi, Mary and Michael Jaharis Associate Curator of Byzantine Art, The Met; Makeda Best, Deputy Director of Curatorial Affairs, Oakland Museum of California; and Mia Matthias, Assistant Curator, Glenstone Museum. I also owe a debt of thanks to Kai Mora, former Research Associate at The Met on this project, who wrote the artist biographies.

Because *Flight into Egypt* occupies the intersection where art history and broader histories meet, the materials brought together here have an extraordinary range, from conventional fine art objects to scientific artifacts. A group of key individuals helped locate work, secure loans and permissions, and identify archival materials for presentation. I am particularly indebted in this regard to Ashton Allen and Tricia Gesner, Associated Press; Rebecca Belarge; Jen Chisholm; Peter Eleey; Yuming Zhang and Katie Fajer, CMG Worldwide; Jim Newman, Comcast; Rosalind Flower, Company Gallery; Laura Hoptman, Executive Director, the Drawing Center; Kim Kent; Isabella Howard, Magnum Photos; Roberto Lugo; Maria Nicolas; Casey Riley, Chair of Global Contemporary Art and Curator of Photography and New Media, Minneapolis Institute of Art; Joeonna Bellorado Samuels; Alice Townsend, Sony Music; Lia Vollack; Jennifer Bertani, WNET; and Motisola Zulu.

For their extraordinary cooperation and willingness to lend works to the exhibition, I extend my thanks to those individuals who prefer to remain anonymous and to the following: John Corbett; Leah D. Daughtry; Beth Rudin DeWoody; George Economou and Skarlet Smatana; Amr Eldib, Mai Eldib and Mohamed Eldib; Walter O. and Linda Evans; Emad Abou Ghazi; AC Hudgins and Lauren Hudgins-Shuman; Richard and Michelle Jeschelnig; Beyoncé Knowles-Carter; Ashra and Merira Kwesi, Kemet Nu Tours; Thomas Lavin; Sophie Mörner; Amy and John Phelan; Robert F. Smith; Mr. and Mrs. Robert D. Summer; and Lisa and Steven Tananbaum.

Colleagues at artist studios and estates were also essential collaborators: I thank Michael Arnold, Eve Arnold Estate; Jesse Roman, Badu World; Erin Gilbert, Barbara Chase-Riboud Studio; Josh Rabineau, Karon Davis Studio; Tatum Dorrell and Summer Perrin, Denim Tears; Maria Larsson, Fred Eversley Studio; Amanda McGough, Lauren Halsey Studio; Rebecca Adib, Simone Leigh Studio; Ursula Davila-Villa and Anna Stothart, Lorraine O'Grady Studio; Michael Handler, Yvette Noel-Schure, and Kylie Gregory, Parkwood Entertainment; Eve-Marie Kuijstermans and Tameka Shockley, Purple; Laura Reinitz and Jane Wissman; Ditte Ravnild, Side Projects; Khaled Abol Naga and Ihab Shawky, TEAM-Cairo; and Diane Shabazz Varnie.

I am deeply indebted to the following colleagues in galleries, foundations, and public collections who have shown their support by lending precious works for the exhibition: Lucy Mulroney, Rebecca Hatcher, and Moira Fitzgerald, Beinecke Rare Book and Manuscript Library, Yale University; Ina Klaassen, Lindy de Heij, and Eefje Breugem, Museum Boijmans Van Beuningen; Anne Pasternak, Shelby White and Leon Levy Director, Kimberli Gant, and Elizabeth Largi, Brooklyn Museum; Danille Taylor, Director, D. Sol Mason, and David S. Clapp, Clark Atlanta University Art Museum; Alexis Johnson, Albert Weaver, Eve Arballo, and Ginevra de Blasio, Paula Cooper Gallery; Sofia Macht, Corbett vs. Dempsey; Shawn Waldron, Getty Images; Mitchell and Emily Rales, Annie Farrar, and Amanda Muhlena, Glenstone Museum; Janavi Janakiraman, Taylor Walsh, Cory Nomura, Lauren Vallese, and Brian Chillemi, Greene Naftali; Aleya Hamza, Gypsum Gallery; Adrienne Chau, Maisey Cox, Amanda Stoffel, Elsa Bruno, Josh Vargas, Jennifer Grimyser, and Sophia Sepperer, Hauser & Wirth; Emma McKee and Jenna Washington, Mariane Ibrahim Gallery; Susan Inglett and Sarah Atwood, Susan Inglett Gallery; Greg Bailey, Lisa Muccigrosso, and Hannah Scates Kettler, Special Collections and University Archives, Iowa State University; Karen Jenkins-Johnson, Jenkins Johnson Gallery; Tina Kim, Pia Sofyanti, Junni Chen, Melissa Celona, and Danielle Lindenbaum, Tina Kim Gallery; Teresa Eggers, Camila Nichols, Amanda Ball, Andy Rosenwald, Shania Naderipour, Molly Everett, Rosa Chung, Reyna Colt-Lacayo, Frederick Coldwell, and Kaelin Keller, David Kordansky Gallery; Wynton Marsalis, President, and Lisa Cohen, Louis Armstrong Educational Foundation; Ricky Riccardi, Louis Armstrong House Museum; Alexander Fang and Jaqueline Tran, Matthew Marks Gallery; Judith Schwartz and Yelena Novitskaya, Charles Evans Inniss Memorial Library Archives, Medgar Evars College, CUNY; Marcelle Polednik, Donna and Donald Baumgartner Director, Liz Siegel, and Jane O'Meara, Milwaukee Art Museum; Mills Morán, Morán Morán Gallery; Sandra Bloodworth, Bridget Donlon, and Andrew Gardner, MTA Arts and Transit; Glenn D. Lowry, David Rockefeller Director, Christophe Cherix, Esther Adler, Elisabeth Thomas, Emily Cushman, Marissa Klein, and Jillian Suarez, the Museum of Modern Art, New York; Roxanne Bucknor, former Senior Director, O'Neil Lawrence, and Javier Gordon, National Gallery of Jamaica; Kevin Young, Andrew W. Mellon Director, Tuliza Fleming, Allison Tolman, Drew Talley, and Mirasol Estrada, National Museum of African American History and Culture; Tsugumi Maki, Director, Tricia Hoffman, Maureen O'Brien, Nicole Priedemann, and Tara Emsley, Museum of Art, Rhode Island School of Design; Michael Rosenfeld and halley k harrisburg, Michael Rosenfeld Gallery; Juan Valadez, Director, and Alexandra Perez, Rubell Museum; Tammi Lawson, Barrye

Brown, and Alexander Garcia, Schomburg Center for Research in Black Culture, the New York Public Library; Bruce Silverstein, Bruce Silverstein Gallery; Stephanie Stebich, Margaret and Terry Stent Director, Randall Griffey, Karen Lemmey, Laura Baptiste, Bridget Callahan, and Katie Hondorf, Smithsonian American Art Museum and Renwick Gallery; Ashkan Baghestani and Yasmeen Gailani, Sotheby's; Marta Fontolan and Hannes Schroeder-Finckh, Sprüth Magers; Thelma Golden, Director and Chief Curator, Connie Choi, Sydney Briggs, Gina Guddemi, Rachel Hansen, and Habiba Hopson, Studio Museum in Harlem; Burt Sugarman and Marlin Prensky, Burt Sugarman Productions; Katy Green, Sylvia Kouvali, and Estelle Renaud, Sylvia Kouvali Gallery; Leslie Willis-Lowry and Diane D. Turner, Charles L. Blockson Afro-American Collection, Temple University Libraries; Kirstin Kay and Isabel Espinal, University of Massachusetts Amherst Libraries; Jesse Palek-Zahn, University of Washington Libraries; Olivia Gauthier, Vielmetter Los Angeles; Alex Nyerges, Director and CEO, Michael Taylor, Sarah Eckhardt, and Nancy Nichols, Virginia Museum of Fine Arts; Adam Weinberg, Alice Pratt Brown Director Emeritus, Scott Rothkopf, Alice Pratt Brown Director, Roxanne Smith, Andrea Zlotowitz, and Barbi Spieler, Whitney Museum of American Art; Anthony Cran and Naomi Wilding, Wilding Cran Gallery; Matthias Waschek, Director, Phyllis Boot, Claire Whitney, Nancy Kathryn Burns, and Ali Rosenberg, Worcester Art Museum; and finally to Bárbara Rodríguez Muñoz, Director of Exhibitions and the Collection, and Begoña Guerrica-Echevarría, Centro Botín, for their willingness to lend.

The earliest phases of this project were undertaken during my tenure at the Museum of Fine Arts, Boston. I thank my former coworkers there for their role in its incubation and for their generous loans of artwork to the exhibition: Matthew Teitelbaum, Ann and Graham Gund Director, and Lawrence Berman, Ian Alteveer, Ethan Lasser, Layla Bermeo, Michelle Millar Fisher, Janet Moore, and Betsy Nelson, as well as former colleagues Ella Huzenis, Emma Rose Rainville, Daniela Sierra, Yutong Shi, Reto Thüring, and Nemo Xu.

Darren Walker, President of the Ford Foundation, was an early and substantial supporter of this project, enabling research, a commission, and acquisitions at both the Museum of Fine Arts, Boston, and The Met.

I am grateful to have had the opportunity to pursue research as the Cynthia Hazen Polsky/Metropolitan Museum of Art Visiting Curator at the American Academy in Rome. At the AAR I thank Aliza Wong, Director, and her colleagues Laura Cabezas and Denise Gavio for their generosity with time, expertise, and contacts, as well as members of the community gathered at the AAR during the Spring of 2023, including Anna E. Arabindan-Kesson, Lisa Cooper, Alex Da Corte, Denva E. Gallant, Todd Gray, Lynn Nottage, Elle Pérez, Alvin Singleton, Elka Stevens, Ashley Teamer, Saskia K. Verlaan, and Alice Visentin.

This project could not have reached fruition without the extraordinary support, talent, and hard work of many individuals at The Met. I wish to thank Max Hollein, Marina Kellen French Director and CEO, for being a steadfast champion of this project. For their sustained support, I am grateful to Inka Drögemüller, Deputy Director for Audience Engagement; Lavita McMath Turner, Chief Diversity Officer; and Andrea Bayer, Deputy Director for Collections and Administration, who also facilitated my research abroad. I am also grateful to Sharon H. Cott, Senior Vice President, Secretary, and General Counsel, and her colleagues Emily Balter, Cristina del Valle, and Amy Lamberti for shepherding the various legal documents that made it possible for this project to come to life.

My heartfelt appreciation to Whitney W. Donhauser, Deputy Director and Chief Advancement Officer; Jason Herrick; and their colleagues in Development Hannah Howe, Jennifer M. Brown, Lewis Levesque, Emma Claire Marvin, John L. Wielk, Evie Chabot, Kim McCarthy, and Jane Parisi, whose shared passion for this project led to fundraising successes. I am deeply grateful to Annie Bailis, Head of Communications, and Alexandra Kozlakowski, as well as Gretchen Scott, Head of Marketing, and her colleagues Taylor Latrowski, Tiffany Lucke, and Micah Pegues for their thoughtful collaboration in sharing the message of this project.

For advice, direction, and support I am deeply grateful to David Breslin, Leonard A. Lauder Curator in Charge, Department of Modern and Contemporary Art, and our departmental colleagues Carey Adler; Lee Berman; Micayla Bransfield; Tiarra Inez Brown; Michaela Bubier; Catherine Burns; Iria Candela, Estrellita B. Brodsky Curator of Latin American Art; Lionel Carre; Mary Chan; Stephanie D'Alessandro, Leonard A. Lauder Curator of Modern Art; Clare Davies; Destinee Filmore; Jordan Frank; Margaret Gaines; Olivia Henry-Jackson; Zach Hewitt; Cynthia Iavarone; Brinda Kumar; Lesley Ma, Ming Chu Hsu and Daniel Xu Curator; Denise Murrell, Merryl H. and James S. Tisch Curator at Large; Jane Panetta, Aaron I. Fleischman Curator; Jane Pierce; Skye Prosper; Alejandro Leal Pulido; Mallory Roark; Brooks Shaver; Tuesday Smillie; Abraham Thomas, Daniel Brodsky Curator of Modern Architecture, Design, and Decorative Arts; Katy Uravitch; Michaela Warshaw; and Nalani Williams; as well as former colleagues Sheena Wagstaff, Curator Emerita, and Pari Stave.

For their generosity in sharing works from their collection, I would like to acknowledge Sylvia Yount, Lawrence A. Fleischman Curator in Charge; Matthew Heffernan; Adrienne Spinozzi; and Thayer Tolles, Marica F. Vilcek Curator, in the American Wing. I am deeply grateful for our ongoing dialogues. I am also grateful to Elyse Nelson in the Department of European Sculpture and Decorative Arts for sharing her research on Edmonia Lewis.

Special thanks for their conservation work are owed to Lisa Pilosi, Sherman Fairchild Conservator in Charge, and Kendra Roth, Department of Objects Conservation; Charlotte Hale, Sherman Fairchild Conservator in Charge, and her colleagues Shawn Digney-Peer and Isabelle Duvernois, Department of Paintings Conservation; Nora Kennedy, Sherman Fairchild Conservator in Charge, and her colleagues Jonathan Farbowitz and Natasha Kung, Department of Photograph Conservation; Janina Poskrobko, Conservator in Charge, and Kristine Kamiya, Department of Textile Conservation; and Rachel Mustalish, Sherman Fairchild Conservator in Charge, and Rebecca Capua, Department of Paper Conservation, as well as Anna Serotta, who pursued research into George Washington Carver's Egyptian Blue with me in collaboration with

Greg Bailey, Head of Special Collections and University Archives, and Lisa Muccigrosso, Collections Conservator, Iowa State University; Susan Buck; Judy Jacob; Edith Powell, retired Tuskegee University Professor and Independent Researcher, Tuskegee University Archives; Jontyle Robinson, Founding Director and CEO, the Alliance of HBCU Museums and Galleries; and Rachanice Candy Tate, Curator and Co-Director, the Legacy Museum at Tuskegee University. I also thank Kenneth Soehner, Arthur K. Watson Chief Librarian, Amy Hamilton, and Fredy Rivera of The Met's Thomas J. Watson Library for research support.

The execution of an exhibition of this size and complexity requires the skill and expertise of many individuals. I extend my deepest gratitude to Quincy Houghton, Deputy Director for Exhibitions and International Initiatives, and her colleagues Jason Kotara, Marci King, and Melissa Klein for overseeing the many moving parts of this project; I am deeply grateful to Meryl Cohen, Chief Registrar, and registrars Aislinn Hyde and Bryanna O'Mara for tracking all of the objects in the exhibition and coordinating their secure transportation with lenders. I'd like to express my gratitude for the opportunity to work with Douglas Hegley, Chief Digital Officer, and his team, especially Skyla Choi, Melissa Bell, Kate Farrell, and Ashliy Sabb, who secured media permissions and produced new content, and Paul Caro, Kaelan Burkett, and Reid Farrington, who seamlessly coordinated the exhibition's several audiovisual installations. Heidi Holder, Frederick P. and Sandra P. Rose Chair of Education, and her team conceived and supported dynamic programs to enhance the impact of this project. I am especially grateful to Laura Arike; Andrew Cappetta; Amy Charleroy; Marie Clapot; Francesca D'Alessio; David Freeman; Kathryn Galitz; Merantine Hens; Zenzele Johnson; Chelsea Kelly; Karina Krainchich; Martina Lentino; Rebecca McGinnis, the Mary Jaharis Senior Managing Educator, Accessibility; Jeary Payne; Elizabeth Perkins; Isaac Pool; Grace Rago; Marianna Siciliano; Zev Slurzberg; Jamie Song; Beth Stolting; Kate Swanson; Christina Vanech; Christina Westpheling; Sherri Williams; and Eleni Zaras, and former colleagues Alexis Gonzalez and Darcy-Tell Morales.

My sincere thanks to Alicia Cheng, Head of Design, and to the exhibition's designer Joachim Hackl and his colleagues Chelsea Garunay, Tiffany Kim, Alexandre Viault, Sarah Parke, Maanik Chauhan, Clint Coller, Amy Nelson, and Laurel Keller, as well as former colleague Christopher DiPietro, for a daring and innovative design appropriate for such a multilayered and multimedia project. For their support of the installation, I am grateful to Tom Scally and his colleagues Deepesh Dhingra, Mike Dominick, Matt Lytle, Taylor Miller, and Maria Nicolino in Buildings; for their meticulous mounts and casework I thank mount makers Fred Sager, Matthew Cumbie, Warren Bennett, and Andrew Estep, and plexi technicians Thomas Zimmerman, Warren Estler, and Chi-Wei Hue. For their meticulous movement and installation of works I am grateful to art handlers Ray Abbensetts, Mike Doscher, Kenny Khan, Luis Negron, Luis Nunez, Todd Rivera, Ray Tablada, and Derrick Williams. I thank Merryl Jamison, Angela Reynolds, and Gordon Hairston for maintaining the galleries.

This project is enriched by an unprecedented curatorial collaboration with MetLiveArts. I am deeply grateful to my gracious thought partner Limor Tomer, Lulu C. and Anthony W. Wang General Manager for Live Arts, and her colleagues Ricardo Barton, Harrison Corthell, Madyson Barnfield, Kerrigan Quenemoen, and Nunally Kersh for programming, coordinating, and documenting performances, and designing the Performance Pyramid with me.

For her exceptional industry, insights, and many and varied contributions in the execution of intellectual, logistical, and diplomatic labors, I offer my deepest thanks to McClain Groff, Research Associate at The Met.

This publication was produced by the outstanding team in The Met's Publications and Editorial Department, headed by Mark Polizzotti, Publisher and Editor in Chief, and including Michael Sittenfeld and Peter Antony. I am grateful to Josephine Rodriguez for her patience and persistence in acquiring images for this book, and to Christina Grillo for so ably overseeing its production. I express my warmest gratitude to Eleanor Hughes and Kayla Elam for their judicious editorial guidance and support; Polymode for their superb design; and Jeanwon Kim and Clarissa Melendez, interns, who provided bibliographic research. I am also grateful to Jennifer Bantz for editing the exhibition materials.

This exhibition is made possible by the Gail and Parker Gilbert Fund, the Jane and Robert Carroll Fund, the Ford Foundation, and the Hobson/Lucas Family Foundation, whose generosity and belief in this project is deeply appreciated. Additional and consequential support is provided by The Hayden Family Foundation, Allison and Larry Berg, The Holly Peterson Foundation, The Andy Warhol Foundation for the Visual Arts, the National Endowment for the Arts, and DeWayne N. Phillips and Caroline A. Wamsler, PhD. The catalogue is made possible by Mellon Foundation and Denise Littlefield Sobel, with generous gifts from The Witten Family Foundation, Lonti Ebers, the Jeffrey and Leslie Fischer Family Foundation, and Kent Kelley. Presentations in the Performance Pyramid are the result of gifts from Cynthia Hazen Polsky and Leon B. Polsky, and the Adrienne Arsht Fund for Resilience through Art. Together, these supporters offered significant endorsements of this project that brought it to life.

I thank my family for their priceless and unrequitable contributions of love, time, space, inspiration, encouragement, nourishment, and understanding.

Akili Tommasino

Lenders to the Exhibition

Beinecke Rare Book and Manuscript Library, Yale University,
New Haven
Brooklyn Museum
Clark Atlanta University Art Museum, Atlanta
Getty Images Gallery
Glenstone Museum, Potomac, Maryland
Iowa State University Library, Ames
Louis Armstrong House Museum, Queens, New York
Medgar Evers College, The City University of New York
The Metropolitan Museum of Art, New York
Milwaukee Art Museum, Milwaukee, Wisconsin
Museum Boijmans Van Beuningen, Rotterdam
Museum of Art, Rhode Island School of Design, Providence
Museum of Fine Arts, Boston
The Museum of Modern Art, New York
National Gallery of Jamaica, Kingston
Nation of Islam Historical Archives
Rubell Museum, Miami and Washington, D.C.
Schomburg Center for Research in Black Culture,
The New York Public Library, New York
Smithsonian National Museum of African American History
and Culture, Washington, D.C.
Studio Museum in Harlem, New York
Temple University Libraries, Philadelphia
University of Massachusetts Amherst Libraries,
Amherst, Massachusetts
University of Washington Libraries, Seattle
Virginia Museum of Fine Arts, Richmond
Whitney Museum of American Art, New York
Worcester Art Museum, Worcester, Massachusetts

Private Collections

The Estate of Terry Adkins
Ghada Amer
Eve Arnold Estate
Estate of Janet Braun-Reinitz
Rashida Bumbray
René Burri Estate
John Corbett and Terri Kapsalis
Renee Cox
Leah D. Daughtry
Damien Davis
The Estate of Noah Davis
Charles Daniel Dawson

Denim Tears
Beth Rudin DeWoody
Emory Douglas
Dream The Combine (Jennifer Newsom and
Tom Carruthers)
The George Economou Collection
The Egyptian Lover
Amr Eldib
Walter O. and Linda Evans
Fred Eversley
Emad Abou Ghazi
Sam Gilliam Foundation
Lauren Halsey
Maren Hassinger
Chester Higgins
Hudgins Family Collection, New York
Madeleine Hunt-Ehrlich
Gregston Hurdle
Iman Issa
Steffani Jemison and Jamal Cyrus
Richard and Michelle Jeschelnig
Armia Malak Khalil
Jas Knight
Solange Knowles
Ashra Kwesi
Thomas Lavin
Maha Maamoun
Senga Nengudi
Lorraine O'Grady
Clifford Owens
Parkwood Entertainment
The Phelan Art Collection
Baaba Heru Ankh Ra Semahj Se Ptah
Ahmed Shehaby
Lorna Simpson
Ming Smith
Robert F. Smith
Robert D. Summer
Lisa and Steven Tananbaum
David Tobey
Tommasino Family Collection, Brooklyn
William T. Williams
Private collectors who wish to remain anonymous

Contributors

Akili Tommasino is Curator in the Department of Modern and Contemporary Art, The Metropolitan Museum of Art, New York.

Andrea Myers Achi is Mary and Michael Jaharis Associate Curator of Byzantine Art in the Department of Medieval Art and The Cloisters, The Metropolitan Museum of Art, New York.

Erykah Badu is a singer, songwriter, actor, activist, producer, and health practitioner/doula.

Makeda Best is Deputy Director of Curatorial Affairs at the Oakland Museum of California.

Barbara Chase-Riboud is a visual artist, sculptor, novelist, and poet.

Awol Erizku is a conceptual artist.

Lauren Halsey is an artist and funkateer.

Iman Issa is an artist based in Paris.

Solange Knowles is a multidisciplinary artist, musician, and founder of Saint Heron.

Mia Matthias is Assistant Curator at Glenstone Museum, Potomac, Maryland.

Julie Mehretu is a visual artist.

Kai Mora is a PhD candidate in African and African American Studies at Harvard University.

Jennifer Newsom is an architect and artist, co-founder of Dream The Combine, and Assistant Professor of Architecture in the College of Architecture, Art, and Planning at Cornell University.

Matthew Shenoda is a poet and Professor and Chair of the Department of Literary Arts and affiliated faculty in Africana Studies and the Brown Arts Institute at Brown University.

Fred Wilson is a visual artist.

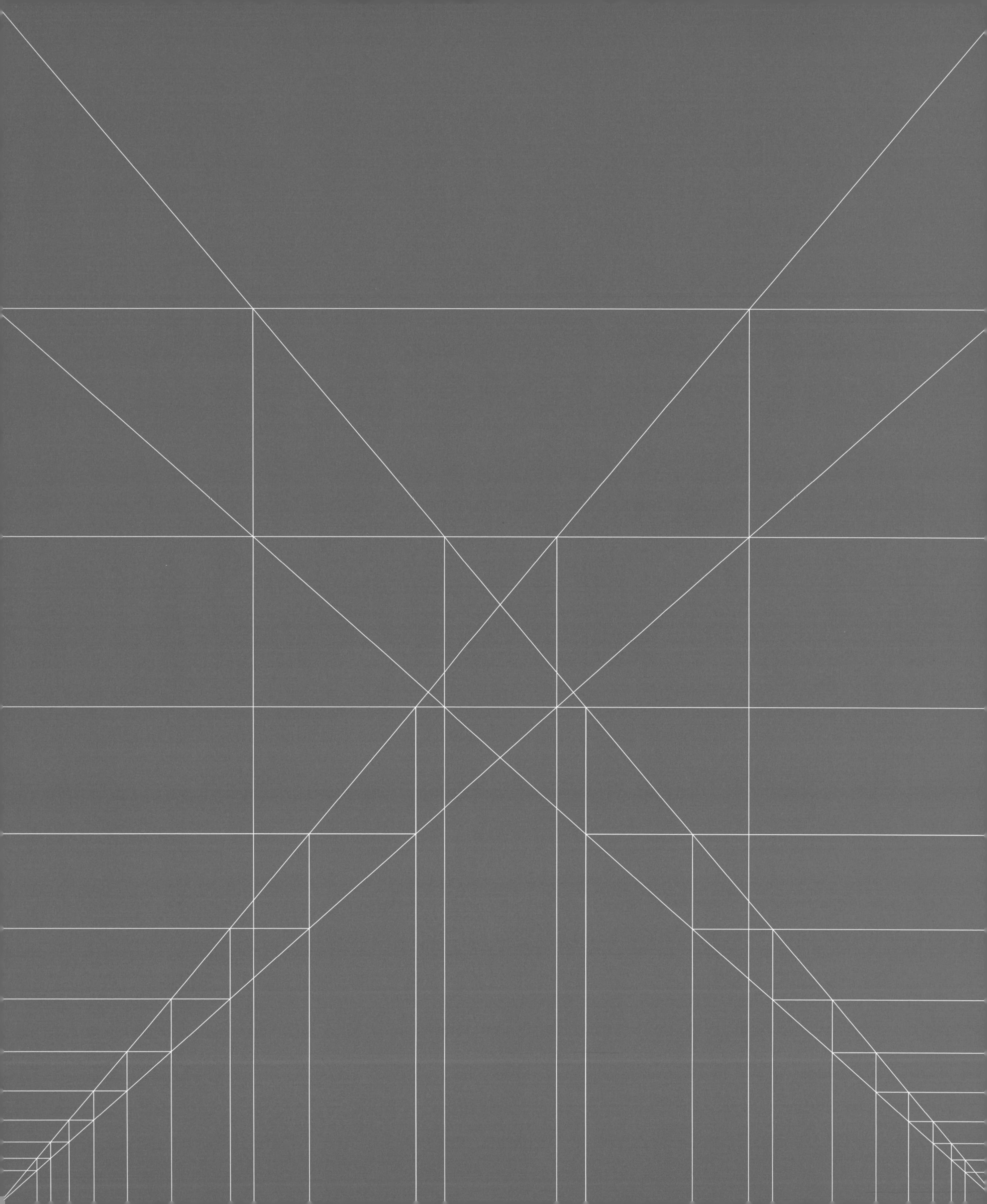

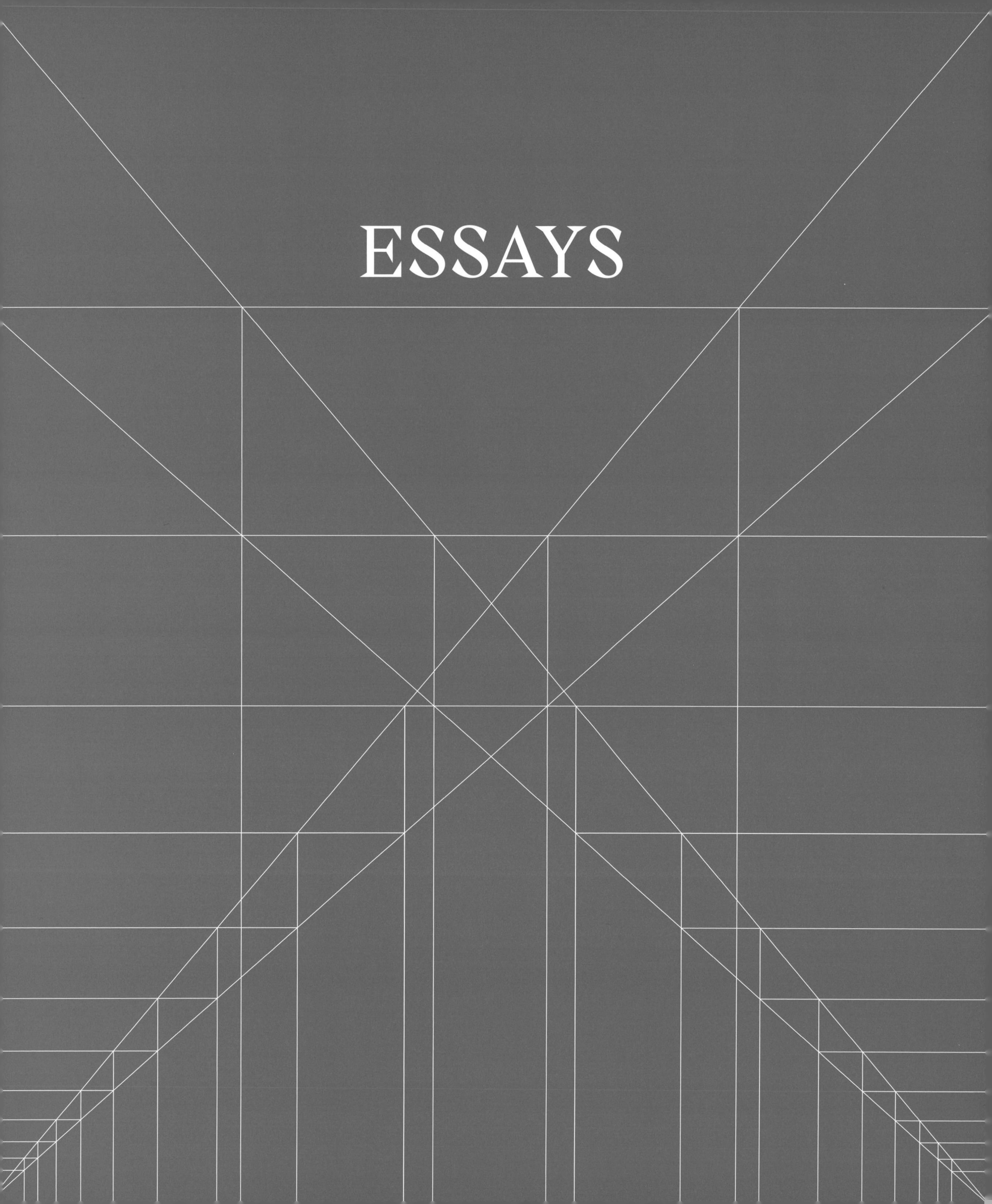
ESSAYS

Flight into Egypt: Black Artists and Ancient Egypt, 1876–Now

Akili Tommasino

Murky blue, tawny yellow, purple, and mauve hues enshroud the twilit faces of the four clandestine travelers in Henry Ossawa Tanner's painting *Flight into Egypt* (pl. 2), who seem to advance quietly into the dense night. Tanner's painting, in the collection of the American Wing at The Met, is "a mature work by . . . the leading early 20th-century African American artist who studied in Paris and resided in France—largely due to the systemic racism he encountered in the United States." In 1891, the year of his departure for Europe, he declared, "I cannot fight prejudice and paint at the same time."[1] Tanner was the first Black American painter to attain international success. Born in Pittsburgh, Pennsylvania, and trained at the Pennsylvania Academy of Fine Arts in Philadelphia, where he studied with Thomas Eakins, Tanner permanently expatriated to France in 1891. Having begun his career painting emotionally resonant images of Black American life, by the mid-1890s he had shifted to biblical themes familiar from his childhood in the African Methodist Episcopal Church, where his father, Benjamin Tanner, was a bishop. To represent these stories, the artist developed an increasingly painterly, highly personal style based on direct observation and imagination. Tanner visited Egypt on his tour of North Africa in 1897, documenting his experiences in paint. *Interior of a Mosque, Cairo* (pl. 1), for example, is an eyewitness souvenir. Tanner's travel to Egypt set a precedent for the cultural pilgrimages of future generations.

Tanner incorporated architectural sketches from his travels into the biblical scenes that would become his best-known works. *Flight into Egypt* depicts Mary, Joseph, and the infant Jesus escaping King Herod's assassins.[2] Their exile in pursuit of safety in Egypt is a New Testament inversion of the Old Testament Exodus of the Israelites necessary to fulfill the messianic prophecy "out of Egypt have I called my son."[3] Egypt is, in the New Testament, a place of refuge rather than of bondage. This

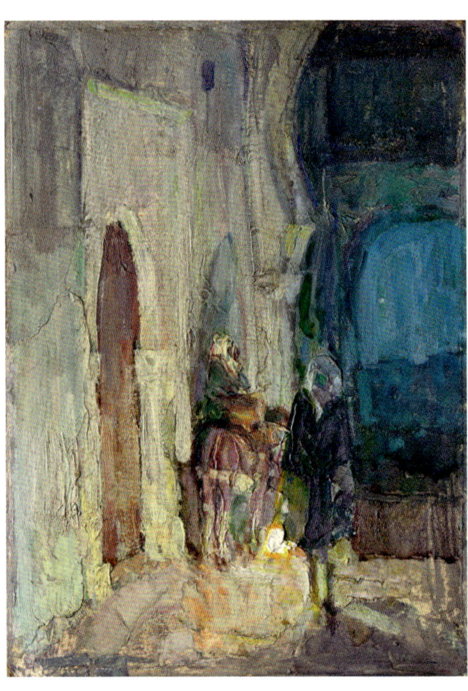

Fig. 1. Henry Ossawa Tanner (American, 1859–1937). **Untitled (Flight into Egypt)**, ca. 1923. Oil on paperboard, 13 x 9 in. (33 x 22.9 cm). The Metropolitan Museum of Art, New York, Marguerite and Frank A. Cosgrove Jr. Fund, 2023 (2023.551)

biblical episode was demonstrably one of Tanner's favorite subjects, and the fact that he produced at least fifteen versions between 1899 and 1932— among them The Met's preparatory oil study (fig. 1)—strongly suggests a sensitivity to issues of personal freedom and mobility, perhaps including the Great Migration of Black Americans from the South after World War I.[4] *Flight into Egypt* certainly resonates with his own experience of fleeing the United States to pursue his career more freely abroad.[5]

"Flight into Egypt" is an apt description of the sustained engagement of Black artists and other agents of culture with ancient Egypt, manifest in visual, sculptural, literary, musical, scientific, scholarly, religious, political, and performative pursuits. Titled after Tanner's painting, *Flight into Egypt: Black Artists and Ancient Egypt, 1876–Now* explores the reception of ancient Egypt within the African diaspora from the late nineteenth century to the present day. Encompassing the poles of abstraction and figuration, documentation and invention, and practices that fall within and outside institutional paradigms, the materials assembled in *Flight into Egypt* embody a continuum of creative and intellectual output reflecting the centrality of this foundational civilization to modern Black imaginations, identities, and ideologies. Ancient Egypt is a symbolic source for people of the African diaspora that continues to inspire. In addition to the urgent act of fleeing described in the biblical episode, flight implies the soaring heights of the imagination—the resource through which the protagonists of this project necessarily engage with ancient Egypt. *Flight into Egypt* is *not* about ancient Egypt per se: rather, it broadly examines how and why Black artists, writers, musicians, and entertainers have employed ancient Egyptian imagery, the contributions of Black scholars and scientists to the study of ancient Egypt, and the importance of ancient Egypt to Black communities over the past century and a half.

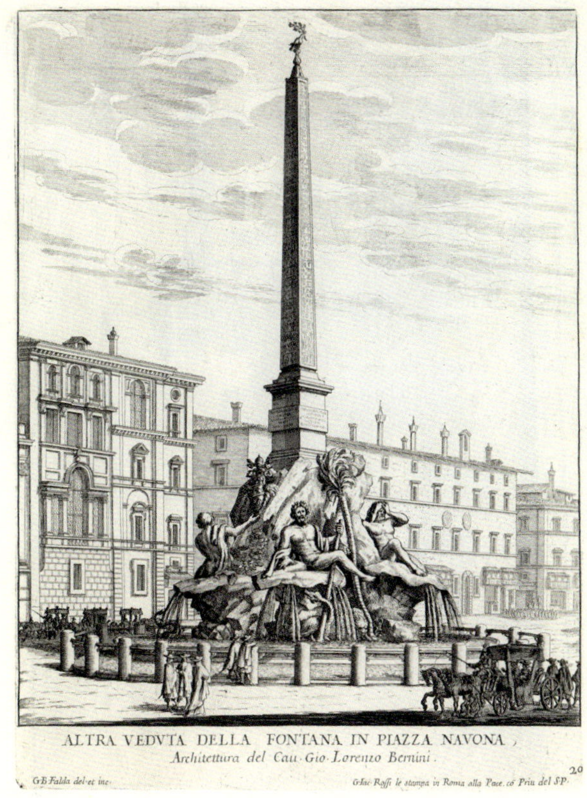

Fig. 2. Giovanni Battista Falda (Italian, 1643–1678). **Another View of the Fountain in Piazza Navona**, in **Le Fontane di Roma nelle Piazze e Luoghi Publici della Città** (Rome, 1691 or after). The Metropolitan Museum of Art, New York, Gift of D. W. Langton, transferred from the Library (1991.1073.145[20])

Furthermore, it highlights the engagement of twentieth- and twenty-first-century Egyptian artists with ancient Egypt, a topic copious and complex enough to warrant its own dedicated exhibitions and book-length studies.

With its abstract passages and coalescent figuration, Tanner's painting evokes a mystical temporality appropriate for a story in which prophecy and history are intertwined. Likewise, the organizational logic of this project involves a cyclical and intergenerational model of history that unites the present and possible future by looking back at multiple layered pasts. While most of the stories in *Flight into Egypt* are about individuals of African descent born and active in the United States, the work of artists of the Caribbean and Egypt, and other African-born artists active in the United States, Europe, and elsewhere, indicates the global resonance of ancient Egypt in the African diaspora—the global dispersion of people of African descent.[6] This project encompasses a wide range of media, from sculpture and painting to applied art, design, fashion, time-based media, performance art as an integral component of the exhibition (not a programmatic corollary), and cultural production—including popular music and various forms of documentation—that are typically outside of the scope of art museum exhibitions. It also includes works that fall literally outside the institution: three permanent sculptural installations

in the New York City Metropolitan Transportation Authority (MTA) subway and Metro-North Railroad evince the quotidian relevance of its subject.

Flight into Egypt challenges Eurocentric constructions of ancient Egypt, offering a revisionist history that focuses on the contributions of Black cultural figures in dismantling prevailing narratives. The contention that ancient Egypt should be characterized as a Black civilization is central to nineteenth- through twenty-first-century Black artists' and other cultural figures' engagement with ancient Egypt. While this essay does not advance that argument from the perspective of archaeology, it does explore Egyptian history as a creative catalyst.

Beginning in the late nineteenth century, the era of emancipation, Black Americans started to look to ancient Egypt as evidence of an undeniably great ancient African culture in order to ennoble Black identities, having been systematically stripped of their knowledge of specific African heritage through the transatlantic slave trade, generational enslavement, and dehumanization in American civic life and society. Prominent individuals began to travel to Egypt, including formerly enslaved abolitionist Frederick Douglass, who visited Egypt as a statesman in 1887. Decades earlier, in a speech titled "The Claims of the Negro, Ethnologically Considered," Douglass had asserted:

> Greece and Rome—and through them Europe and America have received their civilization from the ancient Egyptians. This fact is not denied by any body. But Egypt is in Africa. . . . The ancient Egyptians were not white people; but were, undoubtedly, just about as dark in complexion as many in this country who are considered genuine negroes.[7]

Elsewhere he wrote, "It has been the fashion of [white] American writers, to deny that the Egyptians were Negroes and claim that they are of the same race as themselves. This has, I have no doubt, been largely due to a wish to deprive the Negro of the moral support of Ancient Greatness and to appropriate the same to the white race."[8] This is a bold and early example—before the abolition of slavery in the United States—of a major Black American cultural figure laying claim to ancient Egypt in defiance of widely received notions established by the Egyptology of his era.

OBELISKS IN ROME

If framed as oppositional, to what is the Black reception of ancient Egypt opposed? To set the terms for the exploration of art and cultural history that follows, it is useful to briefly establish the essential timeline, geography, and terminology of ancient Egypt. The period from the emergence of civilization on the banks of the Nile River, which flows from south to north in East Africa, to the establishment of the current political borders of the Arab Republic of Egypt spans over five thousand years. For millennia, the land called *kmt* (Kemet) by its ancient inhabitants ("Egypt" is derived from the Greek *Aigyptos*) has been a dynamic region with confluent populations. The constellation of proximate regions includes Libya to the west, the eastern Mediterranean, the so-called Near East, Nubia (stretching from southern Egypt to northern Sudan), Sudan itself, and

Ethiopia, a term that refers both to a specific territory and, as recently as the early twentieth century, to the African continent as a whole. There are clear distinctions between the art of the pharaonic dynasties, the later Ptolemaic, and the eclectic art of Roman Egypt and Egyptianized Rome. Most of the works by the modern and contemporary artists discussed here feature references to pharaonic Egypt, which began in 3100 BCE and ended when Alexander the Great conquered Egypt in 332 BCE.[9]

When the biblical Holy Family fled to Egypt, ancient Egypt was already ancient. It had become a Roman province in 30 BCE, when Cleopatra was defeated by Augustus (reigned 27 BCE–14 CE). The European and Anglo-American Egyptomania of the eighteenth, nineteenth, and twentieth centuries was arguably preceded by that of Augustan Rome:

> *Ancient* Egypt had a symbolic significance in the Mediterranean that was quite distinct from attitudes toward recent history. Pharaonic Egypt was seen as a repository of deep history, religious solemnity, and civilized knowledge, and as a touchstone for the sanction of world rule. Roman imperialist thought appropriated this existing eastern Mediterranean view of Egypt. Conquering Egypt meant dominion over time as well as space, and possession of the powerful symbolism that the Mediterranean world invested in pharaonic Egypt.[10]

The Roman period both engenders and naturalizes the notion of Egypt as a proto-European civilization, manifest through the physical presence of Egyptian obelisks brought back to Rome and erected in key locations in the city. Eight obelisks of ancient Egyptian provenance now stand in Rome, whereas seven remain in Egypt.[11] Several of those in Rome are adorned with baroque and Catholic ornament at their bases and summits, frilly malapropisms reflecting the multifold process of their assimilation (figs. 2, 3). Like "Egypt," "obelisk" is a word of

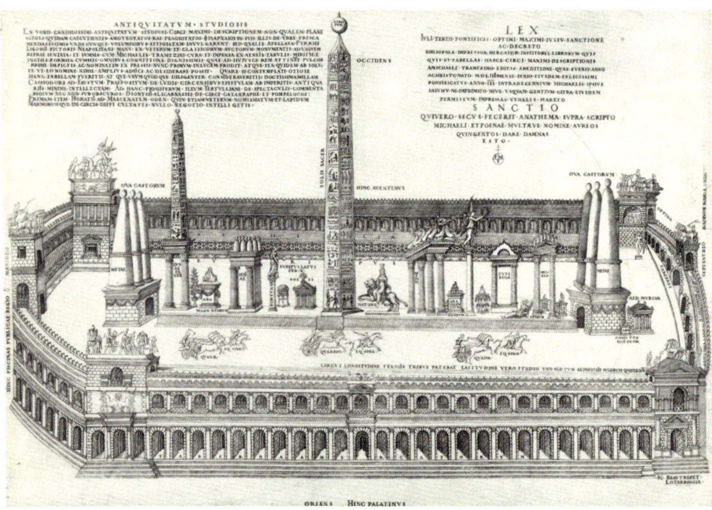

Fig. 3. Nicolas Beatrizet (French, 1515–ca. 1566). After Pirro Ligorio (Italian, ca. 1512/13–1583). **Circus Maximus,** from **Speculum Romanae Magnificentiae**, 1553. Engraving, 14⅞ x 21⅞ in. (38 x 55.5 cm). The Metropolitan Museum of Art, New York, Harris Brisbane Dick Fund, 1941 (41.72[1.67])

Greek origin—it likens the form to needles or skewers; the ancient Egyptian word for the form is *tekhenu*.[12] As Susan Sorek explains, "The obelisks caught the attention of Western civilizations when the Greeks conquered Egypt. The Greeks, and later the Romans, were fascinated by the power and authority that seemed to be imbued in these colossal monuments. This contact would eventually see, as a consequence, the most movable obelisks finding their way to the West.[13] In their original settings, obelisks were usually twin forms, symmetrically installed at the entrances to funerary structures and temples.[14] Roman emperors beginning with Augustus brought Egyptian obelisks to their capital, separating the pairs, recontextualizing them as monolithic trophies and in one case a sundial, and thereby co-opting these primarily religious objects as symbols for strengthening political power. By the Middle Ages, Rome's periodic earthquakes had toppled many of the obelisks. Some were reerected and rededicated as Catholic monuments as part of ambitious papal urban planning campaigns, for example that of Sixtus V (fig. 4).[15] Even today, special papal masses commence around the so-called Vatican obelisk, which is adorned with flowers for the occasions.

Obelisks in Rome (pl. 5), a silent, split-screen video by the polymathic artist Terry Adkins, points to the absorption of ancient Egypt by Rome and to the distortion of African subjectivity in the West. Adkins recorded images of these symbols of syncretism and conquest in 2010 while he was a fellow at the American Academy in Rome, an institution that historically has been supportive of Black artists.[16] *Obelisks in Rome* was displayed as the backdrop for a performance by Adkins's multidisciplinary collective, the Lone Wolf Recital Corps, titled *At Osiris* (2013).[17] Staged at the Studio Museum in Harlem, it featured "live instrumentation and recitation from ancient Egyptian Osirian texts."[18] Adkins's recitals incorporated live and recorded music, video, recitation, and costumed, choreographed movement. For the artist, they were part of "an ongoing quest to reinsert the legacies of unheralded immortal figures to their rightful place within the panorama of history."[19] Symmetrical doubling was a favorite formal strategy of the artist. The split- screen format is also related to Adkins's interest in stereoscopic images and their combination, which creates a third image. In tandem with the contrast of solarized images and their negatives, the doubling of the obelisks in the video points metaphorically to their hybrid identity, born of their displacement. Moreover, it restores the harmonic status of each obelisk as part of a pair. The metabolism of ancient Egyptian symbols, artistic and architectural attainments, religious practices, and social mores was consistent with the cultural voracity of Roman conquest. In an interview with Martha Boyden for the catalogue of his exhibition at the American Academy in Rome in 1993, David Hammons characterized the dynamics of ancient Roman appropriation bluntly: "Most people don't go to look. They go to rob, steal, or borrow. It's very rare for people to look and leave the sculpture where they found it."[20] As Grant Parker asserts, "It would be easy to tell an 'obelizing' version of the grand narrative of Western Civilization, moving from the Fertile Crescent via classical antiquity and the Renaissance to modern times, and touching on colonialism and the nation-state."[21]

EGYPTOLOGY AND THE COLOR LINE

Modern Black cultural figures asserted affinity with ancient Egypt against the prevailing definition established by institutional Egyptology of the ancient civilization as separate from Black Africa, a philosophical distinction discussed at length in Andrea Myers Achi's essay in this volume. Although medieval Islamic writers considered ancient Egypt, the modern discipline of Egyptology was born in the late eighteenth century when Napoleon Bonaparte's invasion of Egypt was accompanied by scientific exploration of ancient sites. Until the establishment of autonomous Egyptian national authorities in the 1950s, the preeminent institutions and protagonists of Egyptology were for much of its history Eurocentric and colonial. In turn, this understanding of ancient Egypt was accompanied by the denigration of sub-Saharan African cultures. The legacy of Eurocentrism is evident in the distinction of ancient Egypt from other African civilizations in the layout of many Western art museums, including The Met. Jas Knight's diptych *The African Origin of Civilization* (pl. 9) depicts objects from the Department of Egyptian Art and the Michael C. Rockefeller Wing, which houses the Museum's collection of sub-Saharan African art, atypically displayed together, as they were in an exhibition jointly organized by those departments that likewise took its title from Cheikh Anta Diop's groundbreaking book, published in 1974 (pl. 14). The departments' physical distance—in opposite corners of the building—is underscored by the historic treatment of the two collection areas during The Met's history. Egyptian art has been considered a pillar of the institution since its founding, becoming a distinct department in 1906 "in response to increasing Western interest in the culture of ancient Egypt," while the sub-Saharan African collection was not on view at The Met until 1982.[22] More than a still life, Knight's painting is an artistic reflection on the problematics of institutional Egyptology. While The Met is now working to address the presentation of these works through a comprehensive renovation of the Rockefeller Wing, the overall floor plan will uphold a division rooted in notions of Egyptian exceptionalism.

Critiques of Egyptology's Eurocentrism and de facto exclusion of Black scholars have even been made manifest in popular culture. The second episode of *The Richard Pryor Show*, which aired in 1977, featured a skit titled "Egypt 1909" (pl. 8). The comedian plays an archaeologist who discovers in an ancient Egyptian tomb "The Book of Life," according to which "the Black gods did leave the spacecraft . . . and man in his Blackness did walk the earth." Pryor's character exclaims, "These were all Black people!" as his three white colleagues balk in denial and shut Pryor—still rapt at his discovery—in the tomb. Pryor's biting sketch parodies the historically Eurocentric and colonial protagonists and institutions of Egyptology and broaches the Black Egyptian Hypothesis, which contends that ancient Egypt was an indigenous Black African civilization as opposed to a proto-European one. The marginalization of Pryor's invented archaeologist—however comical—is reminiscent of the experiences of real Black scholars who faced exclusion from the gatekeepers of the field of Egyptology. Alain Locke, the literary and philosophical

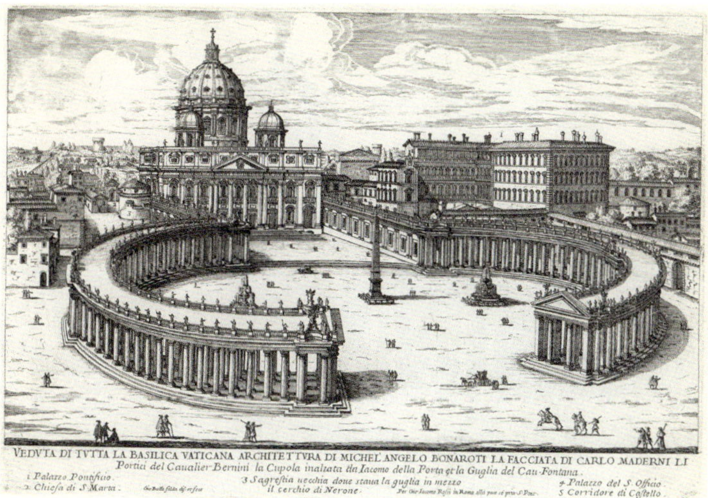

Fig. 4. Giovanni Battista Falda (Italian, 1643–1678). **View of the Entire Vatican Basilica**, from **Il Nuovo Teatro delle Fabbriche, et Edificii, in Prospettiva di Roma Moderna**, 1665–69. Etching, 7 3/16 x 11 3/8 in. (18.2 x 28.9 cm). The Metropolitan Museum of Art, New York, Harris Brisbane Dick Fund, 1931 (31.67.4[53])

father of the Harlem Renaissance, was barred (as were others) from visiting the tomb of Tutankhamun by its British excavator, Howard Carter, in 1923.[23] William Leo Hansberry, another Harvard-trained scholar, was in 1932 deterred by Dows Dunham—the head of the Department of Egyptian Art at the Museum of Fine Arts, Boston—from joining an expedition to Kawa, in northern Sudan, led by British Egyptologist Francis Llewellyn Griffith.[24] In response to Hansberry's request for a letter of recommendation in support of his wish to join Griffith's excavation, Dunham wrote (pl. 10):

> I now come to the racial question, and that, I confess, strikes me as the greatest difficulty. To be perfectly frank with you, if I were in charge of such an expedition I should hesitate long before taking an American Negro on my staff. I should foresee the danger of great difficulty with the native workmen, who would, I believe, find it almost impossible to understand your position, and I should fear that the mere fact of your being a member of the staff would seriously affect the prestige of the other members and the respect which the native employees would have for them. It is, in my judgment, not a question so much of your relations with the white members of the party, but of the effect your presence would have on the relations between natives and staff as a whole.

Dunham continued, "I feel sure that you know me well enough to realize that I do not say this out of any feeling of race-prejudice, but because it is my sincere estimate of the probabilities of the case. For my part I am sure you are the last man who would want to put yourself . . . into a false position." Hansberry went on to become the founder of the African Civilizations course at

Flight into Egypt

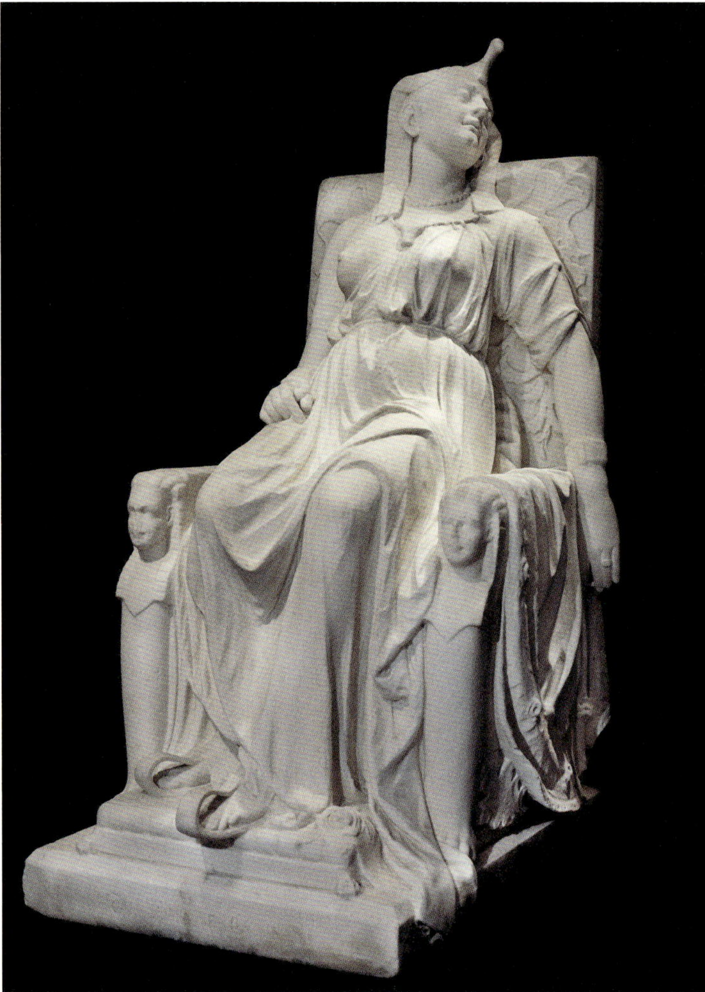

Fig. 5. Edmonia Lewis (American, 1844–1907). **The Death of Cleopatra**, 1876. Marble, H. 63 in. (160 cm), W. 31¼ in. (79.4 cm), D. 46 in. (116.8 cm). Smithsonian American Art Museum, Washington, D.C., Gift of the Historical Society of Forest Park, Illinois (1994.17)

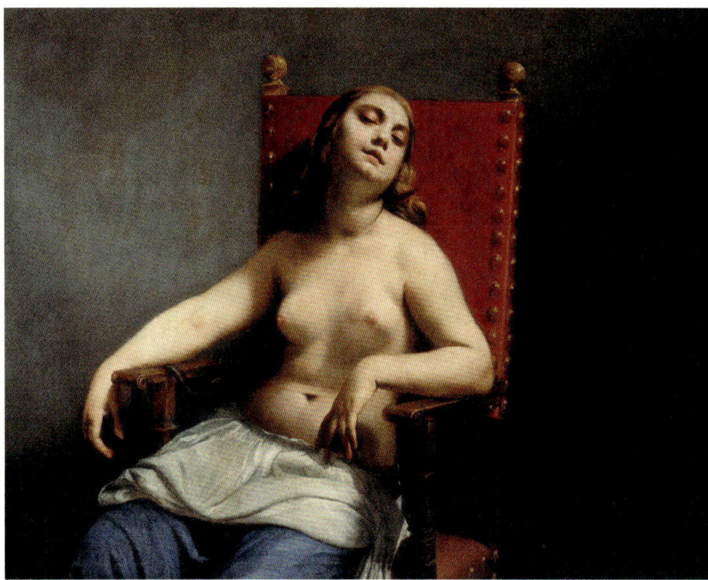

Fig. 6. Guido Cagnacci (Italian, 1601–1663). **Death of Cleopatra**, 1660–62. Oil on canvas, 47¼ x 62¼ in. (120 x 158 cm). Pinacoteca di Brera, Milan (2341)

Howard University, where Locke had founded the philosophy department in 1921; they both taught there for many years (pl. 11).

Black radical scholarship, revisionist pedagogy, and creative counternarratives emerged as parallel responses to the legacy of the exclusions of mainstream Egyptology. Despite being left out of many official channels, Black scholars and scientists have persisted in the pursuit of a better understanding of ancient Egypt, and Black historians have sought self-determination in storytelling. Evoking the glories of ancient Egypt in the title of his history of Egypt from the Ottoman period onward, Dusé Mohamed Ali published *In the Land of the Pharaohs* in 1911 (see fig. 27). Born to a Sudanese mother and an Egyptian father (pl. 12), Ali corresponded with others who advocated for the unity of Africans on the continent and in the diaspora along with the elimination of colonialism and white supremacy, such as Pan-Africanists W. E. B. Du Bois and Marcus Garvey, among others.[25] The artist and agricultural scientist George Washington Carver developed a formula he believed to be Egyptian Blue, an example of diasporic Egyptology that has been largely omitted from the history of conservation (pl. 3) An article published in 1932 quotes Carver claiming that "there is no one of the moderns . . . who uses blue half so well," and describes him producing a jar containing "the richest, purest blue he had ever seen," declaring, "I believe . . . that it's a rediscovery of the old Egyptian blue."[26] New scientific research on Carver's pigment led by Anna Serotta, Conservator, Department of Objects Conservation at The Met, in collaboration with colleagues at Iowa State University and Tuskegee University, has determined that the chemical composition of the pigment in a container labeled by Carver "Egyptian Blue, 9th Oxidation" is Prussian Blue; nevertheless, Carver's naming of his pigment is a significant cultural reclamation.[27] Carver originally filed for a patent for his soil-based formula in 1923; US Patent 1632365A was issued in 1927, and the pigment was marketed as the color found in Tutankhamun's tomb.

The first scholarly publications that assert Afrocentric perspectives on the study of ancient Egypt emerged in the 1970s. Yosef A. A. ben-Jochannan's *Black Man of the Nile and His Family* (pl. 13) argued that the African history of the Nile Valley cultures had been distorted by Europeans.[28] In 1974, Senegalese scholar and humanist Cheikh Anta Diop's groundbreaking book, *The African Origin of Civilization: Myth or Reality* (pl. 14) shocked and challenged historians with the author's assertion that ancient Egypt—whose civilization was a source for the subsequent development of cultural traditions in the rest of the African continent and the Western world—belongs to Africa.[29] In his *Black Athena* (pl. 15), British academic Martin Bernal tied the purported achievements of ancient Greece to ancient Egyptian (i.e., African) precedents.[30] At the time of publication, Solange Ashby, author of the pioneering study of Nubian religion *Calling Out to Isis* (pl. 16), was the sole Black Egyptologist working within an accredited university.[31]

Even as Black scholars faced exclusionary encounters with gatekeepers of Egyptology, developments in the field were catalysts for curiosity and creativity. As momentous as the discovery of Tutankhamun's tomb in 1922 was the massive movement of Nubian monuments in the mid-1960s to preserve them from the flooding that would result from the creation of the Aswan Dam (now called the High Dam at Aswan). The Roman-era Temple of Dendur, housed at The Met, is one such monument. Noah Davis's painting *Untitled* (pl. 17) reinterprets a photograph of the movement by UNESCO of the Great Temple of Ramesses II at Abu Simbel to higher ground between 1963 and 1968. The painting, which hauntingly depicts the removal of the face of a massive pharaonic statue, suggests that the telling of history is as malleable as the shifting sands and that in history's reconstruction there are ghastly distortions.

CLEOPATRA

The connection between expatriation and creative expression is as strong in the career of Edmonia Lewis as it was for Tanner. Born in New York, Lewis studied at Oberlin College. When she was accused of poisoning another student, a vigilante group stripped and beat her viciously.[32] After a period in Massachusetts, she permanently moved to Europe, first settling in Italy. Lewis's masterpiece *The Death of Cleopatra* (fig. 5), created in 1876, is the earliest surviving major example of a Black artist of the modern era engaging with an ancient Egyptian subject. The massive sculpture followed neoclassical models, down to its pastiche of a hieroglyphic inscription. Among the likely sources for Lewis's version of Cleopatra is a painting by Guido Cagnacci (fig. 6), which she might have seen in person during her travels through Italy or as a printed reproduction.[33] Lewis's sculpture has often been read as autobiographical (misread, according to Kirsten Pai Buick), yet there are compelling connections between her experience and the subject of her *Death of Cleopatra*.[34] As the filmmaker Madeleine Hunt-Ehrlich observes in her film *Cleopatra at the Mall* (pl. 19), Cleopatra's reported death by venomous snakebite has resonance with the poisoning of which Lewis had been accused.

The story of Cleopatra VII, queen of Egypt from 51 to 30 BCE and the final ruler of the Ptolemaic Dynasty, which had Macedonian Greek origins, has been an enduring source of visual and literary inspiration; her death signaled the official end of autonomous Egypt in the ancient world. For some artists, Cleopatra became a symbol of the moribund interaction of Africa with Europe. Almost a century after Edmonia Lewis lived in Rome, Philadelphia-born artist Barbara Chase-Riboud took up residency there. Chase-Riboud is noted for having been the first Black woman in the community of fellows at the American Academy in Rome and the subject of The Met's first solo exhibition of a living artist.[35] On a dare from other residents at the academy, Chase-Riboud traveled to Egypt from Rome in December 1957. Of this formative trip, the artist recounts,

> I grew up that year. It was the first time I realized there was such a thing as non-European art. For someone exposed only to the Greco-Roman tradition, it was a revelation. I suddenly saw how insular the Western World was vis-à-vis the nonwhite, non-Christian world. The blast of Egyptian culture was irresistible. The sheer magnificence of it. The elegance and perfection, the timelessness, the depth. After that, Greek and Roman Art looked like pastry to me. From an artistic point of view the trip was historic for me.[36]

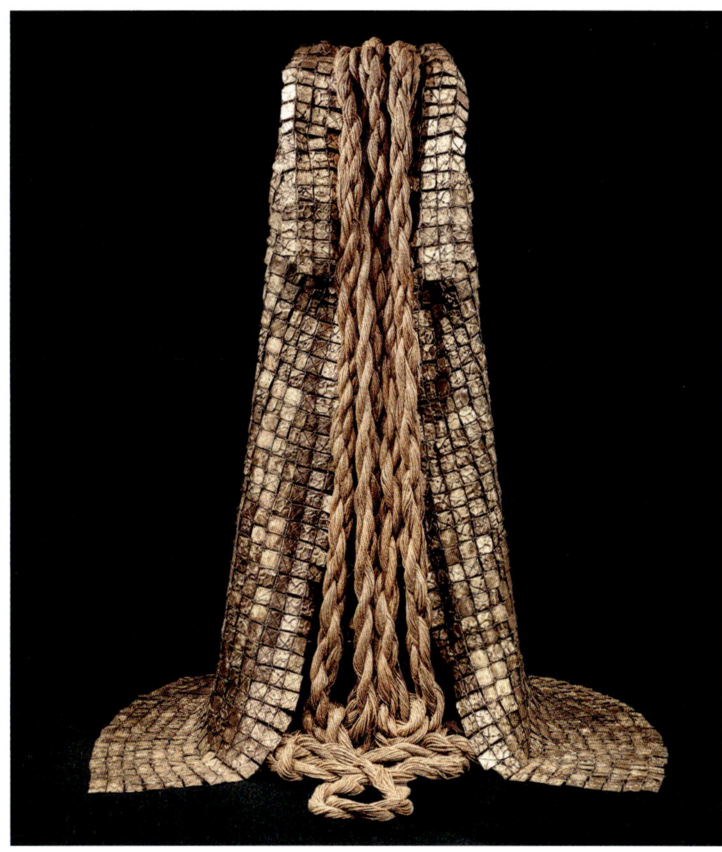

Fig. 7. Barbara Chase-Riboud (American, b. 1939). **Cleopatra's Cape** or **Le Manteau (The Cape)**, 1973. Bronze, hemp rope, and copper, H. 99½ in. (252.7 cm), W. 84 in. (213.4 cm), D. 72 in. (182.9 cm). Studio Museum in Harlem, Gift of the Lannan Foundation (1998.7.4)

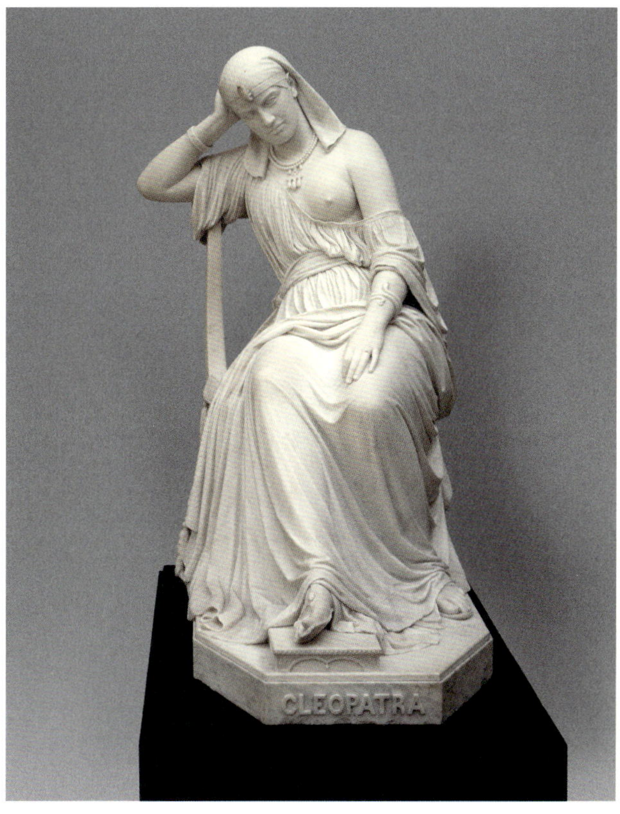

Fig. 8. William Wetmore Story (American, 1819–1895). **Cleopatra**, 1858, carved 1869. Marble, H. 55½ in. (141 cm), W. 33¼ in. (84.5 cm), D. 51½ in. (130.8 cm). The Metropolitan Museum of Art, New York, Gift of John Taylor Johnston, 1888 (88.5a–d)

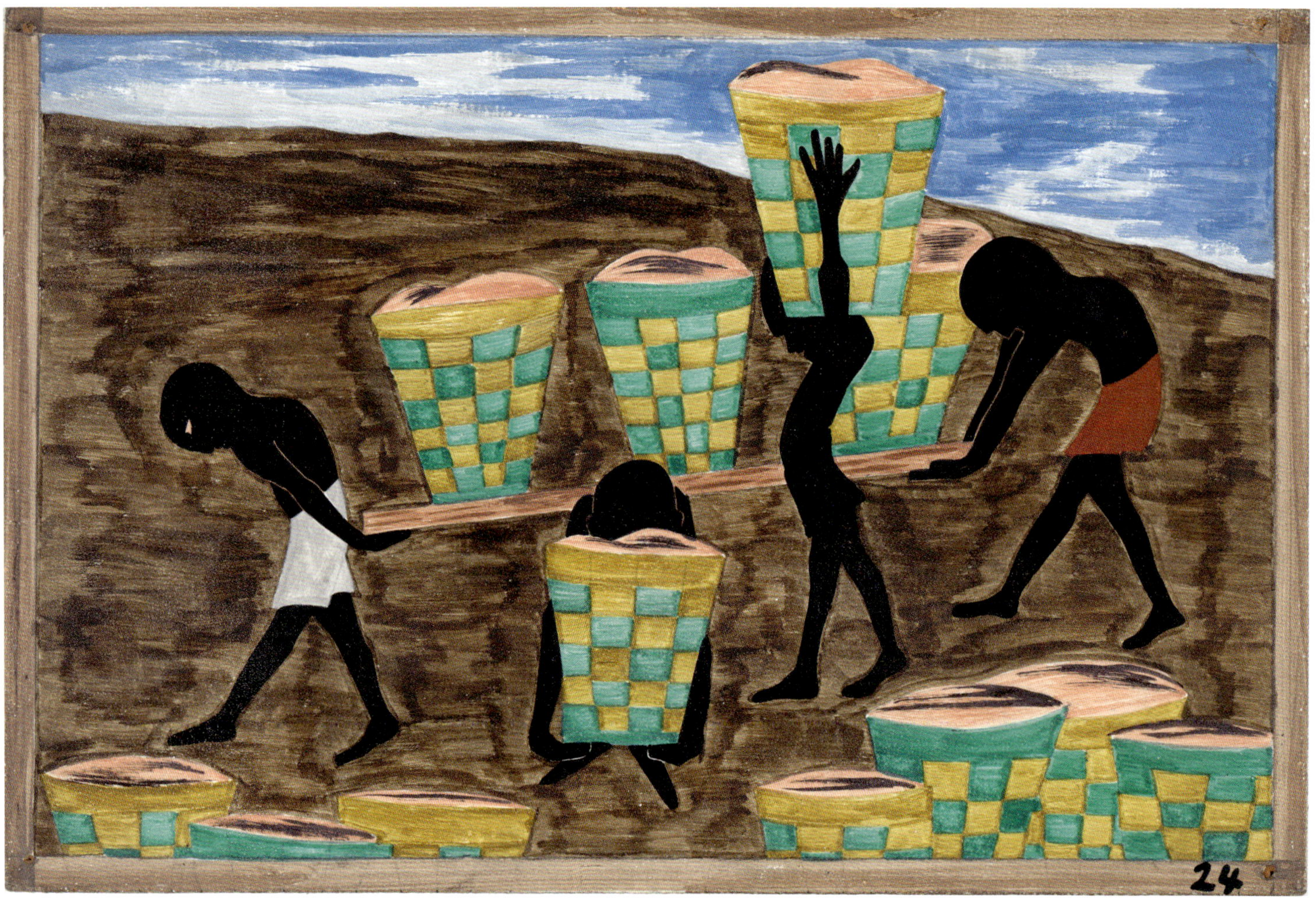

Fig. 9. Jacob Lawrence (American, 1917–2000). **Their children were forced to work in the fields. They could not go to school**, panel 24 from The Migration Series, 1940–41. Casein tempera on hardboard, 12 x 18 in. (30.5 x 45.7 cm). The Museum of Modern Art, New York, Gift of Mrs. David M. Levy (28.1942.12)

Chase-Riboud's sculpture *Cleopatra's Chair* (pl. 21) formally and conceptually resonates with Edmonia Lewis's work. Part of a series of large bronze sculptures dedicated to Cleopatra that was inaugurated in 1973, it evinces the long-standing impact of Chase-Riboud's encounter with Egypt. Chase-Riboud's Cleopatra sculptures occupy a unique position on the representational spectrum for an artist best known for working in the tradition of modernist abstraction. Although *Cleopatra's Cape* or *Le Manteau* (*The Cape*) (fig. 7), *Cleopatra's Door* (1984), *Cleopatra's Chair* (1994), *Cleopatra's Bed* (1997), and *Cleopatra's Wedding Dress* (2003) are not sculptures of a figure, they are sculptures made for a vanished figure. Absent the figure, these objects evade contemporary debates about Cleopatra's racial identity and appearance. Both Edmonia Lewis and Barbara Chase-Riboud engage with an ancient Egyptian subject without explicitly adopting ancient Egyptian modes of representation. With references to ancient Chinese funerary art as well as Egyptian hieroglyphs, *Cleopatra's Chair* achieves a vision of universality based on eclecticism.[37] Lewis is conversant with

her white male neoclassical artist peers like William Wetmore Story (fig. 8) for whom the sculptural subject is a cipher of racial difference.[38] In contrast to these sculptural examples, Irene Clark's painting *Cleopatra* (pl. 39) explicitly demonstrates the influence of ancient Egyptian pictorial conventions such as using flat planes of color and rendering the rudimentary figure in profile. Moreover, she depicts Cleopatra with undeniably dark skin—associating contemporary Black identity with Egypt's last queen.

THE HARLEM RENAISSANCE

The projection of identity through aesthetic emulation is a guiding principle of Afrocentric cultural production, which began in earnest as part of the literary and artistic phenomenon known as the Harlem Renaissance, at the beginning of the twentieth century. As the rediscovery of ancient Roman art (itself based on ancient Greek precedents) was the inspirational source for the Italian Renaissance, ancient Egypt served as a model of

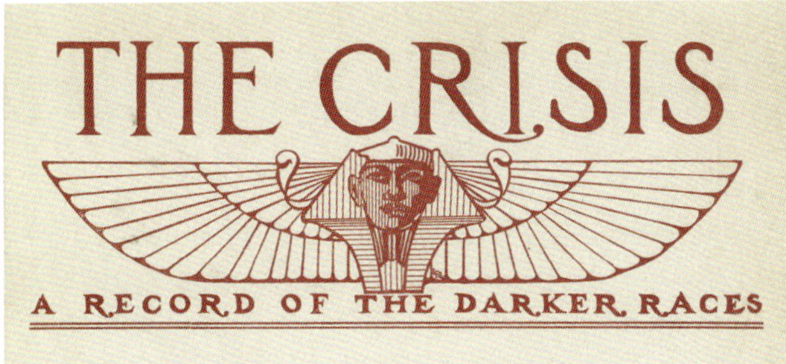

Fig. 10. Masthead of **The Crisis** 3, no. 3, January 1912. Smithsonian National Museum of African American History and Culture, Washington, D.C. (2015.97.14.2)

ancient African aesthetics for "New Negro" artists seeking to craft a unifying identity. Artists of the Harlem Renaissance took up the call to forge a visual identity for the New Negro, which had to be grounded in the art and identity of a putative ancient Negro to give it definition and pedigree. The impact of ancient Egyptian pharaonic statuary and mural decoration on the figurative expression of modern Black artists was tremendous. Meta Vaux Warrick Fuller's emblematic *Ethiopia Awakening* (pl. 22) is recognized by art historians as the first Afrocentric work of art. Such claims are always dubious because of the plethora of undocumented artworks, but Fuller's work is distinguished by the Black American artist's adoption of an African theme as a form of self-identification. Why would a sculpture referring to Ethiopia be dressed like an ancient Egyptian pharaoh? The intersecting regions of Egypt, Ethiopia, Sudan, and Nubia have been conflated in different eras for different purposes. A psalmic prophecy justified the elision of Egypt and Ethiopia: "Princes shall come out of Egypt; Ethiopia shall soon stretch out her hands unto God."[39] Melissa Dabakis writes that in the era of abolition this "psalm was understood to refer to the black race—identified as both Ethiopian and Egyptian—and to herald the glories of the African past. Redeeming the continent as a flourishing center of ancient civilizations, white and black abolitionists refuted the charge that the culture of modern Africans and African-Americans was inherently inferior to that of white Anglo-Saxons."[40] Jamaican-born Pan-Africanist Marcus Garvey adopted the phrase as a slogan of his international Universal Negro Improvement Association (UNIA) movement (pl. 24).[41] A rallying cry for Pan-Africanists, the verse gave its title to the cover designed by Aaron Douglas for the May 1927 issue of *The Crisis: A Record of the Darker Races*, the magazine of the National Association for the Advancement of Colored People (pl. 37). In Fuller's sculpture, Ethiopia is an allegorical figure representing people of African descent globally. She unravels her mummiform bandages in a gesture of self-determination and arousal from unconsciousness. The allegorical Ethiopia also appears in Loïs Mailou Jones's *The Ascent of Ethiopia* (pl. 23), a painterly vision of racial uplift. Jones's Black queen wears a regal ancient Egyptian vulture headdress and observes the progress of her people as they attain creative and economic autonomy. Malvin Gray Johnson's cubistic depiction of an enthroned Black pharaoh, *Negro Pharaoh–Eighteenth Dynasty* (pl. 40), ascribes royalty to ancient Black identity.

The painter Aaron Douglas was perhaps the greatest proponent of adopting ancient Egypt as a source and symbol for images of the Harlem Renaissance zeitgeist of Black uplift. Douglas incorporated circular forms as fractions of color and light—the modernist painterly tendency known as orphism—with a novel adaptation of the ancient Egyptian convention of presenting the figure in profile, often in silhouette, with faceted limbs akin to those shown from multiple perspectives in ancient Egyptian bas-reliefs. *Let My People Go* (pl. 36) is a masterpiece that demonstrates the conflation of the religious and political significance of ancient Egypt for people of the African diaspora. It reflects the Black American affiliation with the plight of the biblical Israelites while understanding the Egyptians to be Black Africans. Douglas's painting *Building More Stately Mansions* (pl. 38), like Jones's *The Ascent of Ethiopia*, presents a reverie of Black progress that synthesizes monumental ancient African symbols like the pyramid, the sphinx, and the triumphal arch with icons of modern America: the skyscraper and the church steeple. Masculine shades wield agricultural and architectural implements while a seated figure leads two children in the study of a globe-like orb that emanates circles of light throughout the composition. Other major artists associated with the Harlem Renaissance, such as Jacob Lawrence, incorporated ancient Egyptian-style figuration into depictions of modern Black subjects, as seen in his *Their children were forced to work in the fields. They could not go to school*, panel 24 from The Migration Series (fig. 9). The ancient Egyptian–inspired Afrocentrism of this era wasn't limited to the United States. In 1923 the Jamaican-born sculptor Ronald Moody moved to London, where at the British Museum he encountered ancient Egyptian art and was inspired to make hieratic wooden sculptures carved from single blocks, like the extraordinary *Tacet (Head)* (pl. 41).

LOOKING BACK

The polemics and aesthetics of the Harlem Renaissance and the activities of the nineteenth- and early twentieth-century Black scholars relating to ancient Egypt would in turn be inspirational for later generations of Black artists. *Harlem Encore* (pl. 6), Terry Adkins's commissioned installation for the Metro-North Railroad Harlem–125th Street station bridge, created in 1999, appropriates a sphinx that Aaron Douglas had designed for the cover of the magazine *Fire!!* in 1926 (pl. 35). Adkins had attended Fisk University, where he regularly encountered Douglas, who had taught there for decades. Adkins's polychromed wood diptych relief *Oxidation Blue 1* (pl. 4) refers both to ancient Egypt, in the doubled forms' evocation of bird sarcophagi and azure patina, and to George Washington Carver's discovery of a formula for "Egyptian Blue."[42] *Langston Hughes' Rivers* (pl. 155), a cosmogram by Houston Conwill, pays homage to "The Negro Speaks of Rivers," an acclaimed poem by the preeminent writer of the Harlem Renaissance, published in the June 1921 issue of *The Crisis*. The protagonist of Hughes's poem boasts, "I looked upon the Nile and raised the pyramids above it." Conwill's design, best known for the corresponding floor mosaic at the New York Public Library's Schomburg Center for Research in Black Culture, under which Hughes's remains are interred, schematically maps the poem's fluvial points of reference: Euphrates, Congo, Mississippi, Nile (see fig. 40).

     Flight into Egypt

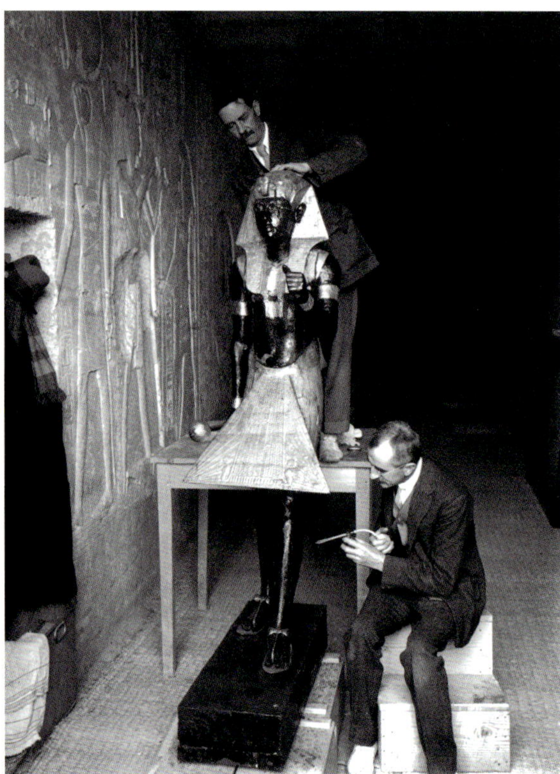

Fig. 11. Harry Burton (British, 1879–1940). Arthur Mace (standing) and Alfred Lucas (sitting) working inside the makeshift "laboratory" (set up in KV 15, the tomb of Sethos II) on the conservation of one of the two sentinel statues from the Antechamber (Carter no. 22), 1924. Griffith Institute, University of Oxford, England

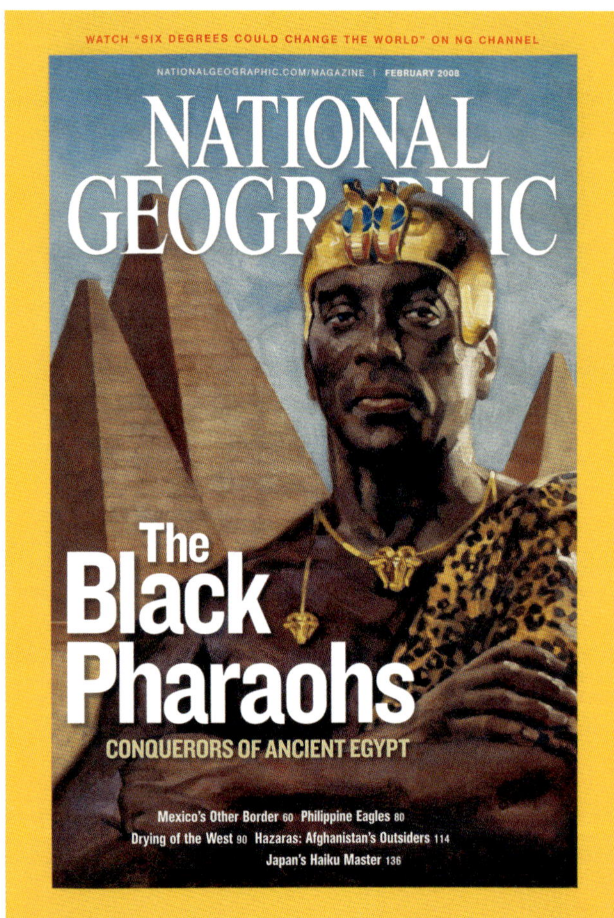

Fig. 12. Cover of National Geographic 213, no. 2 (February 2008)

Similarly, Steffani Jemison and Jamal Cyrus's installation *Alpha's Bet Is Not Over Yet* (pl. 34) is a reading room and discussion space inspired by the energy and politics of historically radical and independent Black publications. The interactive newsstand display features complete reproductions of more than five hundred issues of Black periodicals published between 1900 and 1940, including *The Crisis*; *The Messenger: World's Greatest Negro Monthly*; *Opportunity: A Journal of Negro Life*; and *The Crusader*. These volumes, which include journalistic, literary, and poetic texts, commercial illustrations, and reproductions of artworks in a variety of mediums, collectively encapsulate a major representation of twentieth-century Black modernism. Furthermore, from the pharaonic masthead logo of *The Crisis* (fig. 10) to articles reporting on archaeological activities, much of the imagery and content of these periodicals reflects Black communities' claims to and sustained interest in ancient Egypt. Designed to encourage browsing of the materials, concentrated reading, and conversation, *Alpha's Bet* investigates approaches to language, the written word, self-education, and democratic distributions of knowledge.

GREY AREA

The reception of ancient Egypt is historically contentious and reflects the division of modern society along racial lines. The debate on the racial identity of ancient Egyptians dates to the codification of the modern concept of race by Europeans during the advent of colonization and was further provoked by archaeological discoveries (fig. 11), with anachronism serving as a linchpin in this ongoing discourse. The discussion of race or lack thereof in displays of ancient Egyptian art in Western museums often reflects institutional misgivings on the subject. In 2019, *Ancient Nubia Now*, an exhibition at the Museum of Fine Arts, Boston, addressed how the distinctions between ancient Egypt and its Nubian neighbors to the south (in what is today the Sudanese Nile Valley) ascribed by early Egyptologists echoed their own racial prejudices and asserted that the cultures were more enmeshed than previously understood. Eurocentric archaeologists conceded that ancient Nubians were undeniably Black Africans. In modern times, the ancient Nubians who periodically ruled Egypt were dubbed the Black pharaohs (fig. 12).

Consistent with Anglo-American parlance, the term "Black pharaohs" connotes an alternate form of the linguistic norm, the (non-Black, implicitly white) pharaoh. Popular culture is an extension of societal values and assumptions. Hollywood has promulgated a notion of ancient Egypt inspired by European and American cultural biases, modeling ancient Egyptian royalty on British monarchy and projecting the dynamics of modern racism onto the past. In the iconic film *Cleopatra* (1963), starring white actress Elizabeth Taylor, the titular queen's servile throne bearers are caricatures of Black Africans, played by actors coated in jet-black body paint (fig. 13).

Fred Wilson's provocative yet nuanced installation *Grey Area (Brown version)* (pl. 42) powerfully visualizes the stakes of the color line in the reception of ancient Egypt. Five replicas of the famed bust of Nefertiti, the Eighteenth Dynasty queen and chief consort of the pharaoh Akhenaten, now in the Neues

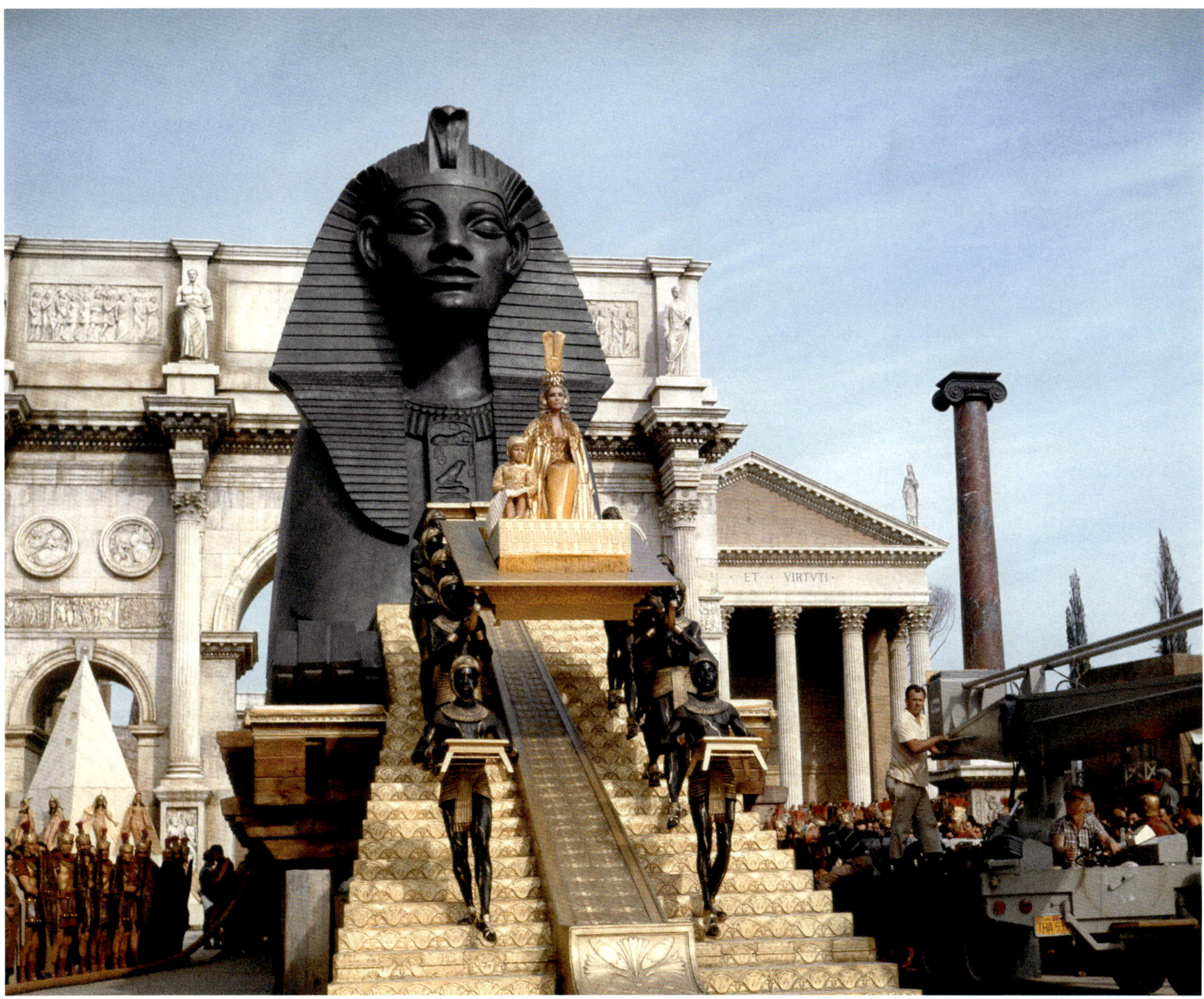

Fig. 13. Production still from **Cleopatra**, directed by Joseph L. Mankiewicz, 20th Century Fox, 1963

Museum, Berlin, ranging from pale beige to dark brown, convey her tremendous value as a symbol of Black beauty and empowerment in contemporary Black culture, while raising—but not settling—the debate around her racial identity (and that of ancient Egyptians generally). Wilson alludes to this historical irresolution in the work's title. The pentaptych sculptural installation is a melanistic alternate to the grayscale version that was the centerpiece of Wilson's installation for the 1993 Whitney Biennial titled *Re:Claiming Egypt*.

ROYALTY AND RACIAL PRIDE

Diasporic Black identity was forged by two major factors: on the one hand, the brutal dispersion of Africans by Europeans— who othered them racially and forced them and generations of their descendants to perform uncompensated labor while stripping them of their specific identities, histories, and cultural and religious practices—and, on the other, the endeavors of self-determination to reconstruct those debased and erased identities. Ancient Egyptian artists modeled images of royalty possessing the same brown skin tones that are demeaned in modern European and American societies. These pharaonic images appealed to Black artists, who used forms of appropriation such as juxtaposition and reenactment to create images of Black royalty that fostered racial pride. *Egyptian Heritage* (pl. 43) proclaims Loïs Mailou Jones's identification with the legacy and lineage of ancient Egypt. The self-portrait—conjoining an image of the artist with a depiction

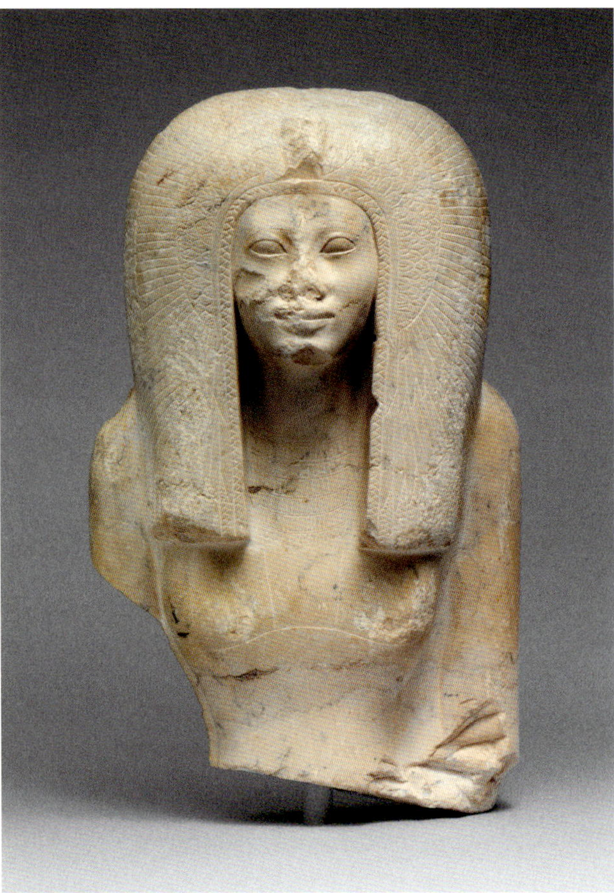

of Nefertiti—incorporates ancient motifs and her own modern Black subjectivity. Jean-Michel Basquiat's prismatic and palimpsestic painting *Kings of Egypt II* (pl. 165) overlays a black ground with textual and graphic references to ancient Egypt, including alternate orthographic manifestations of the name of Ramesses II with Arabic and Roman numerals; a skeletal yellow and blue portrait of the red-crowned pharaoh and schematic depiction of a pyramid in yellow; the artist's signature crown and skull motifs; gestural marks; and both descriptive and cryptic text. Using the photographic language of comparative evidence, Lorraine O'Grady's *Miscegenated Family Album* (pls. 50–53) suggests, through sixteen diptychs, visual resemblances and narrative connections between the family of Nefertiti and that of the Boston-born, New York–based artist. Lorna Simpson's collage *Older Queen* (pl. 56) splices a photograph of a carved wooden statuette of Queen Tiye, the mother of Akhenaten, with the portrait of a Black fashion model. Genevieve Gaignard's photograph *Kings and Queens* (pl. 63) highlights the appropriation of ancient Egyptian motifs of royalty within Black urban landscapes, as do the murals by Jamal Lance, Menelek III, and Kiambu Zawadi for the Bedford Bowling Center, formerly in Brooklyn (pl. 62). In Gaignard's self-portrait, the Los Angeles–based artist leans against a signpost wearing a sweatshirt emblazoned with the word "Queens" and illustrations of Black

women; among the portraits of historically significant Black men in the mural behind her is a depiction of Tutankhamun—colloquially, King Tut.

Reenactment of ancient Egyptian royalty is also a recurrent theme in Black musical history. A captivating poster from 1934 for the pageant *"O, Sing a New Song"* (pl. 105) promises a spectacular musical journey set in ancient Egypt, with an all-Black cast—a feature reflecting both de facto racial segregation and Black solidarity. Black American soprano Leontyne Price broke barriers when in 1957 she debuted in the operatic role of the Egyptian princess Aida, rather than a white woman in blackface as was traditional (pl. 107). From cover illustrations to lyrical content, records spanning the modern musical forms of the African diaspora evince the enduring allure of ancient Egypt to Black musicians and entertainers. Some record cover designs depict key ancient Egyptian sites and incorporate hieroglyphs, like Earth, Wind & Fire's *All 'n All* (pl. 117), which features an illustration by Shusei Nagaoka of the Great Temple of Ramesses II at Abu Simbel, while others portray the musical protagonist in ancient Egyptian guise, as does Danny Hastings's infamous cover for the Nas album *I Am . . .* (pl. 135). Music-related film, specifically the advent of cinematically staged music videos, reflects these tendencies. In an episode of the television series *Black Journal* (pl. 140), the musician Alice Coltrane remarks that playing the harp "makes me recall Egypt, ancient Egypt, it makes me seem to remember that I have a past or a history there somewhere."[43] The video for DJ and music producer The Egyptian Lover's 1986 hit "Freak-A-Holic" features interiors embellished with murals depicting ancient Egyptian gods and goddesses, and replica statuary (pl. 141). Michael Jackson's epic music video for "Remember the Time," costarring Eddie Murphy, Iman, and Magic Johnson, was the first major Hollywood-style film production featuring Black actors as ancient Egyptian royalty. In the opening sequence of Beyoncé Knowles-Carter's award-winning documentary film *Homecoming* (pl. 142), dancers bedecked in bodysuits adorned with the image of King Tut strut in synchrony before Queen Bey appears in a cape bedazzled with the profile bust of Queen Nefertiti. The bust of Nefertiti is a recurrent motif in the expansive iconography that Awol Erizku has employed since the beginning of his artistic career to address race, identity, and contested cultural histories, and which draws on references ranging from culture coded as "urban" to advertising and the art historical canon. Erizku's visually striking *Nefertiti–Miles Davis* (pl. 143), a mirrored bust of Nefertiti suspended from the ceiling and rotating like a disco-ball, draws inspiration from jazz great Miles Davis's 1968 album *Nefertiti* (pl. 111) and embodies the nexus of music and visual art expressing diasporic connection to ancient Egypt.

BLACK POWER

In the 1960s, ancient Egypt was explicitly claimed by the proponents of Black Power and the civil rights movement. The untitled photograph by Louis Draper known as *Girl with Egyptian Mural* (pl. 57) is a compelling image of a young Harlemite raising her fist in the emblematic gesture of the Black Power movement. Draper captures the beautiful alignment of the girl's fist and the raised arm of the pharaoh depicted in the urban mural behind her. In a tender drawing by Emory Douglas, Revolutionary Artist and former Minister of Culture of the Black Panther Party, a pendant ankh adorns a mother's neck, reflecting the popular dissemination of the notion of Black communities' connection with ancient Egypt (pl. 58). Oasa DuVerney's intricate graphite and pulverized gold drawing *Assata Shakur as Ahmes Nefertari* (pl. 60) casts the Black Panther heroine as an incarnation of the first great royal wife of the Eighteenth Dynasty, wearing a headdress depicted in *Upper Part of the Seated Statue of a Queen* (ca. 1580–1550 BCE) in The Met collection (fig. 14).

There are many degrees of reclamation; one can distinguish between efforts to restore Egypt to Africa conceptually and explicit claims to ancient Egyptian heritage within the African diaspora. The fact that transhistorical claims of authenticity linking modern categories of ethnic identity with ancient identities are problematic has been the subject of many an art historical study.[44] What distinguishes the appropriation of—or retreat to—ancient Egyptian aesthetics in Black communities from, say, the Nazi adoption of classical Greece as a fictional forebear, Benito Mussolini's evocation of ancient Rome, or Anglo-American claims to Greco-Roman heritage is the pursuit of a claim for liberation rather than the reinforcement of dominant hegemonies. Moreover, the work examined by *Flight into Egypt* is anathema to the colonial project that attended those social and cultural formations.[45] As Jennifer Trimble comments, "'Distortion' is inherent in any appropriation, and this shift"—here, the engagement of modern and contemporary Black practitioners with ancient Egypt—"involves neither unbroken continuity nor a complete semiotic break," in other words, a rupture with previously signified meanings.[46]

EGYPTIAN ARTISTS AND AFRICA

Especially in the United States, much of the recent informal discourse around ancient Egypt has concerned the diasporic dichotomy of white versus Black interpretations evoked by Frederick Douglass.[47] Makeda Best's essay in this volume discusses the high hopes for Egyptian participation in the Pan-Africanism of the 1950s and 1960s. In Egypt, contemporary artists who engage with ancient themes primarily focus on promoting or interrogating the ownership of Egyptian cultural patrimony and exploring their own identities in relation to the African continent and diaspora. They include the Egyptian and American artist Iman Issa, whose sculpture *Heritage Studies #7* (pl. 69) is one of the most iconic works in an ongoing series that imaginatively recasts ancient Egyptian artifacts and architectural remnants as geometrically abstract, minimal sculptures. A slender tripod topped with an elegant open scissor–like wooden form, *Heritage Studies #7* features an accompanying vinyl wall text that describes a quartzite "Statue of King Ahmose / Unifier of the land who established the country's national borders, which it retains to this day." The discrepancy between the text's apocryphal historical reference and the sculpture's emphatically modern minimalist form—what we might call their speculative temporality—provokes productive questions about the stakes and stewardship of history.

Mahmoud Mokhtar and Mahmoud Saïd are considered the fathers of modern Egyptian sculpture and painting respectively; both made foundational contributions to the promotion of Egyptian identity through art. Mokhtar established

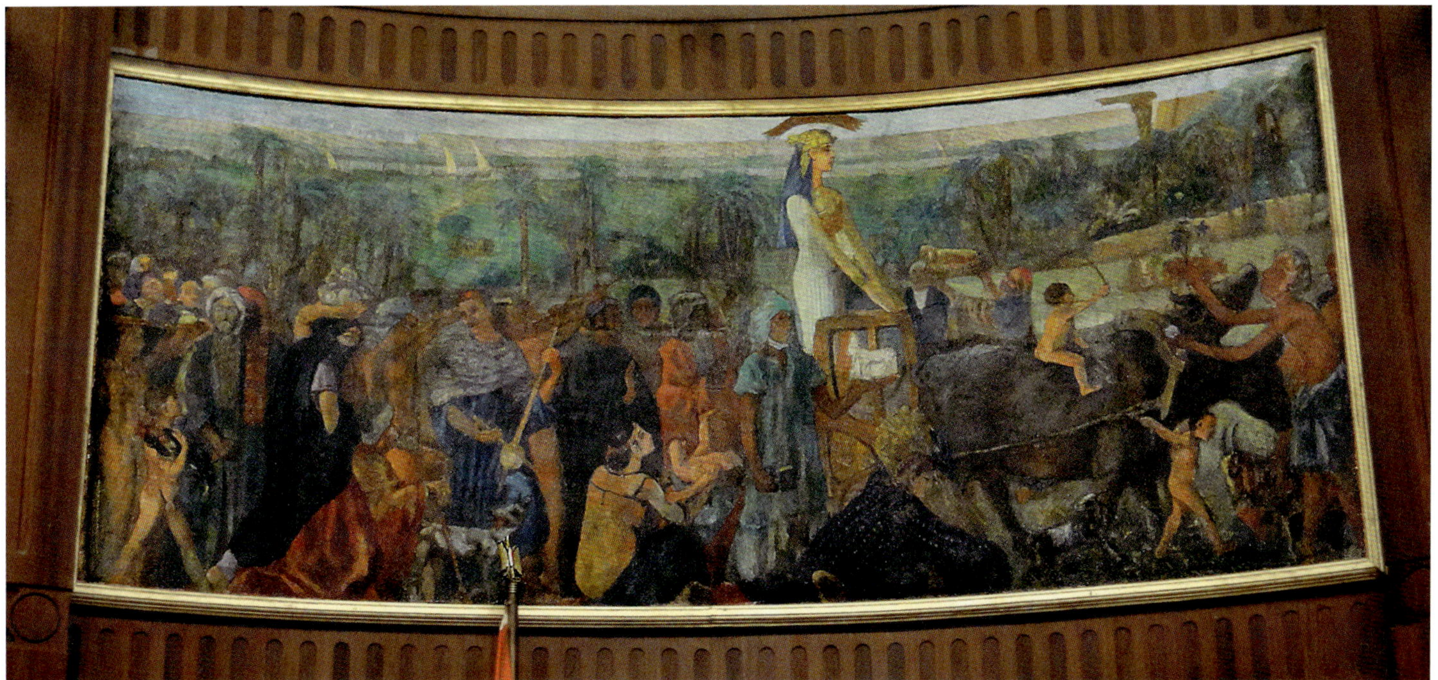

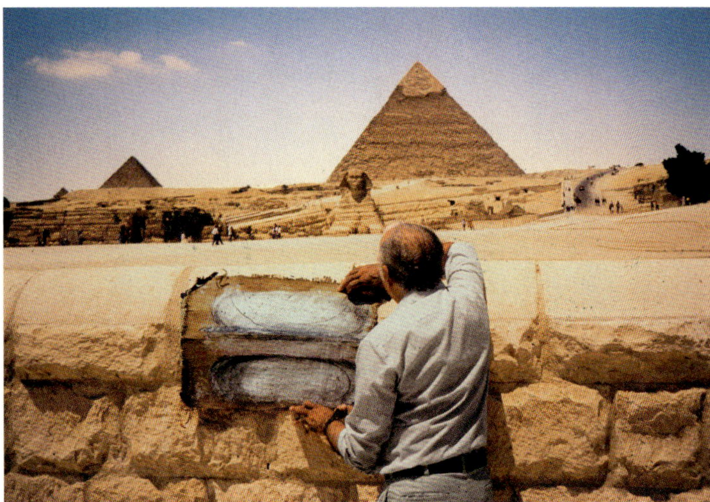

Fig. 16. Unknown photographer. Ed Clark painting en plein air at Giza, 1990s. Estate of Ed Clark

neopharaonism, which is characterized in his artistic practice by the revival of ancient Egyptian sculptural motifs and features idealized modern Egyptian citizens as his subjects. These works asserted a continuity between ancient and modern Egypt, thereby promoting a national self-image free from colonial interlopers. His monumental sculpture *Egypt Awakening (Nahdat Misr)* (pl. 64) is installed in a public square in Cairo. The work celebrated Egyptian independence and, like Meta Vaux Warrick Fuller's *Ethiopia Awakening*, sought to promote a noble history that predated and therefore could supersede recent colonial subjugation. His *Bride of the Nile (Arous El Nil), Bust* (pl. 65) is a more romantically conceived allegory expressing an organic relationship between the people and territory of Egypt. Mahmoud Saïd's *L'invitation au voyage* (pl. 66), a sensual depiction of two figures locked in a shared gaze, is one of the artist's most iconic adaptations of ancient Egyptian figuration. The attenuated features of the figure on the left evoke the hypertrophic anatomies of depictions of royalty mandated during the Amarna period of pharaonic Egypt (ca. 1346–1332 BCE).

Modern and contemporary Egyptian artists work in a range of styles and mediums, from conceptually based practices to traditional craft. Ancient Egypt has been a reference for national symbols in expressly political contexts. Mohamed Naghi's masterpiece *The Egyptian Renaissance, or The Cavalcade of Isis* (fig. 15), a mural-size decoration made for the Parliament of Egypt in 1922, depicts a fete of the cult of Isis as a metaphor for the triumph of the Egyptian state. Maha Maamoun's *Domestic Tourism II* (pl. 68) is a video montage of Egyptian cinema of various genres, from action to comedy to romance, and spanning the 1960s to 1980s. Aggregating scenes that feature the pyramids at Giza, it projects the popular Egyptian imagination of the iconic ancient monuments and adds a dimension to the artist's ongoing exploration of her own identity in the Domestic Tourism series. Iconic ancient Egyptian art has inspired both transgressive and traditional appropria-

tion. Ghada Amer's *Homage à Tut in Black and White* (pl. 67), a painting on bronze, transmutes the celebrated symmetry and frontality of Tutankhamun's funerary mask to a Pop-style portrait of a contemporary Egyptian woman rendered in solid sinuous black lines. New Jersey–based sculptor Armia Malak Khalil began his revival of traditional ancient Egyptian wood carving in Cairo in the 1990s; he continues to be inspired by the archaic sculptures he encounters regularly during his work as a security officer at The Met. *Hope–I Am a Morning Scarab* (pl. 72), a torso-length depiction of a young woman with a large scarab surmounting the crown of her braided hair and a sculpted allusion to painted eyes, was made on the occasion of *Flight into Egypt*.

This desire to connect to the ancient past is also evident in Egyptian media. Two magazines similarly featuring women in the guise of Nefertiti raise questions about the intersection of cultural property and questions of identity. A special issue of the magazine *Al Mussawar*, titled "Nefertiti Speaks" (October 22, 1948), features an illustration of an idealized Egyptian woman wearing the iconic blue crown of Nefertiti (pl. 70). Presented as much a fashion plate as a patriotic symbol, the anonymous model is imbued with the stately bearing and elegant styling of a woman of the newly independent Egyptian state. Almost seventy years later, in November 2017, *Vogue Arabia*'s cover of Barbadian pop singer Rihanna dressed as Nefertiti sparked tremendous controversy (pl. 71). The overwhelming response by Egyptian observers online was that it was inappropriate to portray Rihanna, a Black woman, as the queen. Modern Egyptian perspectives on the relationship between Egyptian society today and ancient Egypt, and on the availability of ancient Egyptian precedents for artistic appropriation vary, with some expressing vehement criticism of creative endeavors by people of African descent—especially Black Americans—that refer to ancient Egypt. Anti-Blackness is a palpable factor in some criticism, as is concern for cultural erasure. Afrocentrism, as explored in *Flight into Egypt*, is a project that does not necessitate denigrating other points of view or identities.

DIASPORIC PILGRIMAGES

Pilgrimage and fellowship are two paradigmatic practices through which peoples of the African diaspora have negotiated the dialectics of distance and proximity, estrangement and familiarity, and distinction from and identification with Egypt and its people, ancient and contemporary, encountered and imagined. The travels of Black Americans to Egypt and their artistic and political engagement with contemporary Egyptian society represent powerful acts of reclamation. A photograph, *Barbara Chase-Riboud at Deir el-Bahri* (pl. 20), is evidence of the artist's adventure in Egypt in 1958. She mimics the crossed-arm gesture of the famous female pharaoh Hatshepsut. Louis Armstrong's visit in 1961, sponsored by the U.S. State Department, is immortalized in an iconic photograph (pl. 73) in which the trumpeter serenades his wife, Lucille, at the Great Sphinx of Giza.[48] Political and religious leader Malcolm X's third trip to Egypt in 1964 was his most thoroughly documented (pl. 75). During this visit he went to pharaonic monuments, Islamic holy places, and modern sites such as the University of Cairo. When he returned to the States, he spoke of both his experience of brotherhood in Egypt and his conviction that ancient Egypt was proof of a noble ancient Black civilization.[49] Malcolm X's travels to Egypt and speeches on the subject were deeply influential to future generations, including artists. Maren Hassinger's mosaic for the MTA Central Park North–110th Street subway station in New York quotes Malcolm X: "I lived in Egypt. I stayed in Egypt, and I was among brothers and I felt the spirit of brotherhood" (pl. 174). Chet Gold's *Mirror Malcolm* (pl. 74) is a screenprint on a mirror that is based on a photograph of Malcolm X's visit to Giza. The title, an imperative to reflect on and emulate the actions, thoughts, and legacy of Malcolm X, points to the work's compelling interactivity; it is complete only in the presence of a viewer. Boxing champion, vocal convert to the Nation of Islam, and political activist Muhammad Ali toured Giza (pl. 76) in 1966, a visit repeated by Mike Tyson in 2019 (pl. 77). Ming Smith's *Womb* (pl. 79) is both a work of art and a document of her travel to Egypt. Embracing an accidental double exposure that layered an image of the artist over one of her son and partner practicing martial arts at the Giza plateau, Smith conflates her identity as a maternal source of life with ancient Egypt as the birthplace of civilization.

The expansion of commercial air travel facilitated access to Egypt for groups in the African diaspora united by profound interest in ancient sites. Since 1980 Ashra Kwesi, co-founder of Kemet Nu Tours with his wife, Merira Kwesi, has led "Know Thyself" excursions through Egypt, teaching groups of Black tourists about Afrocentric cosmology and Kemetology (pl. 80). Some travel to Egypt is motivated by the African diasporic revival of ancient Egyptian spiritual practices. Chester Higgins's vibrant photograph *African American pilgrims dance in honor of ancient spirits. Lake Nasser, Egypt* (pl. 86) captures a ritual scene with practitioners of Kemetic spirituality. Skeptical perspectives are among the diversity of diasporic responses to the notion of connecting or reconnecting with Africa. Glenn Ligon's painting *Gold Nobody Knew Me #1* (pl. 81) cites a Richard Pryor joke that casts doubt on the whole endeavor.[50]

Many in the African diaspora who might never visit Egypt nevertheless had access to ancient Egyptian material culture through museums. The deep connection with ancient Egyptian art felt by Black communities—particularly within urban centers in the United States and Europe—has enabled generations of Black youth to claim their stake in high culture even when these institutions excluded Black artists and audiences by default. The Met in particular has been a catalyst for exploration, creativity, and critique. Eve Arnold's photograph *Black Muslim children at the Metropolitan Museum in New York. They are taught black history* (pl. 88), taken in 1961, shows how a community-based religious group asserted an alternative pedagogy affirming Black identity through local pilgrimages. The group of young learners takes in a seated statue of Hatshepsut.[51] The Black Muslims' Afrocentric teachings deemphasized the history of American enslavement in order to foreground an illustrious ancient African heritage. Rashida Bumbray's video *How High the Moon* (pl. 153), a melodic, visual reverie recorded at The Met featuring the artist's young daughter, reclaims institutional spaces for Black youth.

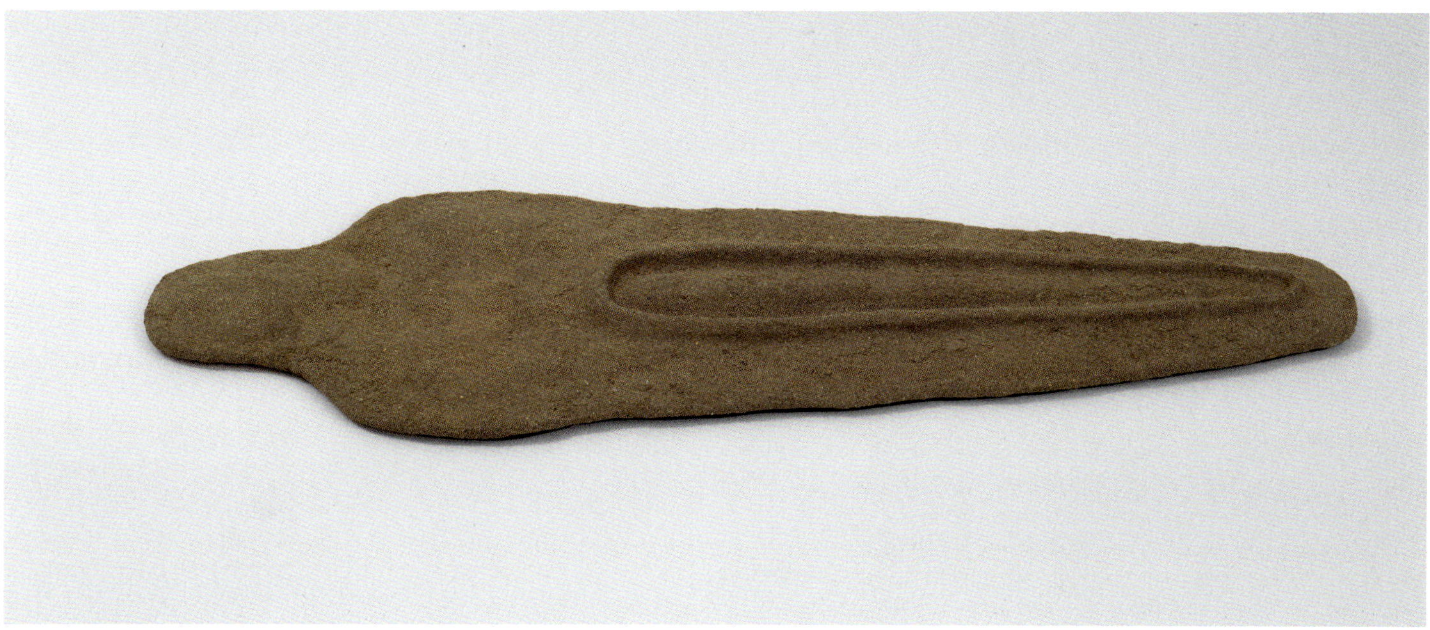

SOCIAL ORGANIZATIONS

The importance of ancient Egypt in the construction of identity
for peoples of the African diaspora is evident in the nomencla-
ture, heraldry, ceremonial practices, and rich material culture of
numerous Black social organizations. The Pyramid Club, a Black
arts and social organization active in Philadelphia from 1937
to 1963, incorporated ancient Egyptian themes in its graphic
identity. The club produced pictorial albums (pls. 82, 83) for its
annual exhibitions (pl. 84). The cover of the 1947–48 album,
for instance, features a photomontage of a fashionable young
woman against the backdrop of the Giza pyramids. Likewise,
the paraphernalia of groups such as the Ancient Egyptian Arabic
Order Nobles Mystic Shrine and the Daughters of Isis amal-
gamate pharaonic logos and masonic garb (pls. 89, 90). Alpha
Phi Alpha, the oldest Black academic fraternity (founded in
1906), prominently features Egyptian imagery in its symbolism, including three heraldic depictions of a sphinx in its logo.
Addison N. Scurlock's *Collage of Photographs of the Alpha Phi
Alpha "Sphinx Club" Fraternity* (pl. 91) features oval portraits of
members of the fraternity surrounded by an illustration of the
Great Sphinx. *Board Meeting* (*Brotherhood Smoke*) (pl. 92), by
artist and fraternity member Derek Fordjour, is a massive and
magnificent painting of a convening of Alpha Phi Alpha members
who clutch pharaonic amulets and practice choreographed step-
ping inspired by ancient Egyptian reliefs under the watch of a
golden bust of Tutankhamun. The influence of ancient Egypt
extends beyond visual motifs to shape even the ethos of these
organizations; the act of surpassing the challenges of joining
Black fraternities and sororities is called "crossing the burning
sands." Beyond fraternal and sororal paraphernalia, esoteric
adornment and commercially available fashion serve as means of
identity projection. The customized creations of Kemetic priest
and jeweler Baaba Heru take inspiration from ancient Egyptian
models (pl. 100). Designer Tremaine Emory's Denim Tears brand
has produced a leather vest and belt embellished with the iconic
bust of Tutankhamun (pls. 97, 98) that pay homage to his father
Tracy's Afrocentric wardrobe from an earlier era.

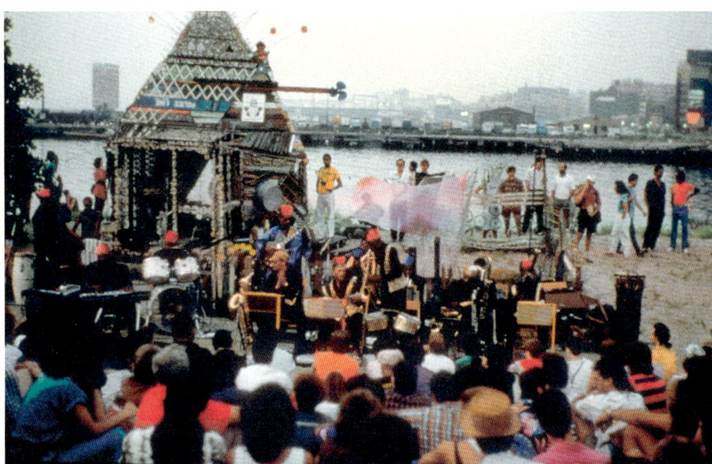

ABSTRACTION AND PERFORMANCE

Although iconographic appropriation dominates the discourse,
abstract forms of appropriation are manifest in Black artists'
evocations of ancient Egyptian movement, materiality, and
space. The history of Black performance art has long been
animated by ancient Egyptian themes. Lorraine O'Grady's
performance *Nefertiti/Devonia Evangeline* (pls. 48, 49), photographed by Freda Leinwand, was an elegant and mournful
elegy to her deceased sister. The images in the slideshow that
served as a backdrop for the performance would later be printed
to form the artist's renowned portfolio *Miscegenated Family
Album* (pls. 50–53). A poster and photographs document *Flying*
(pls. 145–49), a performance in which Maren Hassinger, Ulysses
Jenkins, Senga Nengudi, and Franklin Parker processed through
a Los Angeles park and made synchronized gestures that echoed
those found on ancient Egyptian murals and reliefs. The stage
set designed by musician and multidisciplinary artist Solange
Knowles in 2017 incorporated twin pyramids (pl. 78). Other
contemporary performance artists engaging with this kind
of content include Sidra Bell, Rashida Bumbray, Karon Davis,
Zekkereya El-magharbel, Steffani Jemison, Rashid Johnson,
M. Lamar, Clifford Owens, Kamau Amu Patton, Kaneza Schaal,
and Luke Stewart, all slated to appear at The Met as part of
the *Flight into Egypt* exhibition in recognition of the integral
nature of performance art to the panoply of African diasporic
creative expression.

The textures and sites of ancient Egypt have also
been inspirational to Black artists working in various modes
of abstraction. Ed Clark, a key artist of the generation after
Abstract Expressionism, painted the sweeping strokes of his
Untitled (*Egyptian Series*) (pl. 157) on woven papyrus while
gazing at the horizon of the Giza plateau (fig. 16). The Cuban
American artist Ana Mendieta made *Nile Born* (fig. 17) in Rome
using sand collected from historically and personally significant
locations, including the banks of the Nile. With its mummiform
silhouette evoking rudimentary anthropomorphic glyphs and
ancient burial practices, her sculpture asserts Cuba's African
heritage and affirms the broad diasporic allure of ancient Egypt.
In William T. Williams's monochromatic painting *Nu Nile* (part
of the artist's Shimmer Series) (pl. 154), diagonal clusters of
restrained silver strokes in acrylic paint form a shimmering
moiré pattern evocative of curly hair groomed to form waves.
Williams's cheeky title refers to an iconic Black hair product,
Murray's Nu Nile Hair Slick Dressing Pomade, whose name and
promise of sleekness evoke diasporic affiliation with the Egyptian river. These heterogeneous abstractions connect formal and
conceptual references to ancient Egypt with facets of contemporary Black experience.

The earthbound and the cosmic connect in the work
of gravitationally influential artist, musician, and poet Sun
Ra. In the epic film, *Space Is the Place* (pl. 159; see fig. 41), Sun
Ra plays an extraterrestrial messianic musician who recruits
Black Americans to join a utopian space community inspired
by ancient Egypt. The movie is a hallmark of a creative genre
that has come to be called Afrofuturism, and its striking visu-
als have impacted later generations of artists—Richard Pryor's
aforementioned reference to spacecraft-navigating Black gods is
likely a nod to Sun Ra. Paradoxically, the aesthetics of what has

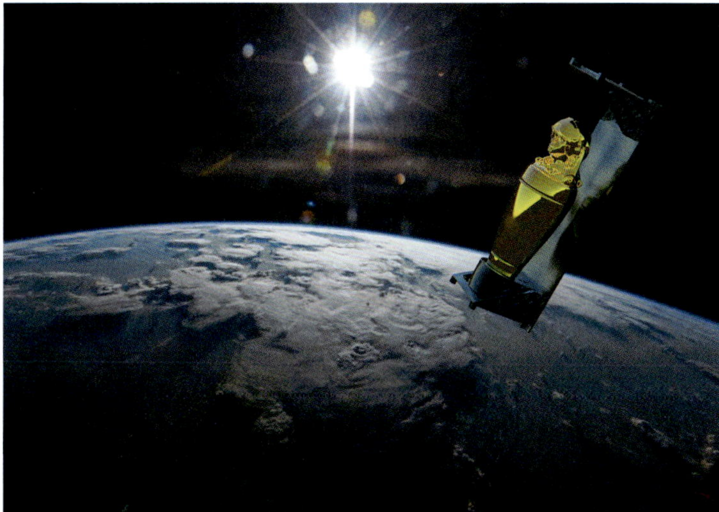

Fig. 19. Tavares Strachan (Bahamian, b. 1979). **ENOCH (Digital Rendering of Display Unit)**, 2015-17. Created in collaboration with the Los Angeles County Museum of Art as part of the Art + Technology Lab initiative

been dubbed "Afrofuturism" are as indebted to the aesthetics of ancient Africa as they are to any Western notion of technologically advanced aesthetics; in other words, Afrofuturism is animated by Afro*past*ism. Rather than wedding a purely modern futurism to the atavistic aesthetics of ancient Egypt, Sun Ra and artists in his wake recognize and amplify the inherently cosmic characteristics of ancient Egyptian art. For Sun Ra, the ways in which ancient Egyptians associated their lives on earth with astral phenomena supersede the aspirations of the twentieth-century space age. In 1985, Sun Ra was invited by David Hammons to perform in front of *Delta Spirit*, an installation created in Battery Park City by Hammons, Jerry Barr, and Angela Valerio that both in form and title refers to the American South, the ancient pyramidal form, and perhaps the Nile (fig. 18). Interdisciplinary artist Kamau Amu Patton's *The Past and Other Dreams* (pl. 152), a sound work incorporating recordings from the archival Sun Ra/El Saturn Collection, underscores Sun Ra's oneiric concept of a regenerative conduit to ancient aesthetics. Ellen Gallagher's *Abu Simbel* (pl. 162), a complex and dimensional collaged print with hand additions, imagines the visitation of Sun Ra's spaceship to the Ramesside Nubian temple. Neatly coiffed nurses beside the monumental pharaohs evoke characters from the film. In the photomontage *Rajé to the Rescue* (pl. 163), the Jamaican-born artist Renee Cox's time-traveling, Afrocentric superheroine alter-ego Rajé witnesses Napoleonic troops taking aim at the face of the Great Sphinx at Giza, visualizing an apocryphal but widely believed narrative that the iconic monument's nose was intentionally shot off in disdain of its phenotypically African features.[52]

Black artists have been likewise inspired by the futuristic qualities—the minimalism, otherworldly scale, and purity—of quintessentially ancient Egyptian structures and forms, as well as by the advanced, code-like system of hieroglyphs. Documentary Polaroids of psychedelic hieroglyphic murals by Ayé Aton, a member of Sun Ra's Arkestra (as his musical ensemble is known), attest to the immersion and seamlessness of art and life in the Arkestra's commune (pls. 160, 161). Jeff Donaldson's *Message from Tehuti* (pl. 164) is a masterful depiction of a drummer cloaked in a shower of hieroglyphs that seem to emanate from his instrument, evoking a computational synesthesia. With calligraphic marks reminiscent of hieratic script and its abstract composition, based on a journalistic photo of a violent uprising, Julie Mehretu's *Stelae 3 (Bardu)* evokes an intermediate state of being as expressed by a term in contemporary Egyptian dialect (pl. 166).

As profoundly as they feel and express affinities for myth and science fiction, contemporary Black artists have also been keen to apply scientific concepts in works inspired by ancient Egypt. Fred Eversley, a former NASA lens engineer, created a sculptural step pyramid comprising gilded sheets of lens-grade plexiglass (pl. 167). Tavares Strachan's sculpture and functional satellite *ENOCH (display unit)* (pl. 168) honors Robert Henry Lawrence Jr. (1935–1967), the first African American astronaut, who tragically died in a crashed flight. Inspired by the ancient Egyptian canopic jars that stored the organs of mummified persons, it features a gilded urn topped with a sculpted portrait of Lawrence; the display unit corresponds to the *ENOCH* satellite launched on a Space X rocket in 2018 (fig. 19). The architects Jennifer Newsom and Tom Carruthers, known as Dream The Combine, conceived *Pyramidion* (pl. 170) as an evolution of the concept for their steam-producing sculpture, *Make it Rain*, which they designed for a public plaza in Vancouver, Canada, in 2014. Ancient Egyptian obelisks emblematized the projection of the sun's rays toward earth. Inverted and reconfigured without steam in its presentation at The Met, Dream The Combine's obelisk connotes movement from the earth to the stars.

NEW MONUMENTS

Generations of Black artists have been inspired by archetypes of ancient Egyptian architecture and monumental sculpture. Mildred Thompson's *Stele* (pl. 169) is the artist's take on the

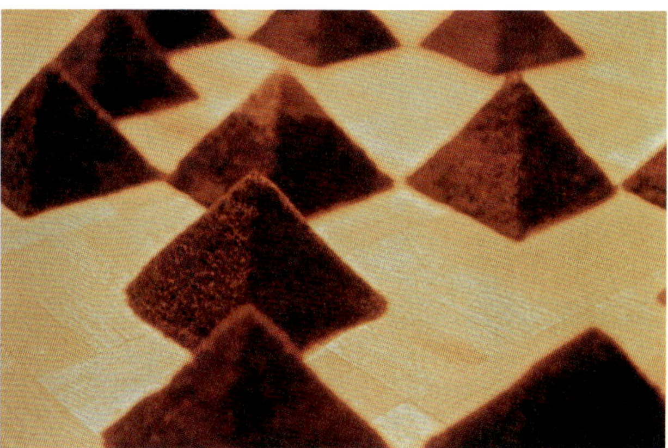

Fig. 20. David Hammons (American, b. 1943). Detail of **Hair Pyramids**, installed at Just Above Midtown, New York, 1976

Egyptian funerary marker rendered in the vernacular mode of domestic architecture of the American South. Its irregularly stacked and painted found wooden slats signal objects of use and evoke labor. The pyramid is perhaps the quintessentially inspirational ancient Egyptian architectural form. David Hammons's 1976 installation *Hair Pyramids* (fig. 20) consisted of a floor-based arrangement of pyramidal piles of hair collected from barbershops frequented by Black men. Hammons's precarious structures merge the phenomenological vocabulary of the modernist grid with essentialist politics. In a trio of contemporaneous untitled two-dimensional works, culled curly hair is enmeshed with pulp to form laid paper pyramids (pls. 171-73). Abstraction serves as a vehicle for exuberance in Maren Hassinger's *Love (Pyramid)* (pl. 175), a floor-to-ceiling installation of pink plastic bags, each inflated by human breath and containing a note that says "love." Rashid Johnson's painterly relief *Pyramid* (pl. 176) features shelves that assemble polyvalent objects and marks, including shea butter, record covers, and spray paint, signifiers of Black culture and consumption. Contemplating the contemporary crisis of African immigration in Europe, Sam Gilliam was inspired to revisit elemental forms of ancient African architecture in a series that includes his stained wood and aluminum sculpture *Pyramid* (pl. 178).

In recent years, leading Black women artists have evoked the monumentality of ancient Egyptian art with ambitious sculptural and architectural works. Kara Walker's massive temporary sculpture *A Subtlety, or the Marvelous Sugar Baby* (fig. 21, pl. 179), displayed in the defunct Domino Sugar Refinery in Brooklyn, New York, in the summer of 2014, conflated the

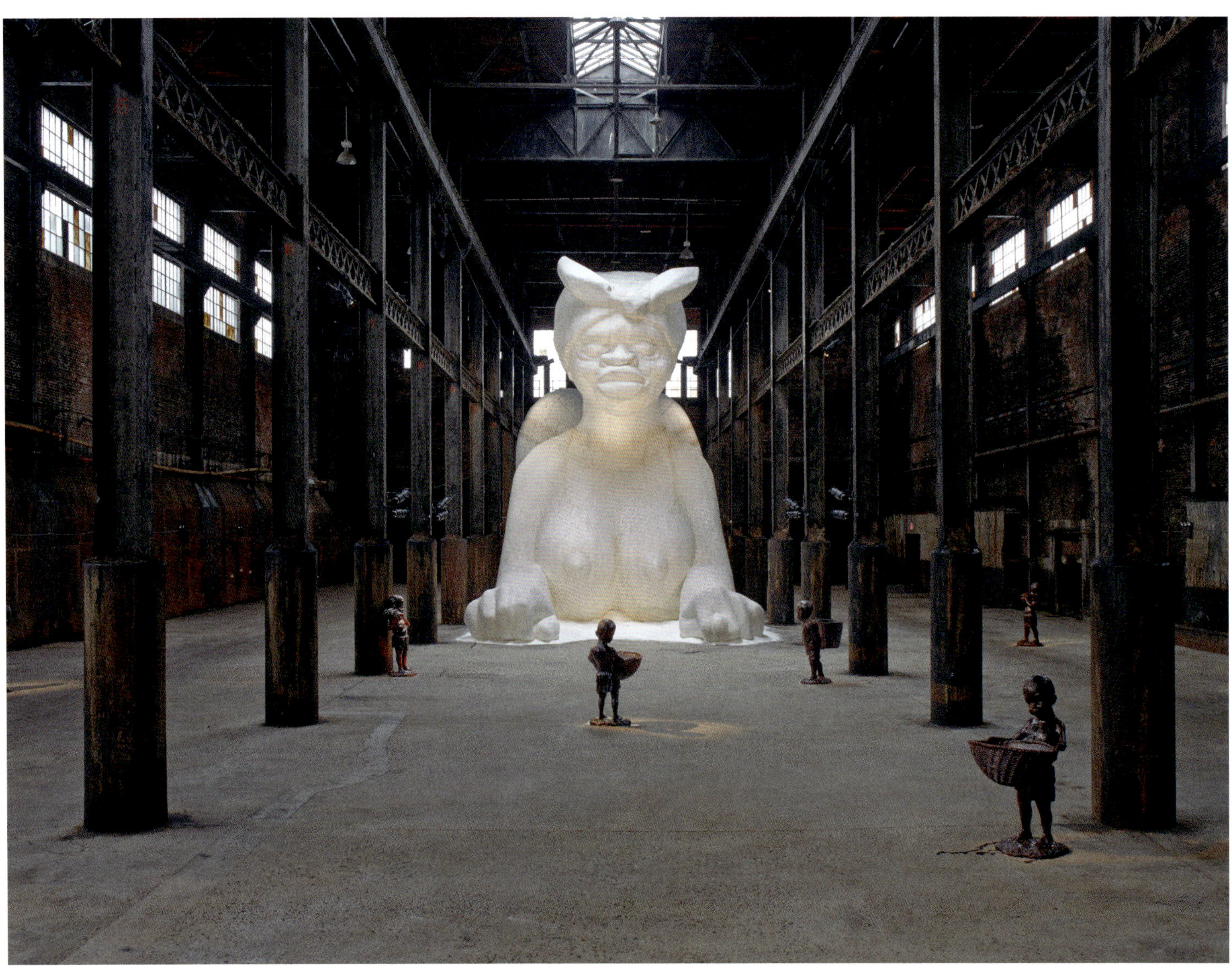

Fig. 21. Kara Walker (American, b. 1969). **A Subtlety, or the Marvelous Sugar Baby: an Homage to the unpaid and overworked Artisans who have refined our Sweet tastes from the cane fields to the kitchens of the New World on the Occasion of the demolition of the Domino Sugar Refining Plant**, 2014. Polystyrene foam and sugar, H. 35½ ft. (10.8 m), W. 26 ft. (7.9 m), D. 75½ ft. (23 m). Domino Sugar Refinery, A project by Creative Time, Brooklyn, New York, 2014

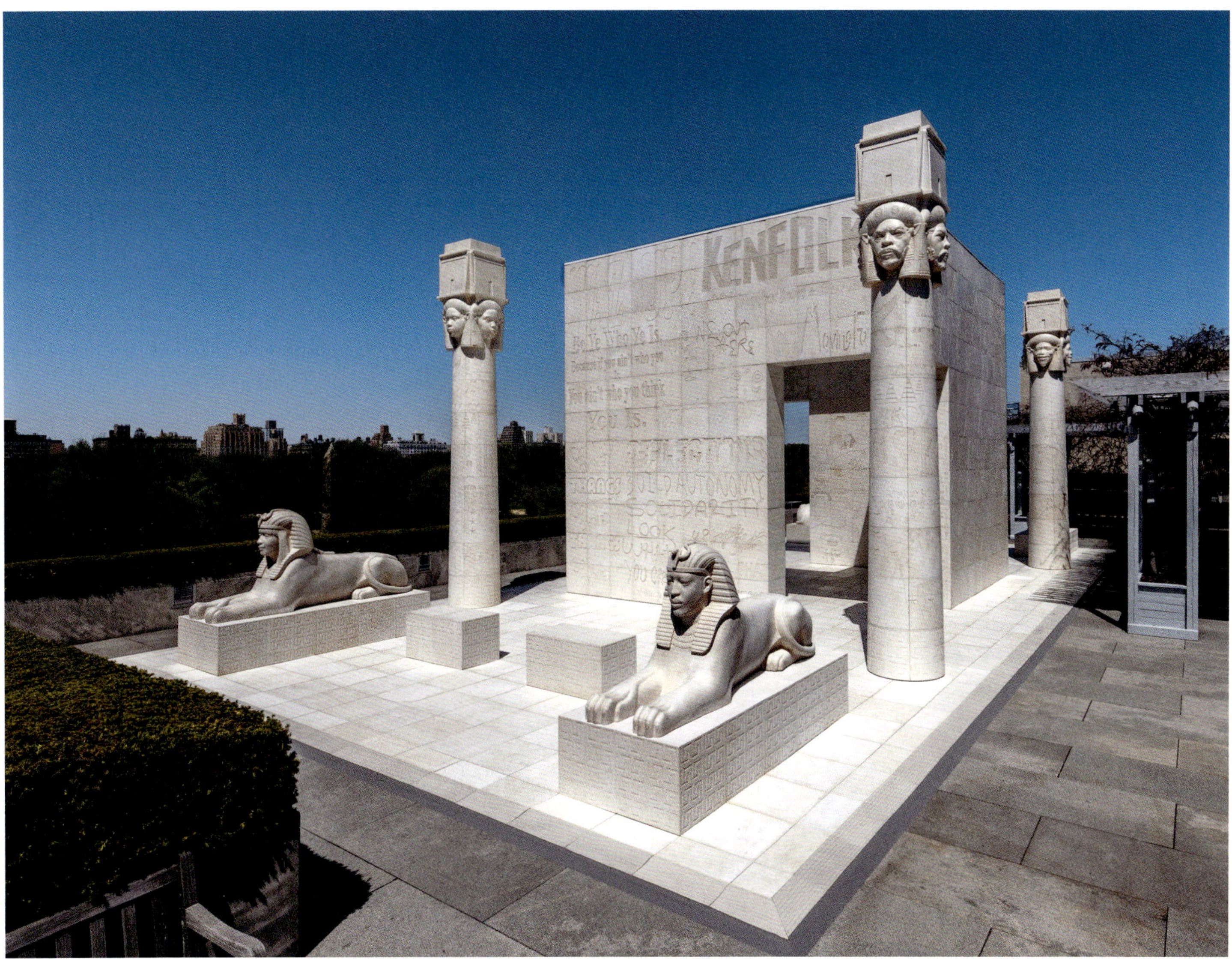

Fig. 22. Lauren Halsey (American, b. 1987). **the eastside of south central los angeles hieroglyph prototype architecture (I)**, 2022. The Iris and Gerald B. Cantor Roof Garden, The Metropolitan Museum of Art, New York

figure of a reclining sphinx, ancient Egyptian symbol of pharaonic might, with a submissive and hypersexualized mammy figure. The hybrid form reconciles poles of experience: the glory of ancient Egypt and the subjugation of Africans in the United States. *Sharifa*, a large standing bronze figure by Simone Leigh, depicts the writer Sharifa Rhodes-Pitts in the guise of an ancient Egyptian official (pl. 181). With the gravitas and grace of an ancient totem, she extends her hands over the skirt that seamlessly falls from her bare chest to the floor as a solid form akin to the long, protruding kilt and extended foot that characterize ancient statues of striding sovereigns. By depicting the female author and scholar in this manner, Leigh's sculpture both adopts and subverts tradition. Lauren Halsey's installation for The Met's Iris and Gerald B. Cantor Roof Garden in 2023, titled *the eastside of south central los angeles hieroglyph prototype architecture (I)*, is a full-scale structure with figurative and textural embellishments inspired by both ancient

Egyptian and modern utopian architectural precedents (fig. 22). Halsey's aesthetic emerges from her community. She is especially attuned to the vernacular expressions of connection with ancient Egypt that are ubiquitous in predominantly Black neighborhoods like her own in South Central Los Angeles. Many of the phrases, fonts, and forms etched into the structure are culled from the street. Halsey's recent squared gypsum columns with painted, collaged, and carved surfaces similarly take inspiration from both ancient Egypt and the artist's contemporary urban environment (pls. 182, 183). Halsey plans to reassemble her building for The Met Roof Garden in her neighborhood, consummating its essence in the realm of public space.[53]

The Problem of the Color Line: Black Americans and the Field of Egyptology

Andrea Myers Achi

In the early twentieth century, many prominent European and American scholars perpetuated the idea that the "darker races" were the least culturally advanced because Africa lacked a deep history, an argument predicated on disavowing the link between the northern regions of the continent (including Egypt) and regions below the Sahara.[1] This bias had deep roots. In his *Lectures on the Philosophy of History* (1837), Georg Wilhelm Friedrich Hegel noted that Egypt was an independent civilization that was isolated singularly in Africa and that the rest of the continent had "no historical part of the World; it has no movement or development to exhibit. Historical movements in it—that is, in its northern part—belong to the Asiatic or European World."[2] In many respects, the question of Egypt's Africanity comes out of the Pan-African movement and the development of Egyptology in the early nineteenth century.

Tensions between notions of race—which itself is not an empirical term and has been used to assume that physical differences equate to cultural differences—and the history of Africa versus the history of Egypt evolved in tandem with the new academic discipline of Egyptology.[3] The field emerged after Napoleon's conquests of Egypt (1798–1801), when primary source material from ancient Egypt became more accessible to European scholars.[4] The scholar and activist W. E. B. Du Bois remarked that the discipline of Egyptology had developed alongside the African slave trade: "Few scientists during that period dared to associate the Negro race with humanity, much less with civilization."[5] Interest in the topic increased in the late nineteenth century following the abolition of slavery in the United States. Colonialism was also deeply implicated: Hegel's denial of Africa as historical and Du Bois's assessment of the impact of racism on the study of history are reflected in the ways that modern scholars have considered the development of Egyptology and more recent conversations about

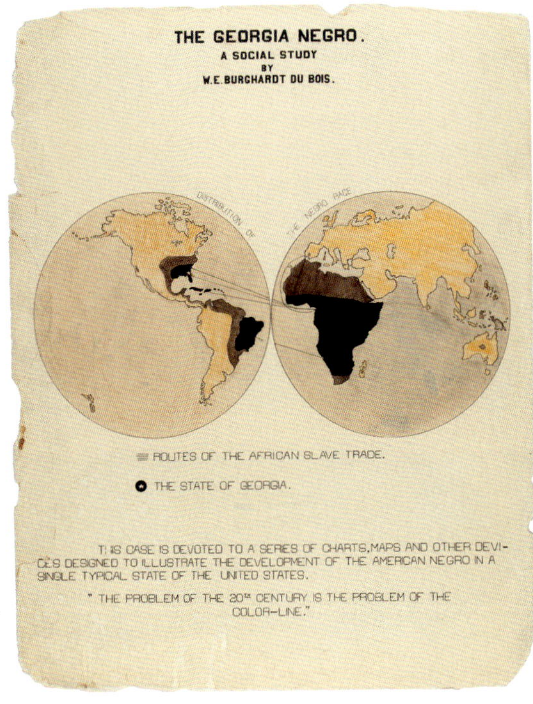

Fig. 23. W. E. B. Du Bois (American, 1868–1963). **The Georgia Negro: A Social Study**, 1900. Ink and watercolor on paper, 28 x 22 in. (71 x 56 cm). Library of Congress Prints and Photographs Division, Washington, D.C. (Lot 11931, no. 1 [P&P])

colonialism and power. For example, as the Egyptian scholar Hany Rashwan has noted, "Egyptology and modern Western imperialism grew up together hand in hand. European scholars created Egyptology as an academic discipline, and they kept watering its branches of knowledge until they thought that this ancient African culture was appearing to them as part of their own Eurocentric world heritage."[6]

Complicating the interpretation of ancient Egypt and Egyptians in the United States were definitions of race and racial purity that were articulated through laws such as the "one-drop rule," which asserted that anyone with "one drop" of African blood was legally Negro, or Black.[7] As Du Bois stated in his address "To the Nations of the World" at the first Pan-African Conference in 1900, "The problem of the twentieth century is the problem of the colour line, the question as to how far differences of race, which show themselves chiefly in the colour of the skin and the texture of the hair, are going to be made, hereafter, the basis of denying to over half the world the right of sharing to their utmost ability the opportunities and privileges of modern civilisation. To be sure, the darker races are today the least advanced in culture according to European standards. This has not, however, always been the case in the past."[8] This color line was visualized in one of the maps produced as part of Du Bois's "Exhibit of American Negroes," displayed at the 1900 Exposition Universelle in Paris (fig. 23). The image also represented how northern Africa had been separated from the regions south of the Sahara through the supposed racial compositions of the regions, redeploying "the Western methods of cartography that had been used to marginalize and exploit black life by inscribing the black world back into history and geography."[9] In the context of these nineteenth- and twentieth-century complexities (or lack thereof), Black and white scholars alike tended to ignore Egypt's actual multiethnic and multicultural heritage,

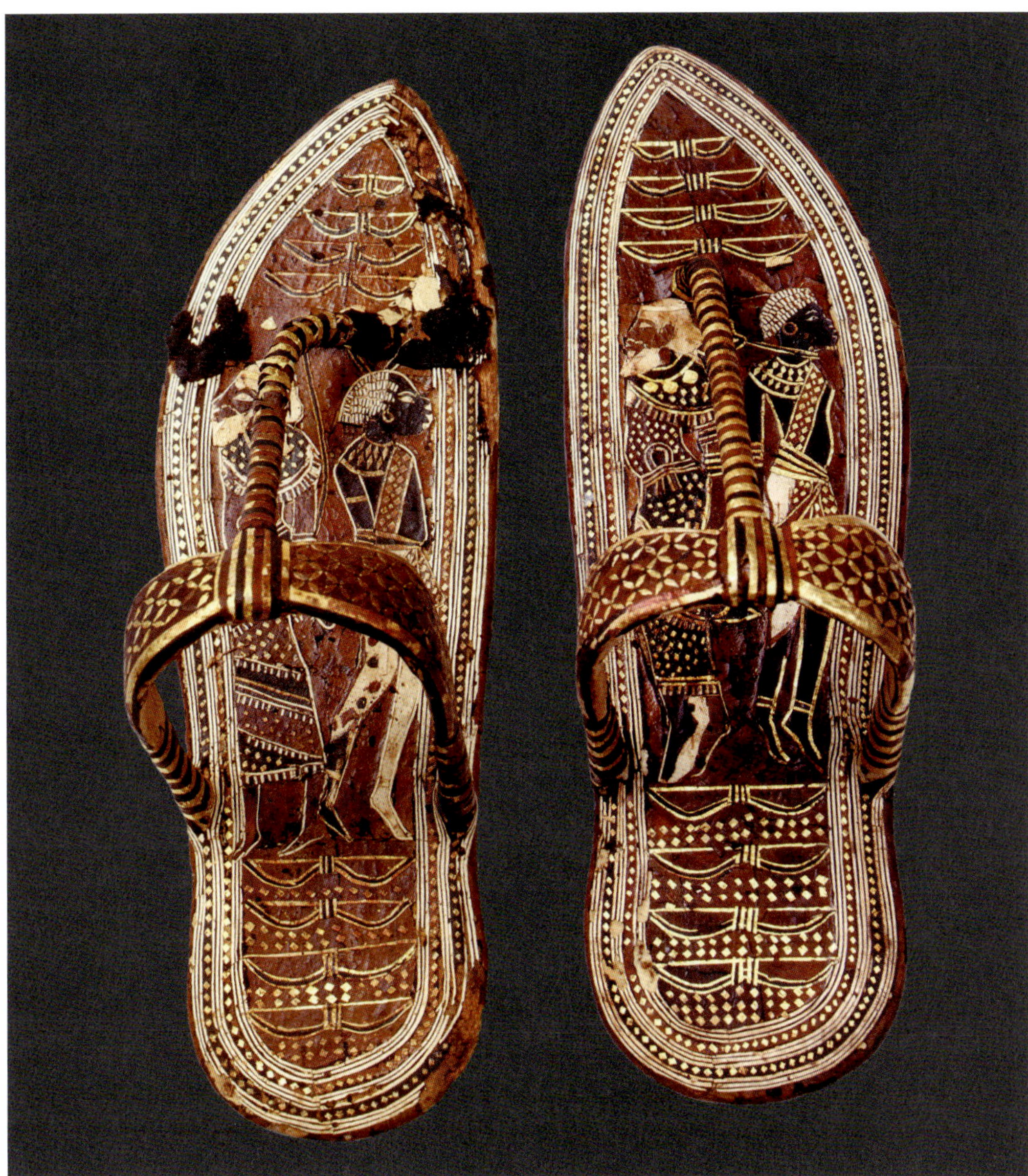

Fig. 24. **Sandals of Tutankhamun**, 18th Dynasty. Excavated from the tomb of Tutankhamun (r. ca. 1336–1327 BCE), Valley of the Kings, West Thebes, 1922. Leather and wood, L. 11⅛ in. (28.3 cm). Egyptian Museum, Cairo (JE 62685)

claiming Egyptian history as a source of Black identity on the one hand and of white Western civilization on the other, which in turn impacted the ways in which these scholars participated within and outside the field of Egyptology.

The discovery in 1922 of the tomb of Tutankhamun in the Valley of the Kings by British archaeologist Howard Carter and his team had an explosive international impact that resonated and refracted in particular ways for Black Americans (as indeed this entire project demonstrates). Many felt an affinity for Tutankhamun's mask as an important part of African history, among them Amy Jacques Garvey, wife of activist Marcus Garvey, who began an essay on the Africanity of Egypt with a description of a photograph of the mask.[10] The tomb

also revealed images of Black Nubians in states of bondage, such as a pair of lavish gold and leather sandals with bound Nubians depicted on its footbed. When wearing them, the Egyptian king actively crushed his captive enemies (fig. 24).[11] These images of Tutankhamun and the enslavement of Black Africans prompted questions of race that rippled across the field for decades.[12] Even in 1987, a *Washington Post* opinion piece quoted Edward Bleiberg, at the time the assistant director of the Institute of Egyptian Art and Archaeology at Memphis State University, as stating categorically that "Egyptians were considered Caucasians."[13]

The accomplishments of Nubia, the ancient civilization stretching from present-day southern Egypt to northern

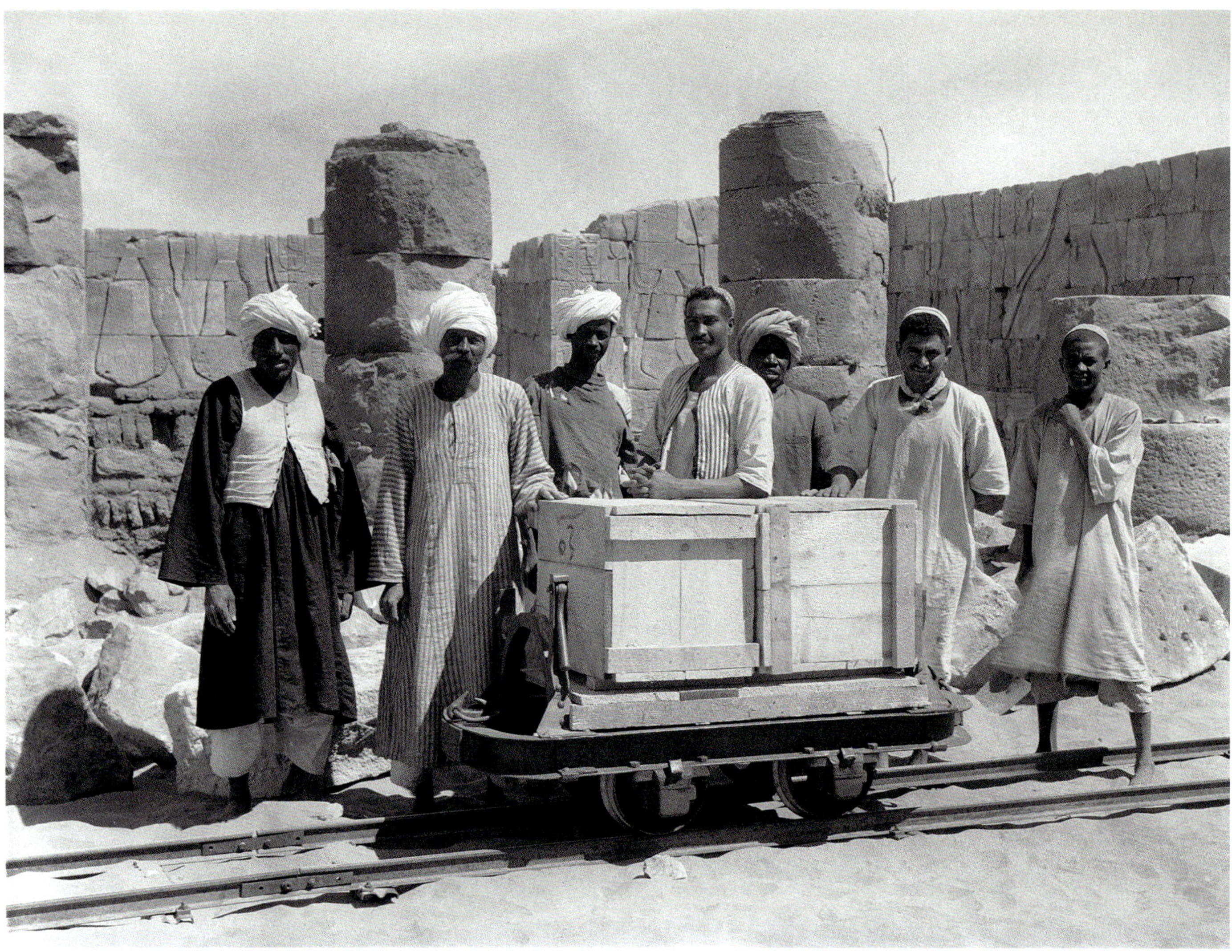

Fig. 25. Reginald St. Alban Heathcote (British, 1888–1951). Workmen transporting wooden crates containing some of the blocks from the Shrine of Taharqa using light railway, 1922–33. Black-and-white negative, 3¼ x 4¼ in. (8 x 10.5 cm). Griffith Institute, University of Oxford, England (N.I 66)

Sudan, and its people were also considered detached from Africa.[14] In the early twentieth century, Nubian studies were subsumed within Egyptology, justified by intellectual acrobatics surrounding the connection (or not) to Black Africans. For example, in the publication of his excavations in the ancient Nubian kingdom of Kush, George Reisner, one of the founders of Egyptology, remarked that the Nubian race was "*negroid*, but not negro."[15] At the same time, archaeologists in Egypt and Sudan noticed physical similarities between the human remains they were excavating and the people then living in local communities. Reisner linked the past to the present, stating, "The population is now, I imagine, much the same in numbers, and much the same in culture, as it was then."[16] Excavation photography produced in the Nile Valley at this time reinforced Reisner's statement, which represents a pressing contradiction in Egyptology (fig. 25). The modern Egyptians or Sudanese represented in his published images, in the era of the one-drop rule, would have been considered Negro or negroid in the United States.[17]

From the early twentieth century, the connection to ancient Egypt within Black communities prompted African American intellectuals to study its long, rich history as African history. Although the racial identity of the ancient Egyptians fell outside of the scope of racial classifications in the United States as defined by the American census, both Black and white Americans tried to grapple with how to address Egypt as a multicultural African society with a mixture of Black ancestry.[18] Popular journals geared toward African Americans included numerous essays on Egypt and race.[19] The teacher, author, and community activist Leila Amos Pendleton wrote, "Some historians tell us very plainly that the Egyptians were not Africans at all and so Negroes need not be proud of what they did."[20]

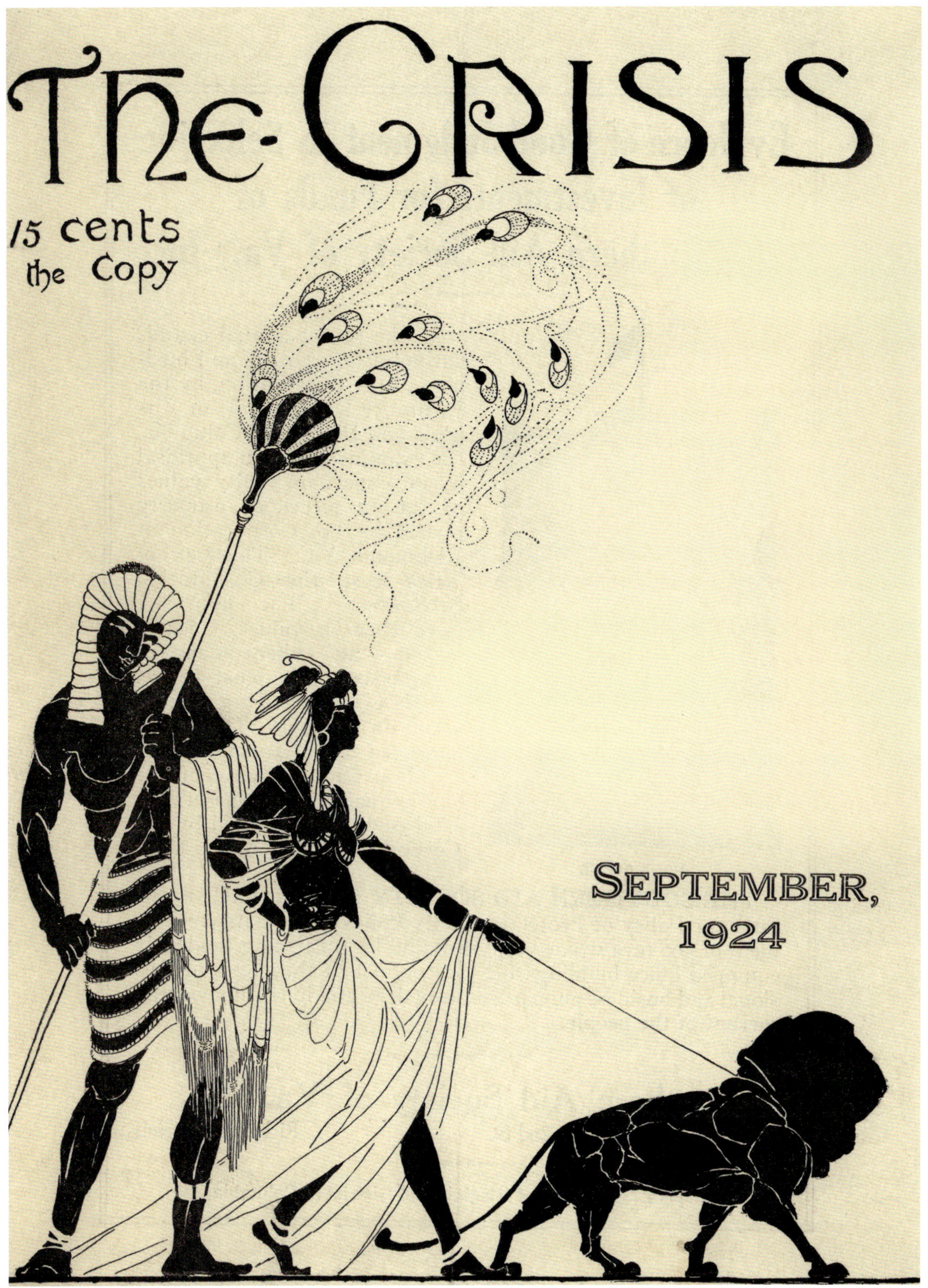

Fig. 26. Detail of Laura Wheeler Waring, **The Strength of Africa**, cover of **The Crisis**, 1924 (pl. 32)

Alongside this increased interest in Egypt was the development of the Pan-African movement, which sought to restore land, nations, and respect to people of African descent.[21] Because of the prevailing Eurocentric perspective that saw ancient Egypt as the only African culture of value, W. E. B. Du Bois understood that the Pan-African project had to include Egypt to reflect the continent's diversity, multiculturalism, and dynamism. Du Bois turned to the history of Africa to show Americans that African heritage was much more than the slavery and oppression faced by people of African descent in America, using his platforms at the Pan-African Conference, the Exposition Universelle, and his journal, *The Crisis*, among others (fig. 26).[22] Other advocates for Pan-Africanism included Marcus Garvey and his wife, Amy Jacques Garvey, who also addressed the question of Egypt in Africa.[23] The Garveys founded the Universal Negro Improvement Association and African Communities League (UNIA-ACL). Their publication, the *Negro World*, consistently presented Egyptian history and culture as part of the history of Africa. Garvey's ideas were influenced by one of his mentors, the Sudanese Egyptian activist Dusé Mohamed Ali, author of *In the Land of the Pharaohs* (fig. 27), who was also a leader of the Pan-African project and wrote for the *Negro World* and his Pan-African publication, *African Times and Orient Review*.[24]

Pan-Africanism was also promoted by Egyptian president Gamal Abdel Nasser, for whom it played a key role, alongside Pan-Arabism, in a vision for Egypt that he laid out in *The Philosophy of the Revolution*. Nasser, who spent a significant portion of his life living in modern Sudan, described the three circles—Arab, the continent of Africa, and Islam—in which he felt Egyptians "must revolve and attempt to move in as much as we possibly can."[25] He contended that Egypt could not turn away from Africa because "we are in Africa" and because "the Nile is the artery of life of our country. It draws its supply of water from the heart of the continent."[26]

African Americans within academic scholarship also sought to make these connections but were discouraged from doing so. William Leo Hansberry studied ancient Egypt at Harvard University, where he was taught by Reisner.[27] Echoing Hegel's description of Egypt and North Africa as related more to Europe (and Asia) than Africa, Reisner told him, "I do not believe that Negroes founded these great civilizations.

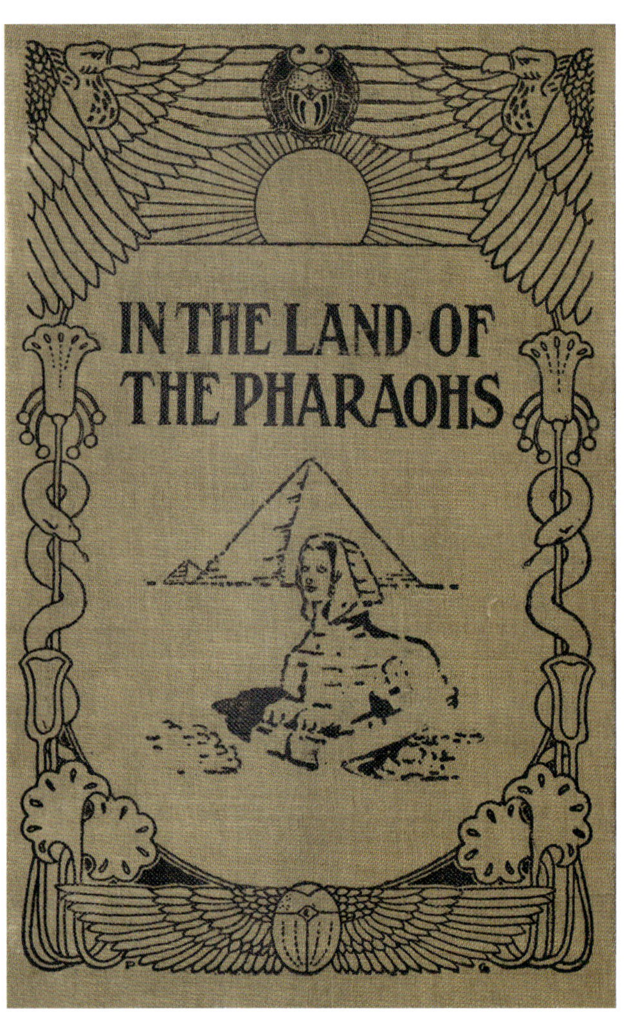

Fig. 27. Dusé Mohamed Ali, **In the Land of the Pharaohs** (London: Stanley Paul, 1911)

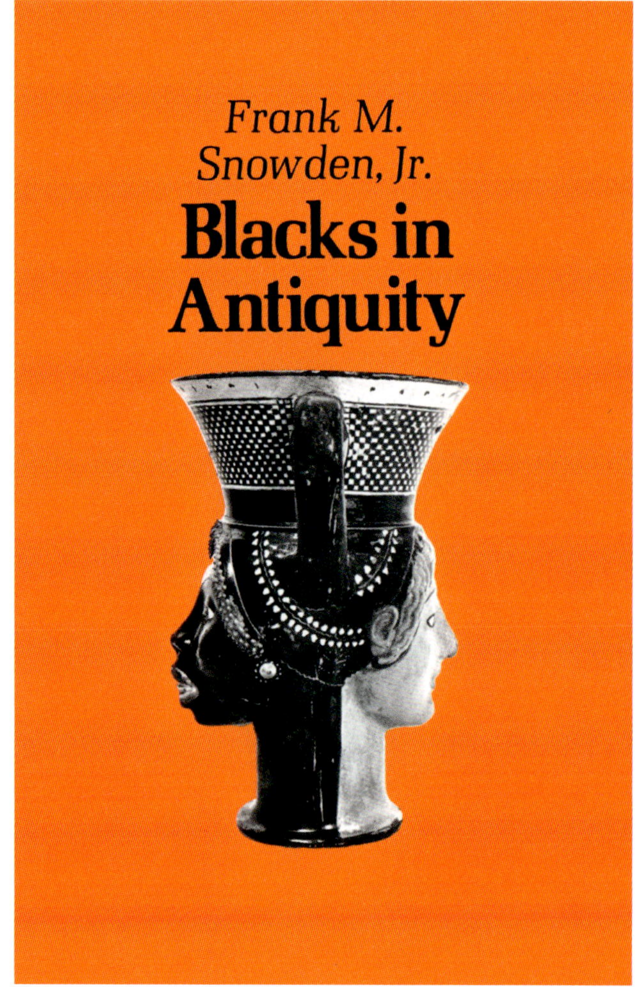

Fig. 28. Frank M. Snowden Jr., **Blacks in Antiquity** (Cambridge, Mass.: Belknap Press, 1970)

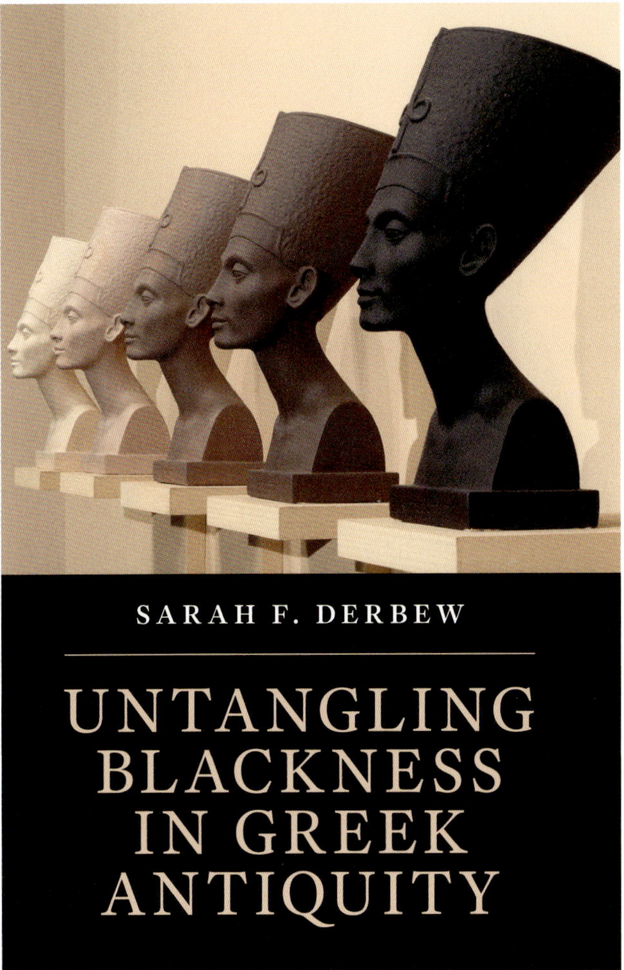

Fig. 29. Sarah F. Derbew, **Untangling Blackness in Greek Antiquity** (Cambridge: Cambridge University Press, 2022)

You are a brilliant student Hansberry, but you are a product of our civilization."[28] Despite this deterrence, throughout his career Hansberry sought to reinterpret archaeological work on the ancient and medieval Nile Valley to privilege the African context of Egyptian and Sudanese material culture.[29]

Black classicists have also considered the question of Egypt in Africa by investigating the presence of Black Africans in ancient Mediterranean societies, including Egypt. American historian Frank Snowden Jr., considered the issue of Egyptians' skin color in his book *Blacks in Antiquity* (fig. 28). He was less concerned with the racial makeup of the Egyptians than to show that Greeks and Romans were unconcerned with skin tone (or race). The thesis of *Blacks in Antiquity* is that racism did not play a role in the reception of "Blacks" in the ancient world.[30] Like those of other Black American scholars before him, Snowden's research interest was influenced by his own academic milieu: educated at Harvard University, he taught classics at Howard University from the 1960s to the 1980s. Whereas Du Bois had tried to show that Africa had a deep history, Snowden explored how Blacks participated in ancient history. Both scholars created space for more people of color

to enter the field. Sarah Derbew's book *Untangling Blackness in Greek Antiquity* (fig. 29) is now the leading resource on understanding the perception of race in the ancient world, including Egypt. Although goals might have differed from Snowden to Derbew, scholars like them have helped shape how the academy views the multicultural communities of Egypt.

Scholars in the mainstream and at the periphery of the field of Egyptology have also recently sought to approach similar topics.[31] Martin Bernal's *Black Athena* (pl. 15) posits that Greek civilization developed through a mixture of influences from many parts of the Mediterranean, including North Africa and Egypt. His thesis is anchored upon Egypt being in the continent of Africa. Although the overall premise is uncontroversial, Bernal made sweeping generalizations about ancient Egyptians colonizing the northern Mediterranean. His claims were not supported by linguistic or archaeological evidence and prompted many critiques.[32] Cheikh Anta Diop's *African Origin of Civilization* (pl. 14) was a precursor to Bernal's book; it argued that the ancient Egyptians were Black Africans, as have other works by African American scholars who sought to connect Egypt with the broader history of Africa.[33] Scholars of African American literature have been able to engage with the topic of ancient Kemet through their field.[34] Such studies have had an influence on the field of Egyptology, which has begun to consider the impact of Egyptians and northern Africans in the ancient world. For example, the Egyptologist David O'Connor's published measured responses to *Black Athena* have illuminated the relationship of Nubia and Egypt to the broader Mediterranean.[35]

Despite Egyptology's shift to topics that Du Bois and Hansberry promoted in the early twentieth century, the field continues to lag in diversity in terms of its practitioners.[36] Classical studies have seen an increase in diversity initiatives beyond those in Egyptology, in part because the courses required to qualify for a PhD program in classics are taught in more undergraduate institutions in the United States than those for an Egyptology program. There are also more classics (or ancient Mediterranean) departments than Egyptology departments, to which the increased diversity in the field can also be broadly attributed. Finally, there are very few Egyptology-specific positions in museums and academia, so entering the field can be discouraging.[37]

However, while most Black scholars who have addressed the topic of color or racism in the ancient world hold doctorates in classics, there has been a significant increase in Black Americans enrolling in Egyptology PhD programs due to the mentorship provided by the William Leo Hansberry Society, a collective for Egyptologists of African descent. Research interests have shifted from understanding racism in—or the race of—ancient Mediterranean peoples to more generative questions that explore the nuances of multiculturalism in antiquity. And although there are few Black American Egyptologists, since the 1990s more Egyptian Egyptologists have received their doctorates. The shift in the field's demographics will define the future of the reception of ancient Egypt. While the topic of Egypt in or of Africa remains fraught, the participation of diverse scholars in the field of Egyptology will further enhance research on the topic.[38]

     The Problem of the Color Line

"We Are Both Myths": Ancient Egypt and Opacity

Mia Matthias

While ancient societies provide fertile ground for the global imagination, their opened tombs and uncovered artifacts spawn as many questions as they answer. Over the course of the century following the New Negro movement of the 1920s, Black artists have continued to engage with ideas, iconography, and rituals inspired by ancient Egypt. Many of these artists blur lines, culling inspiration from various nations and time periods to construct interpretations of ancient Egypt. For these artists, the unknown is generative. Over time, ancient Egypt has helped to fill the gaps in collective and personal histories effaced by time and circumstance. Artists have engaged with ancient Egypt as a means of subverting specificity and developing plastic understandings of themselves, their artworks, and Black identity. Through the lens of Edouard Glissant's opacity, we can understand this connection to Egypt as malleable, shifting, and at times purposefully opaque. Glissant argues against the static Western mode of understanding through transparency and, ultimately, reduction—concepts that serve the equation of knowledge and power that underlies much of the colonialist enterprise. Instead, according to Glissant, what is unknown or illegible can and should exist in its specificity and complexity, continuously changing in relation to context.[1] Engagement with ancient Egypt as an idea, place, and time shifted over the course of the twentieth century; it became a geographically and temporally unmoored site of imagination and mythmaking. This essay analyzes a subsection of artists working over the last century, tracing a shift from outward declarations concerned with collective identities to inward reflections focused on personal histories and finally to conversations across time that fulfill a self-reflexive and self-sustaining Black mythology.

At the turn of the twentieth century, W. E. B. Du Bois traveled to London for the first Pan-African Conference, where, along with a number of international Black leaders, he was instrumental in drafting an address "To the Nations of the World."[2] The letter, addressed to heads of state, monarchs, and leaders throughout Europe, demanded action against racist structures around the world, from colonial strongholds in the Caribbean and throughout the African continent to the ongoing oppression and violence against African Americans in the United States. The scope of the conference and the address signaled a unified identity and purpose for Black populations across nations. Immediately following the conference in London, Du Bois traveled to Paris for the 1900 Exposition Universelle, a sprawling occasion for countries to exhibit their innovations that offered a rare opportunity for pageantry on a global stage. Du Bois, along with Thomas J. Calloway and Daniel Murray, presented an "Exhibit of American Negroes," anchored by almost five hundred photographs by Thomas A. Askew depicting African American culture from a range of vantage points, along with graphs, charts, and maps created and compiled by Du Bois and his students that visualized statistics about the African American population (fig. 30; see fig. 23). The organizers challenged "the scientific 'evidence' and popular racist caricatures of the day that ridiculed and sought to diminish African American social and economic success."[3] As evidence of racial progress Du Bois and his collaborators used empirical data that charted achievements in history, art, and education alongside depictions of upwardly mobile Black people in the United States. The presentation was awarded a gold medal by the Paris Exposition jury.

Du Bois was one of many African American leaders and scholars invested in molding a narrative of progress for the Black community. In 1925, the philosopher Alain Locke published *The New Negro*, a landmark anthology highlighting African American artistic achievement in literature, in which he insisted "that the Negro is not a cultural foundling

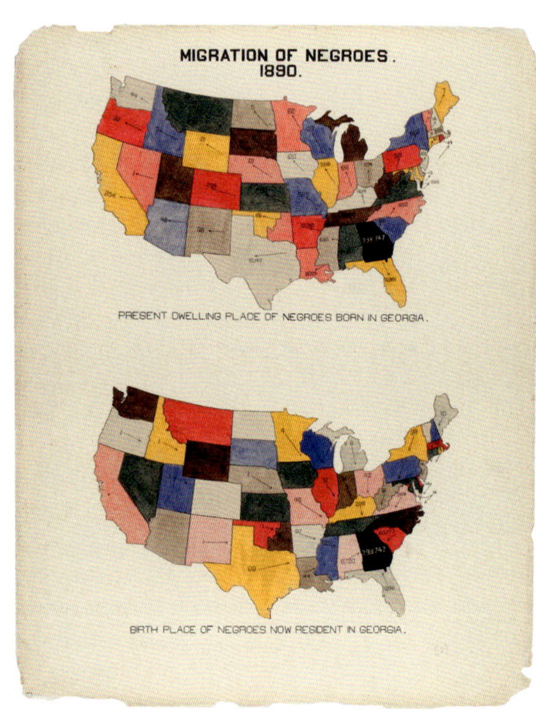

Fig. 30. W. E. B. Du Bois (American, 1868–1963). **The Georgia Negro: Migration of Negroes. 1890**, ca. 1900. Ink and watercolor on paper, 28 x 22 in. (71 x 56 cm). Library of Congress Prints and Photographs Division, Washington, D.C. (Lot 11931, no. 8 [P&P])

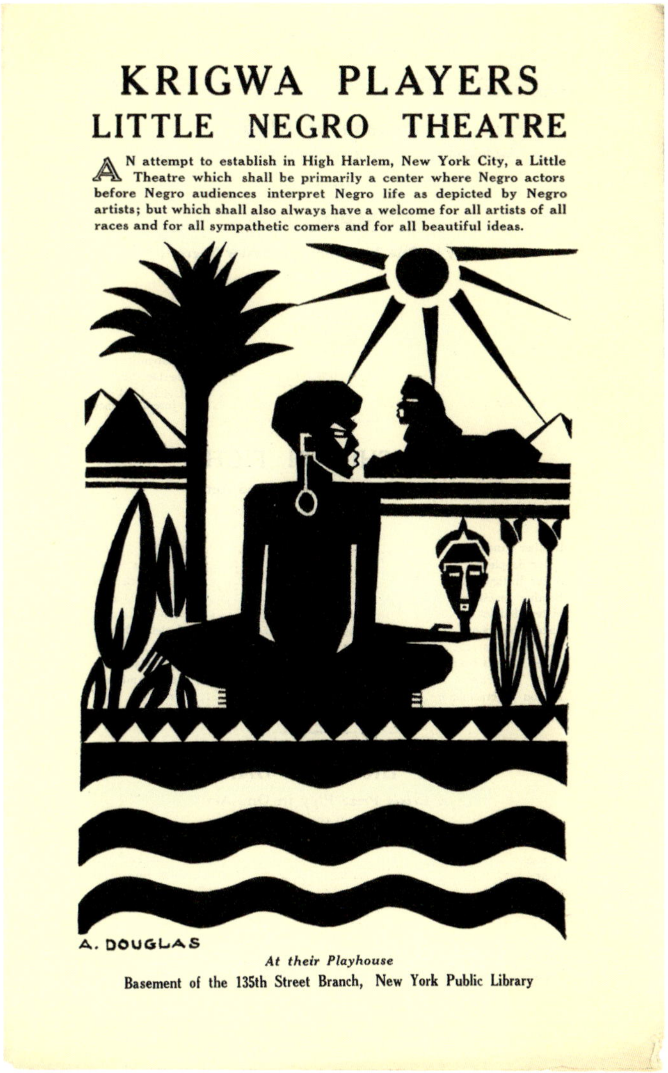

Fig. 31. Aaron Douglas (American, 1899–1979). **Krigwa Players Little Negro Theatre**, ca. 1926. W. E. B. Du Bois Papers, Special Collections and University Archives, University of Massachusetts Amherst Libraries, Amherst, Massachusetts (MS 312)

without his own inheritance."[4] A need for a uniting rhetoric likewise arose in the wake of the Great War, the rising Pan-African movement championed by Marcus Garvey, and the mass migration of African Americans from the Jim Crow South to the industrializing North.

The New Negro of the twentieth century required a cohesive and unifying narrative that would transcend geographic and cultural differences among African American communities nationwide. The effort to build a shared foundation coincided with widespread investment and interest in ongoing archaeological excavations in Egypt, Sudan, Ethiopia, and the surrounding region. These digs revealed artifacts and sacred sites from advanced kingdoms that were created and ruled by nonwhite people. By 1896, the Ethiopian army had thwarted Italian attempts at colonization. In the context of these discoveries and victories, Du Bois, Locke, and many other leaders in the movement turned to the African continent, to the past,

and to artists for a shared foundation. Locke declared, "Nothing is more galvanizing than the sense of a cultural past. This at least the intelligent presentation of African Art will supply to us."[5] Artists across mediums heeded the call, and imagery inspired by the continent abounded. Loïs Mailou Jones and Aaron Douglas created graphic artworks that layered sphinxes and pyramids against the modern urban environment. These images became emblematic of the movement, appearing in newspapers and journals, and on posters (pls. 35–38). Douglas's work is featured on a poster for the Krigwa Players Little Negro Theatre, founded by Du Bois in 1925, in which ancient Egyptian imagery is paired with a description of the theater as a place "where Negro actors before Negro audiences interpret Negro life as depicted by Negro artists" (fig. 31). The connection to ancient civilizations demarcated African American culture as distinct from a broader American identity, resisting assimilation during a period of high immigration and a changing American sociodemographic landscape. It also rooted Black identity in a site understood to be a cradle of modern civilization while sidestepping the ongoing subjugation of the transatlantic slave trade. As the art historian Renée Ater puts it, "To fulfill the desire for a future in American society, the past had to be excavated for signs of the important position of blacks in the creation of civilization."[6] In doing so, Egypt, Ethiopia, and Sudan became sites of allegory, at times interchangeably.[7] This syncretic approach to references laid the groundwork for artists beginning at the turn of the twentieth century and for future generations.

One of the first artists to be engaged in this enterprise was Meta Vaux Warrick Fuller, a sculptor from Philadelphia. At the age of twenty-two, following her studies at the Philadelphia School of Industrial Art, Fuller traveled to Paris, where she earned the acclaim and support of established artists including sculptor Auguste Rodin and painter Henry Ossawa Tanner. She was dubbed the "delicate sculptor of horrors" by the French press for her macabre works such as *Man Eating His Heart* (1900) and *The Wretched* (1903).[8] Warrick Fuller's figures are often writhing and twisted with fraught emotion, their surfaces craggy and rough: "My work is of the soul rather than the figure . . . sometimes the figure must be very crude in order to carry the full strength of the spiritual meaning."[9]

While in Paris, Warrick Fuller attended the 1900 Exposition Universelle, where she would have been exposed to works from artists around the world, including *Egyptian Harpist*, a work by her friend Jeanne Itasse-Broquet (fig. 32).[10] Through the activities around the Exposition, Warrick Fuller was introduced to Calloway, Murray, and Du Bois, who urged the young sculptor to focus on explicitly Black subject matter in her work, a request Fuller initially denied, finding it too limiting.[11]

Upon her return to the United States, Fuller found little audience for her horror-based works. The few opportunities for exhibition and funding offered to the artist were explicitly centered on visualizing the African American experience in the context of the New Negro movement, including *Emancipation* (1913), a seven-foot sculpture that Fuller created for the National Emancipation Exposition commemorating the fiftieth anniversary of the Emancipation Proclamation. As part of the same celebrations, Du Bois wrote and coordinated an elaborate

 "We Are Both Myths"

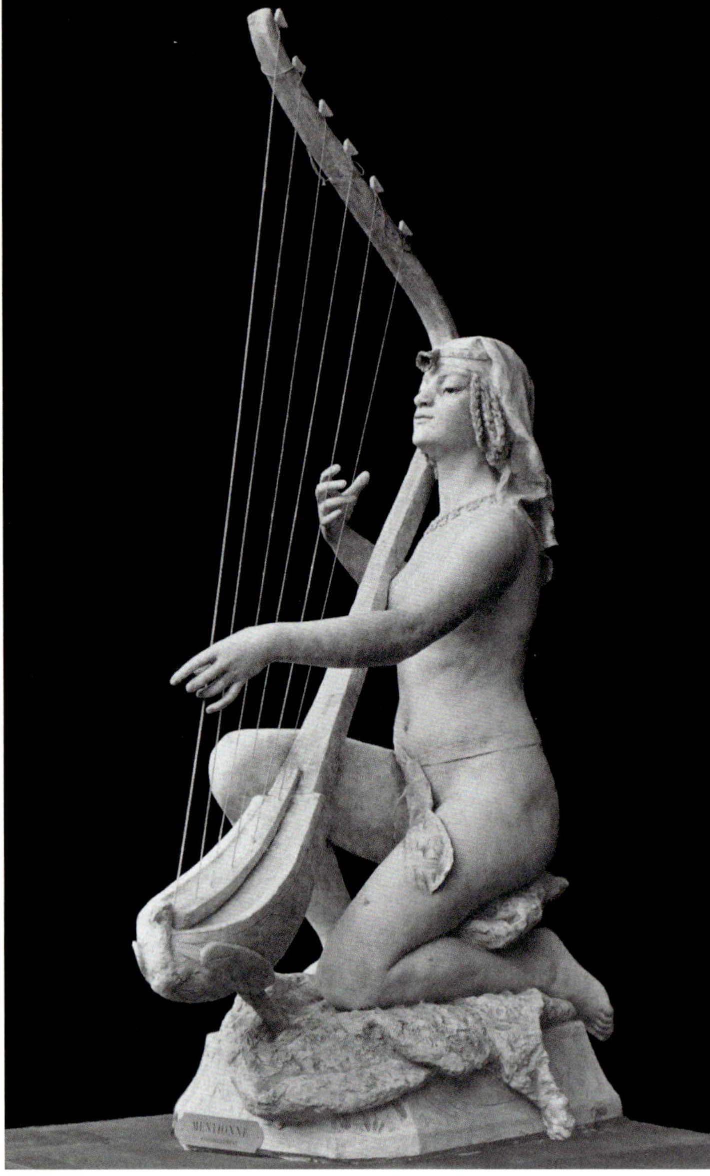

Fig. 32. Jeanne Itasse-Broquet (French, 1865–1941), **Egyptian Harpist**, in Charles-Louis Michelez, **Directorate of Fine Arts: Works Ordered or Acquired by the Department of Fine Arts, Salon of 1891.** Archives Nationales, Paris

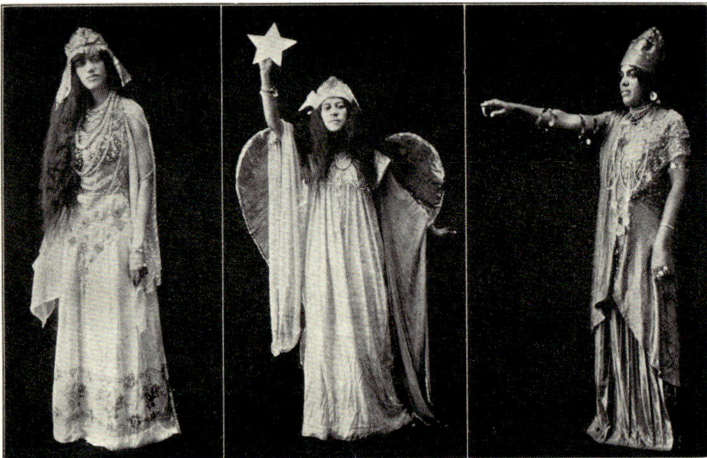

Fig. 33. Unknown photographer, **From the Pageant: "The Star of Ethiopia,"** in **The Crisis** 11, no. 2 (December 1915). Schomburg Center for Research in Black Culture, Jean Blackwell Hutson Research and Reference Division, The New York Public Library

pageant, *The Star of Ethiopia*, staged in New York, Washington, Philadelphia, and Los Angeles (fig. 33; see figs. 43, 44). A broadside describing the pageant advertises the depiction of ten thousand years of Black history, combining "historic accuracy and symbolic truth."[12] It included elaborate sets, costumes, a thousand performers, and a scene in which dancers perform for the Black Pharoah Ra in front of an Egyptian temple. The second act, "Dream of Egypt," showed "how the Egyptians descended from the prehistoric Negroes, evolved a high civilization and met again oncoming hordes of black men from the motherland."[13] The pageant was a resounding success, drawing over thirty-five thousand attendees, among them Fuller. Du Bois declared *The Star of Ethiopia* an opportunity to teach Black people their history and "reveal the Negro to the white world as a human, feeling thing."[14]

Du Bois repurposed the pageant for the America's Making Exposition in 1921, aimed at highlighting the contributions of immigrants to the United States from 1607 onward. Making the considerable leap required to group enslaved people with voluntary immigrants, the organizers designated a section of the exhibition for African Americans. Several key factors contributed to the urgency for Black leaders to establish an identity that claimed a place for African Americans within the wider American narrative. In 1919, the highest rate of lynchings was reported in over a decade. Following World War I, postwar paranoia about foreign subversives led to the overzealous Palmer Raids, which saw more than six thousand people arrested and questioned.[15] It was in this atmosphere of nationwide violence and suspicion that Fuller was commissioned to create *Ethiopia Awakening* as a centerpiece for the America's Making Exposition (pl. 22). In advance of its presentation, Du Bois's journal, *The Crisis,* reported that Fuller's sculpture would be an elaborate, Egyptian-inspired work, "symbolizing the self-emancipation of that race from ignorance into educated, self-reliant citizens and makers of America."[16] The lofty ambitions for the exposition and the sculpture were to provide a vision of upward mobility. At the time of the sculpture's creation, *The Crisis* had published coverage of the archeological excavations in Sudan and Ethiopia, which stressed the reign of the Kushite kings and the ancient city of Meroe.[17] Fuller was among the readers invested in ancient Black dynasties, declaring in a letter to a friend regarding her work for the exposition, "The most brilliant period, perhaps of Egyptian history was the period of the Negro kings."[18]

As with Du Bois's pageant, Egypt is not the sole reference for *Ethiopia Awakening*. Fuller draws from a range of references to the continent. She named the work after Ethiopia, the term used during the period to refer to the continent as a whole as well as to a specific region. She also clothed the figure in a *nemes,* a headdress worn by pharaohs, and colored it in a brilliant blue indicative of ancient Egyptian pigments in the maquette, or study for the full-size sculpture (fig. 34). Several iterations of the sculpture are extant.[19] In all of them the head of the figure is turned to one side, showing the face in profile from a frontal view, as is customary in ancient Egyptian reliefs. The right arm is held to the figure's chest, mirroring Egyptian funerary statues known as *shabti*s, *shawabti*s, or *ushabti*s, small figurines buried with the wealthy deceased to perform labor in the afterlife (fig. 35).[20] She is in the process of emerging from a

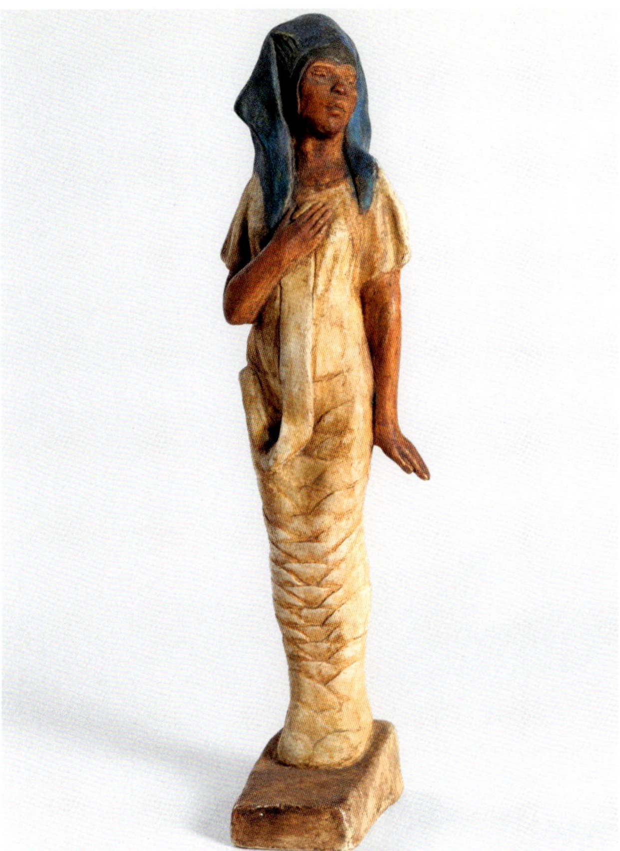

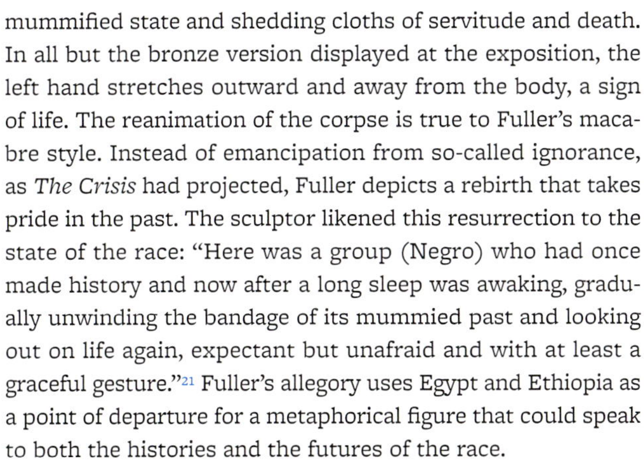

Fig. 34. Meta Vaux Warrick Fuller (American, 1877–1968). **Maquette for "Ethiopia Awakening,"** 1921. Painted plaster, H. 13⅞ in. (35.3 cm), W. 3½ in. (8.9 cm), D. 3¼ in. (8.3 cm). Danforth Art Museum at Framingham State University, Framingham, Massachusetts, Gift of the Meta V. W. Fuller Trust (2006.331)

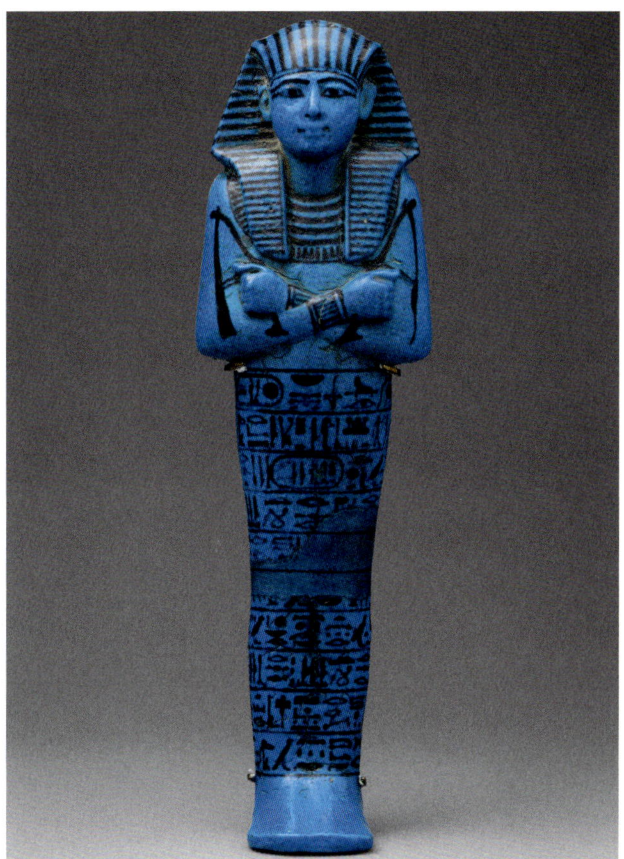

Fig. 35. **Shabti of Seti I,** ca. 1294–1279 BCE. Faience and paint, H. 12 in. (30.5 cm), W. 3⁷⁄₁₆ in. (8.8 cm), D. 2⁹⁄₁₆ in. (6.5 cm). The Metropolitan Museum of Art, New York, Purchase, Edward S. Harkness Gift, 1926 (26.7.919)

mummified state and shedding cloths of servitude and death. In all but the bronze version displayed at the exposition, the left hand stretches outward and away from the body, a sign of life. The reanimation of the corpse is true to Fuller's macabre style. Instead of emancipation from so-called ignorance, as *The Crisis* had projected, Fuller depicts a rebirth that takes pride in the past. The sculptor likened this resurrection to the state of the race: "Here was a group (Negro) who had once made history and now after a long sleep was awaking, gradually unwinding the bandage of its mummied past and looking out on life again, expectant but unafraid and with at least a graceful gesture."[21] Fuller's allegory uses Egypt and Ethiopia as a point of departure for a metaphorical figure that could speak to both the histories and the futures of the race.

Du Bois would eventually declare, "All art is propaganda and ever must be, despite the wailing of the purists. . . . I do not care a damn for any art that is not used for propaganda."[22] For Du Bois, art was a tool, and ancient Egypt was a useful vessel through which a collective yet distinct identity could be established and distributed, as expressed in Douglas's poster for Du Bois's Little Krigwa Players. In an issue of *The Crisis* dedicated to triumphant reflection on the success of the pageant (the "Pageant Number"), Du Bois summarizes the

pageant as "the gown and paraphernalia in which the message of education and reasonable race pride can deck itself." In the same issue, a report from the *Independent* of Elizabeth City, New Jersey, alongside others describing screenings of *The Birth of a Nation* (1915), calls the film, with its racist and derogatory caricatures, "a cruel slander of a weak and helpless race."[23] The contrast makes clear the sense of duty Du Bois and others felt to counter racist depictions and offer uplifting alternate narratives for both Black and white audiences. The connections to an ancient royal past in Egypt, Ethiopia, and the surrounding region rendered the developments of the twentieth century not a new achievement but a long-overdue return to glory.

In the 1950s and 1960s, another generation of African American artists turned to Egypt as a source of inspiration in the context of the civil rights movement. As the leaders of the movement were assassinated and protests for equal rights were met with brutal force, many looked for inspiration in the wave of African and Caribbean countries establishing independence from colonial rule. In 1976, author Alex Haley published *Roots: The Saga of an American Family*, a fictional story that follows a Black family from Africa to the United States over several generations.[24] The novel became a bestseller, and the miniseries adaptation released in 1977 drew more than half

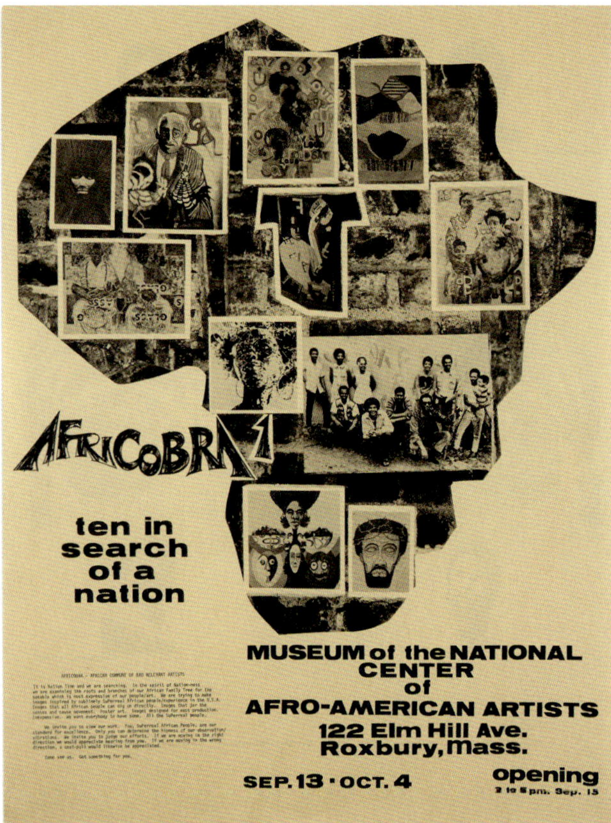

Fig. 36. **AfriCOBRA 1: Ten in Search of a Nation**, exhibition poster, 1970. 22 x 17 in. (55.9 x 43. 2 cm)

the population of the United States as viewers.[25] The series was a part of a larger movement of "roots tourism," or diasporic return, in which African Americans traveled to Africa, adopted African names, and implemented new traditions aimed at establishing a closer connection to their history.[26] While the turn of the twentieth century had encouraged artworks that fostered a collective and unified Black identity, many of these later artists sought a sense of personal connection, their motivations transcending the external validation that had prompted Fuller's commission. Art historian Kellie Jones claims that in the mid-twentieth century, "Rather than a one-to-one relationship between Black people in the United States and those in Africa, a window opened to peoples all over the globe, and metaphysical practices worldwide."[27] Heritage could be explored collectively, and beyond the constraints of linear connections. In 1963, the Kamoinge Workshop, a group of Black photographers with a range of styles and techniques focused on depicting Black communities for Black audiences, was founded in New York City. In 1968, AfriCOBRA (the African Commune of Black Relevant Artists) formed, an artist collective based in Chicago and centered on developing and distributing a transnational Black aesthetic. The AfriCOBRA manifesto read: "In the spirit of Nation-ness we are examining the roots and branches of our African family tree for the seeable which is the most expressive of our people/art" (fig. 36). In these endeavors, didacticism and clarity were frequently eschewed in favor of intuited connections, personal experience, and purposeful opacity. Again, it is

useful to invoke Glissant, who offers: "Opacities can coexist and converge, weaving fabrics. To understand these truly one must focus on the texture of the weave and not on the nature of its components."[28] He continues, "It does not disturb me to accept that there are places where my identity is obscure to me, and the fact that it amazes me does not mean I relinquish it."[29] These artists explored the unknown—and unknowable—parts of their history for themselves without attempting to prove or legitimize their connections. In this atmosphere, ancient Egypt continued to be a recurring theme for artists, now as a prompt for exploring notions of ritual, symbolism, and ceremony.

For decades the artist Betye Saar has used found objects to create sculptures, collages, and assemblages that layer references to spirituality, metaphysics, gender, race, and her personal memories. In 1970, Saar visited the Field Museum of Natural History in Chicago and was struck by its anthropological collections from around the world. She considers the encounter with African, Oceanic, and Egyptian objects a pivotal moment in her development as an artist.[30] The visit prompted her to create her *mojo* series, on which she elaborated in an artist statement for an exhibition in 1974:

> "Mojo" is a positive charm which brings the owner good luck. These works are based on a neo-African concept. The materials used are mostly organic (fur, bones, pods, feathers, leather etc.) which I combine with symbols from Africa, Egypt, and Oceania. I use these elements to construct fetishes related to ceremonies and rituals of unknown mystical ancient beliefs. These works are my personal statement of my evolvement from and the return to the "Essence of Africa."[31]

These artworks are a reaction to the unknown, a manifestation of Saar's constructing bridges to her past. Through layered symbols, motifs, organic materials, and found objects, Saar "felt she could harness the pull of ancestral past and its subconscious memory."[32] In this act of personal world-building, Saar frequently turned to ancient Egypt.

In 1972, the exhibition *Treasures of Tutankhamun* opened at the British Museum in London. Co-organized by the British Museum and the Museum of Egyptian Antiquities in Cairo, the exhibition featured never-before-seen artifacts from the archaeological excavations that had uncovered Tutankhamun's tomb fifty years earlier. The Met organized the tour of the exhibition in the United States from 1976 to 1979, where it drew a total of over eight million visitors.[33] *Treasures of Tutankhamun* fanned the flames of popular fascination with Egypt and made ancient Egyptian references more accessible to the public. Notably, visitors, including artists, encountered these artifacts through the lens of imperialism, which provided the framing, the selection of objects, and the circumstances under which they were extracted from Egypt.

In the same year that *Treasures of Tutankhamun* opened at the British Museum, Saar produced the assemblage *Essence of Egypt* (fig. 37). The central oval three-figure relief, the Eye of Horus, and the green scarab with falcon wings reference a pectoral featured in *Treasures of Tutankhamun*, and the paintings at the top corners are drawn from a New Kingdom tomb wall also included in the exhibition. Similarly, the center

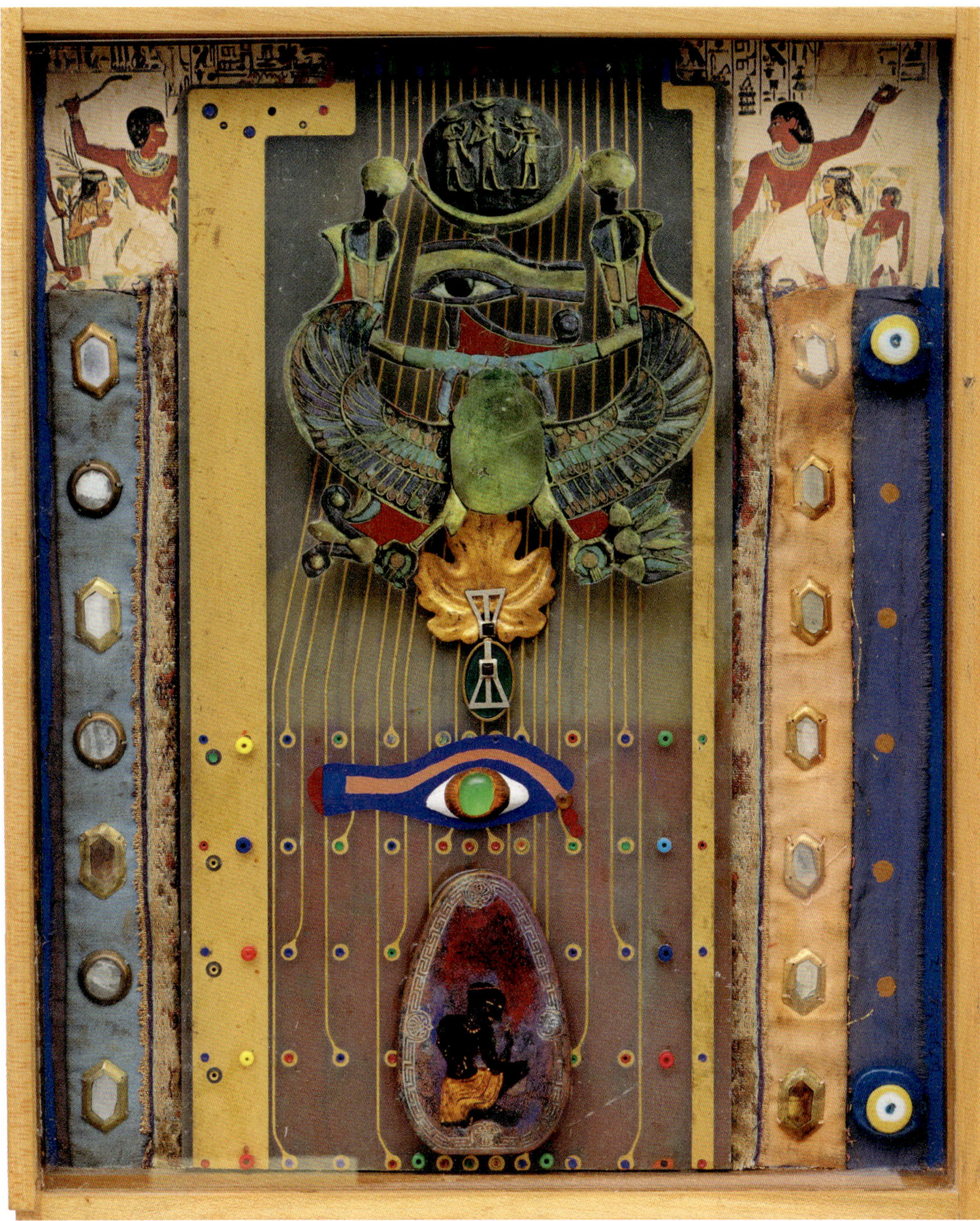

panel of Saar's *Window of Ancient Sirens* (pl. 46) features the golden funerary mask of Tutankhamun. Flanking the mask are two figures of women set against a planetary background, one with the body of a bird. Saar harnesses a personal connection to ancestral tradition through layered references to femininity, cosmology, and ancient Egypt. As scholar Miwon Kwon explains, Saar's work is not "simply trying to illustrate one particular spiritual system. . . . She's . . . piling up all of these emblems of meaning and almost creating her own personal iconography."[34] In Saar's assemblages, the whole is greater than the sum of the parts. In lieu of justifying the inclusion of each element, the artist notes "what the elements were and how they were combined, that made it have a sense of power."[35] This culling of references from different cultures, time periods, and geographic locations is what Saar considers her "ancestral history, that I just made up. Because I can't trace my tribe, and because my family is really mixed and integrated, all I can do is select my tribe and invent my tribe. Part of it is fantasy of maybe civilizations that are even lost. That's where a lot of the sculpture comes from, where I just invent these things."[36] *Essence of Egypt* and *Window of Ancient Sirens* are evidence of Saar building her own lineage through personal resonance.

    "We Are Both Myths"

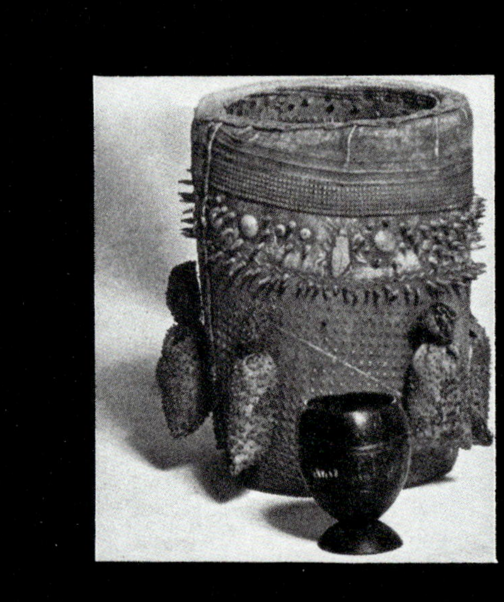

Fig. 38. Houston Conwill (American, 1947–2016). Artist statement, in **Studio Z: Individual Collective** (Long Beach, Calif.: Long Beach Museum of Art, 1977)

Saar's approach was championed by her younger contemporaries, including the artist Houston Conwill, who described himself as "concerned with myth and reality, oral tradition and history, contemporary anthology and the cycles of life and death" (fig. 38). Many explicit references to Egypt can be found in Conwill's early works from the 1970s, including recurring pyramid symbols and insertions of "scripts from the Egyptian *Book of the Dead* into his canvases while wet."[37] Conwill was a self-proclaimed *griot*, a West African keeper of oral tradition through music, stories, and poetry.[38] Conwill's sources of inspiration, like those of Fuller and Saar, were transgeographical: the artist drew from Egyptian, Sudanese, Kongo, Dogon, and Yoruba imagery and rituals.[39] Conwill was likely inspired by the Kongo cosmogram, which alludes to the heavenly origin and destiny of man, the immortality of soul and the eternity of life, and universal salvation.[40] At times, these works required physical navigation or interaction on the part of the viewer. *The Cakewalk Humanifesto*, a work made for the Museum of Modern Art, New York, in 1989, featured an etched-glass cosmogram stretching from floor to ceiling that filtered natural light and cast shadows. Installed adjacent to a courtyard, it implicated viewers in its composition through its transparency. Conwill's cosmograms merged references to geography, poetry, and navigation; the spiral central to the artwork is inspired by ancient Egyptian motifs. A diagram of *The Cakewalk Humanifesto* shows quotations dating from the nineteenth century through to the civil rights era alongside symbols, place-names, and terms describing sensory and bodily experiences (fig. 39).

Rivers, created in 1991 with Conwill's sister Estella Conwill Majozo and architect Joseph De Pace, is a large-scale perma-

nent installation at the Schomburg Center for Research in Black Culture in Harlem (see pl. 155). Constructed from terrazzo and brass, the work is a cosmogram embedded in the floor of the atrium; visitors must navigate around or through it to enter the building. At the center of the circular artwork is a fish overlaid with the phrase "My Soul Has Grown Deep Like the Rivers," drawn from Langston Hughes's iconic poem "The Negro Speaks of Rivers" (1921). For Conwill, the fish was emblematic of "archetypal life, a symbol of transformation. One can interpret entering the fish as a journey into the womb—the idea of immersion, transformation, and emergence. You become linked with the past."[41] Embedded in the circle are six additional fragments of the poem placed alongside geographically significant locations. The outermost circle of the cosmogram is labeled with fragments of Hughes's poem and the four major rivers named in it: the Euphrates, the Mississippi, the Congo, and the Nile, which is paired with the line "I looked upon the Nile and raised the pyramids above it." Two lines running perpendicular to the circles represent the lifelines of historian Arturo A. Schomburg and Hughes, beginning in their respective birthplaces—Santurce, Puerto Rico, and Joplin, Missouri—and intersecting in Harlem, where both men lived and died. Hughes's ashes are buried beneath the center of the cosmogram. The work is a tribute to ancestors and cycles of life, death, and reincarnation.[42] The positioning on the floor of the lobby ensures visitors will physically interact with the work, on occasion using it as a dance floor and a site of celebration, as the poets Maya Angelou and Amiri Baraka notably did at the opening of the library's Langston Hughes Auditorium in 1991, captured in a photograph by Chester Higgins (fig. 40). Through the artwork, Conwill activates a site of collective remembrance. The circular

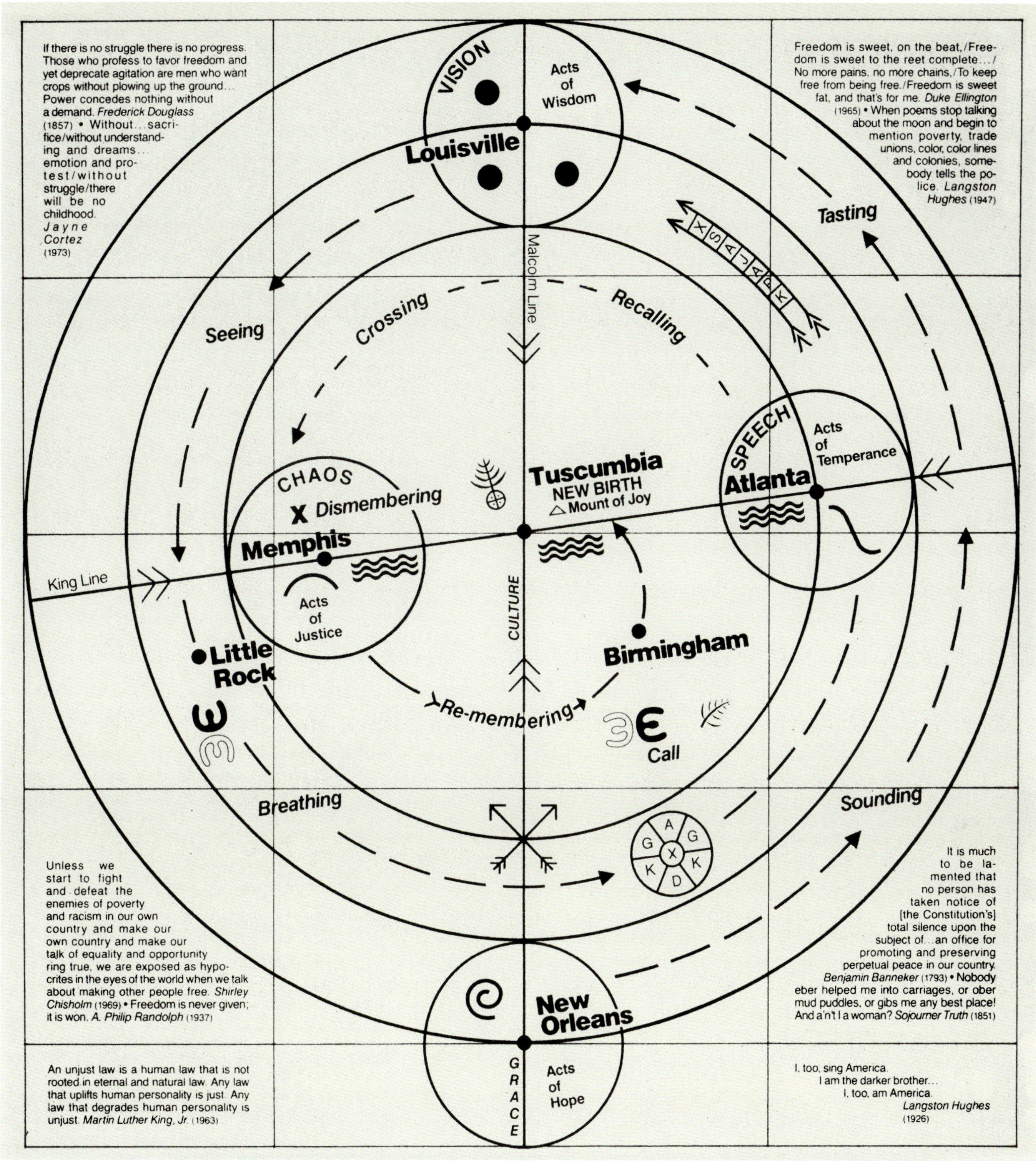

Fig. 39. Houston Conwill (American, 1947–2016). **Diagram of the window from "The Cakewalk Humanifesto,"** 1989. Color slide, 1¹⁵⁄₁₆ x 1¹⁵⁄₁₆ in. (5 x 5 cm). The Museum of Modern Art Archives, New York (ARCH.10416)

format connects these disparate water systems and the lives of two major Black figures, creating a continuous loop that encompasses time and geography, and holds an ancestor at its core. In Conwill's work, ancient Egypt provides an avenue to engage with and honor a past shared with those no longer living.

Lorraine O'Grady also invokes ancient Egypt in her artworks to complicate and extrapolate on her lineage and connections to those who have passed away. In 1980, O'Grady performed *Nefertiti/Devonia Evangeline* at Just Above Midtown Gallery in Manhattan (pls. 48, 49). The performance was partially inspired by O'Grady's trip to Egypt in 1963, where she felt a sense of kinship with those she encountered. The performance was set against sixty-five projected diptychs, each pairing an image from the life of O'Grady's sister, Devonia Evangeline O'Grady Allen, with statues and carvings of Queen Nefertiti of the Eighteenth Dynasty and her family. Images of Allen's family were paralleled by Nefertiti's corresponding family members: daughters with daughters, husband and king. The pairings activated the ancient artifacts, and the modern family photographs filled in gaps of tenderness and vulnerability while simultaneously rendering Allen's family photos stately and regal.

The performance aspect of *Nefertiti/Devonia Evangeline* took place in front of the projected images, riffing on and against the "Opening of the Mouth" ceremony, an ancient Egyptian ritual intended to reanimate the senses of the dead in preparation for the afterlife. The ceremony included a tool used to cut an umbilical cord, evoking a rebirth.[43] O'Grady's sister, Devonia, had died almost twenty years earlier due to complications following an abortion. In the performance, O'Grady moves through motions and gestures inspired by the ritual to explore grief and kinship. O'Grady collapses time, geography, and sacred references by drawing on the customs of Nefertiti's era to honor her sister while blurring the lines between past and present, historic and personal.

O'Grady's *Miscegenated Family Album* (1980/94) was born of the same performance (pls. 50-53). The installation consists of sixteen photographic pairings that originally appeared in *Nefertiti/Devonia Evangeline*. The title references the antiquated terminology for the intermixing of races. In 1967, anti-miscegenation laws were ruled unconstitutional by the Supreme Court in the landmark case *Loving v. Virginia*. O'Grady, born before the ruling, is of Black Jamaican and white Irish descent. She looked to the "dual structures" of ancient Egypt both to understand her own layered identities and to determine the structure of the juxtaposed images. O'Grady has said, "I have been

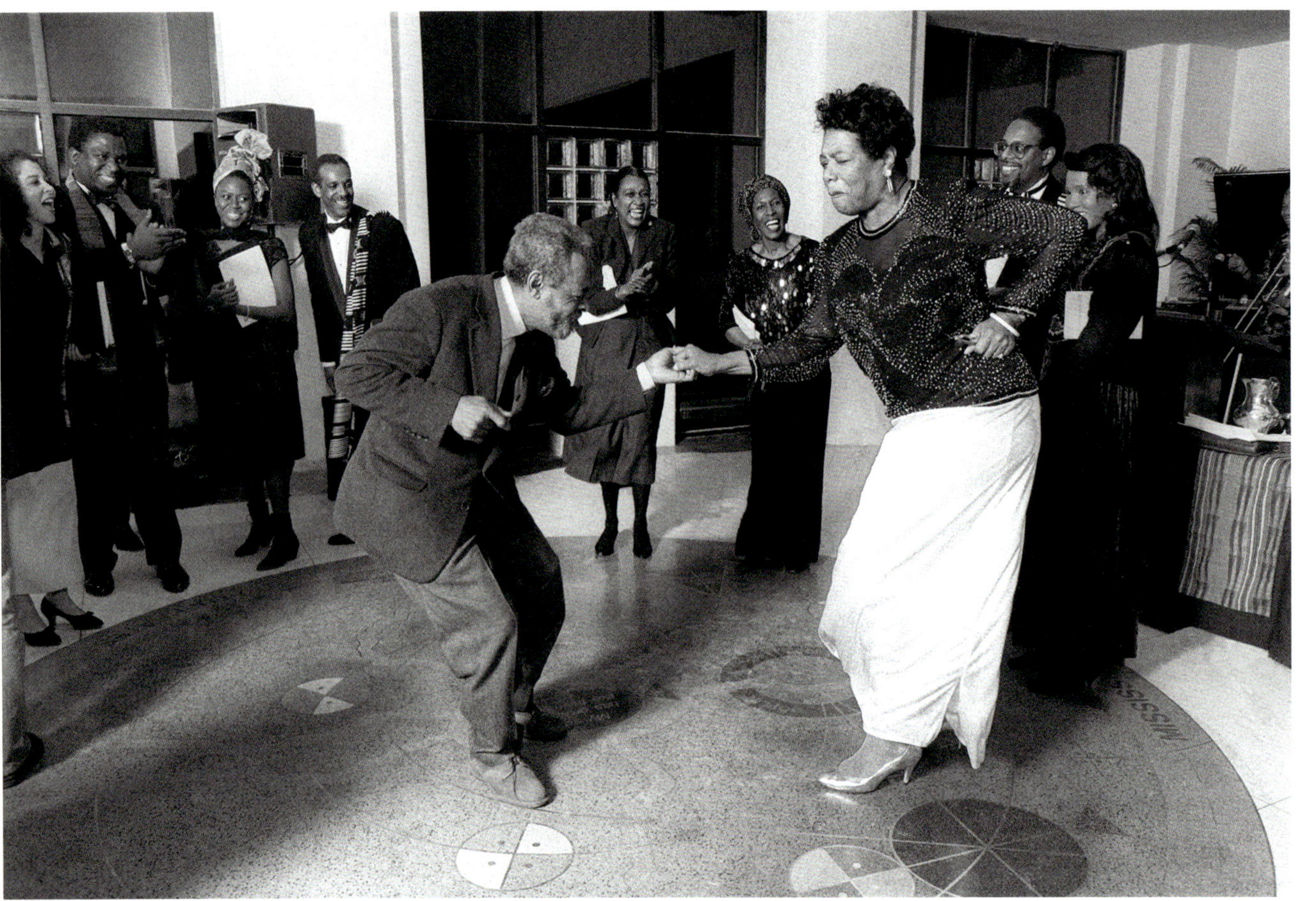

Fig. 40. Chester Higgins (American, b. 1946). **Maya Angelou dancing with the poet Amiri Baraka over the ashes of the poet Langston Hughes at the New York Public Library's Schomburg Center for Research in Black Culture,** in **The New York Times** (December 22, 2014)

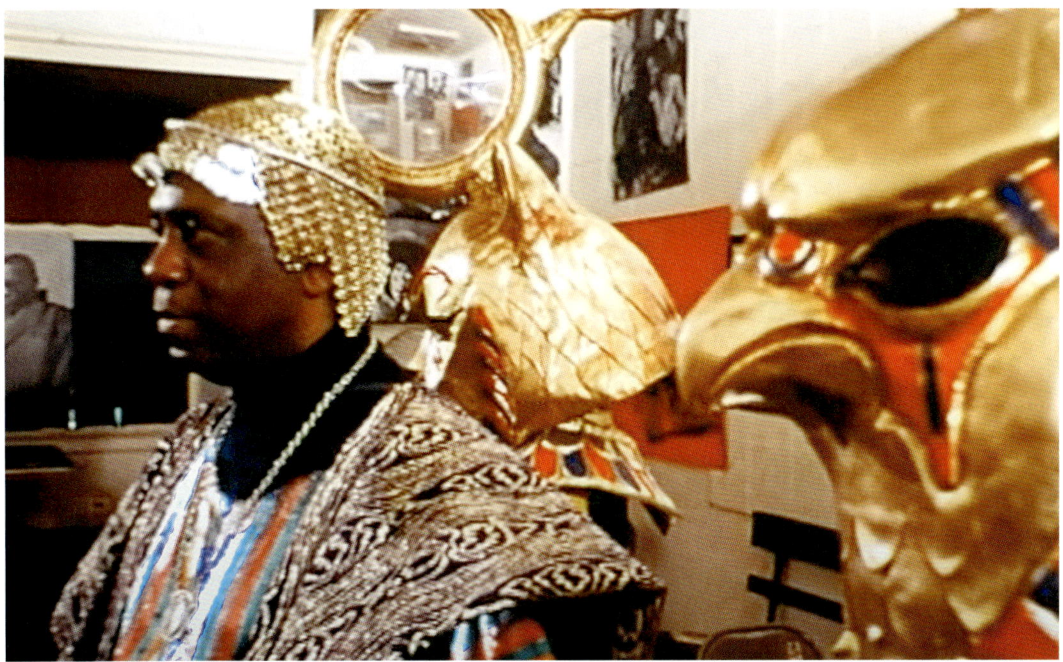

Fig. 41. Still from **Space Is the Place**, directed by John Coney, written by Sun Ra and Joshua Smith, North American Star System, 1974

drawn to the diptych or multiple, where much of the information happens in the space between."[44] The artist anticipates the instinct to draw parallels between the images but is not proposing a one-to-one relationship between the two families so much as a comparison that invites overlaps as well as friction. As Catherine Damman notes, the format of the presentation recalls traditional art historical comparisons as well as the strategies of racist pseudo-scientific practices, such as phrenology.[45] These strategies were used in analyzing the remains extracted from excavations, determining Tutankhamun's royal status based on the shape of a mummified skull, among other indicators. O'Grady emulates the same proof she has been offered, allowing what is implied to be generative. If these image pairings are precarious—in the sense that their similarities are contentious or debatable—then the same must be true of the conclusions drawn from tombs and reported as fact. Unlike the supposedly neat categorizations of art history, genealogy, and ancestry, the artist embraces the dissonance in the subject matter. In reference to the hybrid identities of diasporic people, including herself, the artist notes, "It is diaspora peoples' straddling of origin and destination, their internal negotiation between apparently irreconcilable fields that can offer paradigms for survival and growth in the next century."[46] O'Grady's performance and photographs thus not only establish a personal history but act as a road map for the future. She embraces the "irreconcilability" of the diasporic identity, allowing it to exist in its complexity without reduction in favor of transparency. Between the photographs are oceans, centuries, and continuously shifting versions of lineage.

Like O'Grady, Sun Ra considered ancient Egypt a frame for the past, present, and future simultaneously. Sun Ra named himself after the Egyptian sun deity, Ra. In the 1974 film *Space Is the Place,* written by the artist with Joshua Smith and directed by John Coney, Sun Ra depicts himself as a beacon of hope sent from Saturn to rescue African Americans from their plight in the United States (fig. 41, pl. 159). His signature freewheeling jazz provides both the soundtrack and structure for the film: trance-inducing instrumentals are layered with voices that open portals, cause explosions, and power time travel. The narrative skips between storylines and pauses for interludes, including one that features a robed figure with a mirrored face dancing in front of a wall of Egyptian symbols.[47] Sun Ra merges references to ancient Egypt, Blaxploitation films, and outer space, and in so doing he not only undermines the notion of a mutually exclusive past, present, and future, but also embodies it. He asks that we "consider time ended" and reminds us that "we work on the other side of time," rejecting the normative structures and logics that create distance between his ancient and intergalactic references.[48] When attempting to convince a group of young Black people to accompany him into space, flanked by figures outfitted in ancient Egyptian–inspired paraphernalia, Sun Ra states, "I came from a dream, that the Black man dreamed long ago. I'm actually a present sent to you by your ancestors." He posits himself as manifestation, accepting and celebrating the slippery status of "myth" and rejecting hard-edged "reality":

> How do you know I'm real? I'm not real. I'm just like you. You don't exist in this society. If you did, your people wouldn't be seeking equal rights. You're not real. If you were, you'd have status among the nations of the world. So, we are both

     "We Are Both Myths"

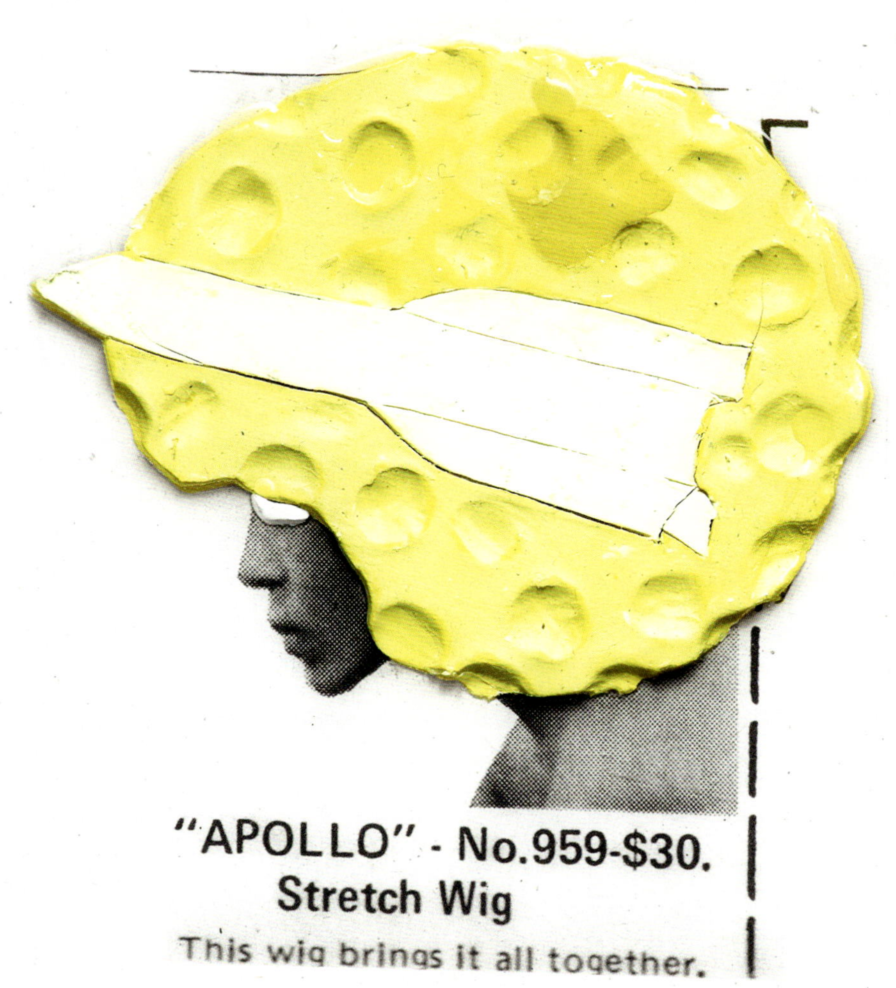

Fig. 42. Ellen Gallagher (American, b. 1965). Detail of **Pomp-Bang**, 2003. Plasticine, ink, and paper mounted on canvas. Museum of Contemporary Art Chicago, Joseph and Jory Shapiro Fund by exchange and restricted gift of Sara Szold

myths. I do not come to you as reality. I come to you as the myth because that's what Black people are: myths.[49]

Sun Ra inhabits a mythical status and invites others to do the same. His invocation of space and ancient Egypt is active and mutable; his references to ancient Egypt, cosmologies, the past, the present, and the future all overlap in a dynamic harmony. Like O'Grady, he looks to the irreconcilable and uses the flawed logics of the world as a prompt. According to exclusive, oppressive, and violent systems, Black people must not be real. If we are not real, we are myths; therefore this world and everything beyond it are ours for the taking. We can land spaceships on the pyramids and reside beyond the constraints of systems that deny and reject us. In response to dominant structures of power, Sun Ra states: "I hate your reality. I hate your cognitive absolute reality."[50] Or, in Glissant's words, "there are limits to absolute truth."[51]

In pushing against the static nature of Western myth-making, Glissant invokes movement as an analogy:

> We are far from the opacities of Myth or Tragedy, whose obscurity was accompanied by exclusion and whose transparency aimed at "grasping." In this version of understanding the verb *to grasp* contains the movement of hands that grab their surroundings and bring them back to themselves. A gesture of enclosure if not appropriation. Let our understanding prefer the gesture of giving-on-and-with that opens finally on totality.[52]

In place of reductive interpretations aimed at knowledge as possession or arrested understanding, Glissant suggests a generosity and malleability that will be generative and continuously evolving. His warning against myth and tragedy is aimed at an opaque and static narrative with an agenda, like the propaganda Du Bois declared useful. In place of these static myths, Glissant encourages a constant flux that is both a response and a prompt.

The artist Ellen Gallagher is the recipient of the future that Du Bois and Sun Ra were building. Through dense art historical and archival references, Gallagher enters into conversation with her predecessors, explicitly referencing and expanding upon their works. In *Abu Simbel* (pl. 162), Gallagher collages a still from *Space Is the Place* with a reprint of a photogravure that hangs in the library of the founder of psychoanalysis, Sigmund Freud, depicting the Great Temple of Ramesses II at Abu Simbel. Gallagher refers to the collaged work as "a tricked-out, multi-directional flow from Freud to ancient Egypt to Sun Ra to George Clinton."[53] The work layers fur, Plasticine, and crystals with images of Black pharaohs, Cadillac grilles, predatory Harlem real estate speculators, nurses representative of the medical staff complicit in the Tuskegee syphilis experiment conducted between 1932 and 1972, and the faces of Black people in pain, waiting to be saved by Sun Ra, who is arriving in a spaceship.[54] Gallagher's engagement with Sun Ra is part homage and part critique. As Robin D. G. Kelley notes, Sun Ra is depicted not as the "'Black Moses' looking to lead the people to the promised land" that he considered himself but as "a strong leader for the people but not of the people."[55] Through his affil-

iation with Egypt, Sun Ra separates himself from the plight of the suffering masses and aligns himself with the pharaohs. A century after the New Negro movement, Gallagher turns to face the artists who came before her with respect—and questions. The leaders of the New Negro movement turned to the continent for an origin story that could anchor them in the New World. They prioritized the histories of pharaohs and pyramids over West Africa, from whence came the majority of people who were captured, enslaved, and transported to the United States. Ancient Egypt offered an inspiration point, but it also offered a convenient sidestepping of the transatlantic slave trade. In Gallagher's work, Sun Ra descends onto multitudes of Black people in pain, a pharaonic messiah figure, detached from their struggle. Adrienne Edwards elaborates on Gallagher's fascination with the site of Abu Simbel, built by Ramesses II in 1274 BCE. In the 1960s, the entire site was painstakingly moved two hundred meters from its original location to make way for the Aswan Dam. Gallagher reconsiders Sun Ra's version of ancient Egypt "brick by brick," understanding both the site and the myths to be in flux and more malleable than they appear.[56]

Gallagher's yellow paintings, such as *Pomp-Bang* (fig. 42), consist of gridded archival advertisements layered with three-dimensional wigs made of yellow Plasticine. In this body of work, Gallagher makes reference to the processional structure and ambitious world-building aims of Du Bois's pageant, *The Star of Ethiopia*. Gallagher explains, "In the yellow paintings the repeat characters . . . are fiction made real. The way historical and fictional characters exist simultaneously in the pageant form. The way history is used in pageantry to illuminate space and time (a way to think through history and race activated by ideas of trans-historical consciousness). . . . [It is] fiction with a stake in real relations between the 'being' of humans and consciousness."[57] In Gallagher's work, Egypt is not invoked to essentialize a collective for outside consumption or explore her own personal narrative. Instead, Gallagher indulges in, pushes against, and further stretches the myths of her predecessors. Ancient Egypt becomes a vessel for building personal and collective mythologies and a self-reflexive mythology for Black people speaking to each other across time and space. By culling a variety of references from across the African continent, the artists considered here continue the precedent of a syncretic understanding of their histories, presents, and futures. The function of the fiction—or myth—as an access point to shared consciousness is as important as the myth itself. Through ancient Egypt, these artists build nonlinear, transhistorical, trans-spatial bridges between themselves and their ancestors, each other, and the diaspora.

Compressive of Ideas: Black Photography and Ancient Egypt

Makeda Best

American photographer Chester Higgins made the photograph titled *African American pilgrims dance in honor of ancient spirits. Lake Nasser, Egypt* in 2006 (pl. 86). Twenty or so figures clad in white move across the frame of the blue-hued picture. Some at the back of the line have upraised arms; another, just at the edge of the frame with arms outstretched, seems to draw the group forward. Blurring elongates and distorts the forms, and elegant, waving fingers are framed graphically against the sky as the camera catches the movements of the bodies through space. Although the figures' backs are turned away from the camera and their faces are unseen, the picture communicates the emotional intensity of the moment.

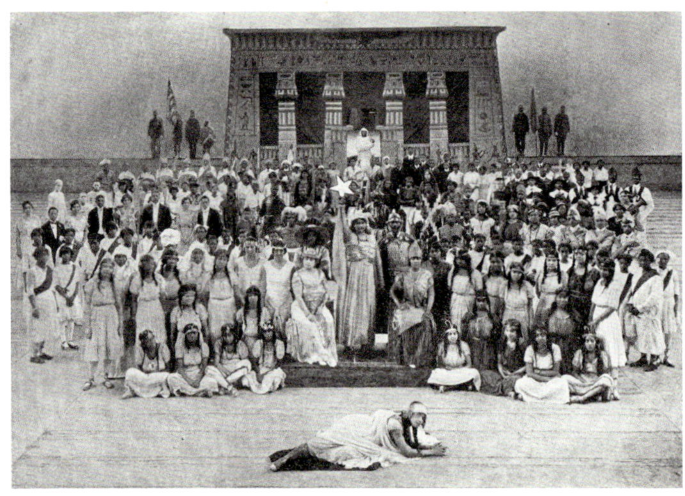

Fig. 43. Addison N. Scurlock (American, 1883–1964). **The Pageant, "Star of Ethiopia," in Philadelphia: A group of 200 of the 1,078 participants**, in **The Crisis** 12, no. 4 (August 1916). Schomburg Center for Research in Black Culture, Jean Blackwell Hutson Research and Reference Division, The New York Public Library

Over the past half century, and uniquely among African American photographers, Higgins has dedicated his lens work to Egypt. Before embarking in the mid-1970s on a decades-long career as a staff photographer at the *New York Times,* Higgins worked on commercial projects, including a commission that first took him to Egypt in 1973 to make photographs for a travel brochure. As part of his extensive and ongoing research, Higgins has made twenty trips to Egypt in his quest to explore relationships between the spiritual and physical worlds of people of the African diaspora—concepts that he views as foundational to the African American experience: "Unseen but ever manifesting itself, the spirit is omnipresent."[1] This essay surveys the visual culture of African American engagement with ancient Egypt through photography, exploring the work of Black photographers and the ways that Egypt figures in the self-fashioning of Black subjects through photography.

Egypt, long a mystical and idealized feature in the Western imagination, played a formative role in the early history of photography, driven by the Enlightenment-era interest in antiquity. With beliefs fed by Egypt's exotic associations, nineteenth-century scholars, geographers, and scientists contributed to the technical development of the medium and demonstrated its cultural utility in examining detailed information and documents related to Egypt and its past. When daguerreotype images were first announced to the world in 1839, astronomer François Arago, director of the Paris Observatory and champion of the inventor Louis-Jacques-Mandé Daguerre, argued for their use. He specifically cited the possibility of copying hieroglyphs by "so exact and rapid a means of reproduction" as one of the great gifts the new image-making process would offer to humanity.[2] Within months of Arago's announcement, a French expeditionary party, including a daguerreotypist, set out for Egypt, driven by a certainty that the study of the country's ancient architecture and languages was integral to understanding the history of Western civilization. Various other government-sponsored photographic projects and commissions soon followed.[3] The British gentleman scientist and intellectual William Henry Fox Talbot also referred to Egypt in the promotion of his independently invented, paper-based photographic process in the mid-1840s. Like other Victorians of his class, education, and background, Talbot counted Egyptology—along with such varied fields as art history, chemistry, mathematics, the classics, and botany—among his preoccupations.[4] As photographic technologies improved throughout the late nineteenth century, images of Egypt found expanded use as tools of colonial rule.

Until recently, histories of photography in the West cast Egypt as a passive subject. More recently, scholars such as Stephen Sheehi and Maria Golia have worked to disrupt this narrative through research on indigenous Egyptian photographers, photojournalists, artists, and studios—and the ways their work has shaped the country's social and political history.[5]

Photography by Egyptians reveals tensions between, on the one hand, the idealized views and perceptions of outsiders, and, on the other, how Egyptians see themselves and their history, their complicated attitudes toward race, identity, the appropriation of Egyptian culture, and the relationship between Egypt and the African continent.

While Egypt became inspirational to many twentieth-century African American artists, photography is perhaps the least represented medium in African American visual culture. Various factors may explain why Egypt appears less often than might be expected in photography, given the wider exploration of Egyptian motifs and symbols in other art forms. The photographic production of portraiture and the documentation of everyday life in the United States have been core aspects of the African American experience since the nineteenth century. While Alain Locke associated African American modernist painting and sculpture with Africa and African art in his 1925 essay "The Legacy of the Ancestral Arts," there was no such figure in photography. These direct connections were not made until the Black Arts Movement of the 1960s and 1970s. With its questioning of the dominance of Eurocentric models in American society, the Black Arts Movement was interested in language and the intimate role of the artist. In photography, these ideas found expression in publications like the *Black Photographers Annual*. In her introduction to the first volume of the *Annual* in 1973, the novelist Toni Morrison wrote that the publication "takes accurate aim and explodes our sensibilities. Telling us what we had forgotten we knew, showing us new things about ancient lives, and old truths in new phenomena."[6]

As opposed to Higgins's decades-long direct engagement with Egypt, the land and sites of Egypt in African American photographic culture are most often imaginatively or symbolically portrayed. Recognizing the pioneering scholarship of the photographic historian Deborah Willis, Maurice O. Wallace and Shawn Michelle Smith observe that, historically, "African American intellectuals, authors, orators, and activists understood, responded to, and utilized photography to create new spaces for self and community."[7] This pluralistic, imaginative interpretation of photography's function is useful when considering how photographers responded to the subject of Egyptian lands, culture, and politics. Photographs related to this topic have often performed a dual function of personal and collective

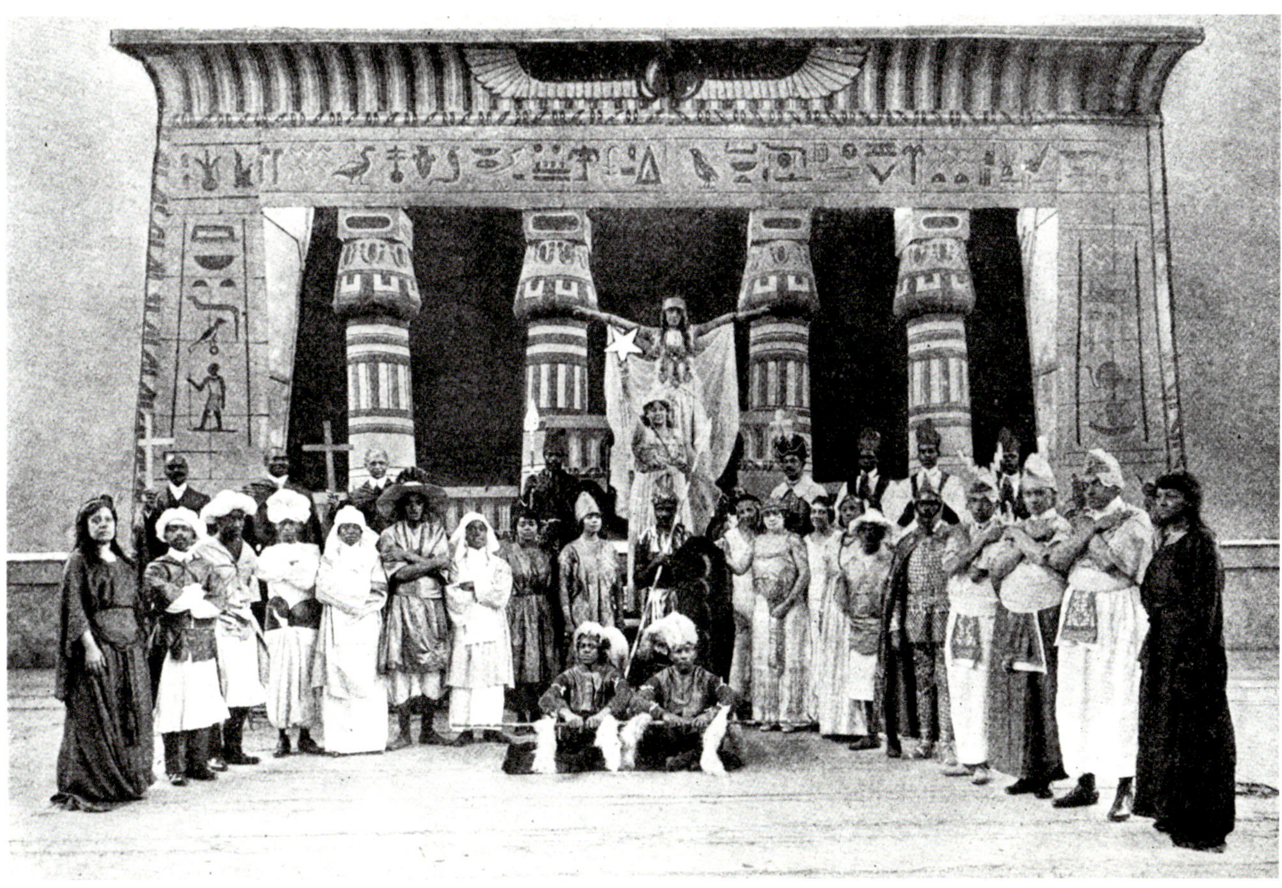

Fig. 44. Addison N. Scurlock (American, 1883–1964). **The Pageant, "Star of Ethiopia," in Philadelphia: Leading characters, and Temple built and decorated by Richard Brown and Lenwood Morris**, in **The Crisis** 12, no. 4 (August 1916). Schomburg Center for Research in Black Culture, Jean Blackwell Hutson Research and Reference Division, The New York Public Library

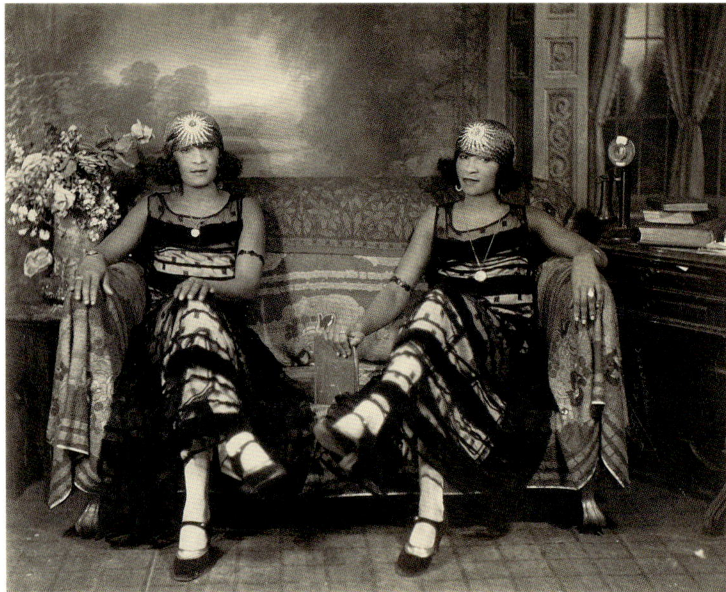

Fig. 45. James Van Der Zee (American, 1886–1983). **Identical Twins**, 1924. Gelatin silver print, 7⅜ x 9⅜ in. (18.7 x 23.8 cm). The Metropolitan Museum of Art, New York, Gift of James Van Der Zee Institute, 1970 (1970.539.2)

spiritual and political placemaking. Since the early twentieth century, this photographic expression has taken many forms, from portraiture to abstraction, and has been produced in different formats, from print journalism to fine art. Africana studies scholar and literary theorist Christel N. Temple offers the concept of "anteriority," which she describes as "an awareness of the continuum from ancient to modern origins" that "informs . . . practices, procedures, guidelines, and techniques."[8] Photography as a medium has a unique potential to engage this concept. The documentary nature of the photograph offers the opportunity both to objectively record details and to affirm perceived spiritual, cultural, and political connections; the medium allows practitioners simultaneously to imagine the existence of the "continuum" of history, capture it, and insist on its presence in the now. African American visual culture's photographic engagement with Egypt can be contextualized within the broader twentieth-century exploration of distinctly African American political identities. In realistic detail, photography could contribute to this work through its capacity to document the process of identity formation in real life.

In the August 1916 issue of *The Crisis,* the official magazine of the National Association for the Advancement of Colored People, readers found full-page photographs from the Philadelphia production of a historical pageant, *The Star of Ethiopia*, written and produced by historian and activist W. E. B. Du Bois, who was also the founder and editor of *The Crisis* and one of the era's leading cultural figures. Du Bois, himself the frequent subject of photographs, had co-curated the "Exhibit of American Negroes" at the 1900 Paris Exposition, demonstrating that he knew how to strategically deploy images. Written in 1911, *The Star of Ethiopia* was first performed in 1913 as part of an exposition in New York commemorating the fiftieth anniversary

of the Emancipation Proclamation. In six sections, the pageant presented symbolic episodes of African and African American history, with ancient Egyptian culture featured prominently. The literary historian Evan Lee argues that Du Bois recognized the potential for Egypt and Ethiopia to function similarly to the classical tradition of ancient Greece and Rome as a rhetorical tool that could be used in order to cement the dignity of a people by establishing their ancient roots.[9]

The first photograph in the multi-page spread portrays "200 of the 1,078" participants in the pageant (fig. 43), and the second features a smaller group of the "leading characters" (fig. 44). Visible in the background of both images is the massive backdrop depicting an Egyptian temple decorated with hieroglyphs, designed and constructed by Richard Brown and Lenwood Morris. The actors positioned aloft at the back center are framed by its pillars, creating depth in the image. The maker of the photographs, Addison N. Scurlock, had opened a studio on U Street, Washington, D.C., in 1911, and began contributing to *The Crisis*. Scurlock deployed the camera as a tool for racial uplift. The power of his large group portraits of *The Star of Ethiopia*, which can themselves be interpreted as a form of pageantry, enforces Du Bois's message concerning the dignity of the past and the present. In these photographs, the stage set is activated by the composition so that it functions as more than just a backdrop. The horizontal orientation of the image, with the actors arrayed across the frame, transports the viewer of the photograph into the theater. Scurlock's skill and attention to detail are evident. Assuming careful poses, the actors are arranged so that each is highlighted. Scurlock graphically juxtaposed the figures against the others that surround them and distinguished them by their costumes. By the time these portraits appeared, *The Crisis* was well on its way toward its peak circulation of one hundred thousand readers. Popular entertainment plays a political function here, just as Scurlock's photographs of everyday life did. Scurlock sought for his work to empower his audiences. His arrangement of the *Star* cast was not unlike his group studio portraits made for private clients. Viewers would have seen commonalities between their personal photographs, celebrating weddings and other occasions, and those of the actors from the Du Bois play.

Du Bois was attracted to the pageantry and ritual of ancient peoples, and photography can be seen as particularly suited to engage those qualities.[10] The production of portraits is itself ritualistic. The "pageant" photograph is an aesthetic that dominates *The Crisis,* creating its own form of visual theater through a regular stream of individual and large group portraits. After the discovery of Tutankhamun's tomb in 1922, the subjects of such images even appeared in the popular Egyptian-inspired clothing of the era. For example, in the 1924 portrait known as *Identical Twins* by Harlem photographer James Van Der Zee (fig. 45), the large appliqué starbursts on the stylish young women's headbands have been seen as "evidence of the women's engagement with a broader African American celebration of Egyptian culture" in the wake of the Tutankhamun discovery.[11]

During the period spanning World Wars I and II, African Americans focused their lenses on domestic life and building a social and political identity, and Egypt once again entered the Black photographic sphere during the civil rights movement of

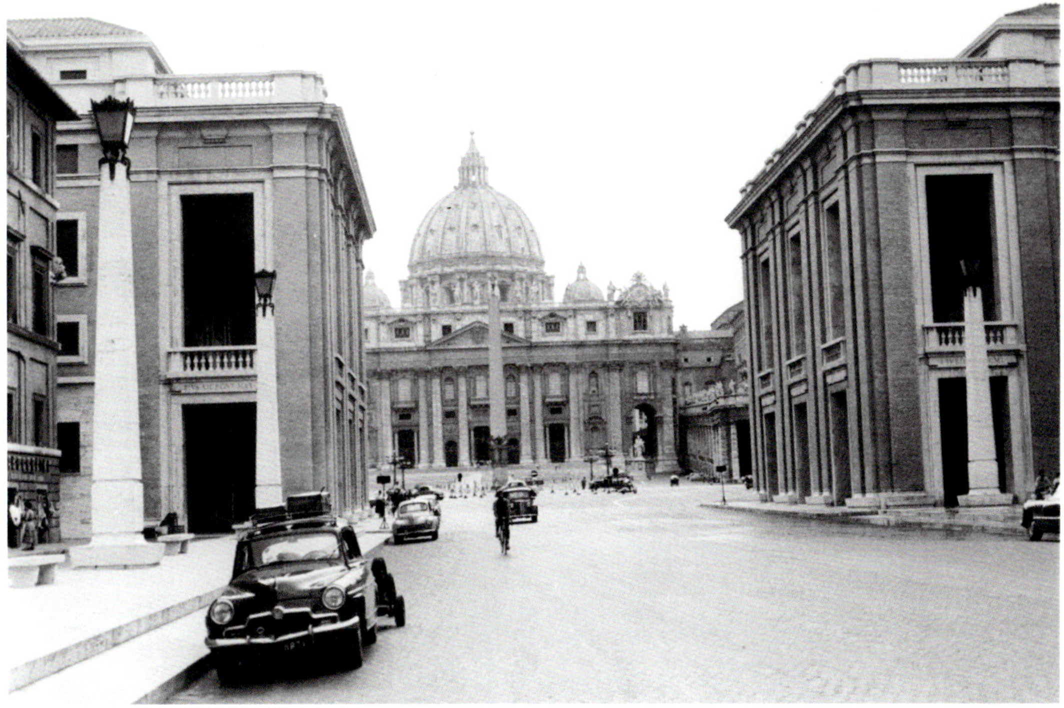

the 1950s and 1960s. Reading Italian newspapers from Rome, author Ralph Ellison learned of decolonization movements in Egypt and referred to these events in his work. His writings also reflected on the "anachronism" of white people who stood against the citizenship of Black people in his own country.[12] Ellison was in Rome from 1955 to 1957 as the American Academy in Rome's first African American writer in residence. He also made photographs, mainly street images. Researchers have only just begun to explore the author's large archive of photographs, which can be interpreted as visual corollaries to various themes present in his writing. Connecting Ellison's frame of mind at the time to the photographs he made in Rome, the Italian studies scholar Sara Marzioli focuses on an image made on Via della Conciliazione (fig. 46). The photograph portrays a street empty except for a lone biker riding toward Ellison. Pointing to the detail of the Egyptian obelisk at the center of the square of St. Peter in the distance—one of eight brought to the capital in ancient times—Marzioli argues that it "functions as a reminder of the long history of relations between Italy and Africa, relations that, until very recently, have been effaced from the official narratives of Italian history."[13] In this way, Marzioli writes, the photograph "reminds us that urban space heightens the visibility of the social and political contradictions of modernity . . . [and] speaks to the history of European imperialism in Africa."[14]

In the mid-twentieth century, Egyptian lands contributed to the self-fashioning of various African American figures. Images of Louis Armstrong in Egypt played multiple roles on the international and domestic stage around the same time that

Ellison made his photograph. Armstrong was enlisted by the U.S. State Department in 1956 as part of a geopolitical strategy to use jazz, by that time an international commodity, as a form of cultural warfare in the competition for influence between the United States and the Soviet Union. Events in Little Rock, Arkansas, in 1957—when white mobs prevented nine African American high school students from integrating Central High School—led the entertainer uncharacteristically to speak out against the actions of American politicians and refuse to participate in a State Department tour.[15] Amid ongoing racial tension in the United States, in January of 1961 he finally embarked on a tour that included Egypt. A photograph shows him standing in front of the Great Sphinx and a pyramid at Giza, serenading his wife Lucille (pl. 73). Personally, Armstrong expressed a growing awareness of his connection to Africa.[16] As emphasized by the sonic references of the trumpet, his photograph triumphantly announces a return, an affinity, a reclamation. The site of the picture is specific, but its "sound" carries across space, as does Armstrong's presence across the land.

El-Hajj Malik El-Shabazz (known as Malcolm X until he changed his name in 1964) was photographed multiple times during his third trip to Egypt, in 1964, by Black Star photographer John Launois. At the time of his trip, Shabazz had recently founded the Organization of Afro-American Unity and earlier in the year had delivered one of his most influential speeches, "The Ballot or the Bullet." By then an internationally recognized figure, he visited Egypt on this occasion as part of a five-week tour of Africa. The images were published in a groundbreaking issue of the *Saturday Evening Post* on September 12, 1964,

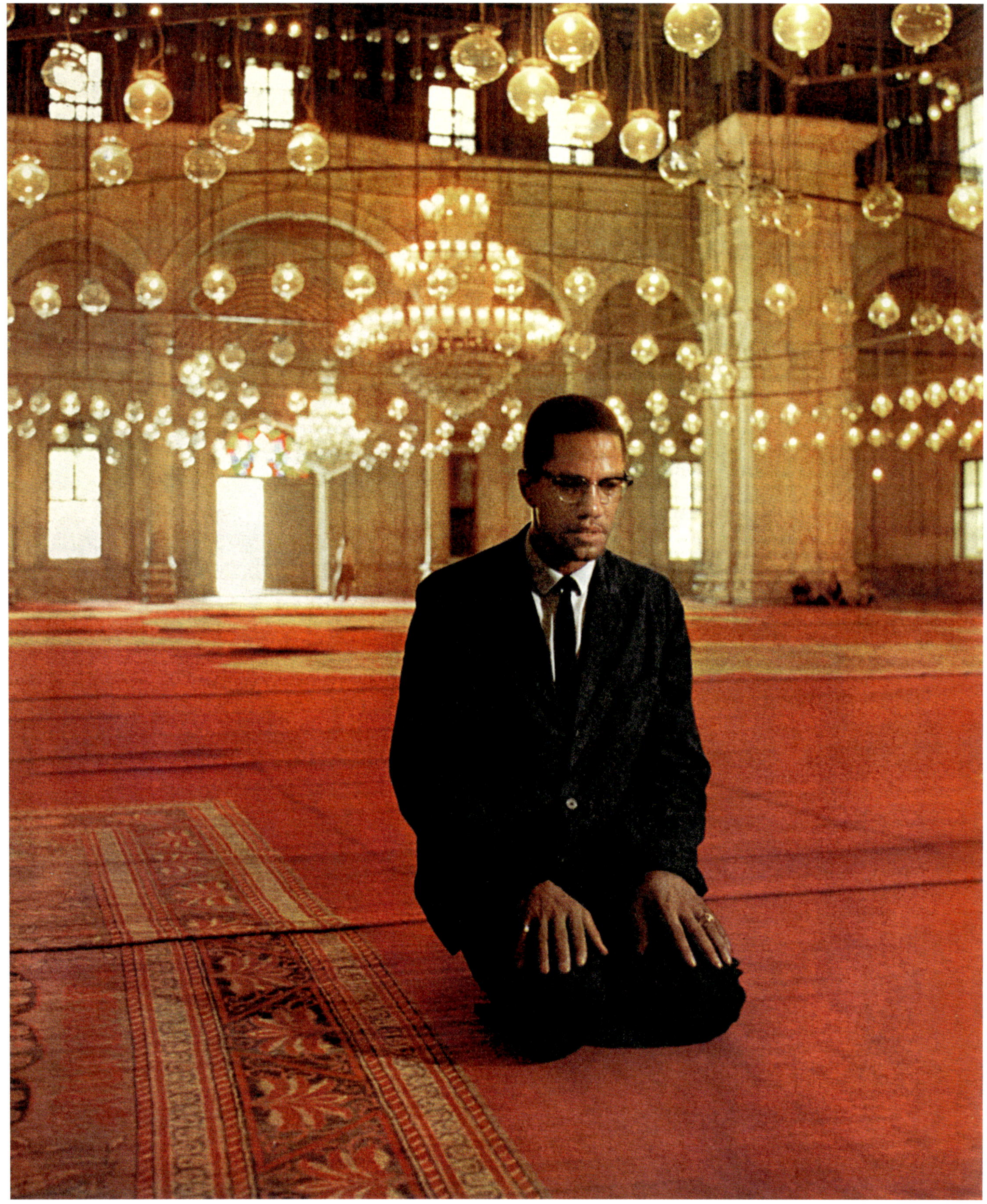

Fig. 47. John Launois (French, 1929–2002). **Malcolm X prays in the great Mosque of Mohammed Ali in Cairo**, in **The Saturday Evening Post** (September 12, 1964)

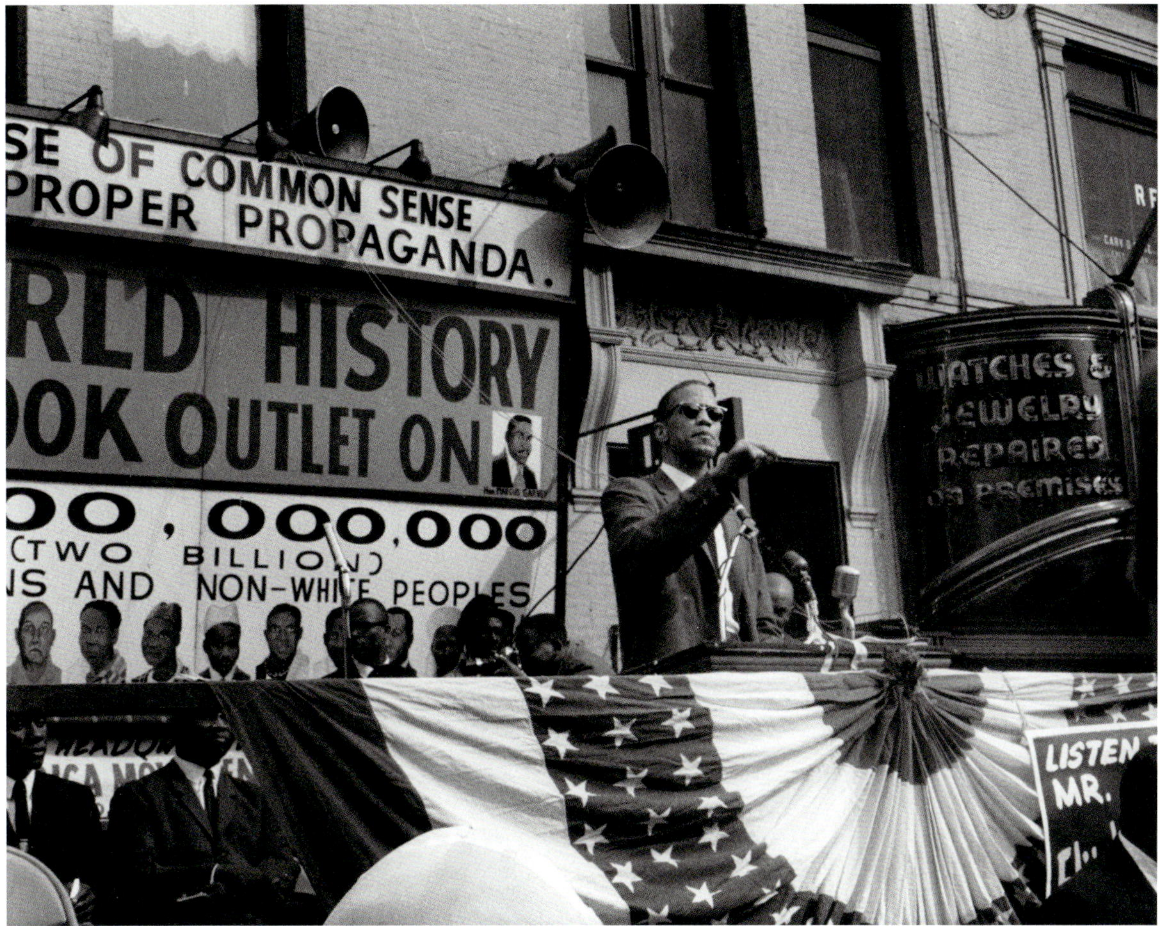

Fig. 48. Beuford Smith (American, b. 1941), **Malcolm X in front of Mr. Lewis Michaux's Bookstore,** 1964, printed 2017. Gelatin silver print, 10¹⁵⁄₁₆ x 13¹⁵⁄₁₆ in. (27.8 x 35.4 cm). Whitney Museum of American Art, New York. Purchase, with funds from the Photography Committee (2020.45)

with the cover story, "I'm Talking to You, White Man," the text of which would later be featured in his autobiography. The intense and intimate cover photograph of the *Post,* made at the mosque of Mohammed Ali in Cairo, depicts Shabazz's face bathed in golden light and features twinkling architectural details blurred in the distance. In another photograph made at the same location, he is kneeling in prayer (fig. 47). Shabazz, in his trademark black suit and tie, is framed by circles of glittering chandeliers, the windows at the back of the mosque, and a vivid red interior. The geometric shapes enhance and provide a contrasting backdrop to Shabazz's deeply contemplative expression. In this way, the composition allows the viewer to see the vast main hall, emphasizing Shabazz's seemingly lone presence and referring to the spiritual quest that had defined his life. These photographs of Shabazz function on multiple levels, casting him as both a subject of the tourist gaze and a tourist. Like Du Bois, the civil rights leader was a frequent subject of images and, as a talented media strategist, a manipulator of images that could address critics and channel and support his ideas (pl. 75).

By the 1960s, inspired by Black independence movements, more African Americans were drawn to Africa, and Egypt played

a new narrative and political function within photographs. At a rally in Harlem, photographer Gordon Parks captured a beaming young man holding a copy of the Nation of Islam's official newspaper, *Muhammad Speaks.* Parks was working on a story for *Life* magazine on Black Muslims. On the front page of the paper the young man holds is a photograph of Akbar Muhammad, son of Nation leader Elijah Muhammad and the newspaper's correspondent in Cairo, standing before the Great Pyramid of Giza (pl. 87). The headline above the image—"Our Freedom Can't Wait!"—refers to the edition's primary feature and is a quotation from Harlem Congressman Adam Clayton Powell Jr., who had joined the Nation in solidarity for an event known as the Human Rights Rally. Parks's photograph captures the dynamic visual, symbolic, and political intermingling of contemporary politics, present-day Egypt, and ancient Egypt in Harlem, where the sense of allegiance with Pan-African independence was also famously on display at Lewis Michaux's National Memorial African Bookstore. A sign on the side of the store, at Seventh Avenue and 125th Street, promised "History of the Negro Retold in Pictures, Busts, Books, Songs," and this plays out across its front, mostly through photographic media. The scrapbook-like facade, covered with texts and photographic images,

     Compressive of Ideas

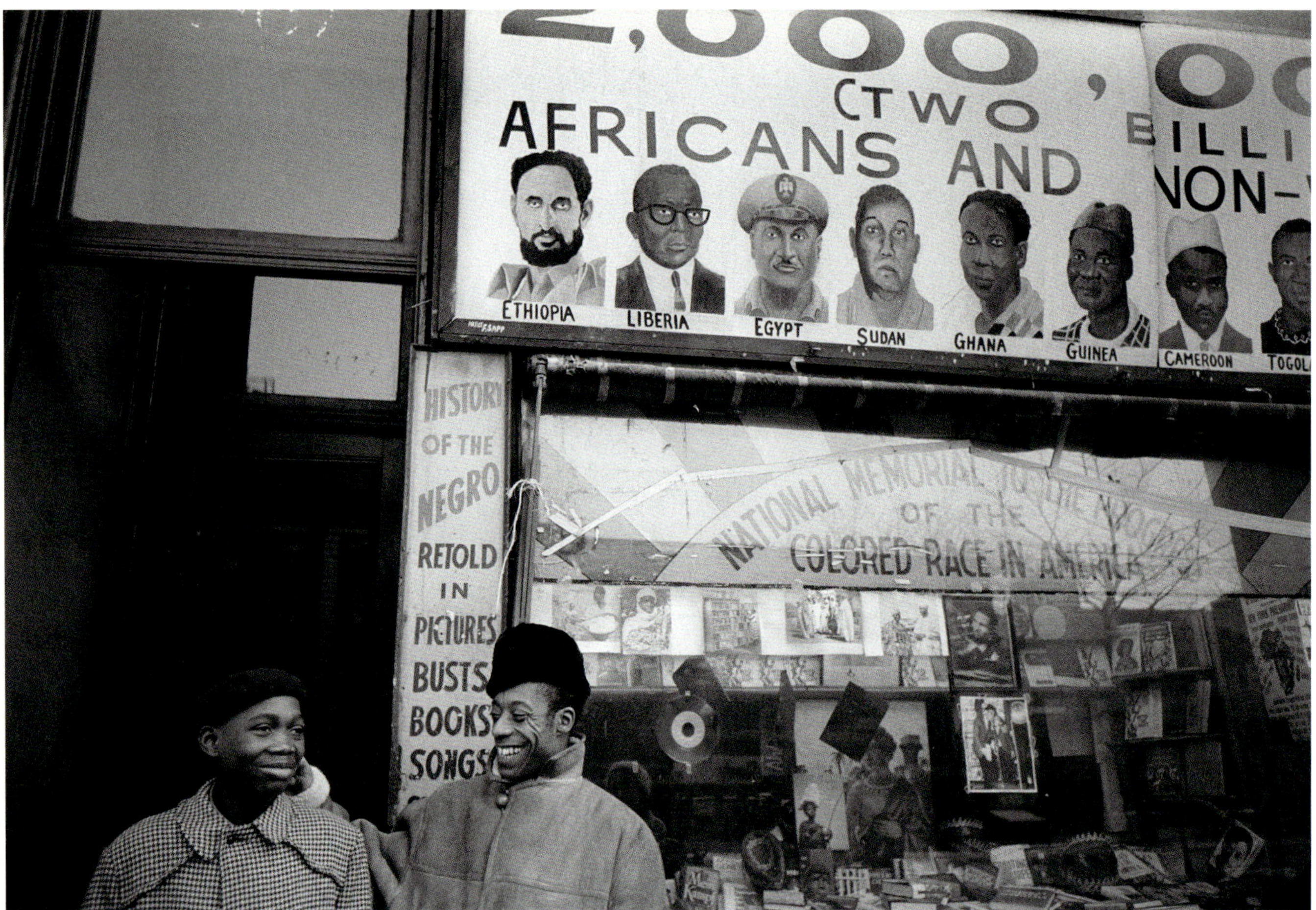

Fig. 49. Steve Schapiro (American, 1934–2022). **James Baldwin with his Nephew and Namesake outside Lewis H. Michaux's National Memorial African Bookstore, Harlem,** January 1963. Silver gelatin print, 15¾ x 19¹¹⁄₁₆ in. (40 x 50 cm). Richard and Carole Cocks Art Museum, Miami University, Oxford, Ohio, Partial Gift of Stephen Schapiro and Miami University Art Museum purchase with contributions from the Kezur Endowment Fund (2019.23.7)

featured a large sign above the door that read "2,000,000,000 (2 billion) Africans and non-white peoples" with a row of twelve portraits titled "African Chiefs of States" that included Egyptian president Gamal Abdel Nasser, Ethiopia's Haile Selassie I, and others. The impact of the state portraits is further bolstered by the words on the sign below that at one point read "With all the facts about all the blacks in all the world over and all the people are invited to come in and browse! Seeing is believing!" The pantheon of leaders offers proof of the end of colonialism's rule. Details such as the cropping of the images, the figures' gazes, and the visible differences in the lighting of each reveal the origins of these painted portraits in photography. Across the facade, Michaux also packed photographs of famous events related to Black history and celebrated Black political and cultural figures. The various styles of the documentary photographs (many of them featuring Harlem's own Shabazz (fig. 48), who held rallies in front of the bookstore) create a visual sense of the action and dynamism of the movement for Black freedom around the world. Shabazz was not the only famous Black

leader to be photographed in front of the bookstore. In 1963, Steve Schapiro photographed the writer James Baldwin and his nephew (fig. 49) standing with, in effect, Nasser and the phalanx of leaders who were reclaiming the African continent.

In mid-twentieth-century photography, Egypt existed beyond its well-known locales, partially embodied in its historic president Nasser, a leader of the 1952 revolution. In 1960, Nasser was one of the many international figures (like India's Jawaharlal Nehru) who visited Cuban leader Fidel Castro when he stayed at the Hotel Theresa in Harlem after leaving a midtown hotel where he and his entourage had originally planned to stay. A large and exuberant crowd turned out to celebrate and support Castro, his choice to recognize the cultural and political significance of Harlem, and the global leaders like Nasser who came to meet with the Cuban prime minister. The crowd included an unidentified woman who appears in a few photographs of the dense crowd (fig. 50). Clutching newspapers under one arm, she has an awkwardly large framed portrait of Nasser affixed by a string around her neck, suggesting the intimacy with

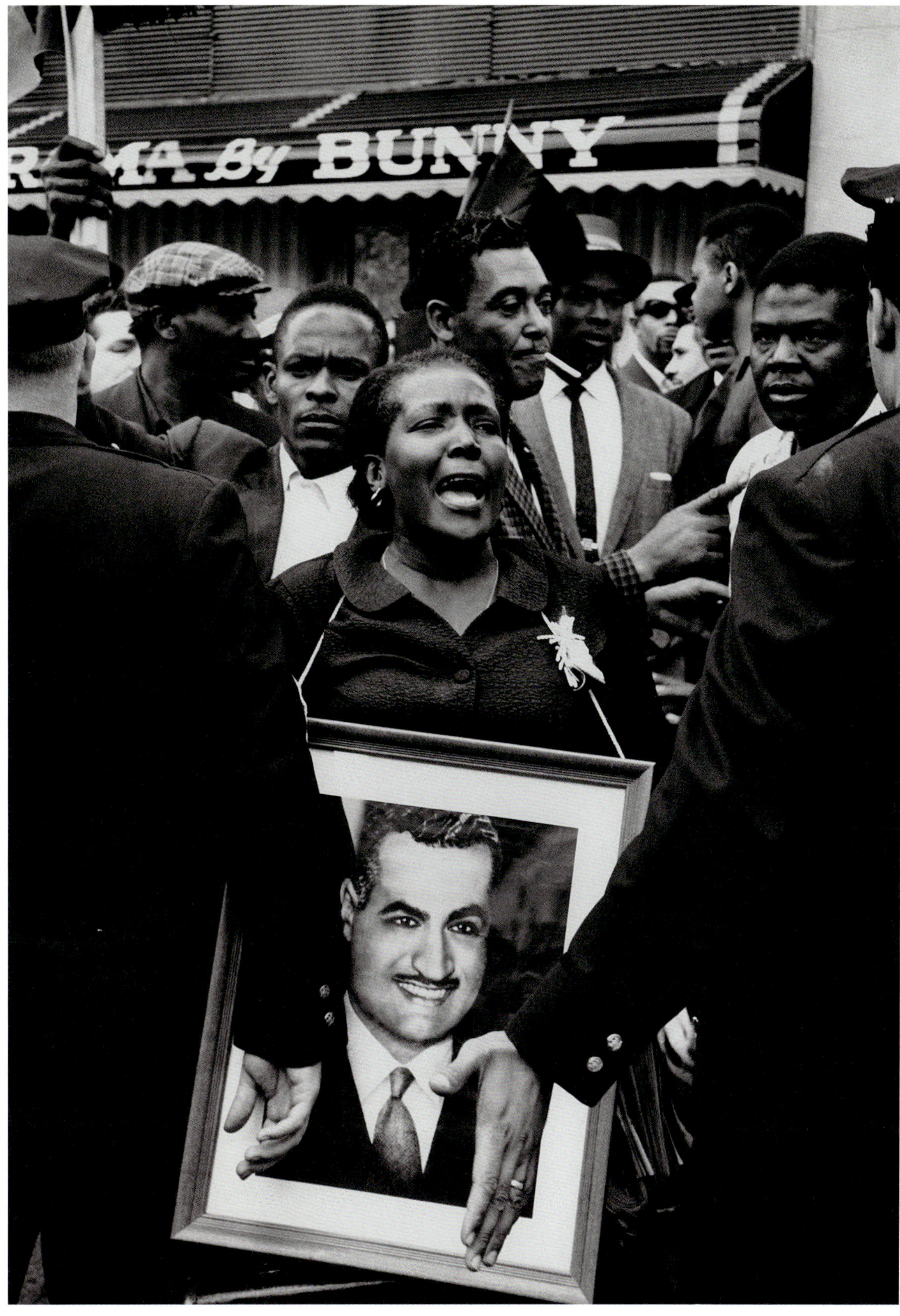

Fig. 50. Andrew St. George (Hungarian American, 1934–2001). **Woman with Portrait of Gamal Abdel Nasser, Harlem, New York**, September 18, 1960

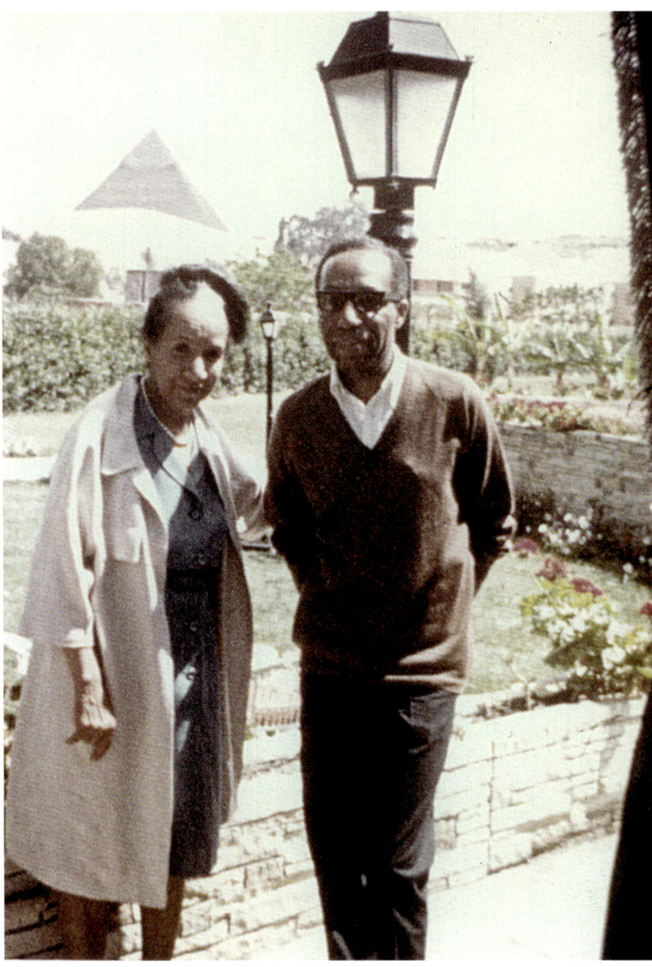

Fig. 51. Unknown photographer. **Shirley Graham Du Bois and Son David Graham Du Bois**, ca. 1968. Special Collections and University Archives, University of Massachusetts Amherst Libraries, Amherst, Massachusetts (MS 906)

beyond the abstract idea of Africa into a real, lived relationship with peoples of African cultures?"[19] During the course of the twentieth century, photographs in African American visual culture reflect a version of that question—that is, how to move from the abstract to the tangible application of ideas modeled in the Egyptian context to the work of African American political empowerment.

While photographs of Ali were widely shared in media markets, mostly lost to history are private images like the one for which Shirley Graham Du Bois and her son David Graham Du Bois posed near the Pyramids of Giza (fig. 51). Shirley Graham Du Bois was a Black Marxist, a Pan-Africanist, and an author, as well as the second wife of W. E. B Du Bois. Seven years after the photograph was taken, David published his novel . . . *And Bid Him Sing*. Set in Cairo in 1964, the book aims to move beyond U.S.–based histories of racism in the Jim Crow South through the presentation of a "global" Jim Crow. The photograph, with its odd cropping (leaving the legs inelegantly truncated and an indecipherable architectural element visible along the side of the photograph) and angled perspective, is touching because of its construction. Within the context of their politics, the vernacular photograph takes on a deeper meaning than a personal memento.

The photographs of Kamoinge, formed in 1963 and based in New York, further engage the complex role of Egypt in 1960s and 1970s in Black American culture. Textual references and photographs pertaining to African anti-colonialist struggles continued to appear in the pages of the *Black Photographers Annual* (1973–80), which was founded and published by photographers associated with Kamoinge.[20] In the photograph known as *Girl with Egyptian Mural*, group member Louis Draper constructed a graphic and symbolic dialogue between a young girl and the wall with Egytian motifs against which she is posed, her profile and raised arm echoed in the figures behind her (pl. 57). The position of the photographer and the slant of the wall distort the pictorial space so that the girl and the pictures seem to merge across time and space.

Textual references to children, Egypt, and twentieth-century political struggles in the built environment occur repeatedly in Draper's photography. In another photograph, a young girl stands in front of a wall. Draper contrasts her clear portrait against the blurred writing on the wall behind her that simply reads "Cuba." The theme of photography as writing and the connection of Black photographers to "ancient" Black "authors" would later be articulated in the pages of the *Annual*. In its fourth edition, John A. Williams wrote: "The mark of a culture, of a people, has always been the ability of that people to create truthful images of itself and what it stands for. We still use the carving tools and the paint brushes, but these have been augmented by the black box. . . . We do this because we are a people still striving for a place under this newer sun. And we do it not because others don't see us, but because we see ourselves better."[21]

Kamoinge member Ming Smith distorts the perception of the built environment in *Street Market, Cairo, Egypt* (fig. 52), a photograph she made while visiting Egypt in the early 1970s. Smith chose to truncate the bodies of her human subjects at the bottom of the composition, emphasizing their roles as

which she feels connected to Nasser and what he represents. The woman with the portrait of Nasser and a large sign visible in another photograph from the same event that reads "Congo for the Congolese"—referring to Congolese independence, which had only been achieved a few months previously—illustrate how the gathering outside of the Theresa had become a temporary "center of Third World negotiation and anticolonial solidarity."[17] But, as the facade of Mr. Michaux's bookstore illustrates, this kind of dialogue already had a permanent home in Harlem through the placement of photographic images.

When the newly crowned heavyweight champion Muhammad Ali made a visit to Egypt in 1964 at the invitation of the Arab Boxing Federation, he made a point of meeting Nasser. In a series of photographs, Ali appears joyful at his meeting with the president, who was widely revered as a champion in his own right. Nasser's 1956 nationalization of the Suez Canal Zone was read by leading Black American writers and presented in the Black press as a powerful act of resistance to colonialism and an inspiration for their own civil rights struggle.[18] In her essay on Pan-African politics and African American art, the art historian Bridget Cooks asks, "How do visual artists move

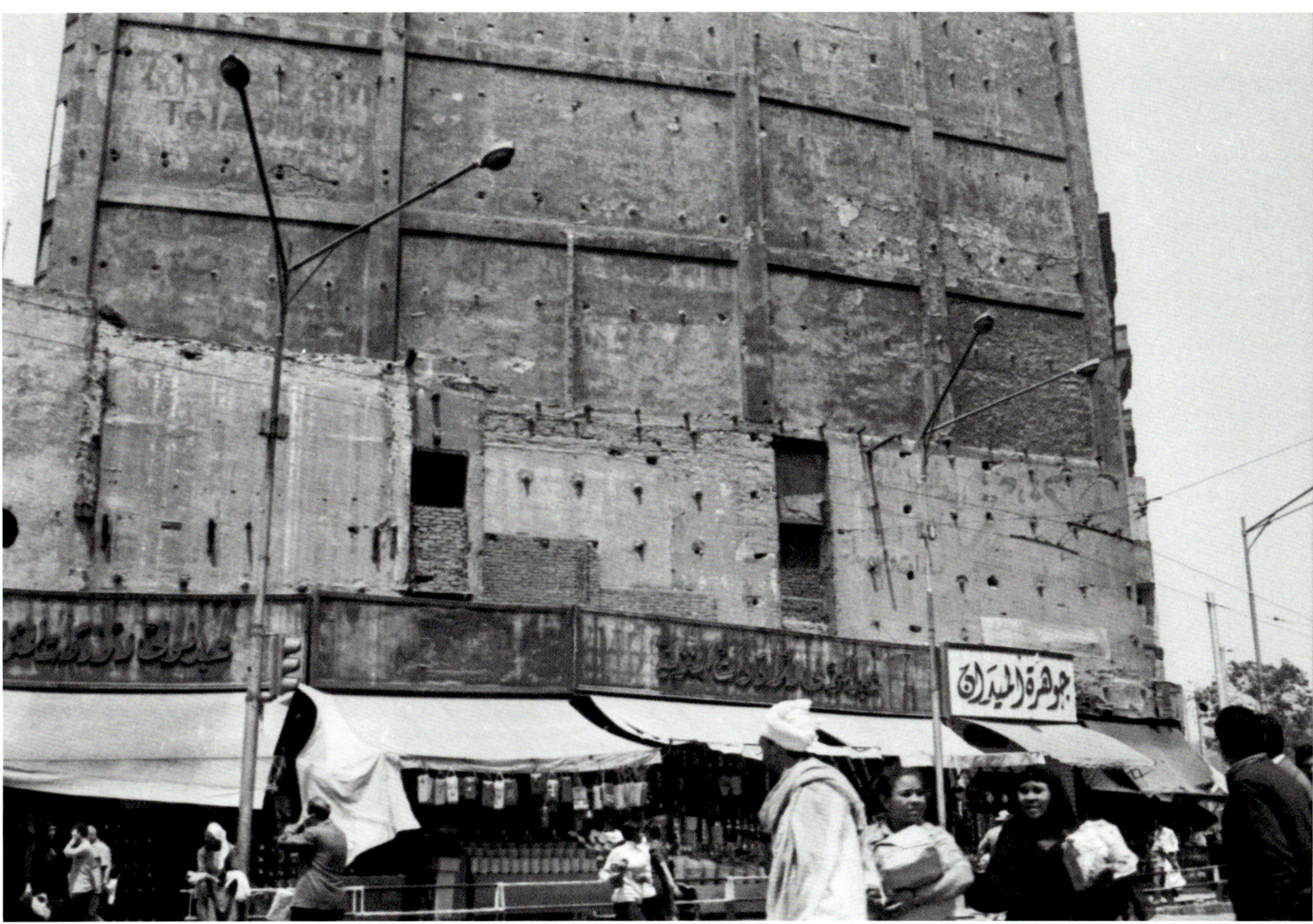

Fig. 52. Ming Smith (American, b. 1947). **Street Market, Cairo, Egypt**, ca. 1973. Gelatin silver print

graphic forms in space. The graphic impact of this compositional choice is heightened by the presence of the large structure in the background; its top is also cut off, and the function of the building is unclear. What is brought into focus are its repetitively graphic qualities—the rectangles that compose its cement skeleton, punctuated with dots, and tips of rebar sticking out of the building. The construction of the composition is disorienting, yet the details and the subject matter make the scene seem both familiar and grand, if mundane.

While Draper delicately merges illusory effects and real-life detail, and Smith transforms an ordinary scene, C. Daniel Dawson creates a purely otherworldly space in *Olaifa and Egypt* (pl. 47). Inspired by what he has described as the "mythopoetics" of the innovative and experimental musician and composer Sun Ra, Dawson in this picture fuses the face of his goddaughter Olaifa with Egyptian statuary in the collection of a New York–area museum.[22] Like Draper's image of the girl, Dawson's participates in Ra's recombinant aesthetic that linked the past and future, and African American and Egyptian cultural motifs, all of which ultimately serve to underscore the origin myths of Egypt and diasporic West African

cultures.[23] As Dawson emphasizes, "You're talking about Egyptian mythology, Black reality, Egypt as being Black, all these things were kind of fused into that, too. So, again, it's kind of compressive of ideas into one piece."[24] Like Draper and Smith, Dawson uses photography as a means through which to ground the historical continuum in the contemporary and in everyday life. His work proposes that it is possible to confront histories of racial oppression while also participating in ritual and in healing. These photographs, like others produced throughout the twentieth century by African American practitioners, speak to the ways in which Egyptian politics and culture inspired, connected, and mobilized people globally.

     Compressive of Ideas

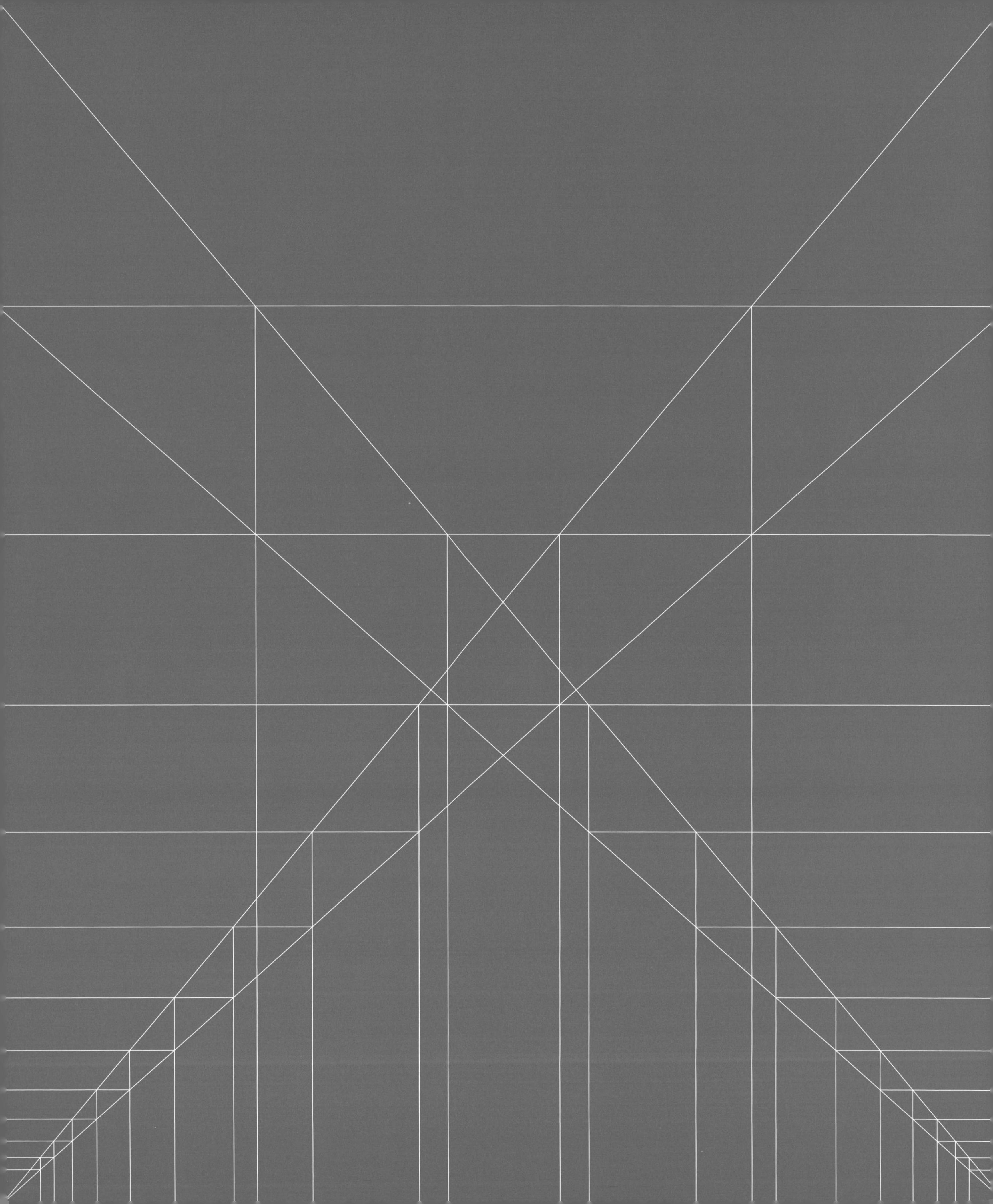

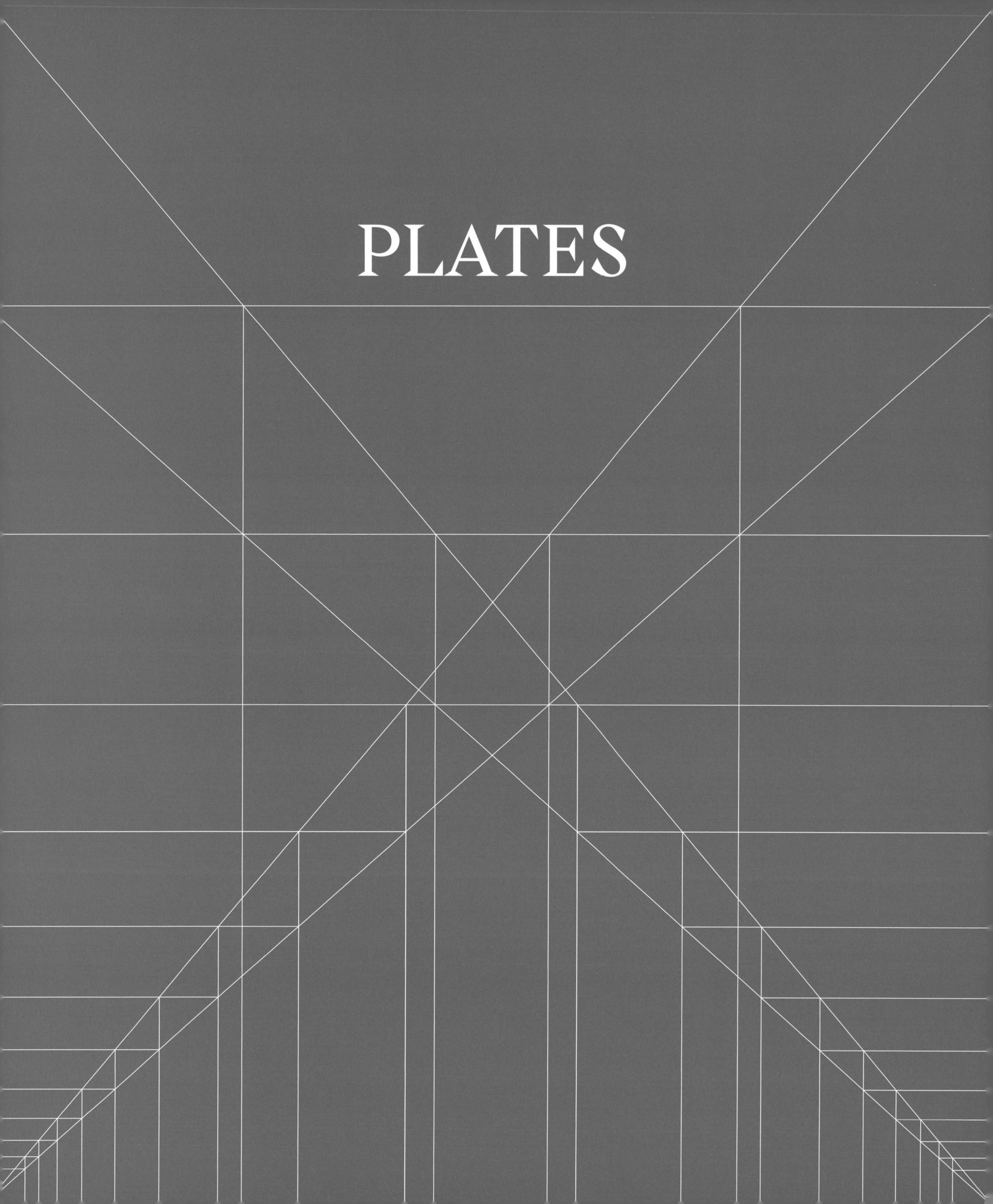

PLATES

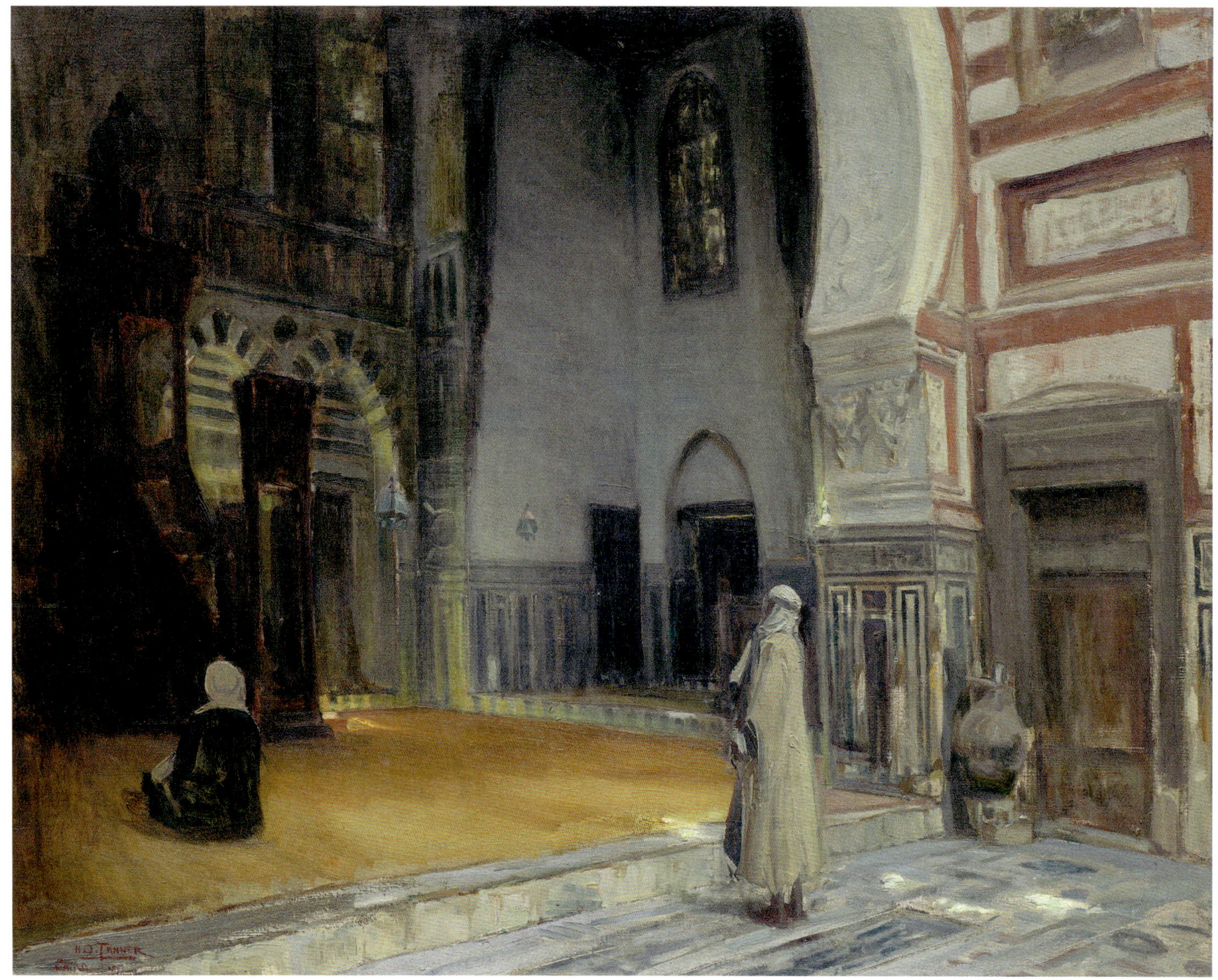

Pl. 1. Henry Ossawa Tanner, **Interior of a Mosque, Cairo**, 1897

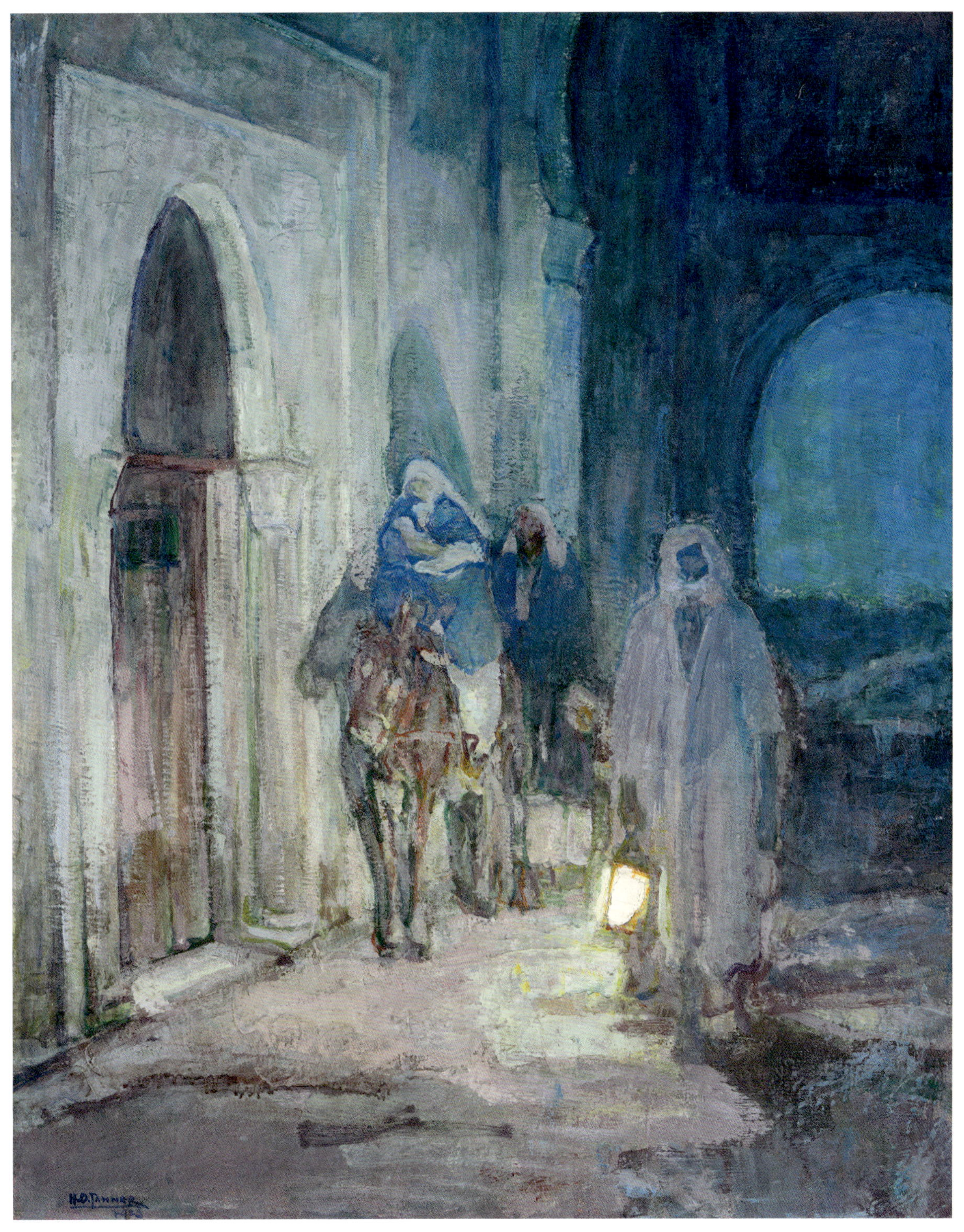

Pl. 2. Henry Ossawa Tanner, **Flight into Egypt**, 1923

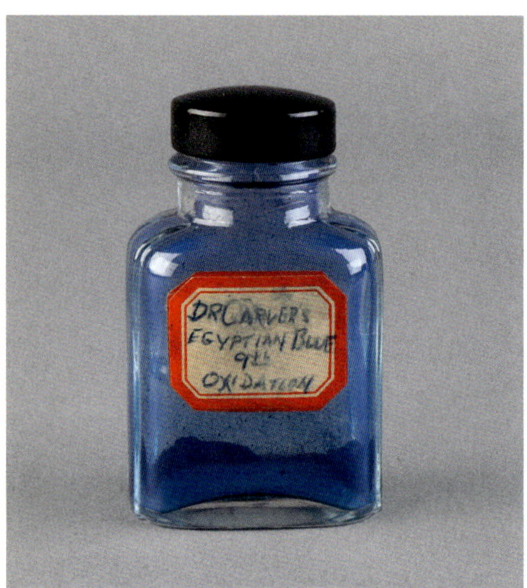

Pl. 3. George Washington Carver, **Dr. Carver's Egyptian Blue 9th Oxidation,** 1930s

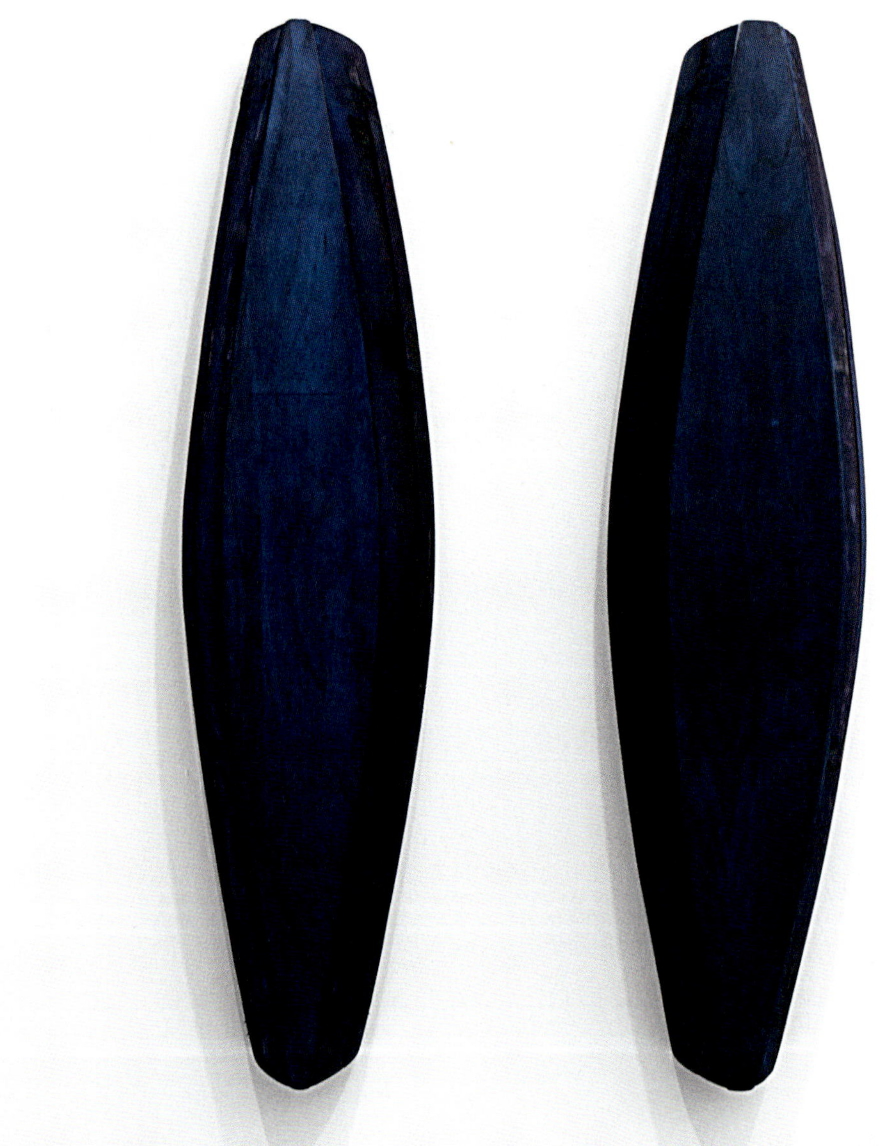

Pl. 4. Terry Adkins, **Oxidation Blue 1,** 2013

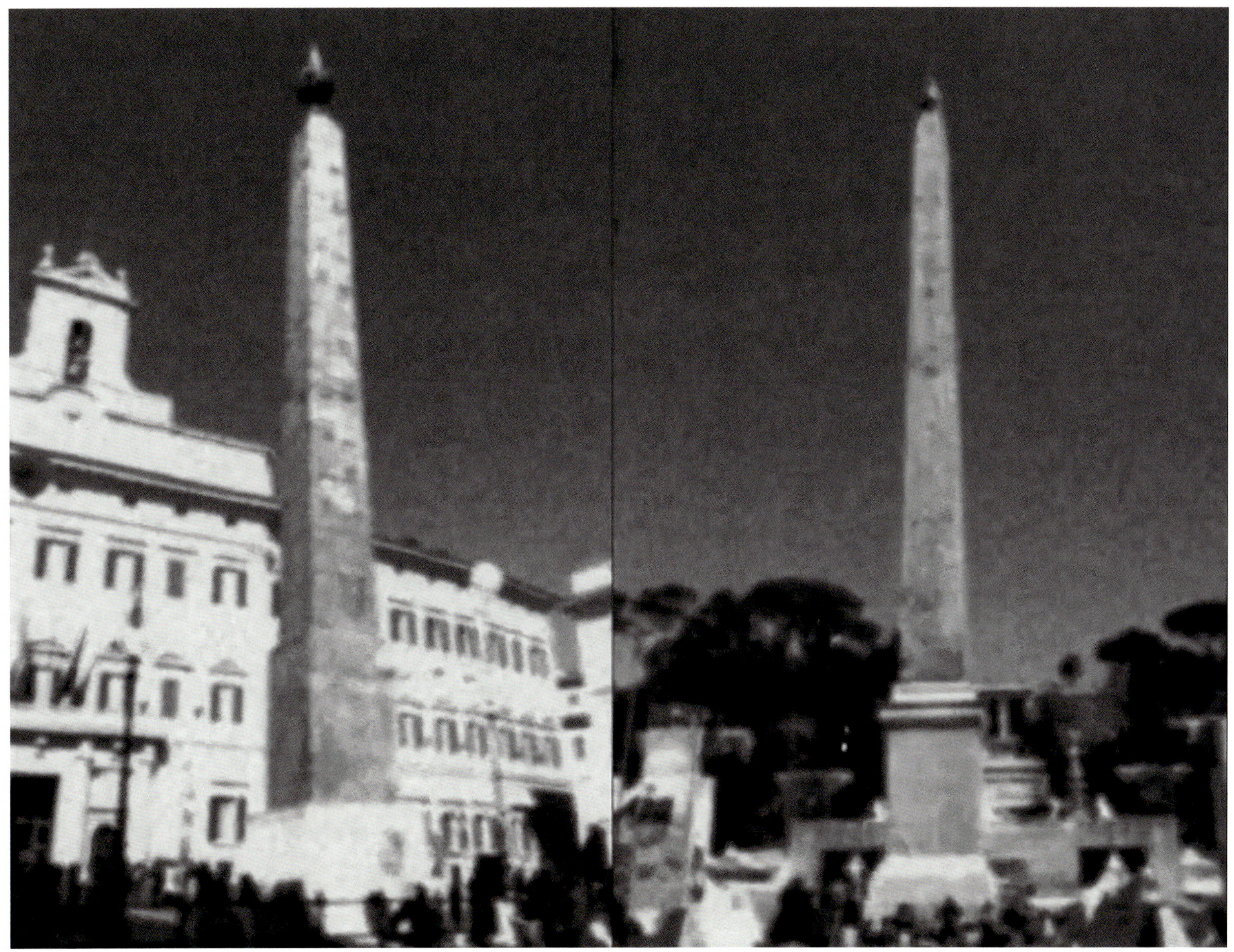

Pl. 5. Still from Terry Adkins, **Obelisks in Rome**, 2010

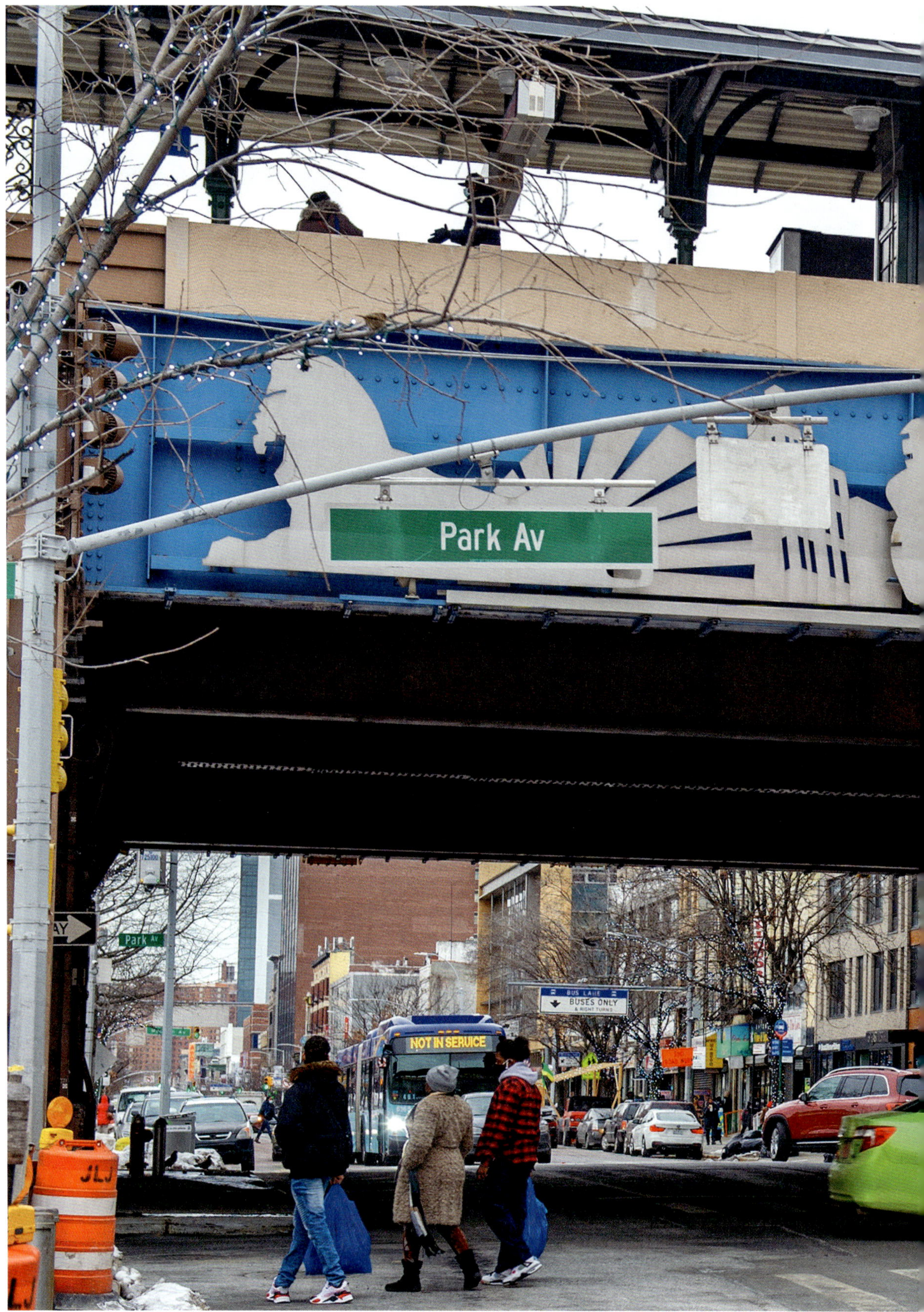

Pl. 6. Terry Adkins, **Harlem Encore**, 1999

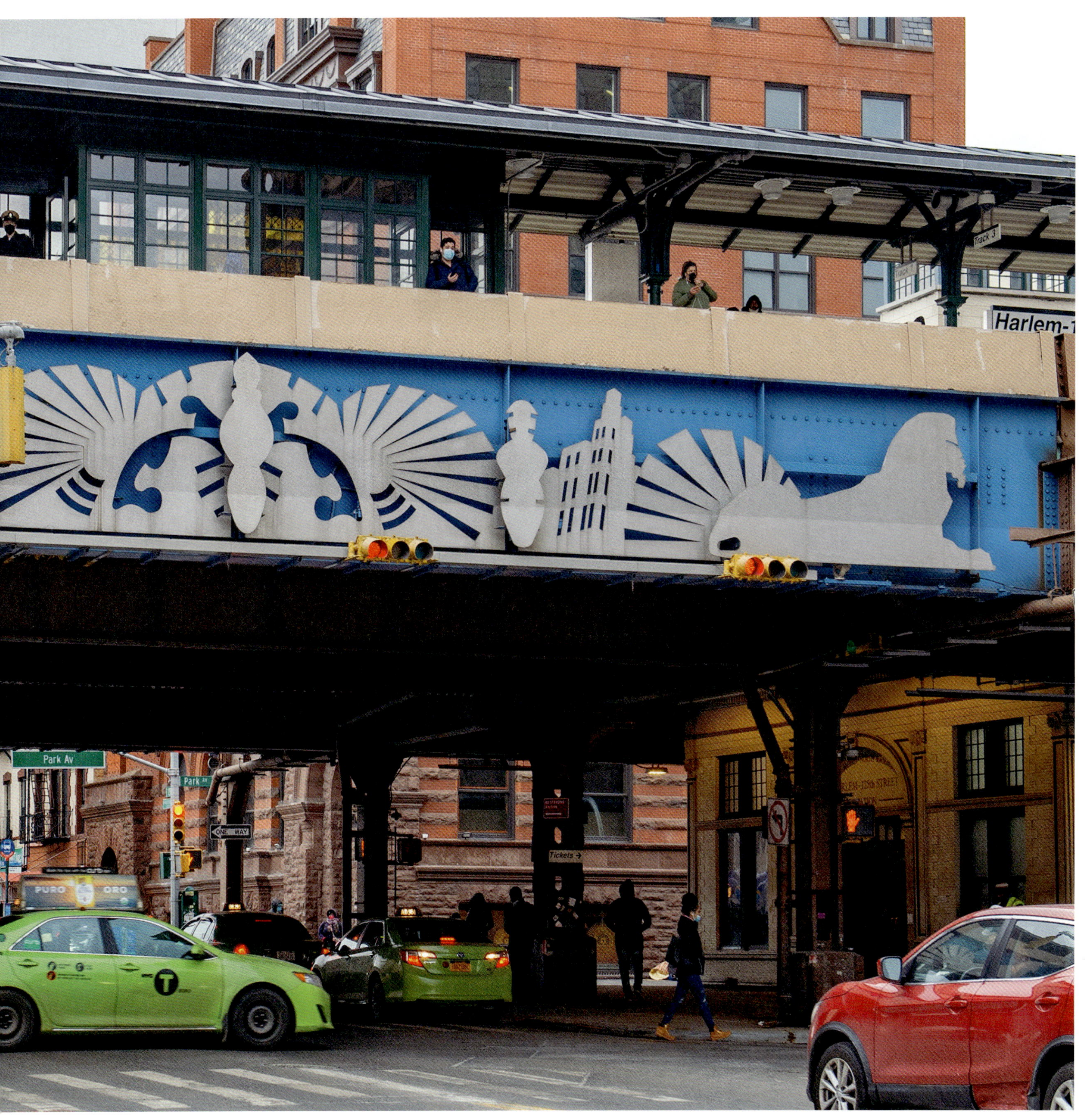
Track 3
Harlem-1
Park Av
Park Av
ONE WAY
PURO ORO
Tickets →
HARLEM-125th STREET
NYC

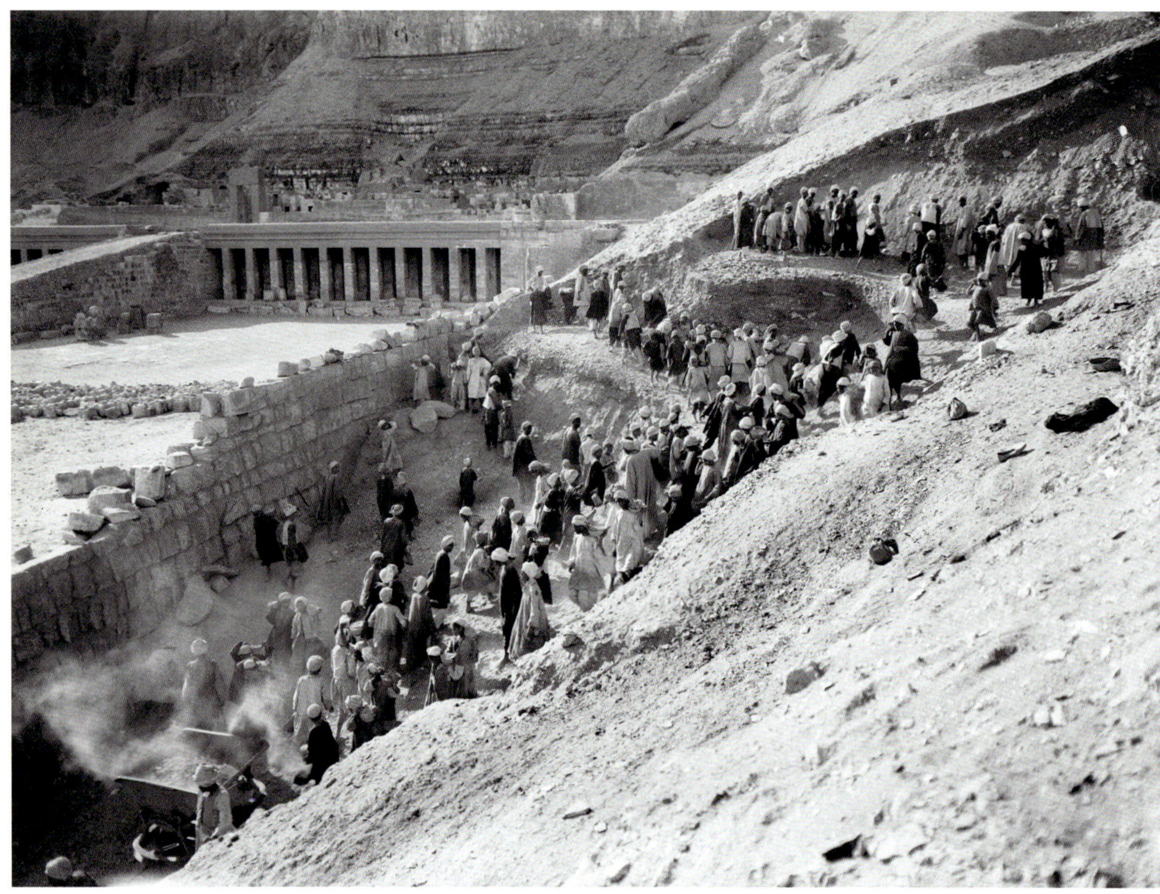

Pl. 7. Harry Burton, **Deir el-Bahri: Progress of the Work, January 1929**, 1929

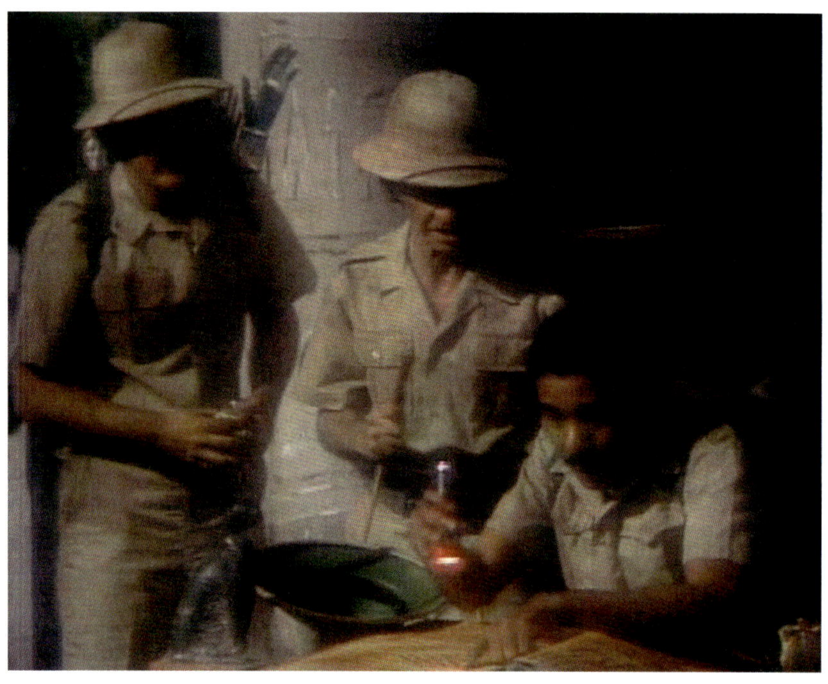

Pl. 8. Still from "Egypt 1909," **The Richard Pryor Show**, 1977

Matthew Shenoda

Theft at the Tomb II

When you had taken it
I had not seen you

My life transmuted by the need to survive
I could not make my way to your place of dour endings
to the freedom you used for caravanning cynicism
for undercutting the breath of life

for stark and naked betrayal of your only true purpose

our only purpose

to love with clarity,
to know God
more than once

to climb the partition of the horizon
and imagine the river meeting the sea.

What else could anyone ask of me?
I have helped prepare the living and the dead
to take the seat of dignity and make it our resting place.

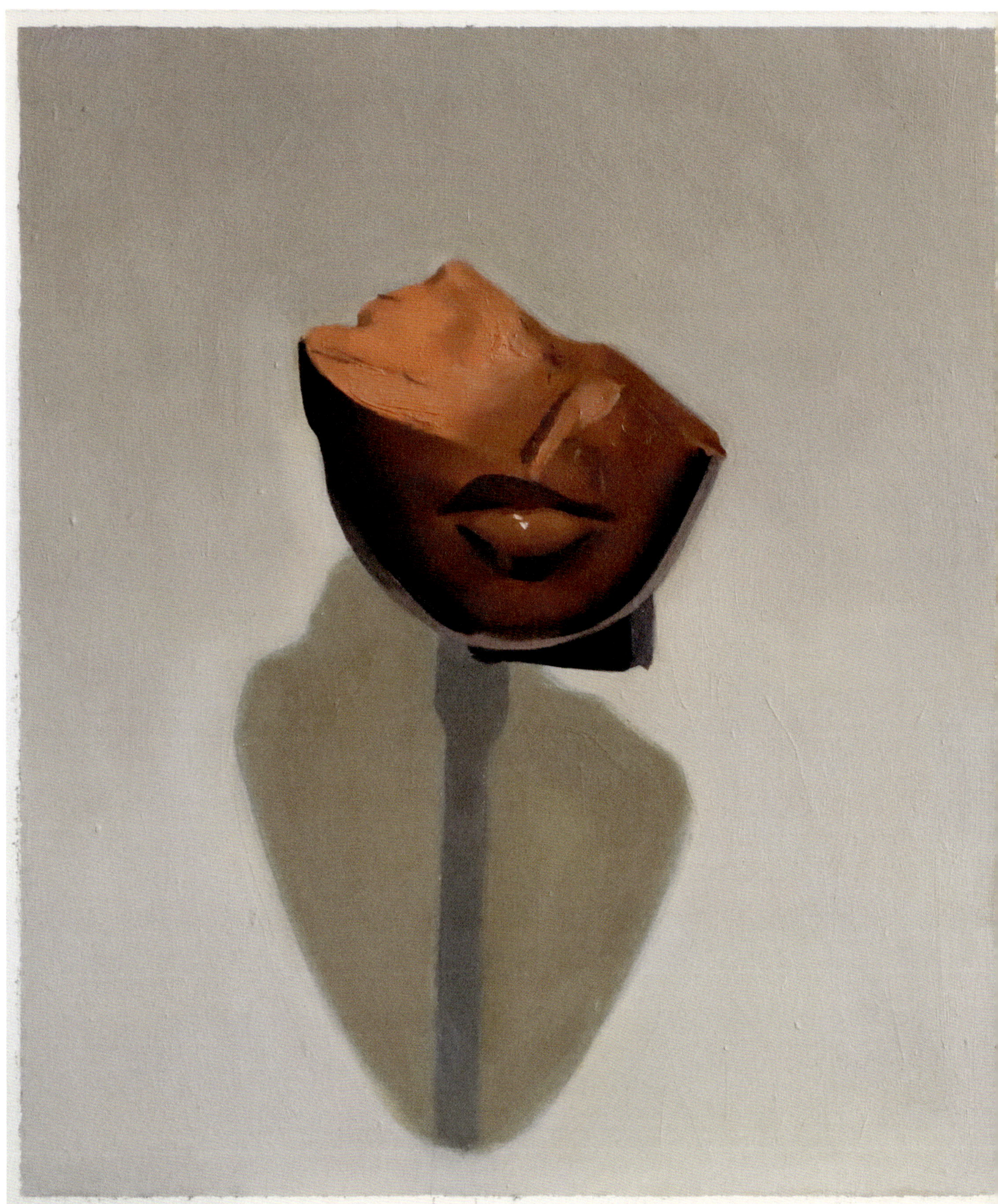

Pl. 9. Jas Knight, **The African Origin of Civilization**, 2023

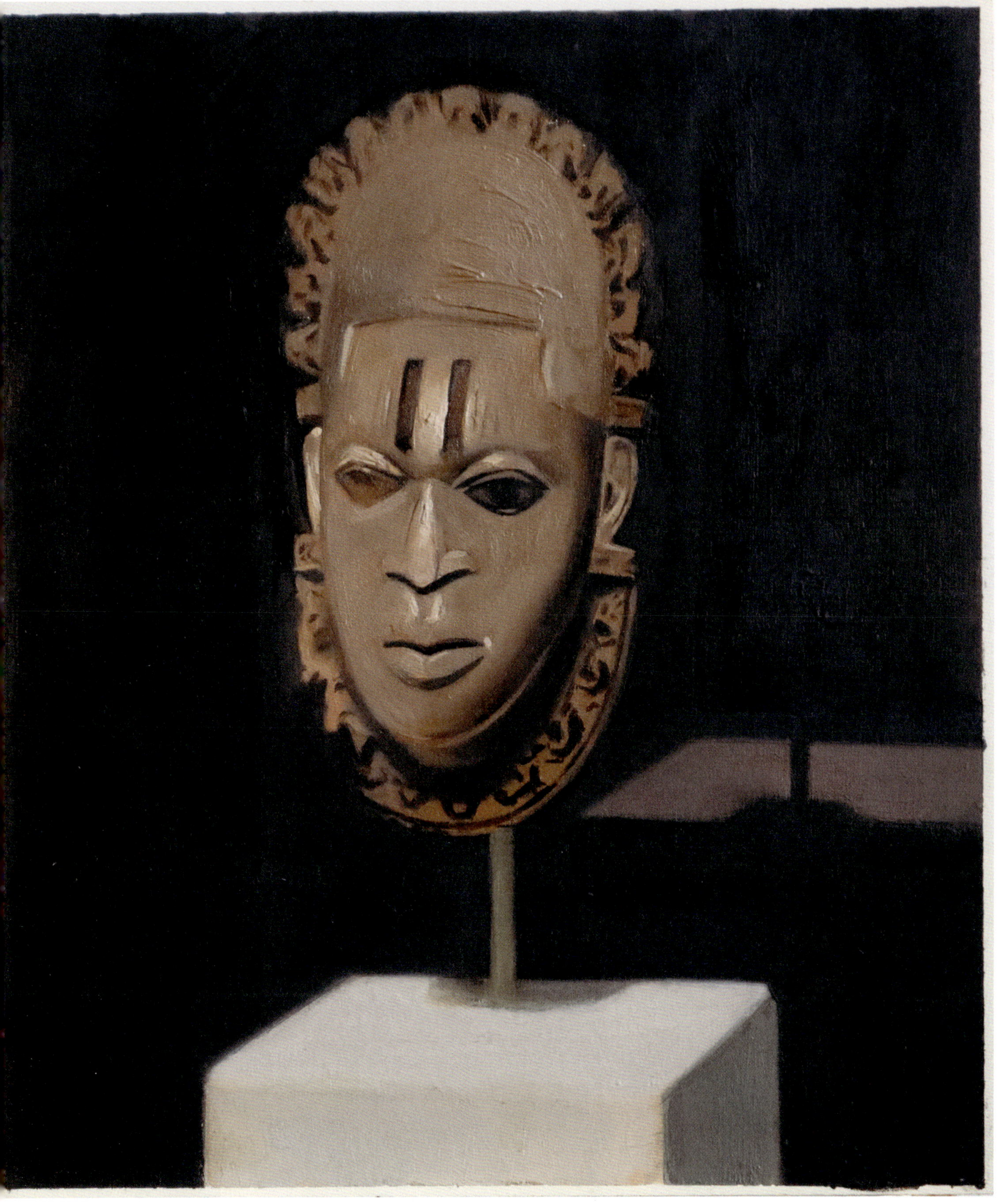

February 2, 1932

Mr. William Leo Hansberry,
Howard University,
Washington, D.C.

My dear Mr. Hansberry;

          I quite understand and sympathize with your
desire to join Dr. Griffith's proposed expedition to the Sudan. Despite
the plan for an expedition mentioned in <u>Antiquity</u>, I should think it very
far from certain that such an undertaking will actually materialize, in
view of the grave financial handicaps which all in England are experienc-
ing these days.   There is also the question as to how you could be useful to such an expedition.   If you paid your own way, that would, naturally, eliminate one difficulty, but would Dr. Griffith be justified in
burdening his party with someone who was without experience in archaeological field work?   You should, I think, give this consideration.   It
goes without saying that your general familiarity with the history and
culture involved would be an asset, but have you any special abilities
which would be useful, such as drawing, surveying, or the like.   You
would, I assume, be prepared to go as a working member of the expedition,
ready to take an active part in the work in whatever capacity you were
best fitted for: only on that basis, I feel sure, would the leader of such
an expedition consider your application.

     I now come to the racial question, and that, I confess, strikes me
as the greatest difficulty.   To be perfectly frank with you, if I were
in charge of such an expedition I should hesitate long before taking an
American Negro on my staff.   I should foresee the danger of great difficulty with the native workmen, who would, I believe, find it almost im-
possible to understand your position, and I should fear that the mere fact
of your being a member of the staff would seriously affect the prestige of

the other members and the respect which the natives employees would have
for them.   It is, in my judgment, not a question so much of your relations with the white members of the party, but of the effect your presence
would have on the relations between natives and staff as a whole.   I can
conceive of an expedition blessed with an experienced group of intelligent
older employees well accustomed to the ways of Europeans, where you might
fit in without great difficulty, but even that would require great tact
and understanding on your part.   Dr. Griffith has not been in the field
constantly enough of recent years to have such a body of men, and my own
experience of the Sudanese workman does not lead me to think him either
particularly intelligent or well versed in European ways.

     I feel sure that you know me well enough to realize that I do not say
this out of any feeling of race-prejudice, but because it is my sincere
estimate of the probabilities of the case.   For my part I am sure you are
the last man who would want to put yourself or Dr. Griffith into a false
position.

     Having said so much for your careful consideration, it is only fair to
add that Dr. Griffith is the best judge of his own business, and that you
would, I feel sure, get a great deal out of joining him.   He may, conceiv-
ably feel differently about the matter than I imagine, and you must decide
yourself whether to write him or not.   If you decide to approach him, use
my name as a reference: then if he wants to consult me about you I shall be
ready to tell him what I know about you, which will not be unfavorable.
But I do not feel that I can write to him now with the appearance of urging
upon him a course which I should be unwilling to take myself.

     With all good wishes, I am

               Sincerely yours,

Pl. 10. Dows Dunham, **Letter to William Leo Hansberry**, February 2, 1932

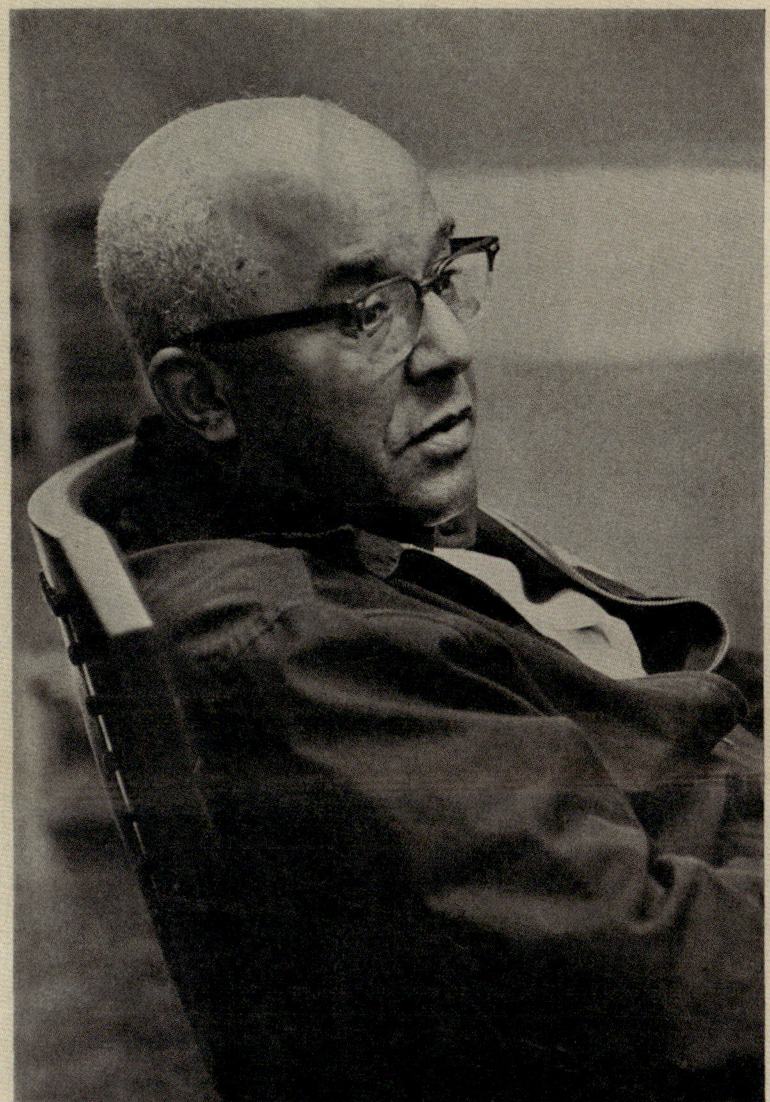

THE SCHOLAR NOBODY KNOWS

Unsung Howard U. Professor is world's best African authority

BY MARC CRAWFORD

FOR MORE than 40 of his 66 years, Howard University's Professor William Leo Hansberry has pursued a lonely study of Africa's history from the dawn of mankind to the coming of the Europeans in modern times. He has done it with that can't-stop-now kind of zeal with which broken old gold prospectors go to their graves; with about as much encouragement as they get in their keeping of the long vigil.

Nearly a quarter of a century ago, the late internationally famous anthropologist Dr. Earnest A. Hooton, his mentor through Harvard undergrad and graduate school days, observed that Hansberry had "passed far beyond the state of detailed knowledge of his problem in which I or any other scholar in the United States can be of any use to him."

And in 1946 Hooton amended his praise to say Hansberry had "made himself certainly the most competent authority upon this subject." Wrote Hooton: "No present day scholar has anything like the knowledge that Hansberry has developed," noted, "he has been unable to take the Ph.D. degree in his chosen subject here (Harvard) or anywhere else because of a lack of proper persons to supervise his thesis and because there is no university or institution, so far as I know, that has manifested a really profound interest in the subject."

A former African student thinks so highly

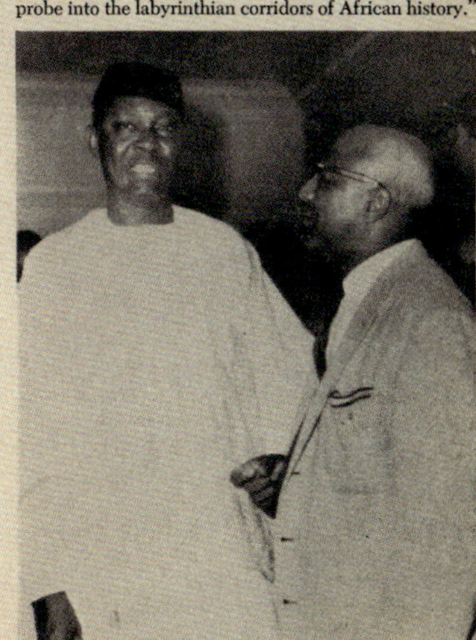

Continued on Next Page

59

Pl. 11. Marc Crawford, "The Scholar Nobody Knows," **Ebony**, February 1961

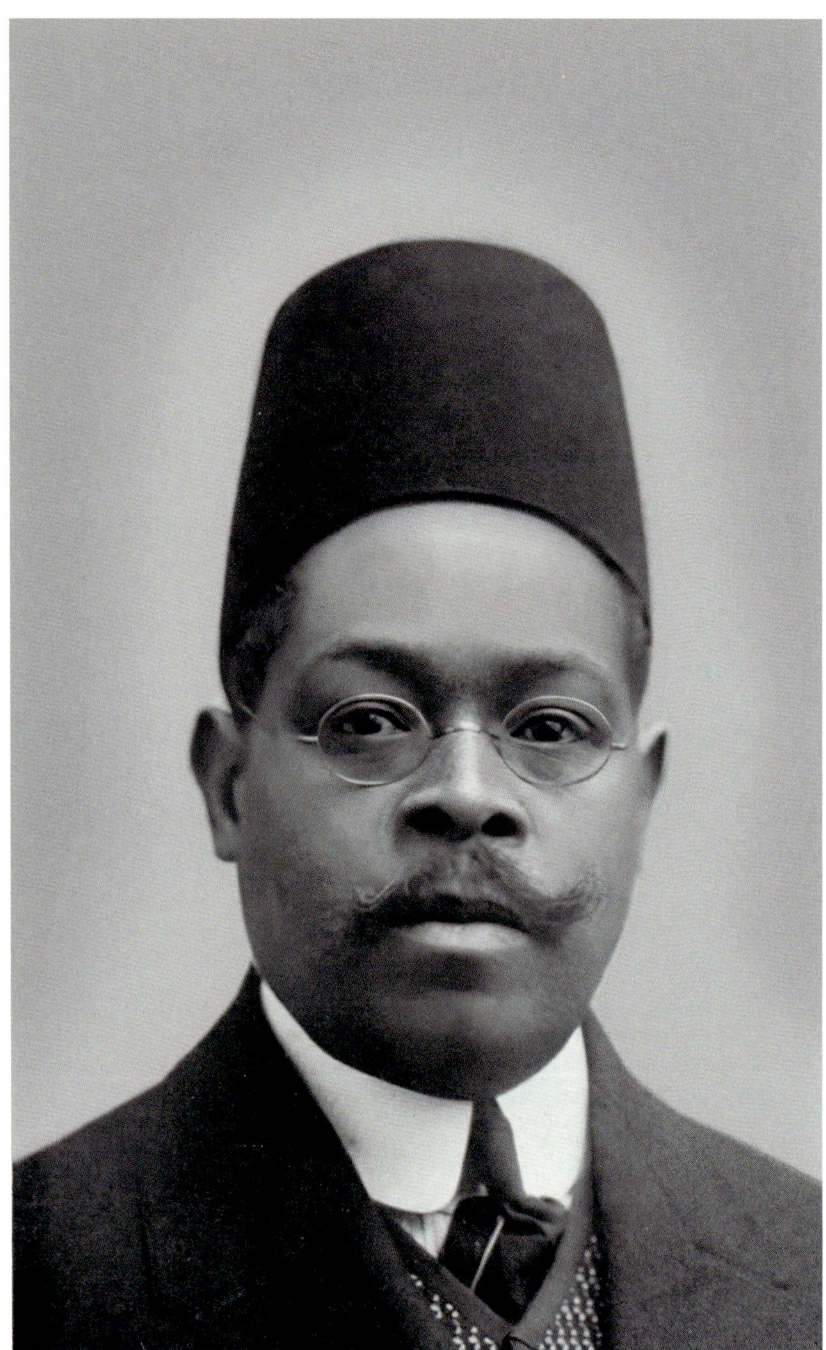

Pl. 12. **Dusé Mohamed Ali**, 1911

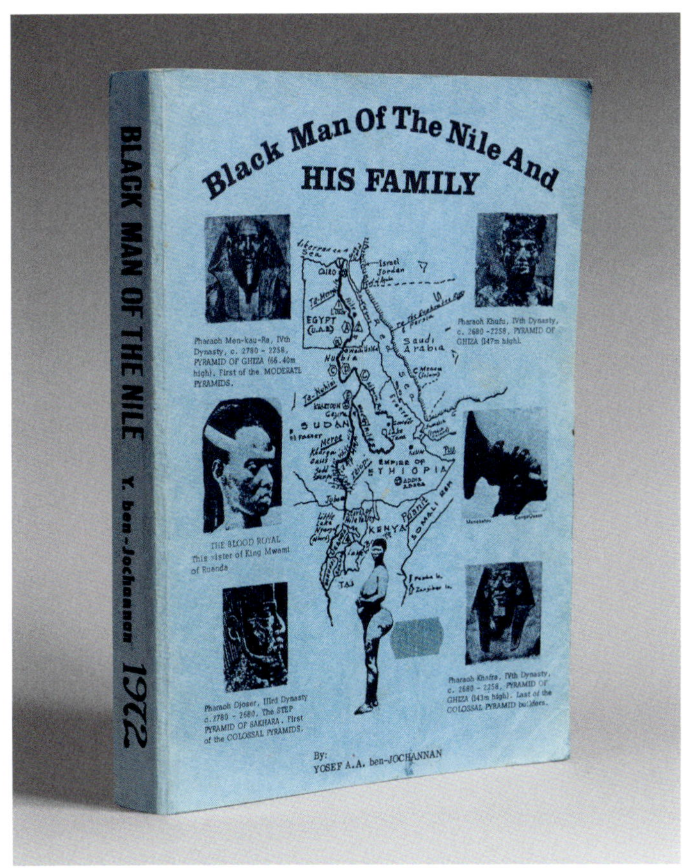

Pl. 13. Yosef A. A. ben-Jochannan, **Black Man of the Nile and His Family**, 1972

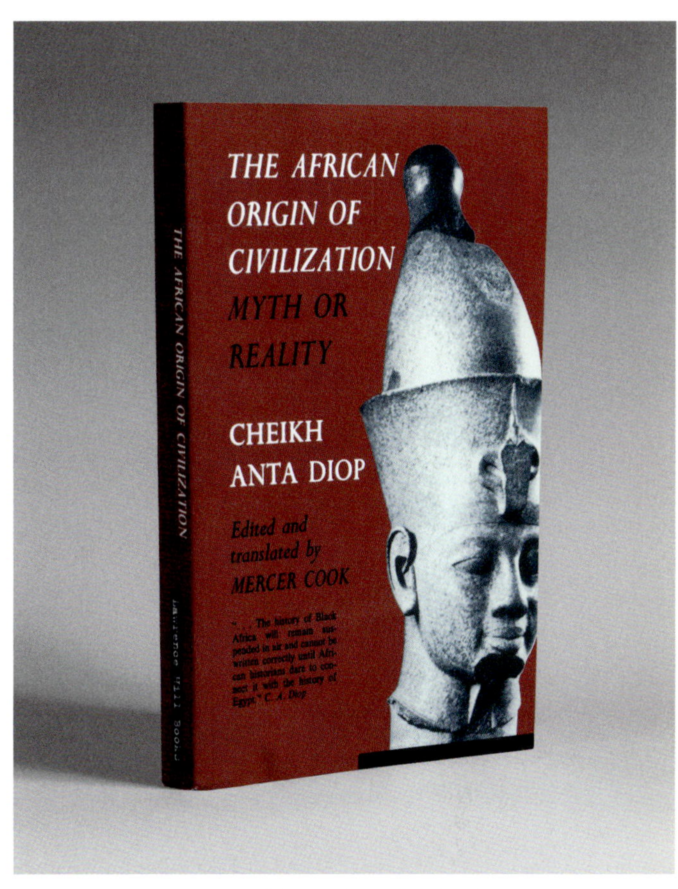

Pl. 14. Cheikh Anta Diop, **The African Origin of Civilization**, 1974

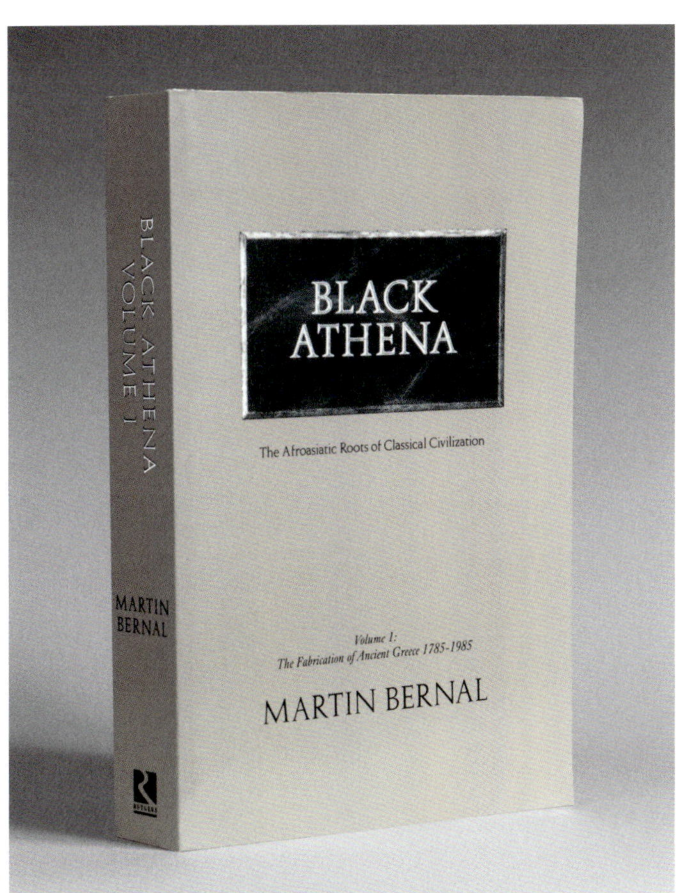

Pl. 15. Martin Bernal, **Black Athena**, 1987

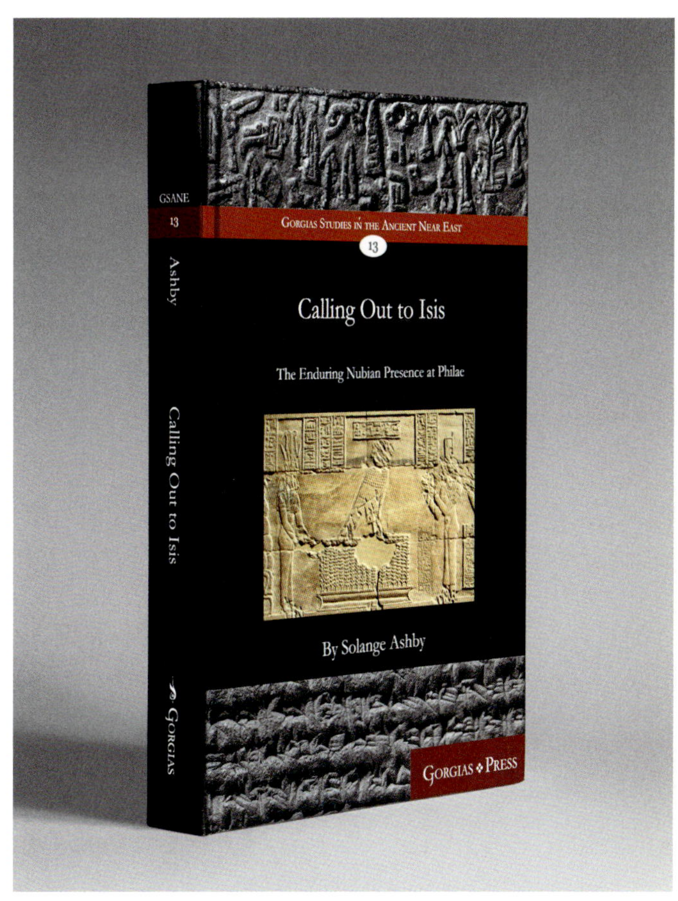

Pl. 16. Solange Ashby, **Calling Out to Isis**, 2020

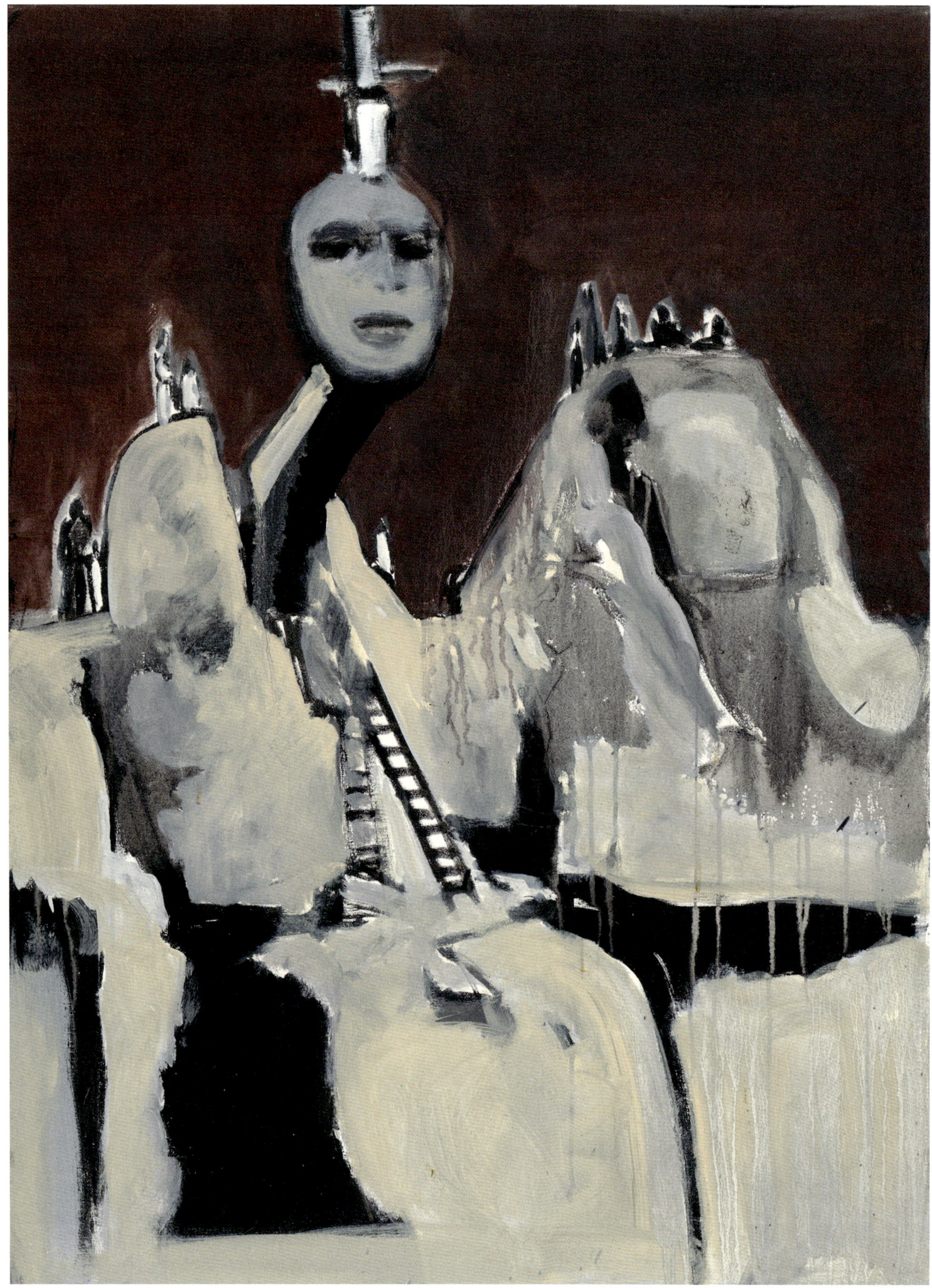

Pl. 17. Noah Davis, **Untitled**, 2010

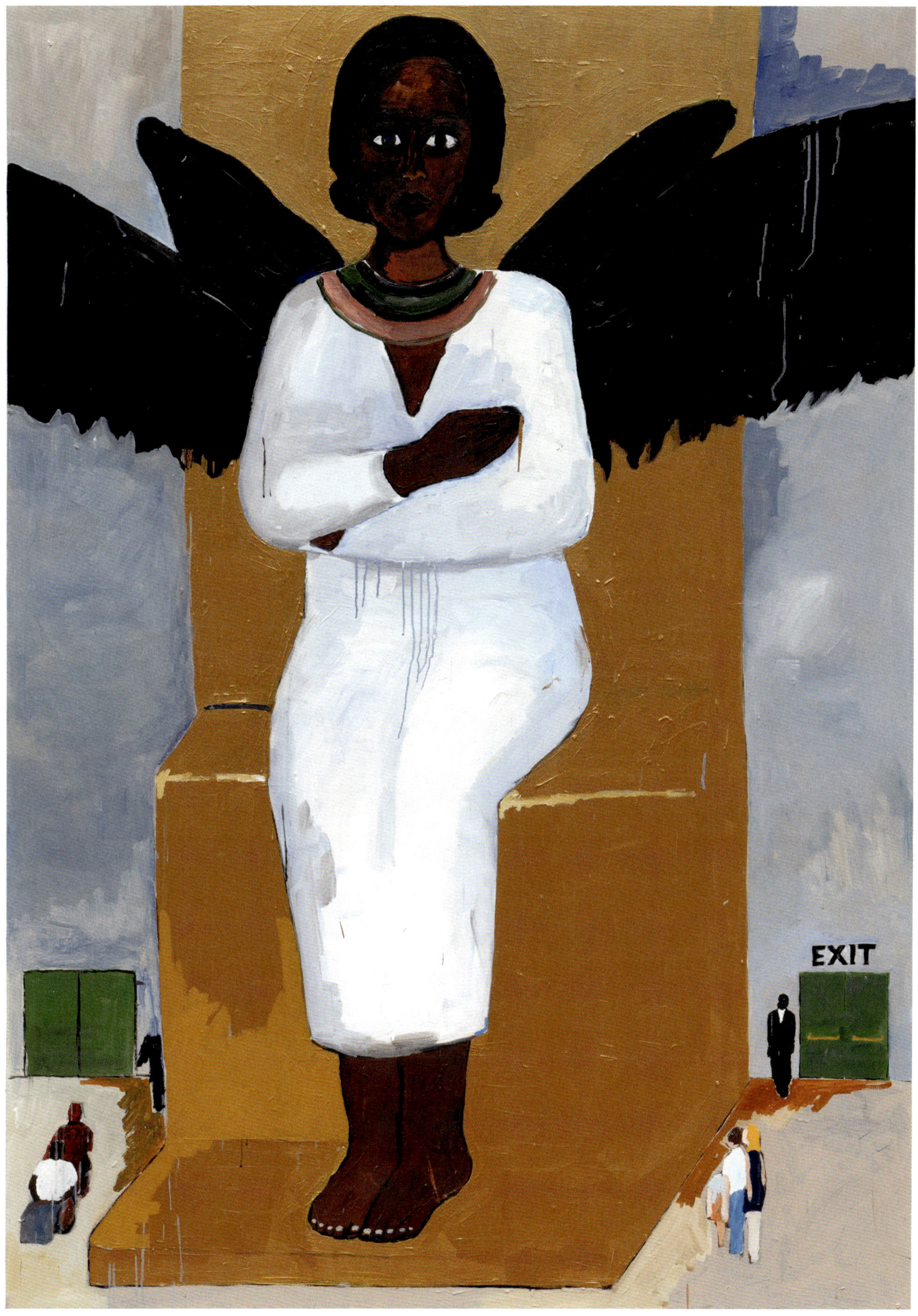

Pl. 18. Henry Taylor, **Michelle**, 2023

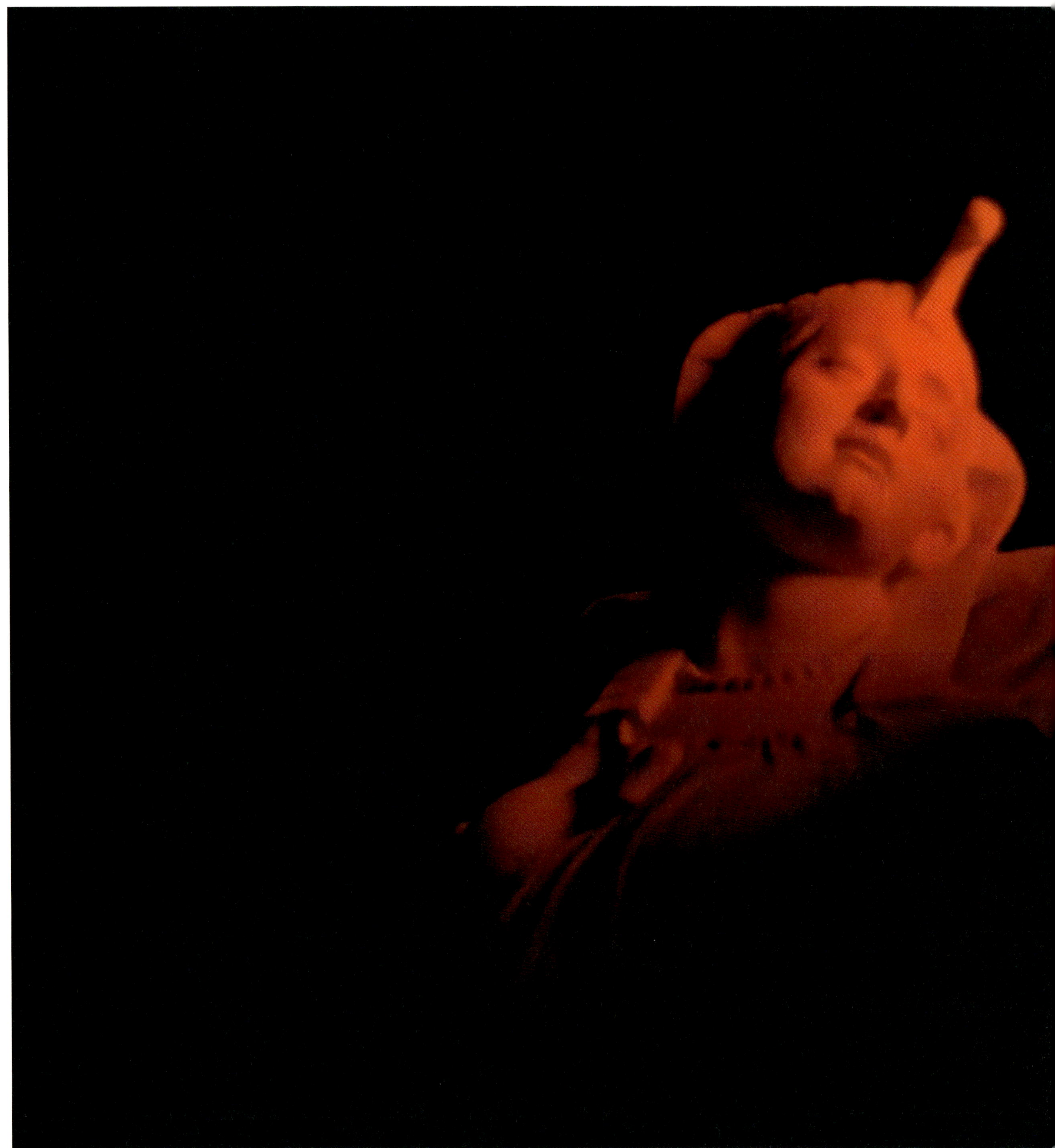

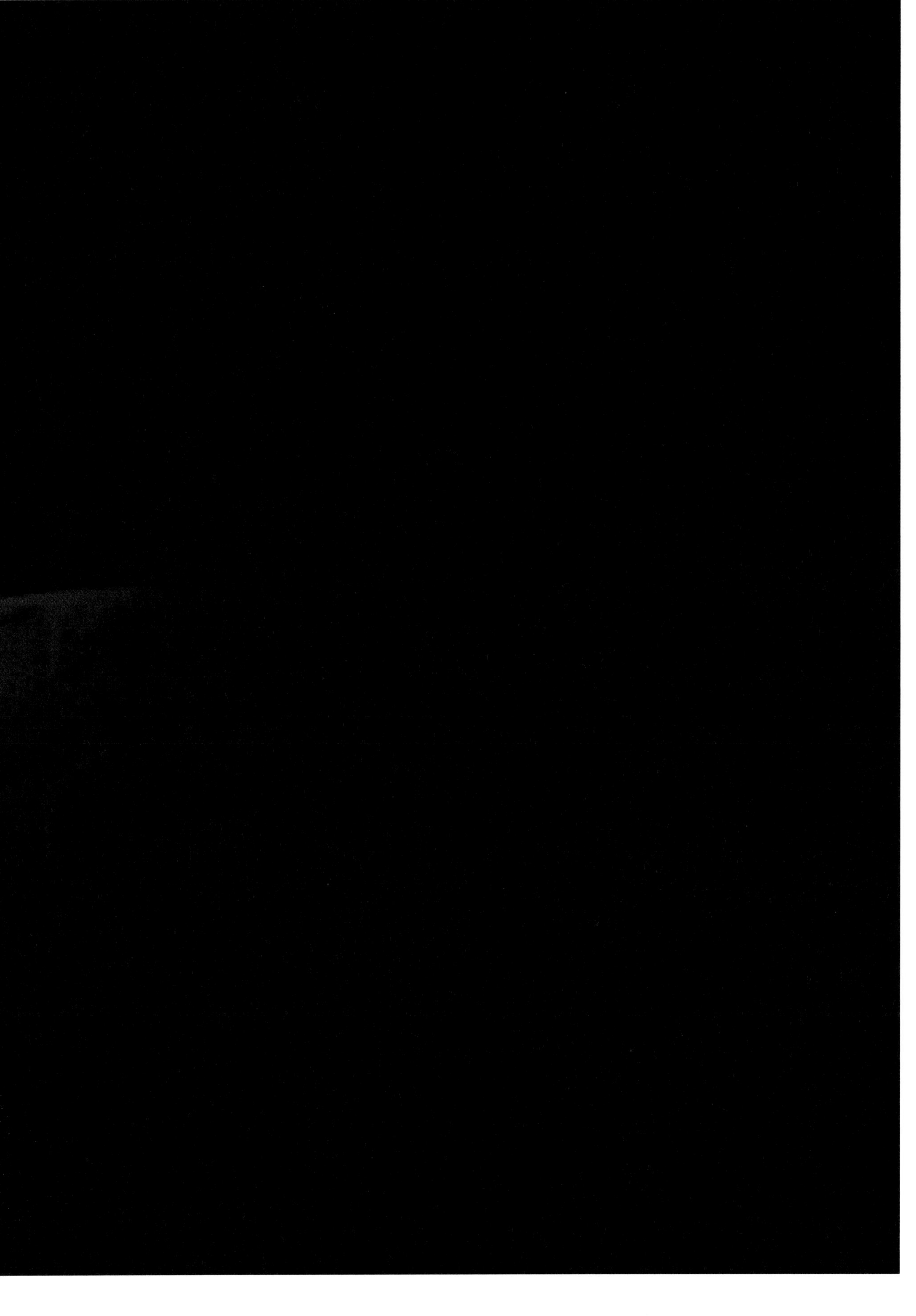

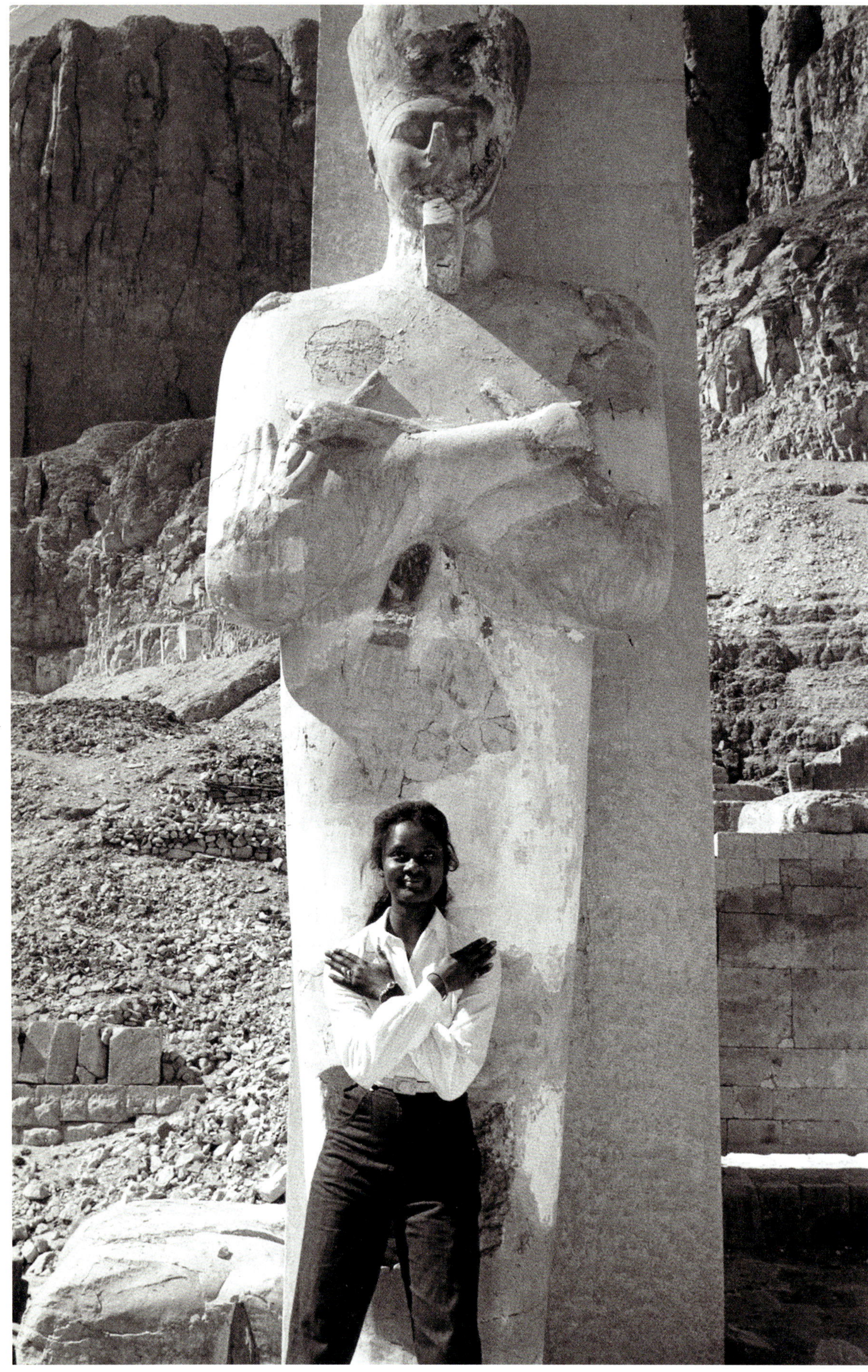

Pl. 20. René Burri, **Barbara Chase-Riboud at Deir el-Bahri**, 1958

Barbara Chase-Riboud

Cleopatra II from *Portrait of a Nude Woman*
as Cleopatra (1987)

In

A   f   r   i   c   a

The strange beasts

Wonder & worry at familiar

Lakes & watch reflections of

Egyptian Gods wade & speak to

Them in a meticulous tongue which is

Not our own nor any we have ever heard

But those who understand it say there is

No   sound   like   their   brilliant   dialogues

Rustling savannah grass, composing mirages &

Miracles   alike   with   bewildering   urgency,   as

Urgent   as   the   pressed   flesh   of   our own language

Which   might be as beautiful if Caesar were in Africa

Pl. 21. Barbara Chase-Riboud, **Cleopatra's Chair**, 1994

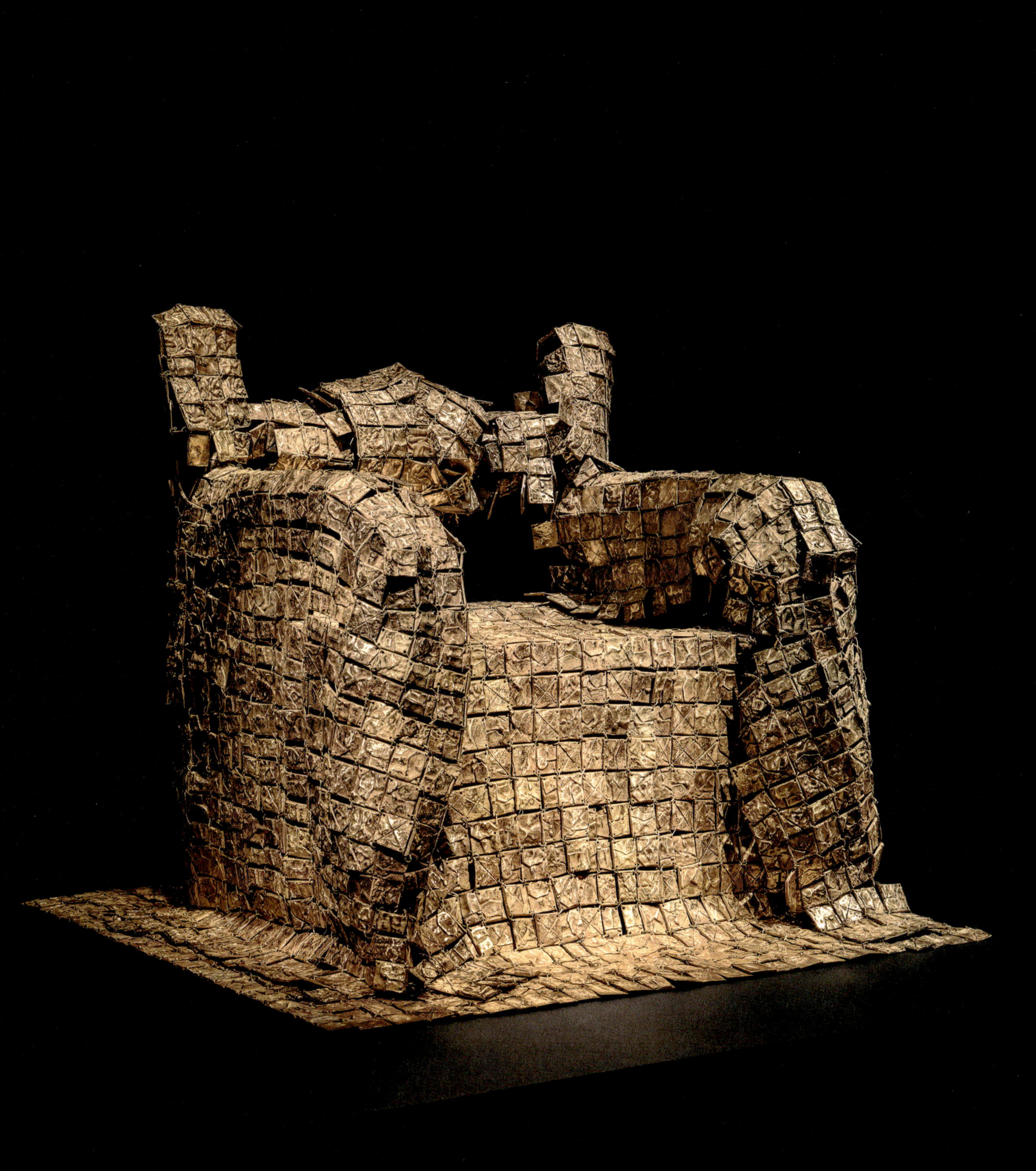

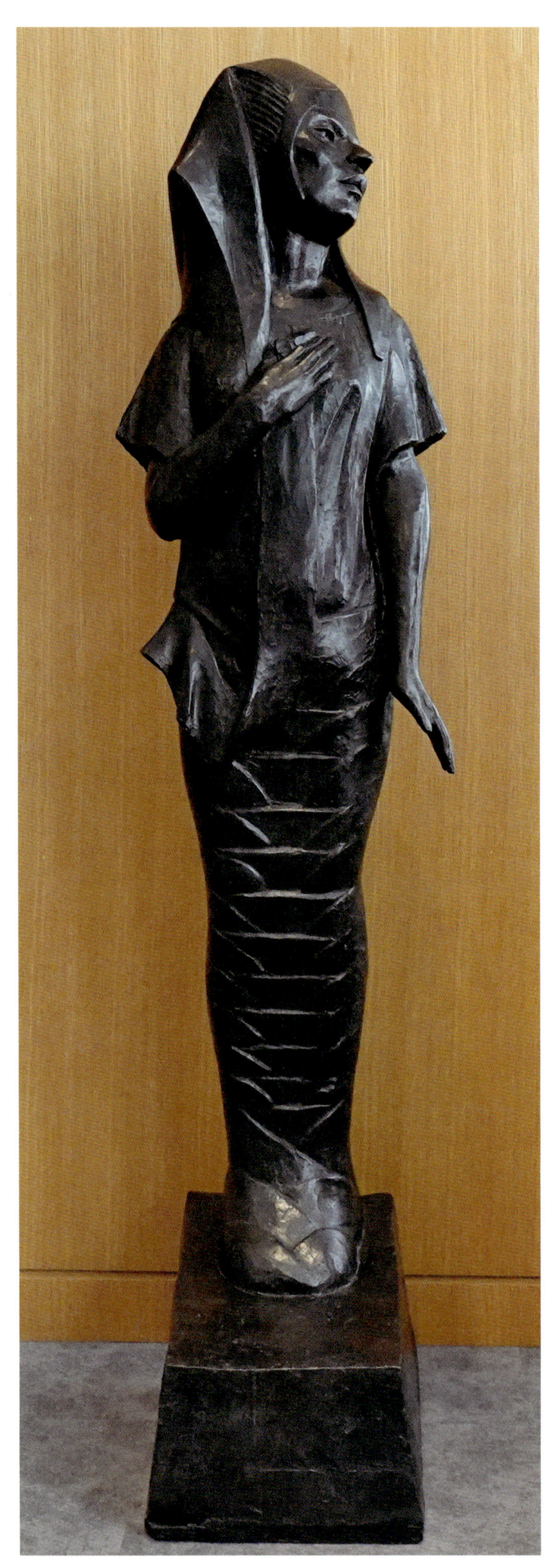 Pl. 22. Meta Vaux Warrick Fuller, **Ethiopia Awakening**, ca. 1914–21

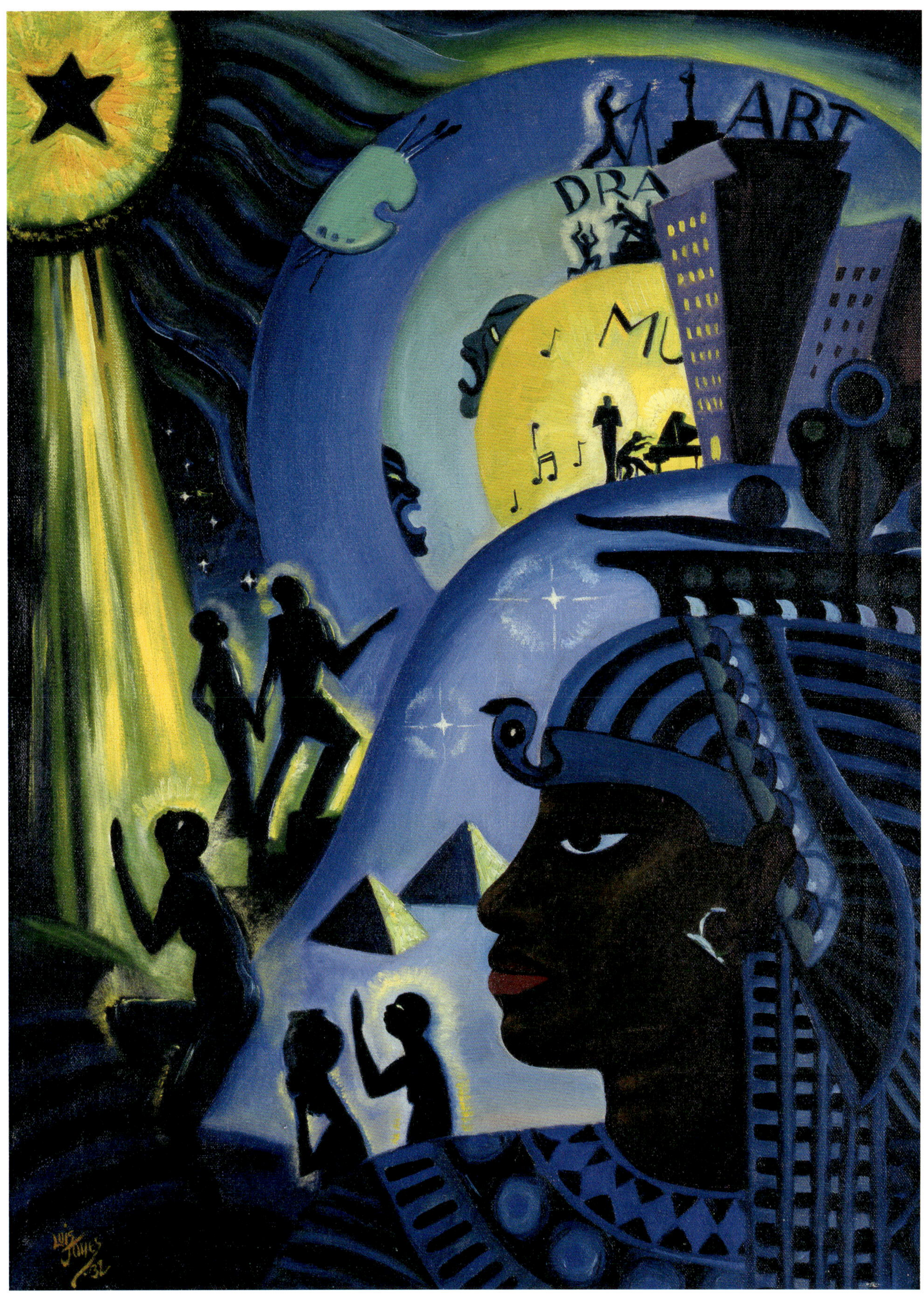

Pl. 23. Loïs Mailou Jones, **The Ascent of Ethiopia**, 1932

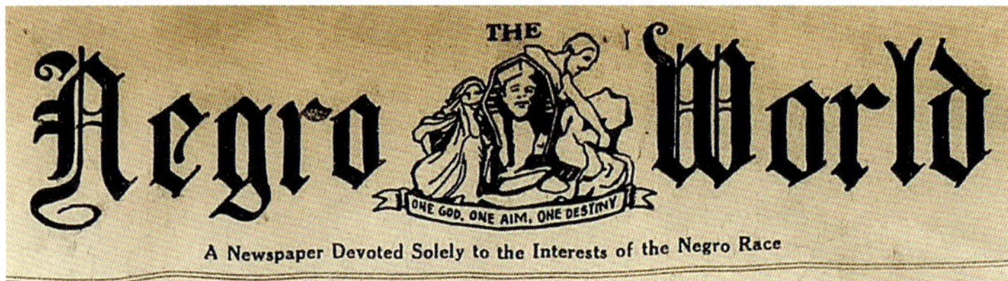

Pl. 24. **The Negro World**, detail of masthead, 1923

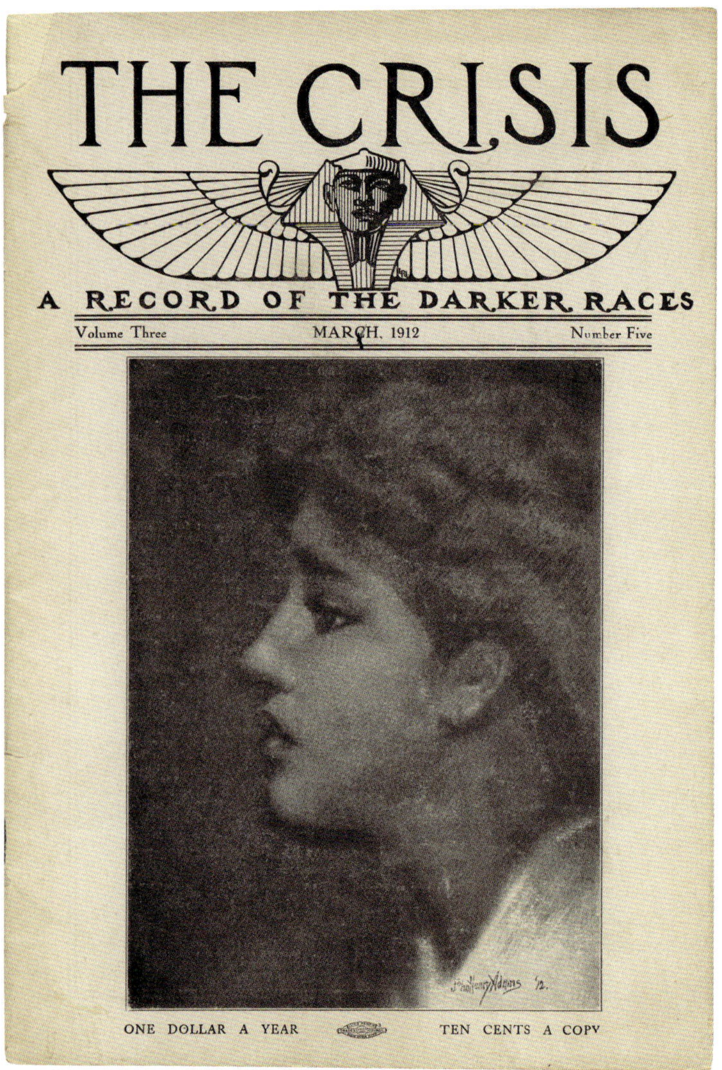

Pl. 25. John Henry Adams Jr., cover of **The Crisis**, March 1912

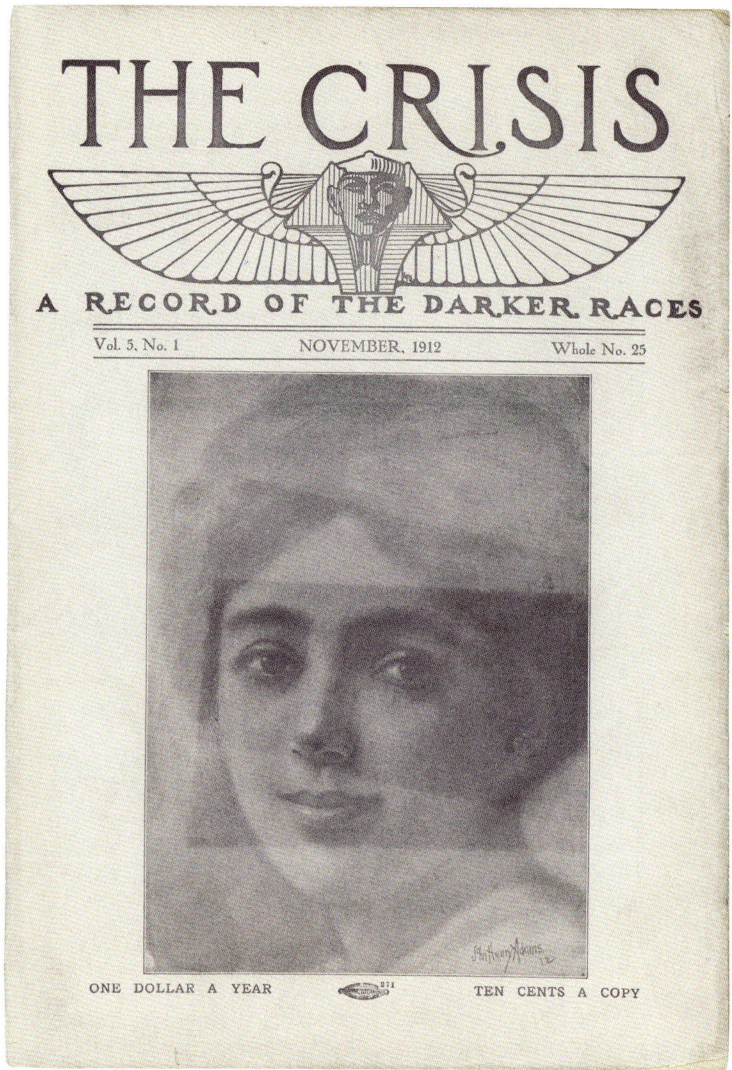

Pl. 26. John Henry Adams Jr., cover of **The Crisis**, November 1912

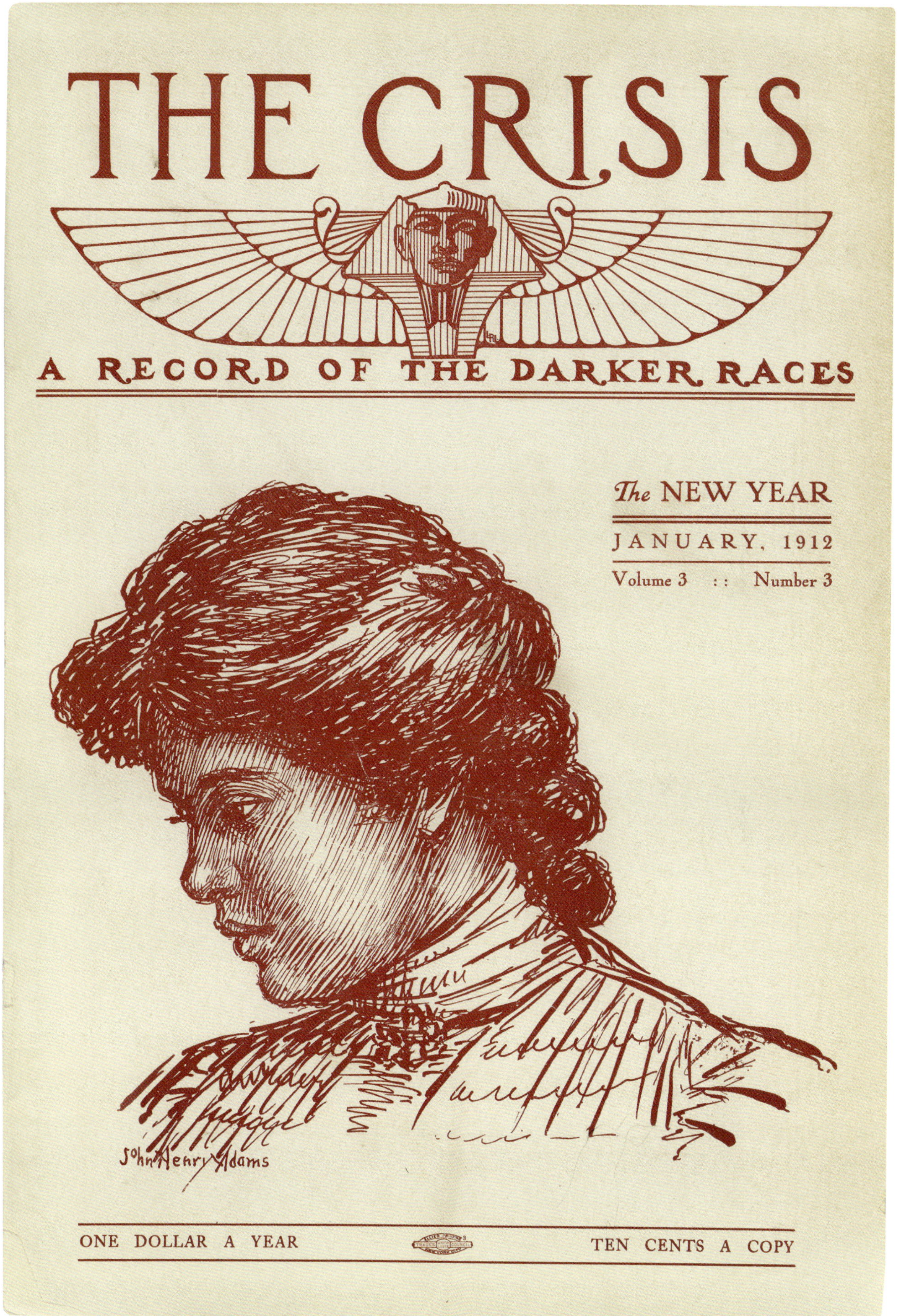

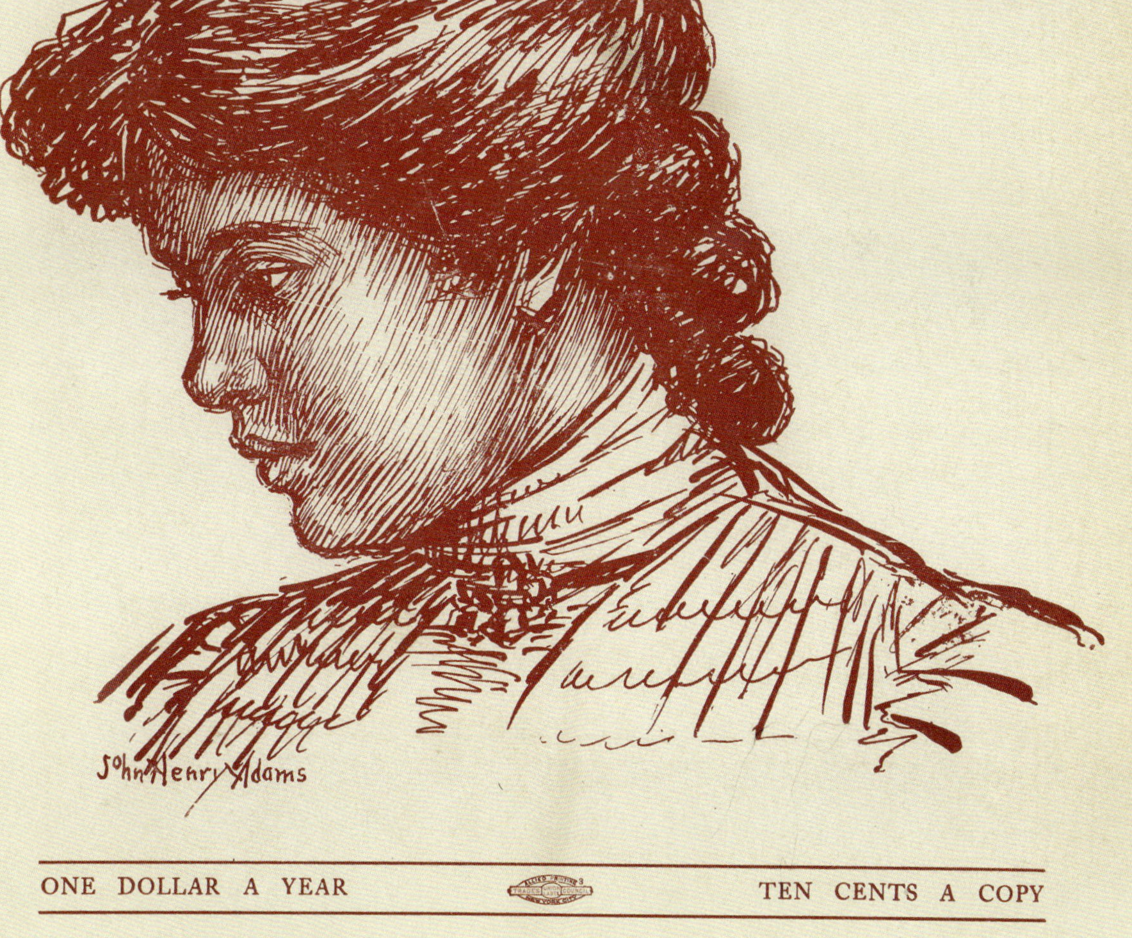

Pl. 27. John Henry Adams Jr., cover of **The Crisis**, January 1912

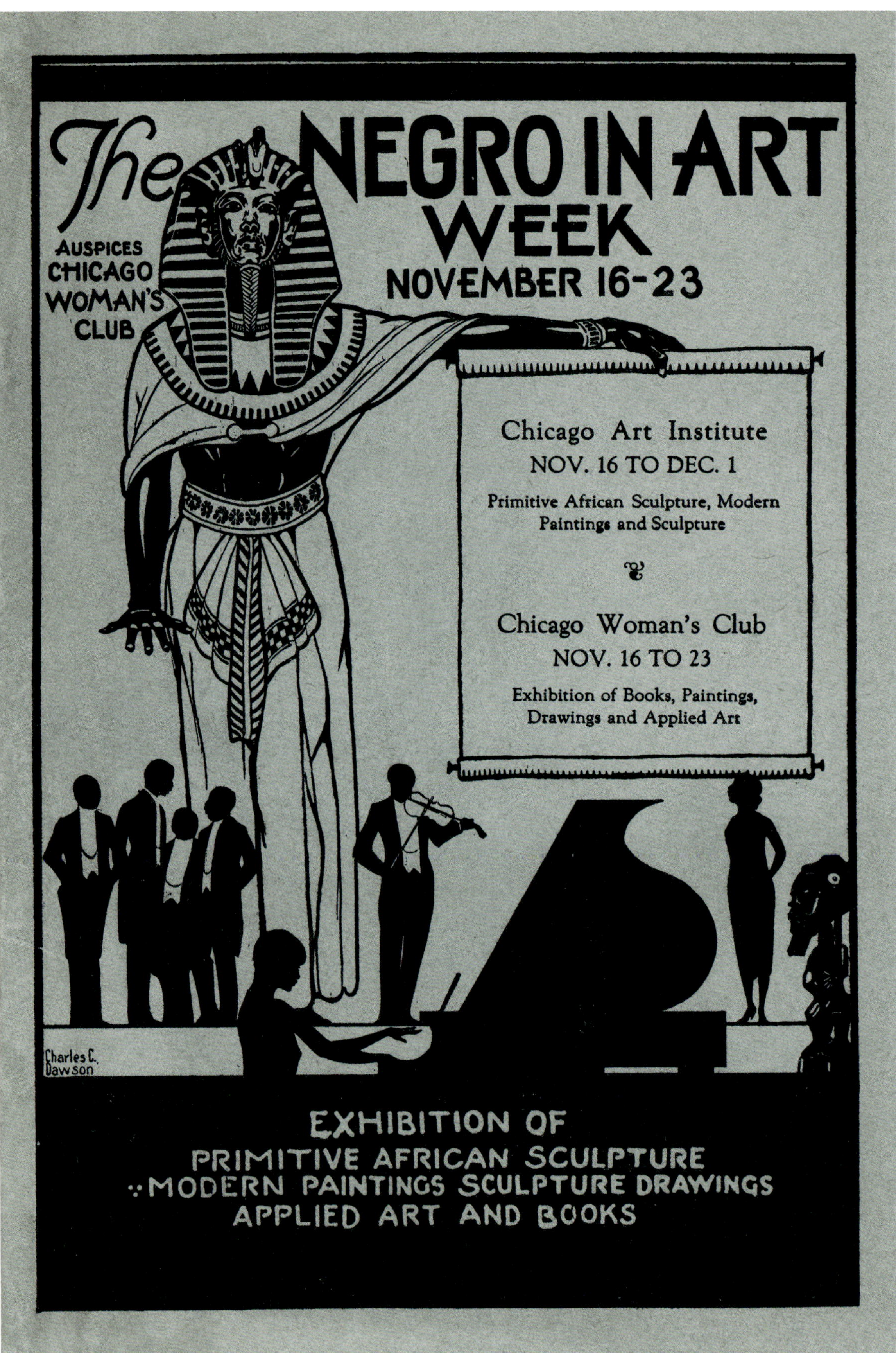

Pl. 28. Charles Clarence Dawson, cover of **The Negro in Art Week**, 1927

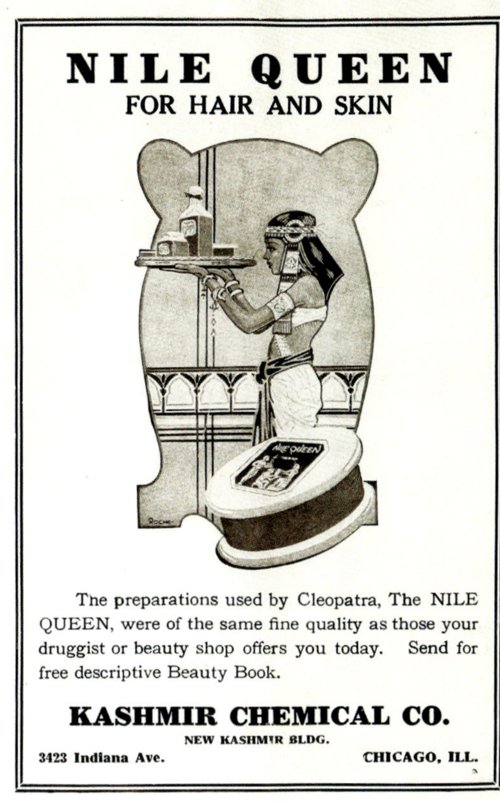

Pl. 29. Roche, **Nile Queen for Hair and Skin**, in **The Crisis**, August 1920

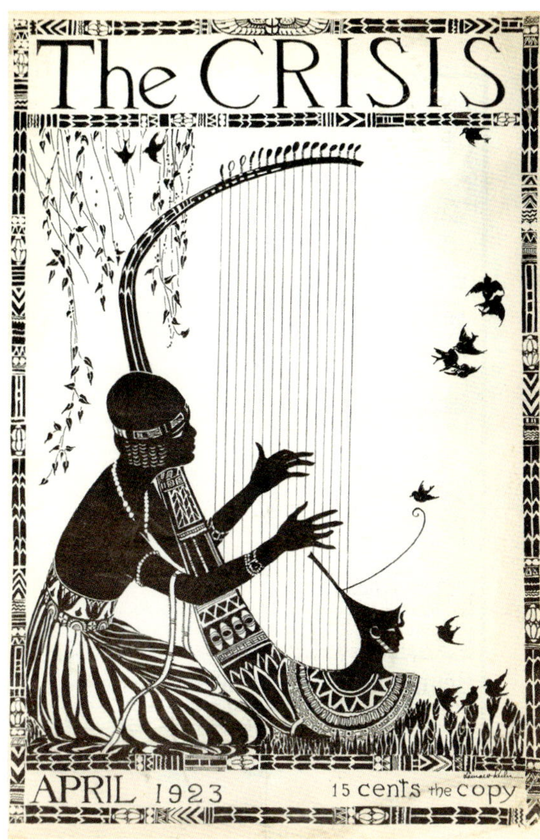

Pl. 30. Laura Wheeler Waring, **Egypt and Spring**, cover of **The Crisis**, April 1923

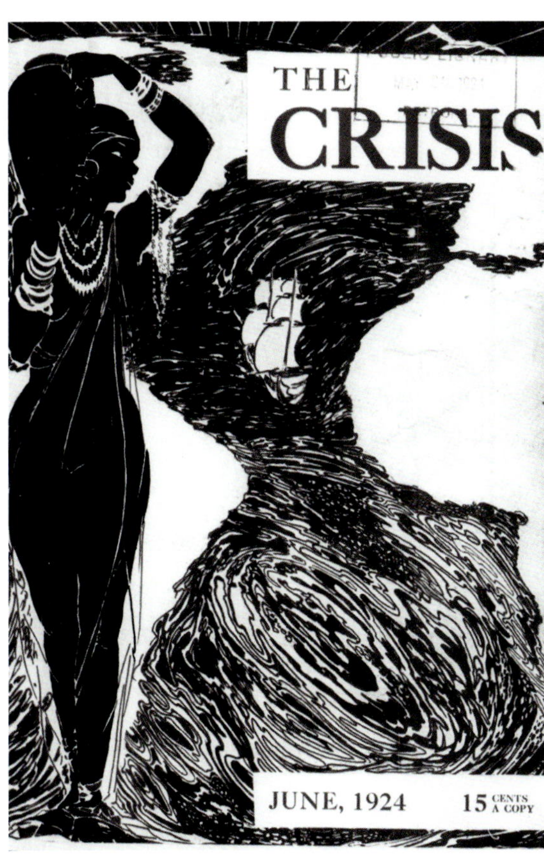

Pl. 31. Laura Wheeler Waring, **Africa in America**, cover of **The Crisis**, June 1924

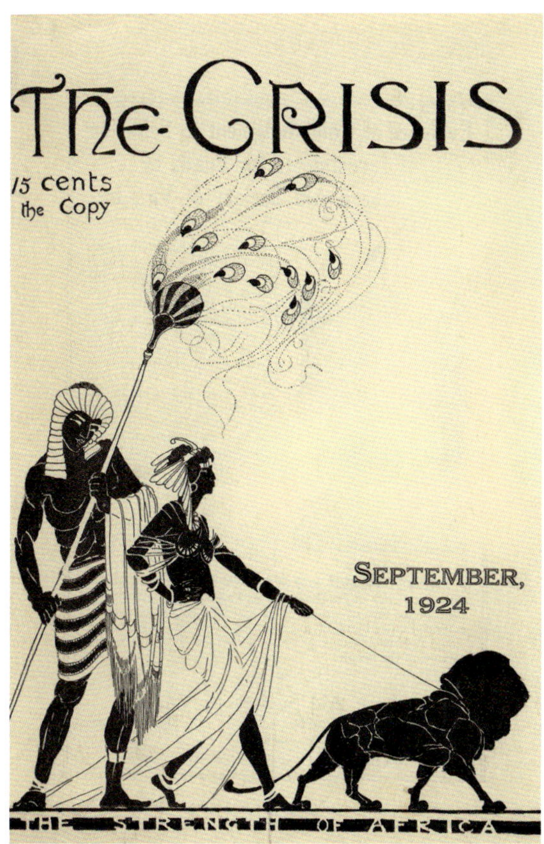

Pl. 32. Laura Wheeler Waring, **The Strength of Africa**, cover of **The Crisis**, September 1924

open' de big blade, an' wanted eve'body to have a good time.

'Bout time de fun wuz at de highes' in de big house, Phillis heared somebody knock-in' at huh cabin do'. She did n' know who it could be, an' bein' as dere wa'nt nobody e'se 'roun', she sot still an' did n' say nary word. Den she heared somebody groan, an' den dere wuz anudder knock, a feeble one dis time, an' den all wuz still.

Phillis wait' a minute, an' den crack' de do', so she could look out, an' dere wuz somebody layin' all crumple' up on de do'-step. An' den somethin' wahned huh what it wuz, an' she fetched a lighterd to'ch fum de ha'th. It wuz huh son Isham. He wuz wownded an' bleedin'; his feet wuz so' wid walkin'; he wuz weak from loss er blood.

Phillis pick' Isham up an' laid 'im on huh bed an' run an' got some whiskey an' give 'im a drap, an' den she helt camphire tuh his nost'ils, meanwhile callin' his name an' gwine on like a wild 'oman. An' bimeby he open' his eyes an' look' up an' says—"I'se come home, mammy,"—an' den died. Dem wuz de only words he spoke, an' he nevuh drawed anudder bref.

It come tuh light nex' day, when de slave-ketchers come aftuh Isham wid deir dawgs an' deir guns, dat he had got in a 'spute wid his marster, an' had achully *hit his marster!* An' realizin' what he had done, he had run erway; natch'ly to'ds his mammy an' de ole plantation. Dey had wounded 'im an' had mos' ketched him, but he had 'scaped ag'in an' had reach' home just in time tuh die in his mammy's ahms.

Phillis laid Isham out wid her own han's—dere wa'n't nobody dere tuh he'p her, an' she did n' want no he'p nohow. An' when it wuz all done, an' she had straighten' his lim's an' fol' his han's an' close his eyes, an' spread a sheet ovuh him, she shut de do' sof'ly, and stahted up ter de big house.

(Continued in the January CRISIS)

TUTANKH-AMEN AND RAS TAFARI

KANTIBA NEROUY

IF you take your map of Africa and look on the extreme east near the end of the Red Sea, you will note a circular country about ten times the size of the state of Ohio, called Abyssinia. The history of this part of Africa is bound up with the history of Egypt because one branch of the Nile rises high in the Abyssinian mountains.

Nefertari, "the most venerated figure of Egyptian history", was a black woman of great beauty and with her husband drove the Shepherd Kings out of Egypt about 1700 years before Christ. Nearly 300 years later one of her descendants married an-other black woman, Mutemua, whose son was the celebrated Amenhotep III, the builder of the great temple of Luxor. The granddaughter of this great mulatto Pha-raoh married Tutankh-Amen and by this marriage raised her husband to royal rank. It is then this husband of a royal colored woman whose tomb, lately discovered, has aroused the civilized world to a new reali-zation of the splendor of Egyptian civili-zation during these years. Tutankh-Amen reigned 1350 years before Christ and the

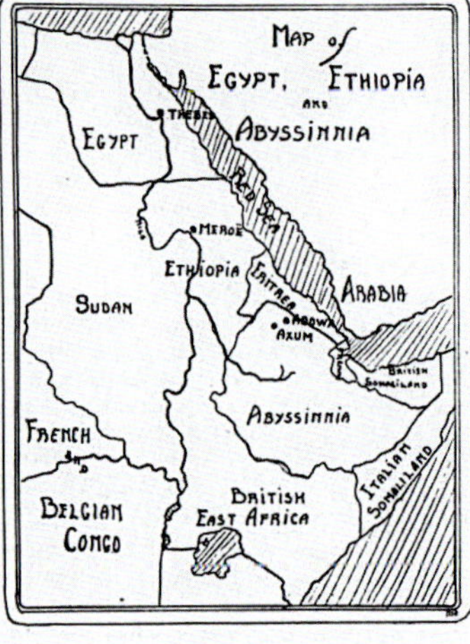

Egyptian empire continued in the ascend-ant for 700 years.

Then it was that the power of Egypt, which had originally flowed from central Africa, began to move back and in southern Egypt the black kingdom of Ethi-opia gained such power that it overthrew the Pharoahs of Egypt and established black kings upon the throne who ruled the world for 150 years. Afterward, the Persians came in and conquered northern Egypt, but Ethiopia maintained its power in southern Egypt and drove back the great Persian Emperor, Cambyses, in 500 B.C.

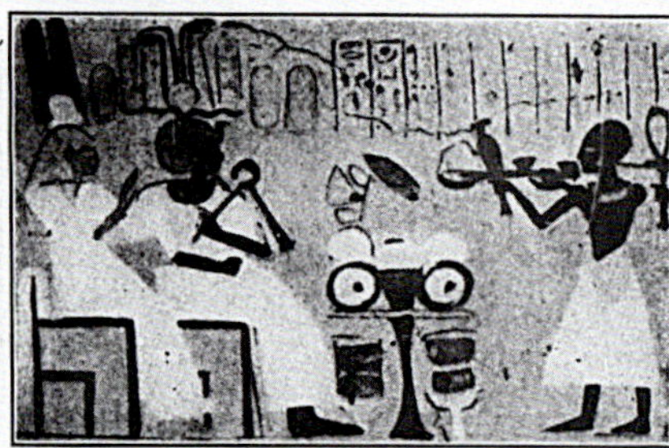

A BLACK PRINCESS

The history of Ethiopia for the next thousand years is not well-known. Various forces helped in her development. The Greeks, the Romans, the Arabians, the Su-danese and finally the Mohammedans pressed in upon her. We hear of great cities like Meroe with 400,000 artisans and 200,000 soldiers. We hear of the queens called by the title Candace who beat back the power of both Greeks and Romans and one of them is said to have declared that Alexander the Great "is not to scorn her people because they are black since their souls are whiter than those of his white folk".

After a time in the part of Ethiopia which we call Abyssinia, there arose at Axum a new center of power. The Greeks consecrated a Christian bishop there and in the sixth century after Christ the Abys-sinians were ruling both their own country and the adjacent shores of Arabia. Then Mohammedanism pressed down upon Chris-tian Abyssinia, north, east and west and as Gibbon says, "encompassed by the enemies of their religion the Ethiopians slept for nearly a thousand years, forgetful of the world by whom they were forgotten". Nevertheless during the middle ages there persisted throughout the Christian world the legend of a certain priest or Prester John, a black African king of a Christian nation; and when the Portuguese began their celebrated discoveries they found and came into contact with the Christian kings of Abyssinia. Later, Portugal, England, France and Italy began to press in upon Abyssinia.

Meantime Abyssinia had been going through various internal vicissitudes. In the 11th century there was a Queen Ma-queda who ruled one of the states, Sheba, and visited Solomon, King of the Jews. Later a Queen Judith reigned. The rulers gradually took the title of "Negus Negusti" meaning King of Kings; that is, king of the various smaller kingdoms which divided up Ethiopia. In the 18th century there came a number of powerful rulers extending from Yesu to Asfa Nassen, who reigned until 1807. Rivalry was now beginning between the French and the English and there arose to power the great Emperor Theodore III who finally proclaimed himself not only King of Kings but "Emperor of Abyssinia" in 1855 and ruled until 1868. Under him the influence of the English waxed and but for the insult of not answering his letter of

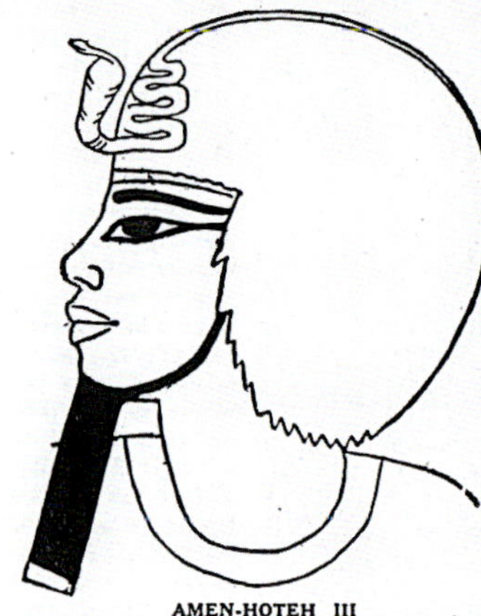

AMEN-HOTEH III

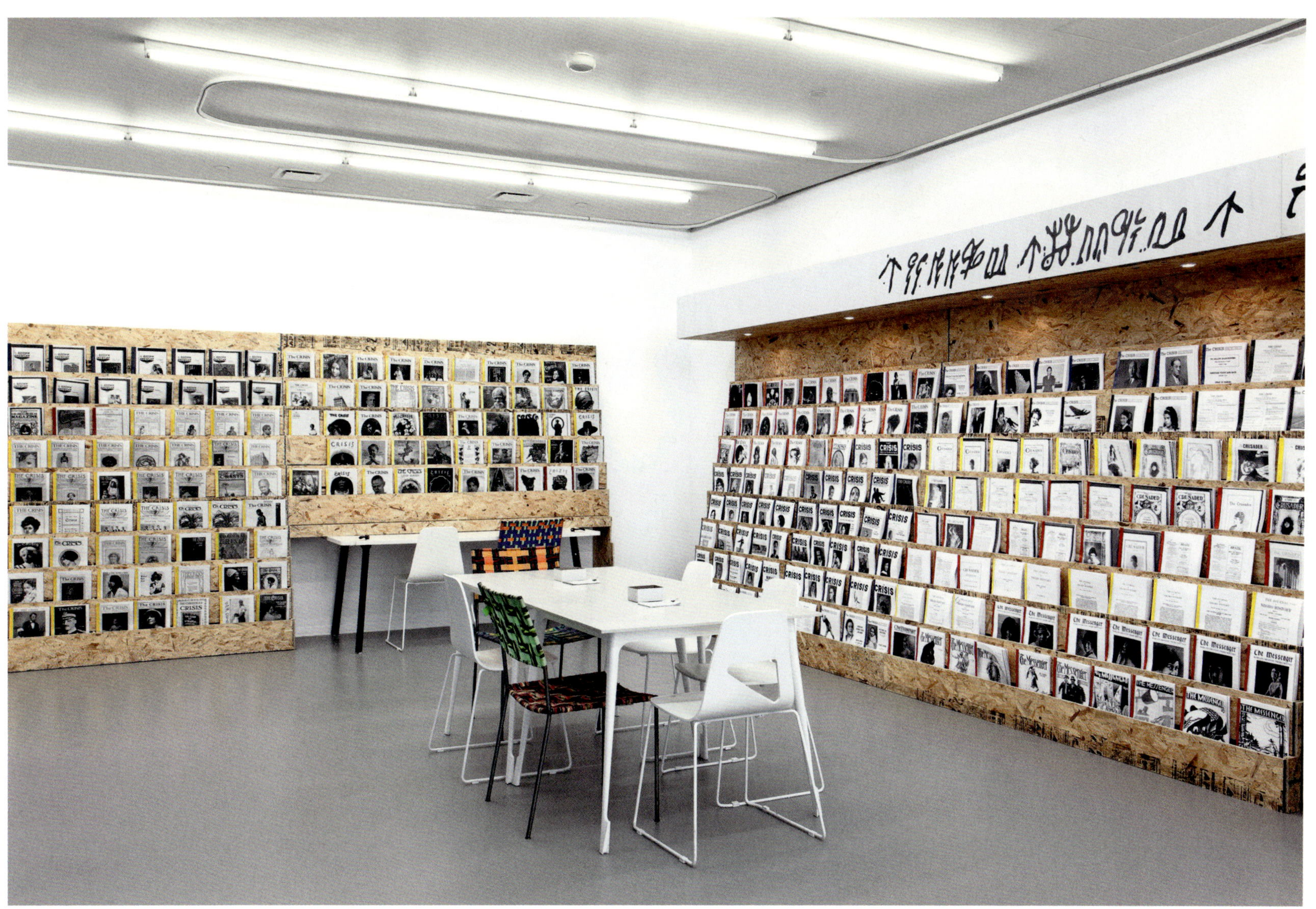

Pl. 34. Steffani Jemison and Jamal Cyrus, **Alpha's Bet Is Not Over Yet**, 2011

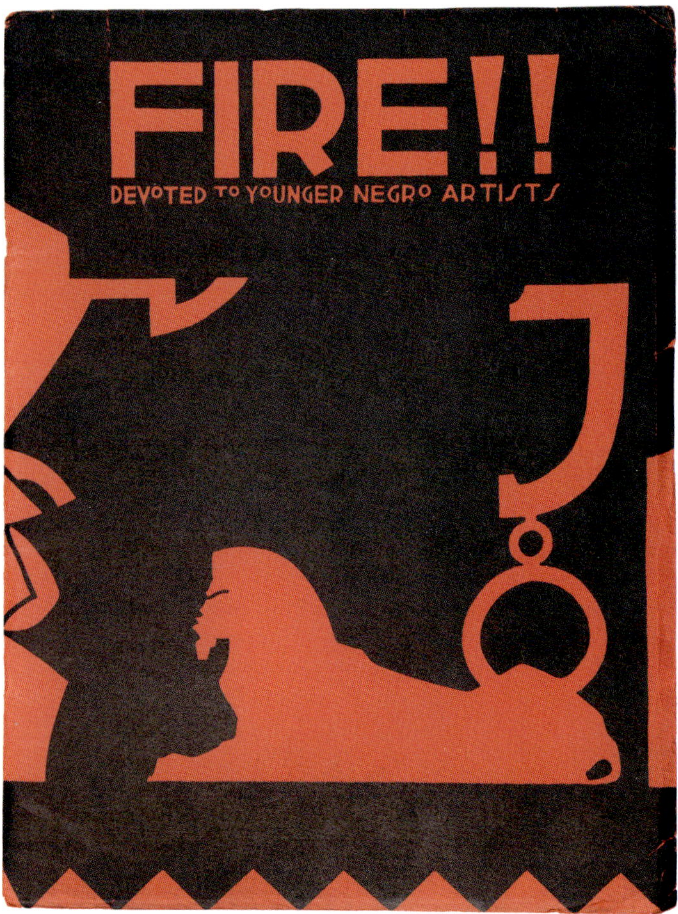

Pl. 35. Aaron Douglas, cover of **Fire!!**, November 1926

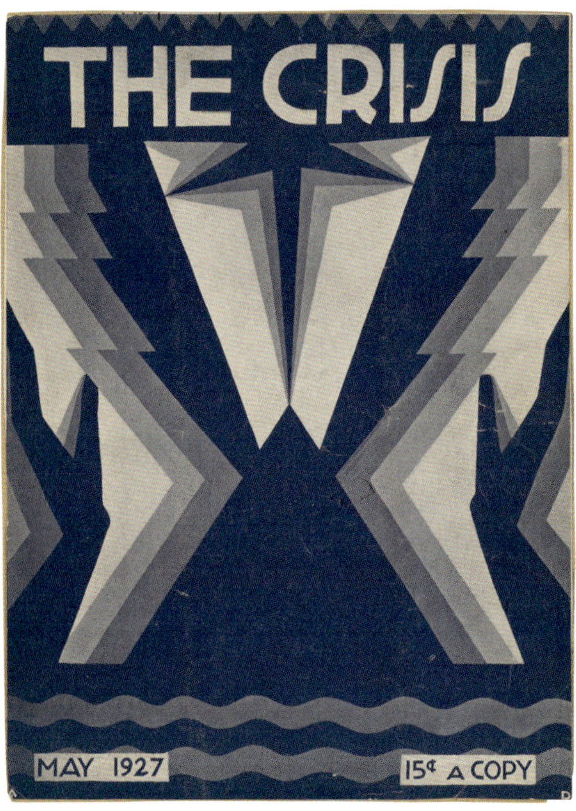

Pl. 37. Aaron Douglas, **Princes shall come out of Egypt;
Ethiopia shall soon stretch out her hands unto God**,
cover of **The Crisis**, May 1927

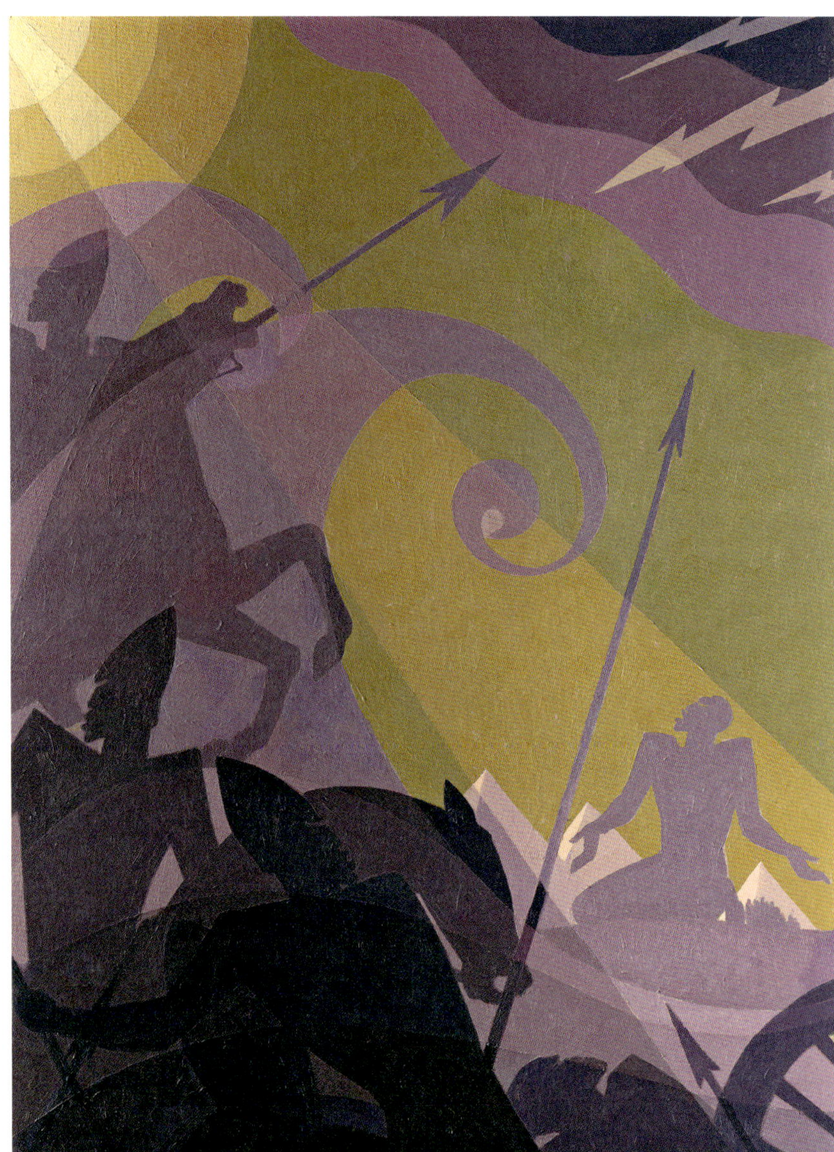

Pl. 36. Aaron Douglas, **Let My People Go**, ca. 1935-39

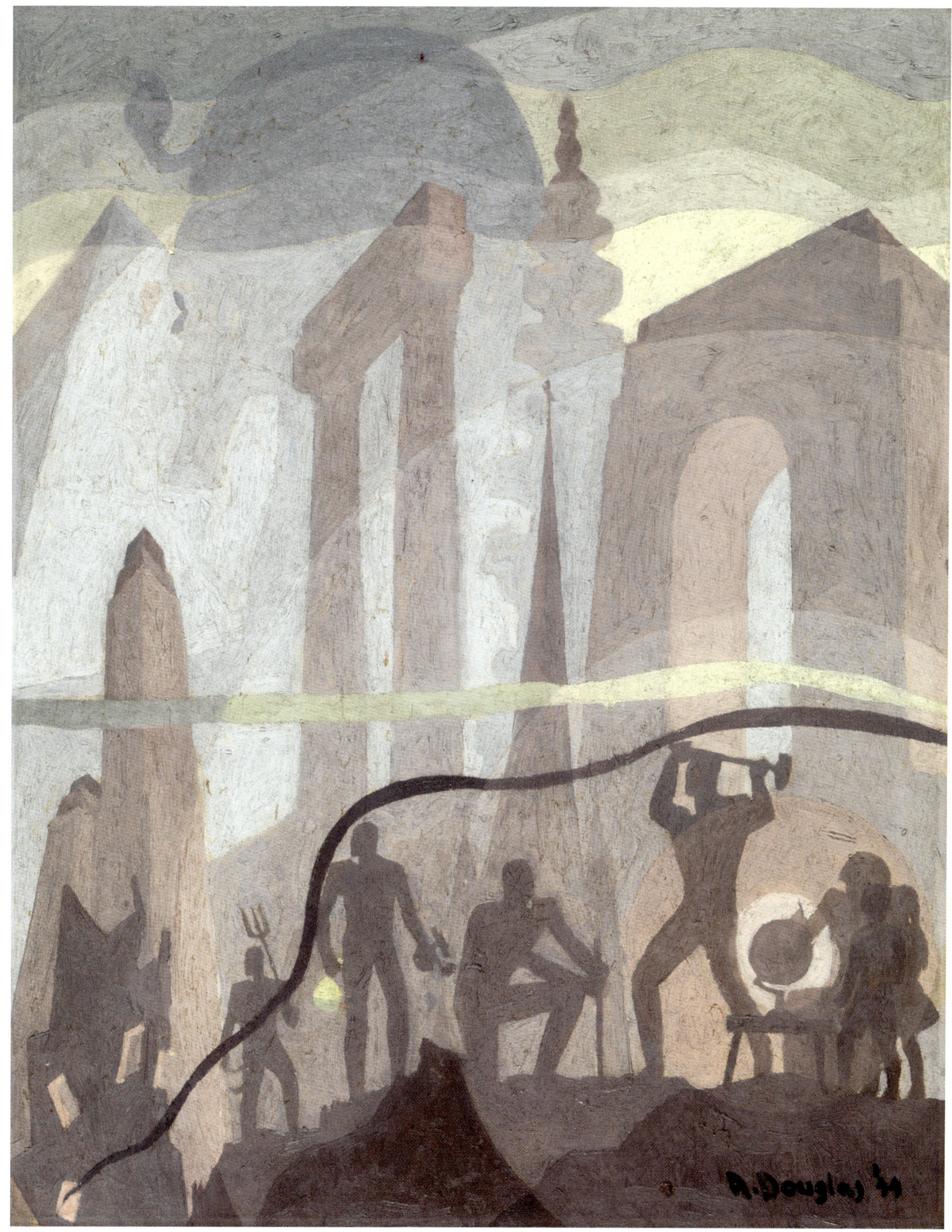

Pl. 38. Aaron Douglas, **Building More Stately Mansions**, 1944

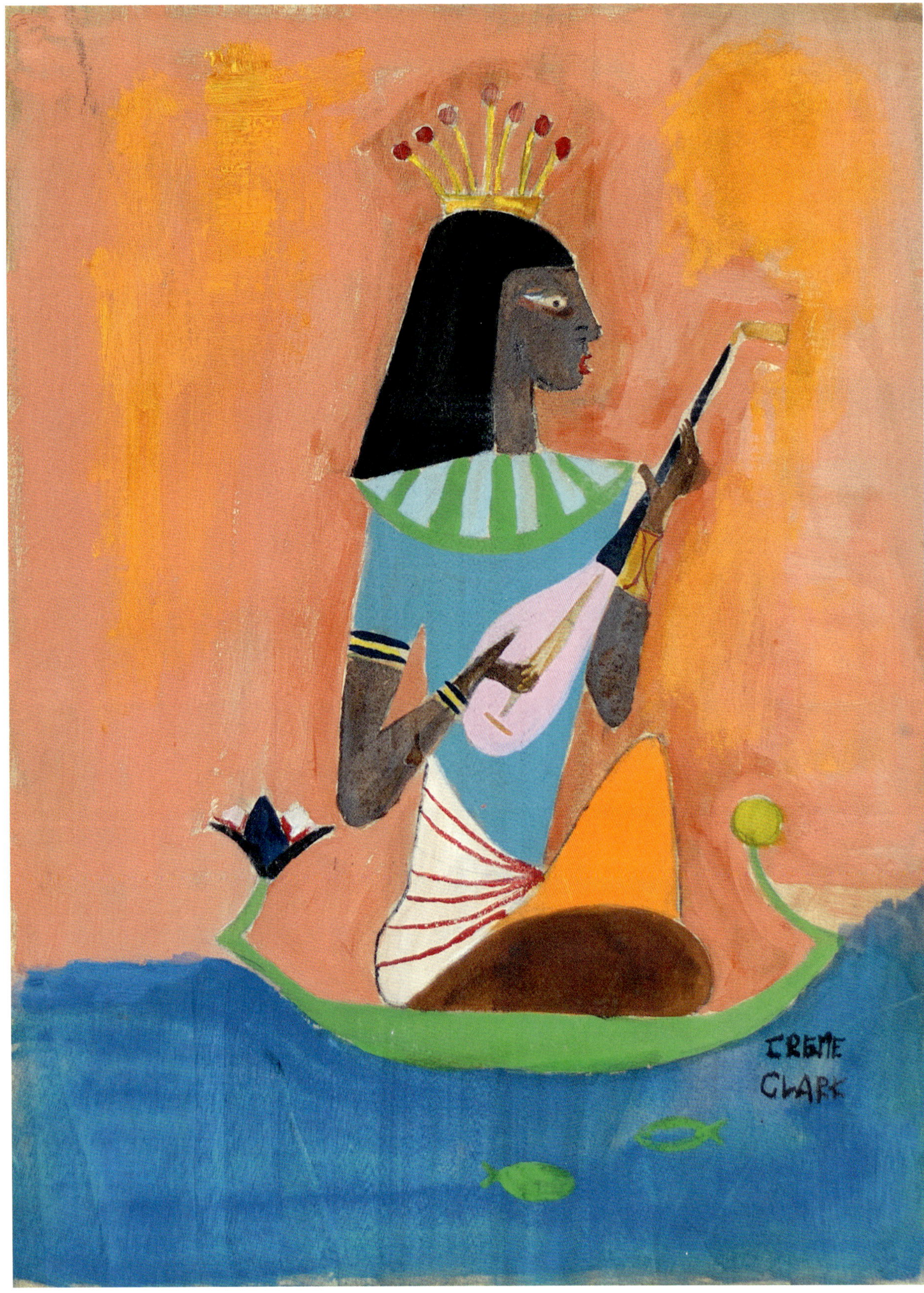

Pl. 39. Irene Clark, **Cleopatra**, ca. 1940-50

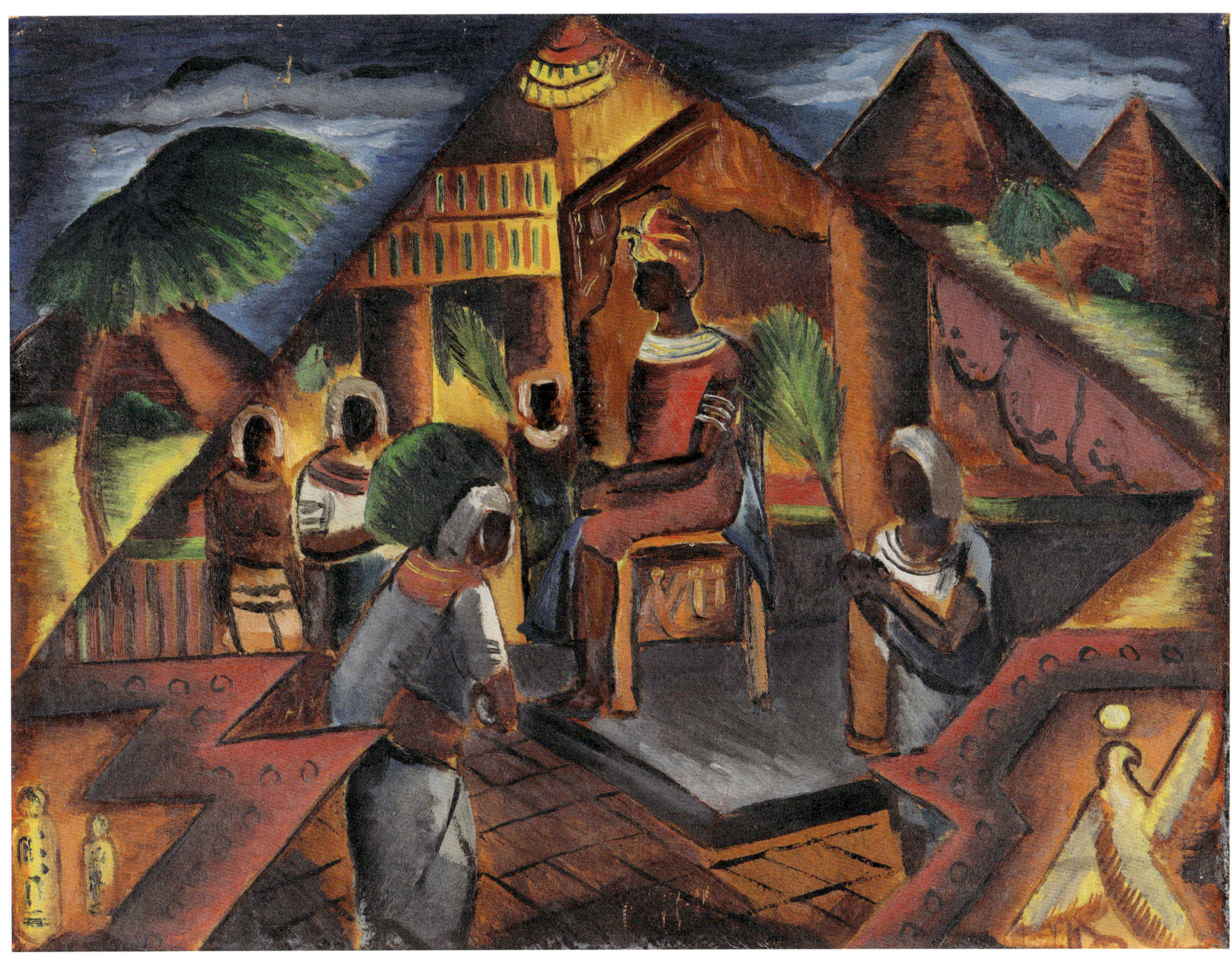

Pl. 40. Malvin Gray Johnson, **Negro Pharaoh-Eighteenth Dynasty,** 1934

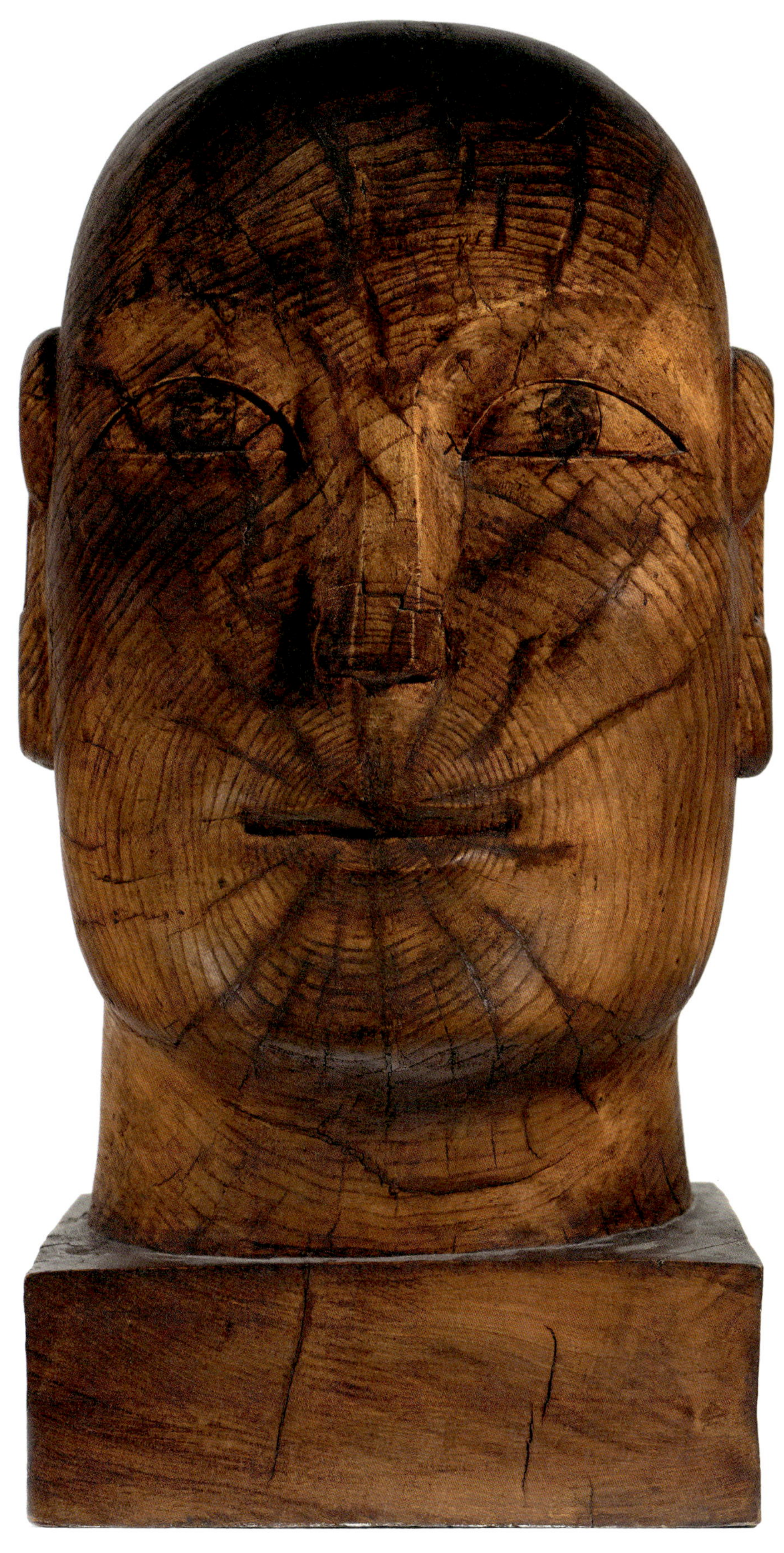

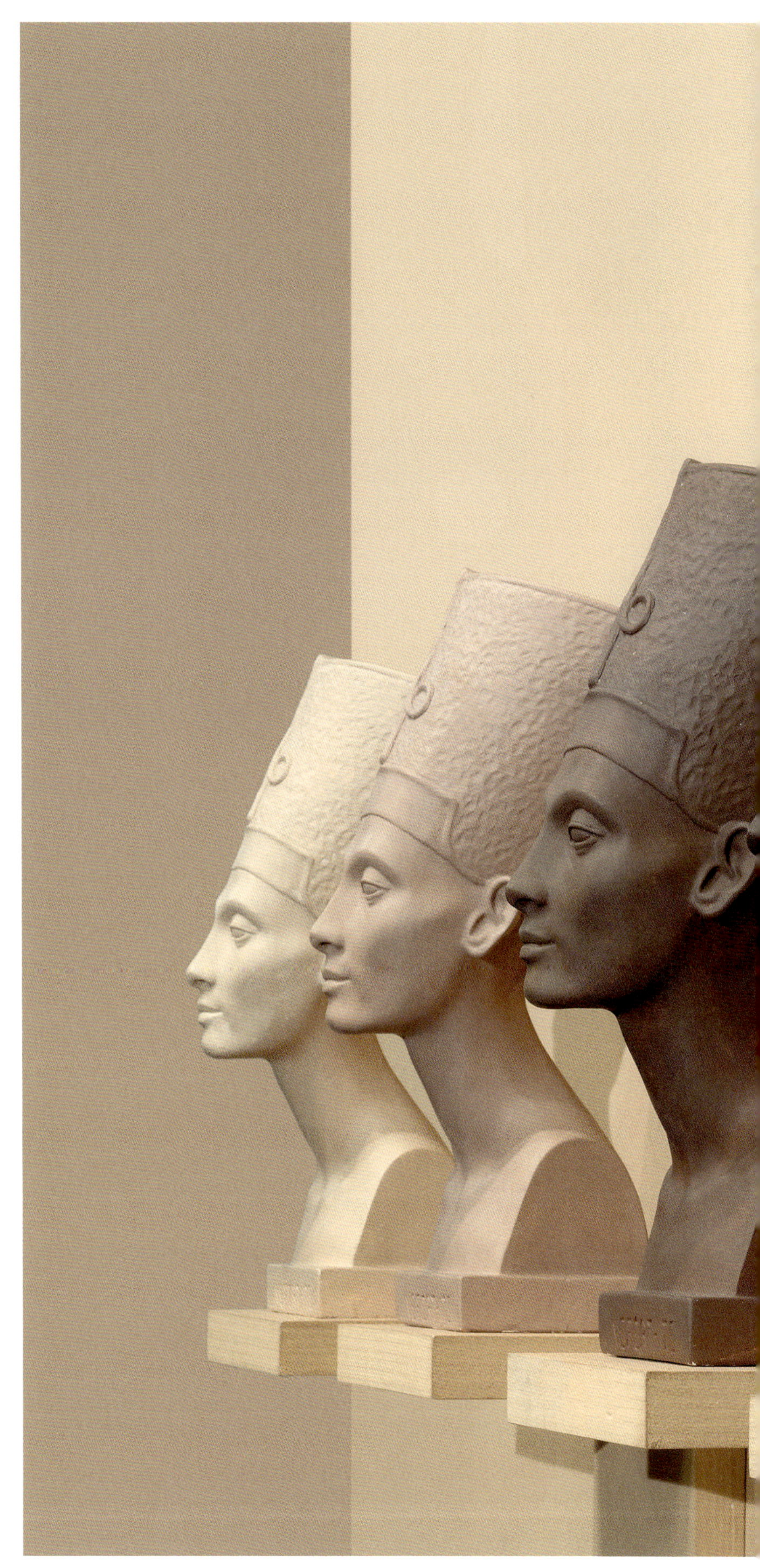

Pl. 42. Fred Wilson, **Grey Area (Brown version)**, 1993

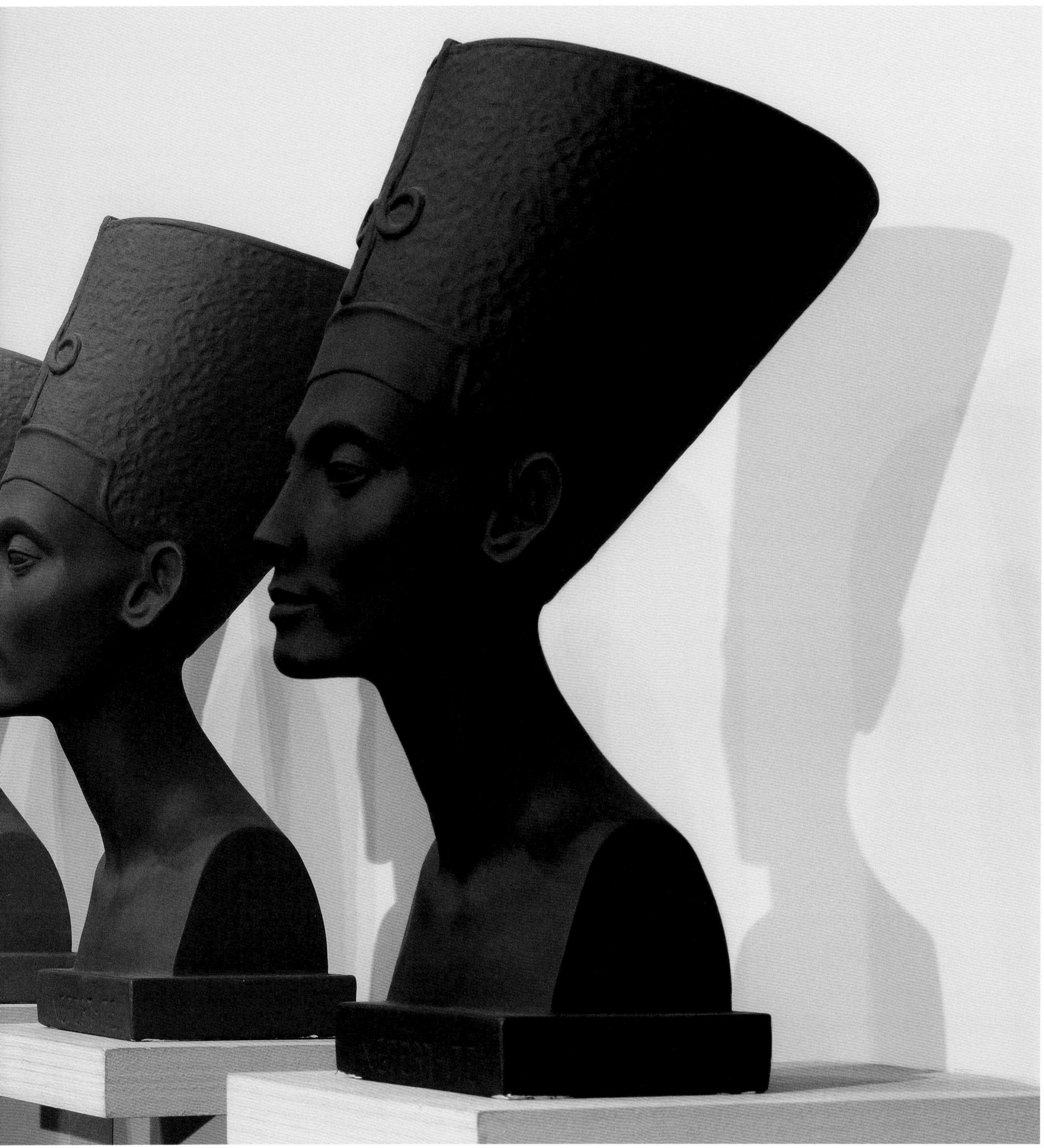

Fred Wilson

Egypt is in my history and in my heart. My father was a civil engineer who worked internationally. He traveled to many parts of the world, heading up projects in various countries in Africa, Asia, and the Middle East. I visited him in Egypt when he was involved with the rebuilding of Port Said. He lived in Cairo at the time, and Anwar El-Sadat was president. While I was there, I traveled throughout Egypt on my own and sometimes with a friend. Being in my youth (early twenties) gave me a perspective that was very different from my three subsequent visits. While I have traveled to Europe, sub-Saharan Africa, and Peru on other trips, Egypt was the only country I have visited where I blended in, to a degree, because of my general appearance. If they didn't think I was from there (and most didn't), they assumed I was from a neighboring country. They'd ask me: "Where are you from?" I'd reply "America." Looking confused or as if I was hiding something or just a bit dumb, they'd ask me, "But where are you REALLY from?" When I'd reply, "the United States," they'd pause and politely say, "Ask your father!"

After that initial experience in Egypt, I was hooked. When Martin Bernal's book *Black Athena* (1987) was on the bookshelves for the first time, I clamored for it. While I did not weigh in on the thesis of the book, I felt strongly that the story of that region had not been objectively told in previous tomes on the subject. I believed that only one perspective had been codified through an imperfect and sometimes historically racist lens. *Black Athena* offered a different viewpoint to revisit, test, and contest what had become the sleeping norm.

It must be understood that my early works related to Egypt as well as my works in the 1992 Cairo Biennial and the 1993 Whitney Biennial were a way to reveal the varying interpretations of this history—ancient, colonial, and contemporary. I laid them out there for audiences to digest and see in relationship to each other, as prior to the Internet and the defining DNA test the various perspectives never collided. It is my belief that, as the science of DNA has now revealed, the ancient Egyptians were unique: their DNA was like that of no other group of humans, then or now. In *Grey Area* and *Grey Area (Brown version)* (pl. 42), for example, I intended neither to present or espouse a final thesis. I just found it fascinating that so many points of view were occurring at the same time.

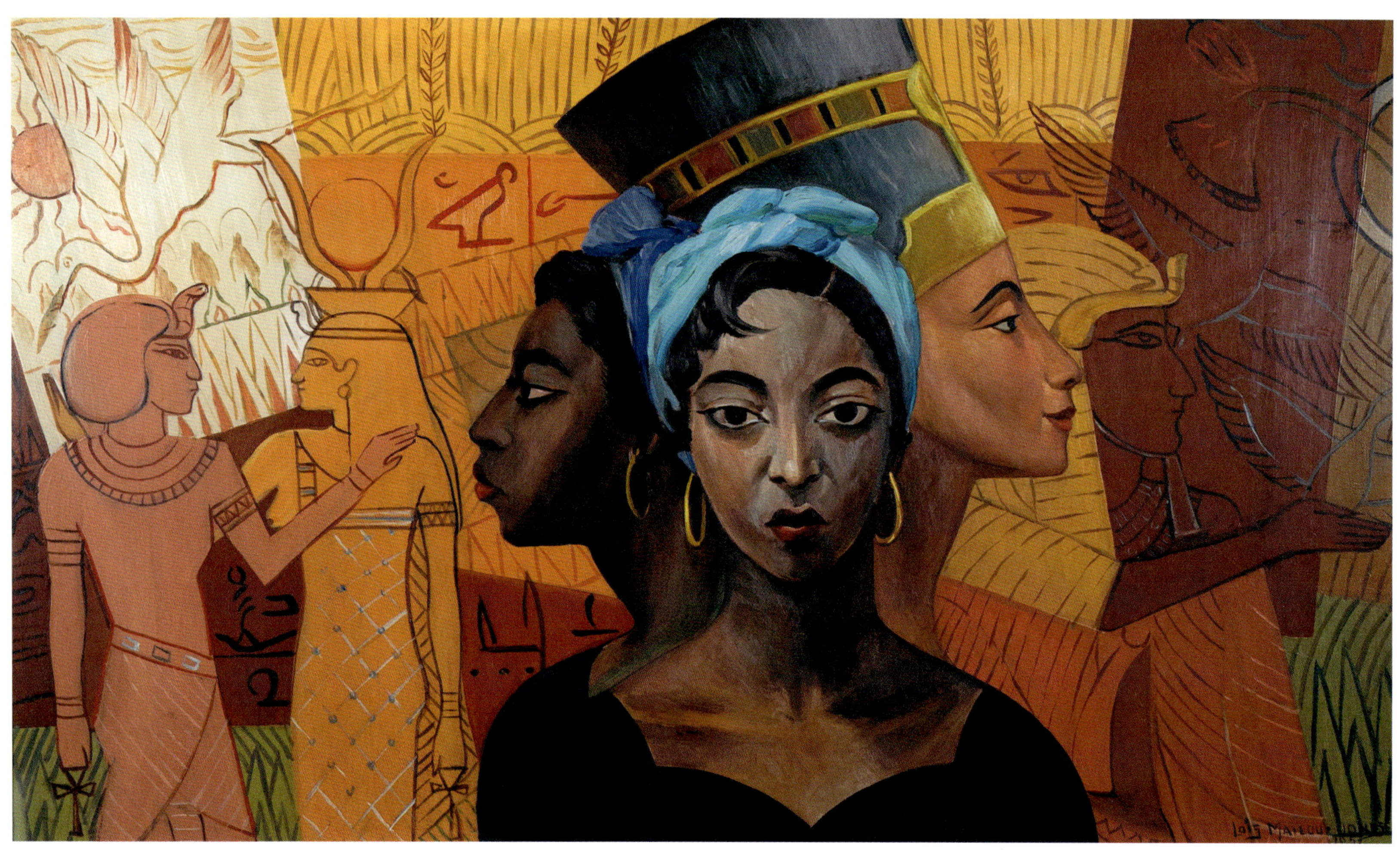

Pl. 43. Loïs Mailou Jones, **Egyptian Heritage**, 1953

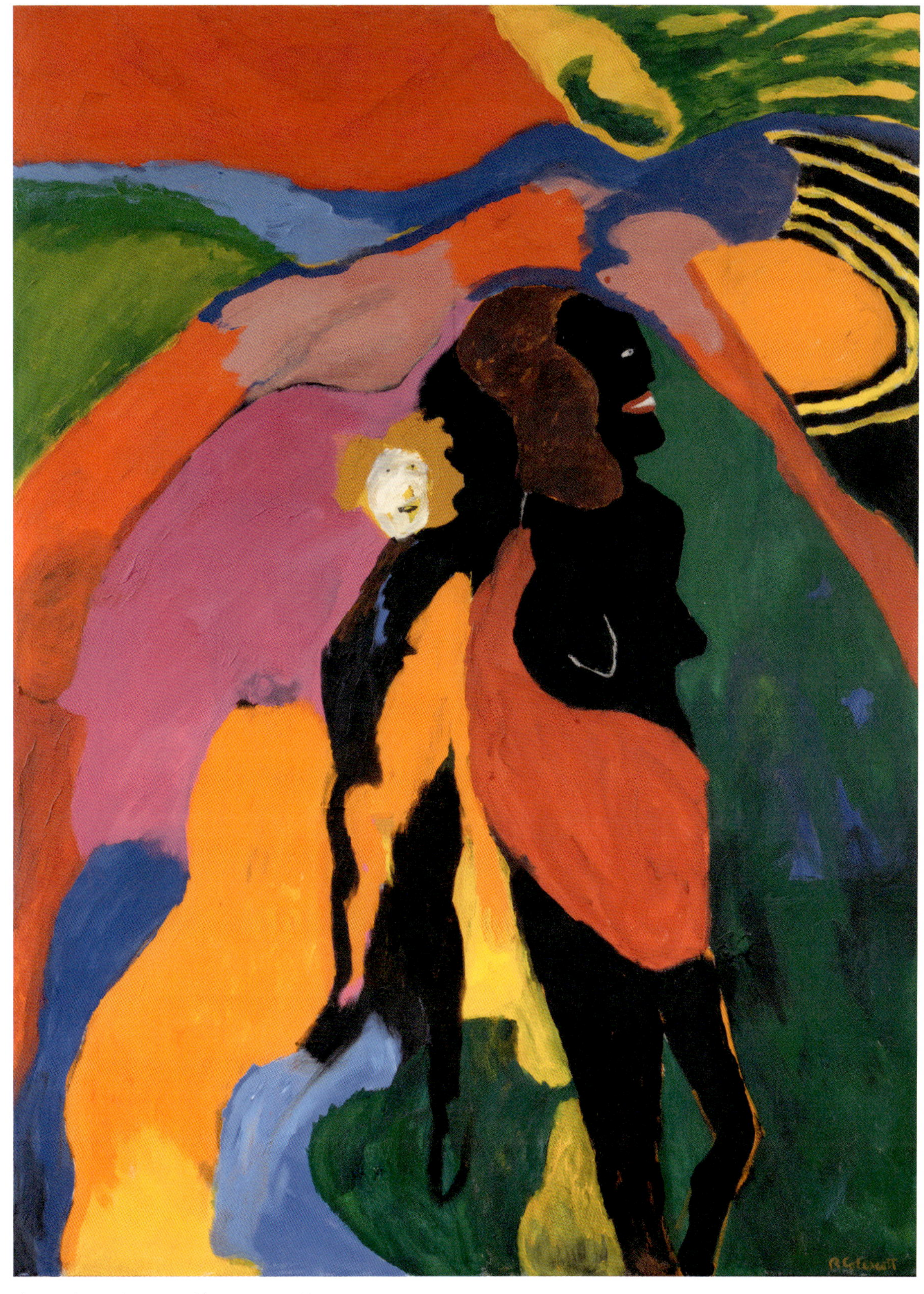

Pl. 44. Robert Colescott, **Nubian Queen**, 1966

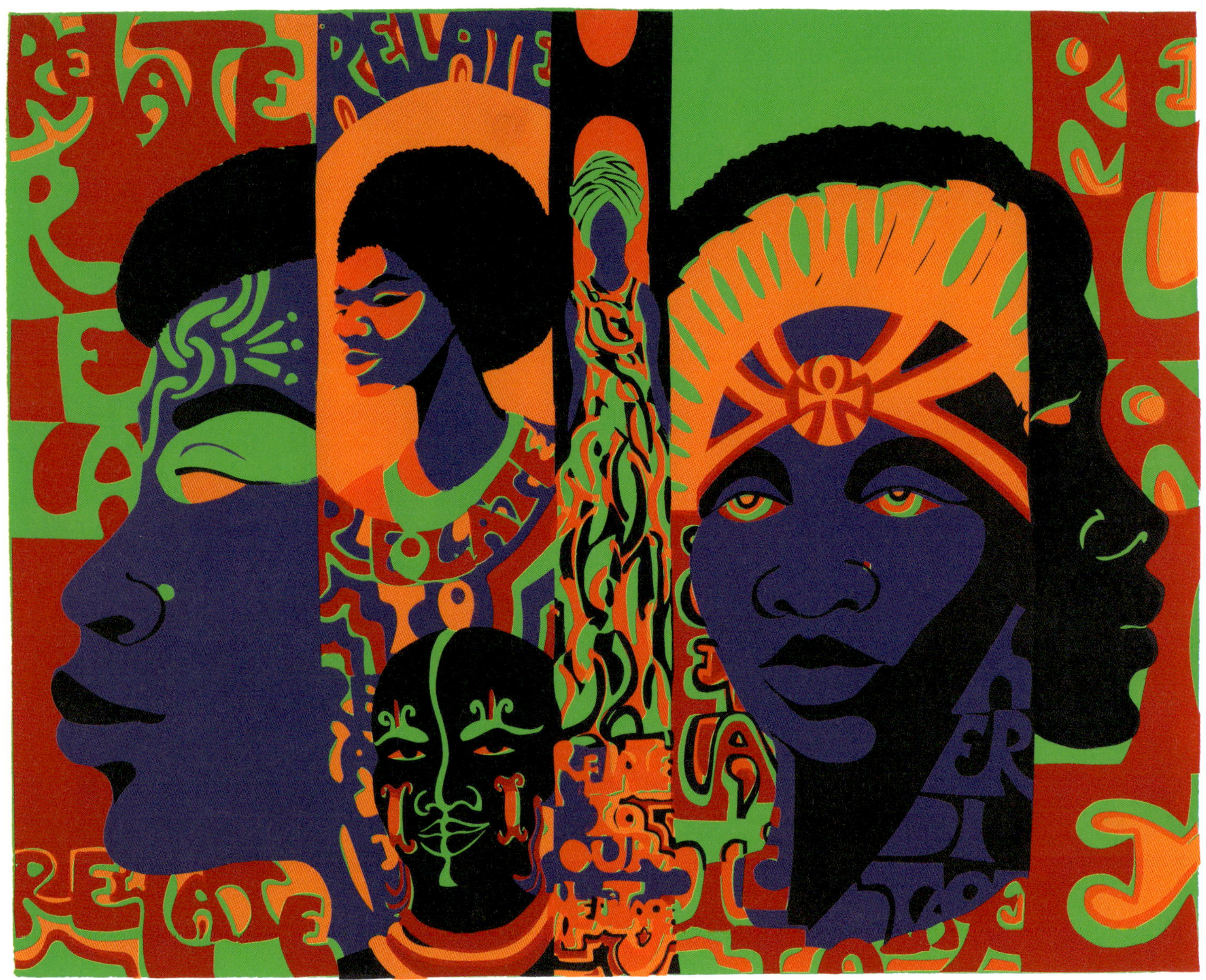

Pl. 45. Barbara Jones-Hogu, **Relate to Your Heritage**, 1971

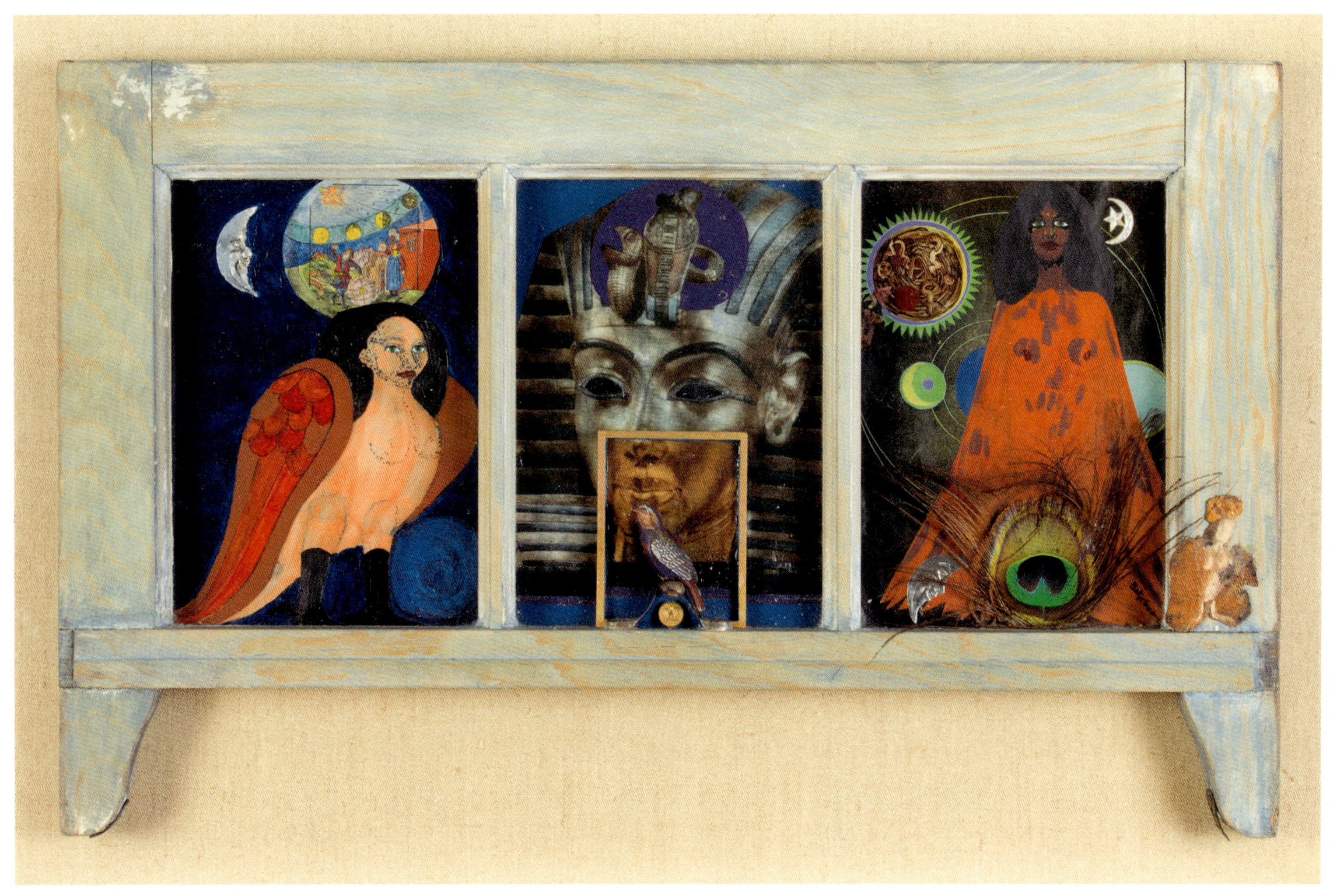

Pl. 46. Betye Saar, **Window of Ancient Sirens**, 1979

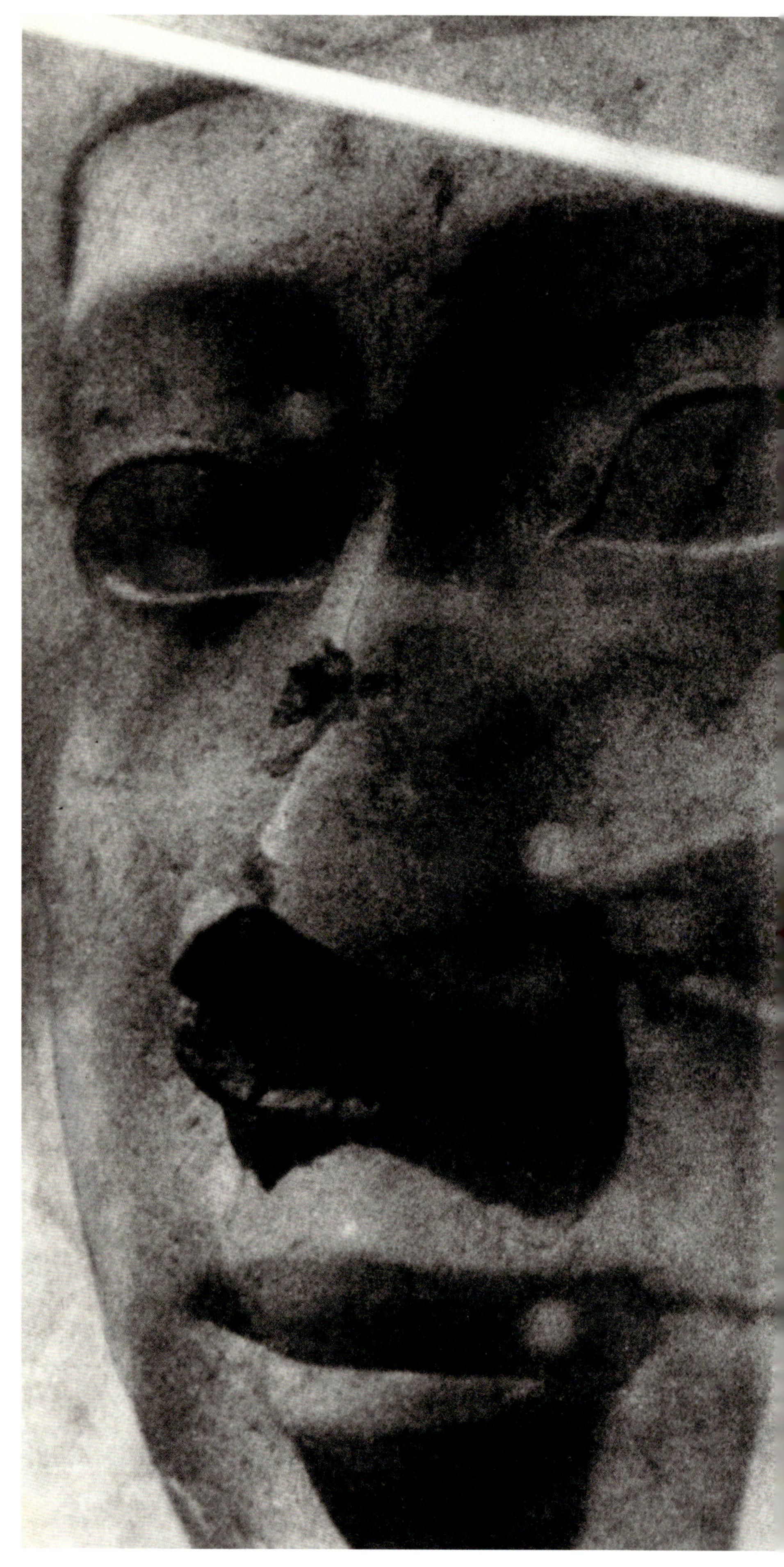

Pl. 47. C. Daniel Dawson, **Olaifa and Egypt**, 1978

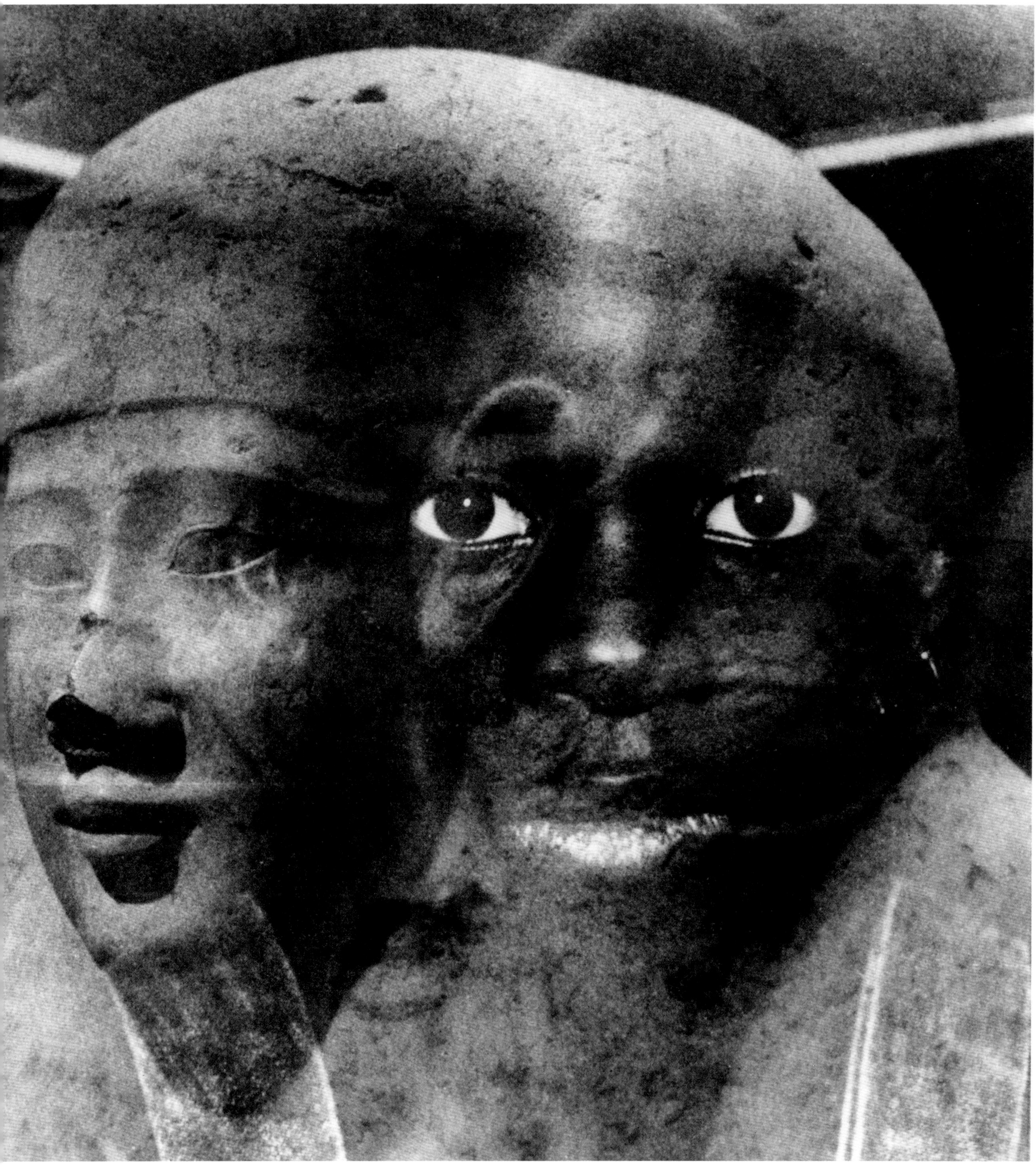

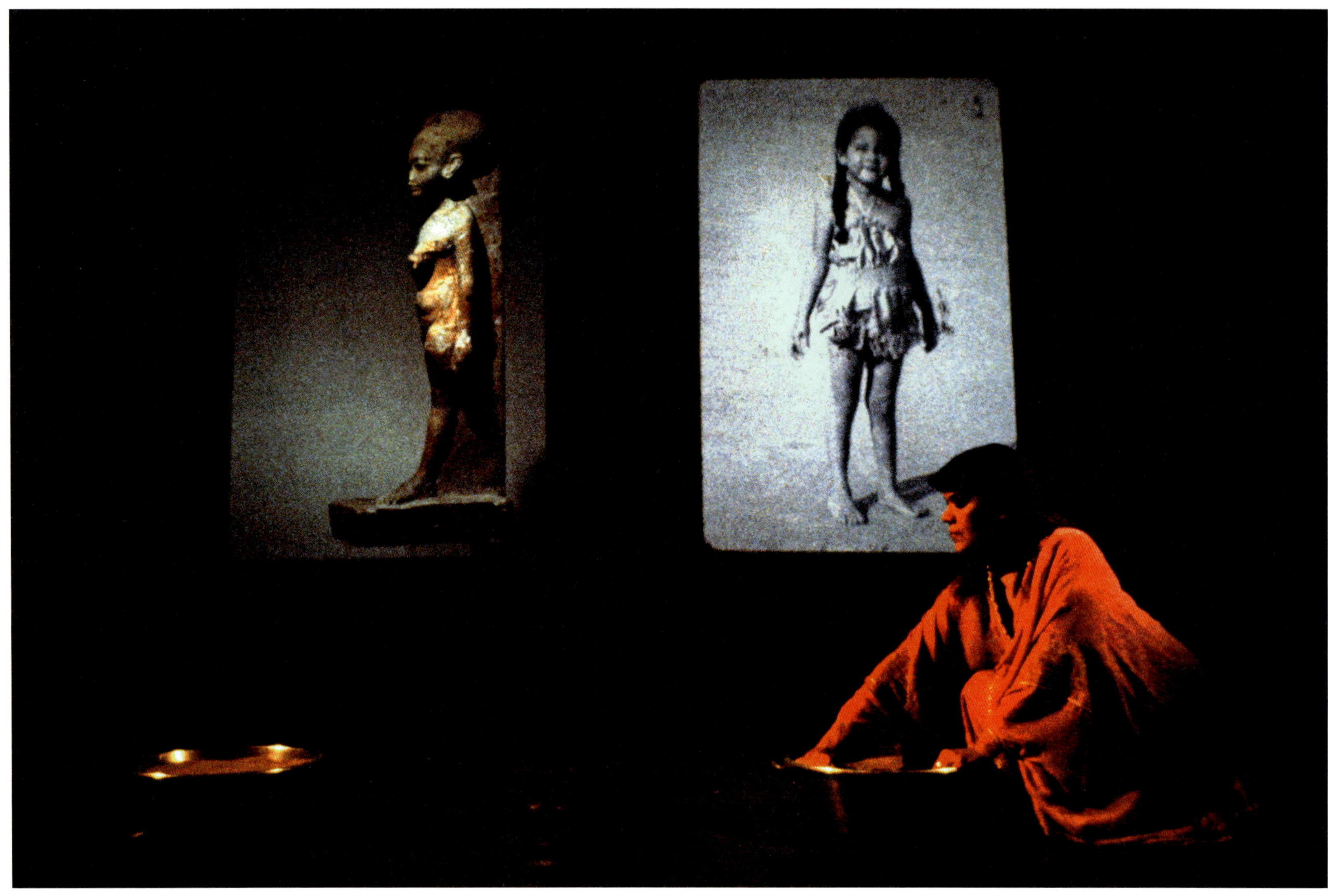

Pl. 48. Lorraine O'Grady, **Nefertiti/Devonia Evangeline: Told to swing an incense censer, she stirs sand instead**, 1981

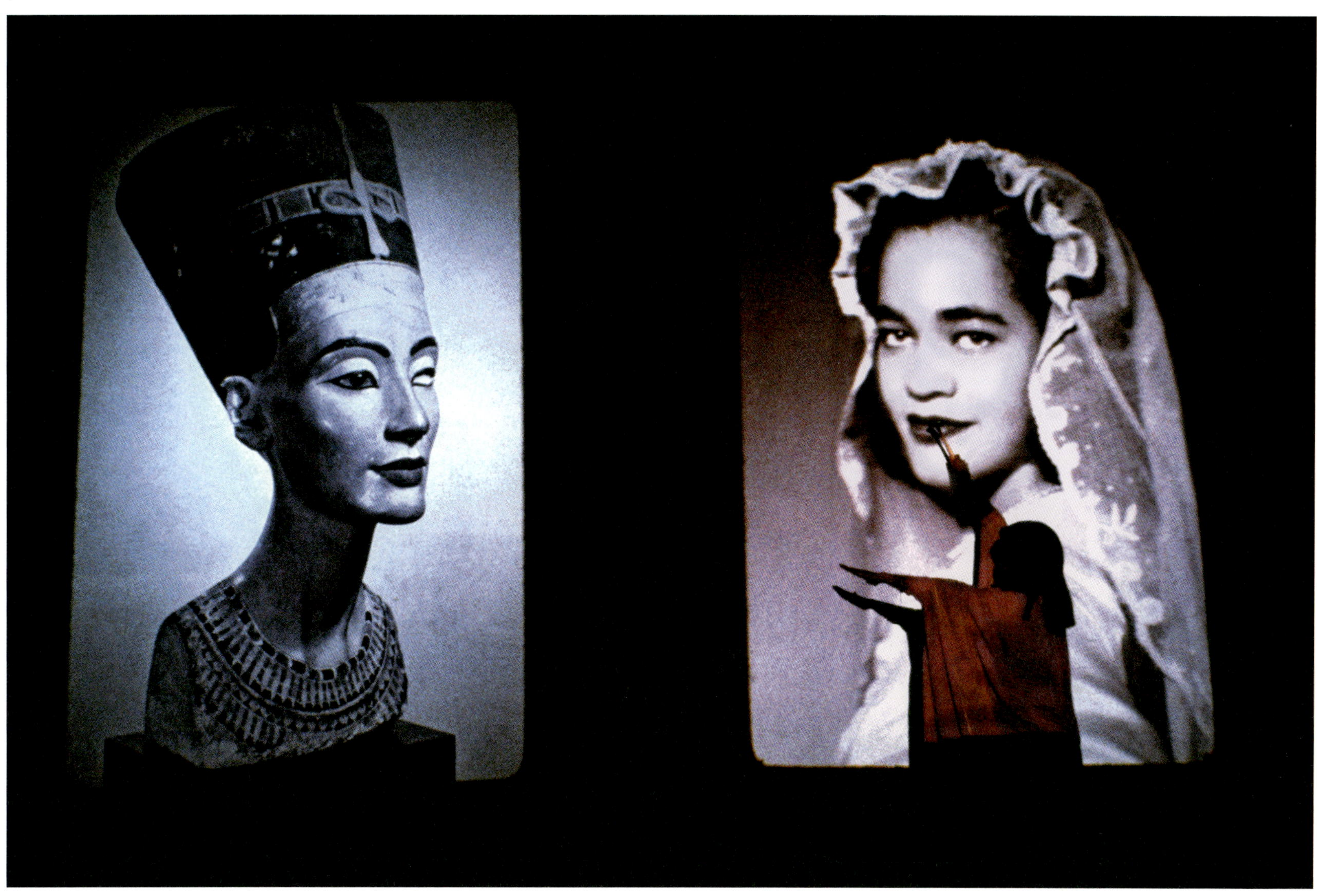

Pl. 49. Lorraine O'Grady, **Nefertiti/Devonia Evangeline: You are protected, and you shall not die**, 1981

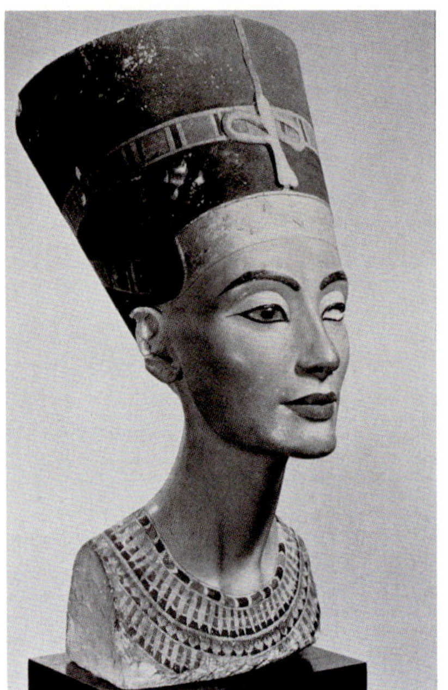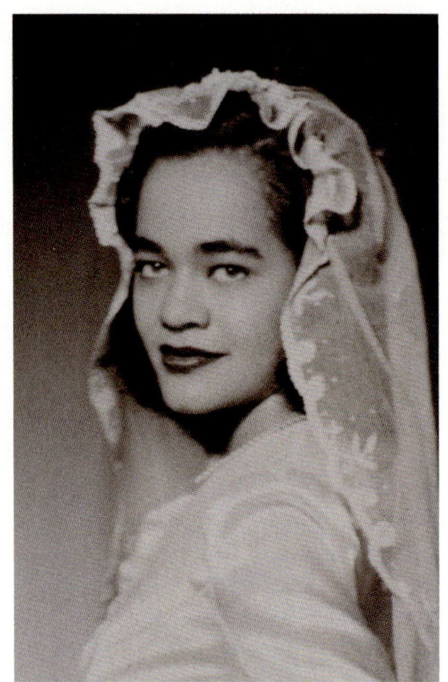

Pl. 50. Lorraine O'Grady, **Miscegenated Family Album (Sisters I), L: Nefernefruaten Nefertiti; R: Devonia Evangeline O'Grady**, 1980/94

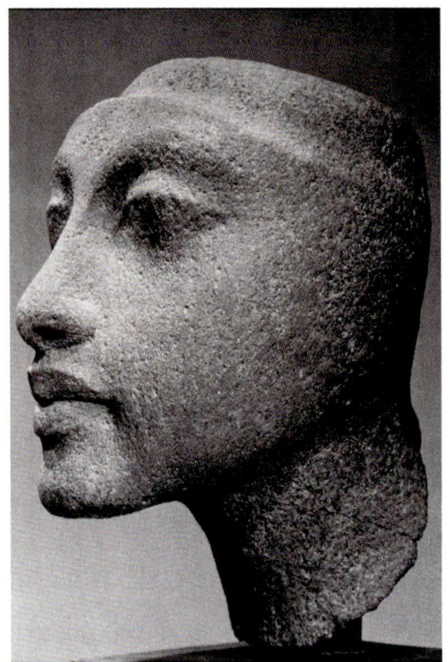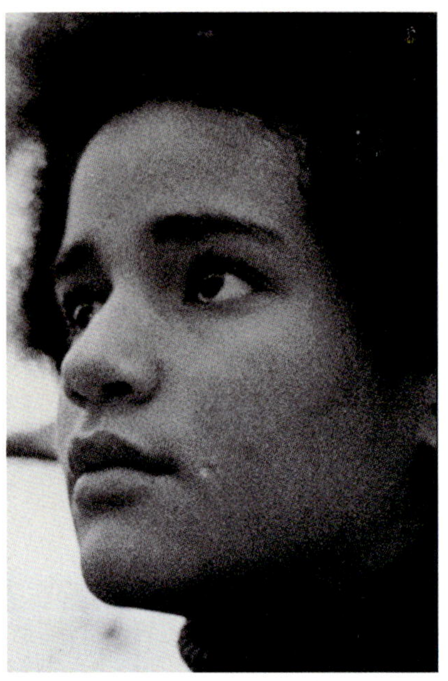

Pl. 51. Lorraine O'Grady, **Miscegenated Family Album (Sisters III), L: Nefertiti's daughter, Maketaten; R: Devonia's daughter, Kimberley**, 1980/94

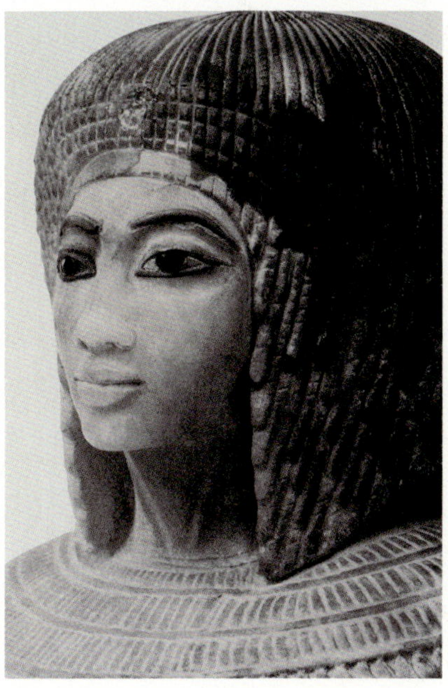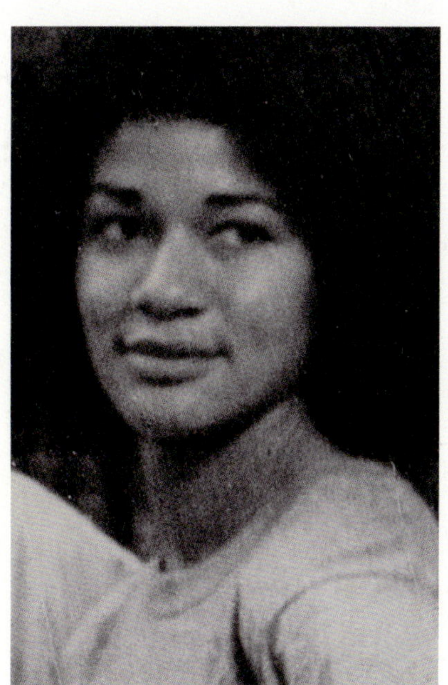

Pl. 52. Lorraine O'Grady, **Miscegenated Family Album (Sisters II), L: Nefertiti's daughter Merytaten;
R: Devonia's daughter**, 1980/94

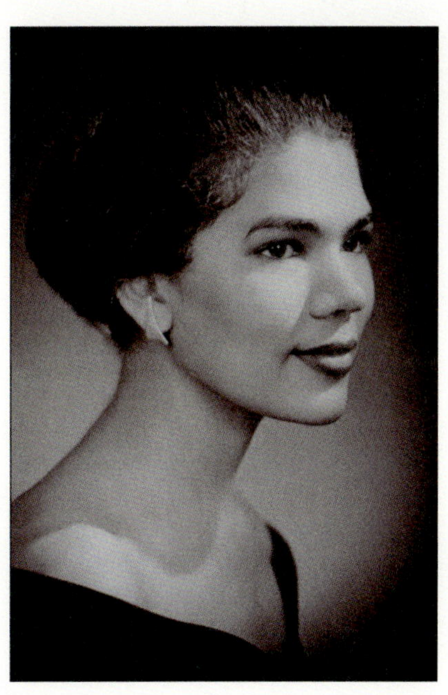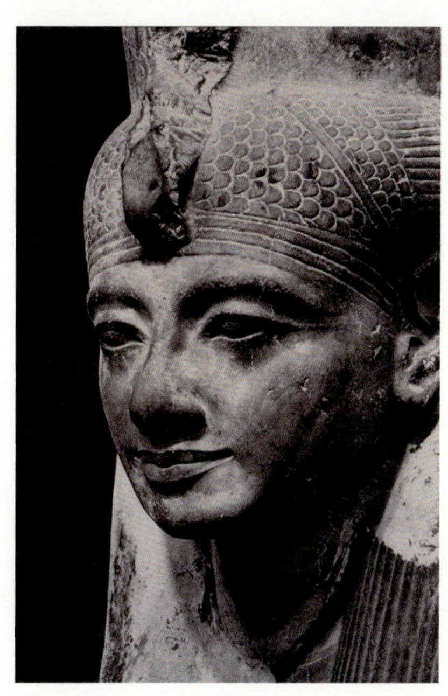

Pl. 53. Lorraine O'Grady, **Miscegenated Family Album (Sisters IV), L: Devonia's sister, Lorraine;
R: Nefertiti's sister, Mutnedjmet**, 1980/94

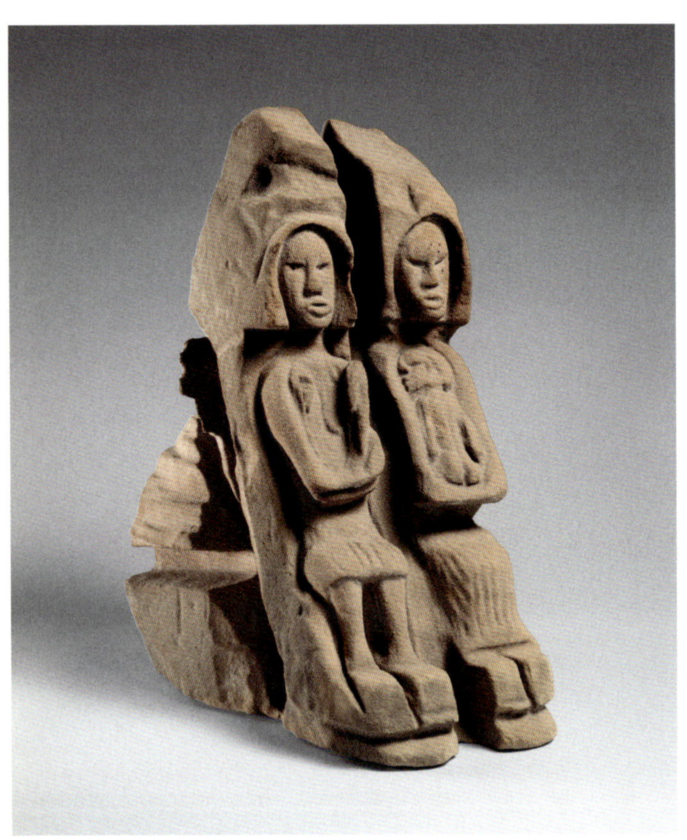

Pl. 54. Lonnie Holley, **Ruling for the Child**, 1982

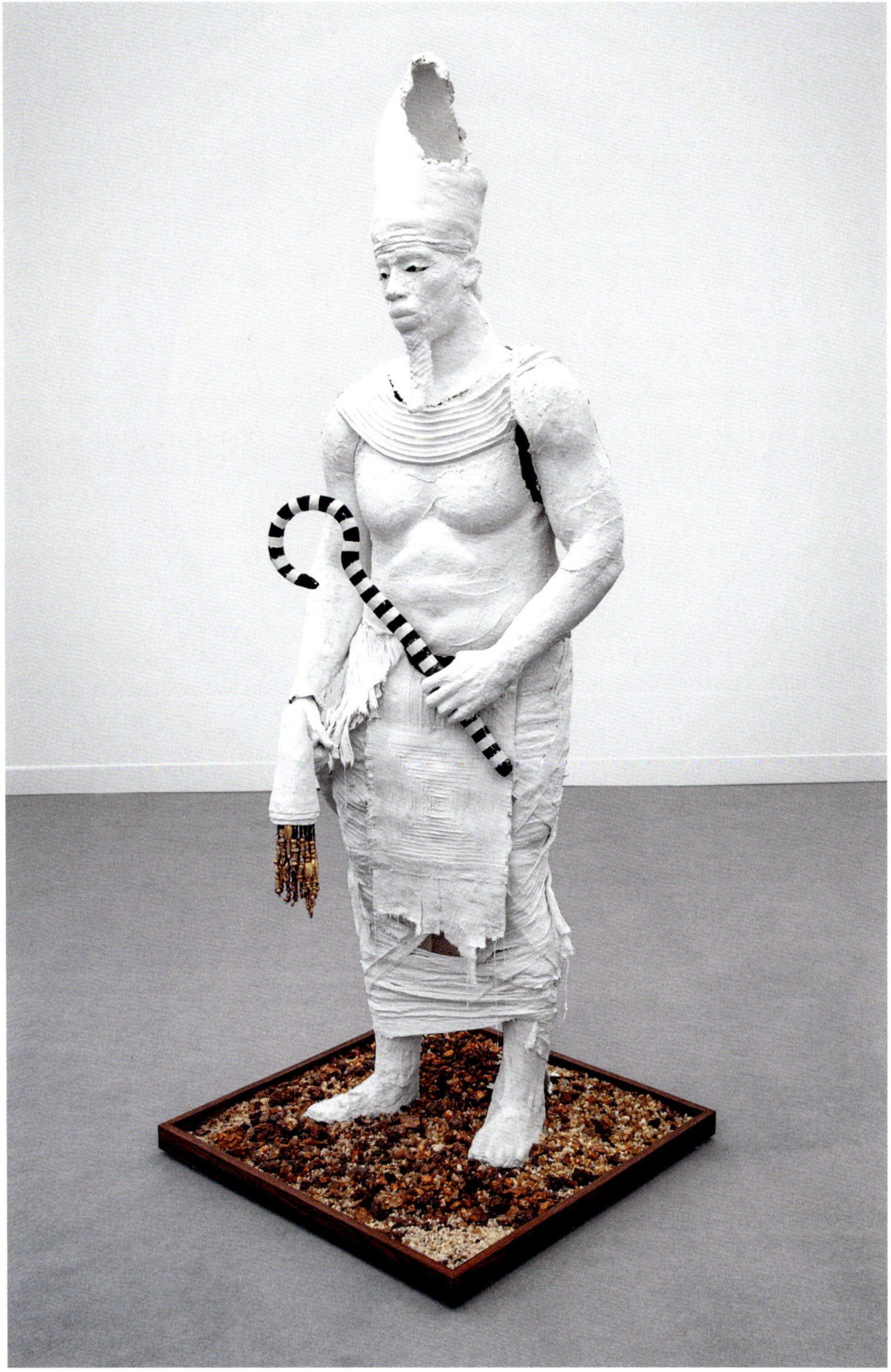

Pl. 55. Karon Davis, **He Who Floods the Nile**, 2019

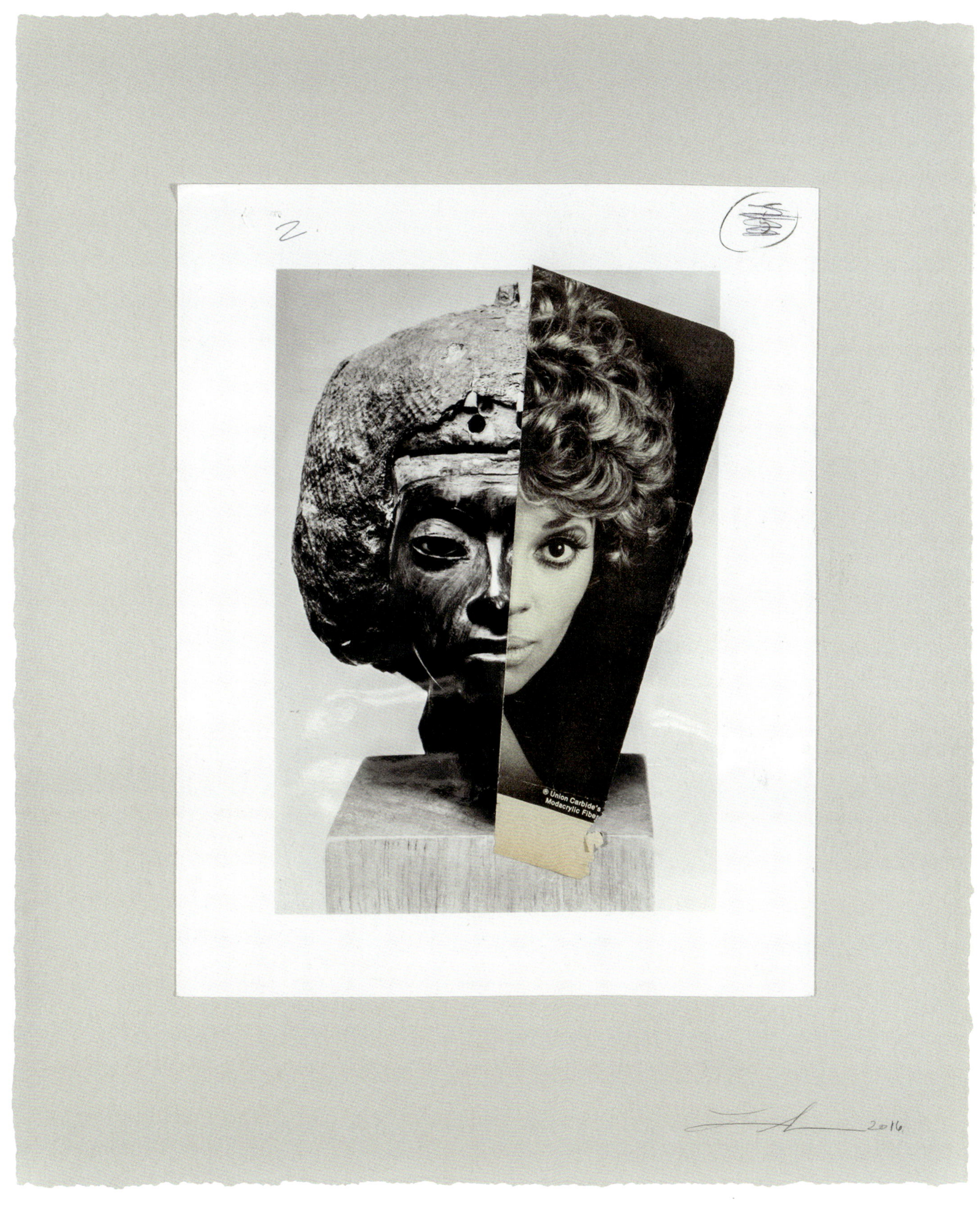

Pl. 56. Lorna Simpson, **Older Queen**, 2017

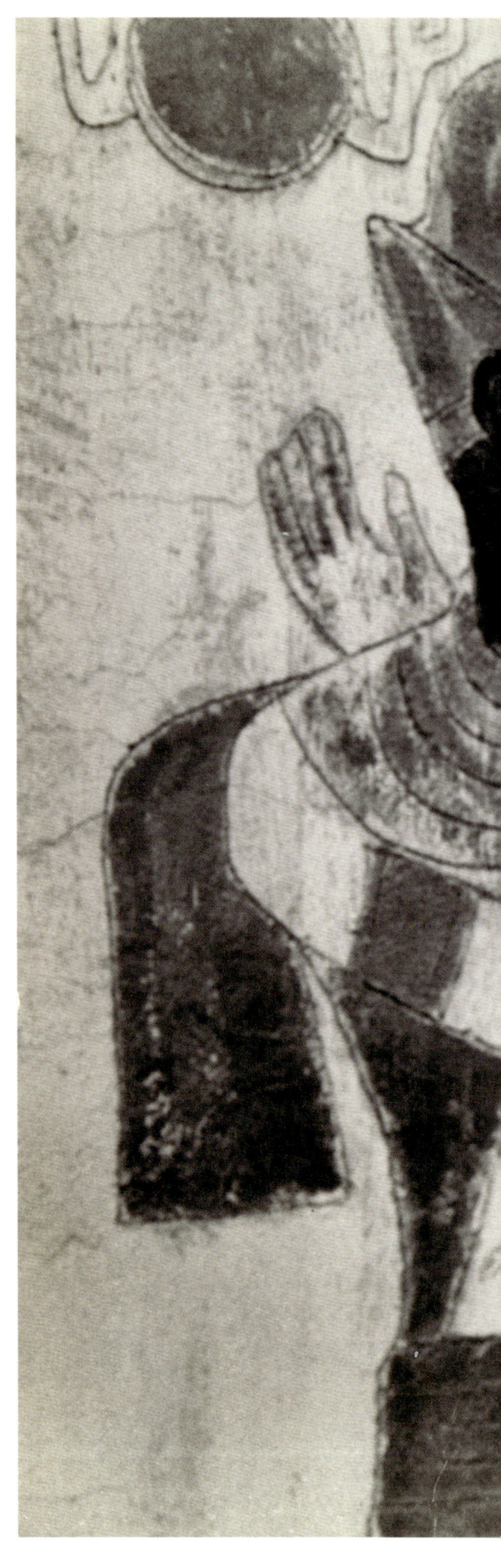

Pl. 57. Louis Draper, **Untitled (Girl with Egyptian Mural)**, ca. 1965

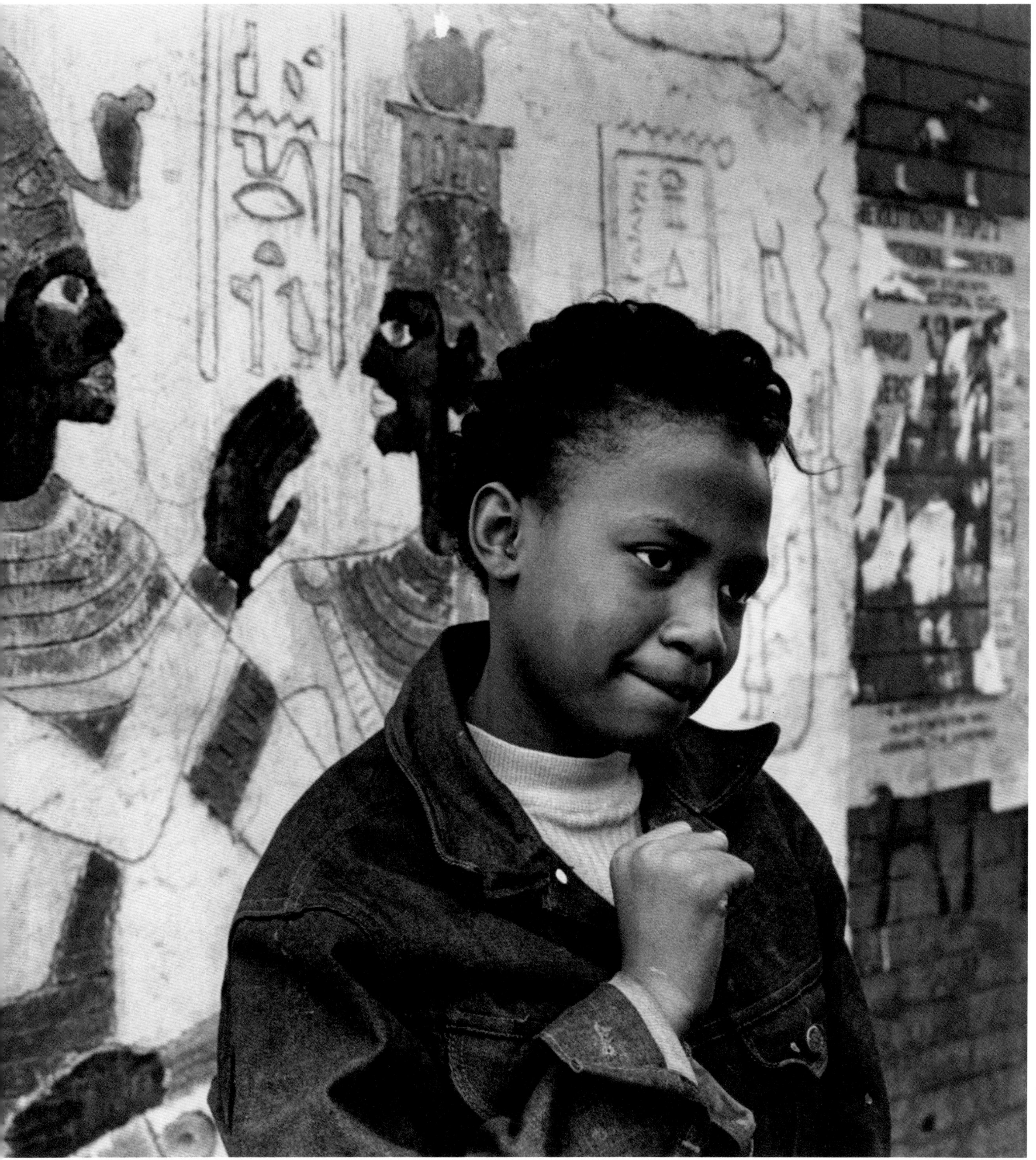

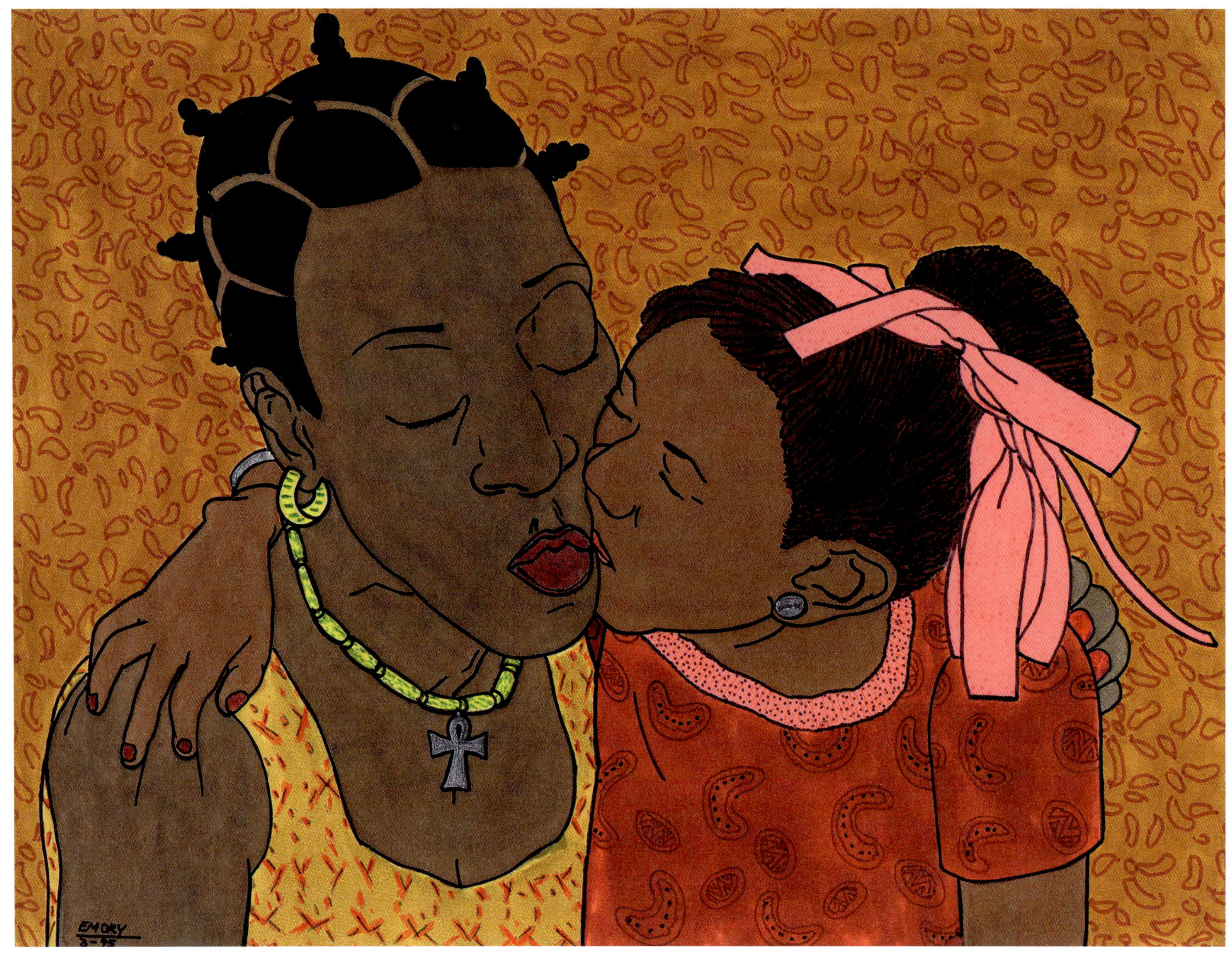

Pl. 58. Emory Douglas, **Mother and Daughter**, 1995

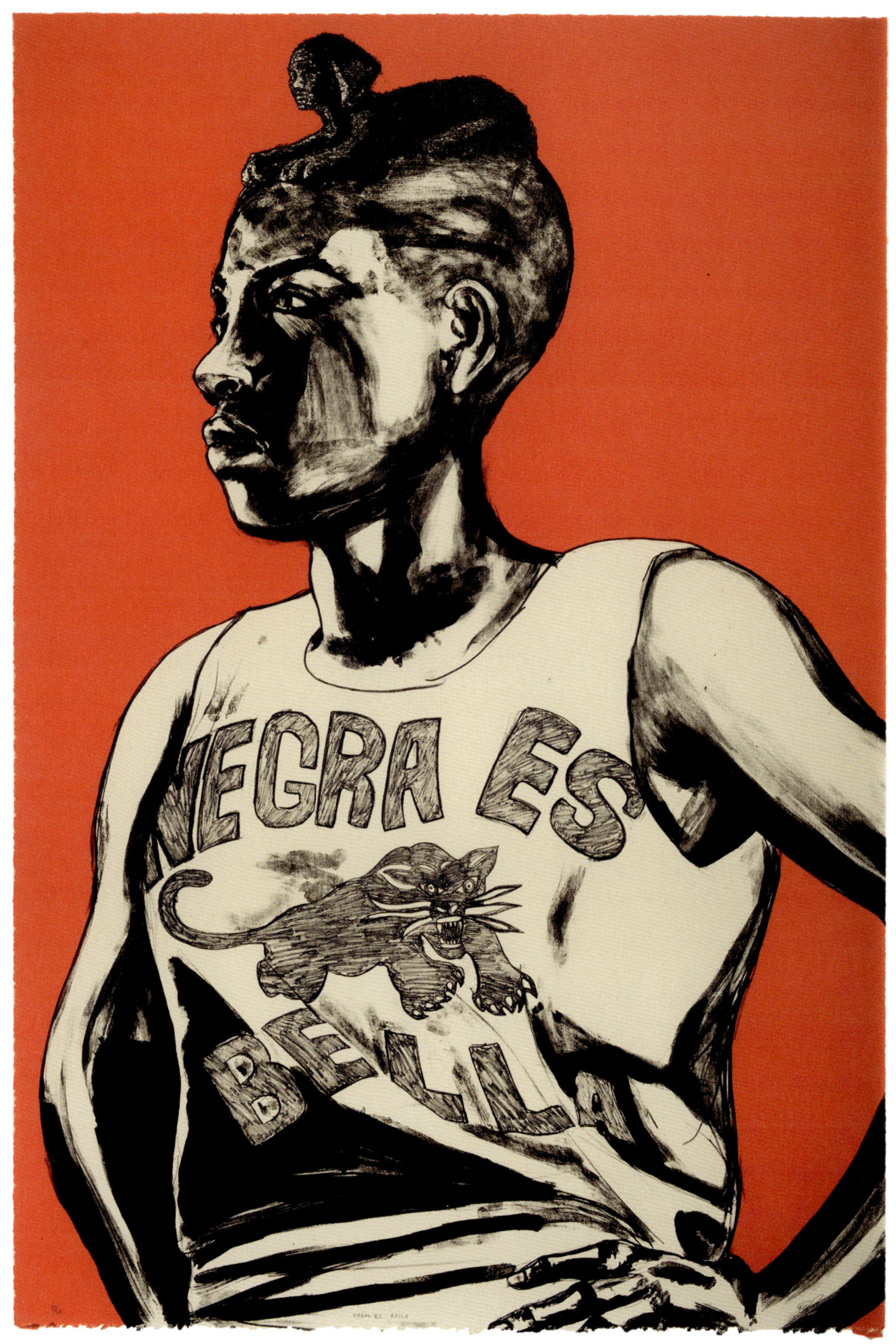

Pl. 59. Robert Pruitt, **Negra Es Bella**, 2015

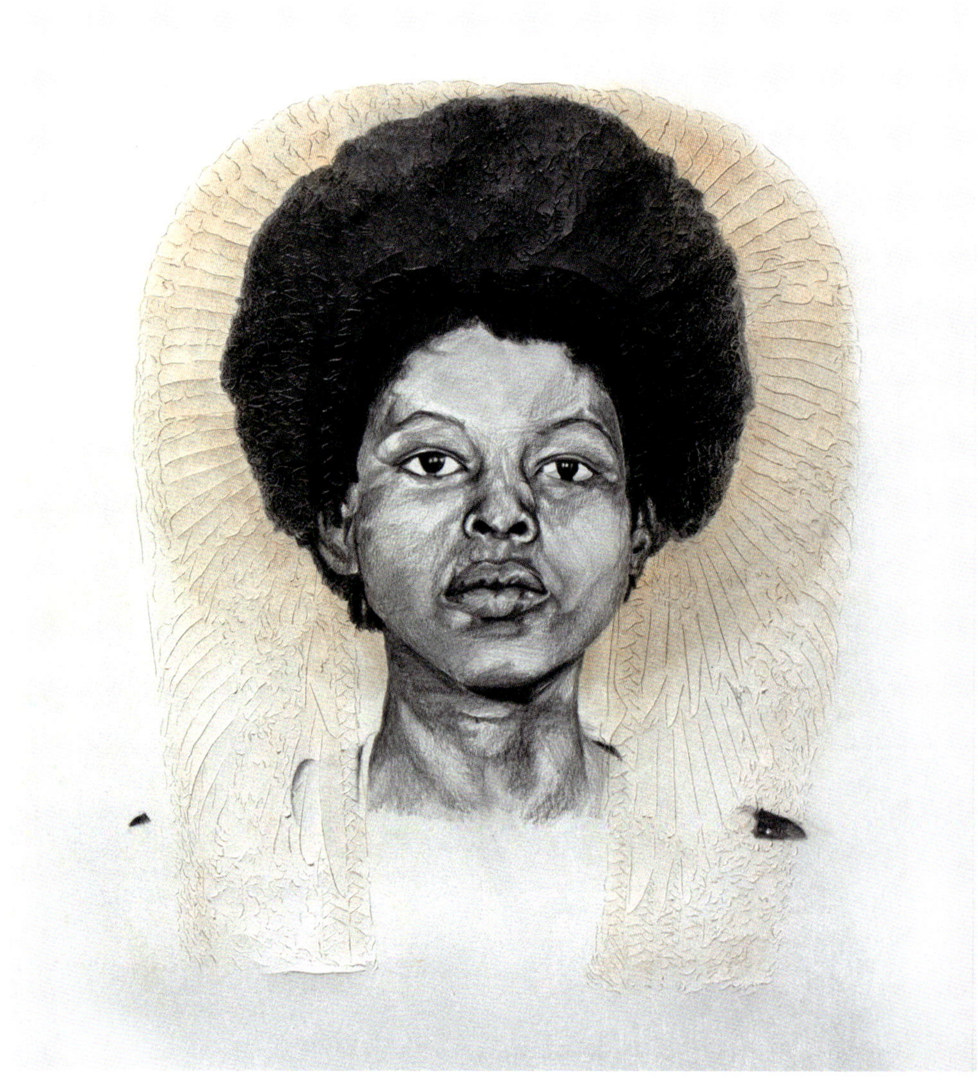

Pl. 60. Oasa DuVerney, **Assata Shakur as Ahmes Nefertari**, 2018

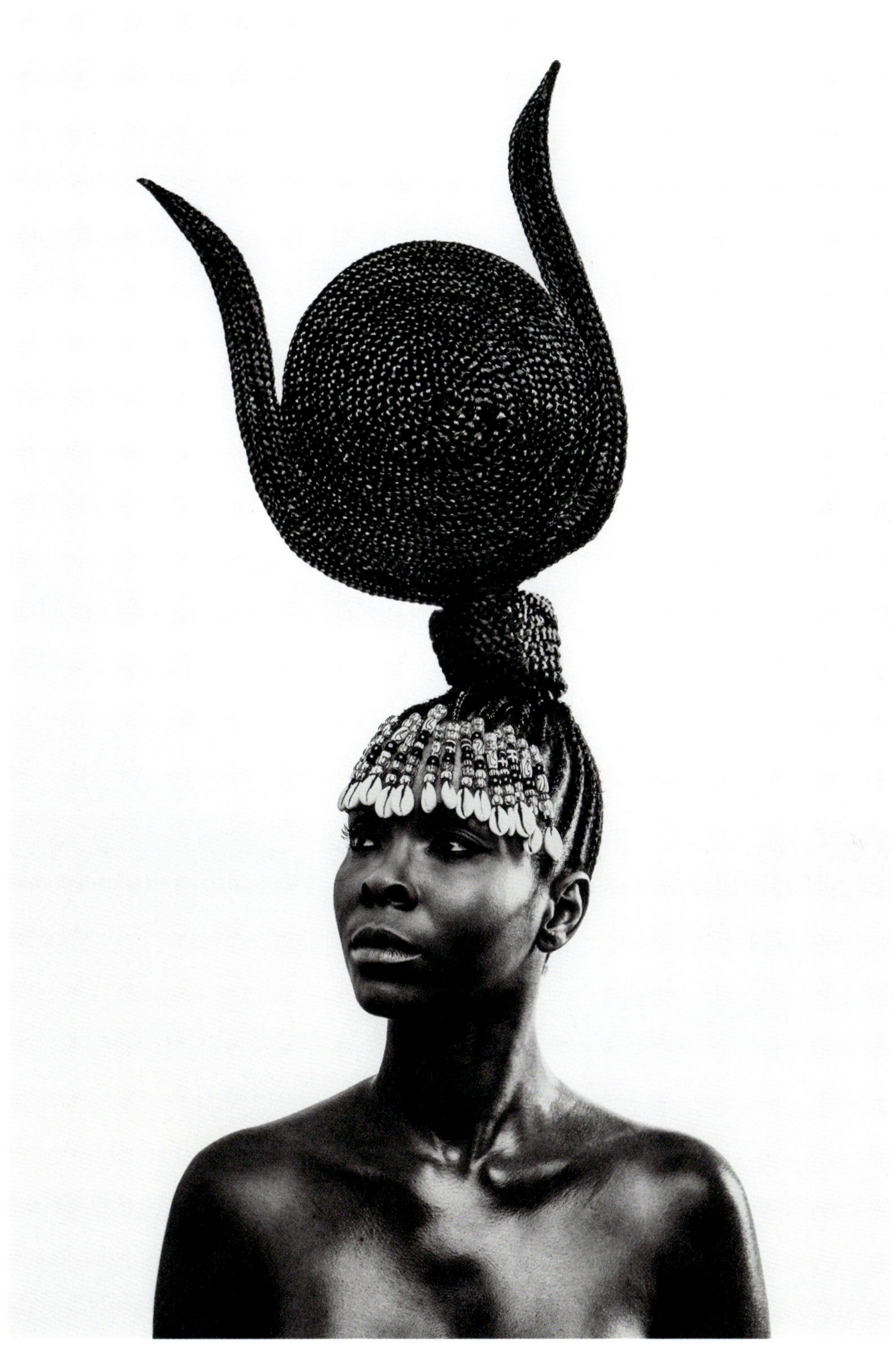

Pl. 61. Shani Crowe, **Sun Trust,** 2016

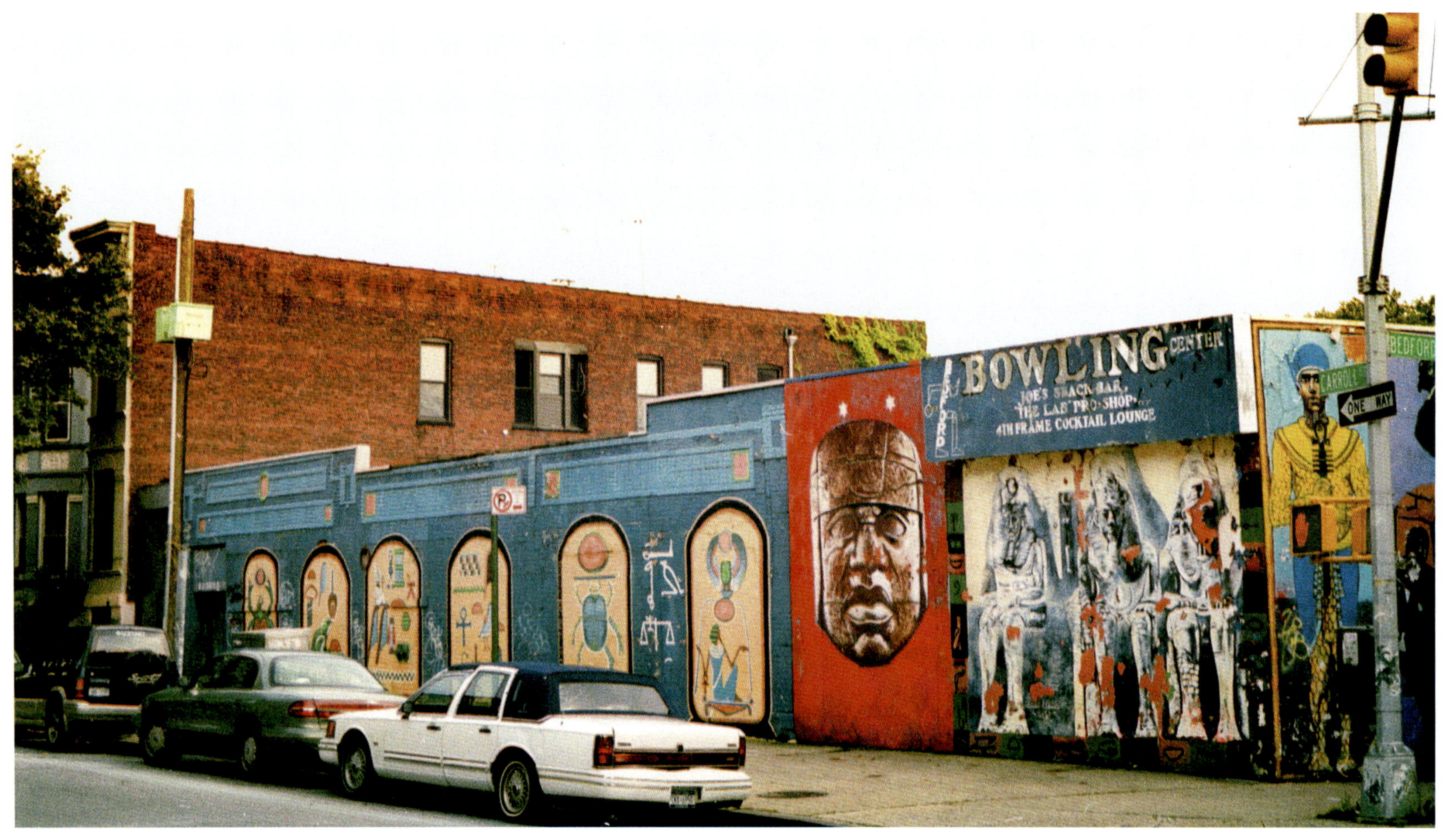

Pl. 62. Jamal Lance, Menelek III, and Kiambu Zawadi, **Egypt Symbols in Arches**, **Olmec Head**, and **Three Pharaohs**, from Bedford Bowling Center murals, 1980–94, photograph by Janet Braun-Reinitz

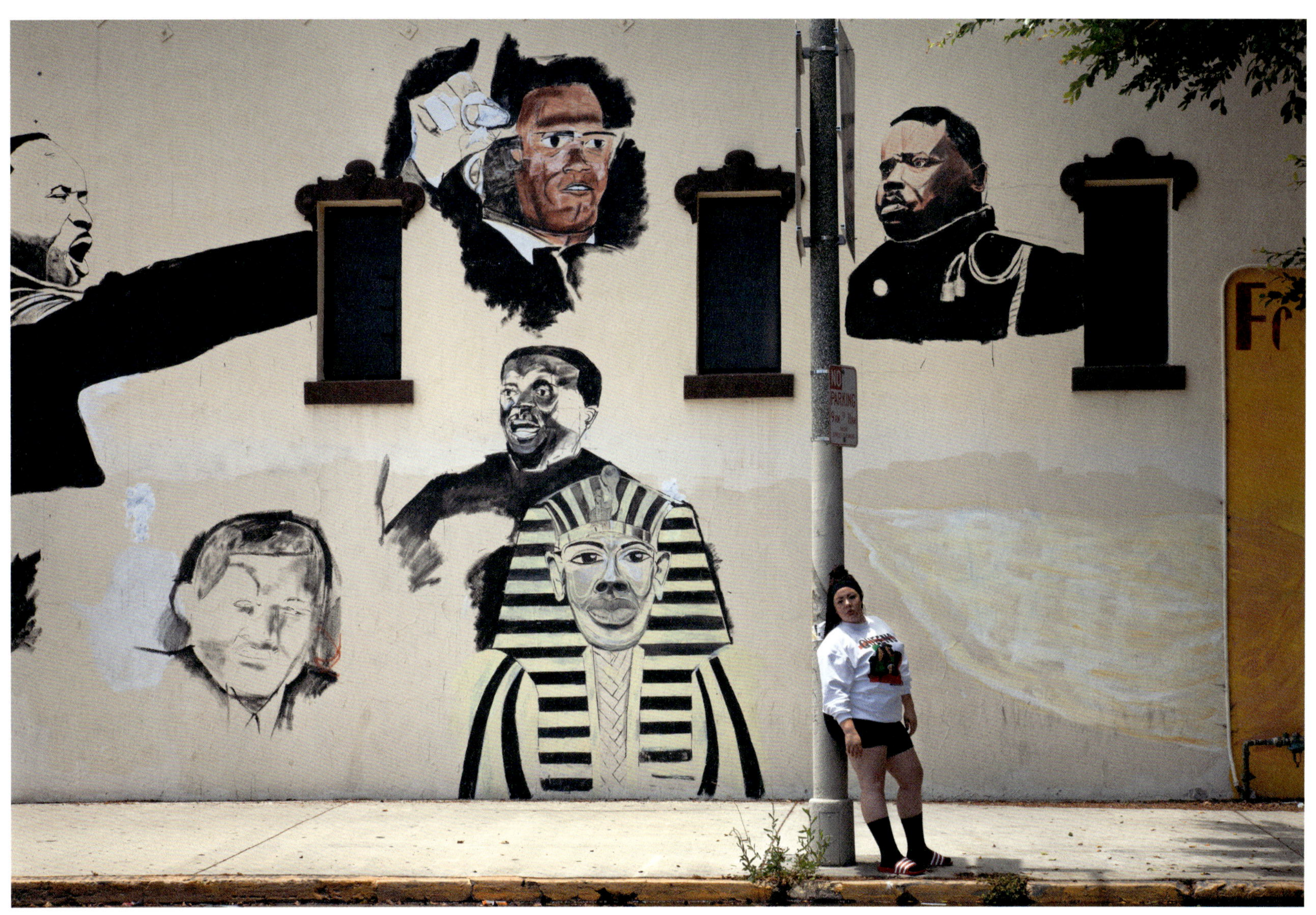

Pl. 63. Genevieve Gaignard, **Kings and Queens**, 2017

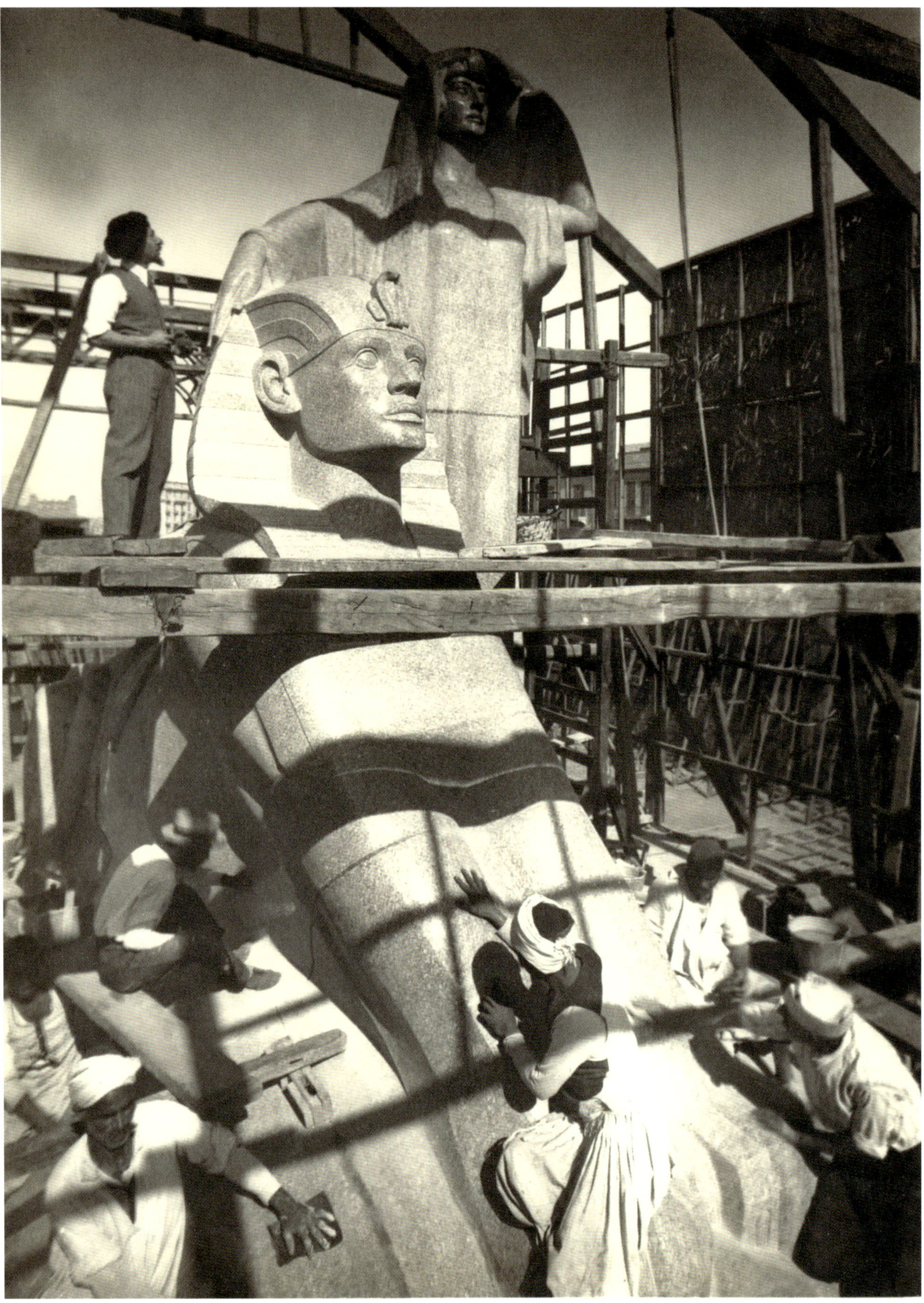

Pl. 64. **Mahmoud Mokhtar Supervising the Installation of "Egypt Awakening" (Nahdat Misr),** ca. 1926

Pl. 65. Mahmoud Mokhtar, **Bride of the Nile (Arous El Nil), Bust,** ca. 1930

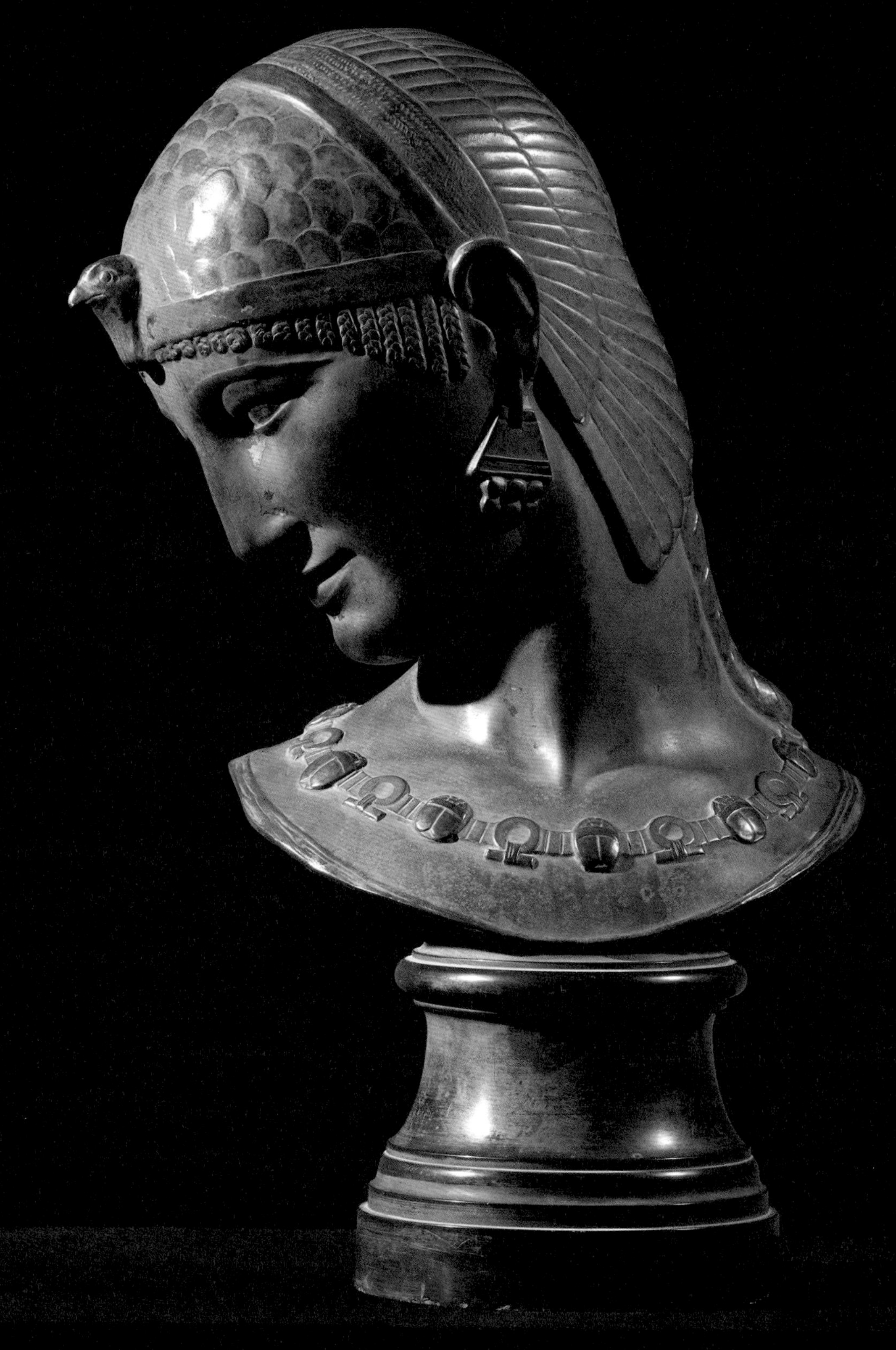

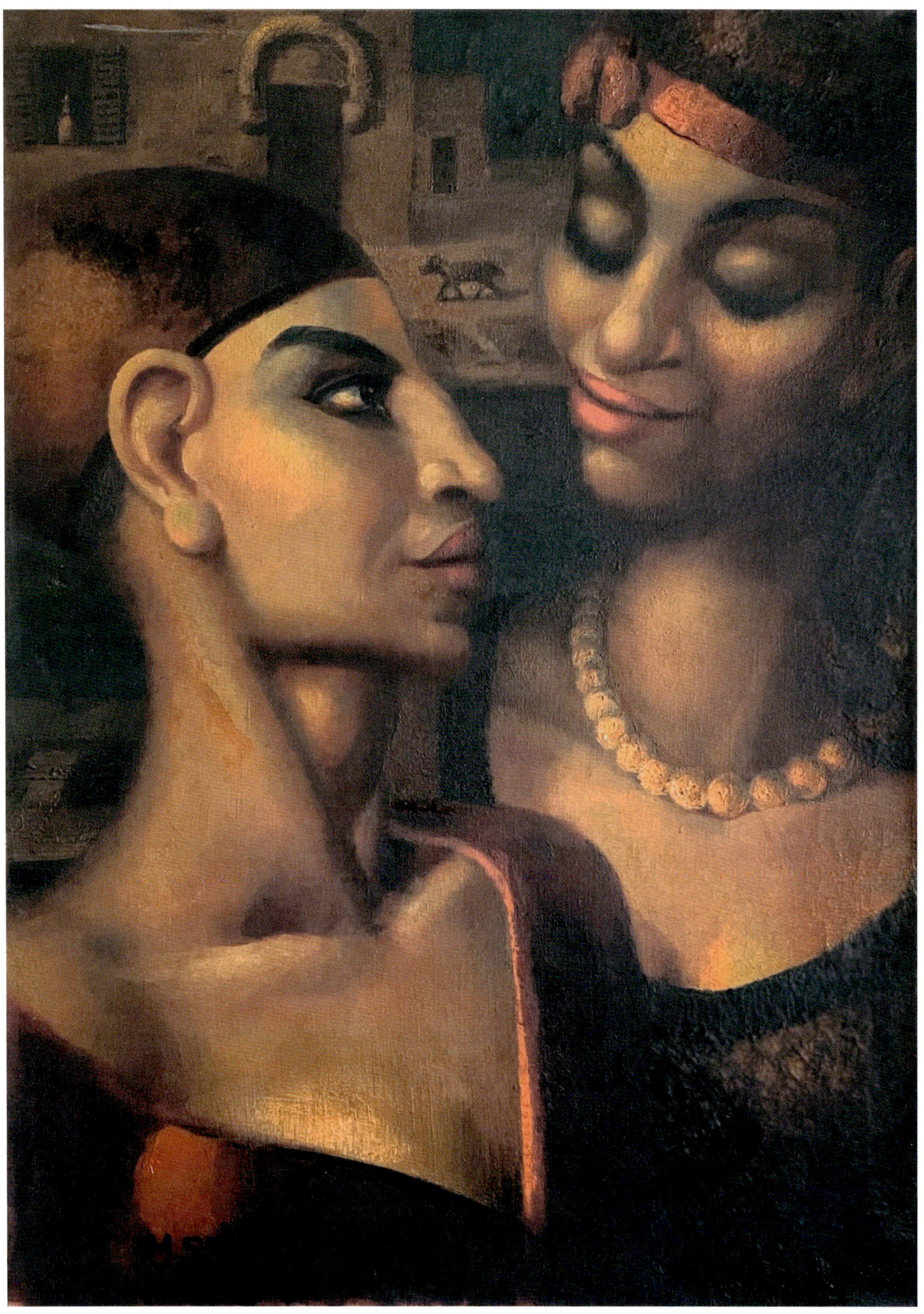

Pl. 66. Mahmoud Saïd, **L'invitation au voyage**, 1932

Pl. 67. Ghada Amer, **Homage à Tut in Black and White**, 2021

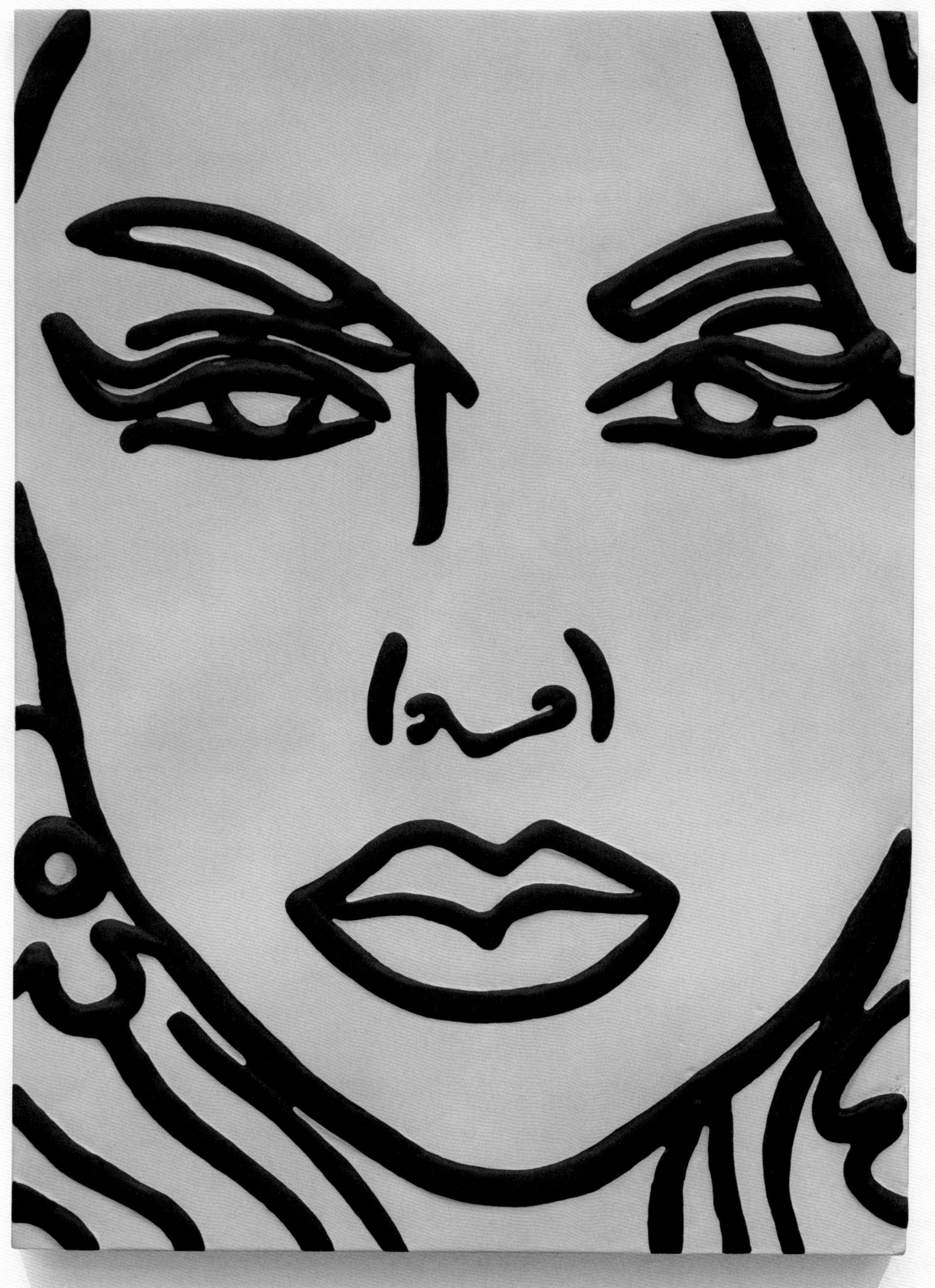

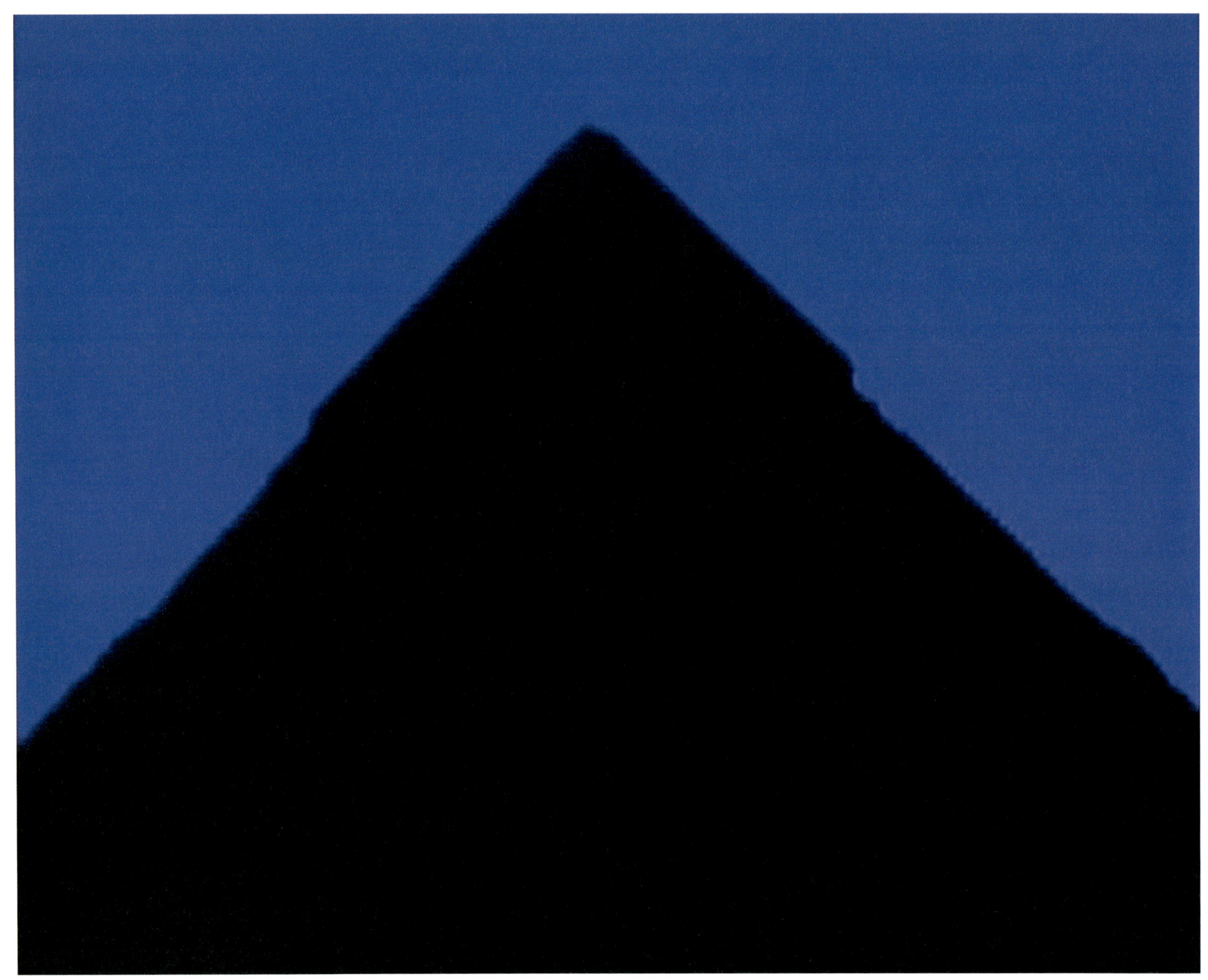

Pl. 68. Maha Maamoun, **Domestic Tourism II**, 2009

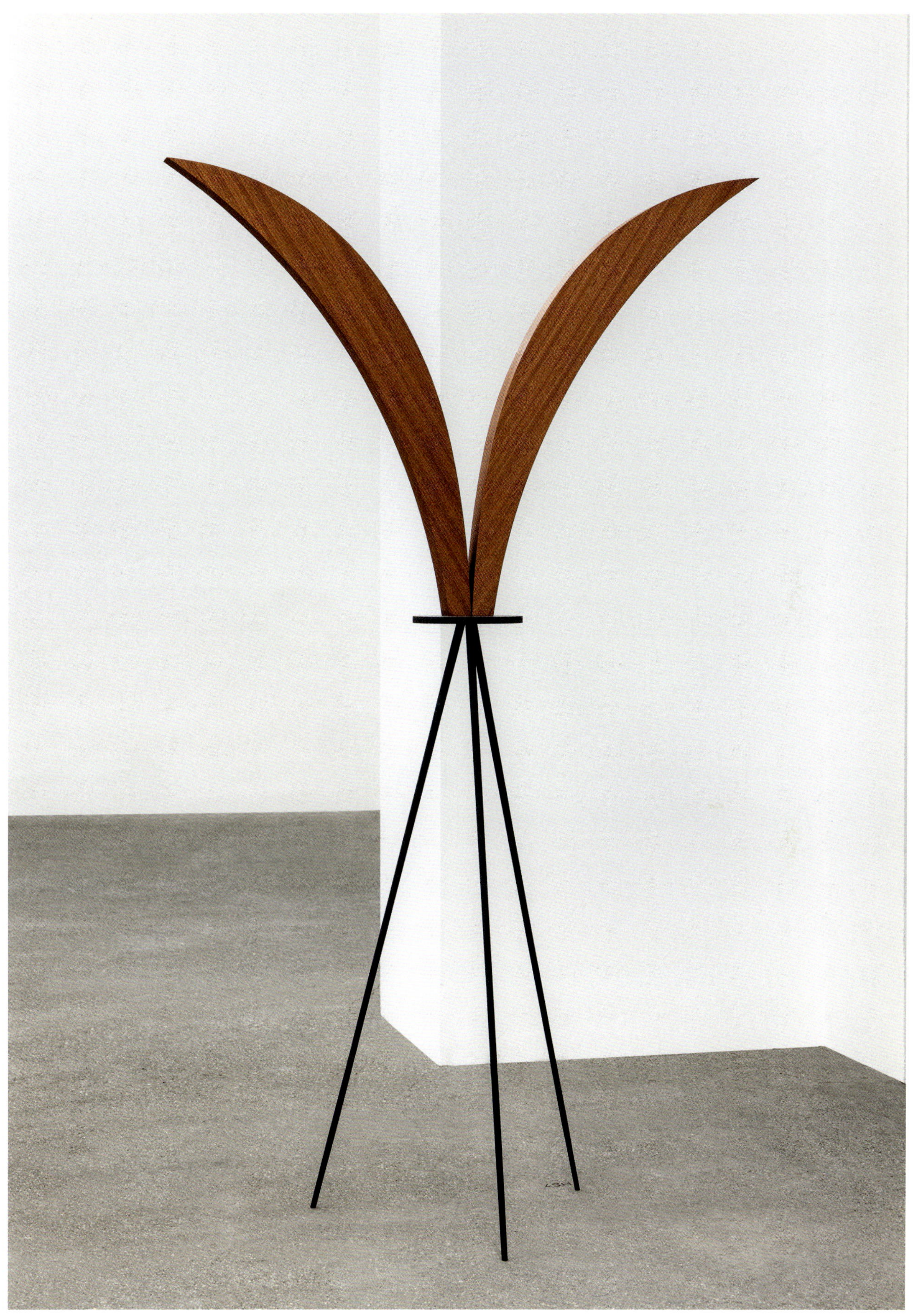

Pl. 69. Iman Issa, **Heritage Studies** #7, 2015

Iman Issa

Ancient Egypt is not a location (a country based in the continents of Africa and Asia) or a time period (one separated from us now, in the early 2020s, by thousands of years). Ancient Egypt is a historical concept. And, like any historical concept, any attempt to pin it down—to speak of it as it might have been back then or there—goes against its very grain.

As a concept, ancient Egypt could be likened to a photograph. One that at first look appears to have captured an event, frozen it in time, laying it bare for someone to look at, to study, and extract knowledge from, but which on closer inspection reveals itself to be a ruse—a mirrored sphere with an infinite number of faces. It is a photograph continuously relating little to the one it just was, with what has been interpreted as its essence, its content, its *punctum*, seeming to have disappeared— either to have never been there or to have been replaced by a completely different essence, content, and *punctum*.

It is perhaps the nature of all photographs to present dormant elements that at different moments in time are awakened, or awaken for reasons no one can fully articulate or comprehend. Elements taking turns, some shining brightly while others are hiding, seemingly dead, but actually only receding from view while breathing heavily, waiting their turn (at some other point in time) to take over their frame, dominating it clearly and completely, giving birth to a singular and definitive reading of themselves and by extension to the container in which they are housed.

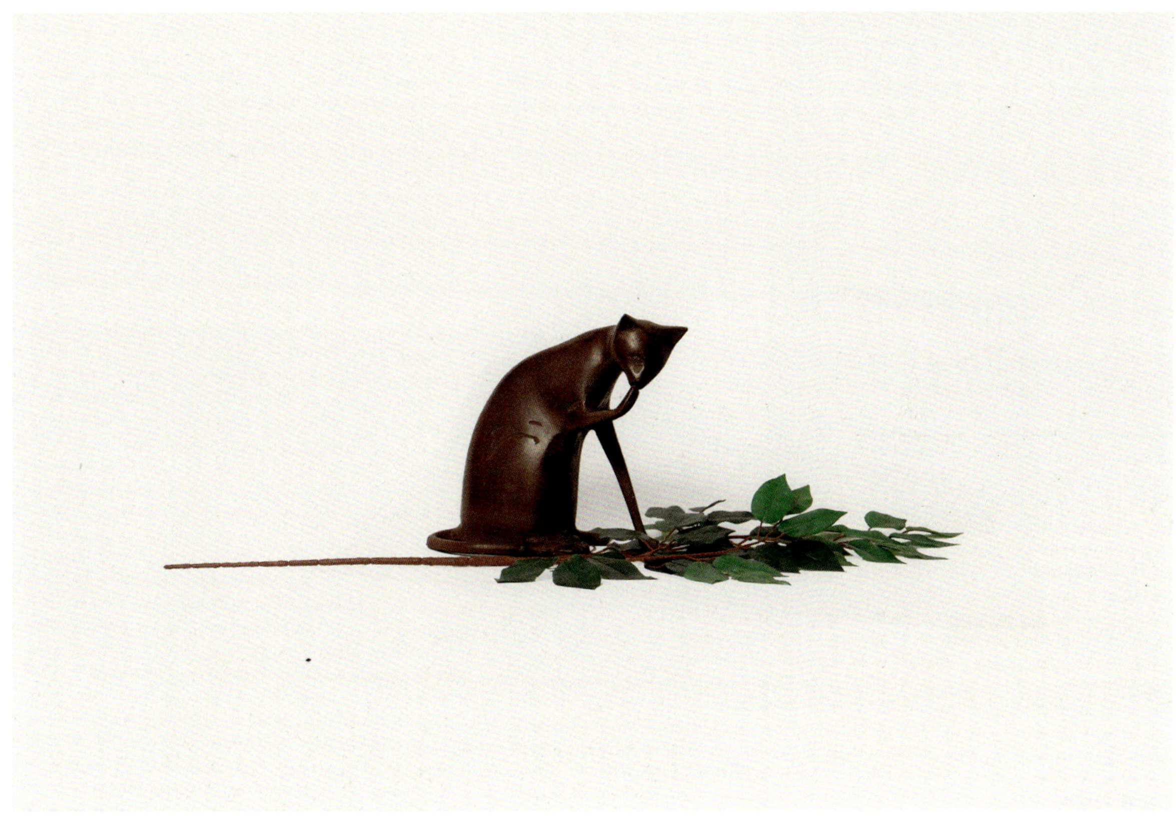

Iman Issa. **No Title—No Date**. Photograph, dimensions variable, 2025

Yet, just as this happens, someone, somewhere, realizes that actually the photograph at hand is not the right one. That there is another, better copy of it with a brighter or fainter shadow, or a different color palette, or a blurrier or sharper subject matter—one that, unlike the one at hand, can truly present its referent.

And as the copies start to multiply, the twenty or more versions collapse into one—one in which little attention is now paid to the nature of the shadows, or color palette, or sharpness of its depicted elements. This is how an ahistorical version of the photograph is born. A version that may or may not be related to itself, waiting to be pointed out by someone, somewhere, at some point in time, as the fraud it is. And so the story goes.

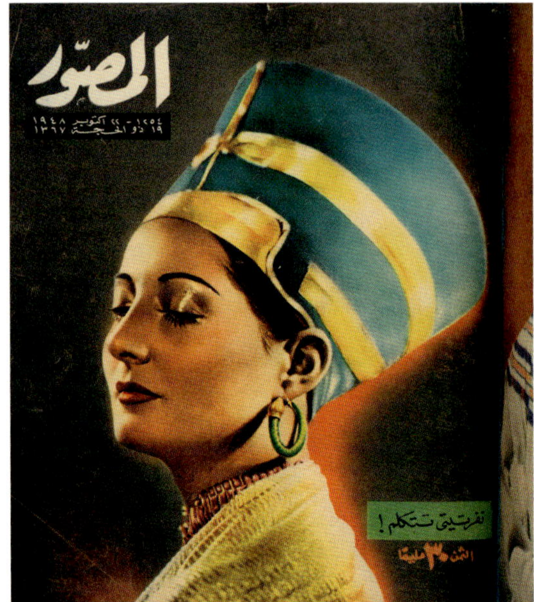

Pl. 70. Cover of **Al Mussawar**, October 22, 1948

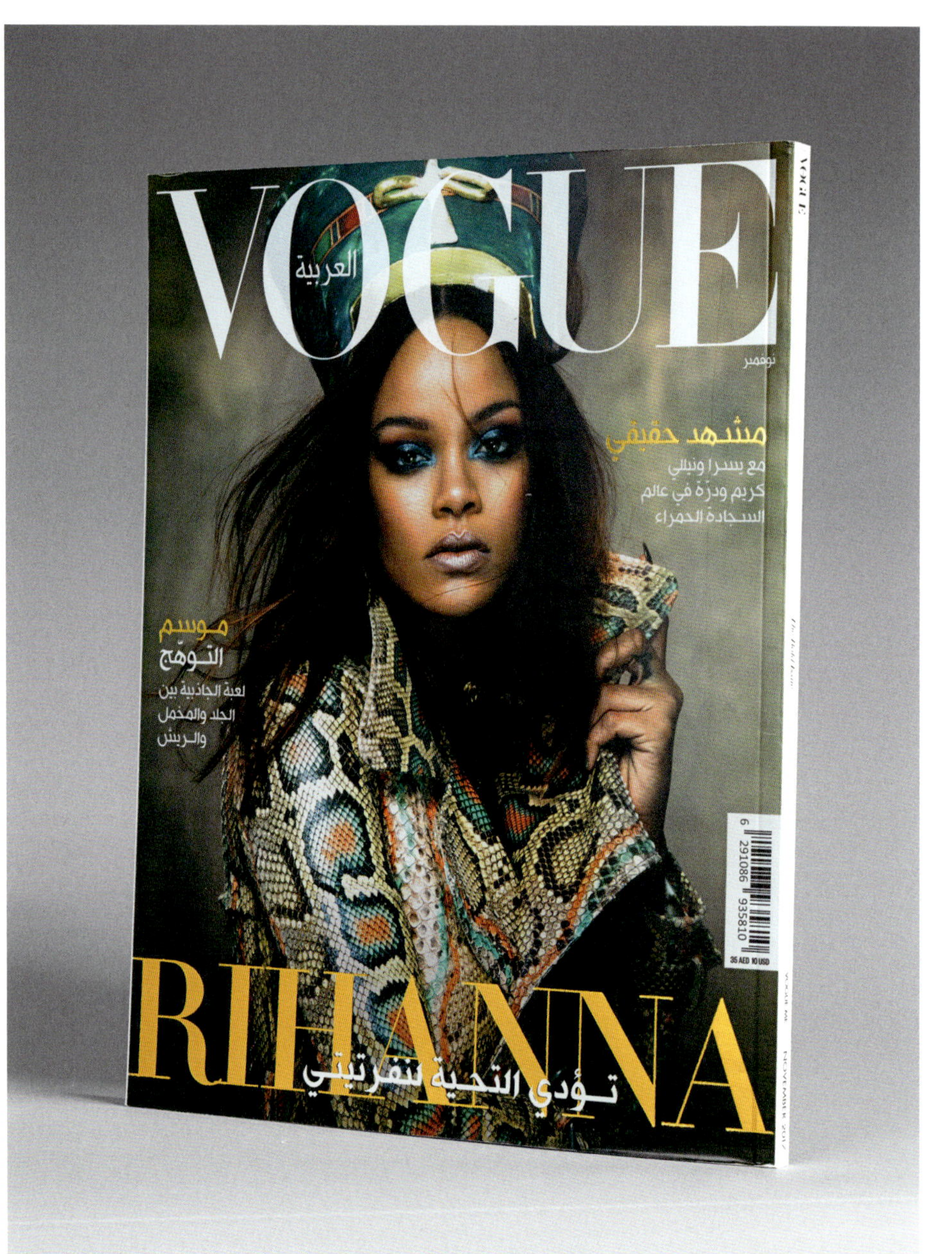

Pl. 71. Cover of **Vogue Arabia** featuring Rihanna, November 2017

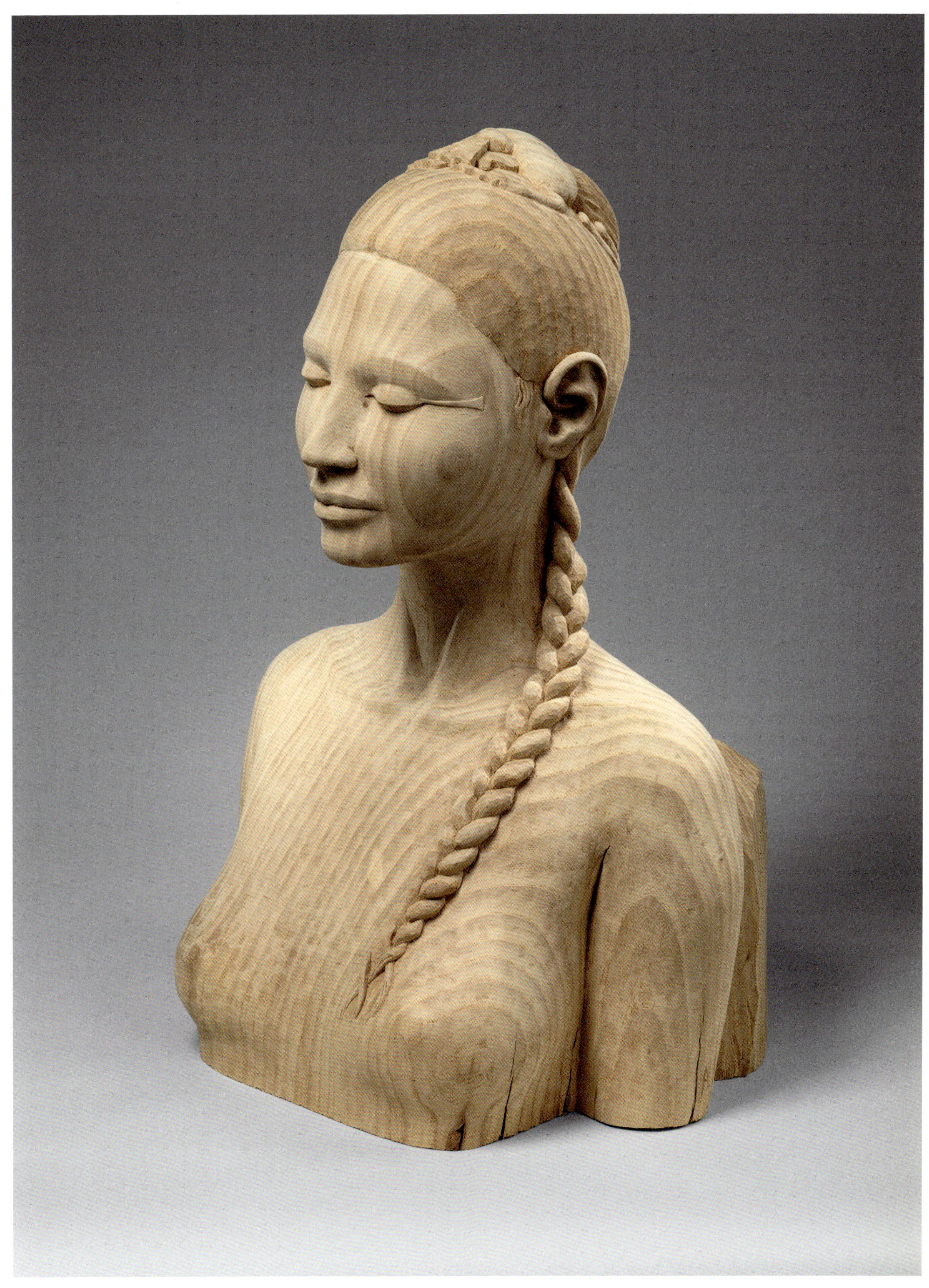

Pl. 72. Armia Malak Khalil, **Hope-I Am a Morning Scarab**, 2024

Pl. 73. Artin DerBalian, **Louis and Lucille in Egypt at the Sphinx**, 1961

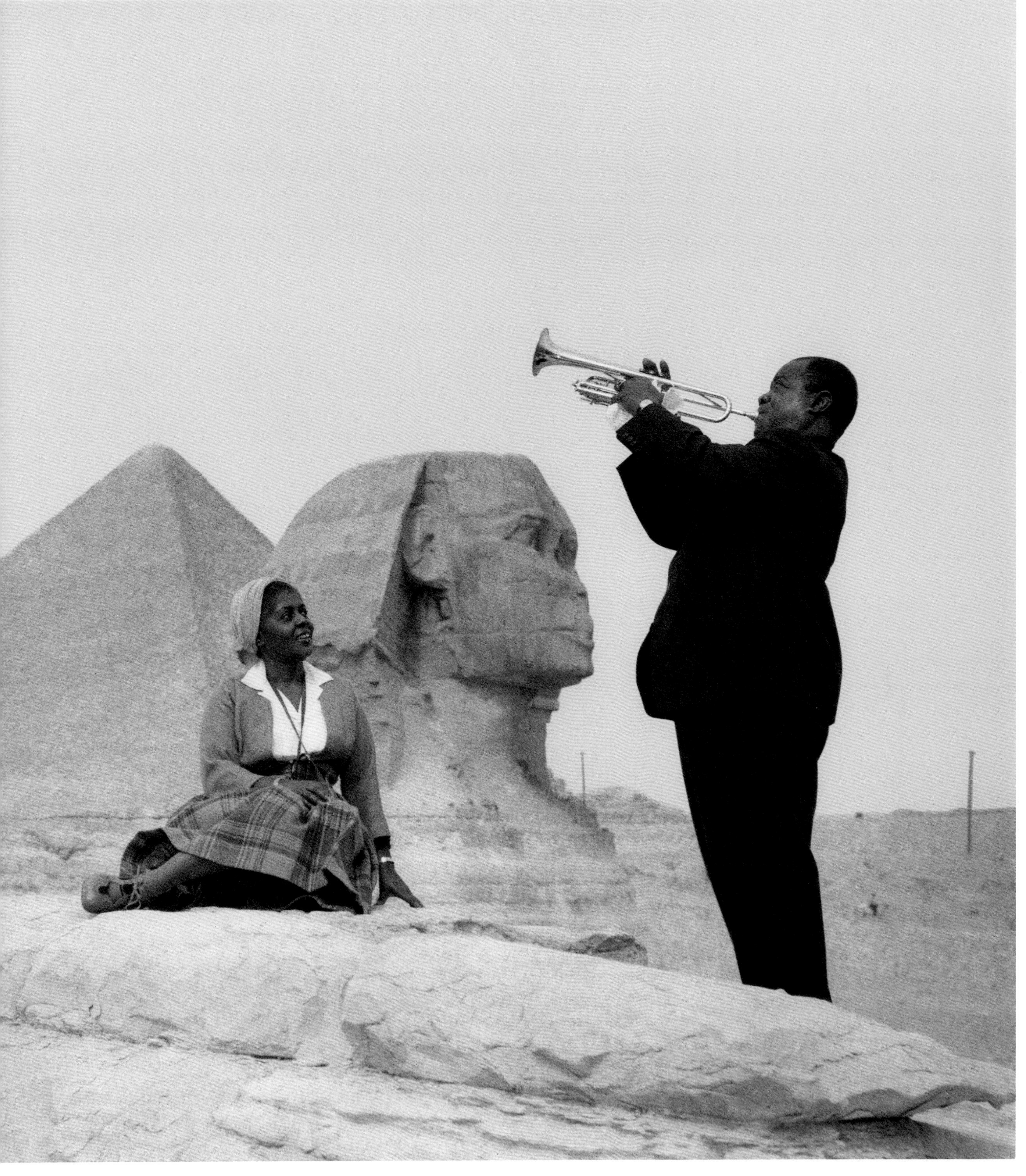

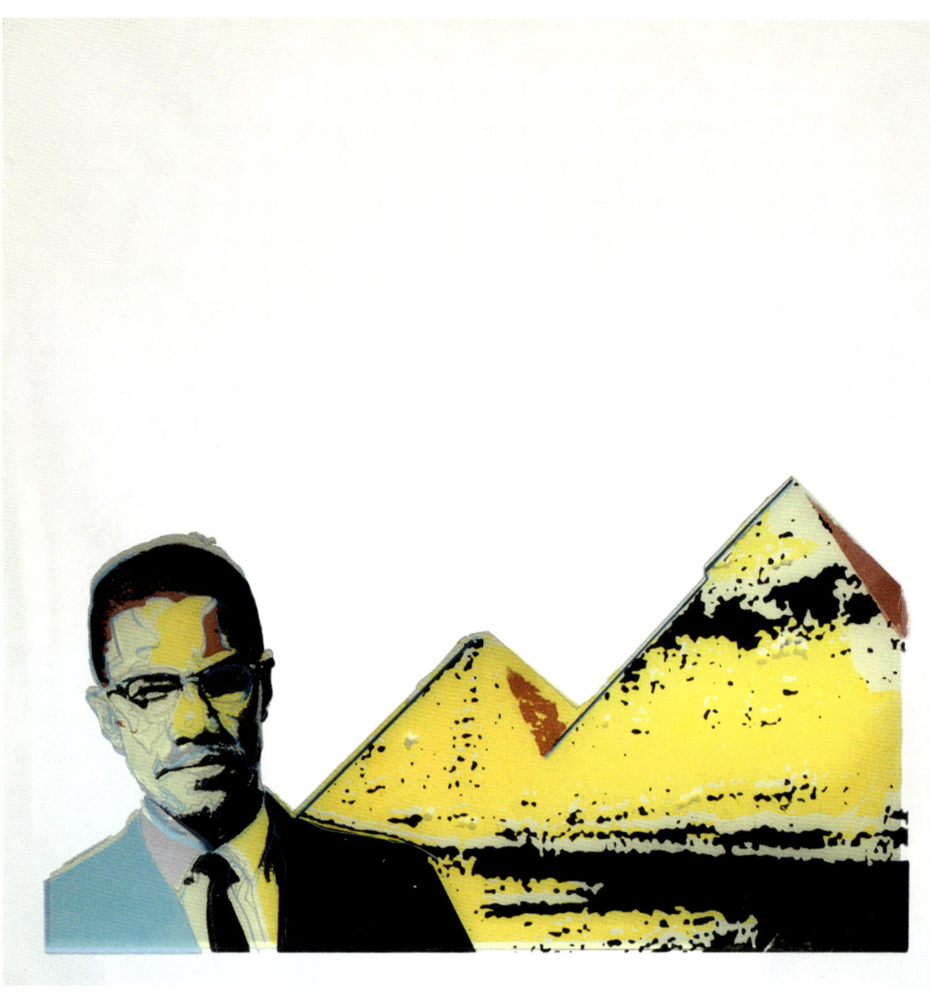

Pl. 74. Chet Gold, **Mirror Malcolm**, 2011

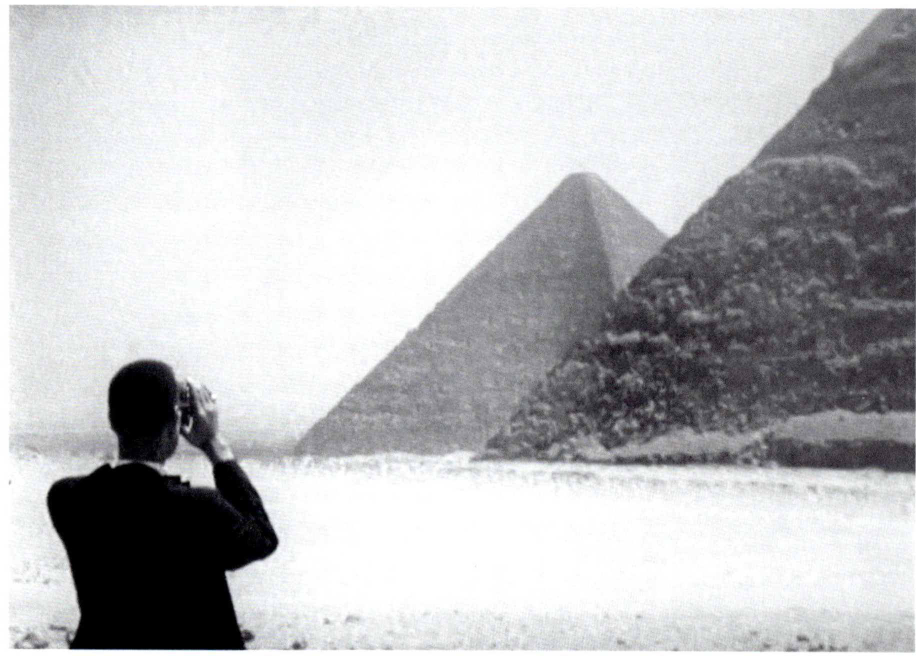

Pl. 75. Still from **Malcolm X in Cairo**, 1964

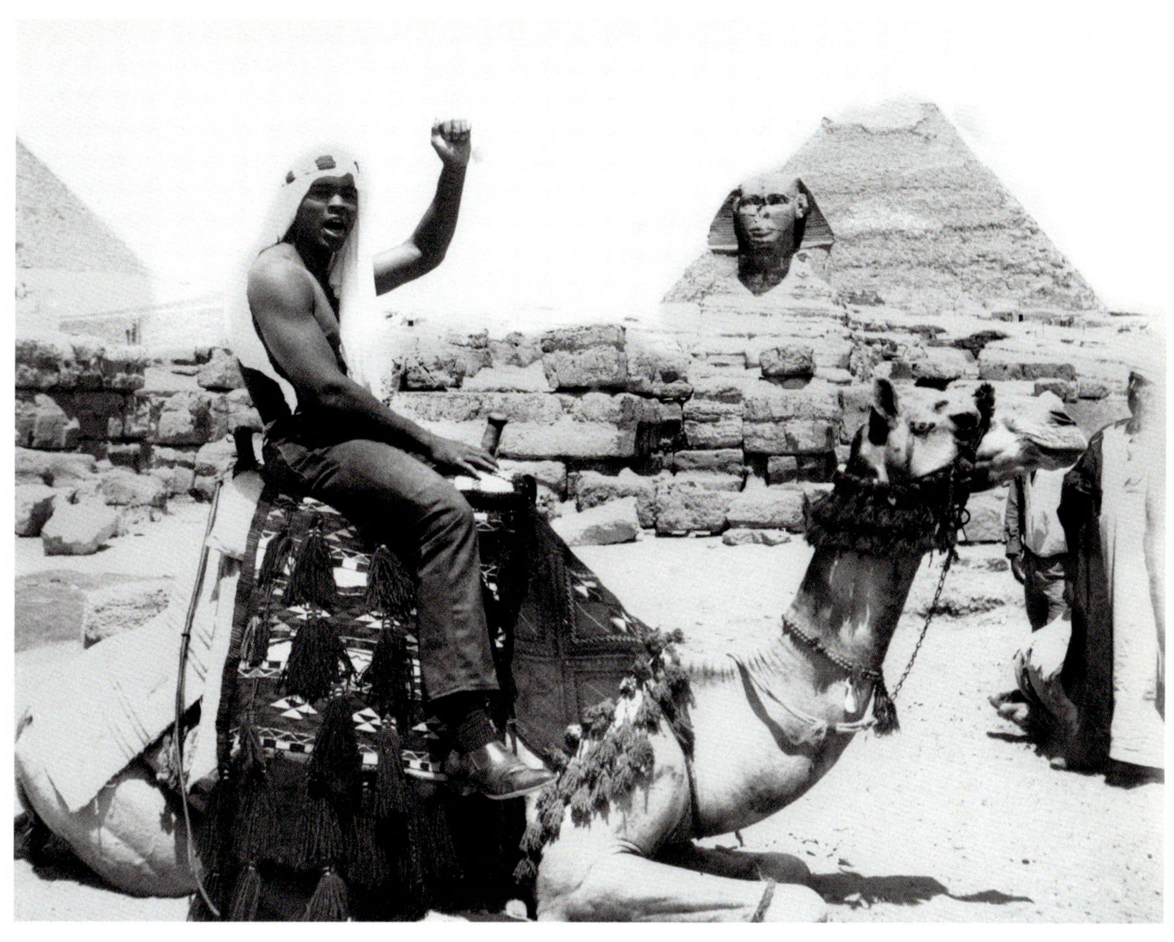

Pl. 76. **Muhammad Ali at Giza**, 1966

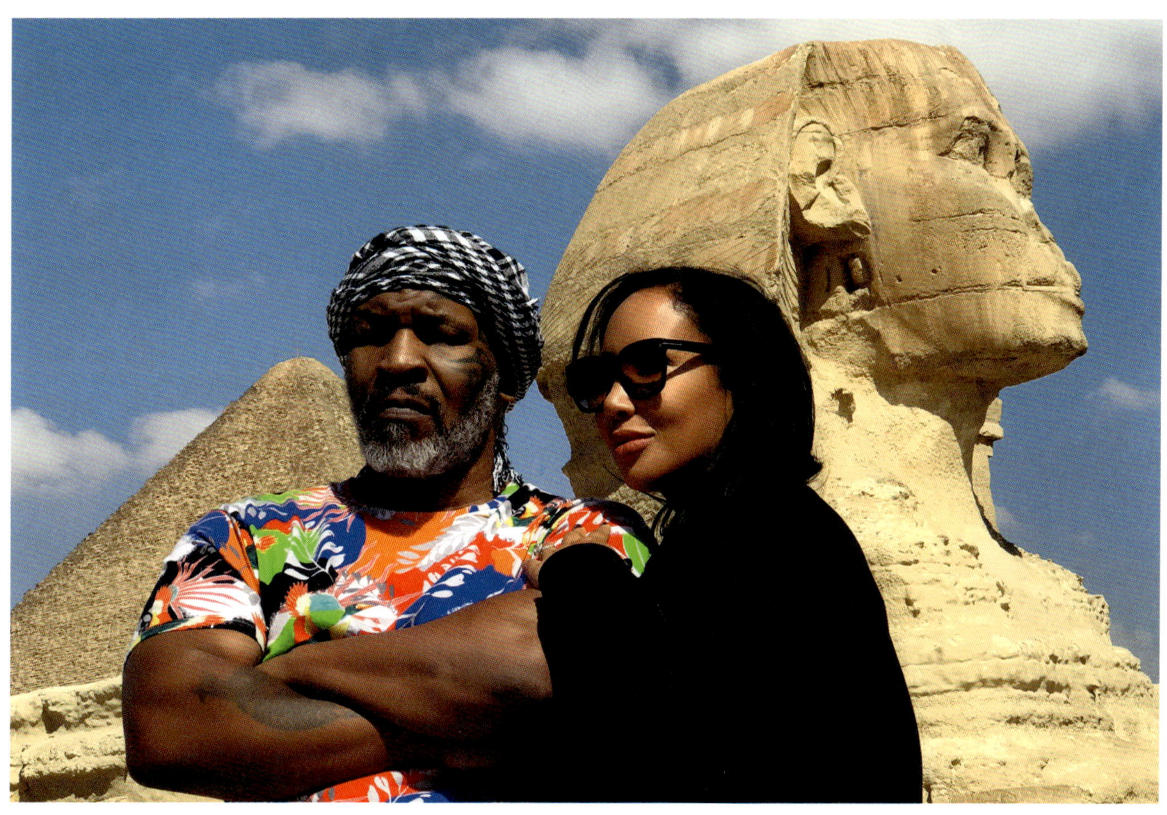

Pl. 77. Ahmed Shehaby, **Mike and Kiki Tyson at Giza**, 2019

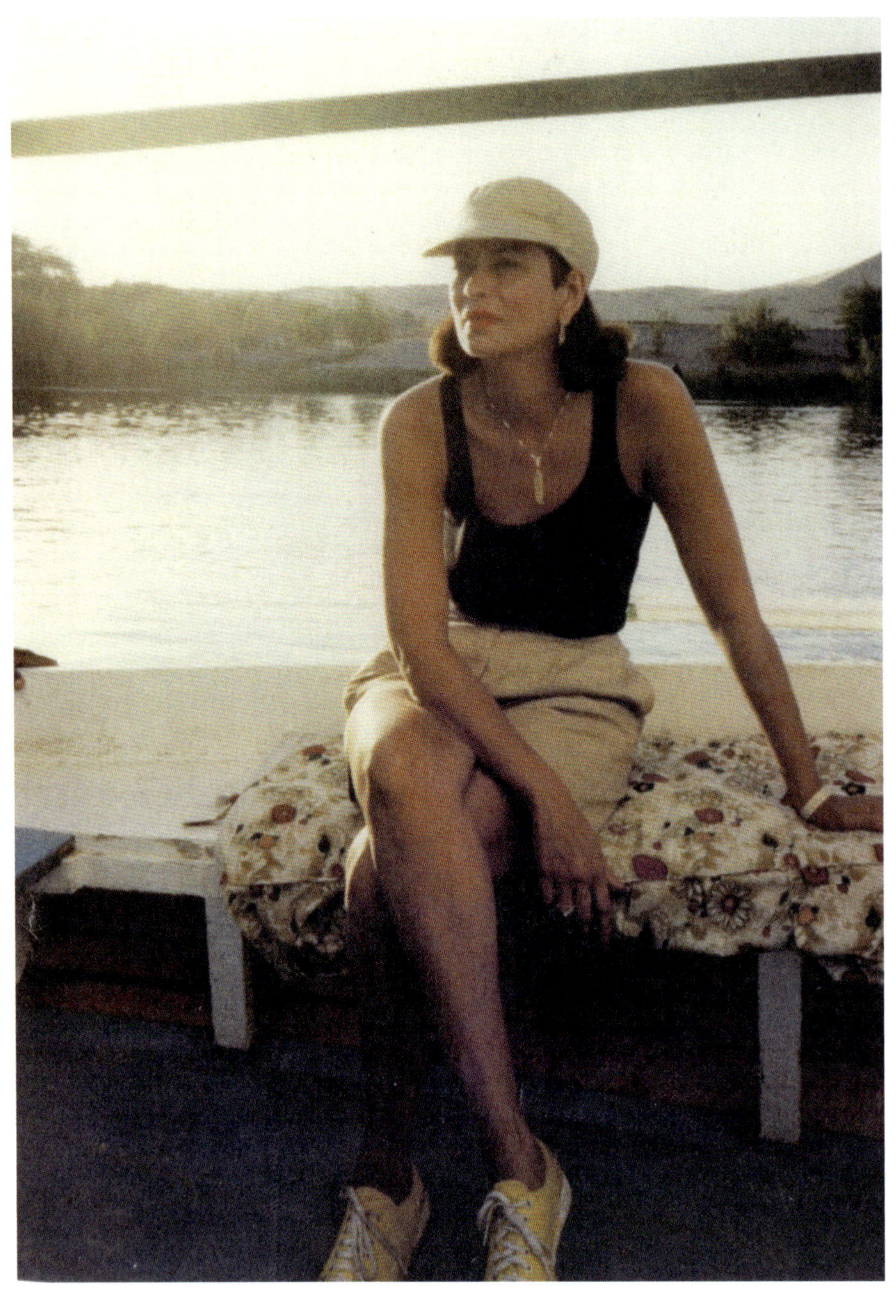

Solange Knowles

I was conceived in Egypt.

On a riverboat cruise on the Nile River to be exact. 1985.

My father, who worked for Xerox, sold a lot of MRIs that year. The company's top salesmen were awarded a trip to sail from Cairo to Aswan. My mother packed lots of white linen and a gold link metal dress. She prayed to get pregnant. I have a photograph of the two of them one evening at a party on the river, in which my mother is dressed up as Cleopatra, my father, a Pharaoh.

Swami Kriyananda describes the moment of conception as "a flash of light in the astral world."

I'd like to imagine my flash in hieroglyphics, decoding life into me, showing me the way.

Some of my favorite people throughout history have spoken about having their lives changed by their time in Egypt. Barbara Chase-Riboud speaks of a visit to the sphinxes of Khartoum, and it revealing to her she was born to make monuments of her own. She wrote in her memoir, "The cool breath of the Valley of the King's tombs told me I had been born to make architecture and sculpture." Sun Ra once told the story of how he declared "Ra" nine times in the King's Chamber at the Great Pyramid, and all of the lights mysteriously went out. He left with his own epiphany that "Jazz was birthed by the sun priests of Egypt." Tina Turner speaks of the revelation, upon seeing a figure of Amenhotep, that she was reincarnated as Hatshepsut in another life. She later recorded the song "I Might Have Been Queen" about the experience. In the book of Matthew, during a time when Bethlehem saw a brutal massacre of infants, an angel appears and tells Joseph to bring baby Jesus to Egypt for his survival. Even the Holy Spirit knew that it was a sanctuary, for refuge.

I've never returned to Egypt, because I'm too afraid of its power. Not ready to hear what it will tell me about my own. Not ready to return to myself. Not ready to rest in my own wounds.

I've only ever felt safe in water. Never on land. I don't think I wanted to come here. Had too much trauma as a baby. Witnessed too much warfare. Too much passing around from arm to arm. I imagine I would look up at the ceiling between fits of tears, trying to make maps of how to get back to the waters. Be it the womb, or Anuket's rivers.

I've only ever felt joy in the sun. They say to name your children who you want them to become. My mother named me Solange, Sol-Ange, angel of the sun. On dark days, I imagine myself traveling west across the sky on the Mandjet just like Ra, rising at dawn to light the day again.

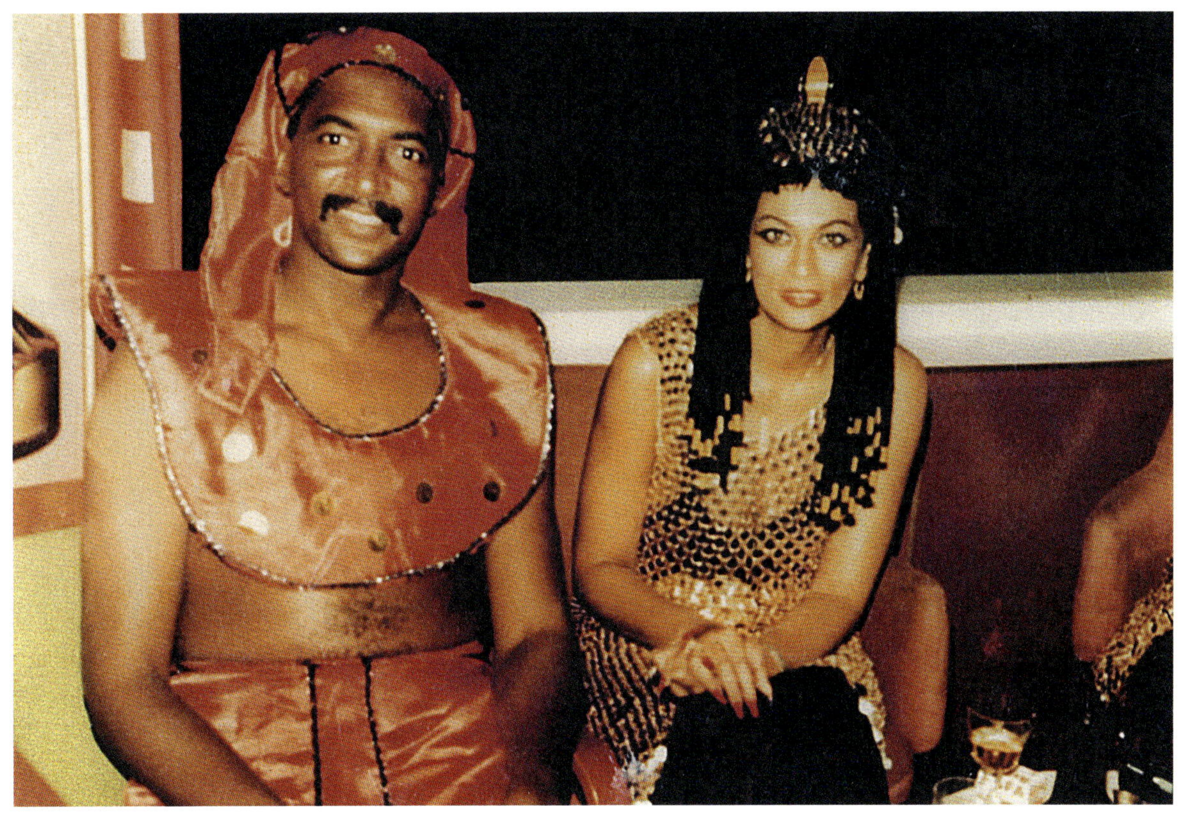

When I was seven, I spent most of my days after school in my mother's hair salon. To pass the time I'd play DJ on her six-disc CD player. My selections were purely based on album covers. When I saw Earth, Wind & Fire's *Spirit*, something moved in me. I saw something in my tiny mind of who I would become and the pyramids I would one day build of my own, the sacred geometry and symmetry I would use to tell my own stories. I saw the radiance of Blackness and how Egyptology could guide us in our own awakenings.

In 2017, I learned that if I called to Egypt, it would answer. Suddenly mysteries started to unfold, and I accepted no coincidences.

I needed protection as I traveled the world telling the stories of my deepest fears and the secrets my ancestors held to get me there. The Orions, *Sah*, were the answer.

I saw the signs everywhere I went. Street signs, movie posters, books I read, suddenly I couldn't go a day without seeing the word Orion. When I learned that the ancient Egyptians designed the Giza Pyramids to align with the Orion constellation, I knew I was on the right path, a path calling me to the beginning.

I embarked on my only, and last, tour of the past decade, "Orion's Rise," featuring the Sun Ra Arkestra, Earl Sweatshirt, Chassol, and Flying Lotus, as a reflection of my origin story into the future. I designed the scenography to build my own civilization using bodies, architecture, and, yes, pyramids. Verdine White joined me one night to play bass, and I thanked him for showing me the way, for being a mirror of myself before I even arrived. I commemorated the moment with two tattoos, Orion's belt and, of course, a small pyramid on my forearm.

A few years later I looked up my Egyptian zodiac sign, and it was no surprise to me, I am the sign of the Nile. I am a daughter of Satis. One day I will return to my waters, return to the womb.

I will seek what those rivers teach, and honor how they show up in my veins. I will return ready. For Egypt is a planet in which my mother's dreams and the cosmos aligned. Egypt is a satellite, connecting the stars with the lands I've built and the ones I've yet to discover.

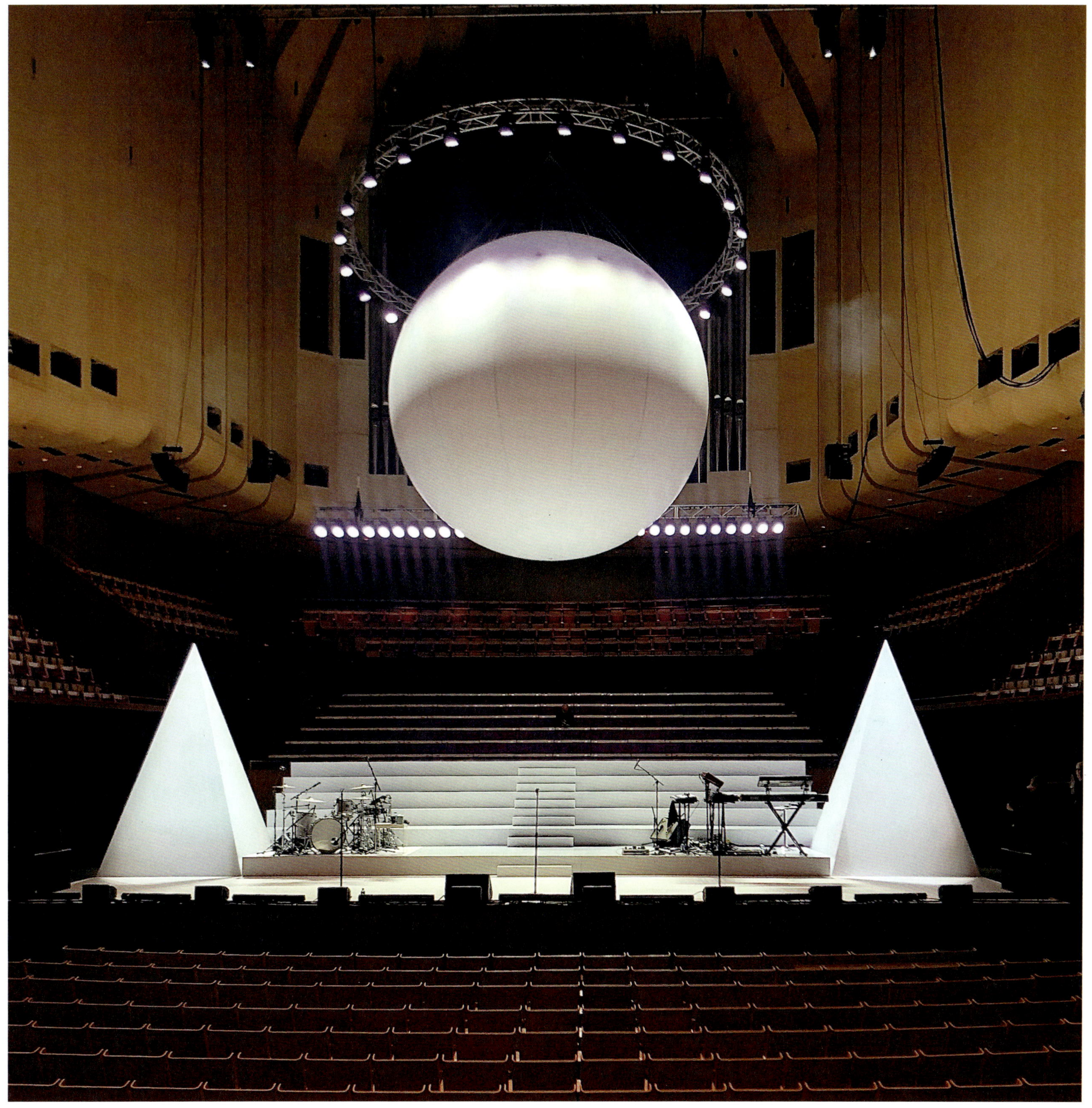

Pl. 78. Solange Knowles, **Orion's Rise**, 2018

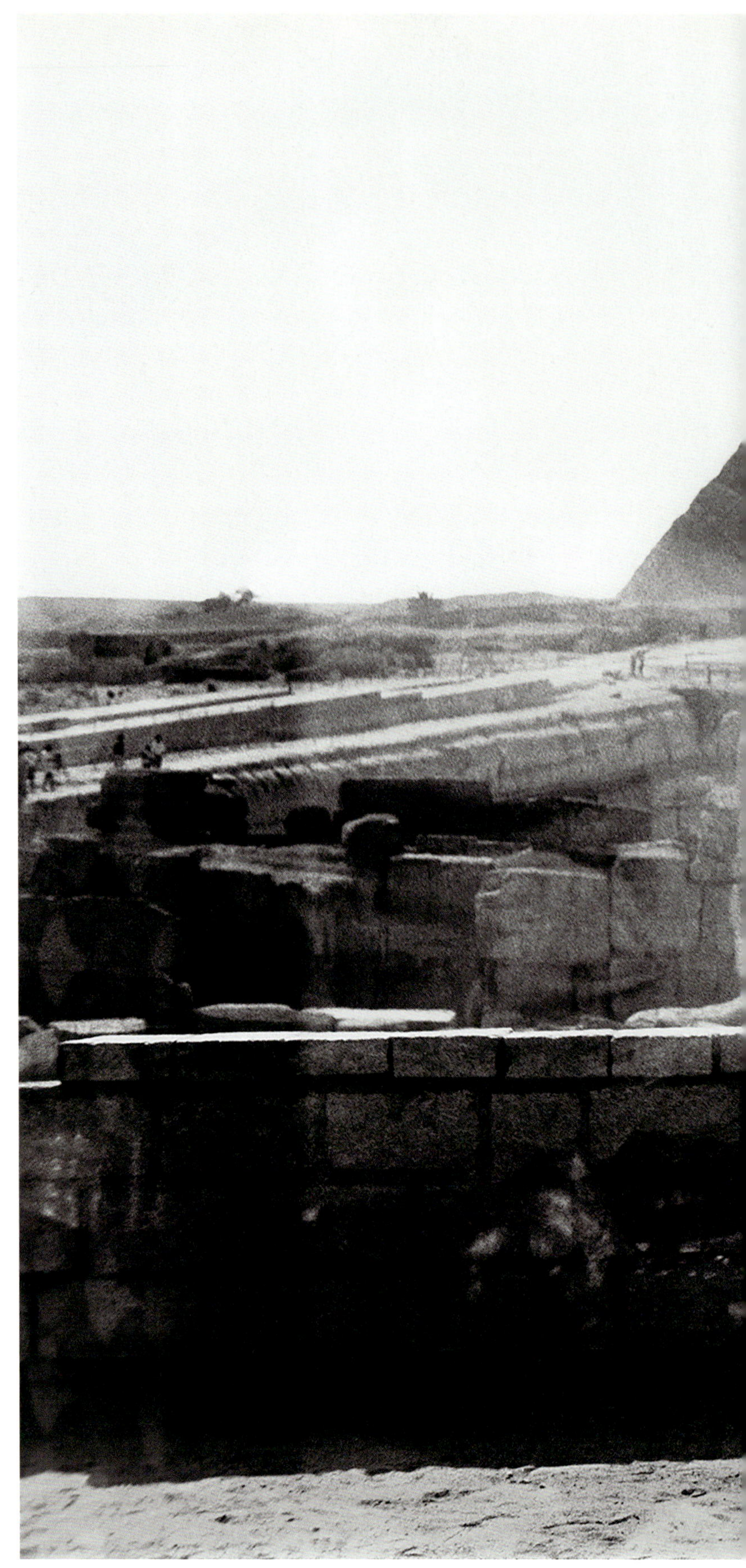

Pl. 79. Ming Smith, **Womb**, 1992

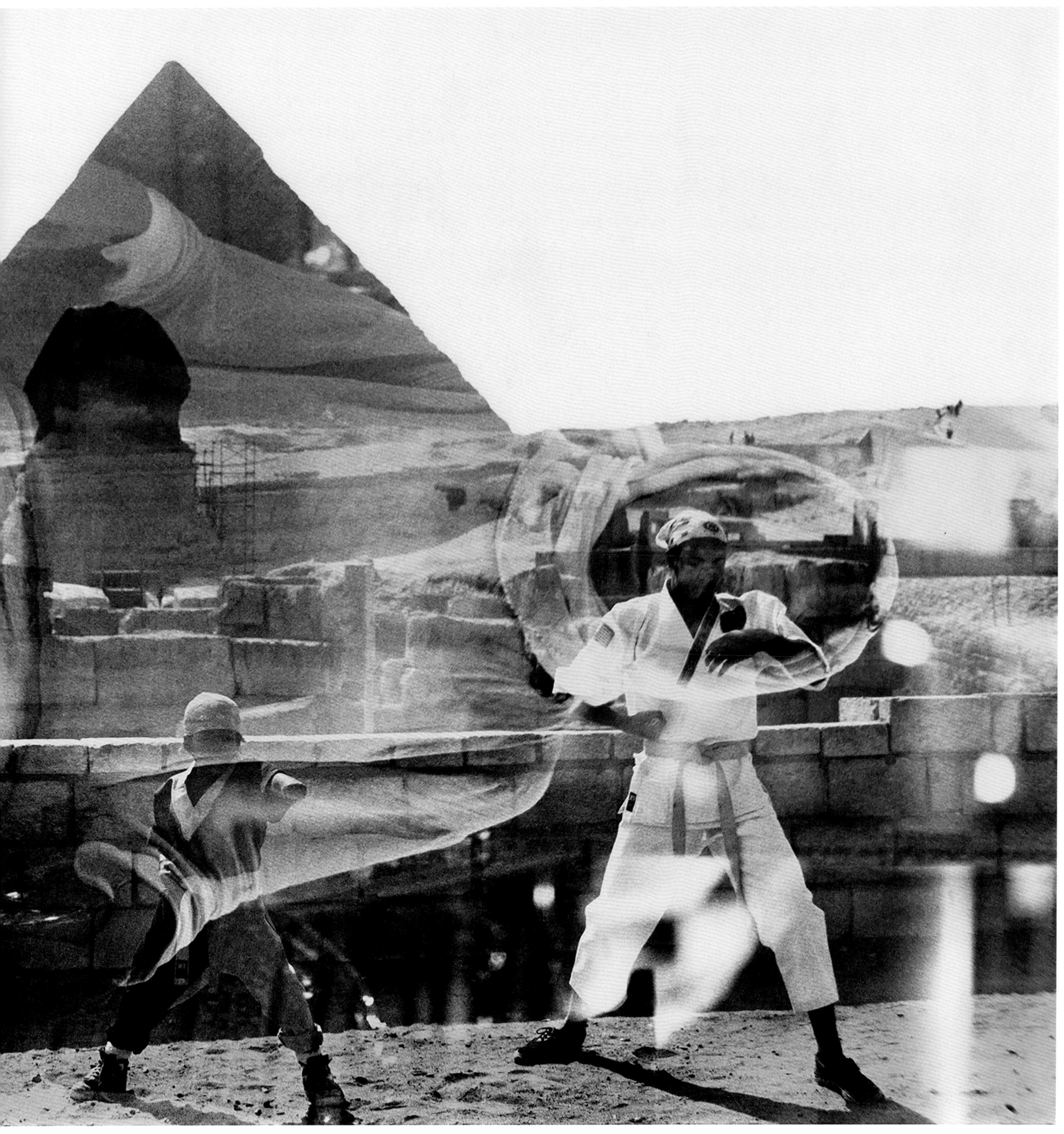

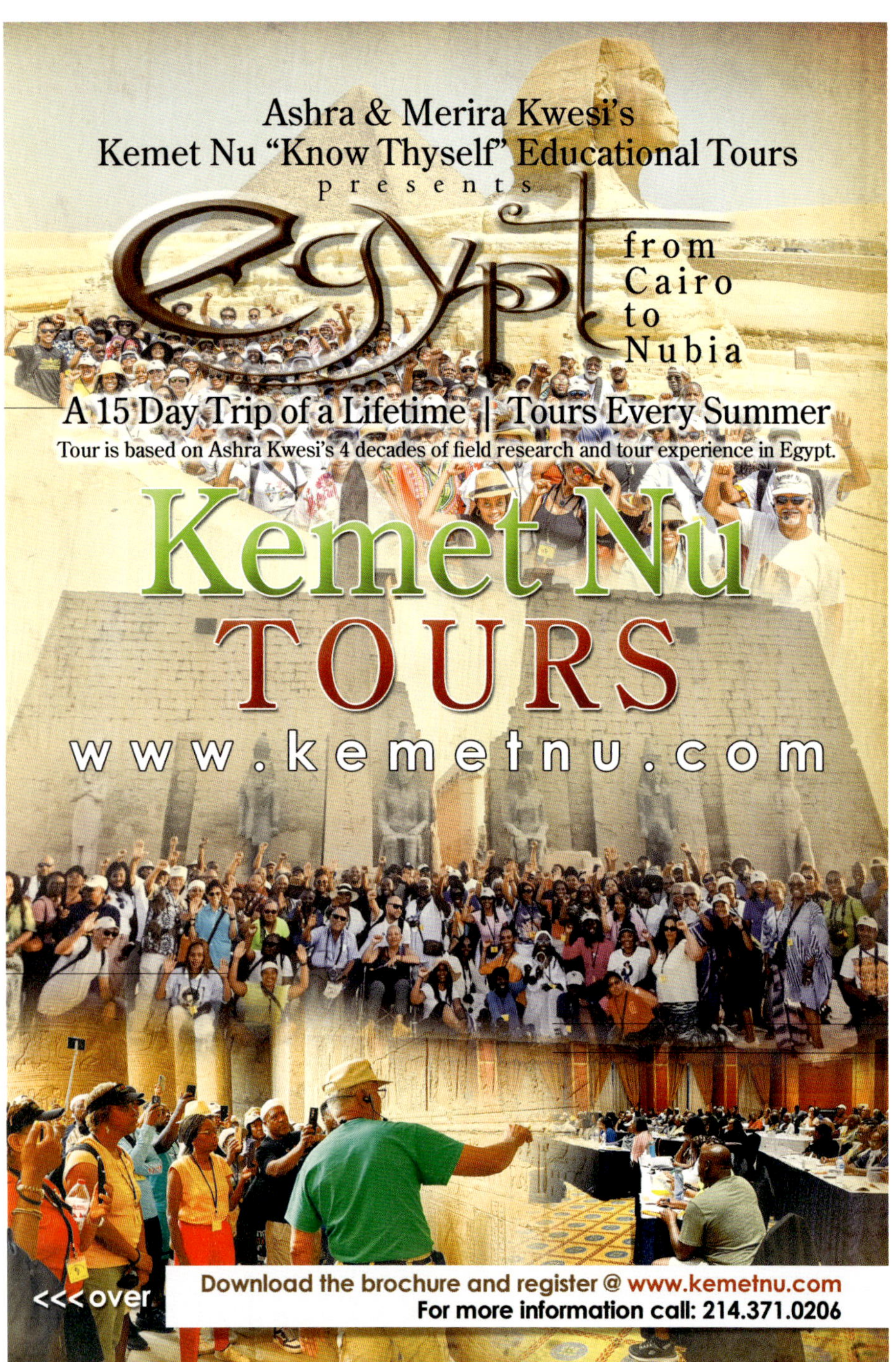

Pl. 80. Ashra and Merira Kwesi, **Kemet Nu "Know Thyself" Educational Tours presents Egypt, from Cairo to Nubia**, ca. 2019

Pl. 81. Glenn Ligon, **Gold Nobody Knew Me #1,** 2008

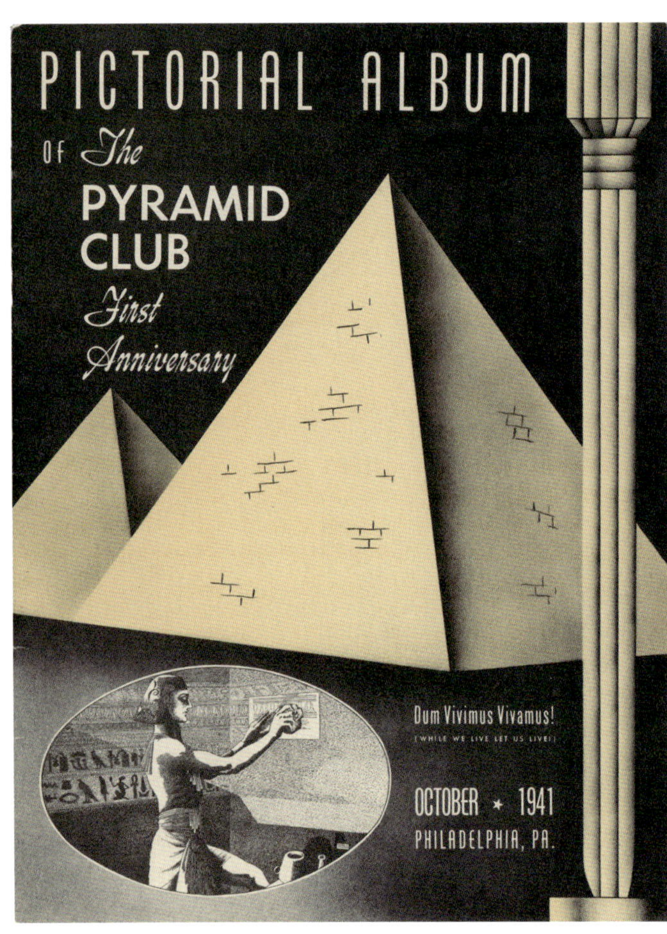

Pl. 82. Pyramid Club, **Pictorial Album of the Pyramid Club**, October 1941

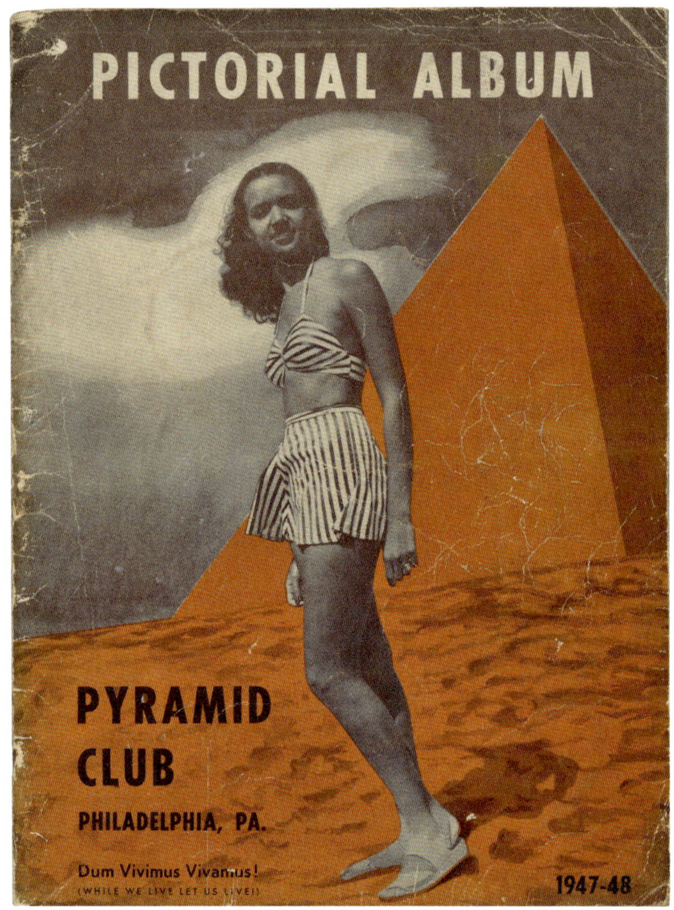

Pl. 83. Pyramid Club, **Pictorial Album of the Pyramid Club**, 1947-48

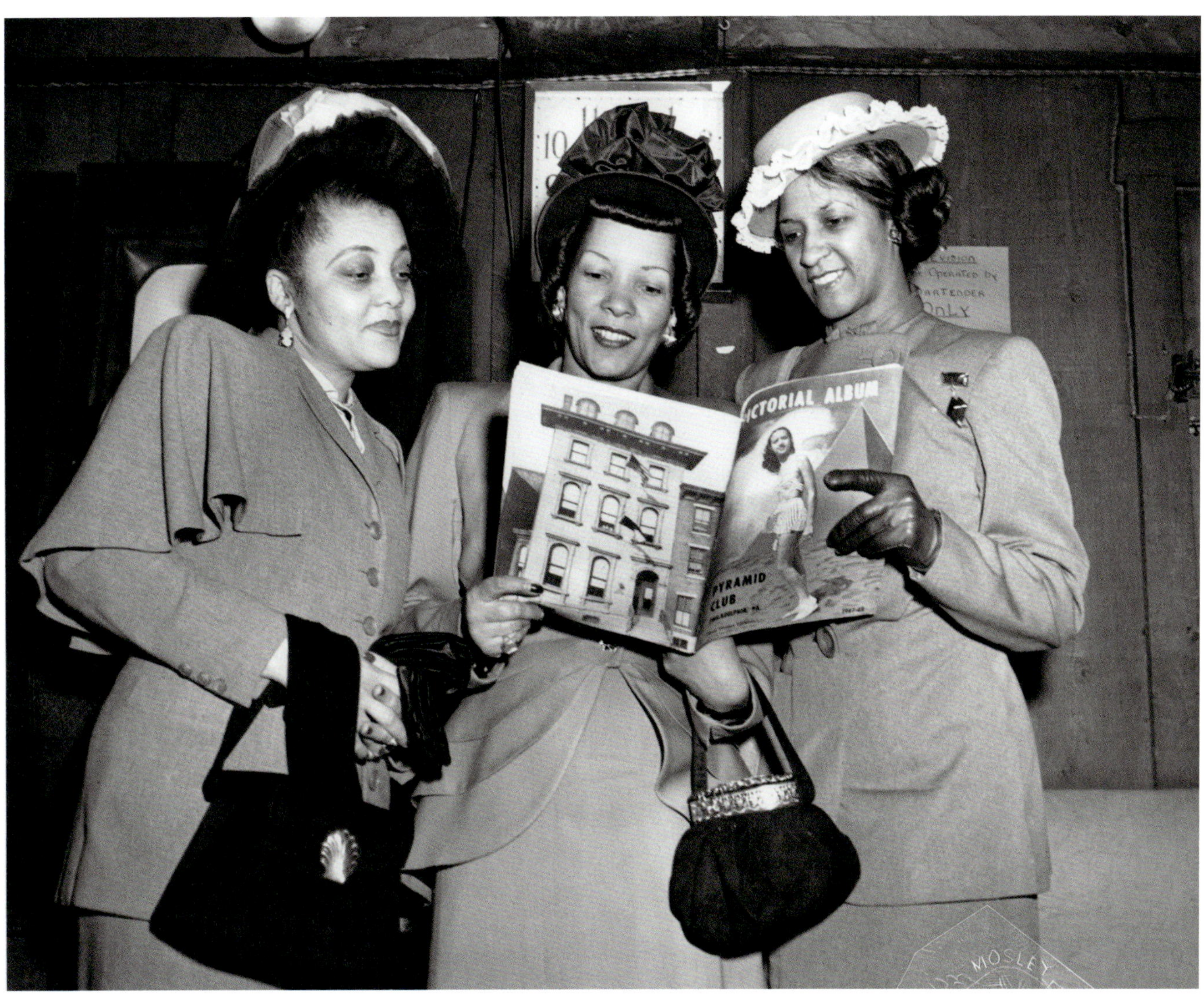

Pl. 84. John W. Mosley, **Guests at Pyramid Club Art Exhibition**, 1947

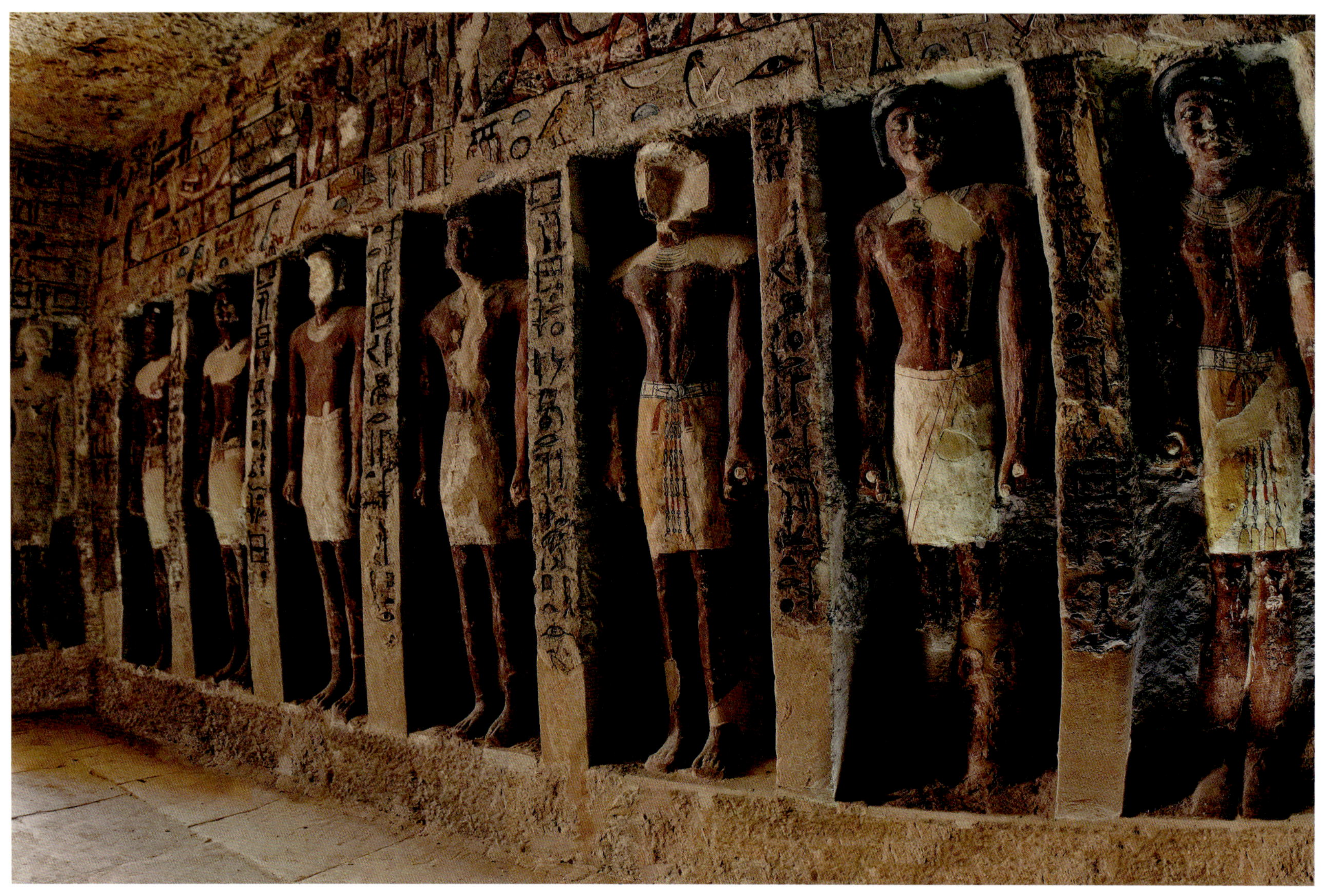

Pl. 85. Chester Higgins, **Tomb of Irukaptah, A Libationer. Saqqara Necropolis, Egypt,** 1979

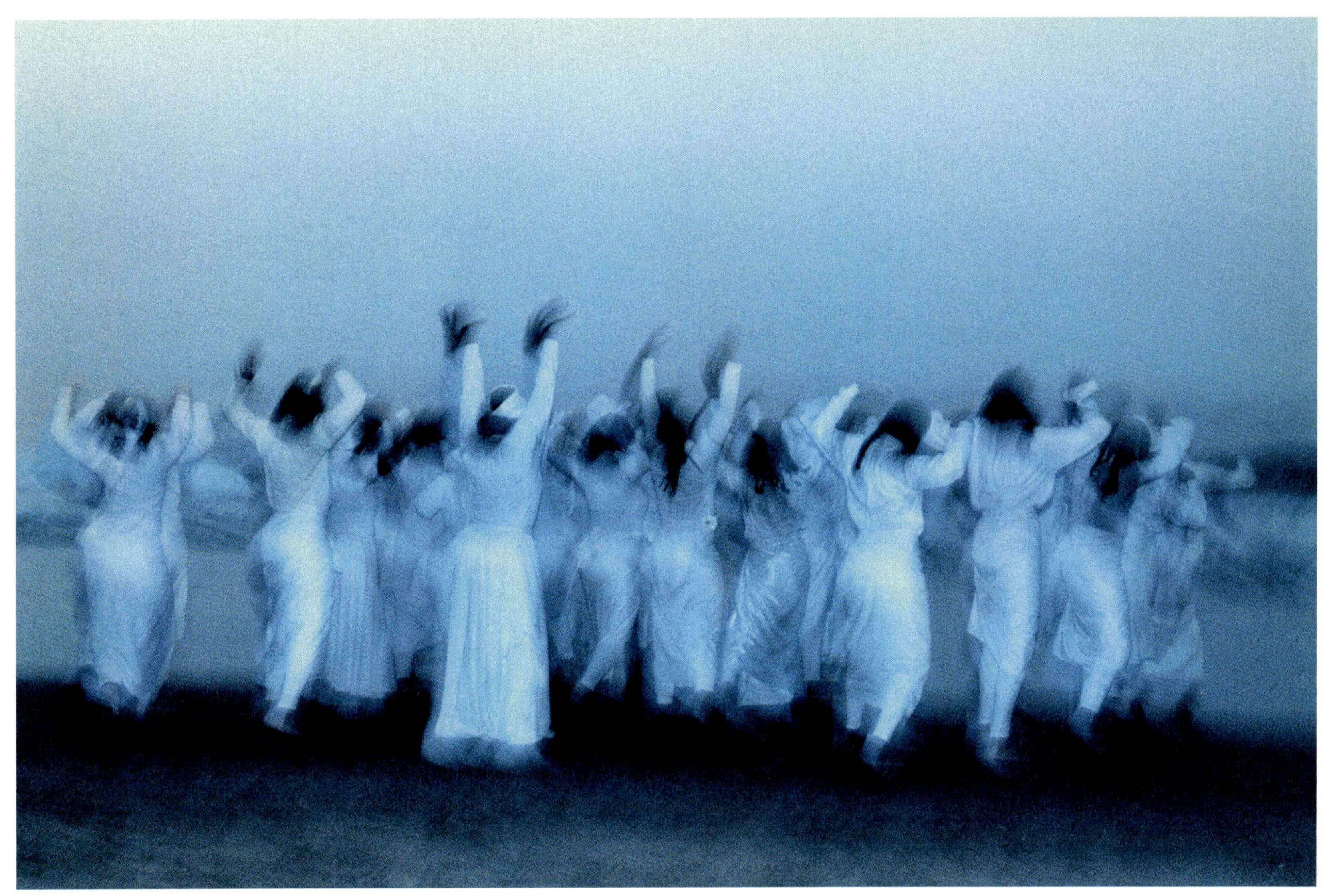

Pl. 86. Chester Higgins, **African American pilgrims dance in honor of ancient spirits.
Lake Nasser, Egypt**, 2006

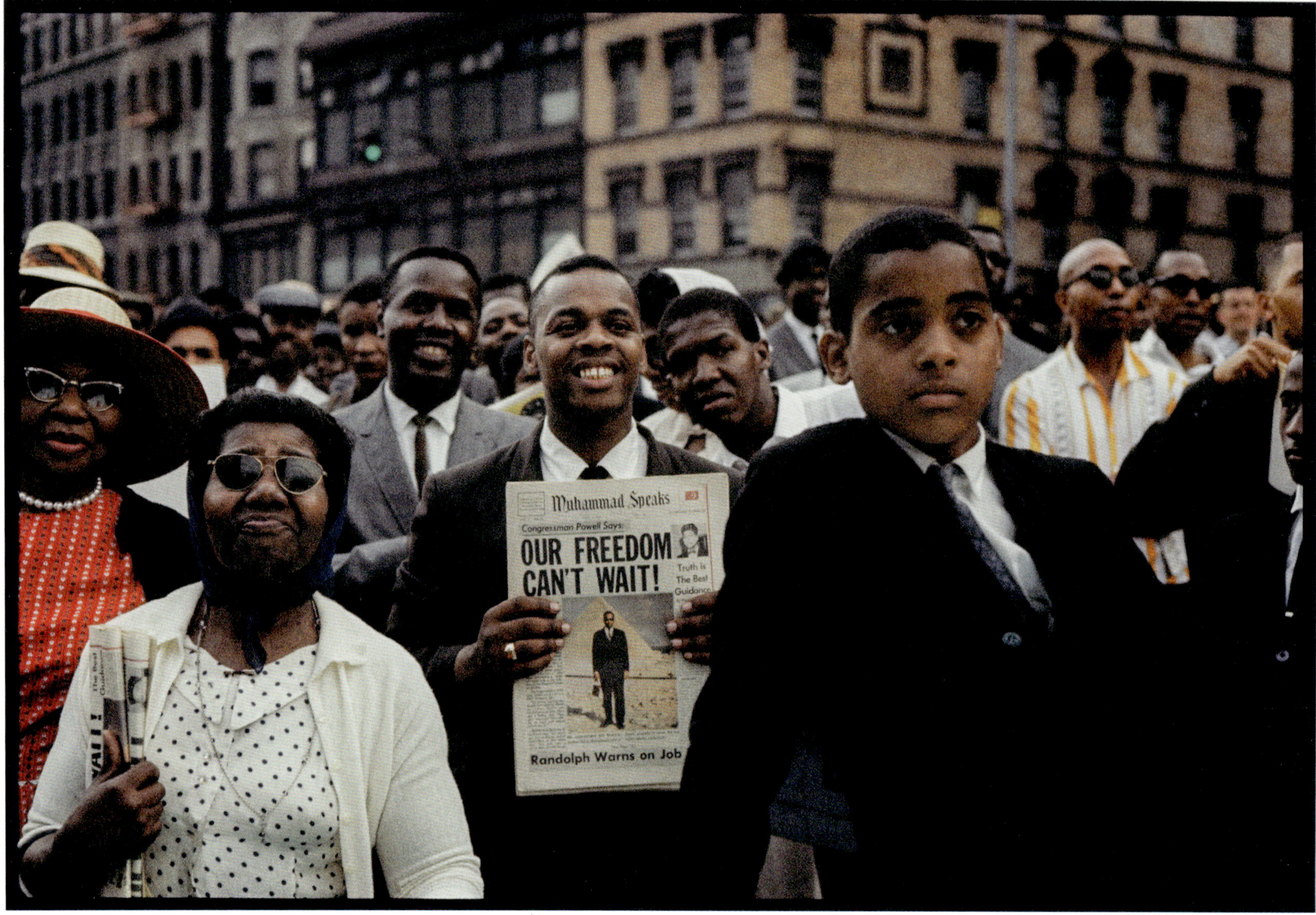

Pl. 87. Gordon Parks, **Untitled, Harlem, New York**, 1963

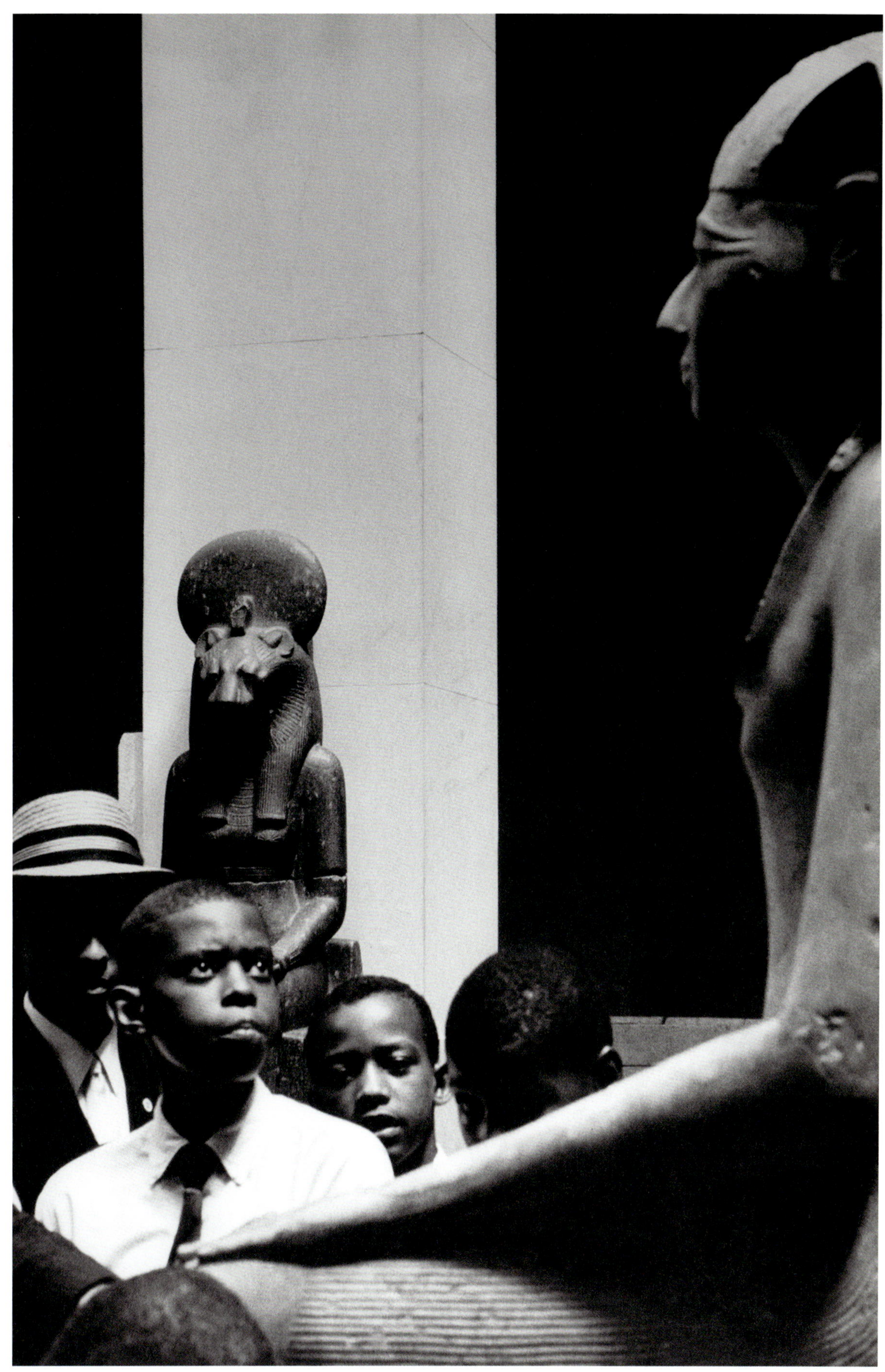

Pl. 88. Eve Arnold, **Black Muslim children at the Metropolitan Museum in New York. They are taught black history**, 1961

153

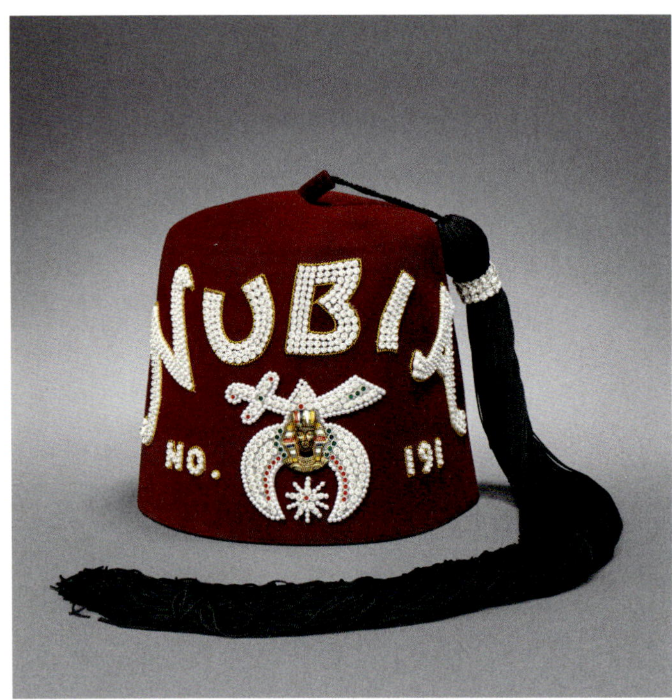

Pl. 89. **Ancient Egyptian Arabic Order Nobles Mystic Shrine Red Fez**, 2024

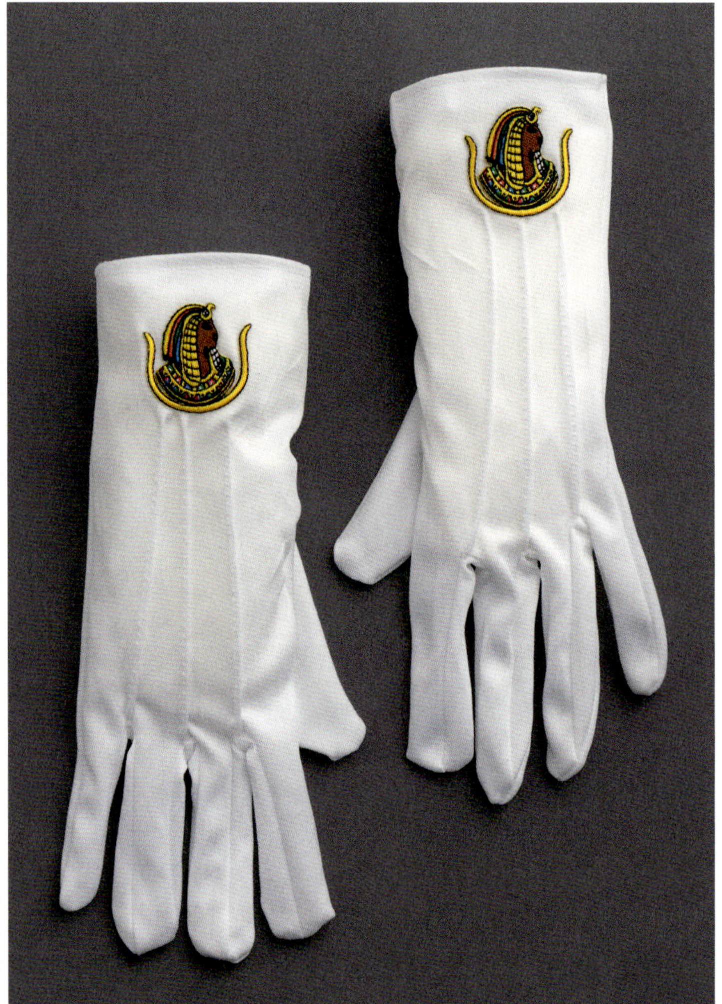

Pl. 90. **Daughters of Isis Gloves**, 2024

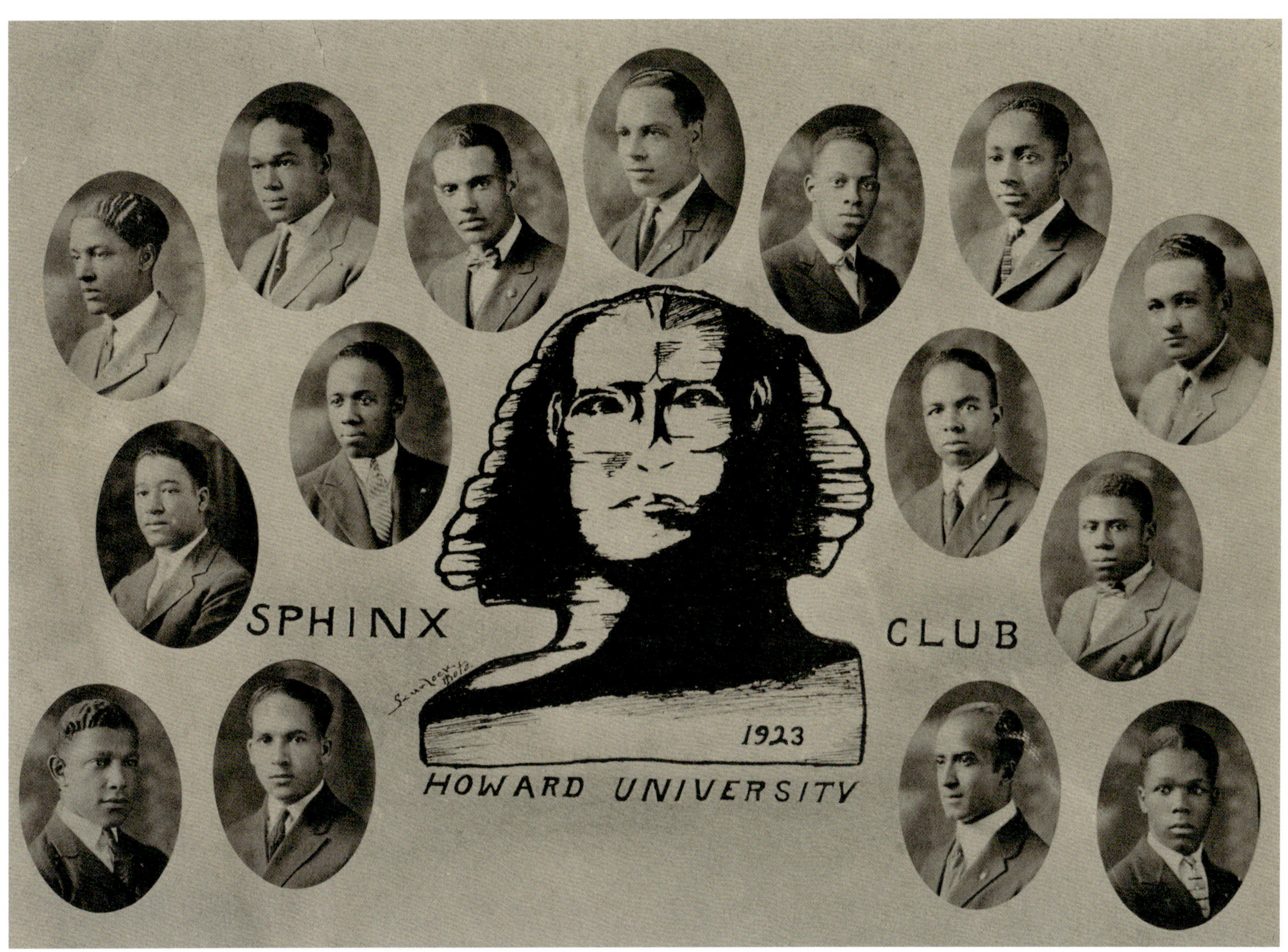

Pl. 91. Addison N. Scurlock, **Collage of Photographs of the Alpha Phi Alpha "Sphinx Club" Fraternity**, 1923

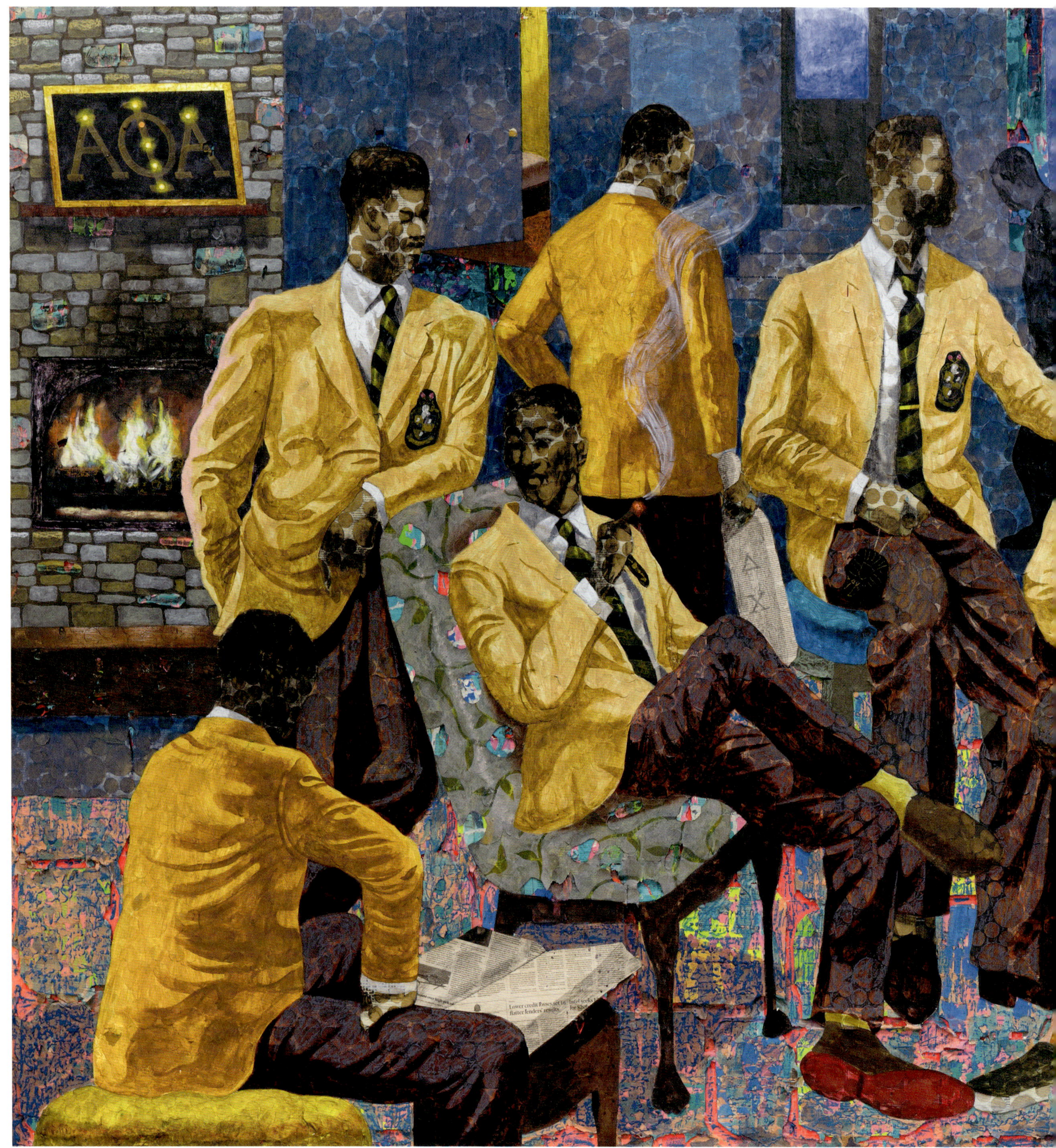

Pl. 92. Derek Fordjour, **Board Meeting (Brotherhood Smoke)**, 2021

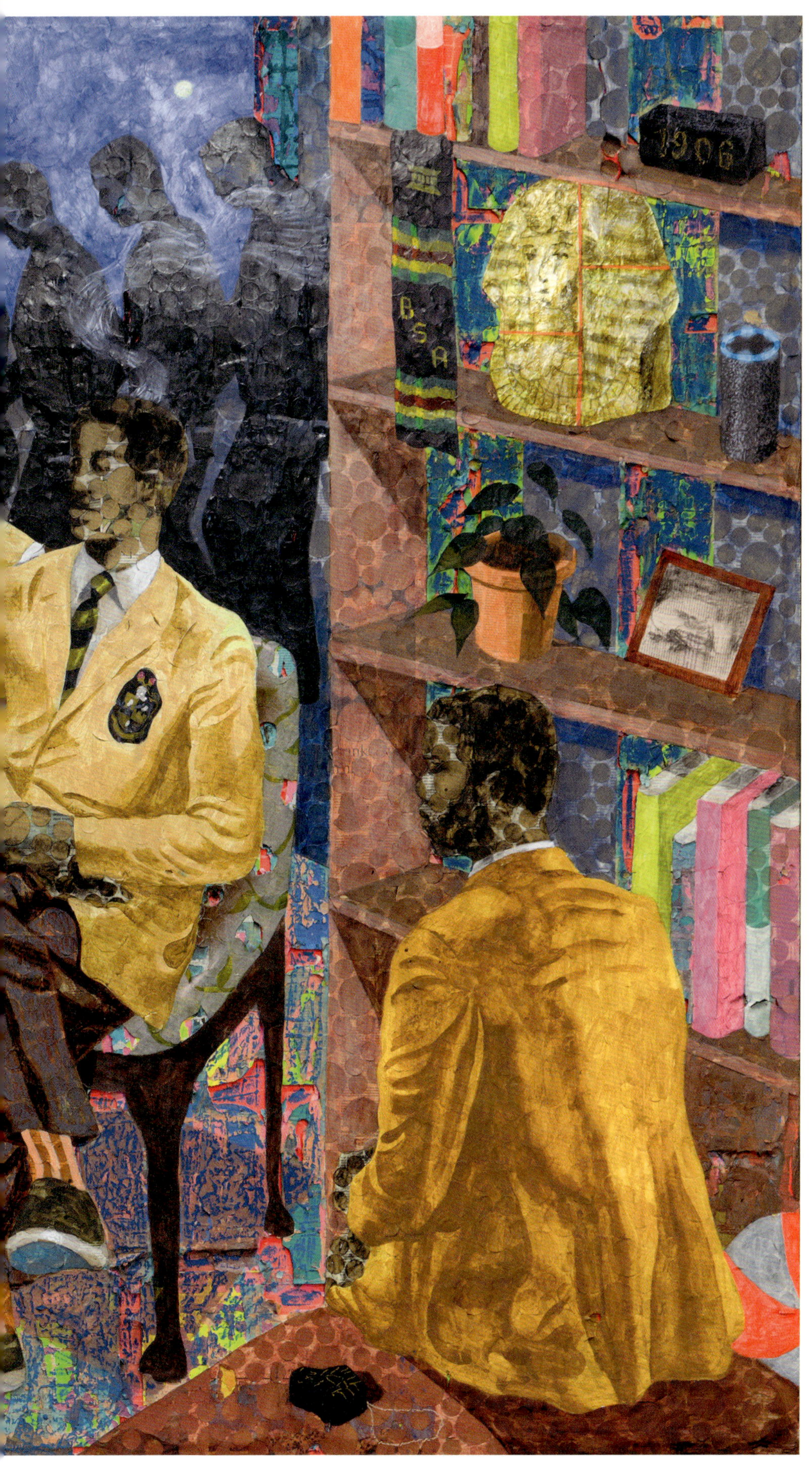

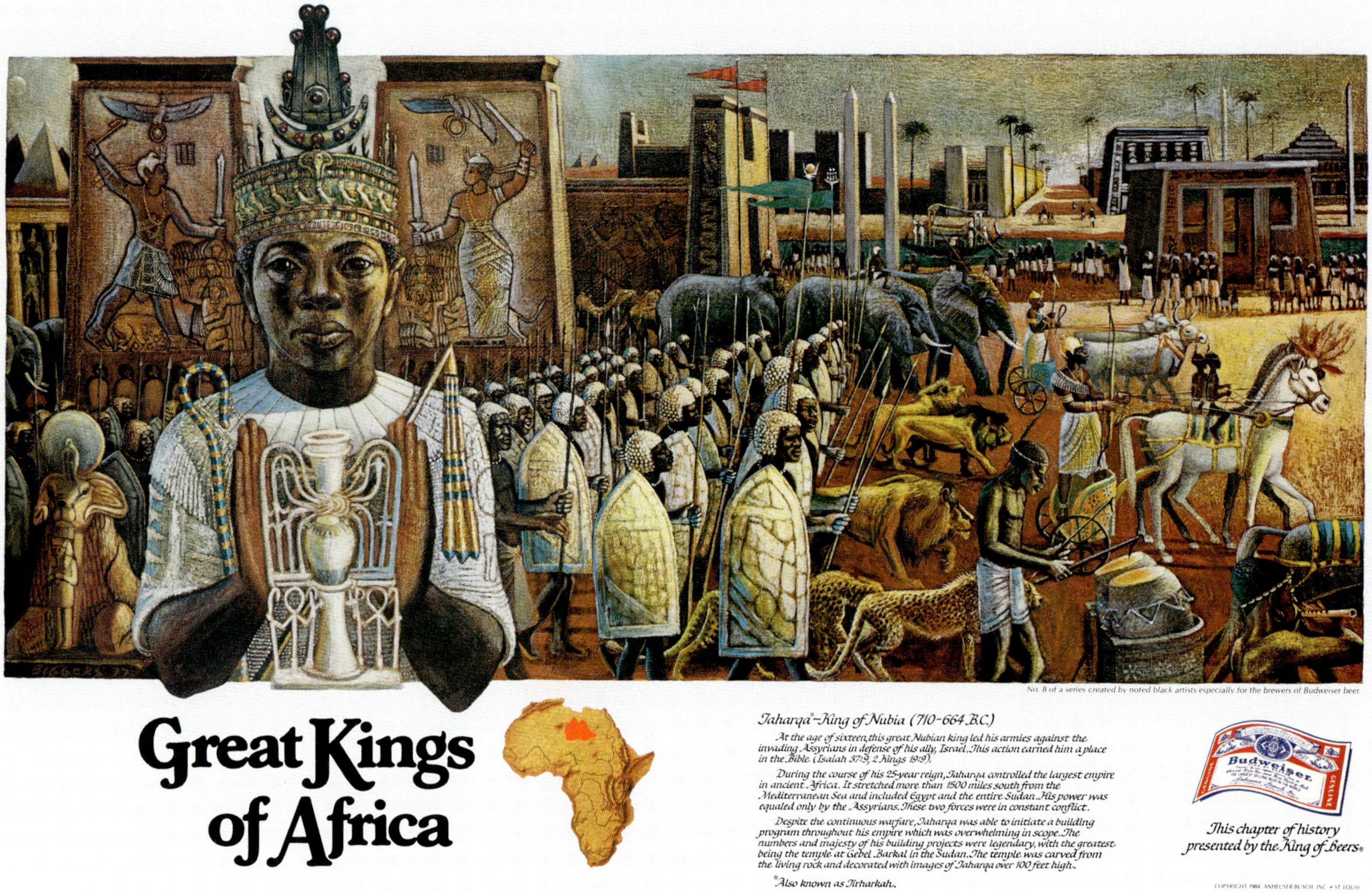

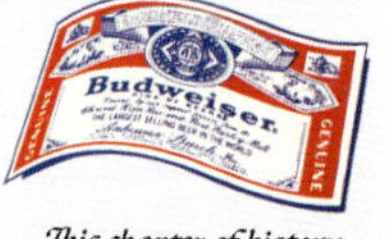

Pl. 93. John Thomas Biggers, **Taharqa King of Nubia (710–664 BC)**, 1984

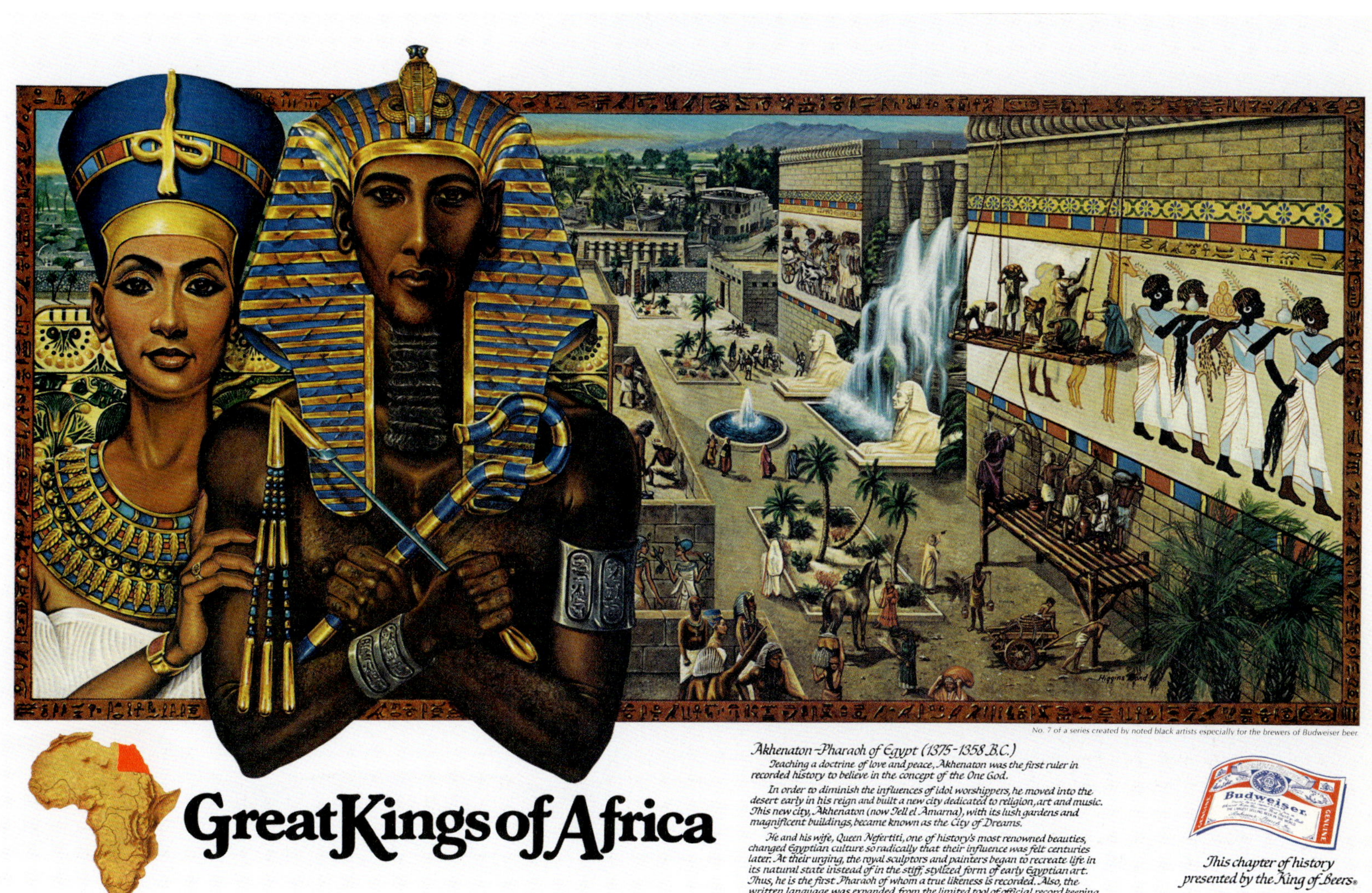

Pl. 94. Barbara Higgins Bond, **Akhenaten Pharaoh of Egypt (1375–1358 BC)**, 1984

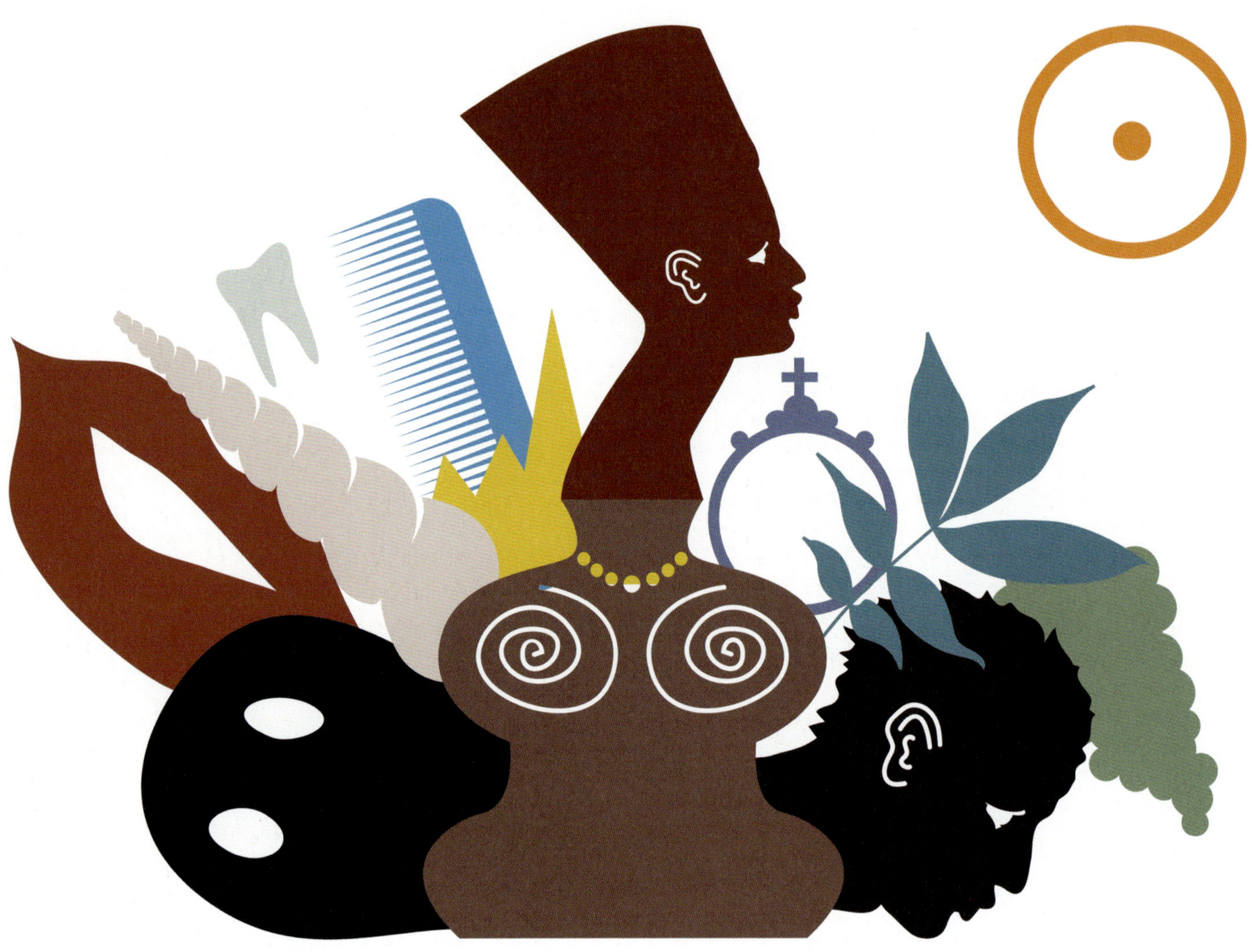

Pl. 95. Damien Davis, **Ancient Still Life**, 2015

Pl. 96. Lakela Brown, **Triangle Pairs with Pharaoh Heads and Nefertiti Recesses**, 2018

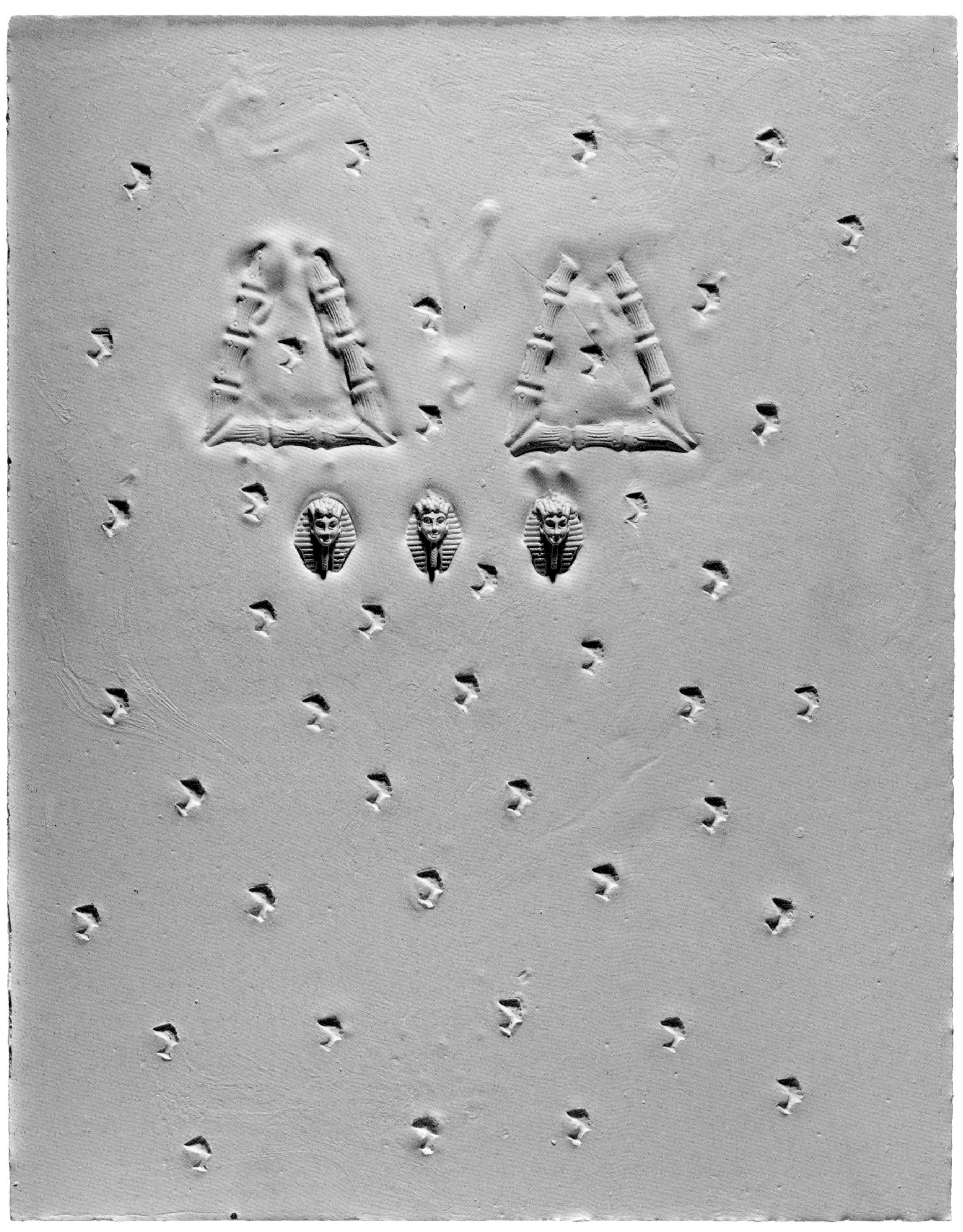

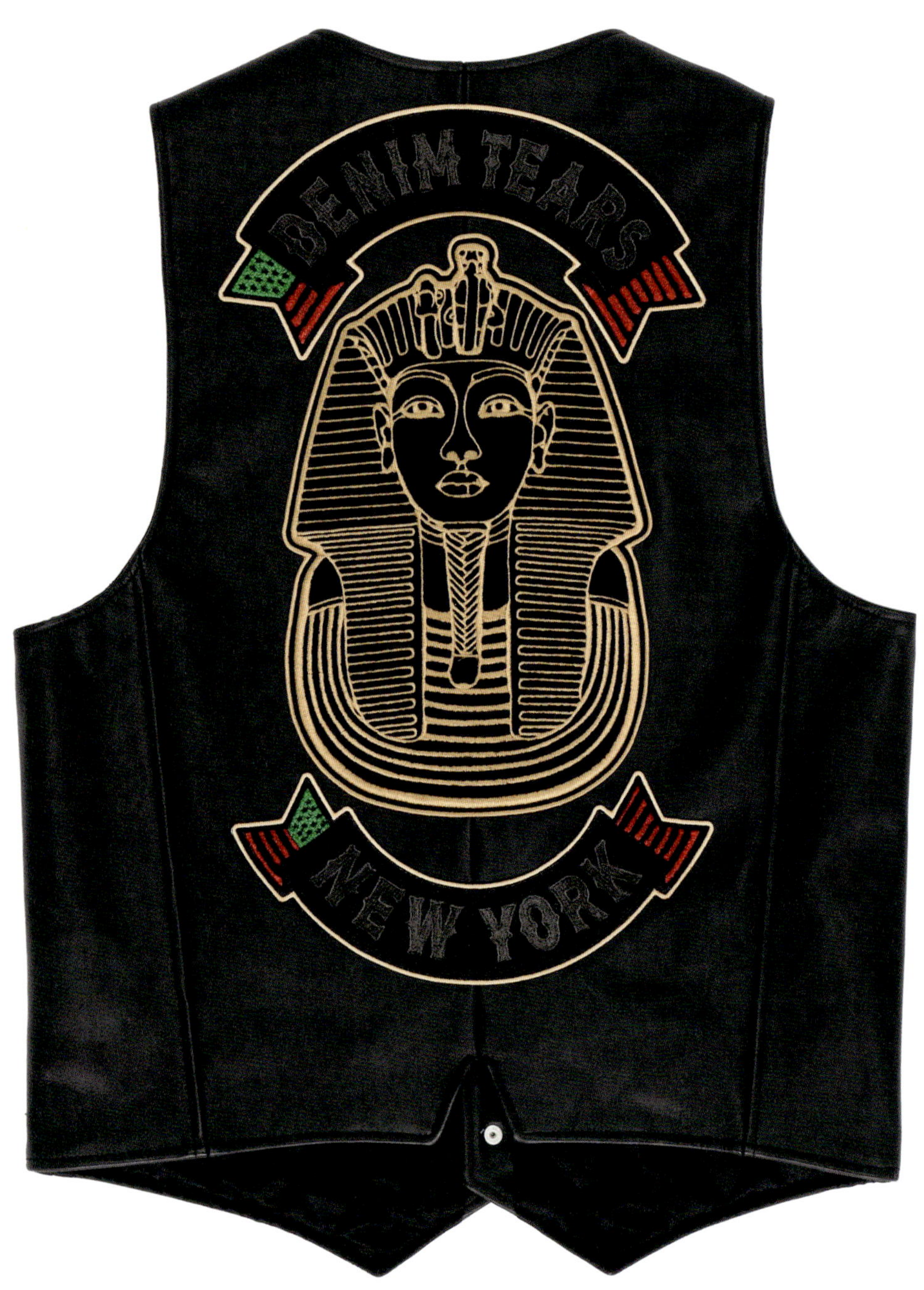

Pl. 97. Denim Tears, **Tracy's king Tut Vest**, 2023

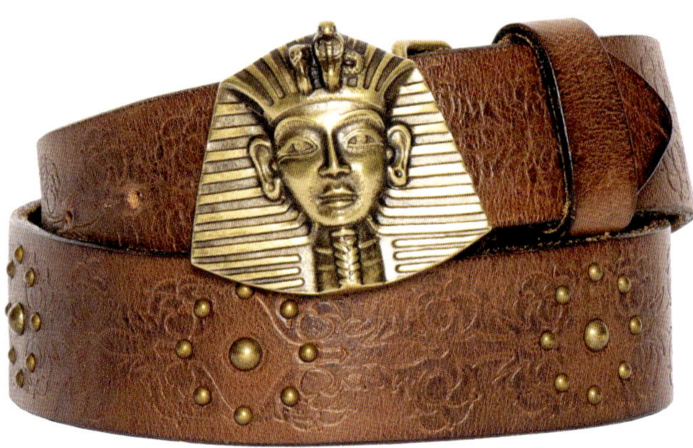

Pl. 98. Denim Tears, **Tracy's king Tut Belt**, 2023

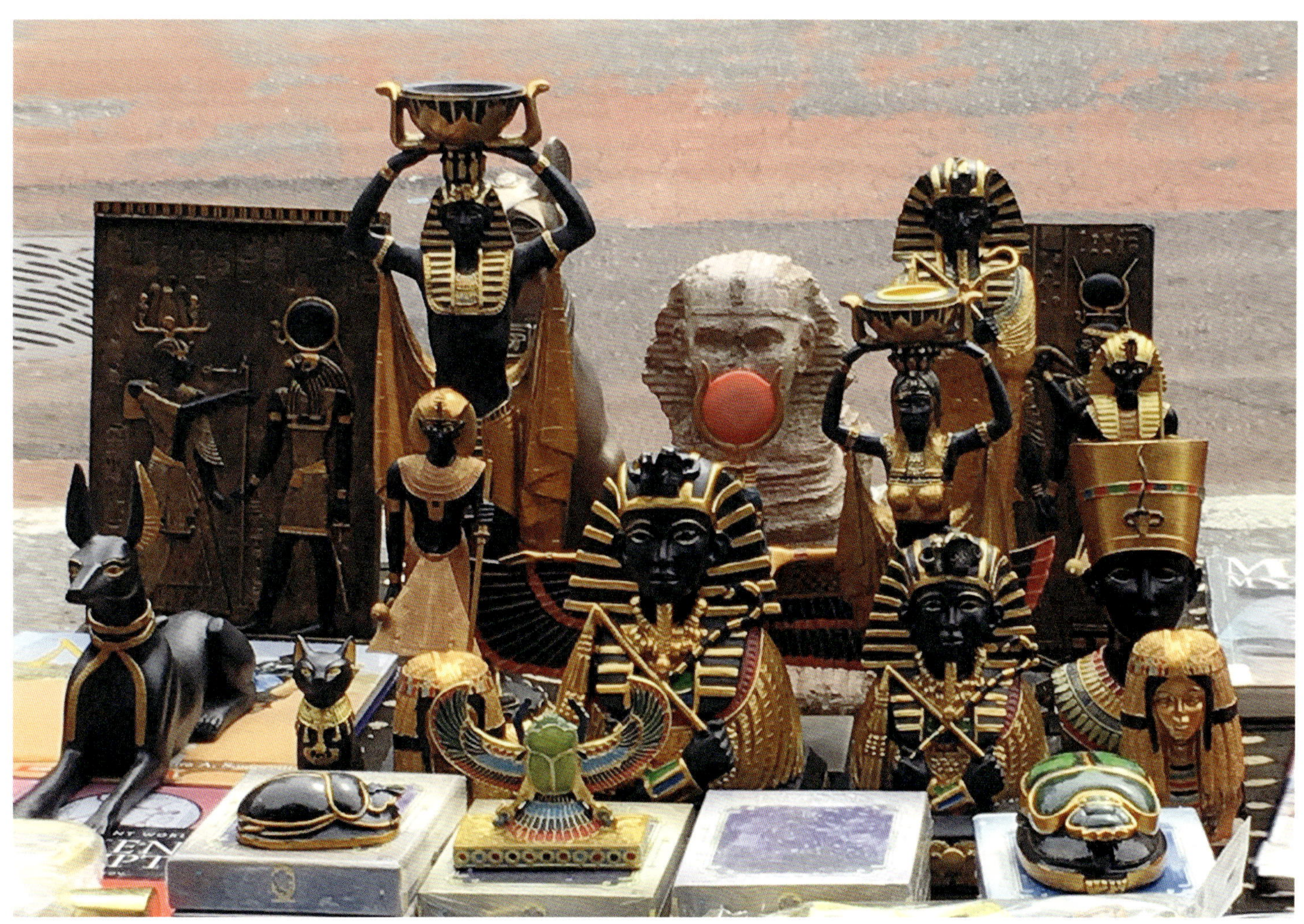

Pl. 99. Fred Wilson, **Black Egypt**, 2019

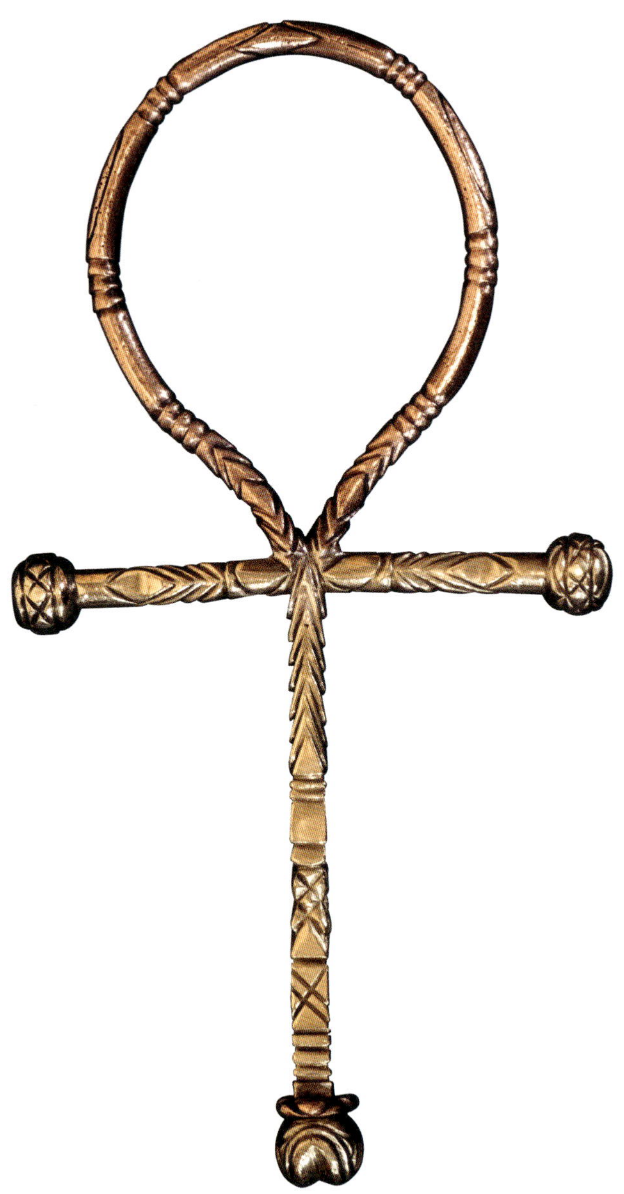

Pl. 100. Baaba Heru Ankh Ra Semahj Se Ptah, **The Ankh of Love**, ca. 1975

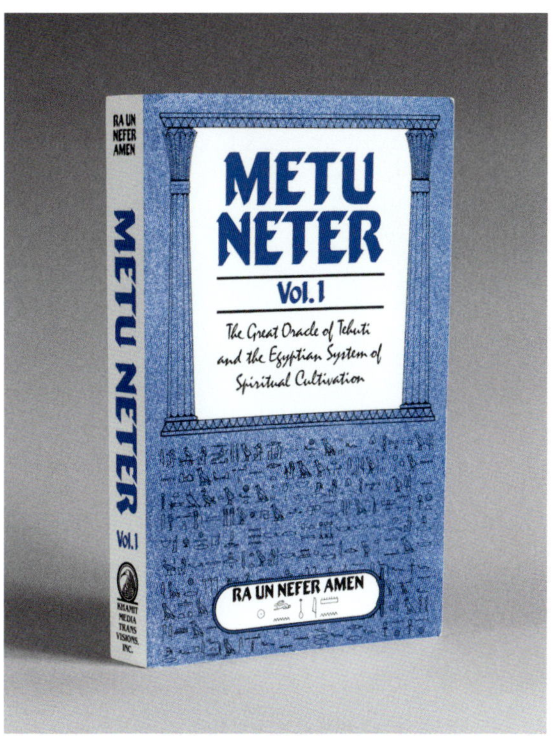

Pl. 101. Ra Un Nefer Amen, **Metu Neter**, 1990

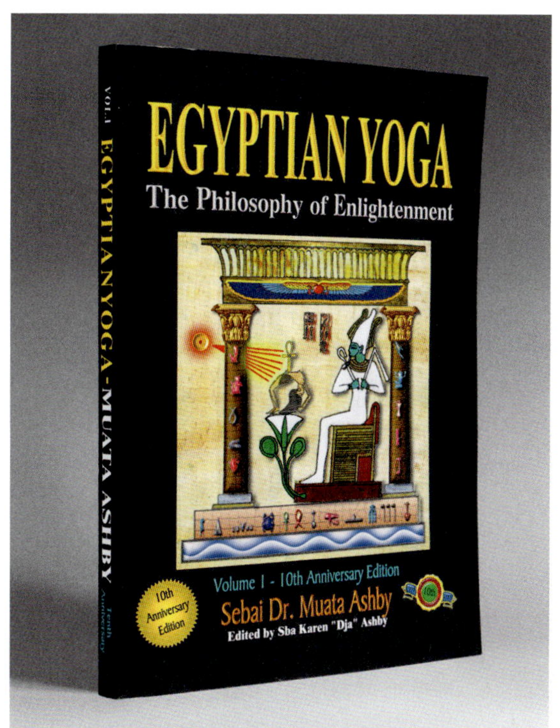

Pl. 102. Muata Ashby, **Egyptian Yoga**, 1995

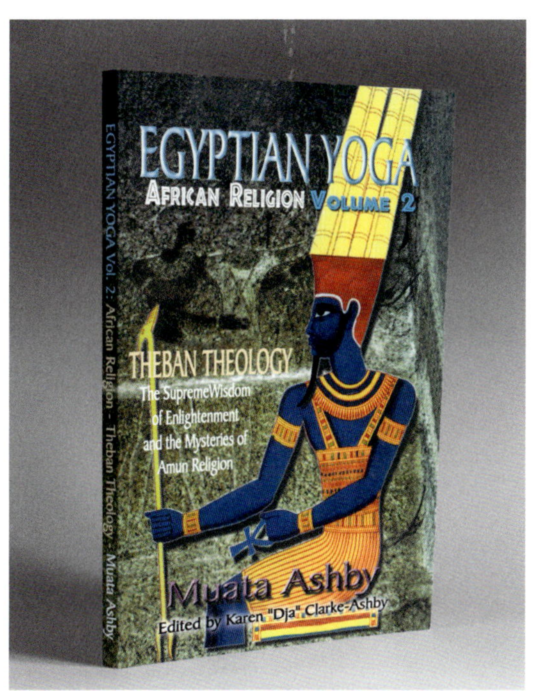

Pl. 103. Muata Ashby, **Egyptian Yoga**, 1998

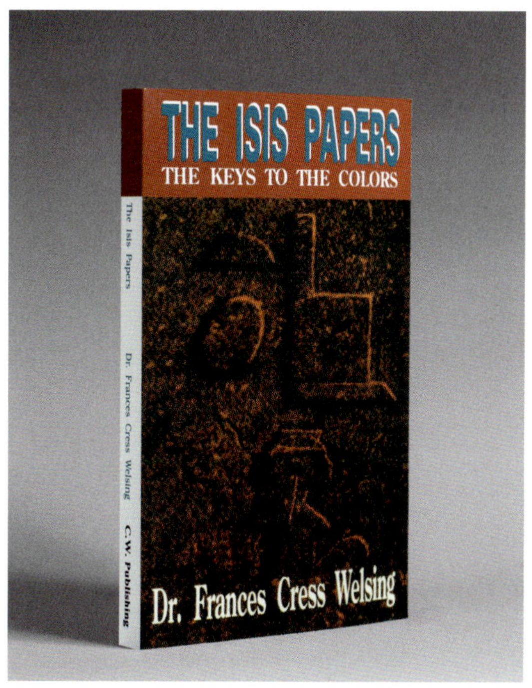

Pl. 104. Frances Cress Welsing, **The Isis Papers**, 2004

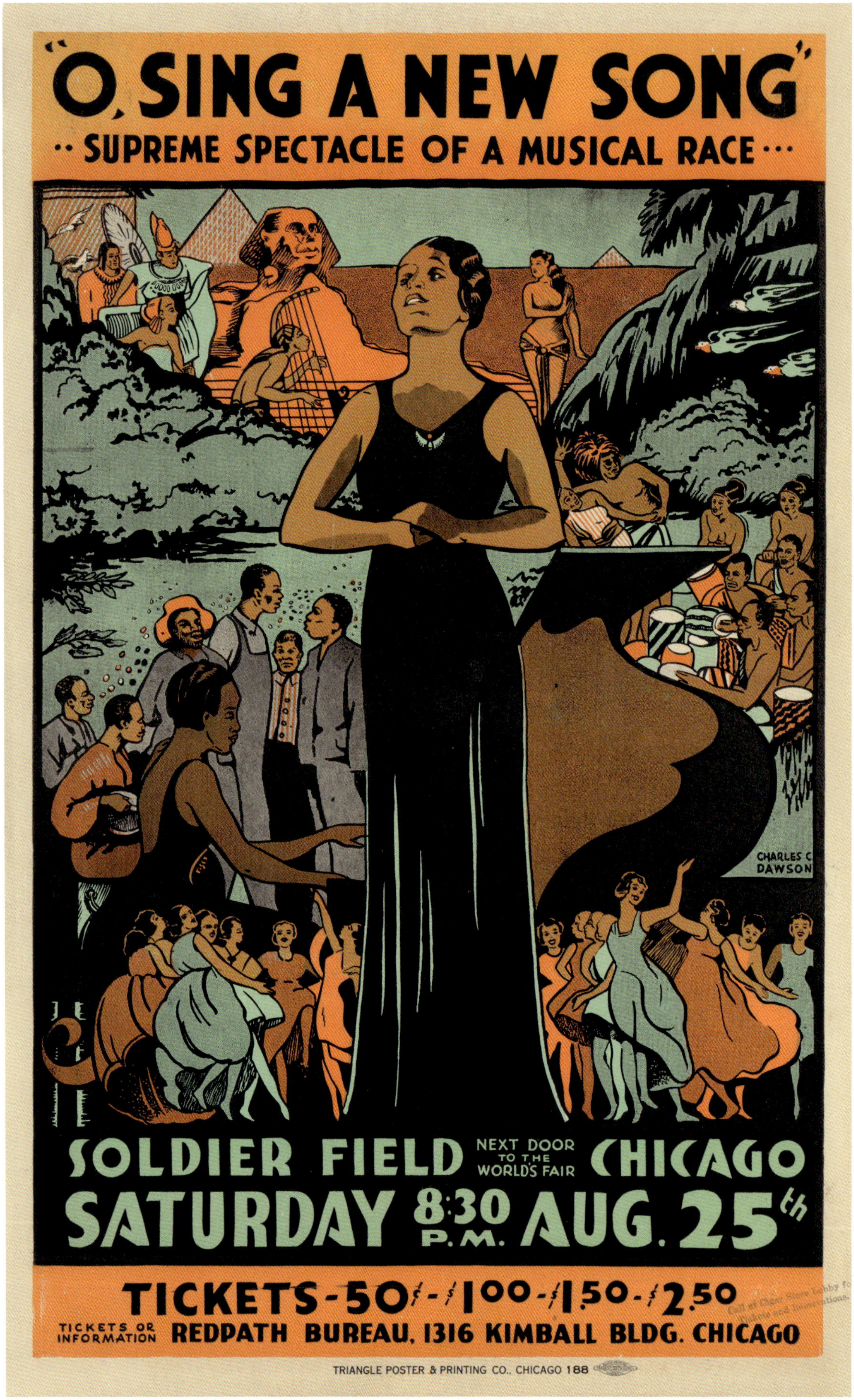

Pl. 105. Charles Clarence Dawson, **"O, Sing a New Song,"** 1934

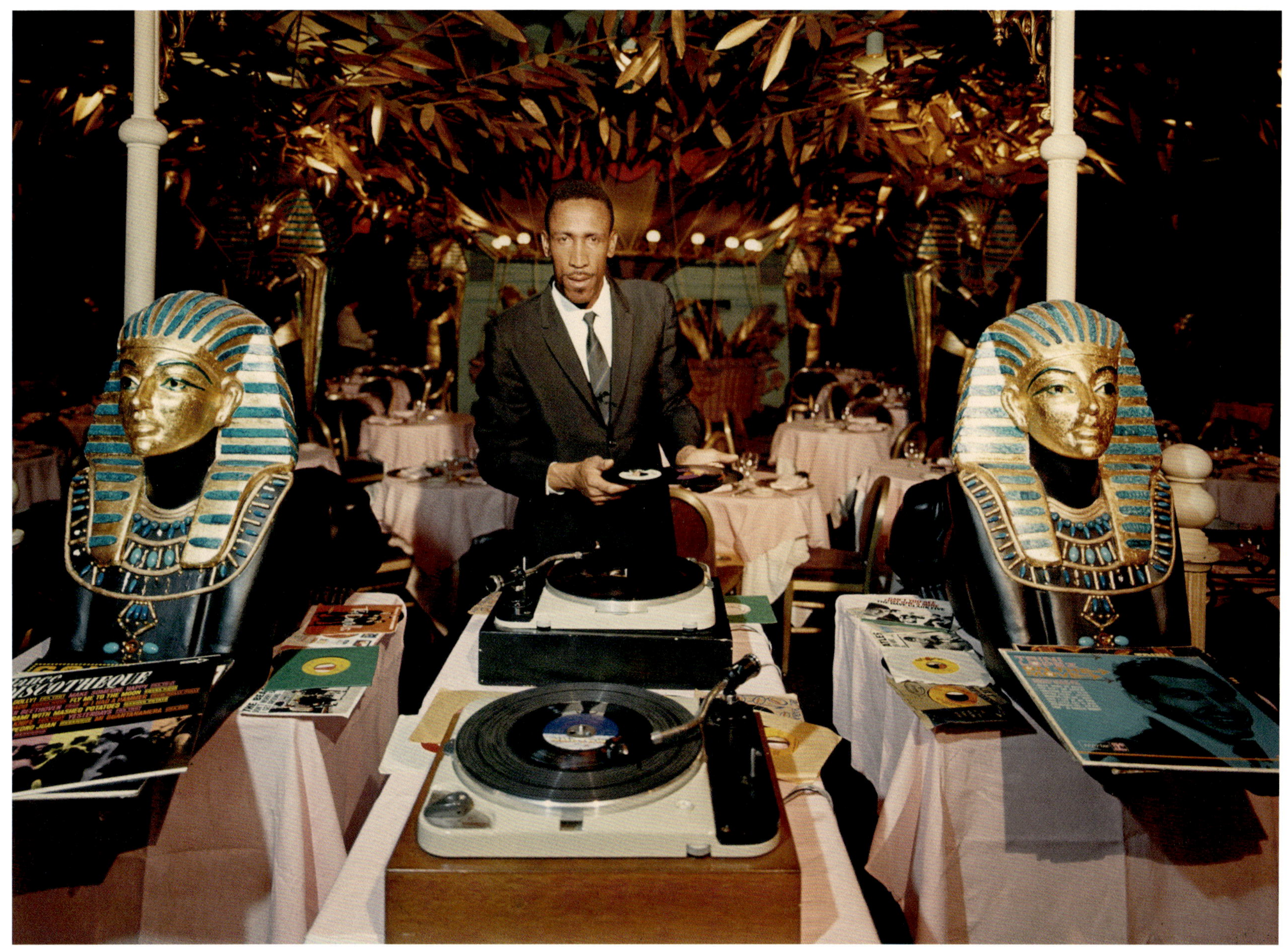

Pl. 106. Slim Aarons, **Slim and Sphinx**, 1964

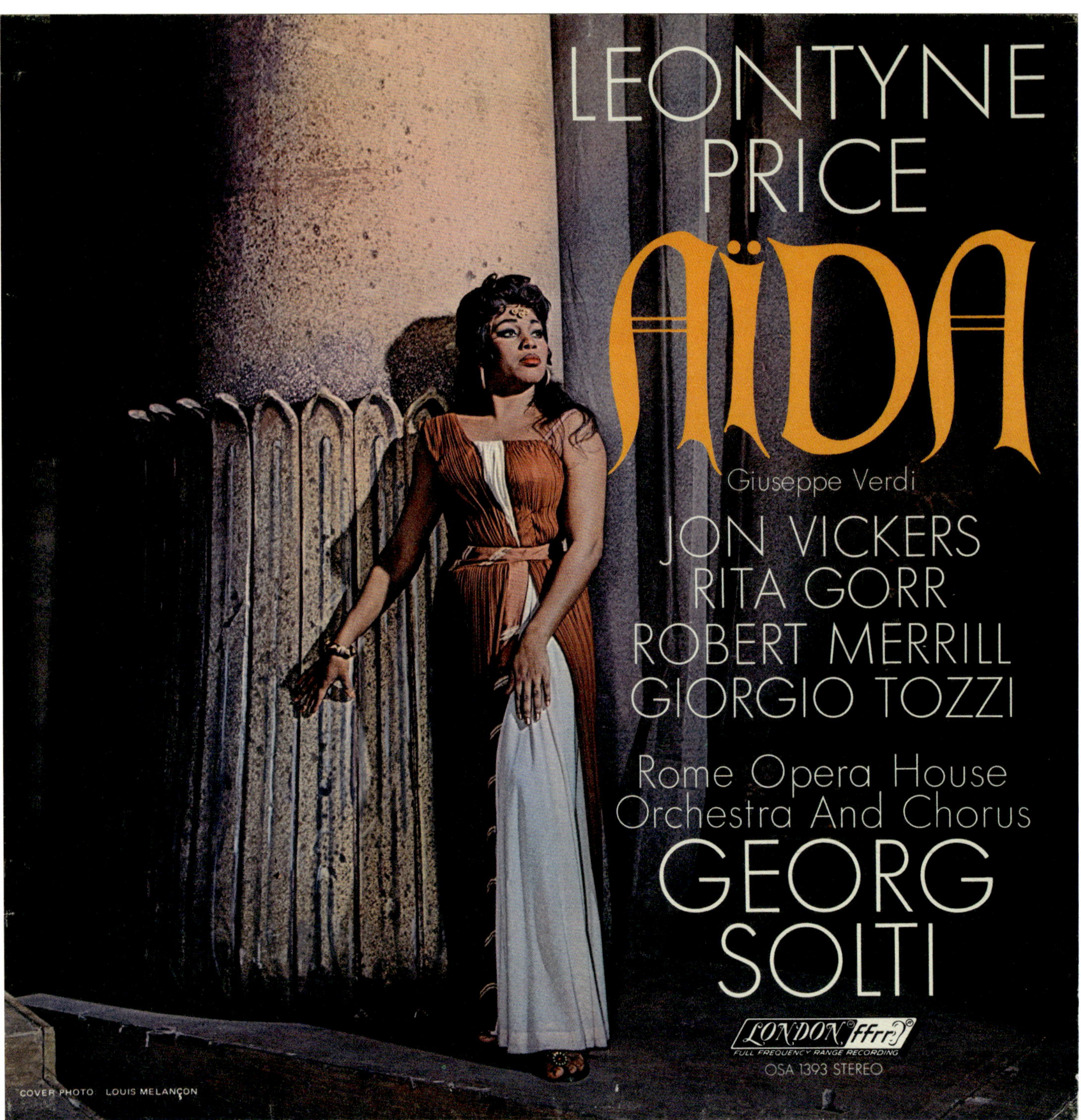

Pl. 107. Leontyne Price, **Aïda,** 1962

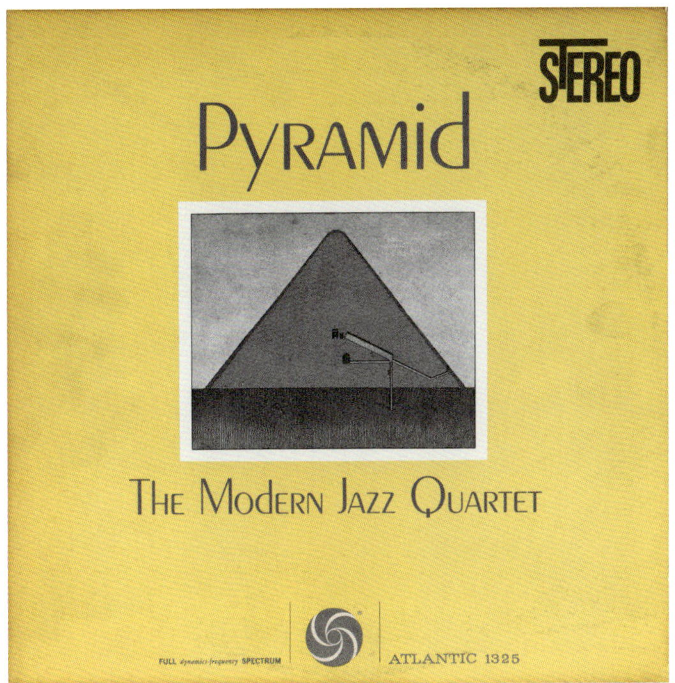

Pl. 108. The Modern Jazz Quartet, **Pyramid**, 1960

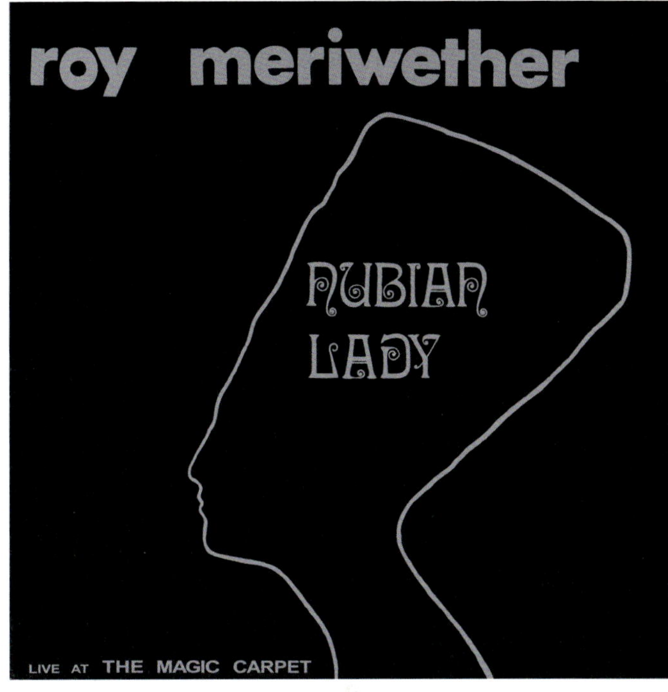

Pl. 109. Roy Meriwether, **Nubian Lady**, 1973

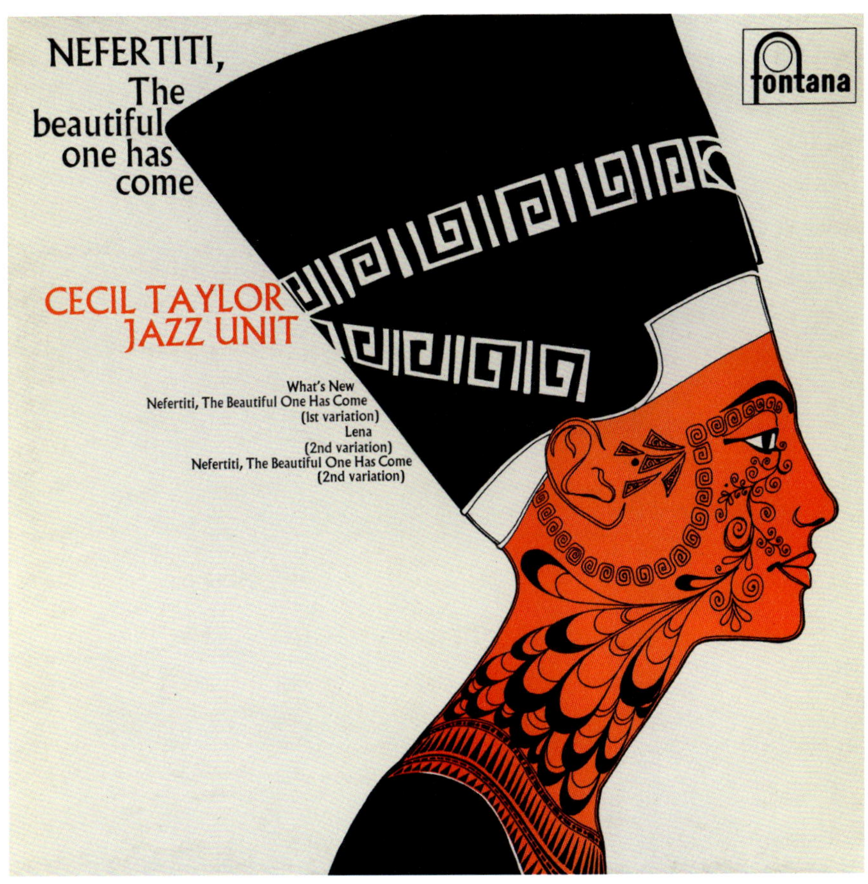

Pl. 110. Cecil Taylor Jazz Unit, **Nefertiti, The Beautiful One Has Come**, 1969

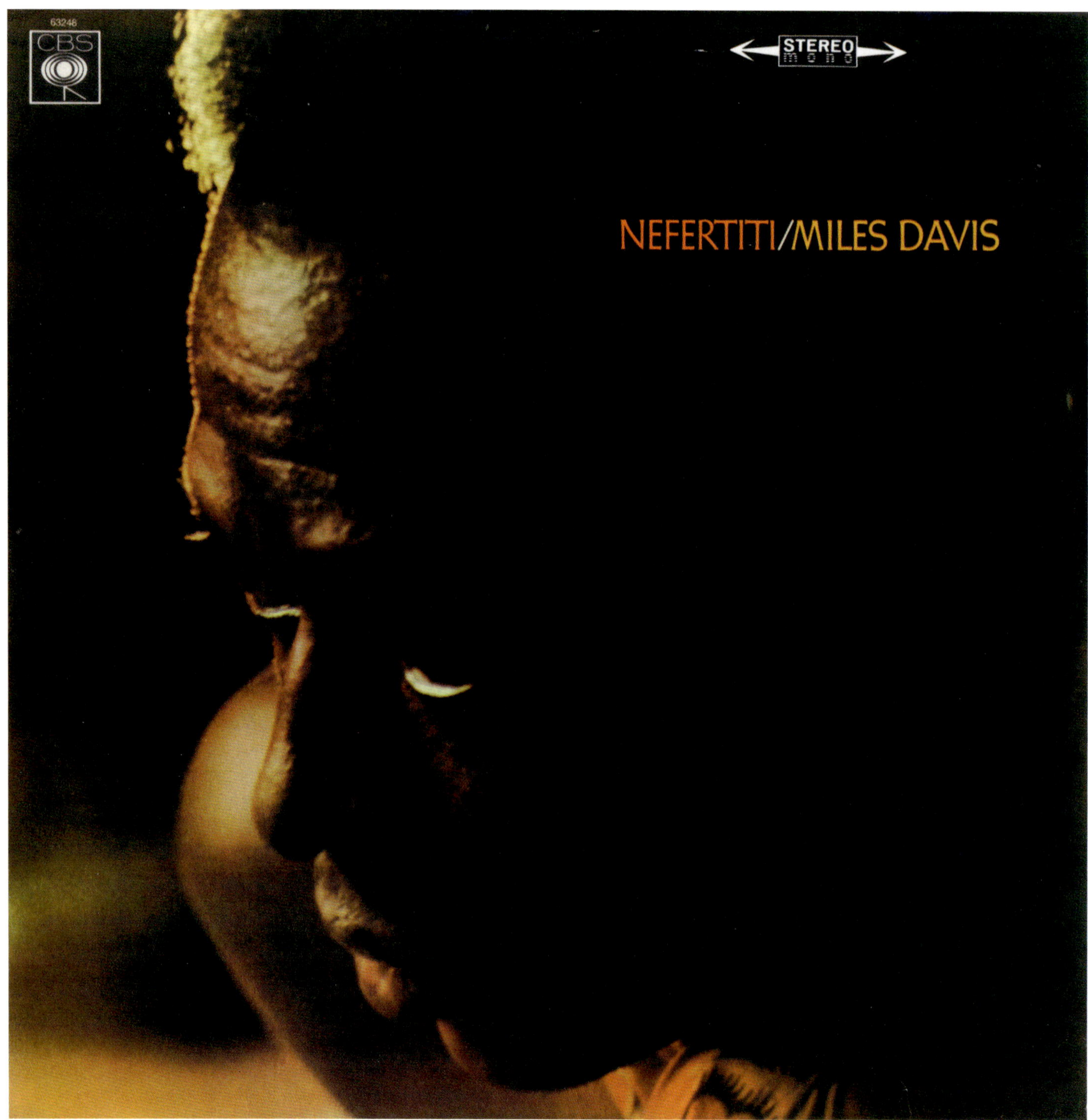

Pl. 111. Miles Davis, **Nefertiti**, 1968

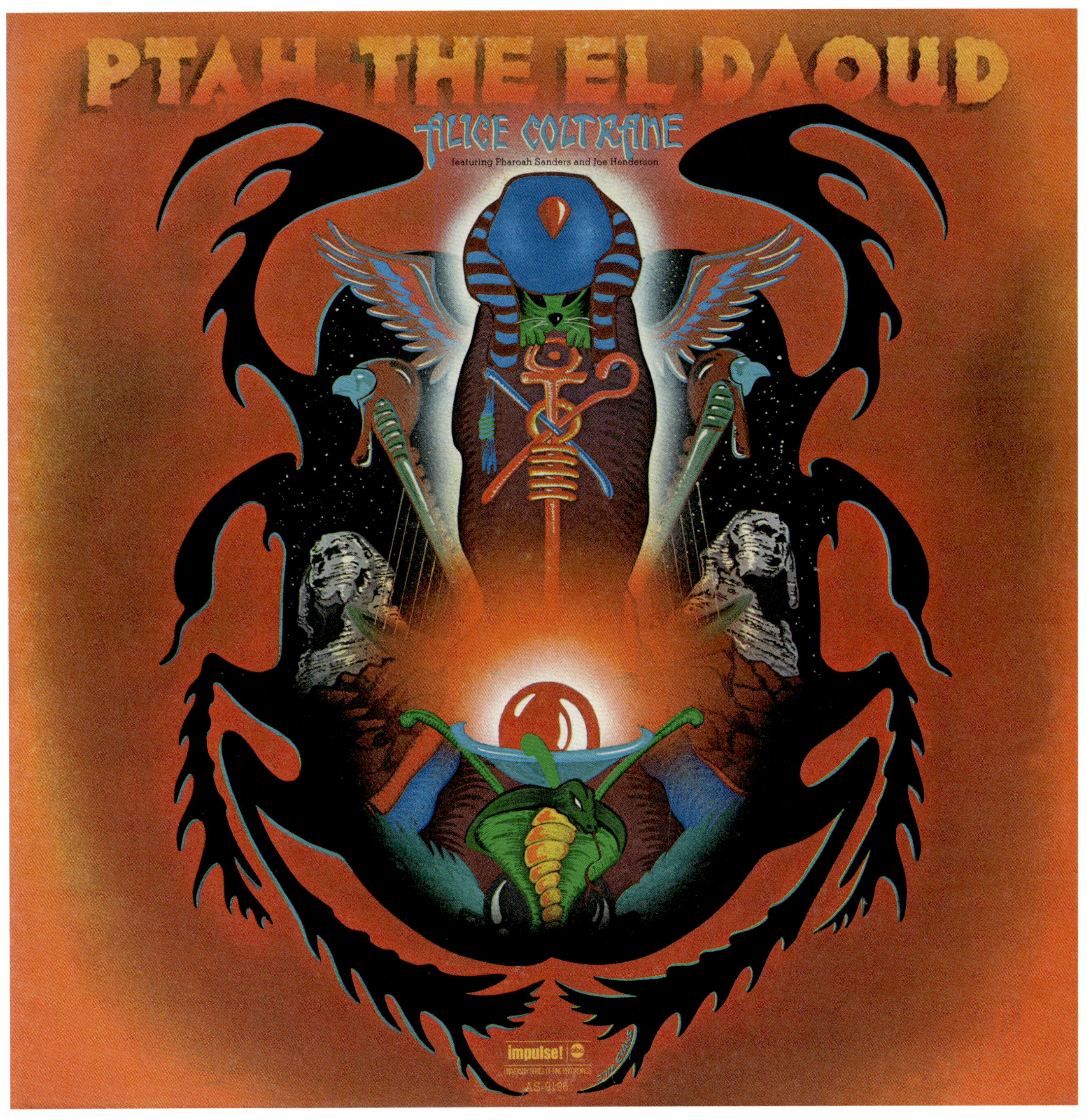

Pl. 112. Alice Coltrane, **Ptah, the El Daoud,** 1970

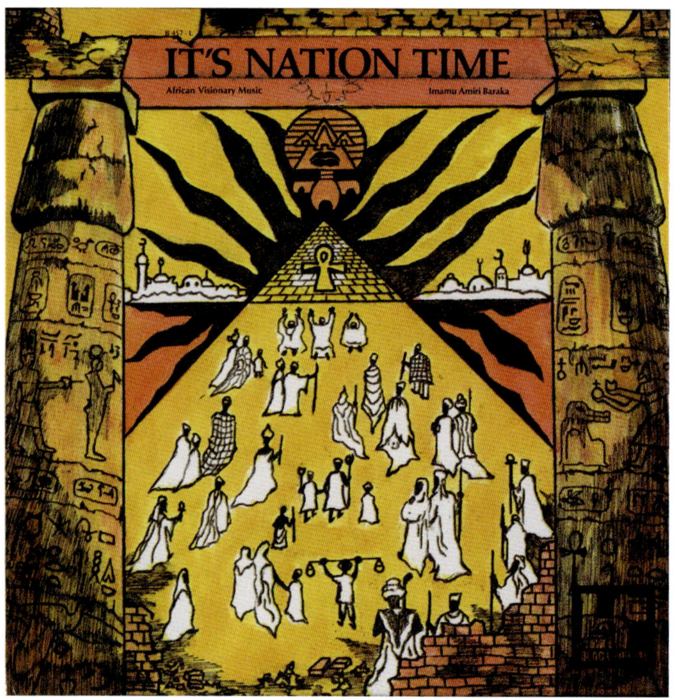

Pl. 113. Amiri Baraka, **It's Nation Time—African Visionary Music**, 1972

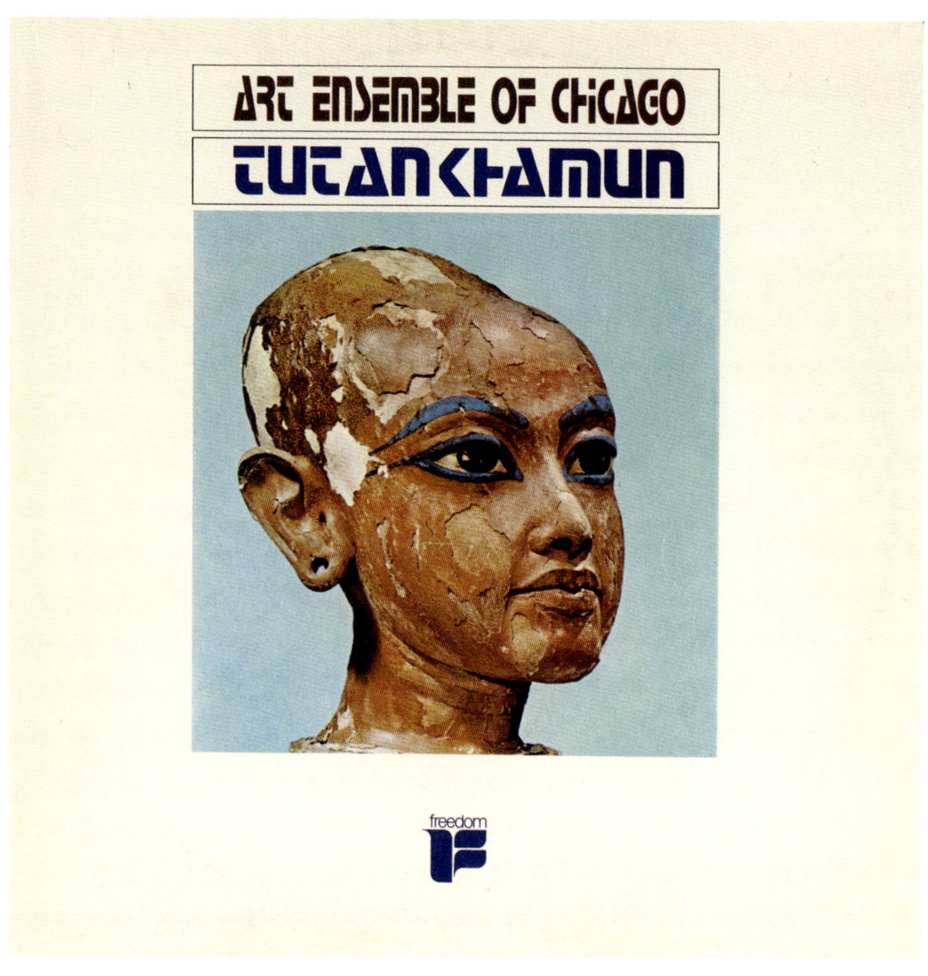

Pl. 114. Art Ensemble of Chicago, **Tutankhamun**, 1974

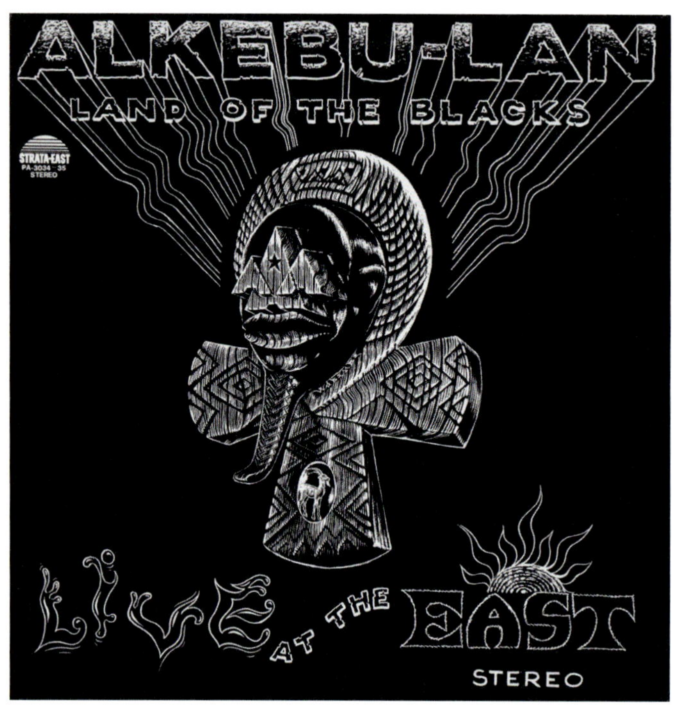

Pl. 115. Mtume Umoja Ensemble, **Alkebu-Lan: Land of the Blacks**, 1972

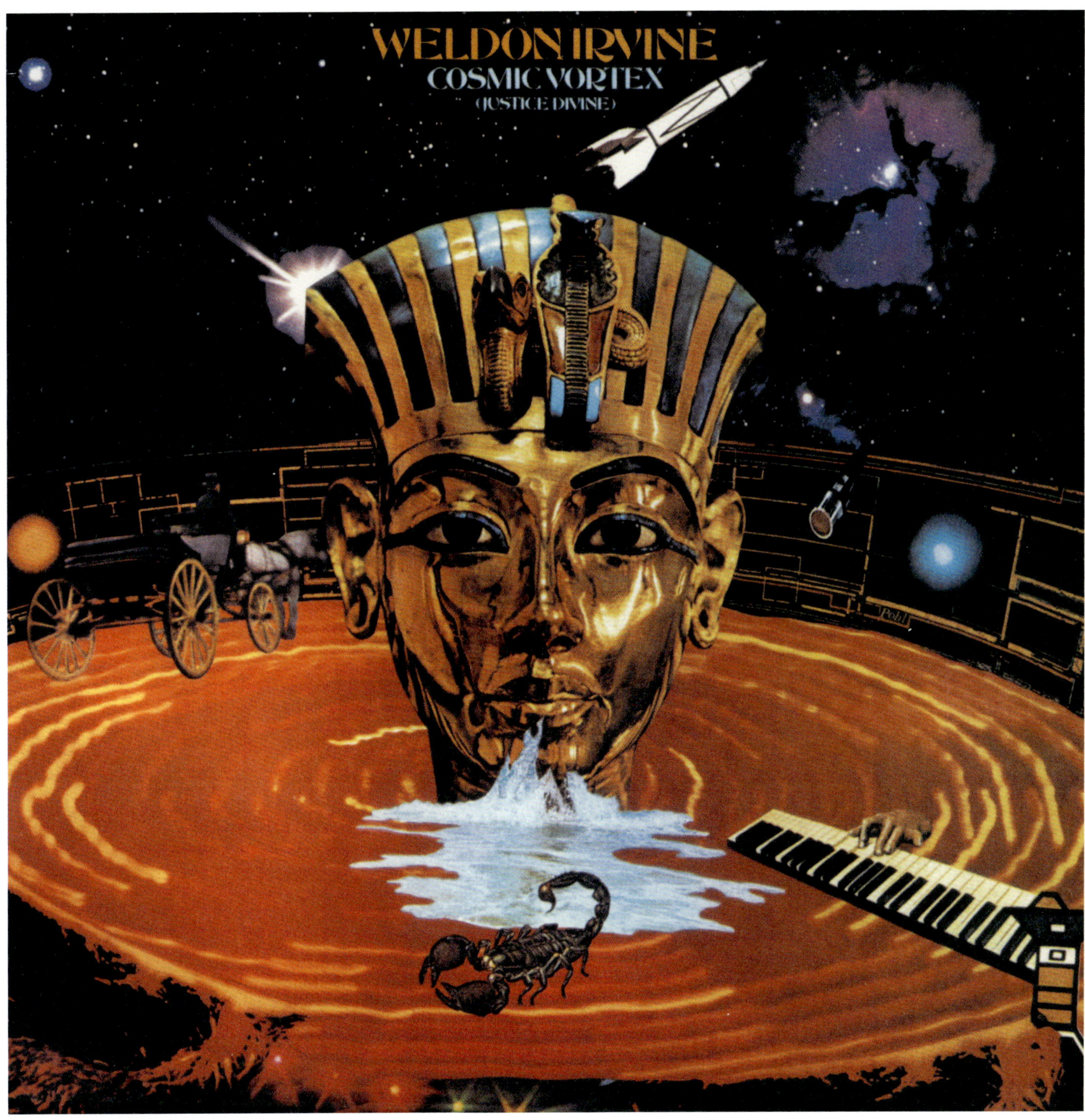

Pl. 116. Weldon Irvine, **Cosmic Vortex (Justice Divine)**, 1974

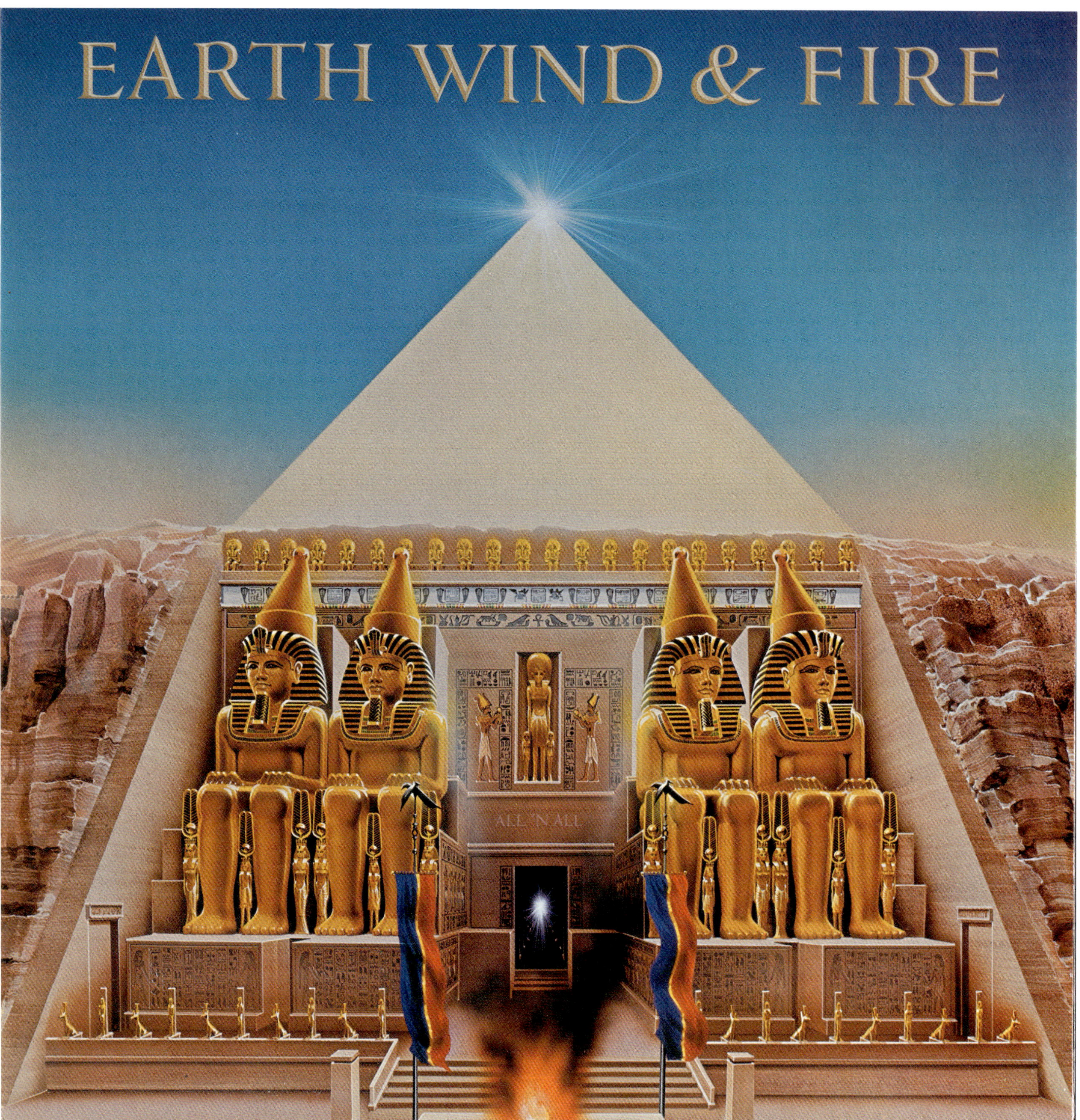

Pl. 117. Earth, Wind & Fire, **All 'n All**, 1977

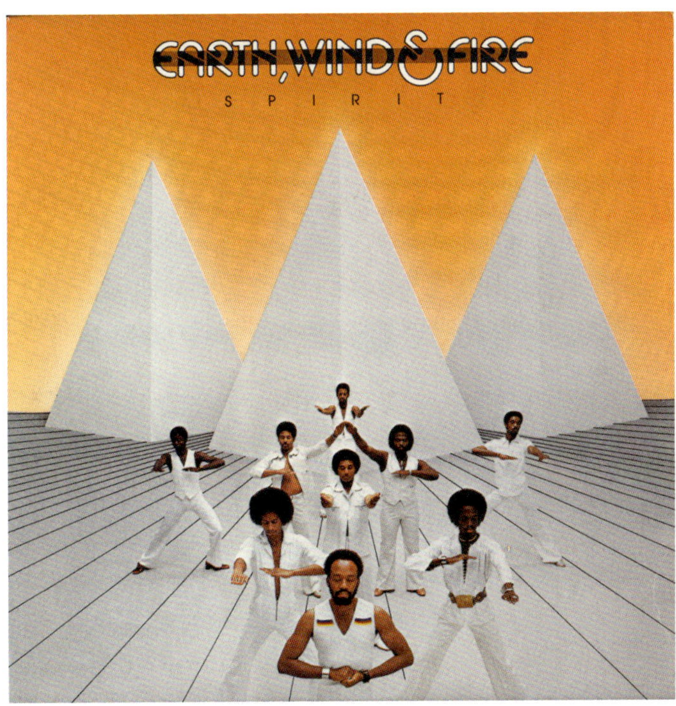

Pl. 118. Earth, Wind & Fire, **Spirit**, 1976

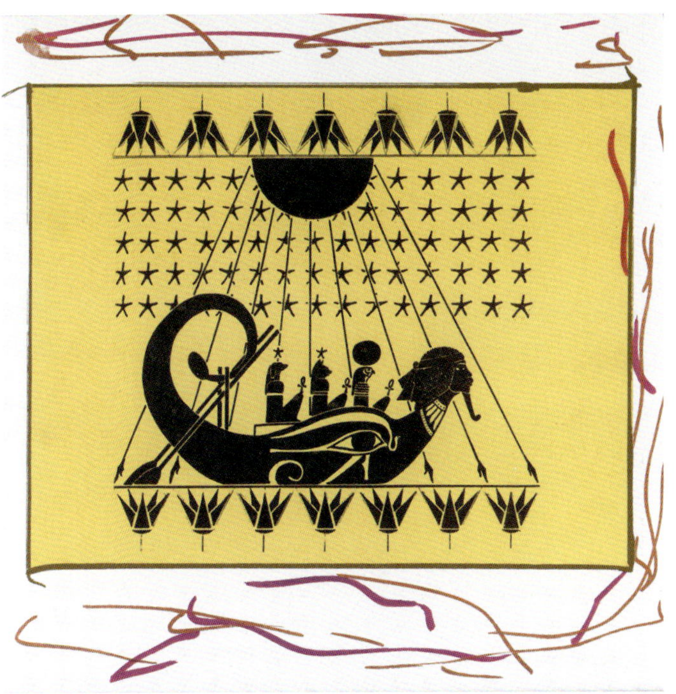

Pl. 119. Sun Ra, **Horizon**, 1972/2020

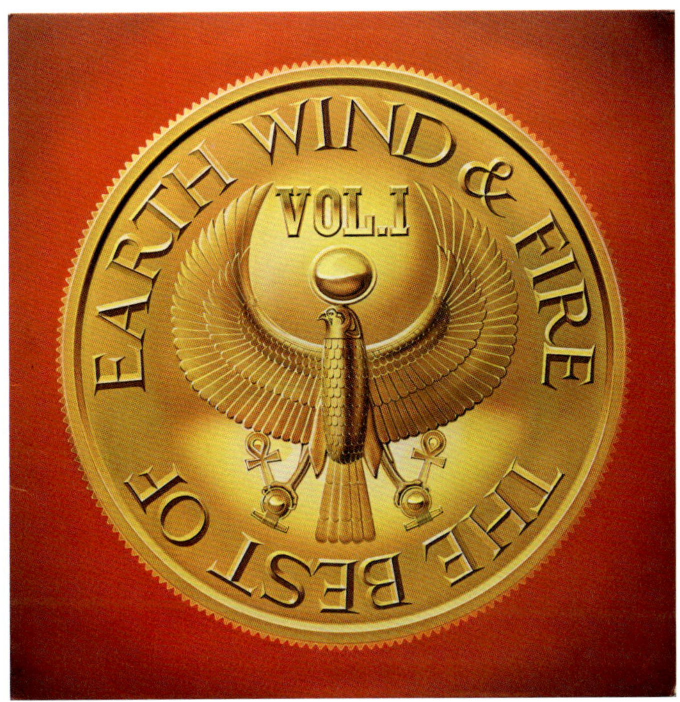

Pl. 120. Earth, Wind & Fire, **Best of Earth, Wind & Fire, Vol. 1**, 1978

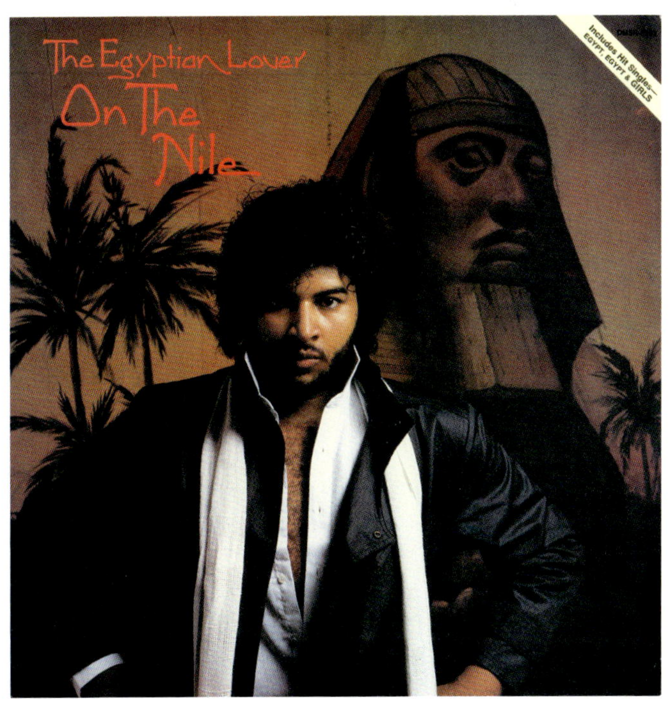

Pl. 121. The Egyptian Lover, **On the Nile**, 1984

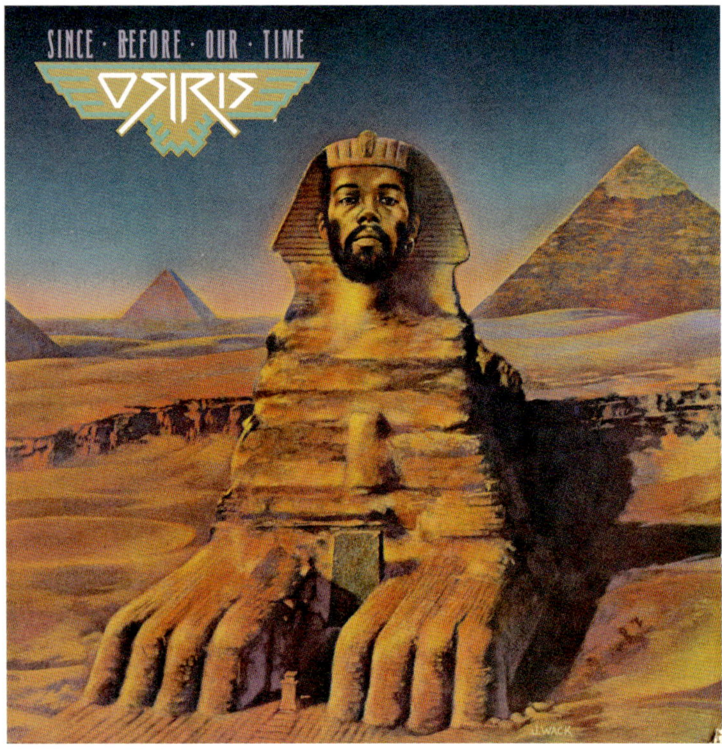

Pl. 122. Osiris, **Since Before Our Time**, 1979

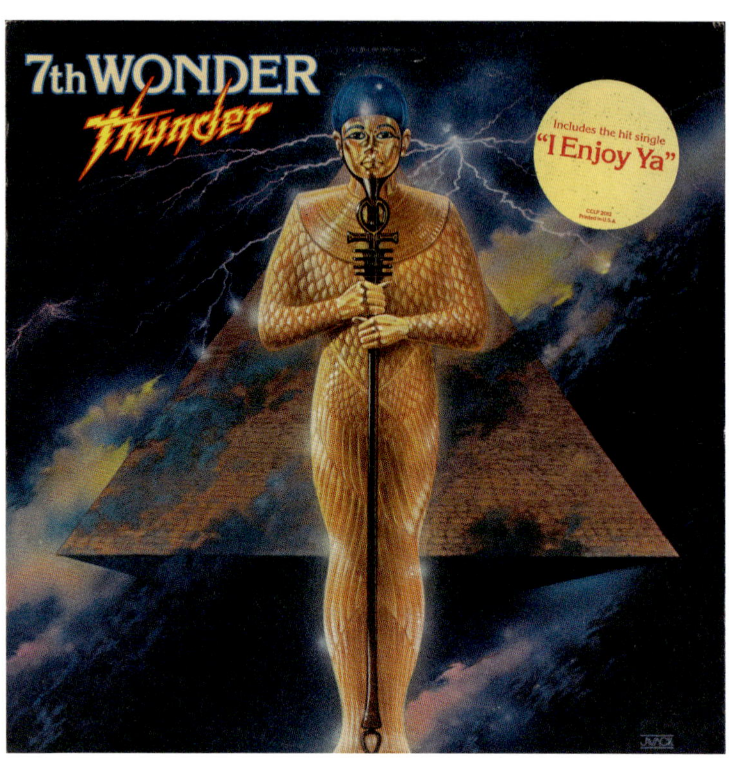

Pl. 123. Thunder, **7th Wonder**, 1980

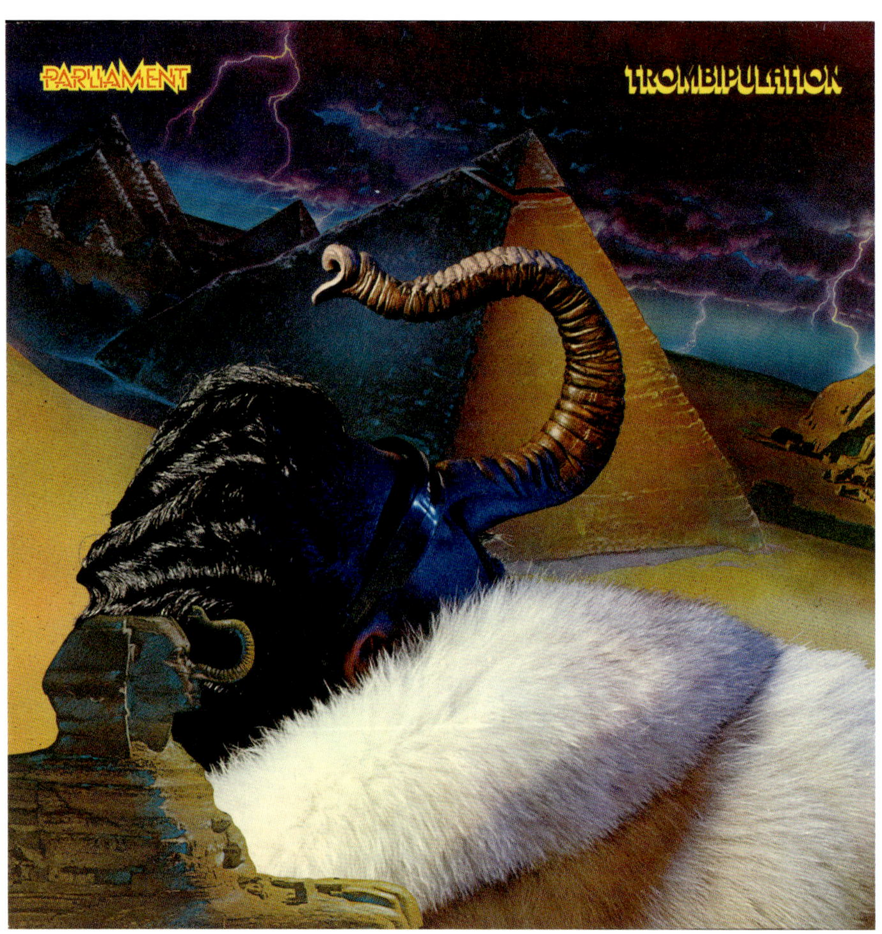

Pl. 124. Parliament, **Trombipulation**, 1980

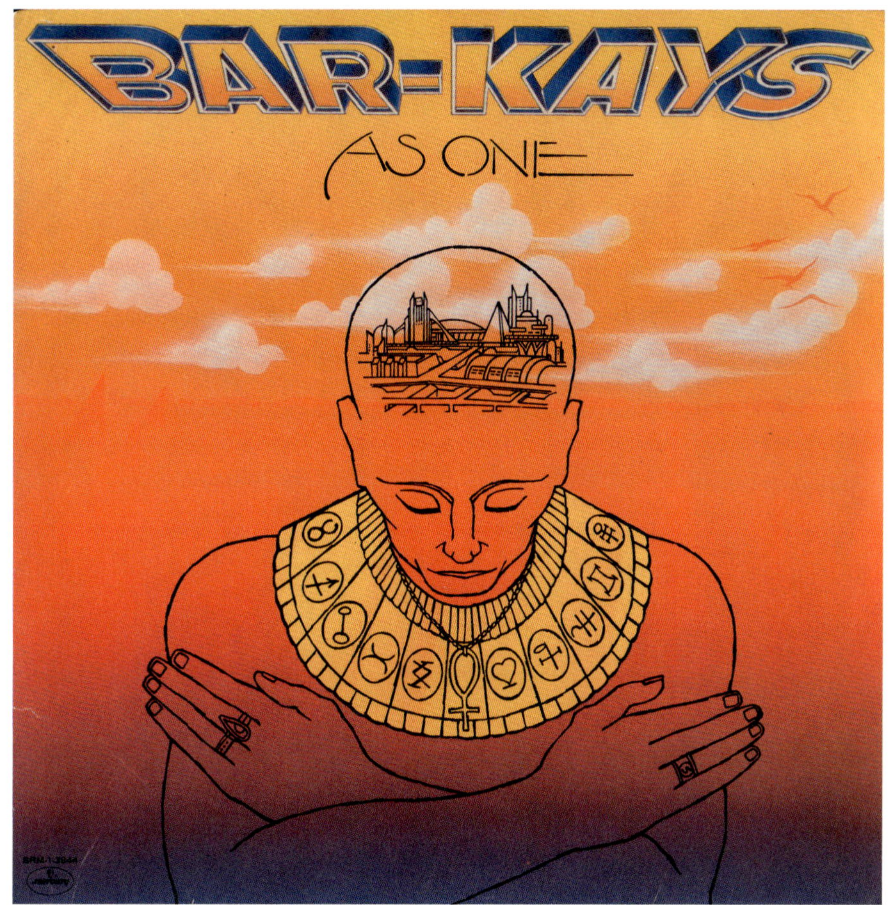

Pl. 125. The Bar-Kays, **As One**, 1980

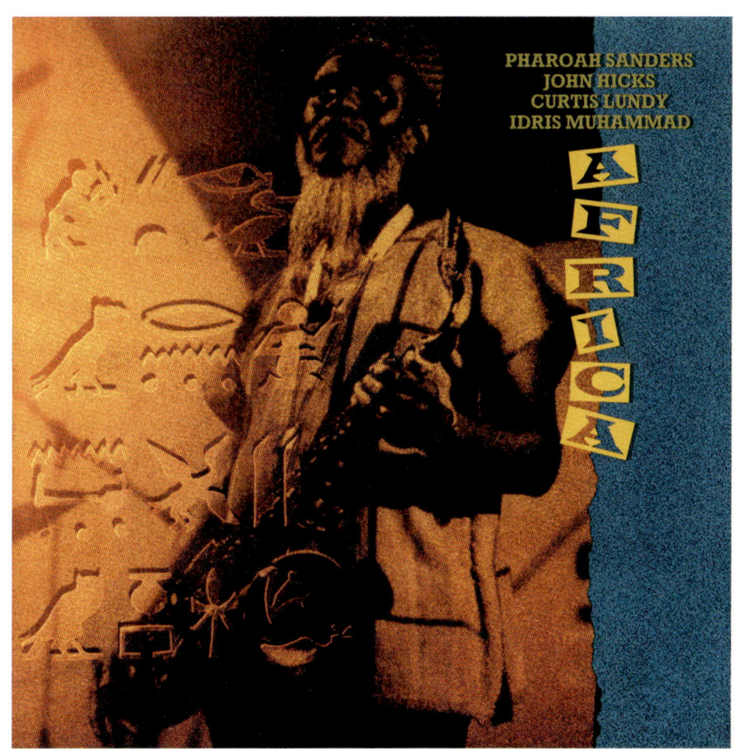

Pl. 126. Pharoah Sanders, **Africa**, 1987

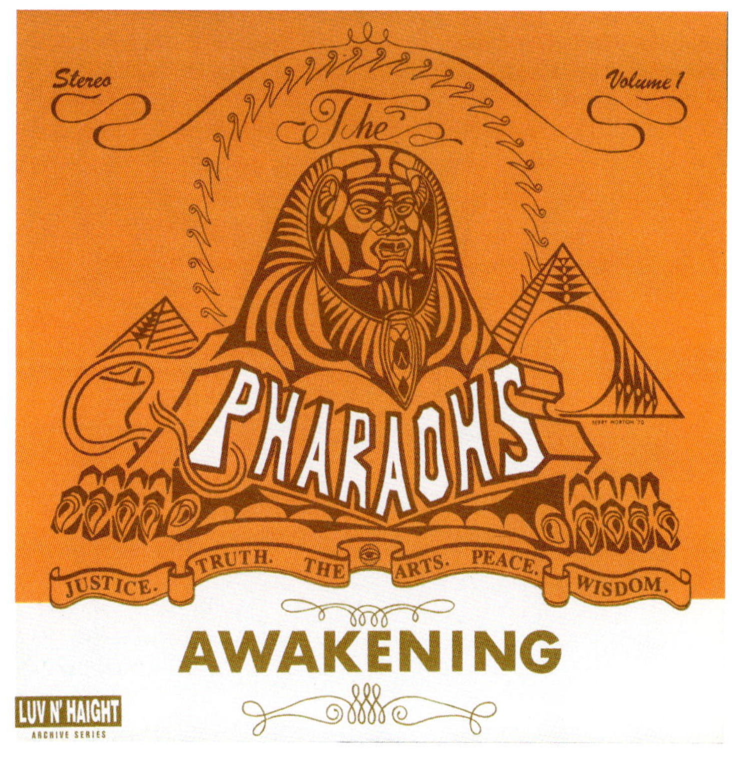

Pl. 127. The Pharaohs, **The Awakening**, 1971/1996

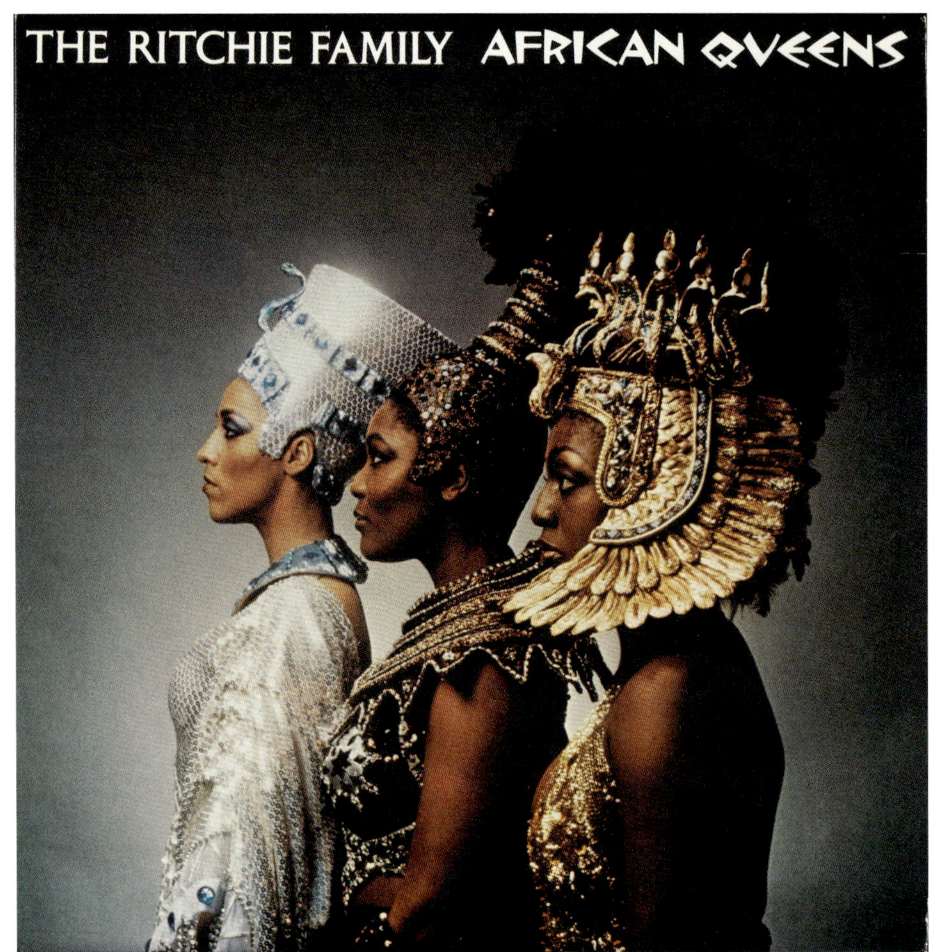

Pl. 128. The Ritchie Family, **African Queens**, 1977

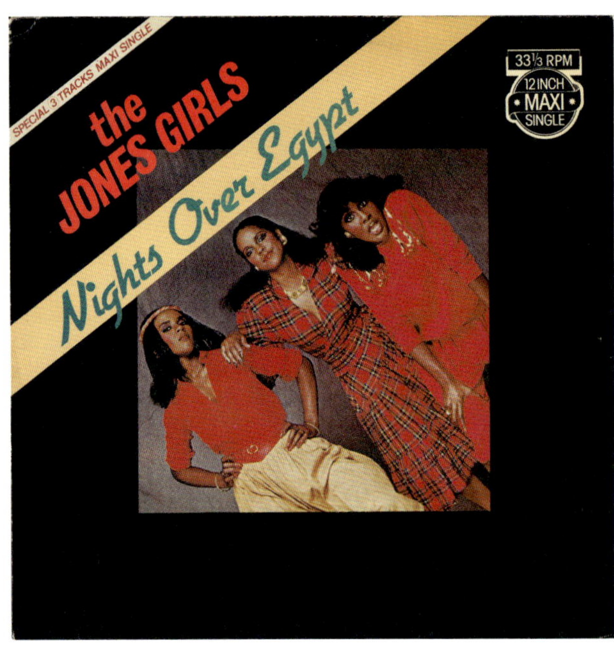

Pl. 129. The Jones Girls, **Nights Over Egypt**, 1981

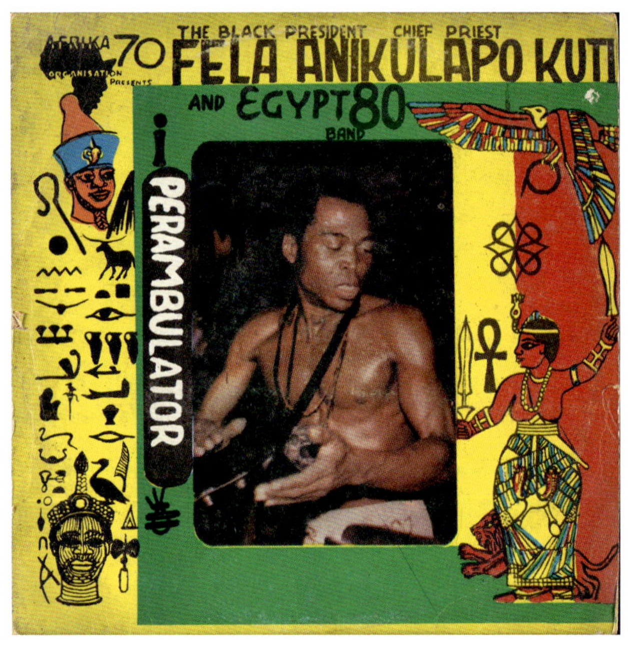

Pl. 130. Fela Kuti and Egypt 80, **Perambulator**, 1983

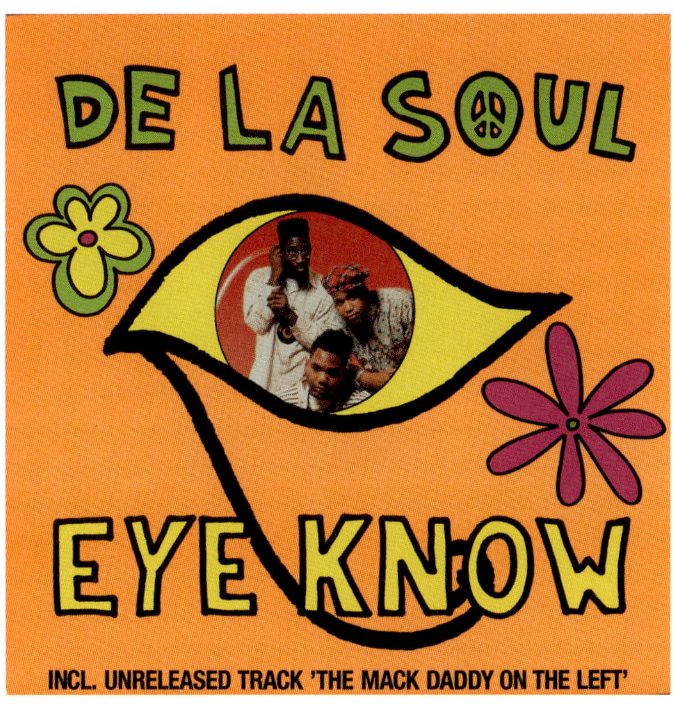

Pl. 131. De La Soul, **Eye Know**, 1989

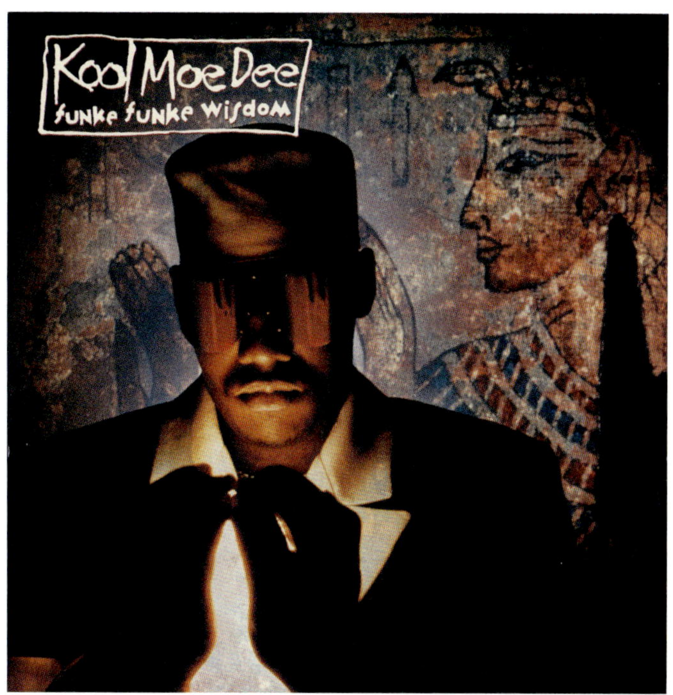

Pl. 132. Kool Moe Dee, **Funke Funke Wisdom**, 1991

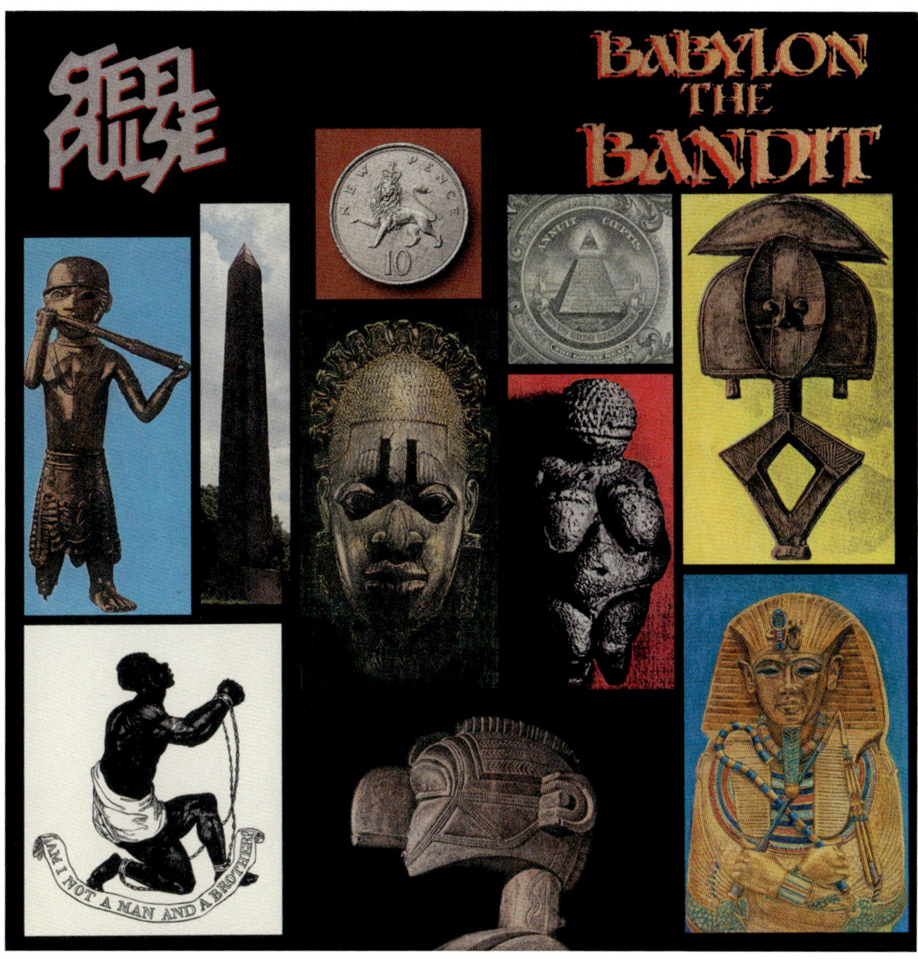

Pl. 133. Steel Pulse, **Babylon the Bandit**, 1985

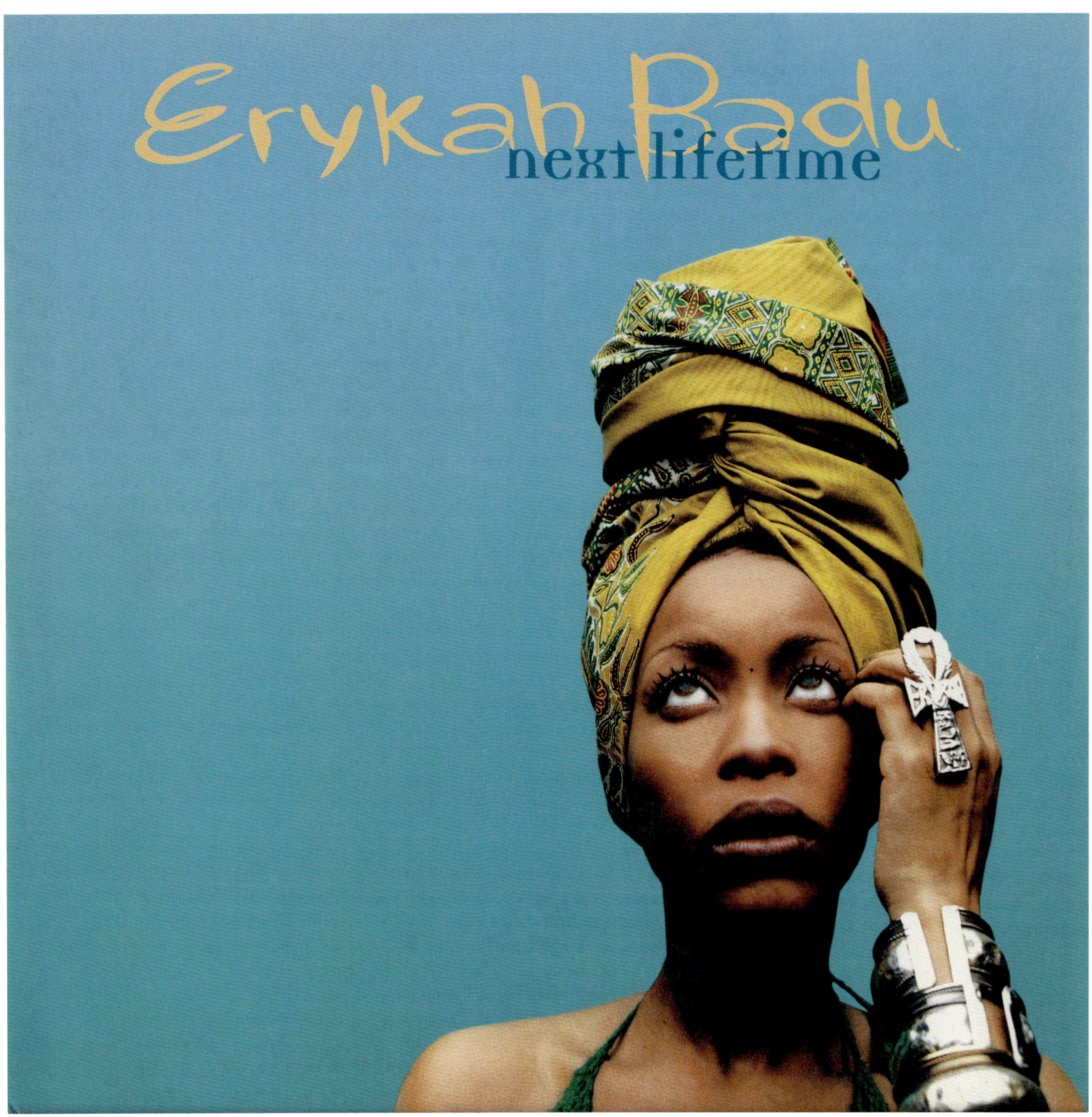

Pl. 134. Erykah Badu, **Next Lifetime**, 1997

Erykah Badu

I was eight years old. I lived in Dallas, Texas. I'm five generations Dallas, Texas, and all I'd ever seen aesthetically, in my view, had been us in our modern way. And I always thought there had to be something else.

I was riding in a car with my grandmother, and we were in our neighborhood, South Dallas. There was an African braiding shop, and the sign was a painting, just black paint on a white background, of two ladies in profile with long flowing thick coils of wavy hair depicting braids. I asked my grandmother if I could get my hair braided like that. When I went into the shop, there was a lady there who called herself Isis. There was African drumming and there were masks from the Pan-African Connection store. Instead of chairs, there were little stools made of wood. Later, I found out they were little altars, and I felt like I walked into the rest of my life.

We had a lot of community events. Harambee Festival was one where all of the Afrocentric people would get together from your city in one block to sell their goods and natural African products, oils, and incense. Little girls would dance African dances that they had learned from their teachers. That's when I was introduced to the idea of "it" (the place).

With the Afrocentricity of the late '80s, the leather medallion took the place of the fat gold chain, and hip-hop went to Africa. This is when I really began to be curious about who we are. I went to Grambling State University, a Historically Black College/University. There were people just like me fighting for the right to know who we were. Because, at that age, that's what you want to do: you want to fight. I was approached by the Five Percenters, an organization started in the mid-1970s as a spin-off of the Nation of Islam. It was created out of the need that Black people had to belong or to remember or to gather the pieces. We were taught that the Black man was God—not Almighty God, but his or her God—because we had all the choices and things we needed to build whatever we needed inside of us. From there, we naturally went into Kemetic studies because once you learn Jesus is Black, you want to know, "Who else is Black?"

I left college and started my music career, taking all these things with me: the headwrap and the Ankh and those things I had learned in school. I took just little pieces of each thing, like Heru, and gathered them together to make my own Baduizm, who I was. Now I am still hungry because that center thing, "it," hole, is still not filled. Now I want to know the history. Now I

want to touch the walls. Now I want to understand the theories.
I met Baaba Heru and his wife, Queen Afua, who is our holistic
guru, and their son Supernova when, after college, I got a record
deal and I moved to Brooklyn, New York. I went right back
into school in their house, where we learned the language, the
glyphs, the colors, the coding, the sacred geometry, the origins,
how other things were derivatives of this ancient culture, how it
was all over the continent, remnants of it, and were encouraged
to study it. Heru taught me Kemet 101 from the ancient *Book
of the Dead*, the *Metu Neter*. Once you get immersed in it, you
become a part of it. And I've never even been to Egypt to this
day. But I'm so in tune with it. I don't know if it belongs to me
or if it belongs to us, but it calls to me, its symbols, its language.
When I speak the language, I feel the vibration in my spine as
it's supposed to be. I named my children in accordance with
those stars. So, as it's calling to me, I am also calling back to
it, and when it's time to go, I'll be ready.

Baaba Heru brought some things to my attention when he
made a ring for me. There was no way I would know that it
would become a symbol that quietly made an impact all over
the world. The symbol itself is a word and the word is life. My
creative imagination wants to believe that I had something to

do with opening a portal in the world, no matter how quirky I am or what people think of me. My mission, one of them, was to open this portal with the key. The key is little by little seeping into the minds of everyone, and we're getting closer and closer to the day of freedom. Freedom for the slaves and the slave masters through the key.

Every album that I have released has Kemetic coding in it. I'm very cryptic with the things that I say, and I feel in my mind that at some point there will be some magical cue for me to release it all and reveal the truth. It's my creative imagination that also got me to this point where I am, closer to Kemet, closer to my best work in music that's still in me, you know? So, it all goes together somehow, and when I find out the truth, I'll let you know.

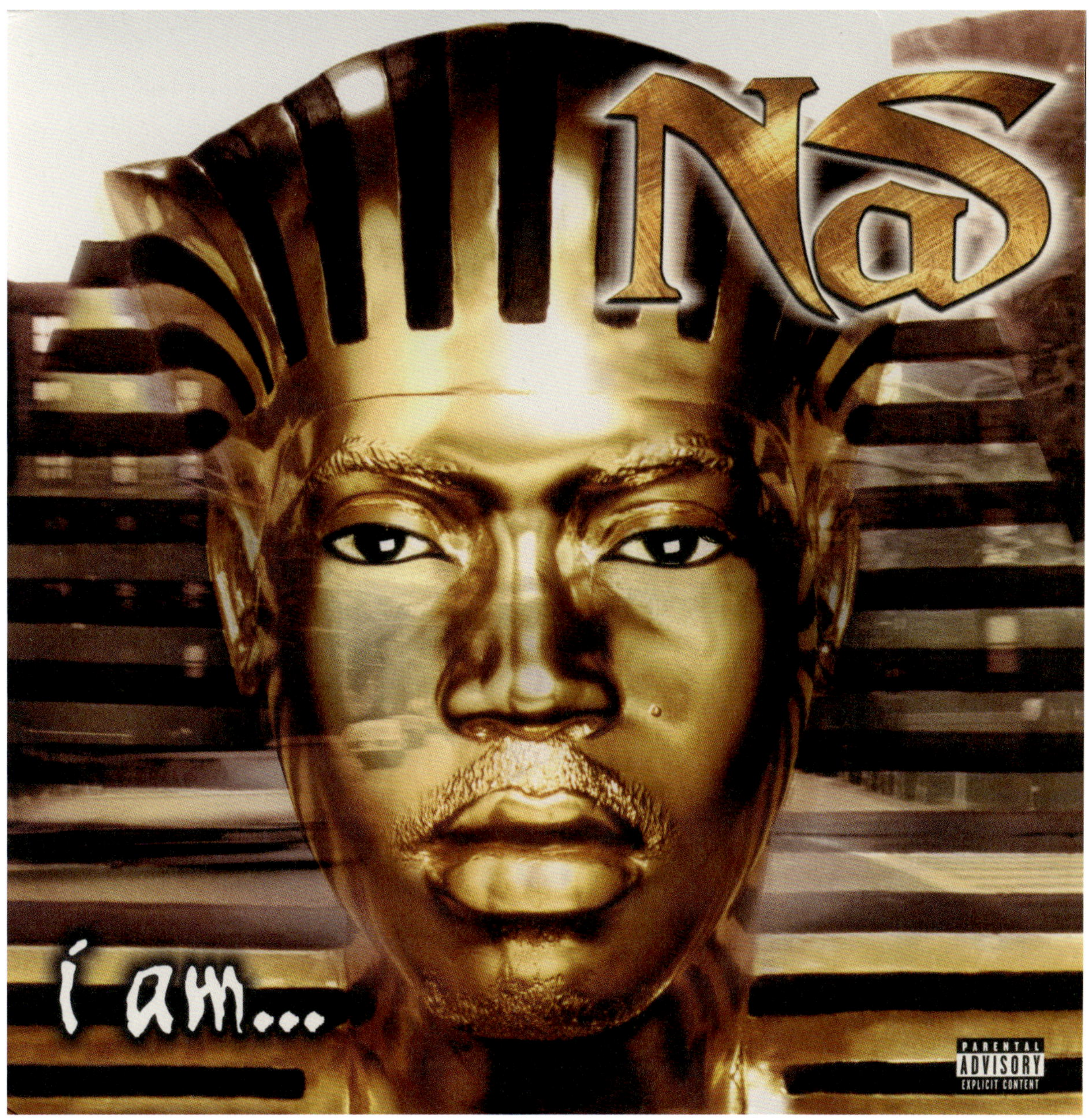

Pl. 135. Nas, **I Am . . .** , 1999

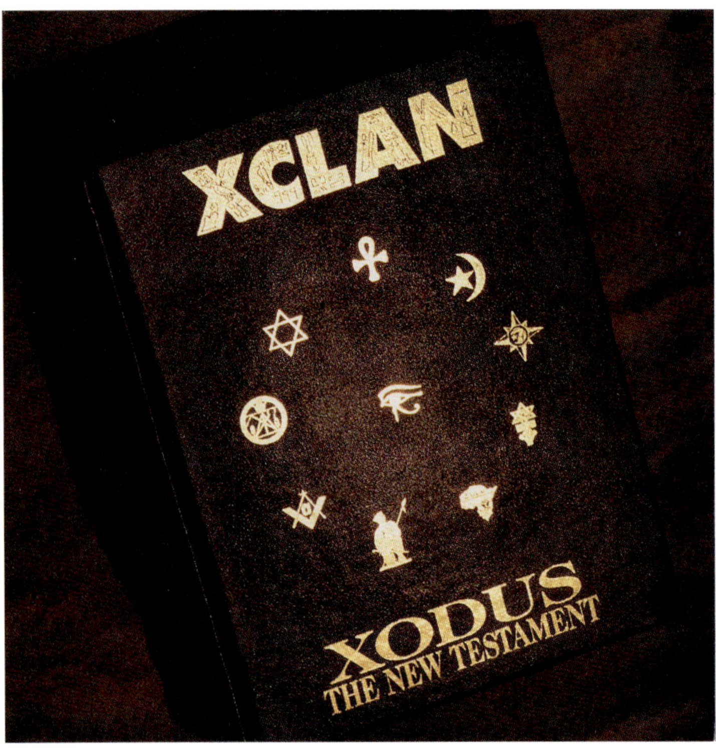

Pl. 136. X Clan, **Xodus (The New Testament)**, 1992

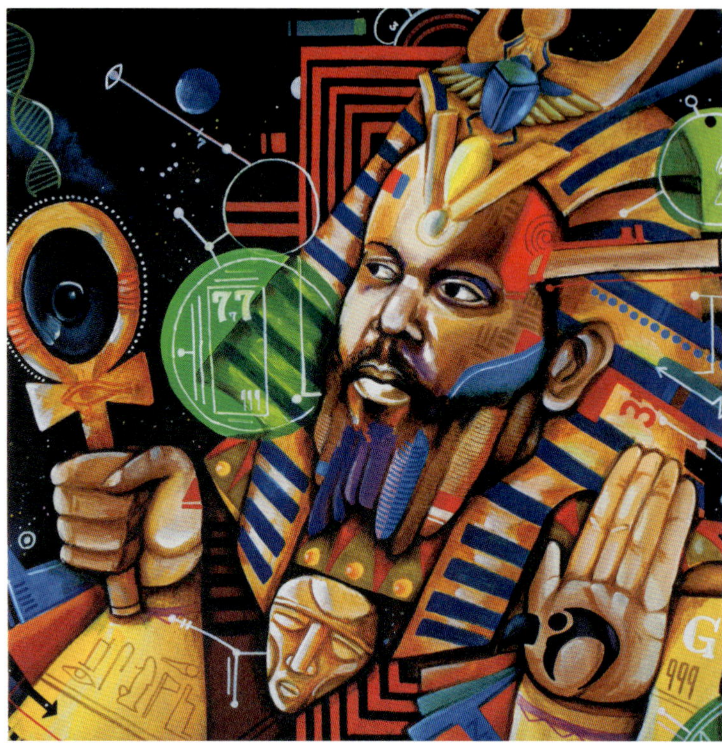

Pl. 137. Ras G and The Afrikan Space Program, **Back on the Planet**, 2013

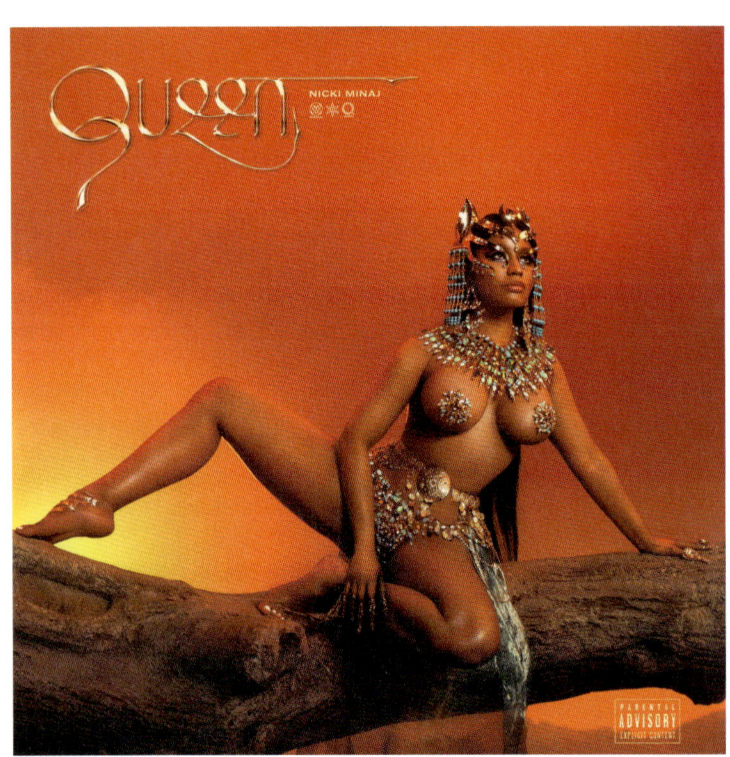

Pl. 138. Nicki Minaj, **Queen**, 2018

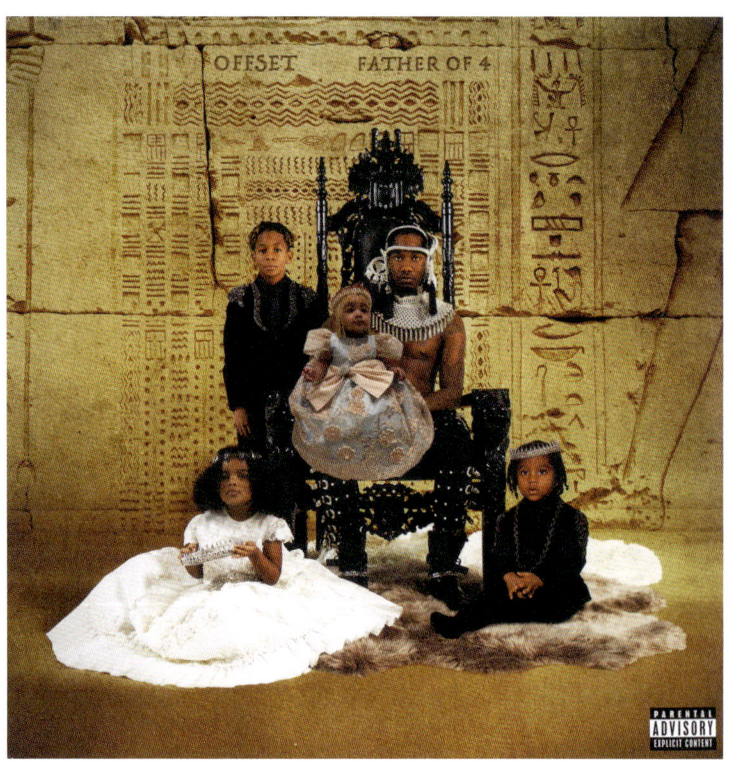

Pl. 139. Offset, **Father of 4**, 2019

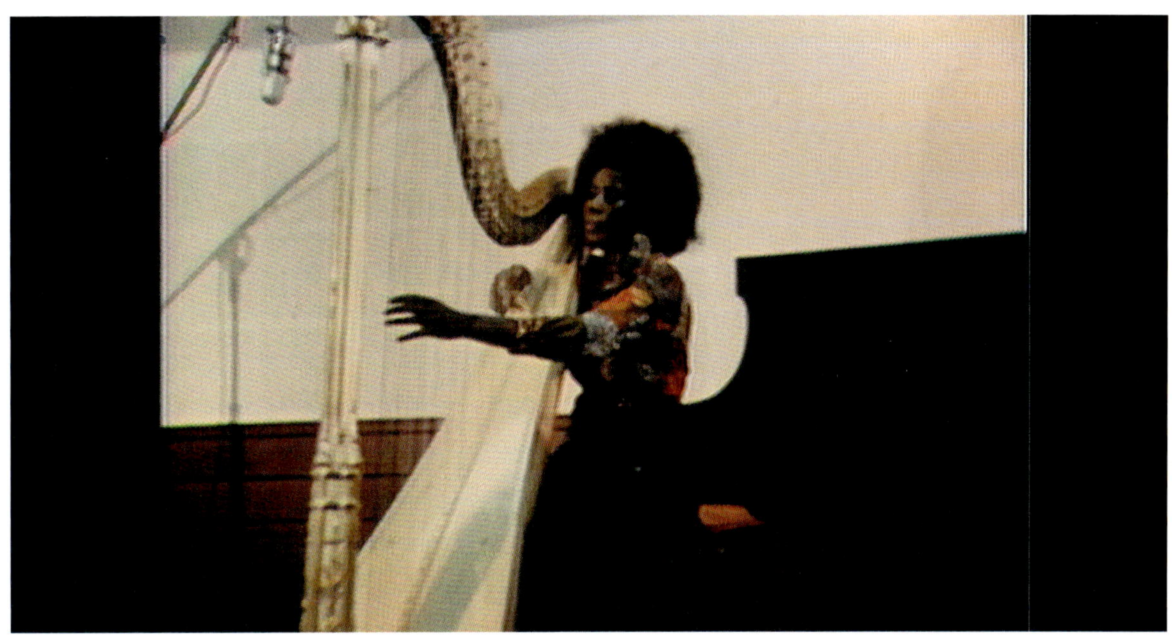

Pl. 140. Still from "Alice Coltrane," **Black Journal**, 1970

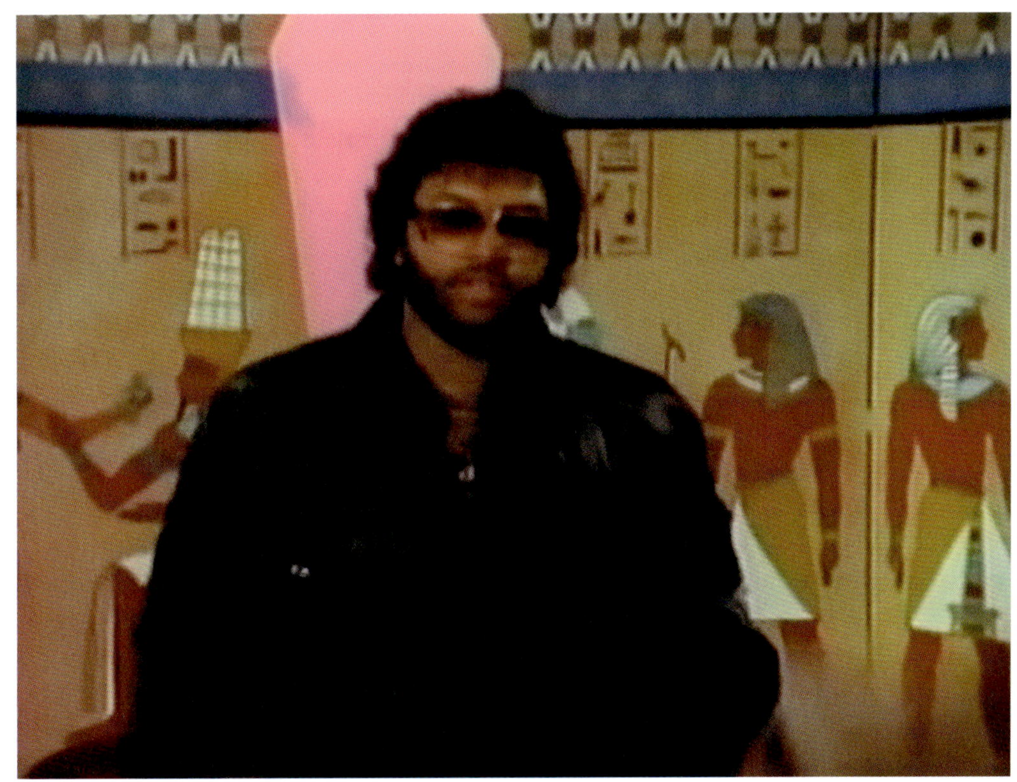

Pl. 141. Still from The Egyptian Lover, **Freak-A-Holic**, 1986

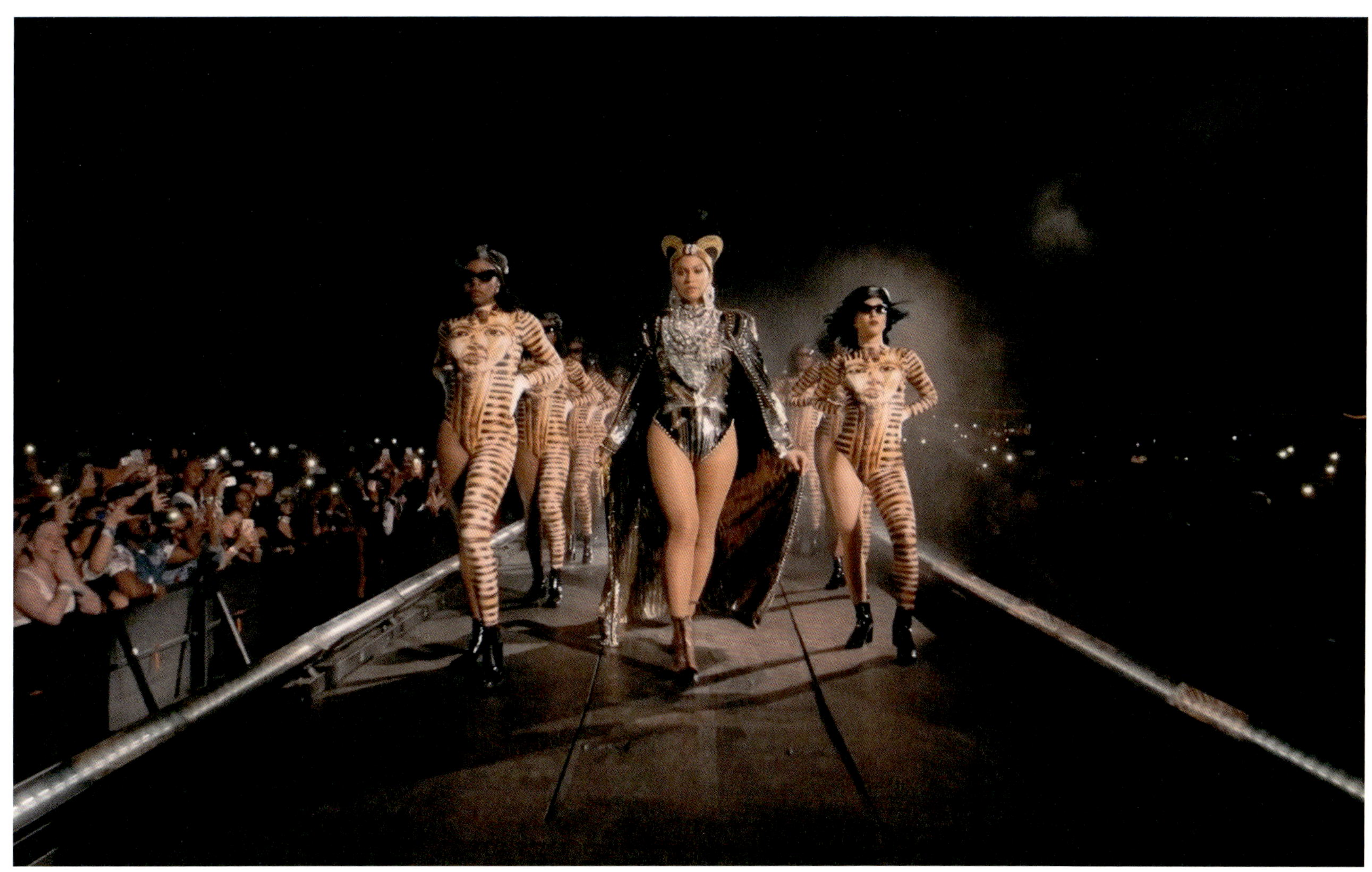

Pl. 142. Still from **Homecoming: A Film by Beyoncé**, 2019

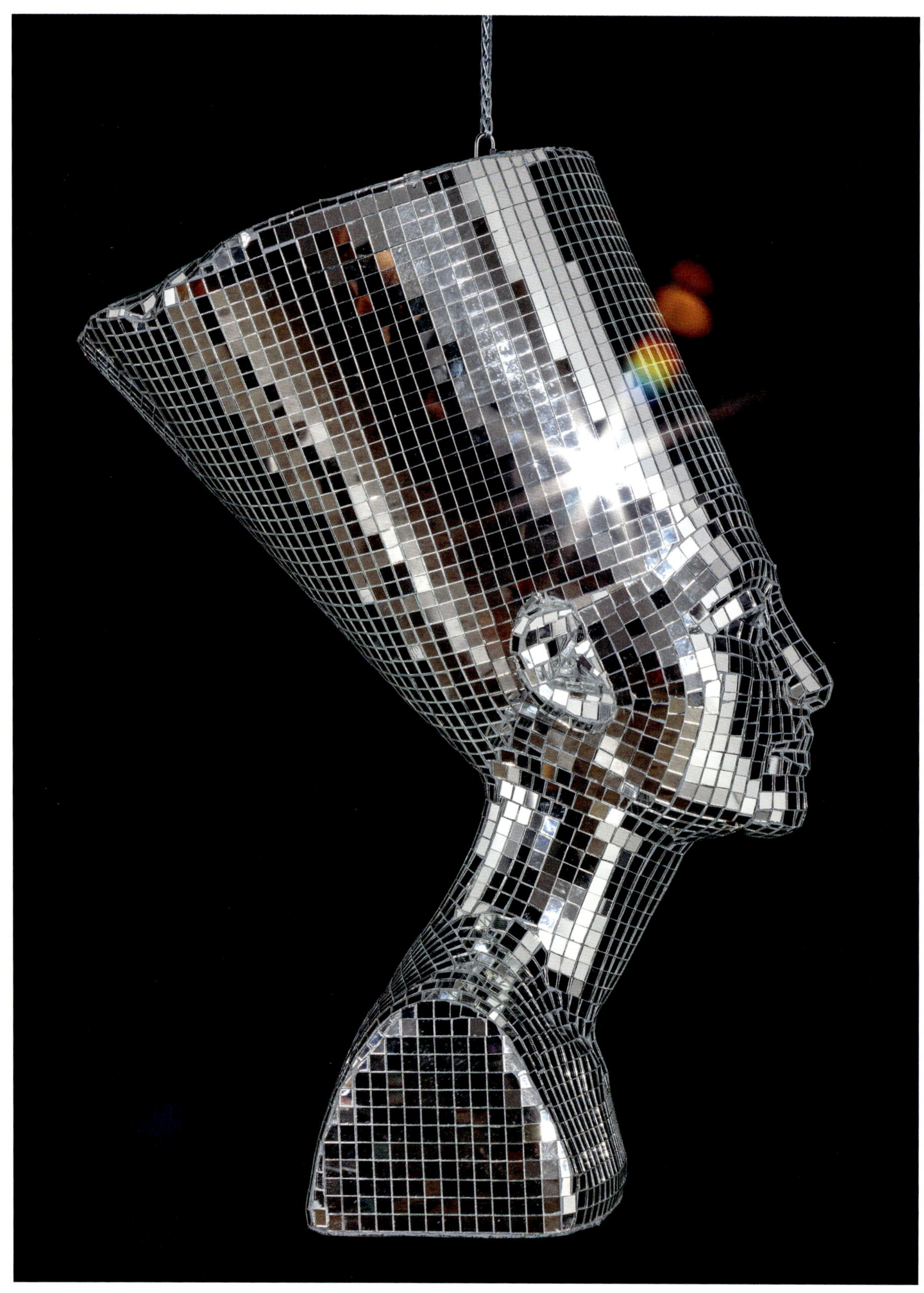

Pl. 143. Awol Erizku, **Nefertiti–Miles Davis**, 2017

Awol Erizku

Viva Egypt (Tahyā Misr)

The allure of ancient Egypt remains undiminished, from its towering pyramids that pierce the horizon to the enigmatic hieroglyphs etched intricately upon temple walls and the regal pharaohs who once ruled its lands. This civilization continues to captivate the global imagination, its significance transcending temporal boundaries to hold profound sway over diverse cultures across both time and space. In the vein of historian Cheikh Anta Diop's intellectual zeal, I aim to embark on an exploration of the multifaceted reasons behind ancient Egypt's vitality and influence, illuminating its role in shaping our comprehension of history, culture, spirituality, and human identity.

Egypt emerges as a testament to the shared African heritage interwoven into the fabric of humanity. In his book *The African Origin of Civilization: Myth or Reality* (1974) and other writings, Diop fervently championed the notion that the cradle of civilization did not rest within the confines of the Greco-Roman world, as Eurocentric theories had propagated, but rather at the heart of Africa itself. Egypt, in Diop's perceptive view, served as the bridge connecting antiquity with the modern era—an intellectual and cultural fulcrum that magnificently showcased the splendors of African accomplishments.

To Diop, Egypt stood as a living testament to the advanced scientific knowledge and spiritual profundity that thrived within African societies. The architectural marvels of the pyramids, the meticulous precision of the calendar, and the mastery of medical arts all bore witness to the intricate ingenuity of Egypt's people. Moreover, the hieroglyphs and inscriptions unveiled a unique vista into the Egyptian worldview, reflecting their veneration for cosmic harmony and their ceaseless quest for eternal truths. Egypt, according to Diop, embodied the African spirit of innovation, resilience, and sagacity, making its reclamation a pivotal endeavor to dismantle the fetters of historical misrepresentation.

More than an archaeological wonderland, Egypt stands as a reservoir of wisdom—a cultural tapestry interwoven with threads of diversity and complexity. It symbolizes the enduring potency of human creativity. The grandeur of its pyramids, the Sphinx, and its temples does not evoke awe solely due to their monumental stature, but because they encapsulate the timeless human ambition to etch an indelible legacy upon the annals of existence. These colossal structures, meticulously engineered, symbolize the relentless human pursuit of knowledge and innovation—an inspiration that resonates with artists, architects, engineers, and dreamers alike.

Withal, ancient Egypt emerges as a historical crossroads—a melting pot of cultures, faiths, and philosophies. Positioned as a conduit between Africa and the Middle East, it fostered a rich exchange of ideas and commodities, culminating in a synthesis of diverse influences. This amalgamation is manifest in the diversity of religious observances, artistic expressions, and languages that adorn the cultural mosaic of ancient Egypt.

In an equally profound manner, Egypt embodies the intricate interplay between the temporal and the eternal. Its intricate belief systems and elaborate funerary customs reflect a nuanced comprehension of life's impermanence and humanity's yearning for transcendence. The sarcophagi and artifacts whisper tales of lives lived, providing glimpses into antiquated eras while inciting introspection regarding the universal themes of mortality and existence. In this essence, ancient Egypt serves as a mirror, reflecting our shared human journey and our inherent quest to comprehend the time that we experience.

In closing, I would like to offer the following: Egypt's magnetic charm persists as a vessel of inspiration, an intellectual voyage that continues to stir profound reflections. Much like the protagonists in the parable of the blind men and the elephant, even seasoned Egyptologists find themselves perpetually discovering new facets of its allure. As the artifacts of ancient Egypt remain a collective legacy bestowed upon humanity, their resounding importance echoes most potently among those of African descent. From these remnants, a rich historical narrative unfolds, inviting individuals to connect with the distant reverberations of their ancestral roots. While Hollywood's lens may inadvertently misrepresent history, it is imperative that individuals of African heritage claim their rightful engagement with Egypt's depictions and sculptures—acknowledging them as poignant symbols of their own legacy, akin to how a Eurocentric observer engages with the relics of Greece. Through this journey, we honor the perennial resonance of ancient Egypt and its enduring role as a beacon of wisdom and cultural brilliance.

Pl. 144. Awol Erizku, **Nefertiti (Black Power)**, 2018

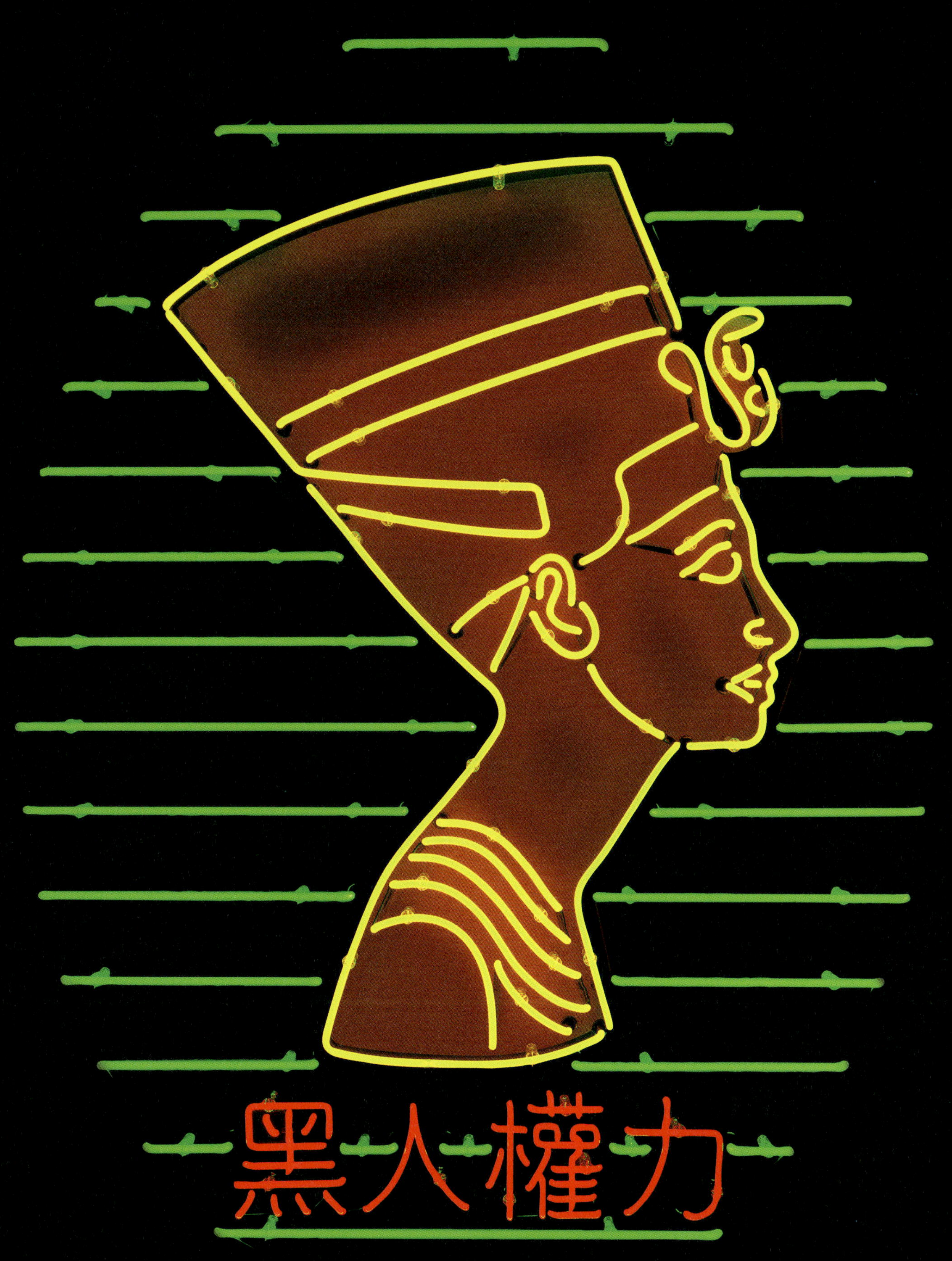
黑人權力

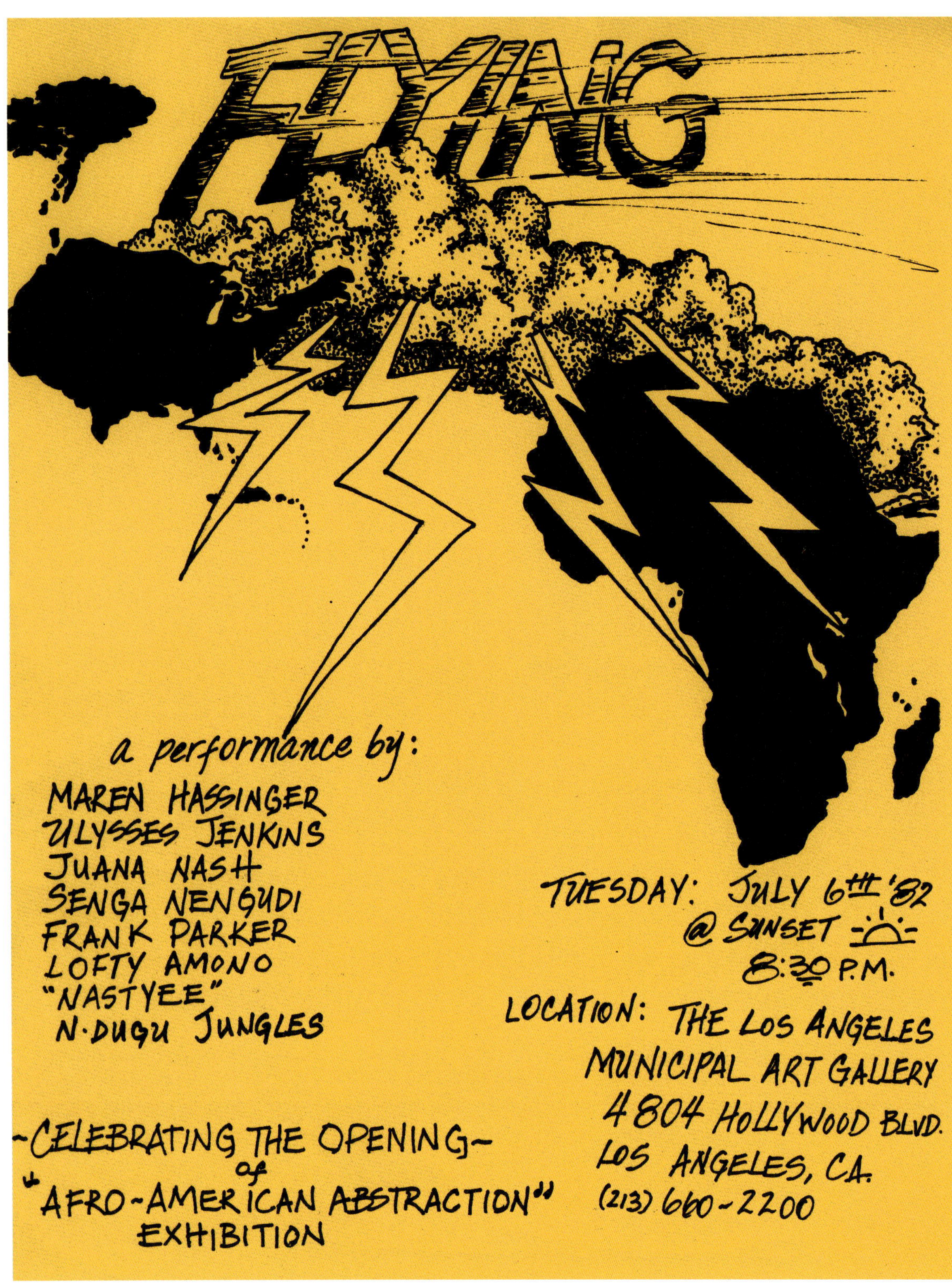

Pl. 145. Maren Hassinger, Ulysses Jenkins, Senga Nengudi, and Franklin Parker, flyer for **Flying**, 1982

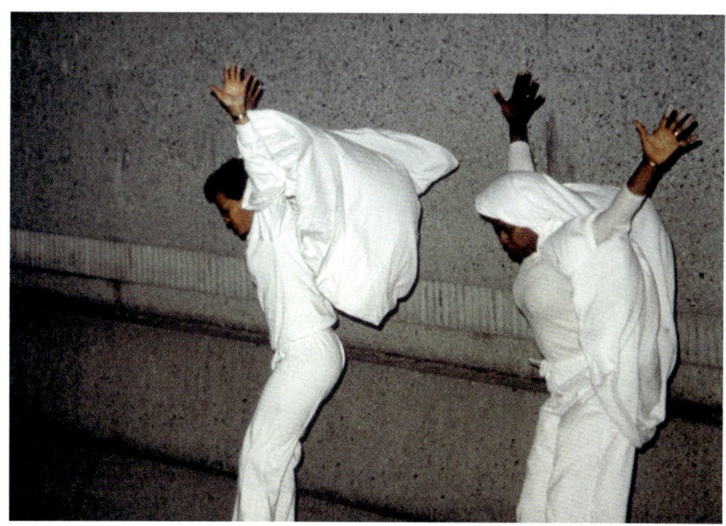

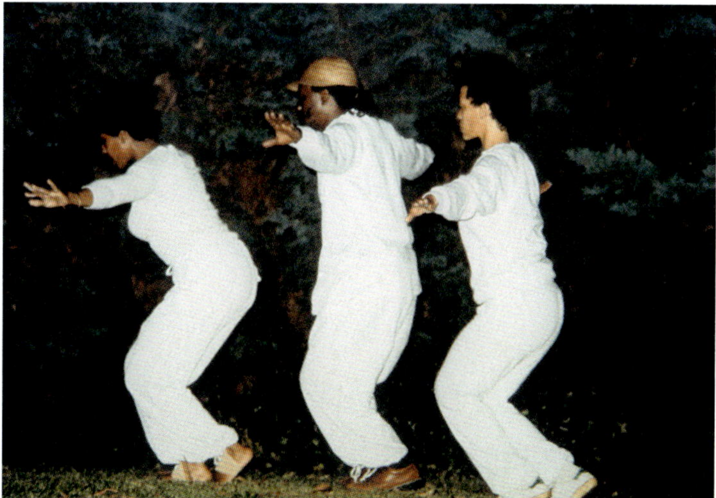

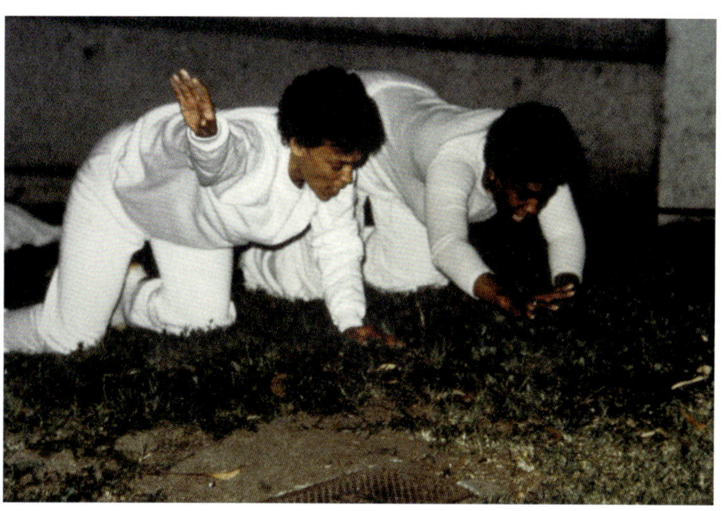

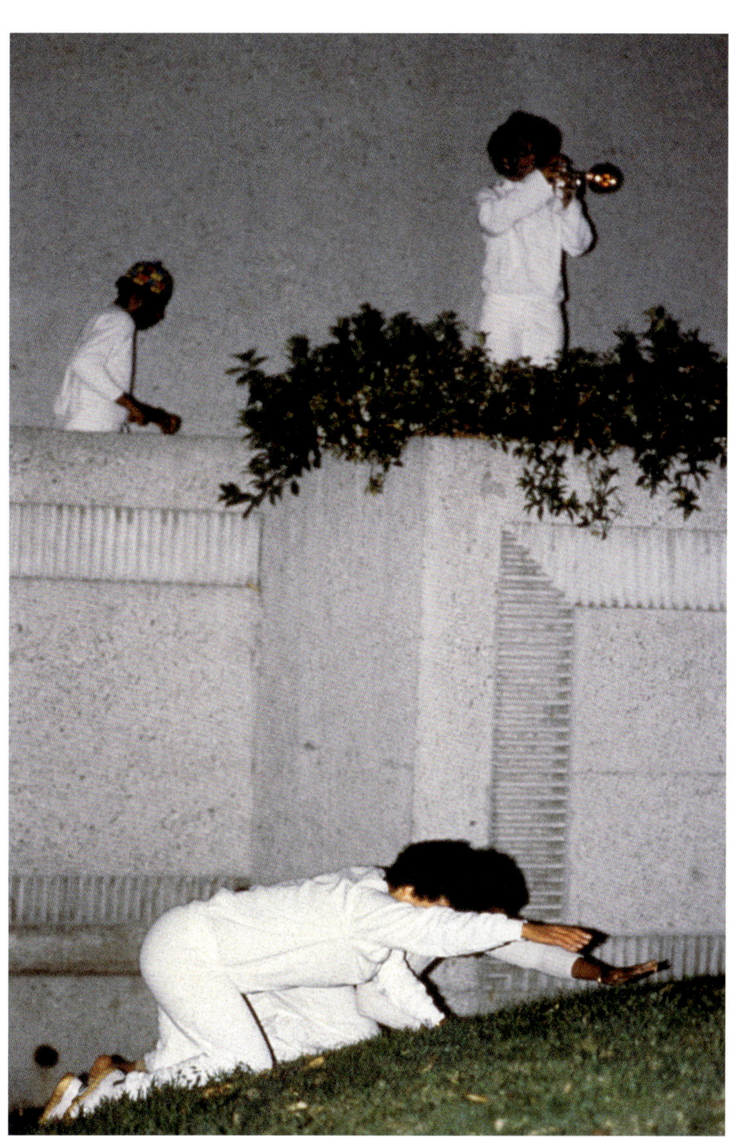

Pls. 146-49. Maren Hassinger, Ulysses Jenkins, Senga Nengudi, and Franklin Parker performing **Flying**, 1982

Terry Adkins
Luxor Solo (Mystical Score for the Ghost of Bud Powell)

Luxor Solo attempts to recover and reenact luminous aspects of
some mystical idiosyncrasies associated with the living spirit
of pianist/composer Bud Powell. It is scored for a solo male
performer wearing a black suit with white shirt and black tie,
black shoes brilliantly shined and a red fez. He stands in
a corner with a potted plant on a stand that is equal to his
height.

After a 90 second period of silence standing next to the
plant with his hands in his pockets, the performer repeats
the words "Bud" and "Powell" slowly at first and gradually
and periodically (surrendering to intuition) building into a
cacophonic stutter of the name spoken as quickly as possible.
Below is the rare image of Bud Powell that sparked this score:

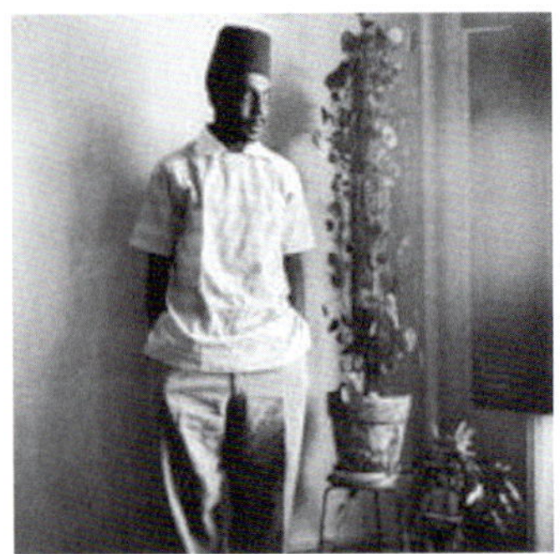

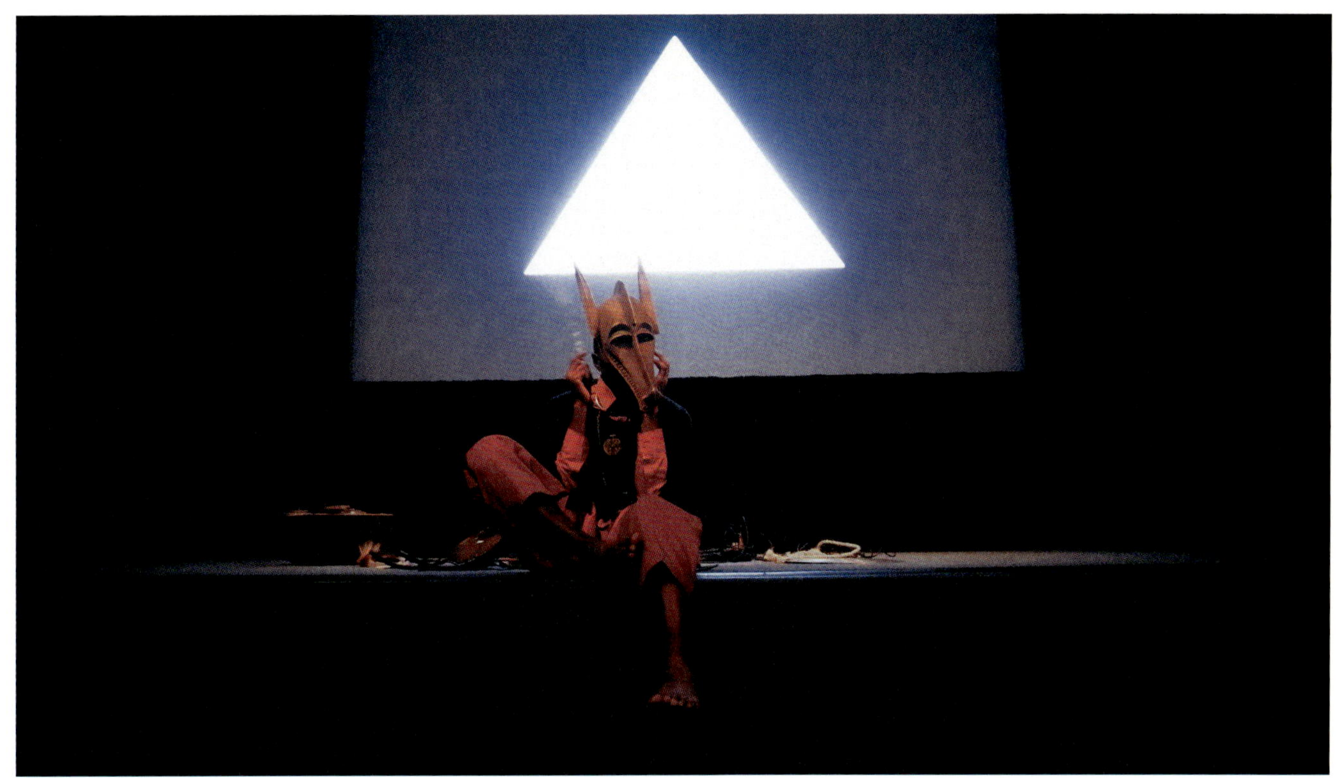

Pl. 151. Gregston Hurdle, **Kamau Amu Patton performing "Amun (The Unseen Legends),"** 2017

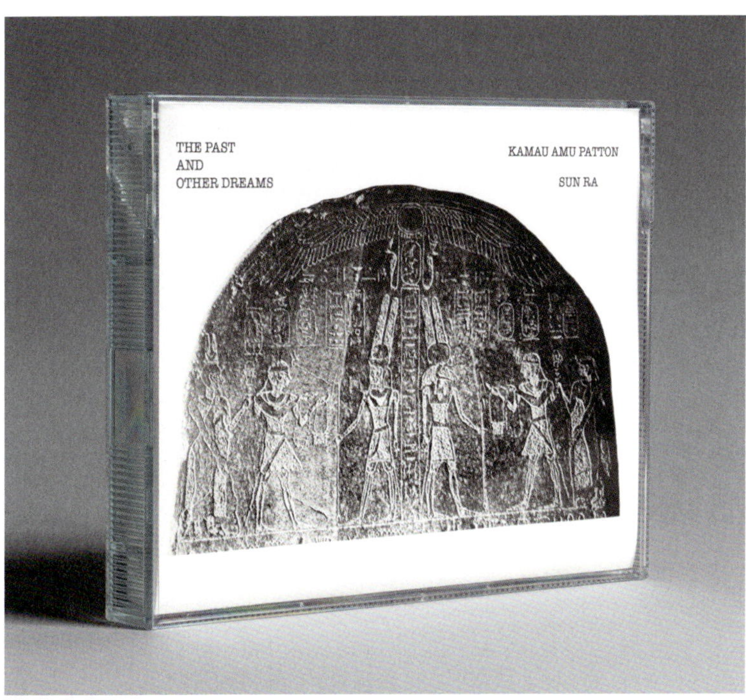

Pl. 152. Kamau Amu Patton, **The Past and Other Dreams**, 2020

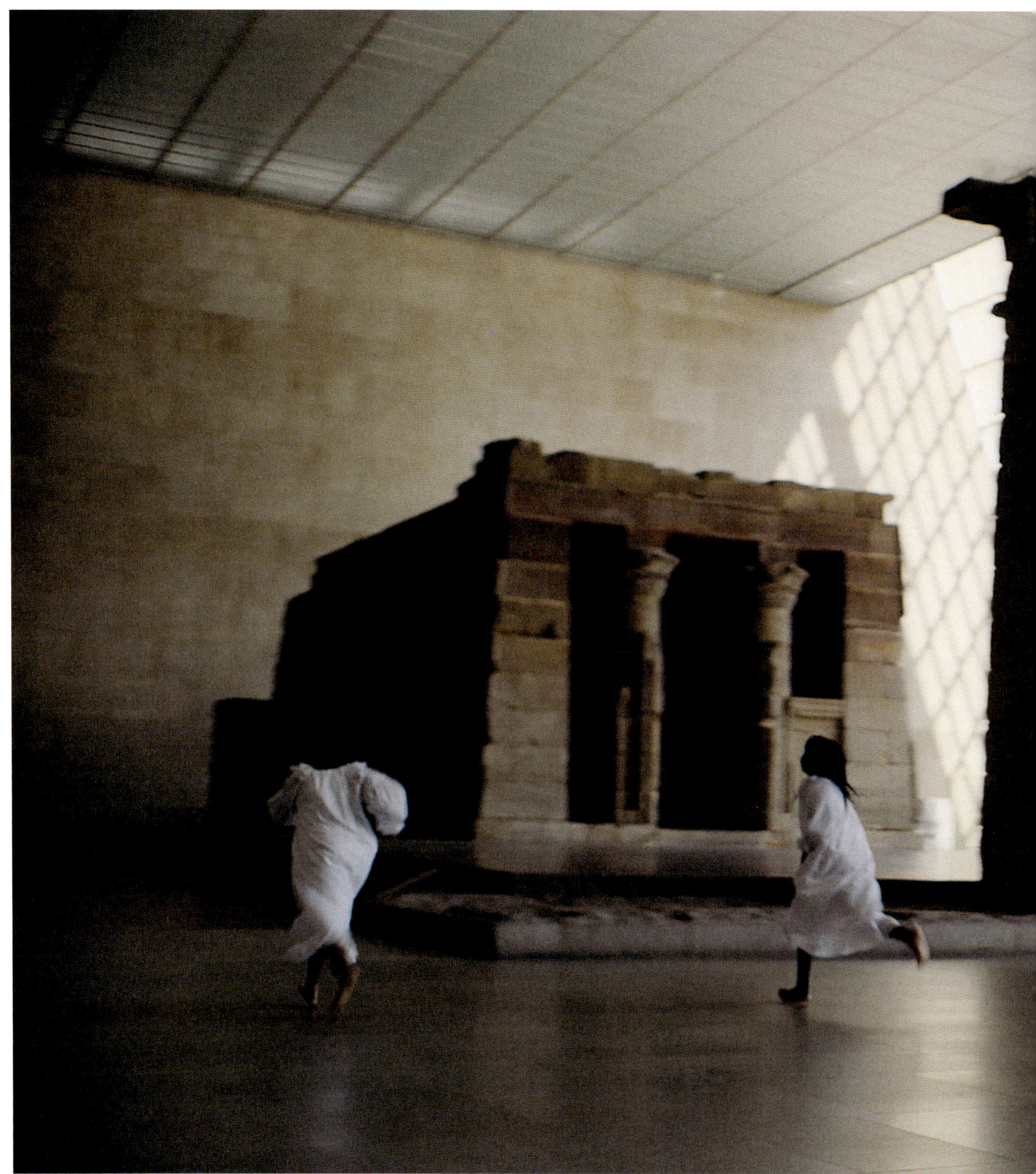

Pl. 153. Still from Rashida Bumbray, **How High the Moon**, 2024

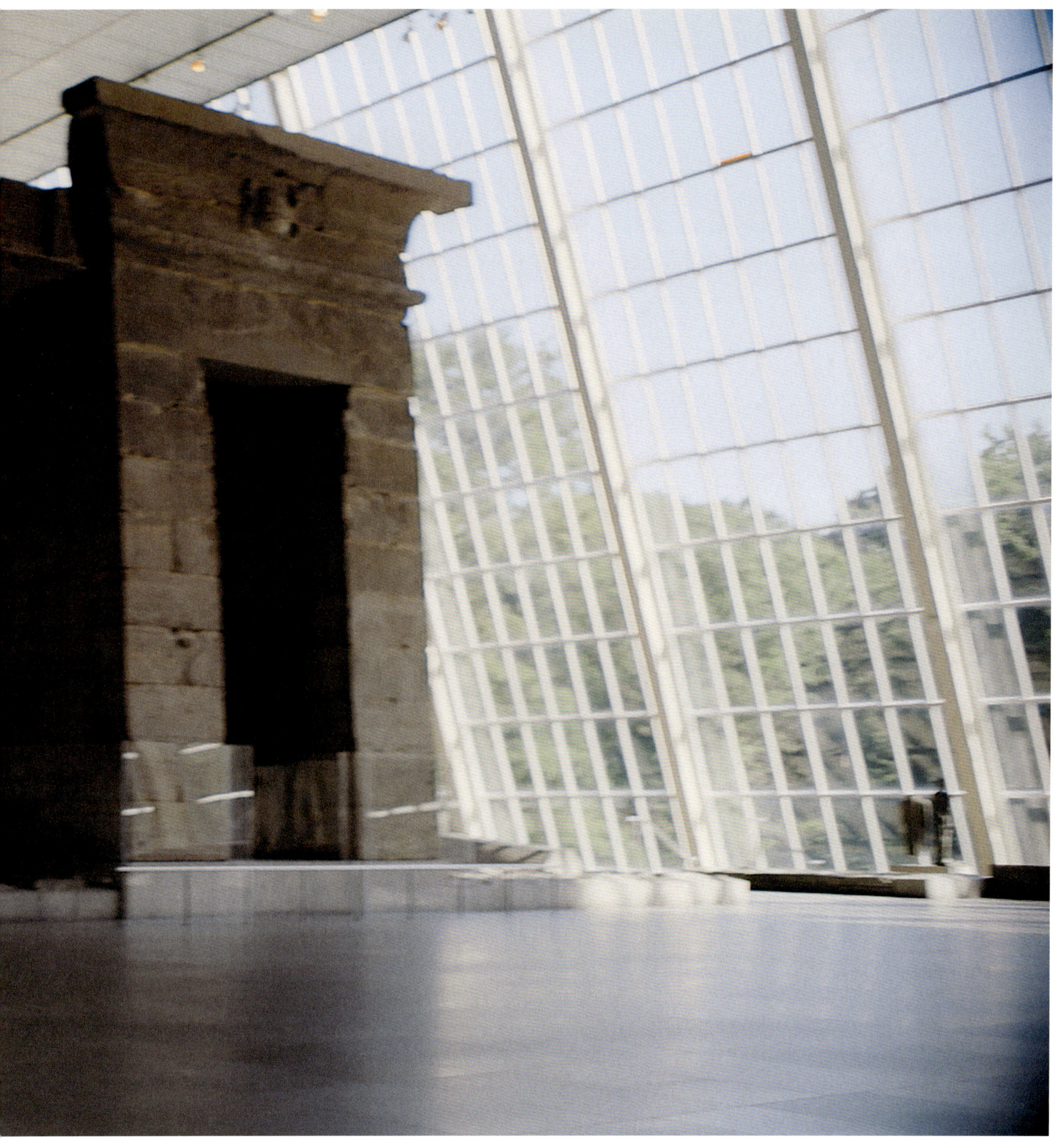

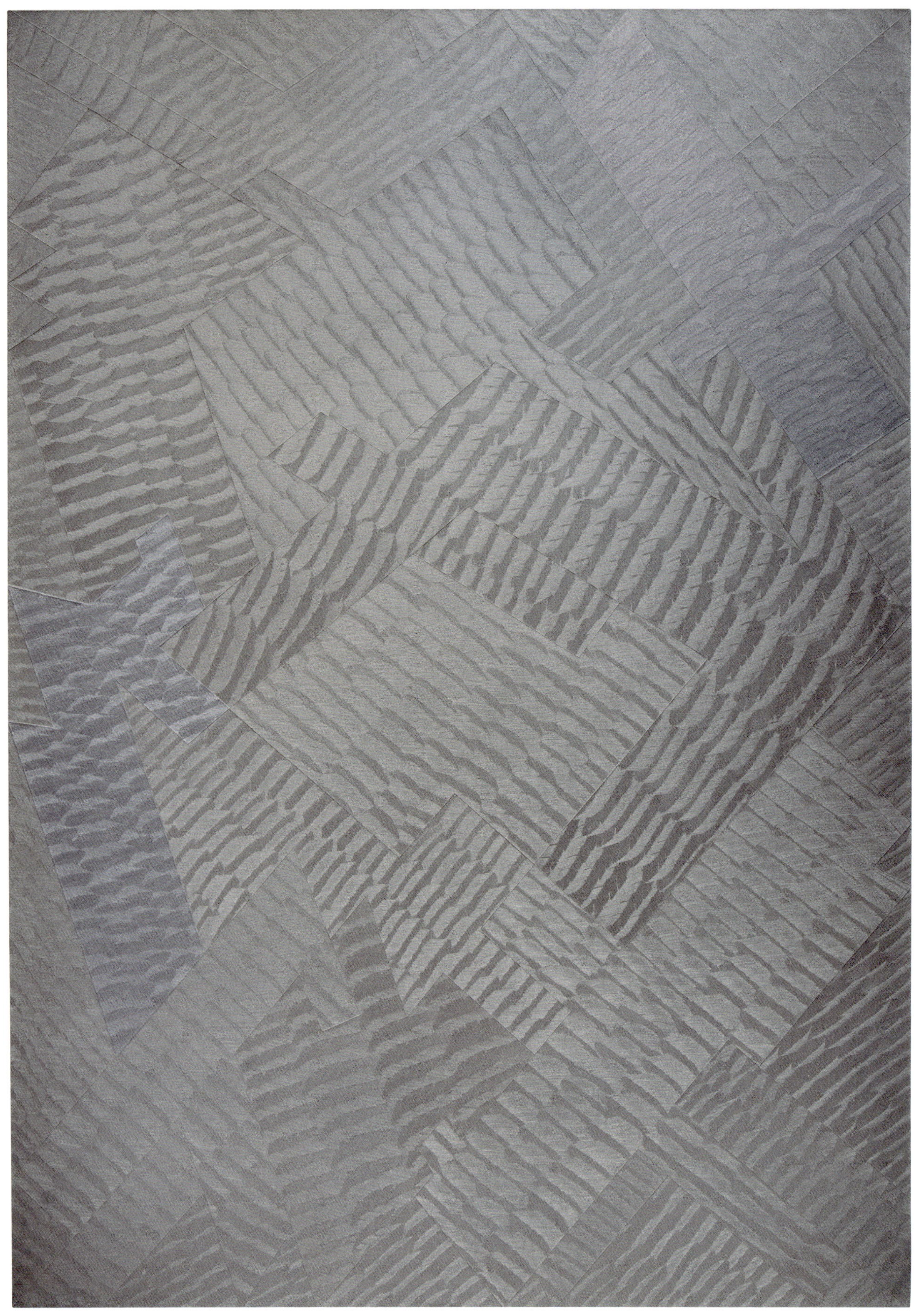

Pl. 154. William T. Williams, **Nu Nile**, 1973

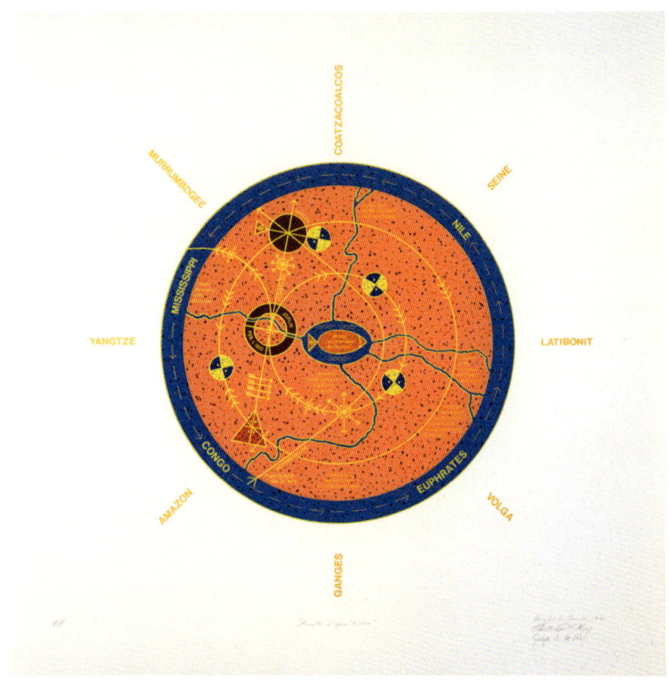

Pl. 155. Houston Conwill with Joseph De Pace and Estella Conwill Majozo, **Langston Hughes' Rivers**, 1991

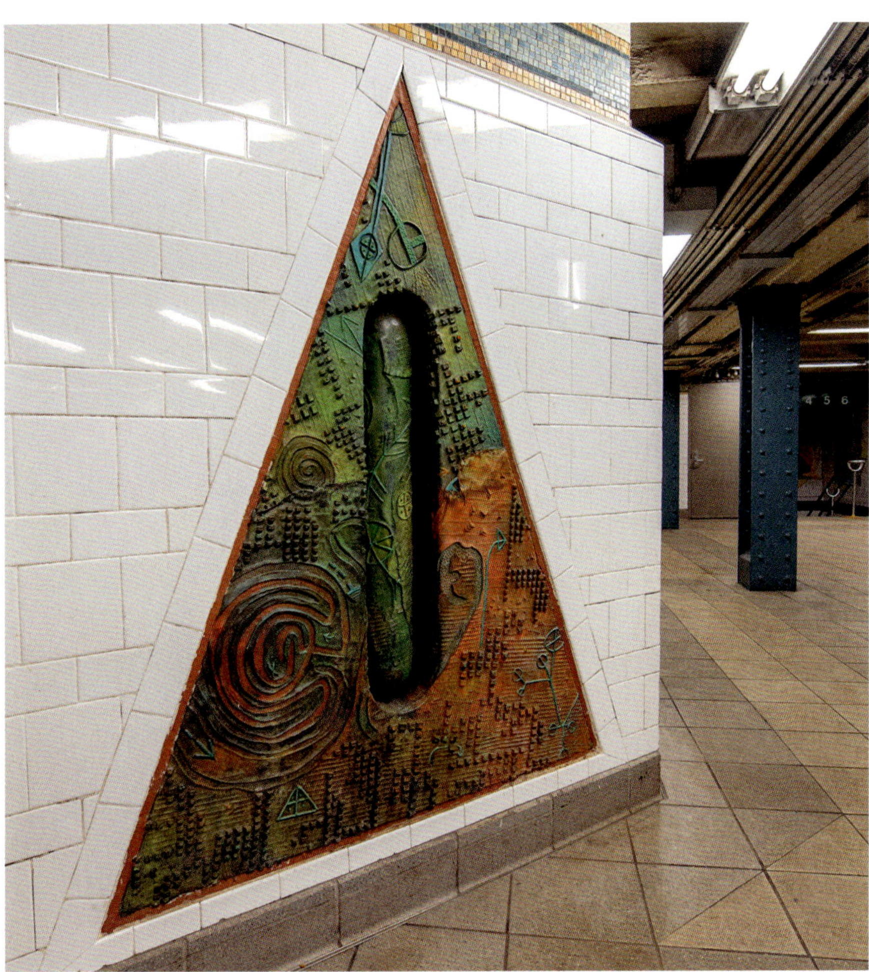

Pl. 156. Houston Conwill, **The Open Secret**, 1986

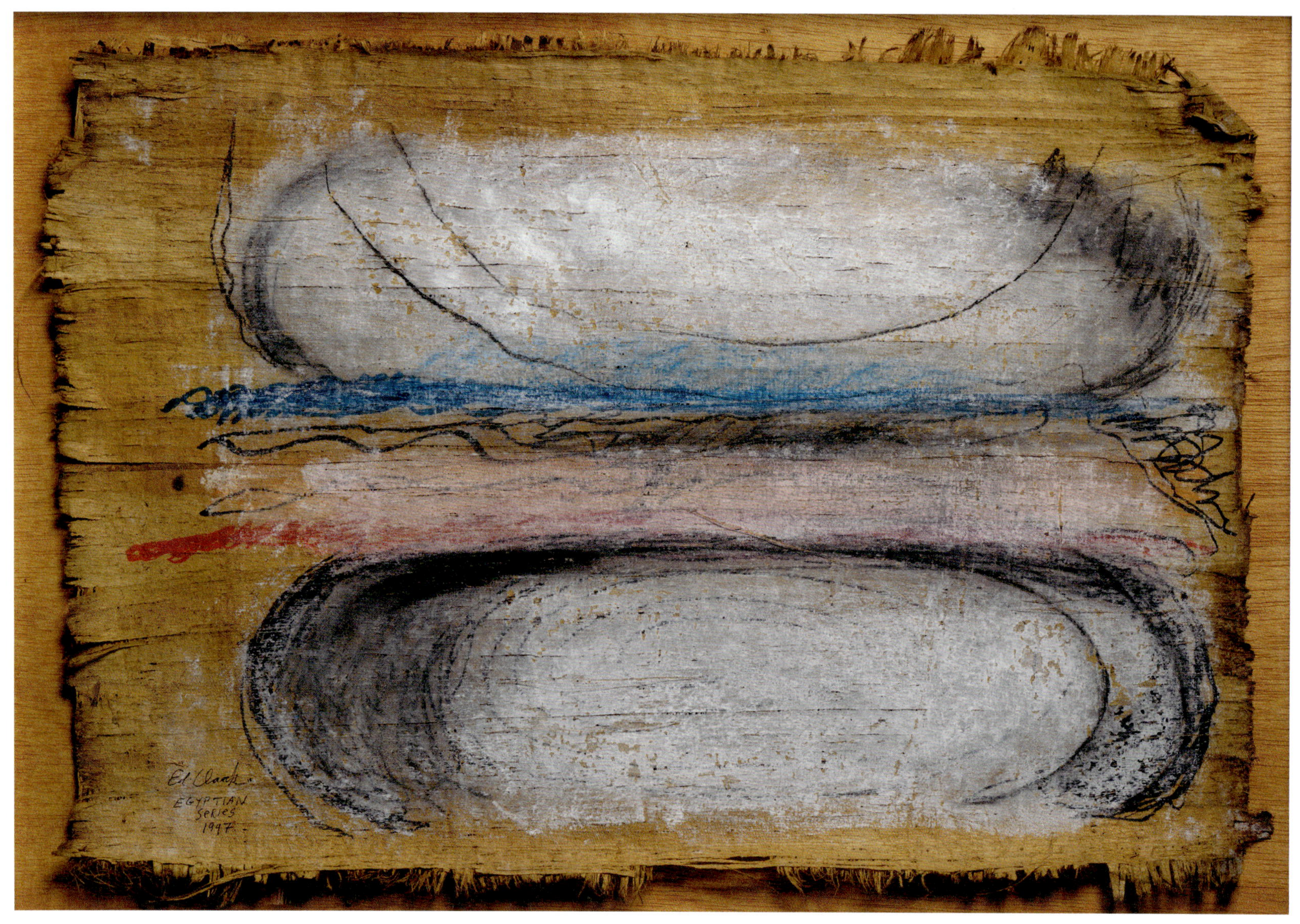

Pl. 157. Ed Clark, **Untitled (Egyptian Series)**, 1997

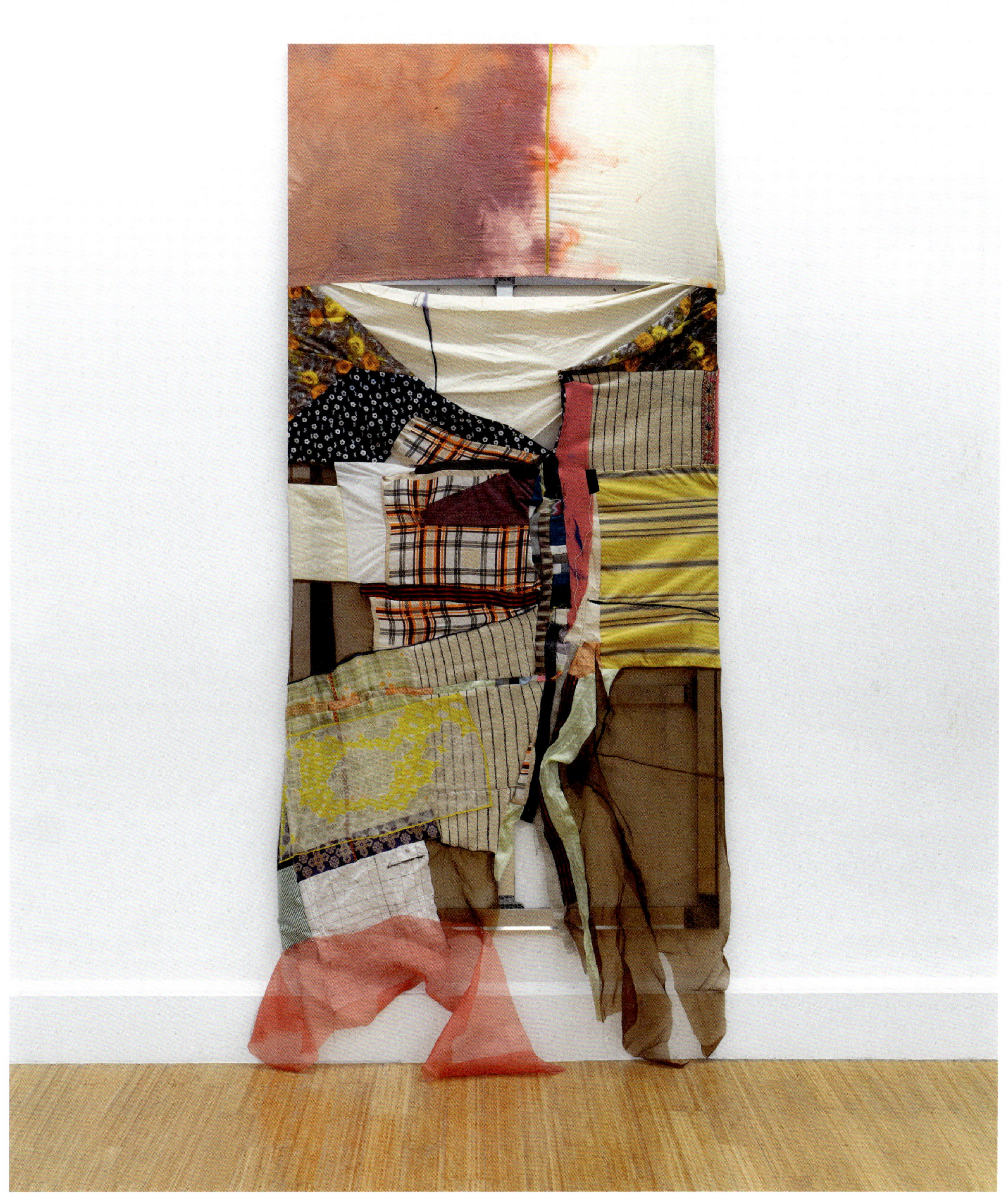

Pl. 158. Eric Mack, **See, The Sarcophagus Is Moot, Too**, 2022

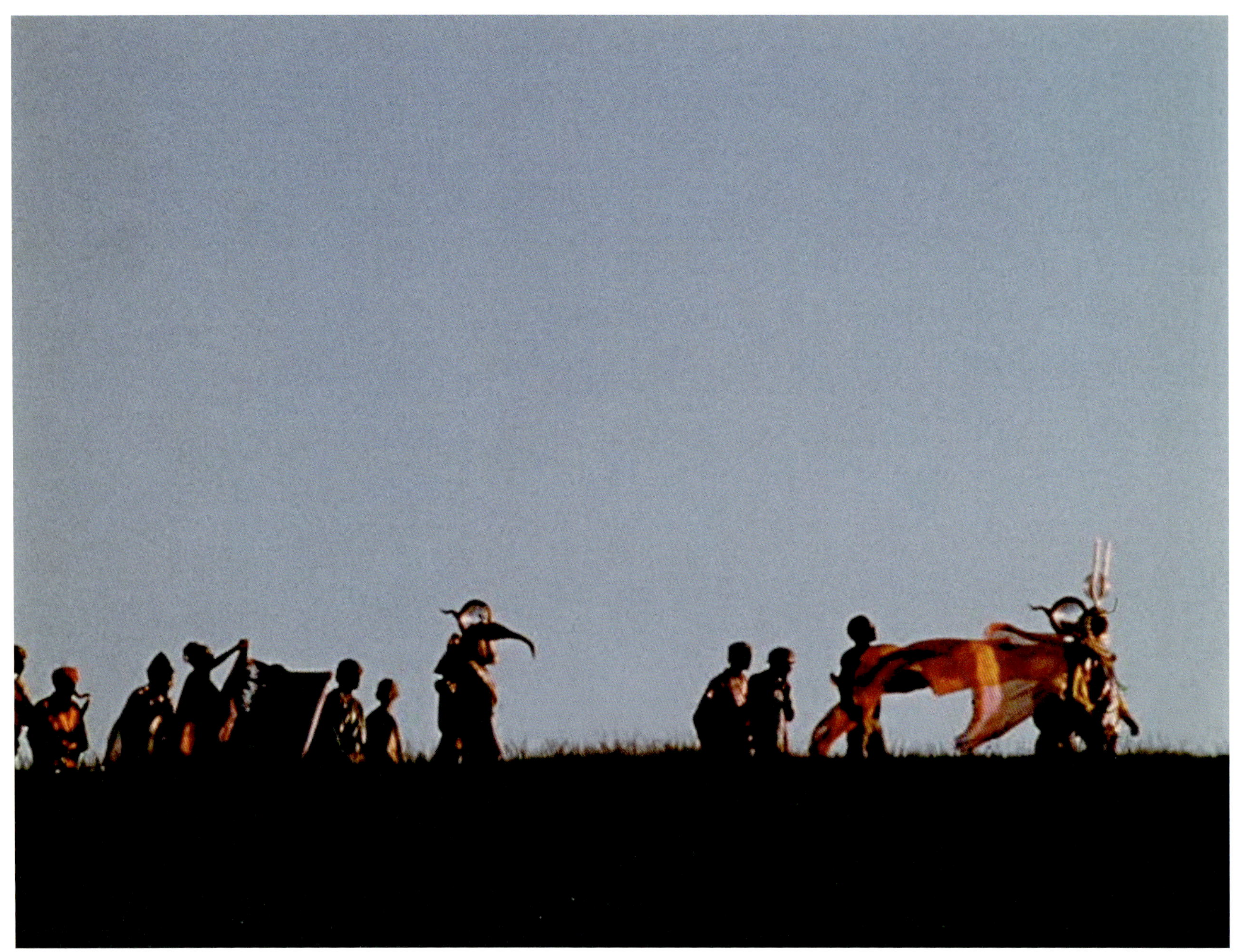

Pl. 159. Still from **Space Is the Place**, 1974

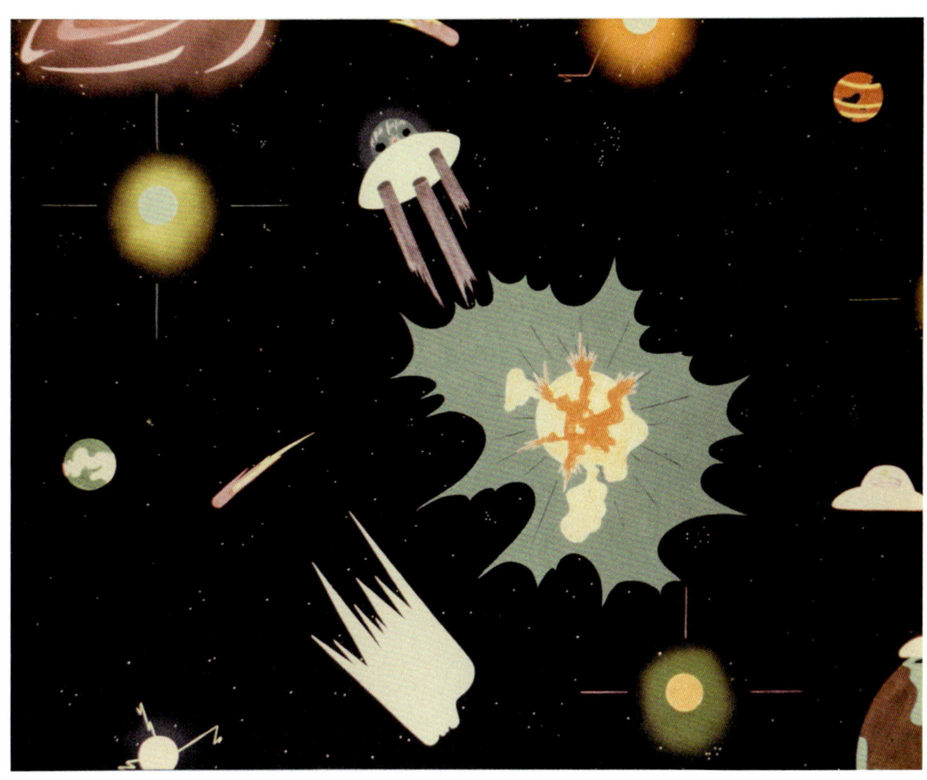

Pl. 160. Ayé Aton, **Untitled**, ca. 1975

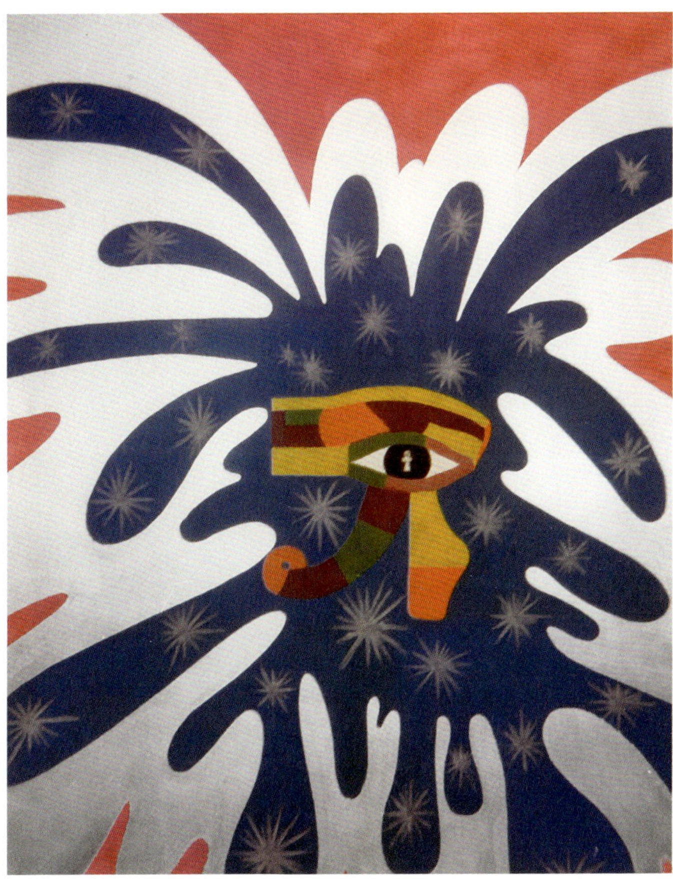

Pl. 161. Ayé Aton, **Untitled (wall mural)**, 1972

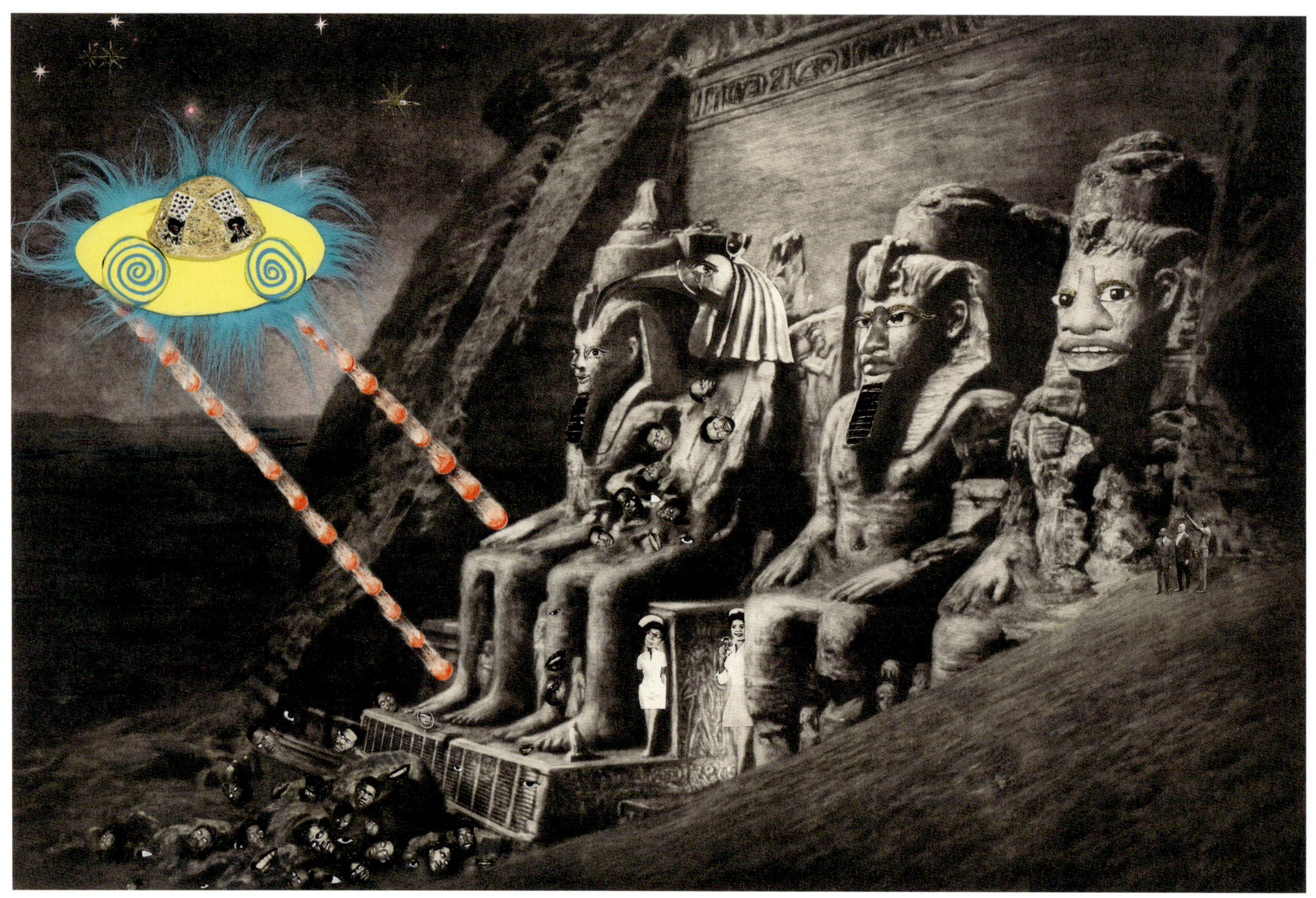

Pl. 162. Ellen Gallagher, **Abu Simbel**, 2005

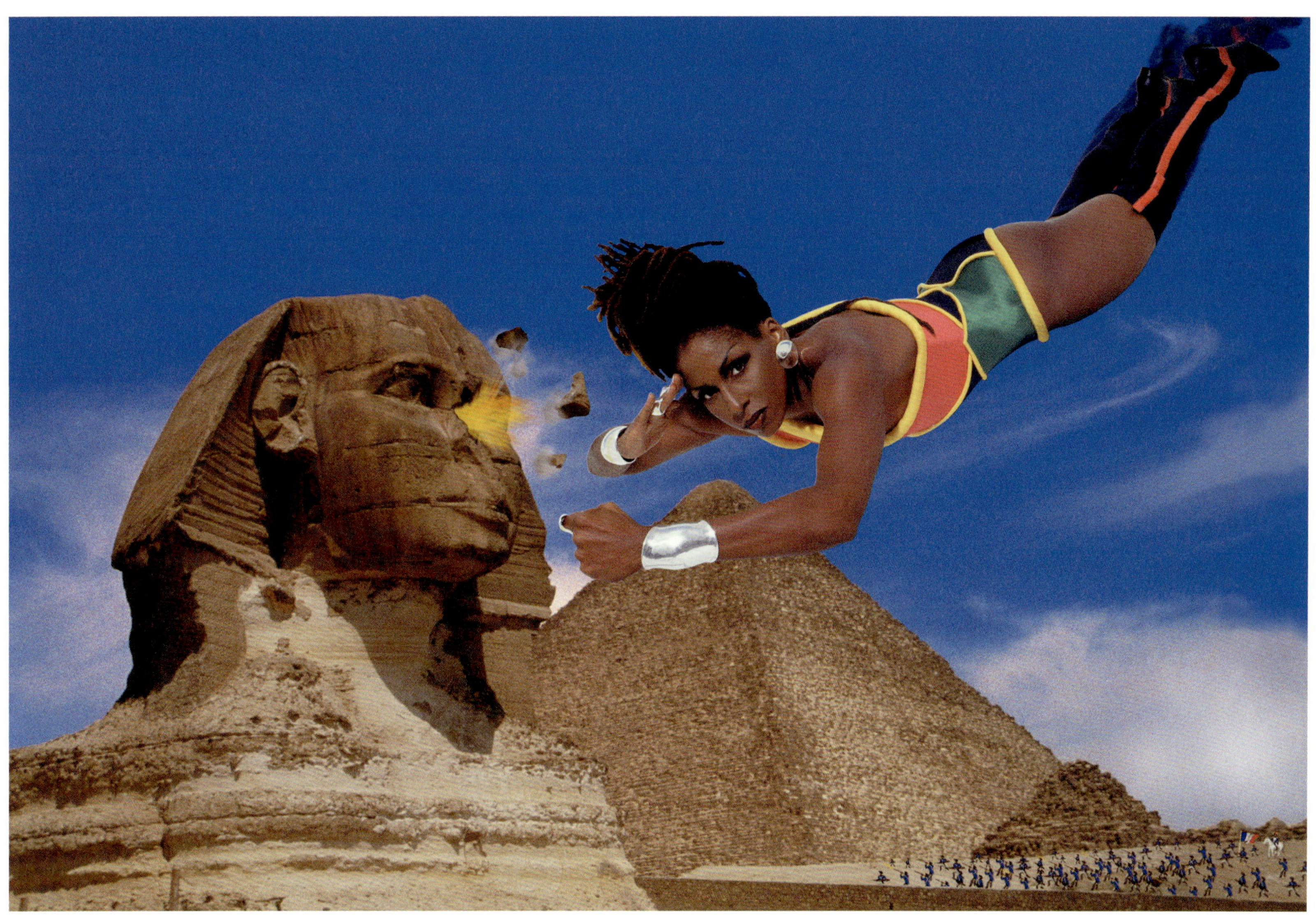

Pl. 163. Renee Cox, **Rajé to the Rescue**, 1998

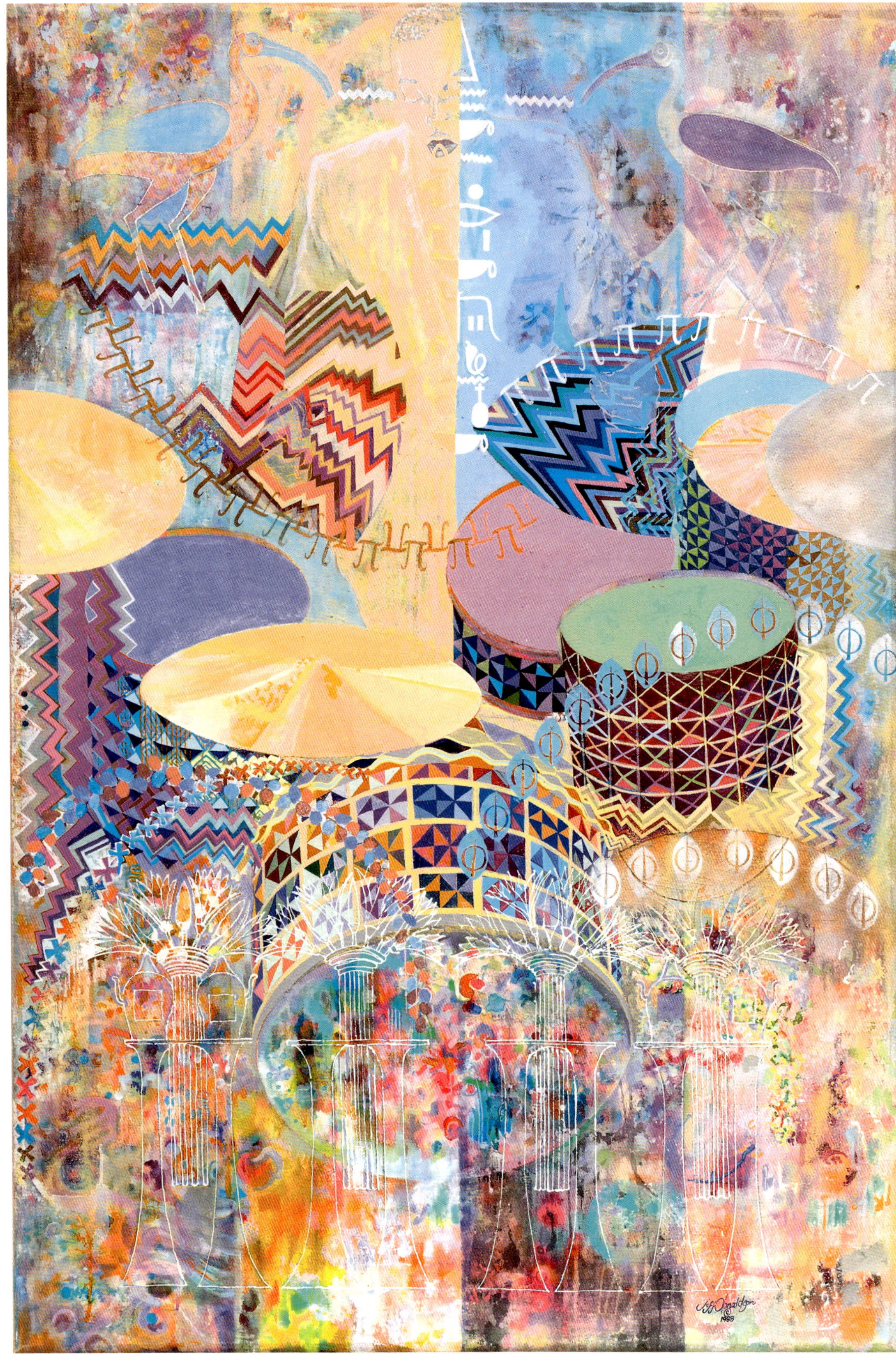

Pl. 164. Jeff Donaldson, **Message from Tehuti**, 1988

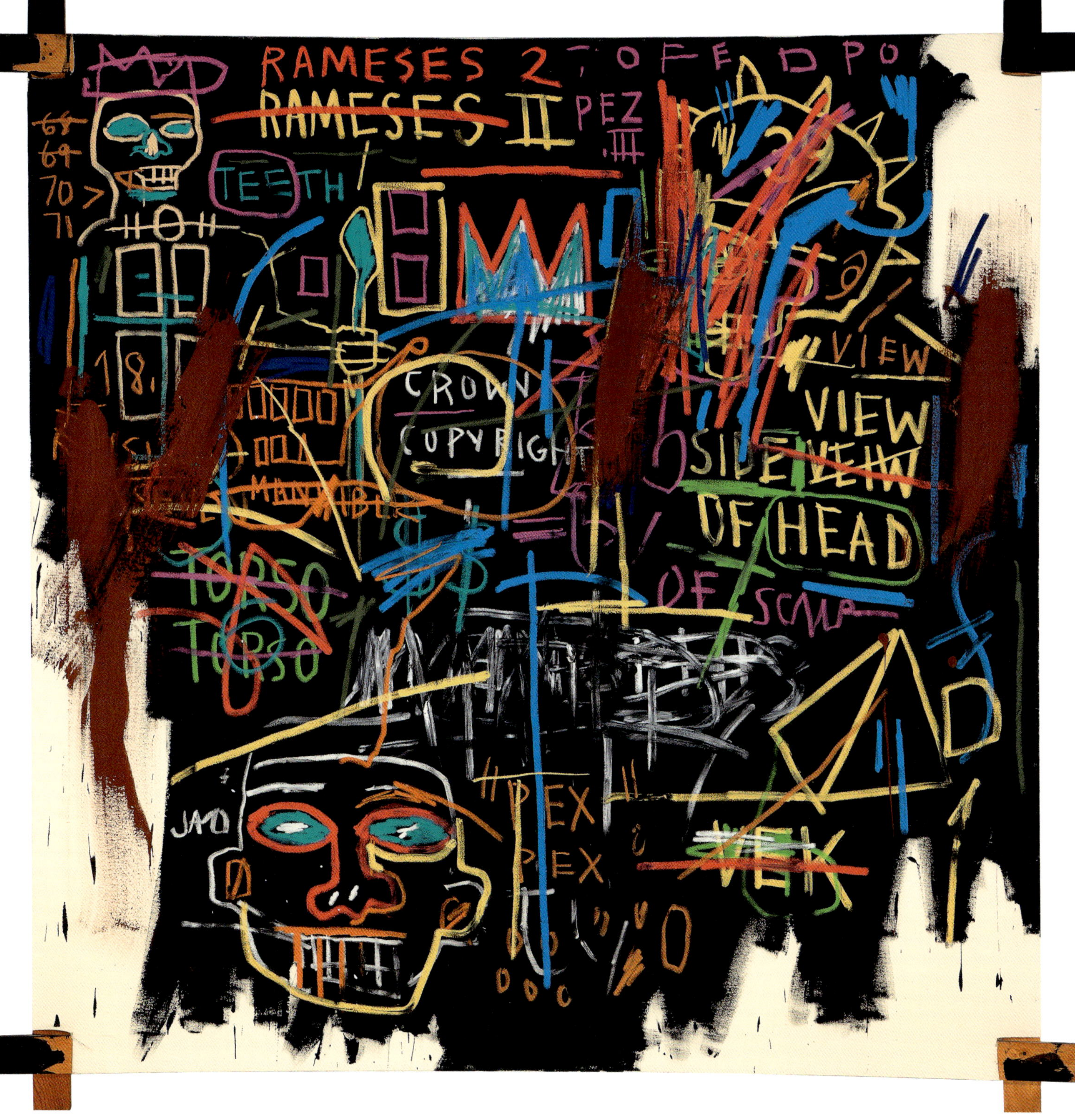

Pl. 165. Jean-Michel Basquiat, **Kings of Egypt II**, 1982

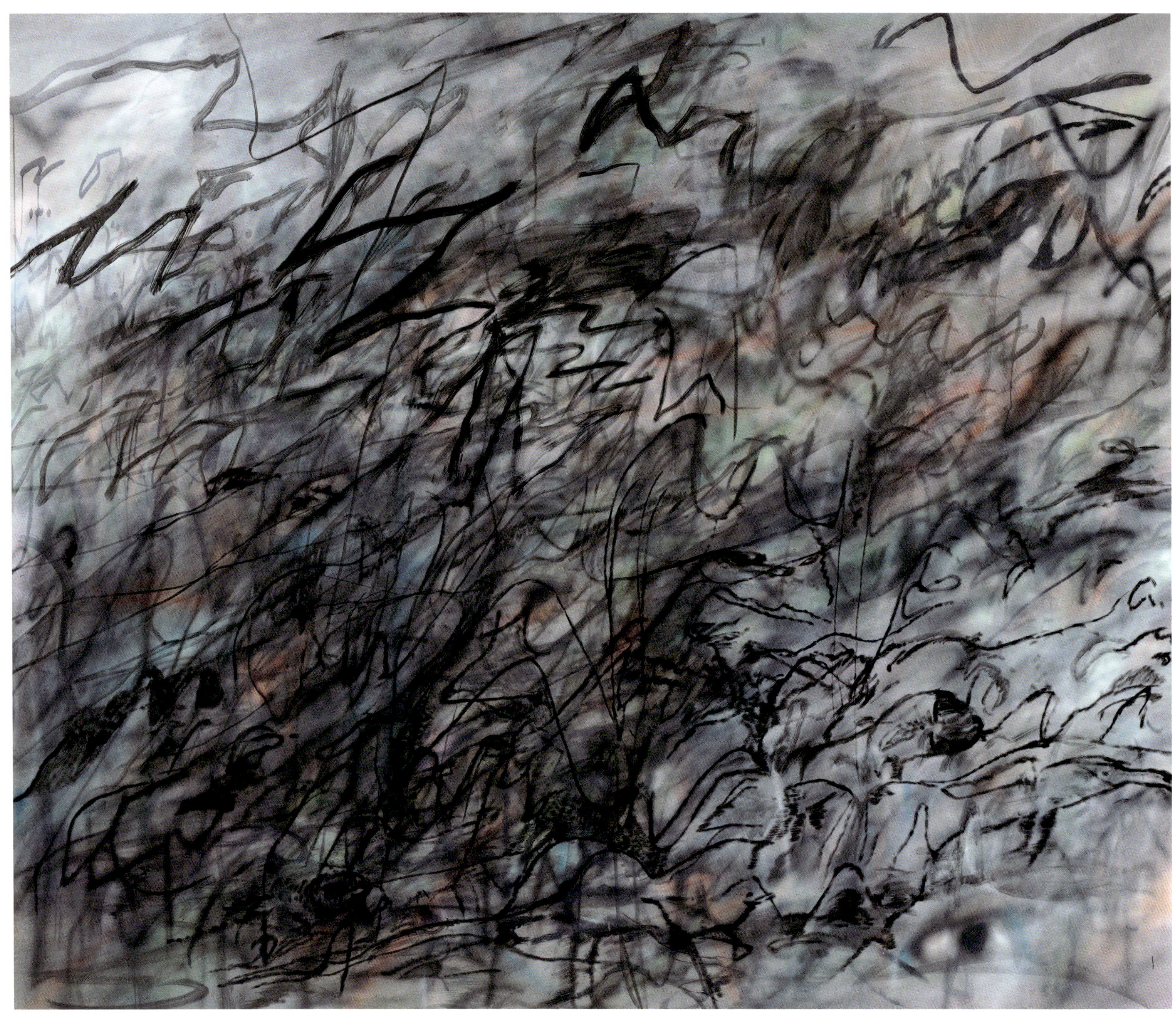

Pl. 166. Julie Mehretu, **Stelae 3 (Bardu)**, 2016

Julie Mehretu

For thirty million years the Nile has been flowing from Lake Tana in the Ethiopian highlands, through Sudan, where the Blue Nile meets the White Nile in Khartoum, through the Nubian desert, past Abu Simbel, Aswan, past Luxor, via Cairo, and finally emptying out of the delta of Alexandria into the Mediterranean. These waters gave rise to all of ancient Egypt, the pharaohs, the kingdoms, and the agriculture. The silt and soil of Ethiopia fed the artists, sculptors, priests, slaves, and pharaohs who created the wealth of ancient Egyptian art. The connection between Lake Tana, not far from where my grandmother is from, and ancient Egypt runs deep.

I was born the child of Africanists of the 1960s. In the smoke-filled bars, clubs, and hotels of Addis Ababa gathered modernists, revolutionaries, socialists, activists, and futurists during the height of the belle époque Ethiopian jazz scene. Whether to the sound of the Walias at the Addis Ababa Hilton or the funkier Dahlak Band at the Ghion hotel, Mulatu Astatke, Getatchew Mekuria, and others created what became the soundtrack of radical imagination, development, and modernization in Ethiopia and across the continent.

North of us, in Cairo, Umm Kulthum's voice, kerchief, and bosom inspired audiences and made them swoon, while Omar Khorshid and his magical guitar serenaded us with love and revolution through Cairo theaters, the radio waves, and the LPs played at home. Like the waters that have bound us over millennia, the music of Egypt and Ethiopia ricocheted back and forth as psycho-funky reverberations of the new postcolonial Africa. Cairo, Khartoum, and Addis are bound by the Nile waters, but also as historic sources of love, art, music, empire, and revolution.

Visiting from Zimbabwe (where we were living in 1984–85) in its early post-revolutionary days, I saw the pyramids of Giza for the first time when I was fourteen and became completely enchanted with ancient Egypt. Not only for the astounding inventions of these ancient Africans that preceded ancient Greece, Rome, and so on, but also for the experiences I had in my encounters with the work. I have returned many times since, to study at the Egyptian Museum in Cairo (one of my favorite museums in the world), the Temple of Karnak in Luxor, the Valley of the Kings and Queens in the desert, and the pyramids of Dahshur. But also, more times than I can count, I have studied the Egyptian collections of the Neues Museum in Berlin and the British Museum in London.

I vividly remember a sculpted head at the Egyptian Museum in Cairo that felt as if it was inhaling through its nose, while I was standing in front of it. That experience expanded my understanding and altered my perception of art. It felt as if that person from over five thousand years ago had just taken a breath with me; it gave me goose bumps. An artist, thousands of years ago, had made black granite stone breathe, and breathe with me.

Much is misunderstood about ancient Egyptian sculptures. These are not approximate, stylized iconographic symbolic images—rather, they are observationally descriptive and vivid portraiture. Each piece, with its specific features—wide ears, elongated chin, broad cheekbones, narrow face, severe expression or bright smile, thin or full lips—each piece is unique in its likeness. Braided heads and sculpted Afros that look like the heads of my aunts, great-aunts, my grandmother, and great-grandmother. We can see Akhenaten, Nefertiti, Hatshepsut, Ramesses II, Thutmose III, and Amenhotep III as distinct individuals. These Nubian and Asiatic Africans of immense power, capability, creativity, and beauty are our collective historic humanity. Whether in the poems of Sappho or the eyes of Hatshepsut or the slightly parted mouth of Akhenaten, we feel them empathetically, and through them, we breathe, their breath that, in the words of Adrienne Edwards, "exalts the real."

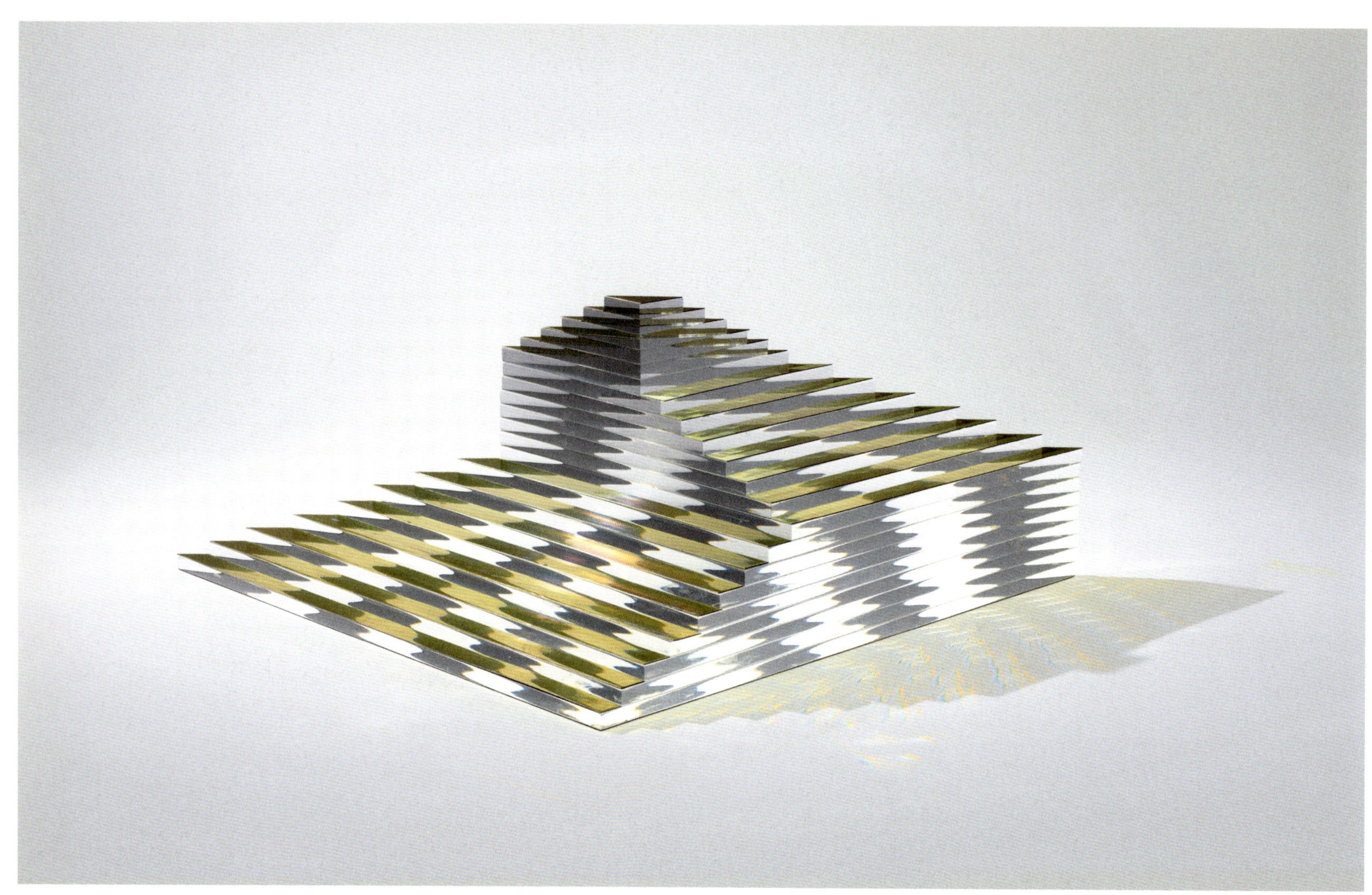

Pl. 167. Fred Eversley, **Untitled (gold layered step pyramid)**, 1983

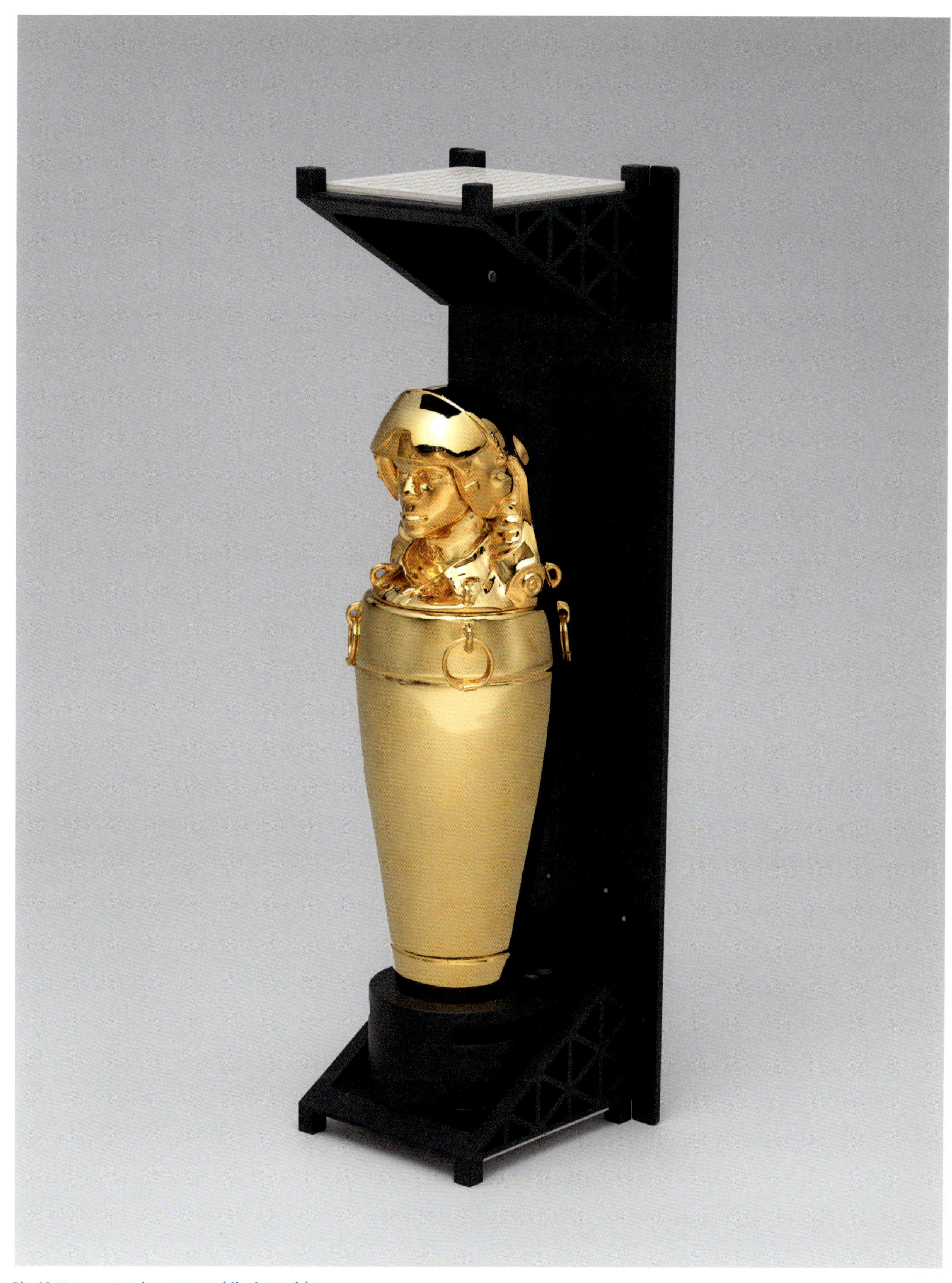

Pl. 168. Tavares Strachan, **ENOCH (display unit)**, 2015-17

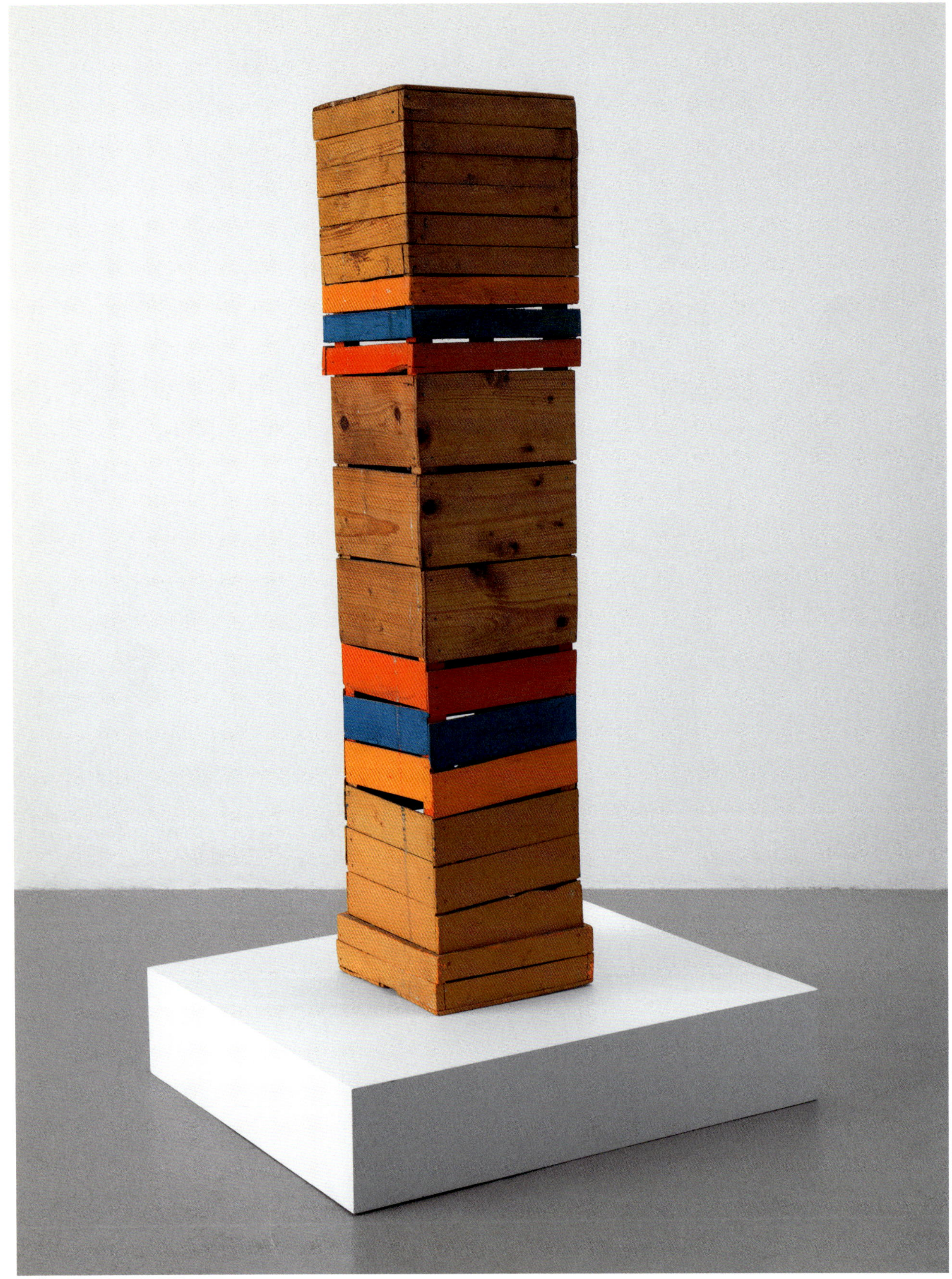

Pl. 169. Mildred Thompson, **Stele**, ca. 1963

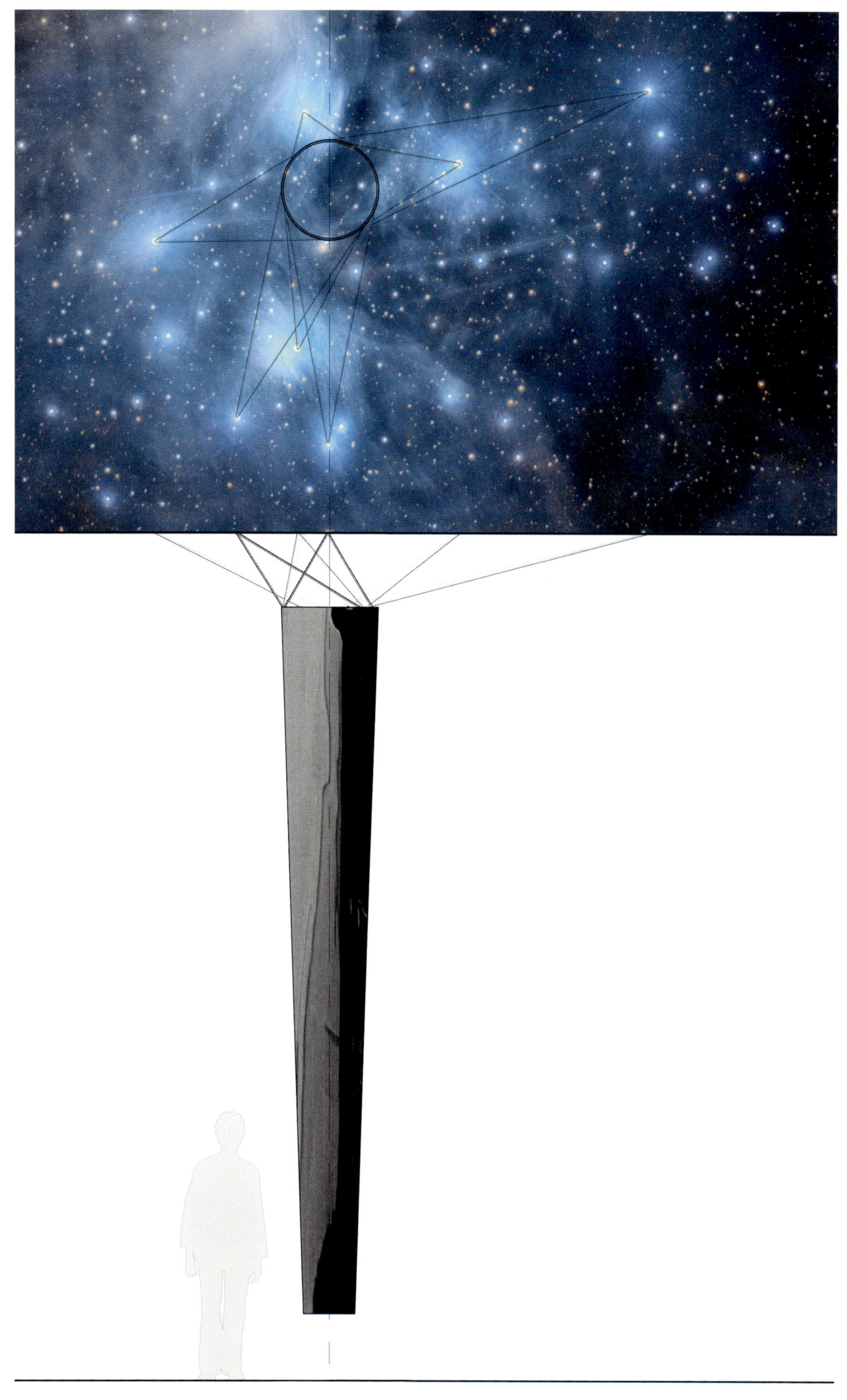

Pl. 170. Dream The Combine, **Design drawing for "Pyramidion,"** 2024

Jennifer Newsom

Flight into Egypt: Phantom Photons

"It's yellow out there." These were the first words spoken by my son on his second birthday, after waking up in Cairo on an October morning. My creative and life partner, Tom, and I had landed with him the previous evening, seeking refuge from burned-out architecture careers. Our son could ascertain that something special awaited us on this journey—a change in the very atmosphere that sustains a life. We flew to Egypt to be inspired and to connect with each other and our selves.

As architects educated through a limited, Westernized canon, we studied Egypt only as a non-site. It was a symbolic projection for desires and power, the greatness of a civilization without its people, contours, smells, and sounds. Without its yellowed air. Pope Sixtus, in his reimagining of Rome that overlaid Augustus's planning, used Egyptian obelisks to mark urban axes throughout the Eternal City, solidifying it as a locus of pilfered strength. He said the quiet part out loud—that Africa is at the center and present always, even if we only see it through the eyes of others. In the words of Ralph Ellison's *Invisible Man* (1952), "When they approach me they see only my surroundings, themselves, or figments of their imagination—indeed, everything and anything except me." The obelisk is both panopticon and blind spot.

Contrary to that displaced gaze, our trip changed my conception of time, ancestral presence, scale, and material. We spent the day at Djoser's funerary complex in Saqqara, following our desire and our son's wish to ride a donkey as a birthday gift. Our son is named after my father, Ogden, who was born in Cairo, Illinois, a provident convergence. My father passed away in 1996, long before his namesake was born. Kꜣ had left the body, yet presence remained in Imhotep's space, created for after life. In Egypt I connected to generations on either side of my own. I can notice the air, spirit-hued light, breathe it in, and let it move through me.

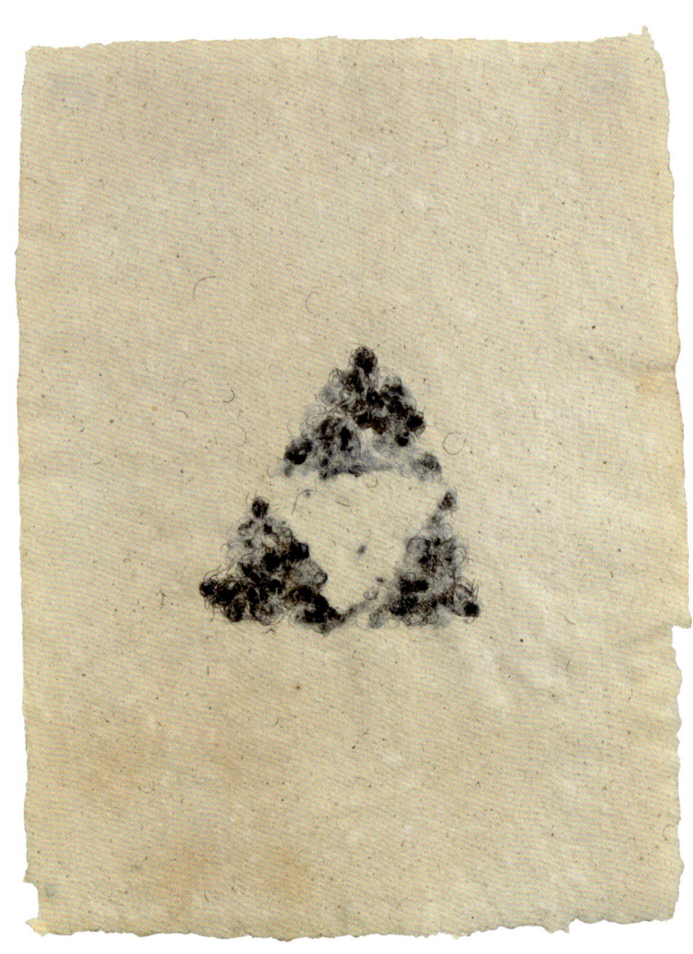

Pl. 171. David Hammons, **Unknown**, ca. 1977

Pl. 172. David Hammons, **Unknown**, ca. 1977

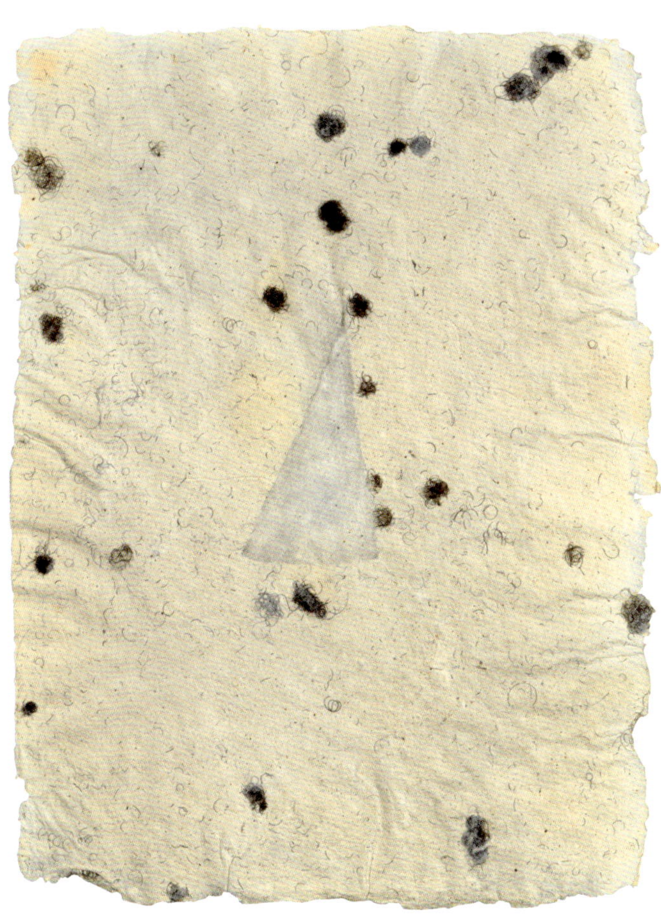

Pl. 173. David Hammons, **Unknown**, ca. 1977

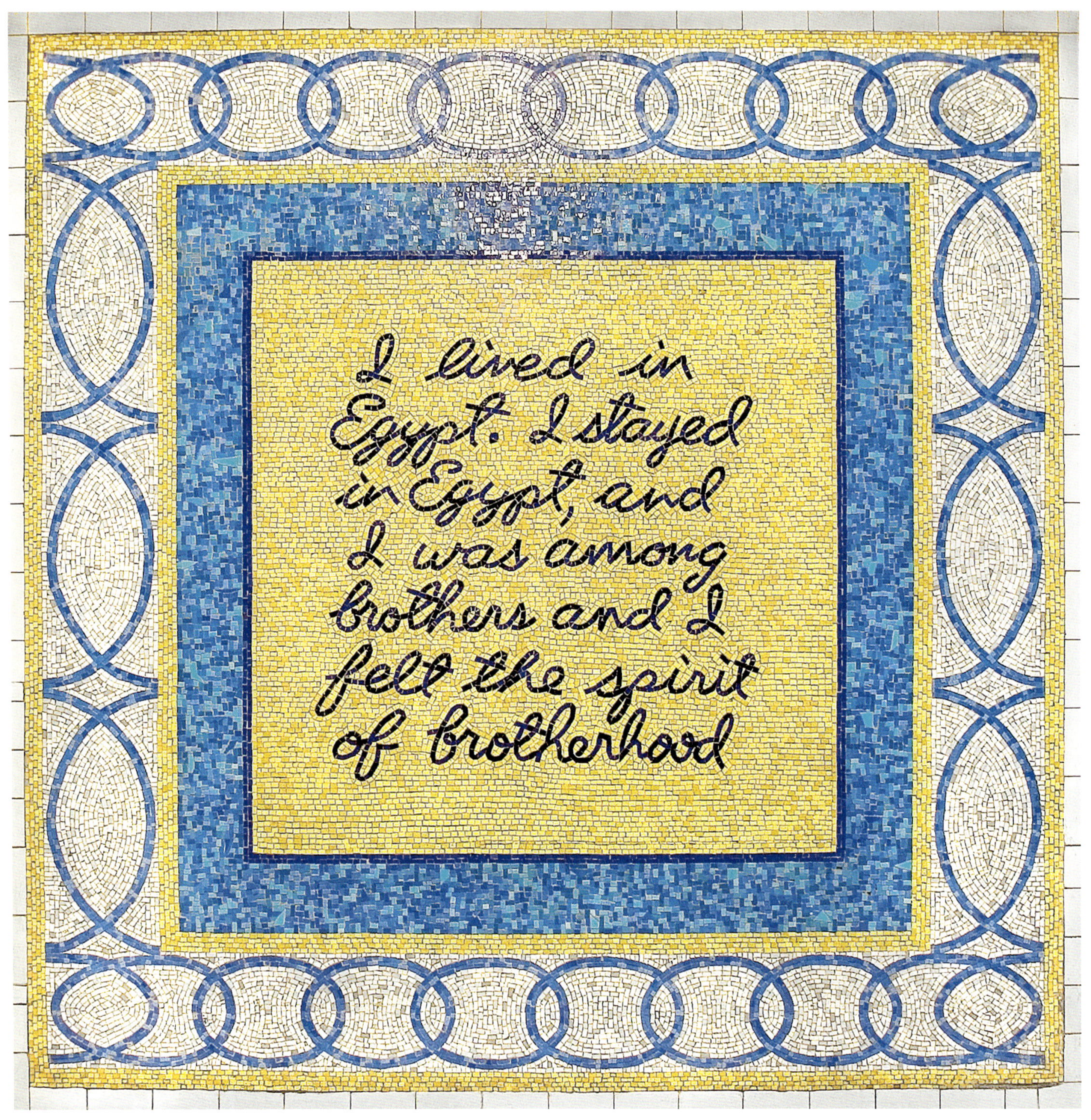

Pl. 174. Maren Hassinger, **Message from Malcolm**, 1998

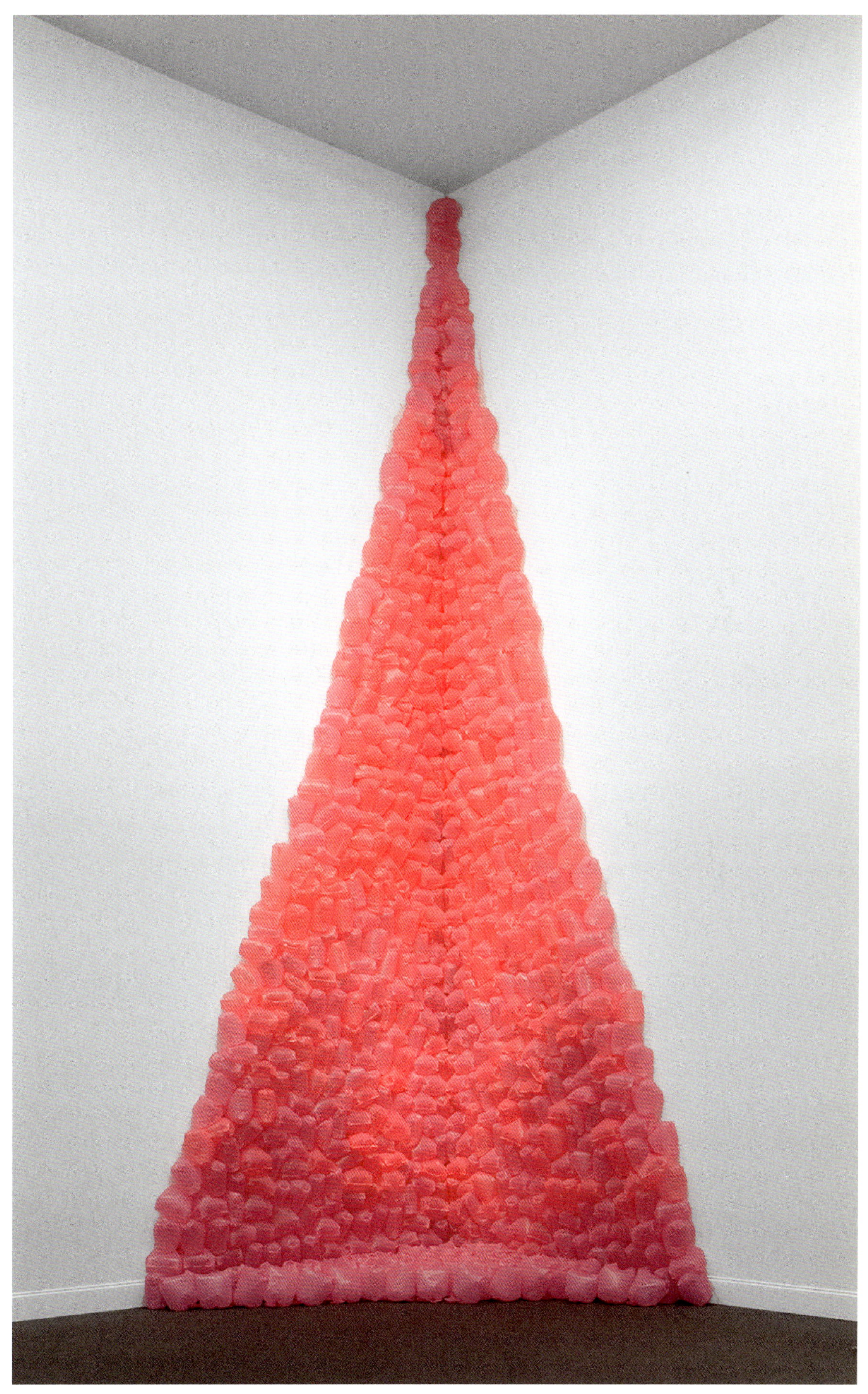

Pl. 175. Maren Hassinger, **Love (Pyramid)**, 2008/24

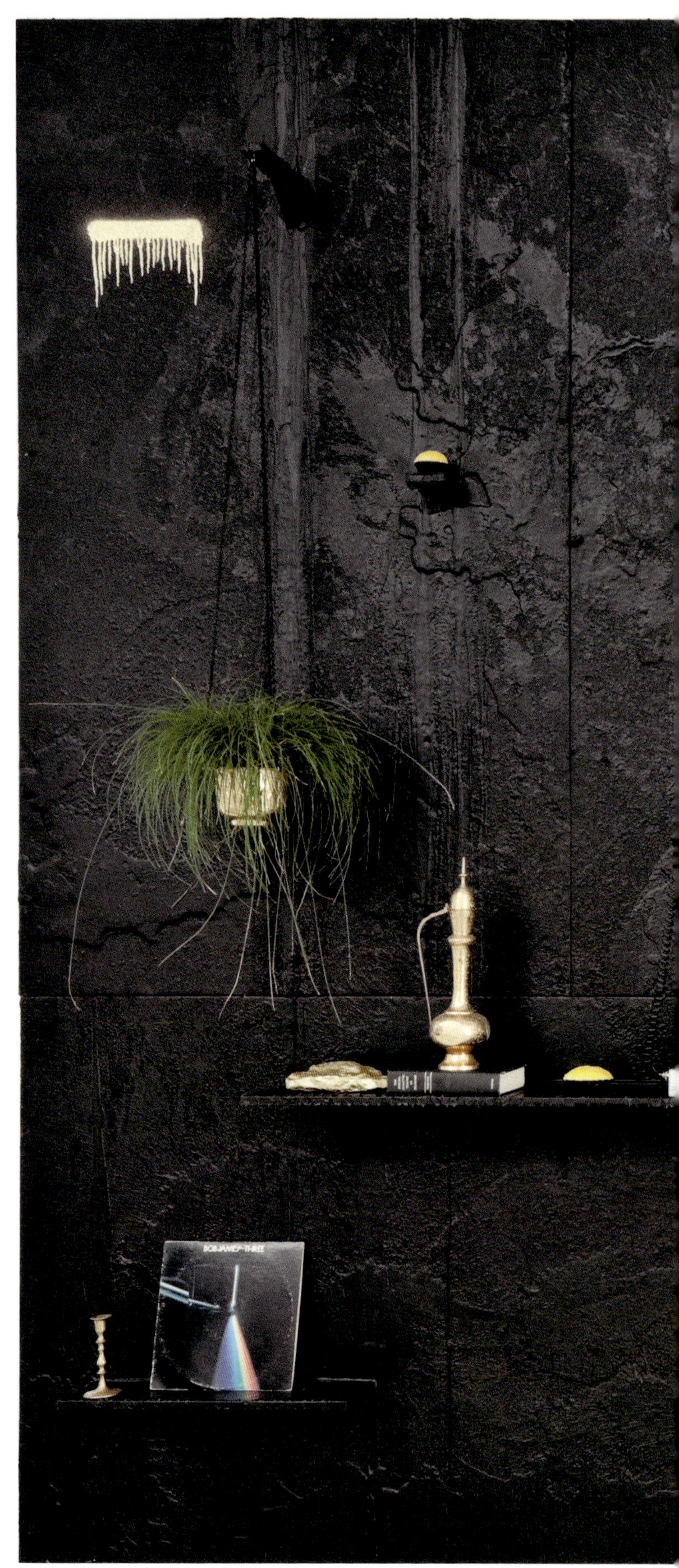

Pl. 176. Rashid Johnson, **Pyramid**, 2009

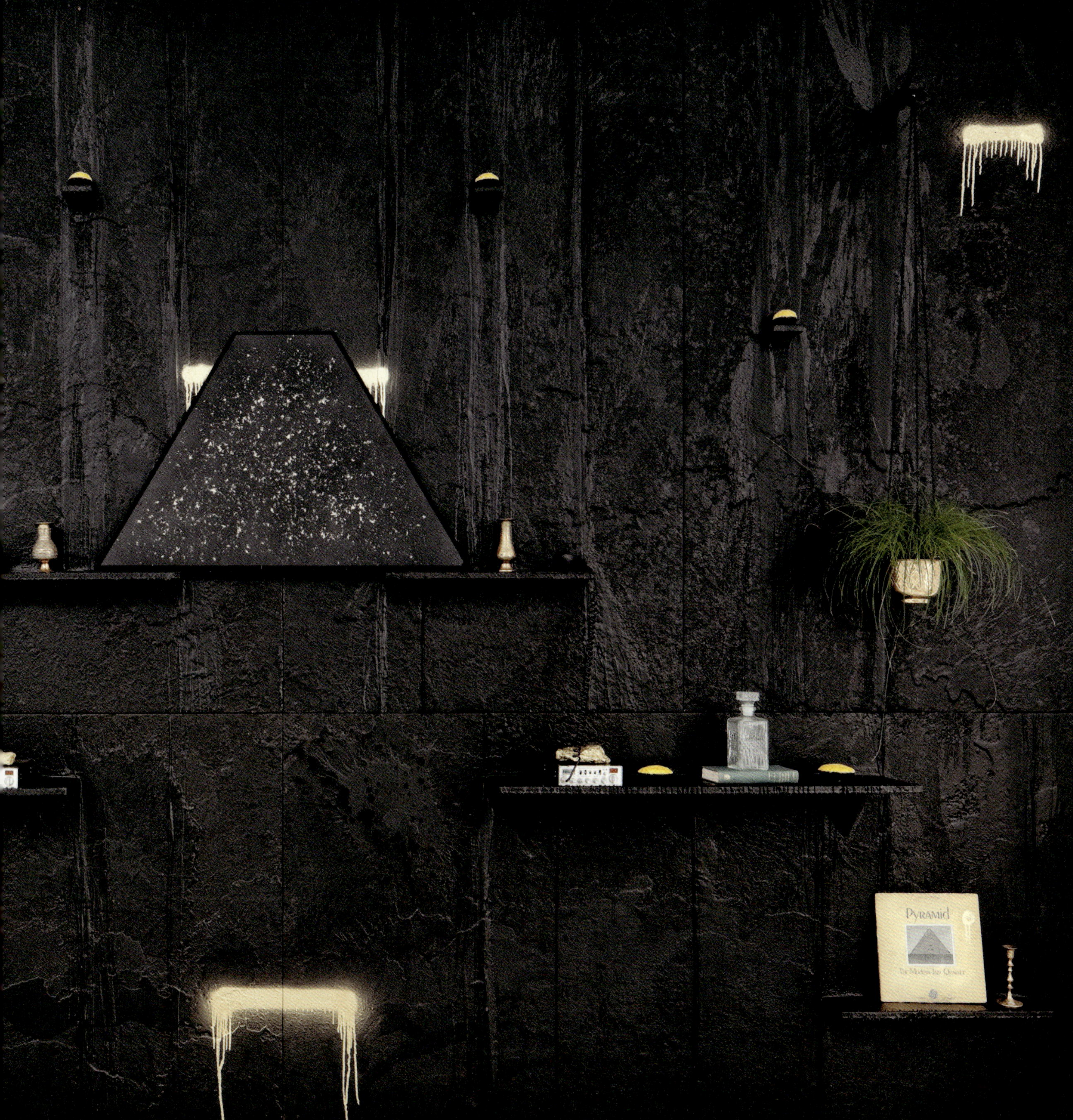
Pyramid
The Modern Jazz Quartet

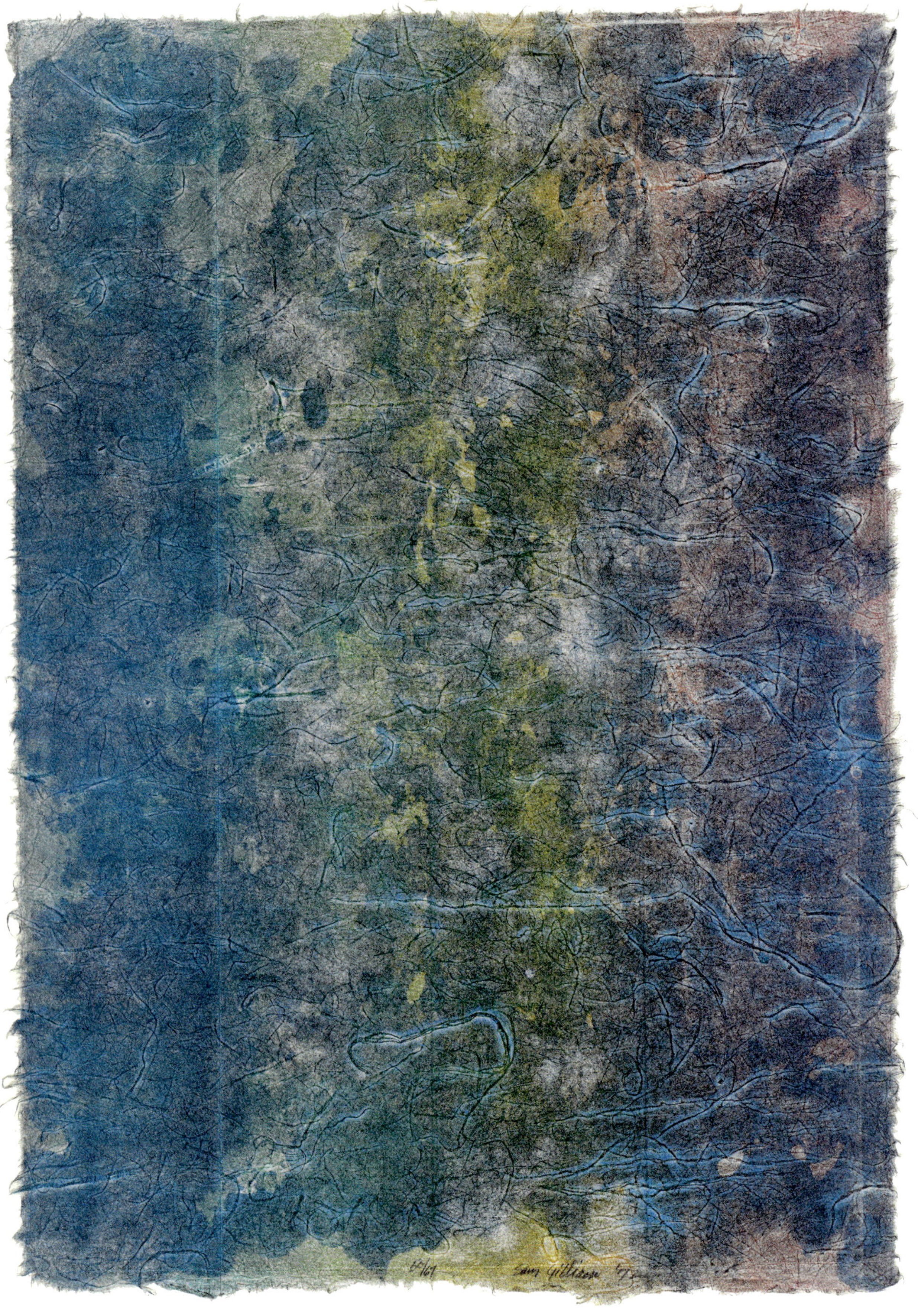

Pl. 177. Sam Gilliam, **Nile**, 1972

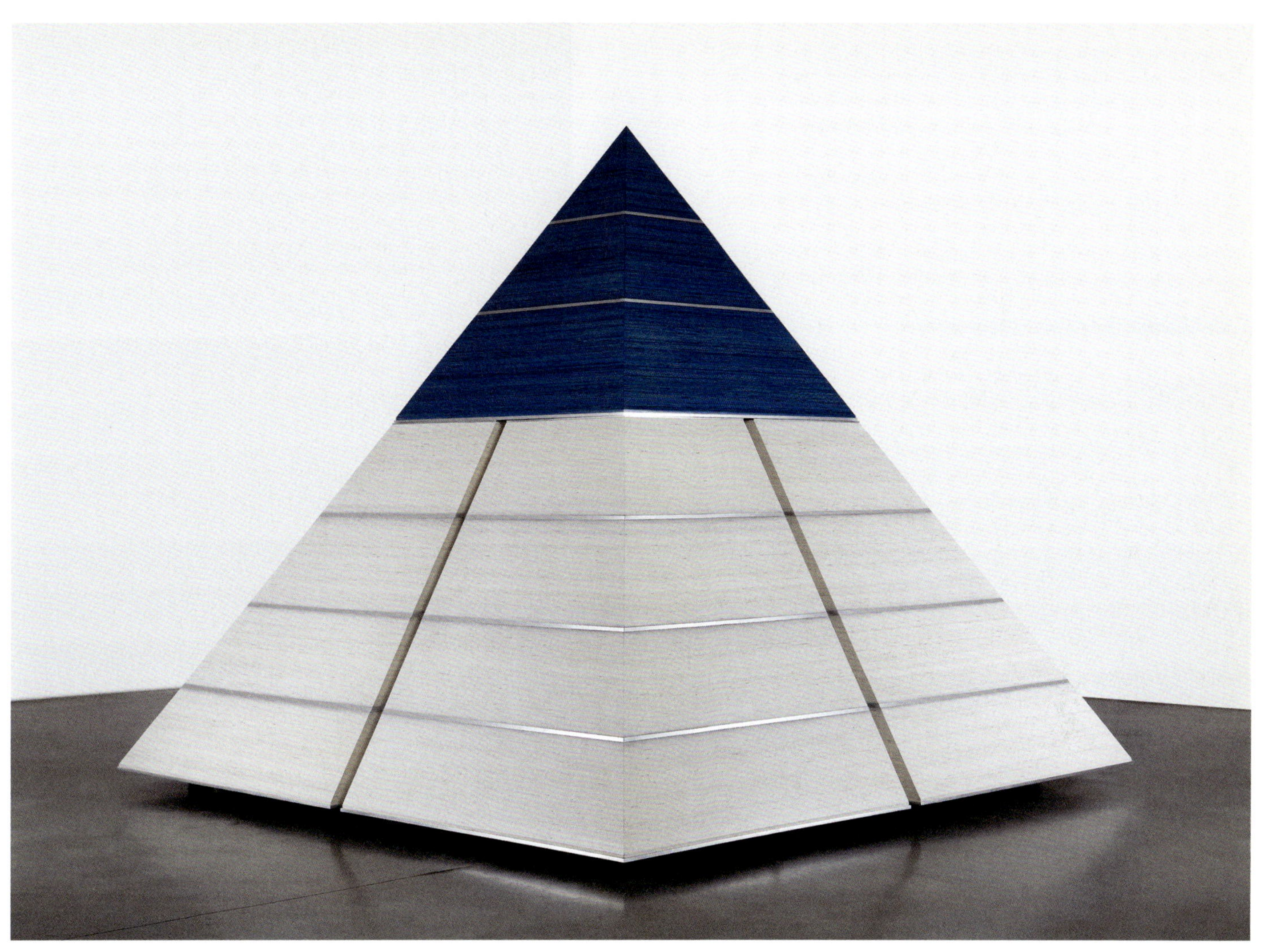

Pl. 178. Sam Gilliam, **Pyramid**, 2020

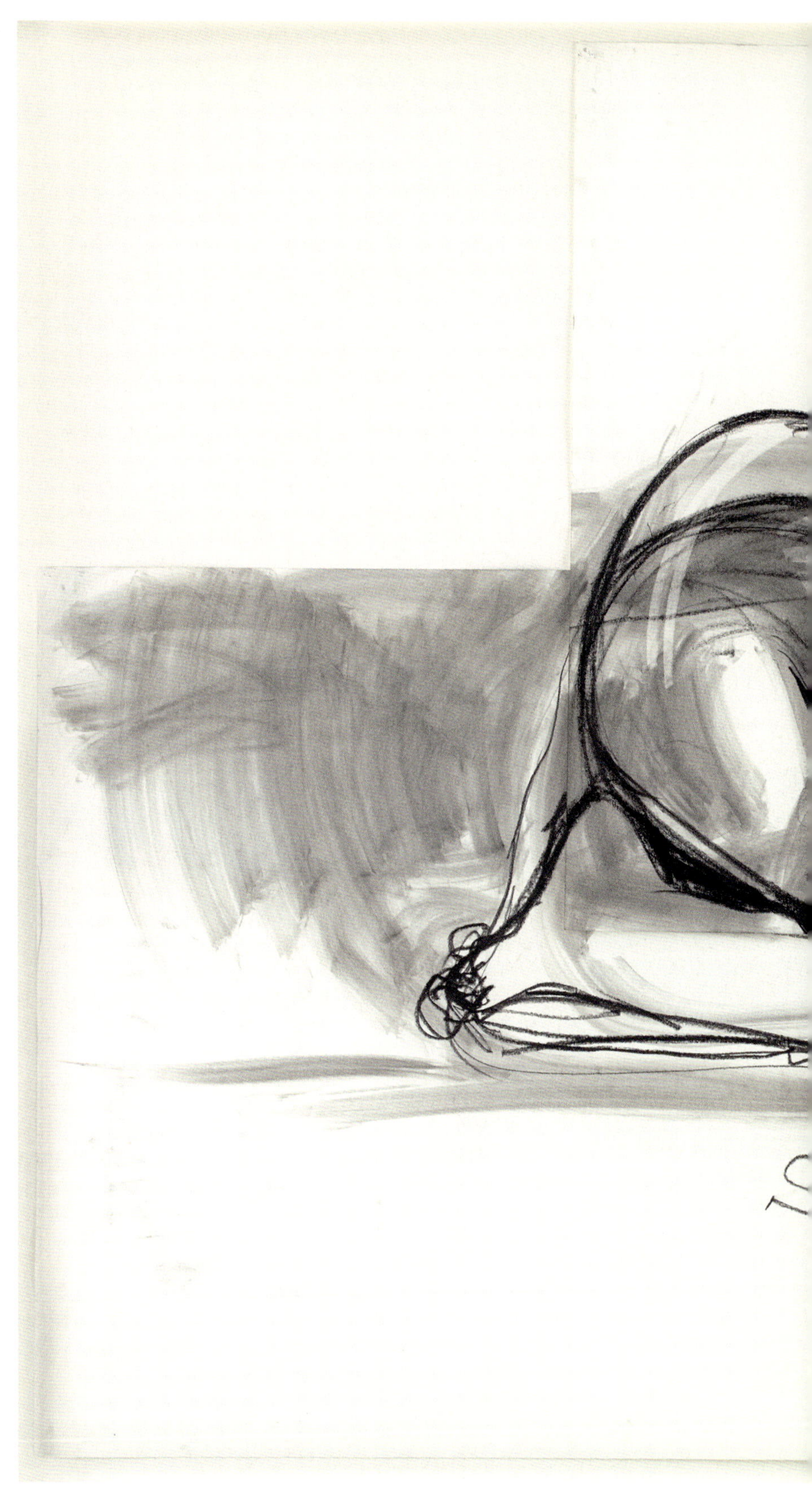

Pl. 179. Kara Walker, **Untitled (Study for A Subtlety, or the Marvelous Sugar Baby)**, 2013–14

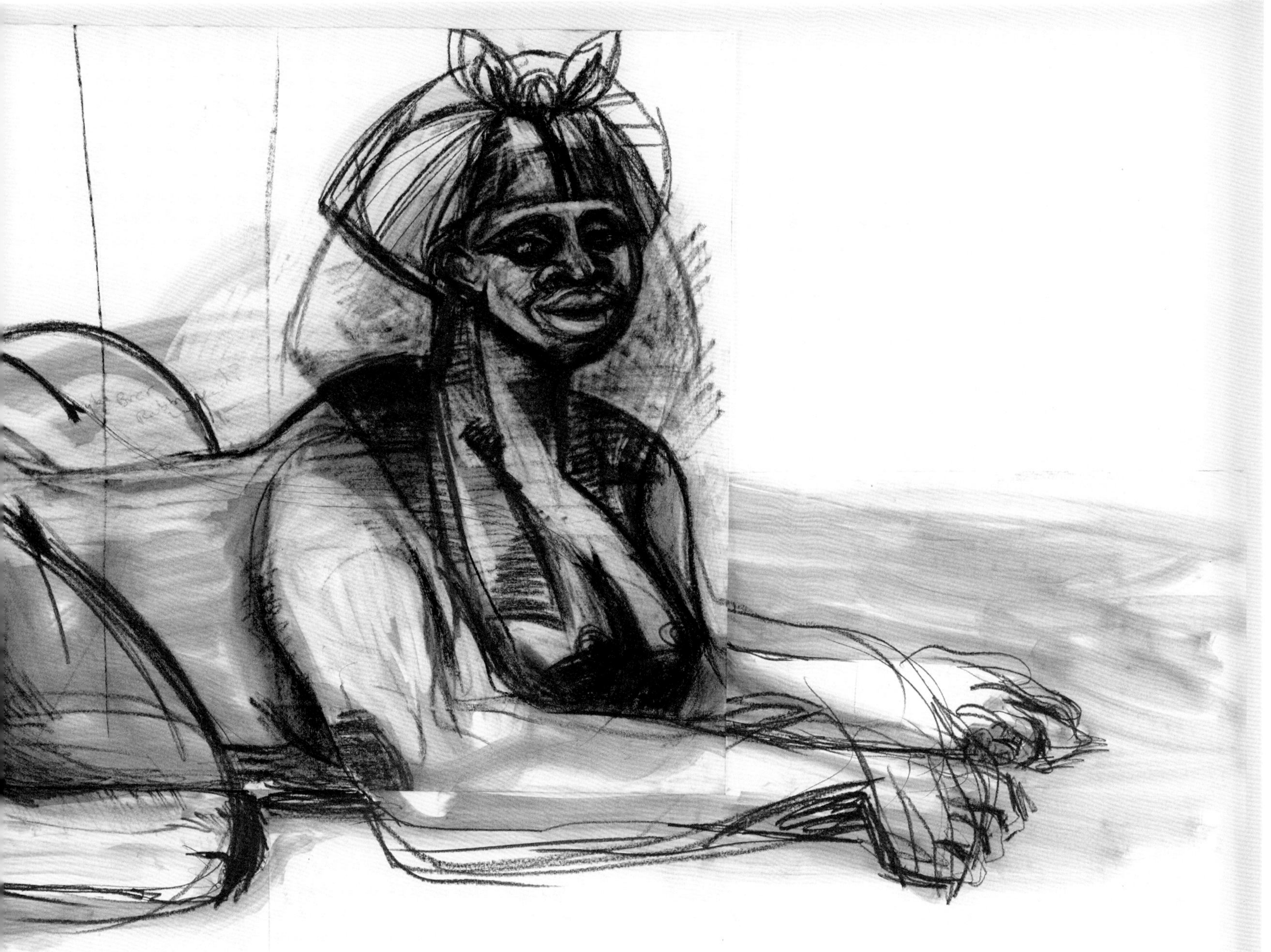

UGAR REFINERY

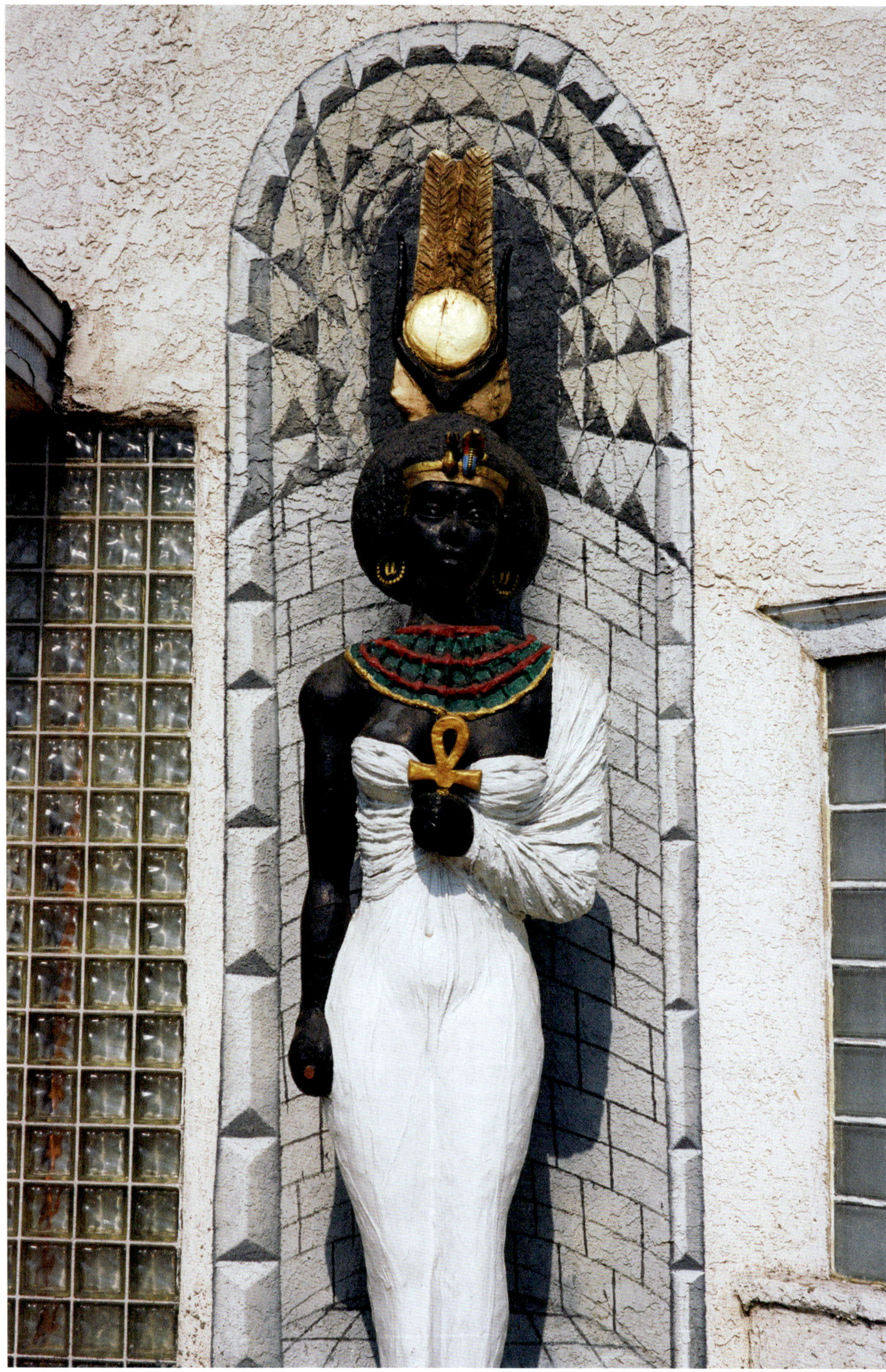

Pl. 180. EJ Hill, **A Divine Mother (after Charles Dickson)**, 2018

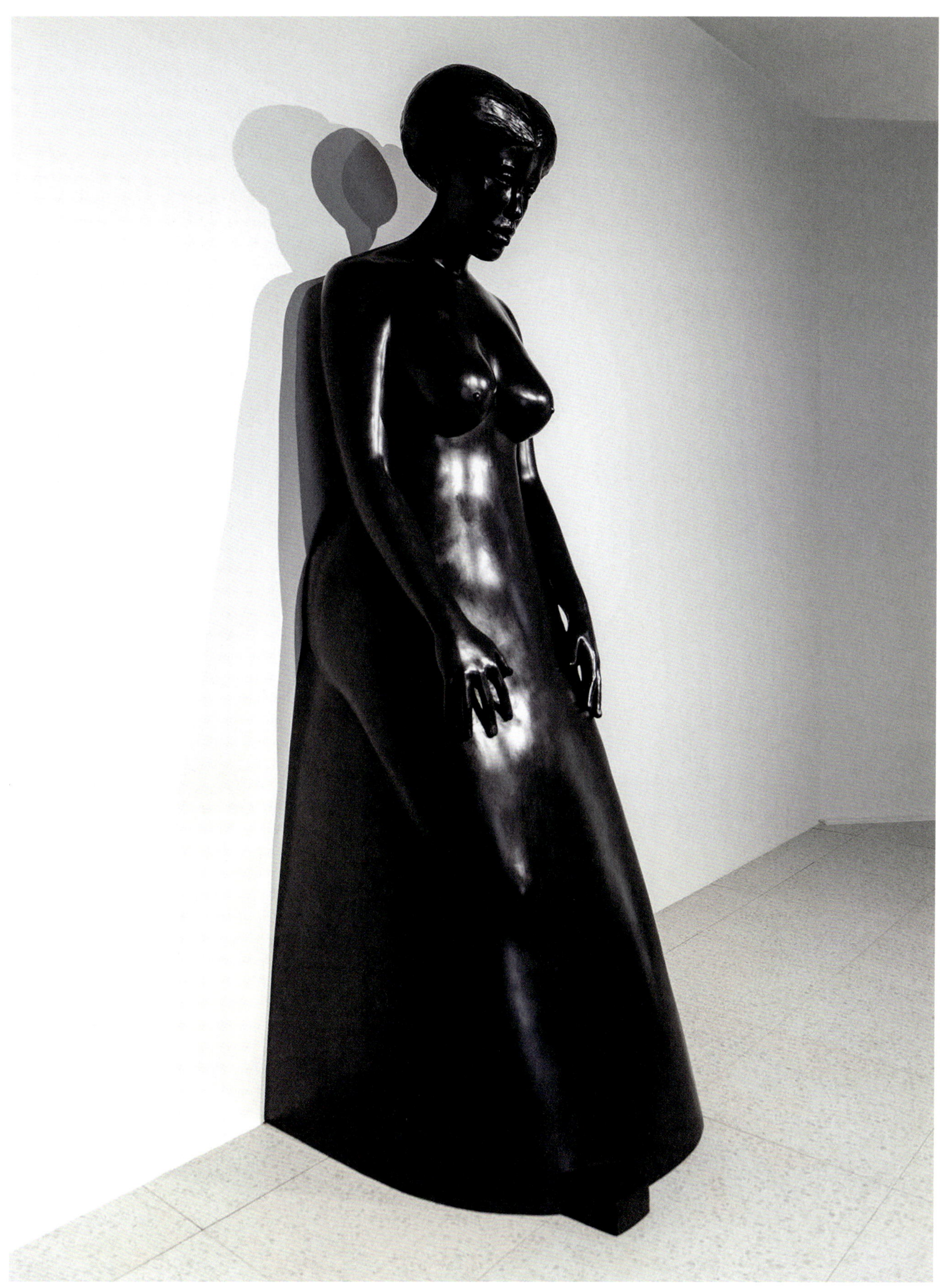

Pl. 181. Simone Leigh, **Sharifa**, 2022

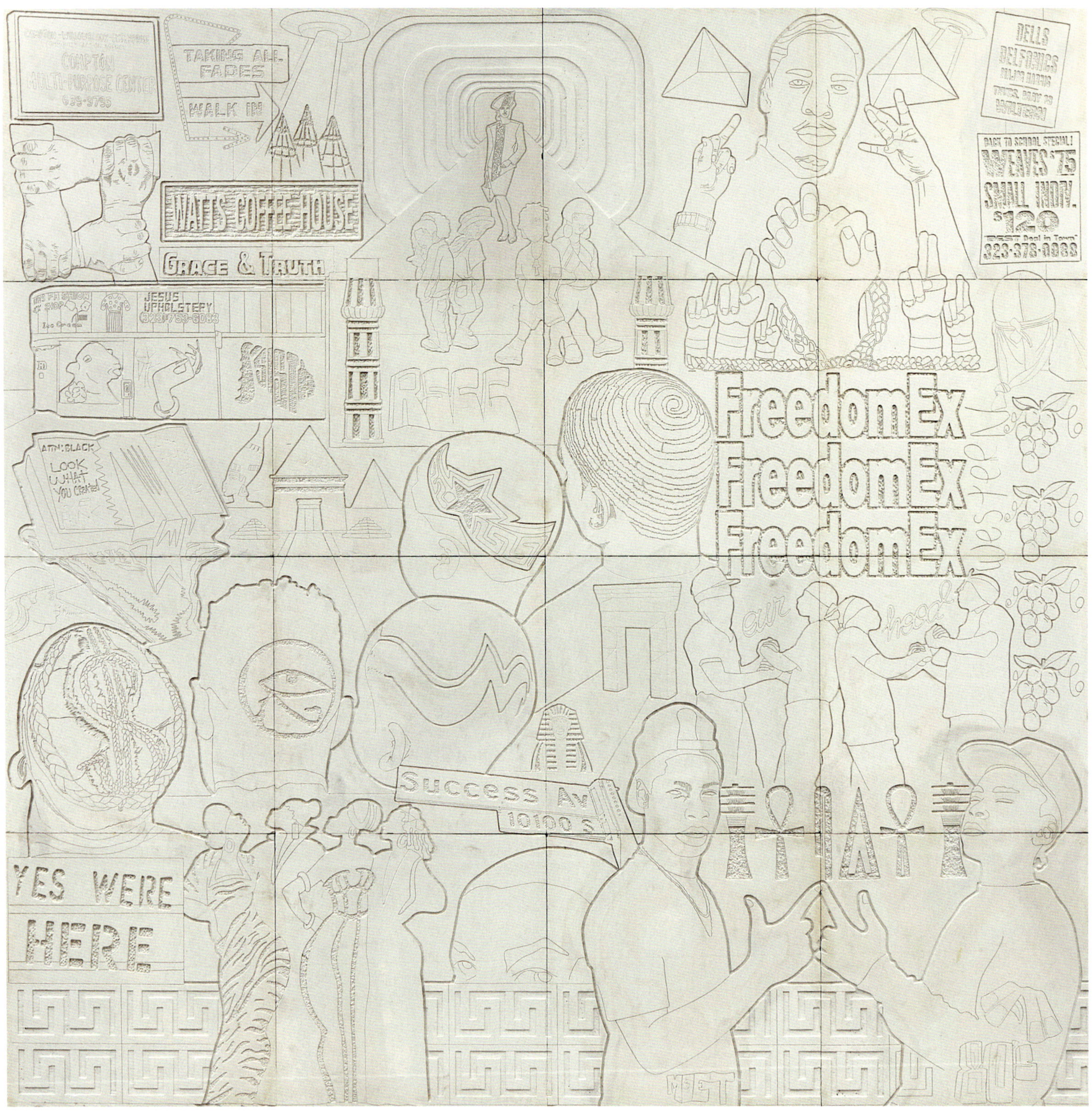

Pl. 182. Lauren Halsey, **FreedomEx**, 2022

Lauren Halsey

My interest is conflated by ancient Egyptian n Nubian antiquities, george clinton's Funk operas, post civil right aesthetics in south central la, my father's testifying on pyramid worlds n pharaoh such n such during fight parties n halftime during raiders games and lastly, ideological groups i was in touch with during my time in Harlem.

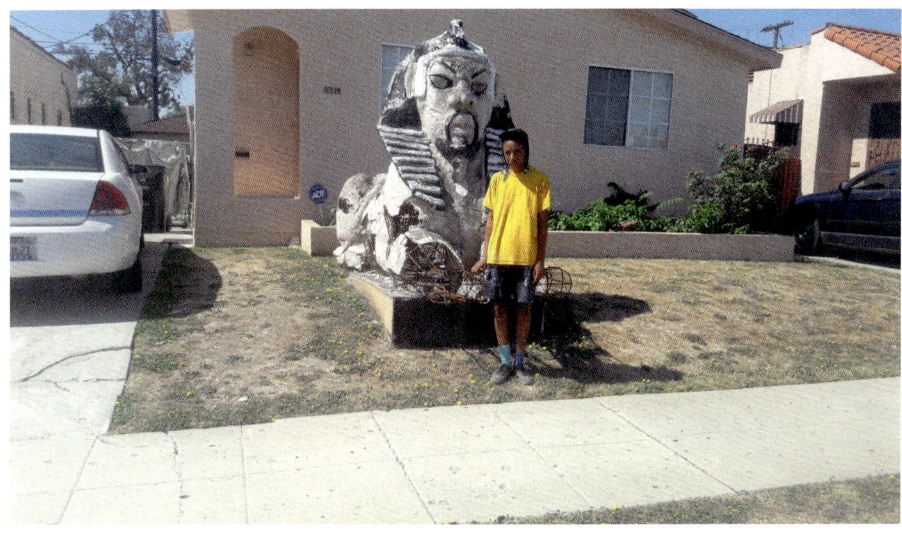

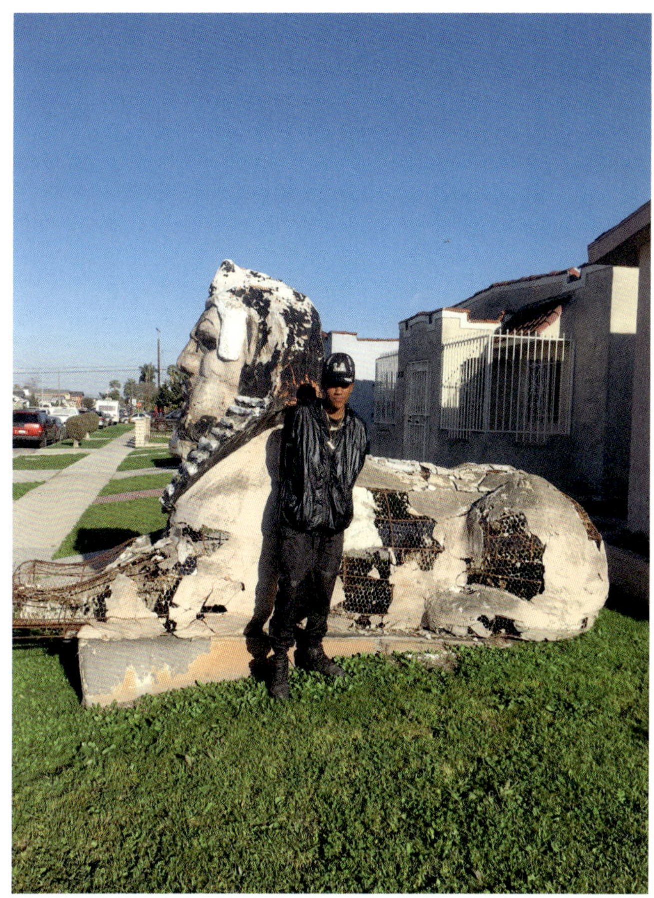

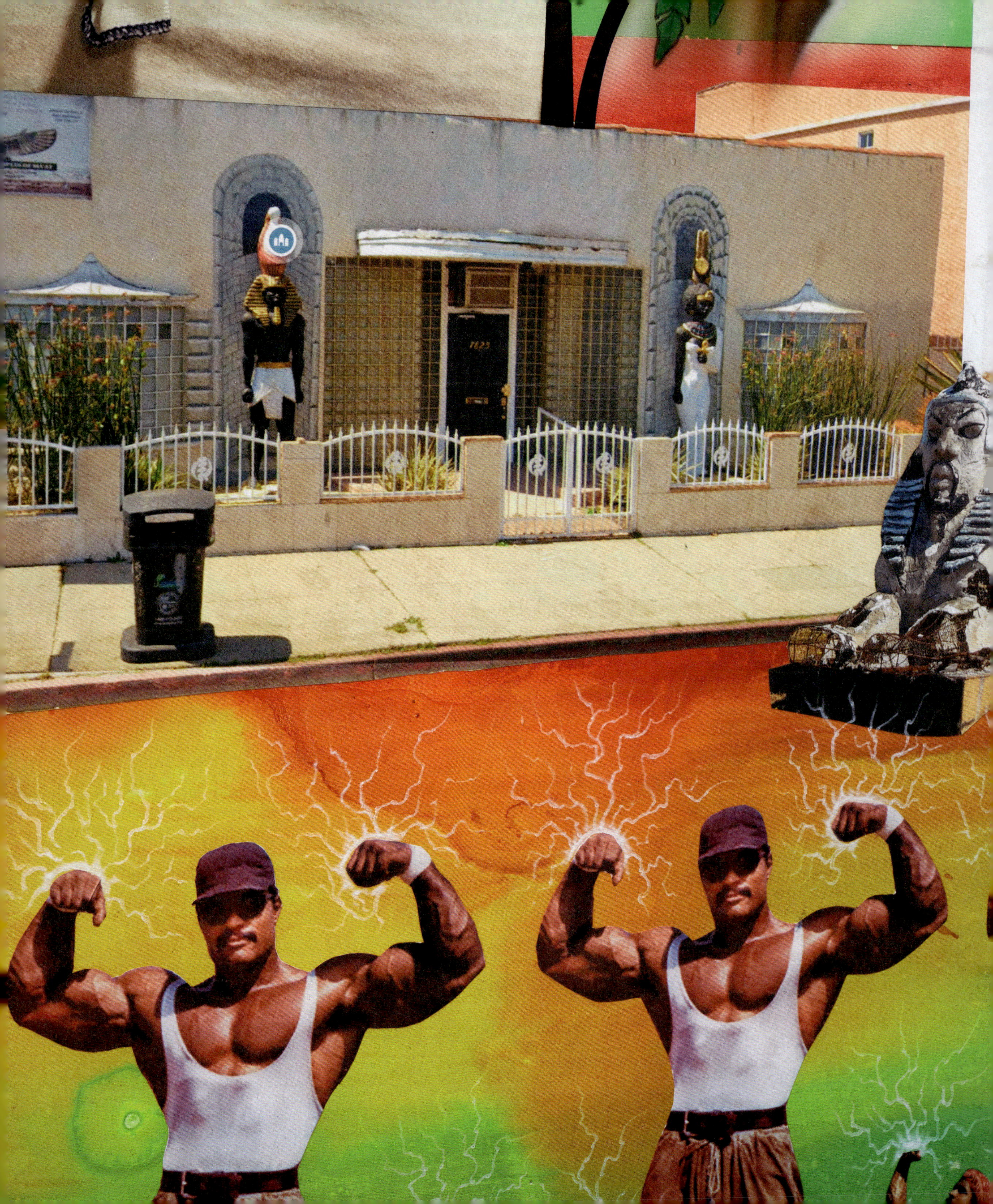

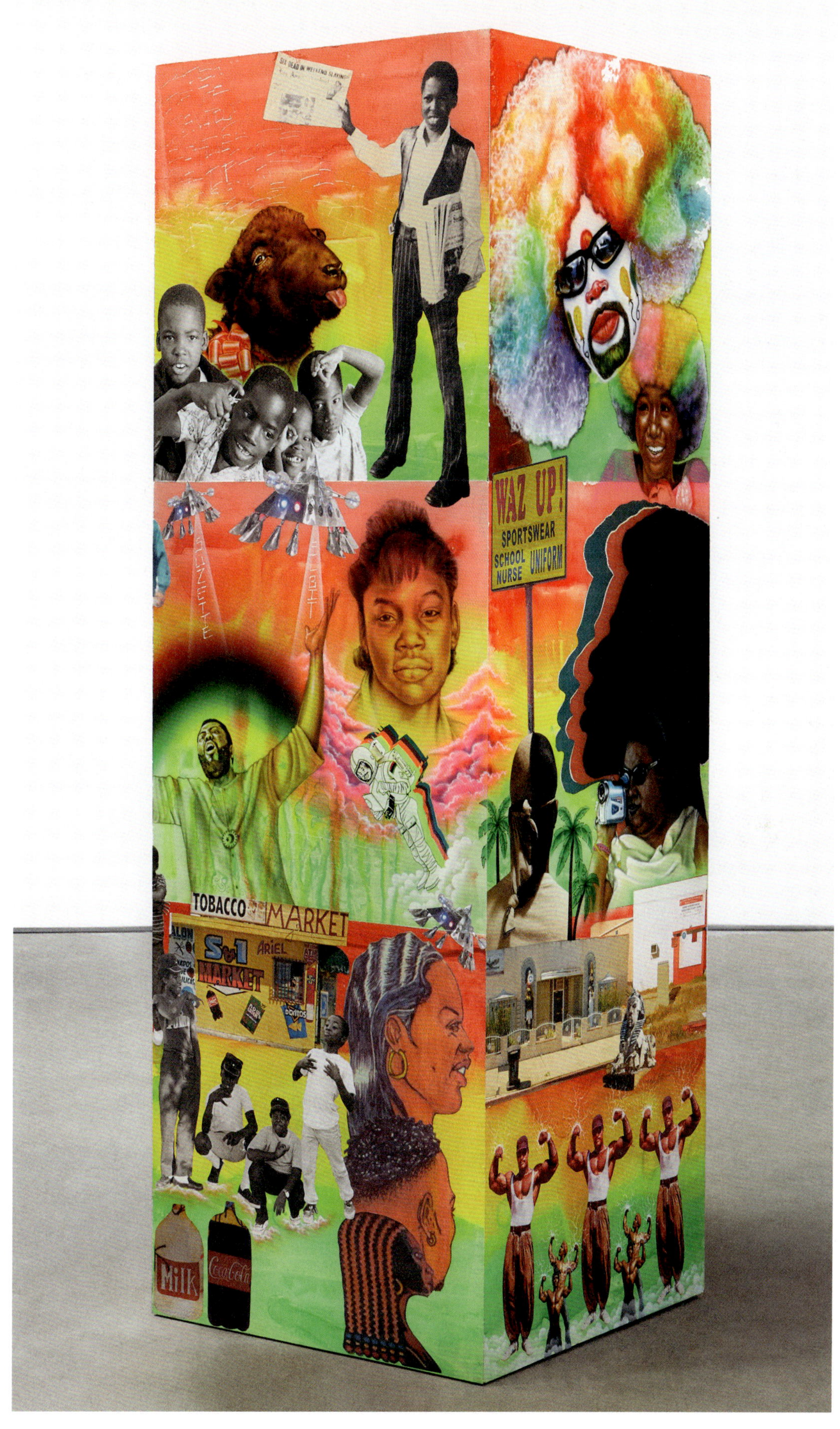

Pl. 183. Lauren Halsey, **Untitled**, 2024

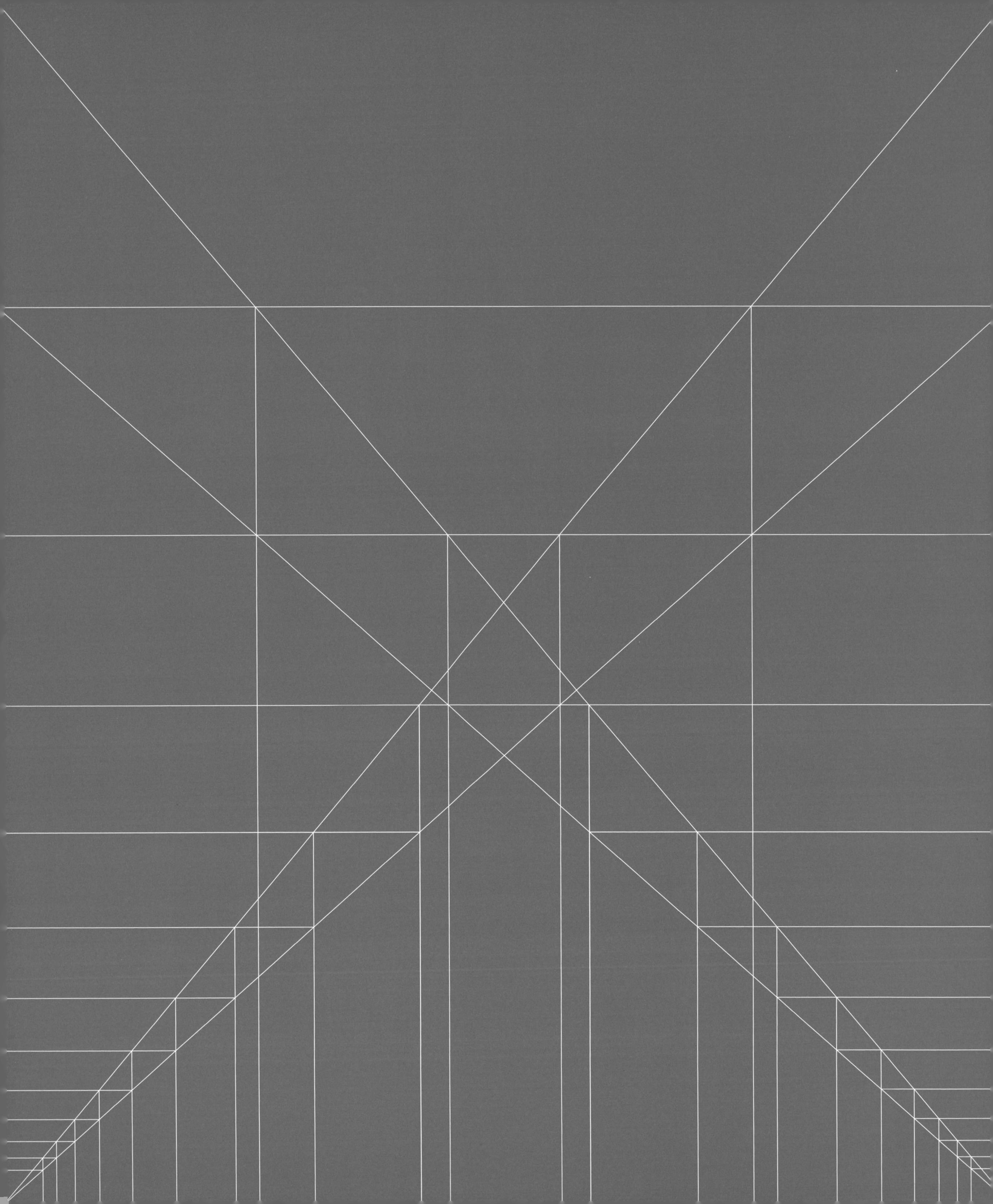

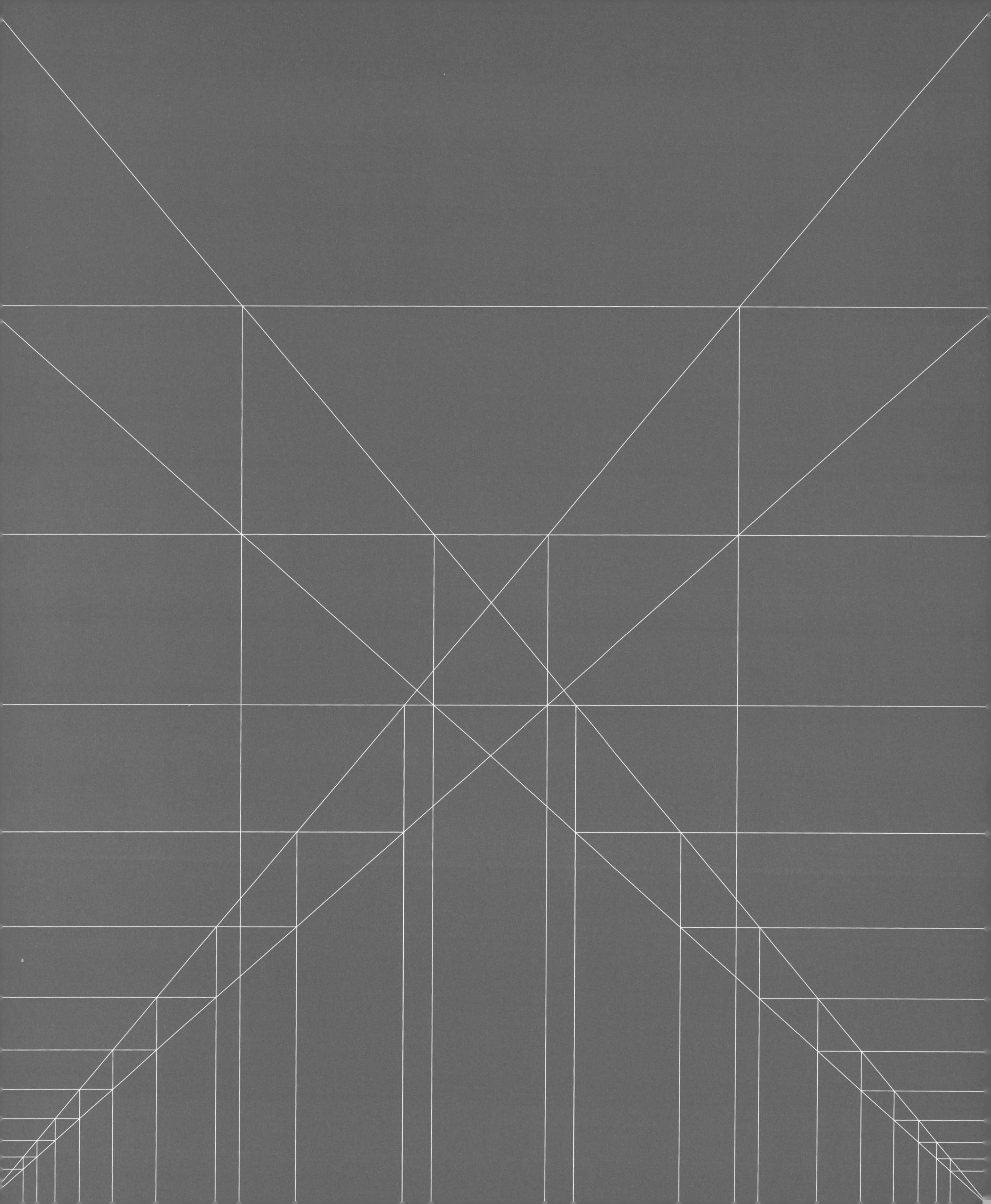

Artist Biographies
Kai Mora

The following brief biographies include less widely known figures whose works are illustrated in the publication but not discussed at length and those who are not usually associated with an interest in ancient Egypt.

TERRY ADKINS
(Washington, D.C. 1953–2014 Brooklyn, New York)

Adkins's artistic interest in the Eurocentric influence on Black identity was catalyzed by his experience in an all-Black Catholic school before attending Fisk University in the early 1970s, where he was mentored by Aaron Douglas. In 1986 Adkins founded the Lone Wolf Recital Corps, which bridged visual and performance art, underpinned by explorations of Greek and Roman classicism within Black history. This sensibility was heightened by his residency in 2009 at the American Academy in Rome, which fed a sustained engagement with both European and Afrocentric Egyptology. In 2010 Adkins completed *Obelisks in Rome* (pl. 5), and in 2013, *Oxidation Blue 1* (pl. 4). In 2013, months before his death, Adkins and his Lone Wolf Recital Corps presented *At Osiris,* which paired *Obelisks in Rome* with live music and recitation from texts that invoked the ancient Egyptian god's assistance as guardian of the afterlife.

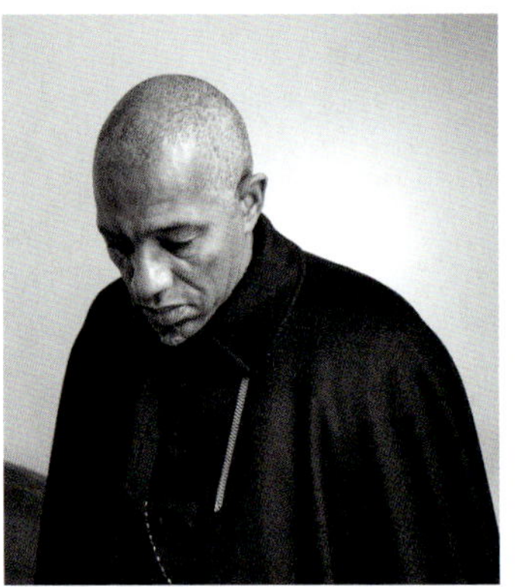

Luca Nostri (Spanish, b. 1976). **Terry Adkins, Lugo,** 2012

ALICE COLTRANE
(Detroit 1937–2007 Los Angeles)

Born Alice McLeod, Coltrane was a composer, musician, bandleader, and pioneer jazz harpist. Starting as a pianist and organist for local churches, by the 1950s she was a regular in Detroit's jazz scene and had studied music in Paris. In 1965 she married musician John Coltrane, joined his band, and began studying the harp, which became central to her role as bandleader after John's death. In a documentary filmed in 1970 for the WNET series *Black Journal*, Alice explained that "the harp . . . makes me recall Egypt, ancient Egypt—it makes me seem to remember that I have a past or history there somewhere" (pl. 140). Her album *Ptah, the El Daoud* (1970) expressed her encounters with Egyptian spirituality, Islam, and Hinduism (pl. 112).

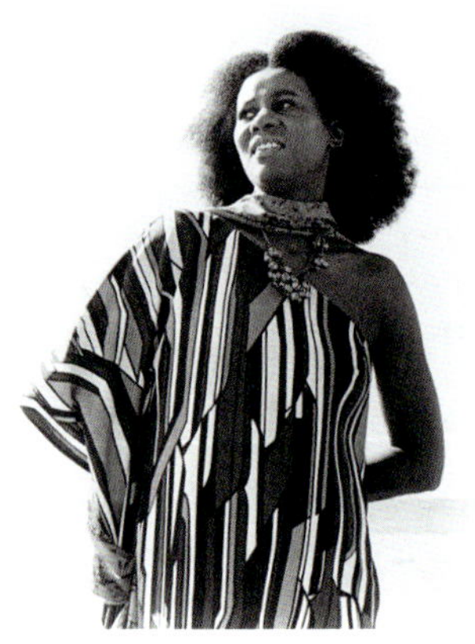

Unknown photographer. **Alice Coltrane,** ca. 1970. Michael Ochs Archives

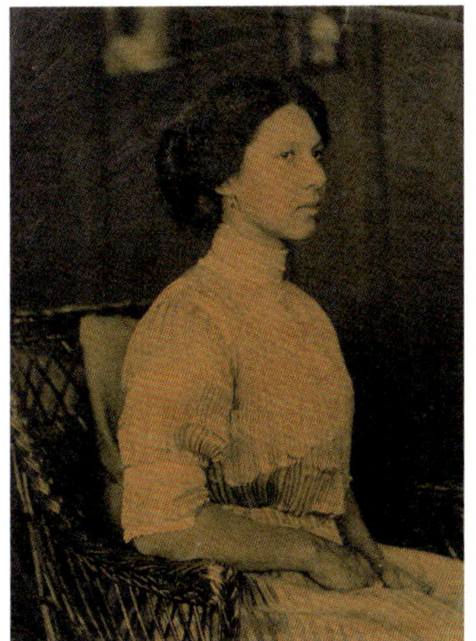

Carl Van Vechten (American, 1880–1964). **Aaron Douglas**, April 10, 1933. Gelatin silver print, 9⅞ x 8 in. (25.2 x 20.2 cm). Carl Van Vechten Papers Relating to African American Arts and Letters, James Weldon Johnson Collection in the Yale Collection of American Literature, Beinecke Rare Book and Manuscript Library, Yale University, New Haven (2019633)

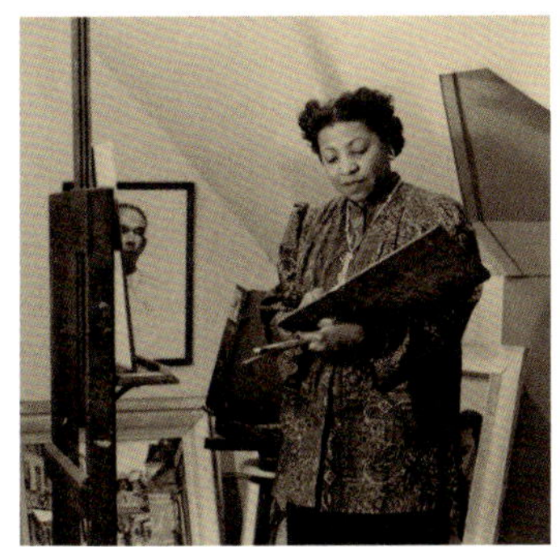

Unknown photographer. **Meta Vaux Warrick Fuller**, ca. 1910. Cyanotype, 9½ x 7½ in. (24.1 x 19 cm). Schomburg Center for Research in Black Culture, Photographs and Prints Division, The New York Public Library

Robert S. Scurlock (American, 1916–1994). **Loïs Mailou Jones**, 1950. Gelatin silver print, 7¹⁵⁄₁₆ x 9¹⁵⁄₁₆ in. (20.2 x 25.3 cm). National Portrait Gallery, Smithsonian Institution, Washington, D.C. (S/NPG.2009.9)

AARON DOUGLAS
(Topeka, Kans. 1899–1979 Nashville, Tenn.)

An illustrator, painter, and educator, Douglas was one of the leading visual artists of the Harlem Renaissance. His early work caught the attention of Charles S. Johnson, a sociologist, the first Black president of Fisk University, and the editor of the National Urban League's periodical *Opportunity: A Journal of Negro Life*. Douglas arrived in New York City in 1925 at Johnson's invitation and was immediately embraced by the community of notable artists and intellectuals of the Harlem Renaissance, including W. E. B. Du Bois and German painter Winold Reiss, who introduced Douglas to Cubism and encouraged him to study African art. He later met Henry Ossawa Tanner in Paris. Douglas's illustrations appeared on the cover of the era's most important periodicals, including *Opportunity* and Du Bois's *The Crisis* (pls. 35, 37). He blended European modernism with West and Central African and ancient Egyptian aesthetics as well as elements of Ethiopianism, which became critical to the emergence of Afrocentric art. In 1940 Douglas accepted a position in Fisk University's art department; he became department chair before retiring to Kansas in 1966.

META VAUX WARRICK FULLER
(Philadelphia 1887–1968 Framingham, Mass.)

Fuller was a leading sculptor of the Harlem Renaissance. After graduating from the Pennsylvania Academy of Fine Arts in 1898, she traveled to Paris, where she was mentored by Henry Ossawa Tanner. In Paris she met W. E. B. Du Bois, who would later aid in commissioning one of her seminal works, *Ethiopia Awakening* (pl. 22), for the 1921 America's Making Exposition in New York. The sculpture reflected her experience as an artist amid the archaeological recovery of ancient Egyptian artifacts in the early 1900s and the literary-religious tradition of Ethiopianism that emerged from the biblical prophecy of Psalm 68:31, "Princes shall come out of Egypt; Ethiopia shall soon stretch out her hands unto God." Ethiopianism featured prominently in the political program of contemporary influential leaders such as Marcus Garvey.

LOÏS MAILOU JONES
(Boston 1905–1998 Washington, D.C.)

Endearingly referred to as the "Grande Dame of African American Art" by fellow visual artist Jeff Donaldson, Jones worked as a painter, designer, and educator during a career spanning more than forty years. Initially she was influenced by Impressionism, which she encountered while living in Paris, and by her mentor Meta Vaux Warrick Fuller, who inspired her work *The Ascent of Ethiopia* (pl. 23). However, a trip to Haiti in the late 1940s and two trips to Africa in the 1970s led her to incorporate Afrocentric motifs into her art. This shift was underpinned by her connections to key figures such as Aaron Douglas and Alain Locke, who asserted that Western art movements were inspired by African art and encouraged its reclamation. At the end of her life, in an interview with Mildred Thompson for the periodical *Art Papers*, Jones reflected on her sense of ownership of the legacy of African art: "It's my heritage—I mean I can make it mine, because I'm more a part of it than [white artists] were."

EDMONIA LEWIS
(Greenbush, N.Y. 1844–1907 London)

Raised in her mother's Ojibwe community in New York State, Lewis entered Oberlin College to study sculpture but was forced to leave because of racially motivated violence against her that obstructed her education. She moved to Boston, where she benefited from the patronage of influential abolitionists. Their support and her earnings enabled Lewis to go to Rome in 1866, where she began sculpting figures related to her native heritage and Catholic faith in her trademark neoclassical style, doing her own stone carving—a rarity for the era. In 1875, she created *Hagar*, a depiction of the biblical Egyptian woman, and her largest work, *The Death of Cleopatra* (fig. 5), for the Philadelphia Centennial Exposition in 1876. Lewis remained in Rome for most of the rest of her life, moving to London shortly before her death.

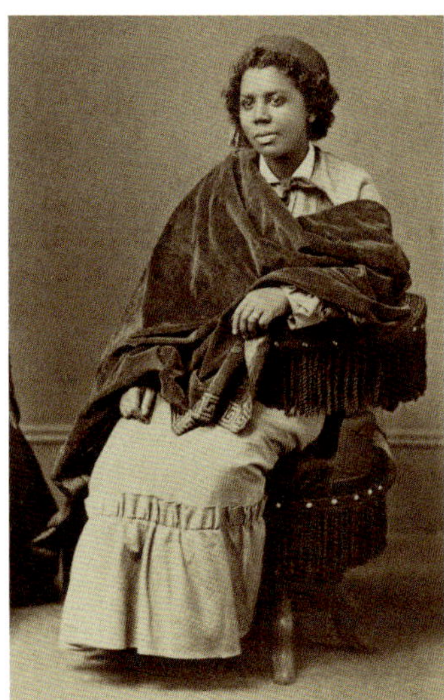

Henry Rocher (German, 1826–1887). **Edmonia Lewis**, ca. 1870. Photograph, 3⅝ × 2¹⁄₁₆ in. (9.2 × 5.2 cm). National Portrait Gallery, Smithsonian Institution, Washington, D.C. (NPG.94.95)

MALCOLM X
(Omaha, Neb. 1925–1965 New York)

Spending almost a decade in the carceral system as a young man, Malcolm X was there introduced to the Nation of Islam in the 1940s, altering his life's path. By the early 1950s, his position as an emerging leader in the Nation led to an invitation by Egyptian officials to visit the region in 1959, his first trip to Africa. Already convinced that ancient Egypt was a Black civilization, Malcolm X began to assert racial and historical links between African and Arab worlds after his visit, subsequently demonstrating a strong dedication to Pan-Africanism, Islam, and Afro-Asiatic unity. In 1964, Malcolm X took his third and last visit to Egypt just months before his death, writing "my heart is in Cairo" in a letter to Muhammad Taufik Oweida, the United Arab Republic's minister of religious endowment. On this last visit, Malcolm also made hajj (the pilgrimage required of all Muslims) to Mecca in western Saudi Arabia, where he was given the name El-Hajj Malik El-Shabazz.

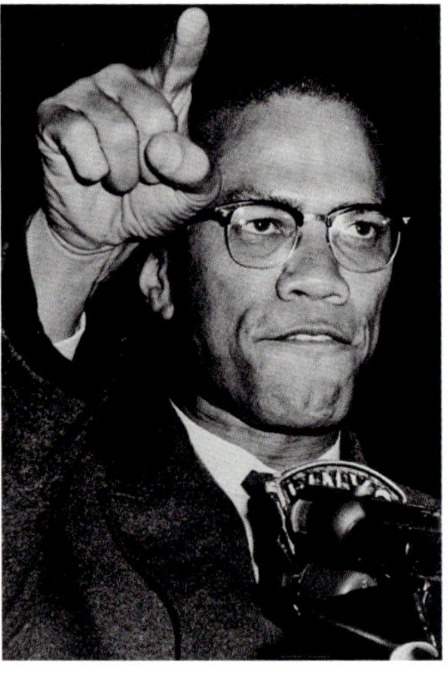

Unknown photographer. **Malcolm X**, 1967. Halftone poster, 2³⁄₁₆ × 29⁷⁄₁₆ in. (107.2 × 74.8 cm). National Portrait Gallery, Smithsonian Institution, Washington, D.C. (NPG.95.36)

MAHMOUD MOKHTAR
(Nile Delta, Egypt 1891–1934 Cairo)

Although his career was relatively brief, Mokhtar is recognized as the progenitor of modern Egyptian sculpture. In 1908 he entered the newly established Egyptian School of Fine Arts in Cairo, a linchpin in the cultural and intellectual renaissance of early twentieth-century Egypt, then occupied by the British. He studied at the Ecole des Beaux Arts, Paris, and stayed there to eke out a living doing menial jobs while making sculptures. A maquette displayed at a Paris salon in 1920 drew the attention of Egyptian revolutionaries. They raised funds for a monumental version of the sculpture *Egypt Awakening* (*Nahdat Misr*), installed in 1928 in Bab el-Hadid Square (pl. 64). It embodied of nationalist sentiments in the country. Mokhtar was instrumental in

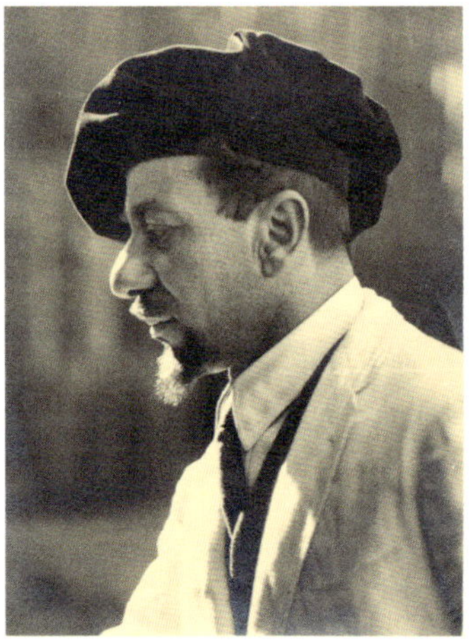

Unknown photographer. **Mahmoud Mokhtar**, n.d. Collection of Emad Badr el-Din Mahmoud Abu Ghazi

catalyzing support for the Egyptian nationalist movement by giving visual form to the struggle for independence. In the following year, Mokhtar exhibited *Bride of the Nile (Arous El Nil)*, another monumental sculpture, in which he continued to juxtapose neoclassical references with ancient Egyptian motifs, also highlighting his sustained choice to depict unveiled or unveiling women subjects as a critical part of his commentary on Egypt's emerging national identity (see pl. 65).

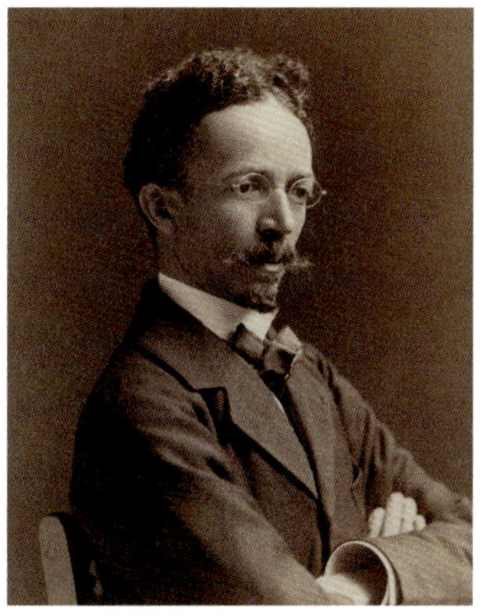

Frederick Gutekunst (American, 1831–1917). **Henry Ossawa Tanner**, ca. 1897. Albumen silver print, 5⁵⁄₁₆ x 4⅛ in. (14.2 x 10.4 cm). National Portrait Gallery, Smithsonian Institution, Washington, D.C. (NPG.2011.10)

HENRY OSSAWA TANNER
(Pittsburgh, Pa. 1859–1937 Paris, France)

Tanner was a painter noted for his depictions of Christian religious subjects. Tanner's father became a bishop in the African Methodist Episcopal Church (AME), the first independent Black denomination in the United States, and was a friend of Frederick Douglass. His mother was a formerly enslaved woman. Tanner attended the Pennsylvania Academy of Fine Arts, studying under Thomas Eakins. After immigrating to Paris in 1891, he pivoted from genre paintings with African American subjects to religious scenes. In 1897 he visited Egypt and Palestine, where he painted several works, including *Interior of a Mosque* (pl. 1); he later painted *Flight into Egypt* (pl. 2), a biblical reference that he would revisit throughout his career.

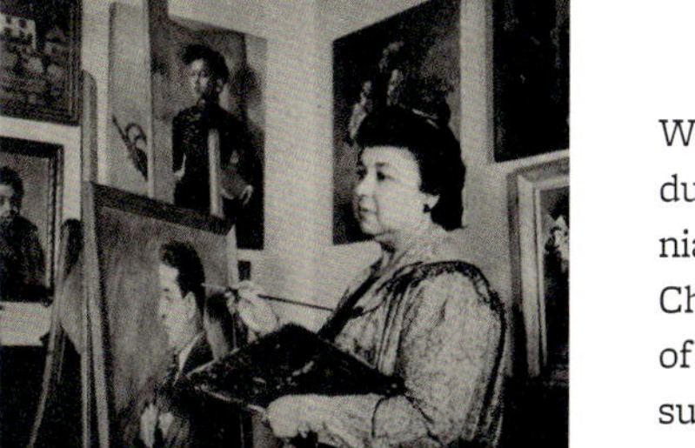

Unknown photographer. **Laura Wheeler Waring: Portrait Painter**. Schomburg Center for Research in Black Culture, Art and Artifacts Division, The New York Public Library

LAURA WHEELER WARING
(Hartford, Conn. 1887–1948 Philadelphia)

Waring was a prominent painter, illustrator, and educator during the Harlem Renaissance. She entered the Pennsylvania Academy of Fine Arts (PAFA) and began teaching at the Cheyney State Teachers College (now Cheyney University of Pennsylvania) in 1906. While in college, she also taught summer drawing classes at Harvard and Columbia. In 1914, she graduated from PAFA and won a scholarship to tour Western Europe, where, in Paris, she met several influential Black artists and leaders, including Henry Ossawa Tanner and W. E. B. Du Bois. After returning to the United States in the early 1920s, Waring contributed to Du Bois's *The Crisis*, becoming the magazine's most featured female illustrator (pls. 30-32). Influenced by the discovery of Tutankhamun's tomb in 1922, she became known for her use of ancient Egyptian iconography in her illustrations. She continued to pursue the arts and taught at Cheyney State Teachers College until her death in 1948.

Notes

Flight into Egypt: Black Artists and Ancient Egypt, 1876–Now Akili Tommasino

1. "*Flight into Egypt*, Henry Ossawa Tanner, American, 1923," The Met Collection, accessed April 8, 2024, https://www.metmuseum.org/art/collection/search/16947.

2. Matthew 2:12–14.

3. Matthew 2:15.

4. "*Untitled (Flight into Egypt)*, Henry Ossawa Tanner, American, ca. 1923," The Met Collection, accessed April 8, 2024, https://www.metmuseum.org/art/collection/search/904568.

5. Although the artist had visited Egypt in 1897, most Tanner scholars associate the painting at The Met with his 1912 trip to Morocco, based in part on his transposition of the architecture he encountered there. I am grateful to Sylvia Yount, Lawrence A Fleischman Curator in Charge of the American Wing, The Met, for this information, communicated in an email message on November 16, 2023.

6. While the African diaspora is global, this exhibition does not engage extensively with the histories of Black cultural figures of Asia or South America; nor does it explore the networks of cultural exchange between modern Egypt and other parts of Africa.

7. Frederick Douglass, "The Claims of the Negro, Ethnologically Considered: An Address before the Literary Societies of Western Reserve College, At Commencement, July 12, 1864" (Rochester: Lee, Mann, 1854), p. 17, https://www.loc.gov/resource/rbaapc.07900.

8. Frederick Douglass to Lewis H. Douglass, February 20, 1887, quoted in William S. McFeely, *Frederick Douglass* (New York: W. W. Norton, 1991), pp. 331–32.

9. According to The Met's Heilbrunn Timeline of Art History, https://www.metmuseum.org/toah.

10. Italics in original. Jennifer Trimble, "Appropriating Egypt for the Ara Pacis Augustae," in *Rome, Empire of Plunder: The Dynamics of Cultural Appropriation*, ed. Matthew P. Loar, Carolyn MacDonald, and Dan-el Padilla Peralta (Cambridge: Cambridge University Press, 2018), p. 116.

11. Ironically, a major publication on the subject signals that "apart from an introductory chapter on their cultic significance, we shall consider the obelisks here as Roman rather than Egyptian monuments." Erik Iverson, "Preface," *Obelisks in Exile*, vol. 1, *The Obelisks of Rome* (Copenhagen: G. E. C. Gad, 1968).

12. Susan Sorek, *The Emperor's Needles: Egyptian Obelisks and Rome* (Bristol, U.K.: Phoenix Press, 2010), pp. 10–11.

13. Sorek, *The Emperor's Needles*, pp. 26–27.

14. Sorek, *The Emperor's Needles*, p. 11. Sorek's is the first major work to link the great civilizations of Egypt and Rome through the "eccentric preoccupation shown by Roman emperors for these monuments," p. i.

15. Sorek, *The Emperor's Needles*, p. 68.

16. In addition to Adkins, other artists whose works are represented in *Flight into Egypt* have also been Rome Prize Fellows: David Hammons, Dream The Combine, Eric Mack, and Fred Wilson. Barbara Chase-Riboud's residency is discussed later in this essay.

17. See Akili Tommasino, *Projects 107: Lone Wolf Recital Corps*, exh. brochure (New York: Museum of Modern Art, 2017).

18. Description accompanying "Terry Adkins, Blanche Bruce and the LWRC: At Osiris (2013)," Studio Museum of Harlem, November 26, 2013, YouTube video, 46:27, https://www.youtube.com/watch?v=Lyhzys9nH-U.

19. Third Streaming, LLC, "The Lone Wolf Recital Corps: Atum (Honey from a Flower Named Blue)," press release for a performance on May 27, 2012, https://artguide.artforum.com/uploads/guide.001/id26496/press_release.pdf.

20. *David Hammons, Janis Kounellis*, exh. cat. (Rome: American Academy in Rome, 1993), p. 8.

21. Grant Parker, "Monolithic Appropriation? The Lateran Obelisk Compared," in Loar et al., *Rome: Empire of Plunder*, p. 145.

22. The Metropolitan Museum of Art, "The African Origin of Civilization," press release, updated August 11, 2022, https://www.metmuseum.org/press/exhibitions/2021/african-origin.

23. Diana Craig Patch and Alisa LaGama, "The African Origin of Civilization," special issue, *The Metropolitan Museum of Art Bulletin*, n.s., 79, no. 4 (spring 2022), p. 11.

24. Lawrence Berman, email message to author, July 6, 2023.

25. See, for example, Ian Duffield, "Dusé Mohamed Ali and the Development of Pan-Africanism, 1866–1945" (PhD diss., Edinburgh University, 1971), p. 205; and Dusé Mohamed Ali to W. E. B. Du Bois, May 25, 1921, W. E. B. Du Bois Papers (MS 312), Special Collections and University Archives, University of Massachusetts Amherst Libraries, https://credo.library.umass.edu/view/full/mums312-b016-i218.

26. "Something Out of Nothing is Negro's Gift to Science," *Virginia Register*, November 2, 1932.

27. Information shared at an online meeting convened by Anna Serotta on June 10, 2024.

28. Yosef A. A. ben-Jochannan, *Black Man of the Nile and His Family* (New York: Alkebu-Lan Books, 1972).

29. Cheikh Anta Diop, *The African Origin of Civilization: Myth or Reality* (Chicago: Lawrence Hill Books, 1974).

30. Martin Bernal, *Black Athena: The Afroasiatic Roots of Classical Civilization* (New Brunswick, N.J.: Rutgers University Press, 1987).

31. Solange Ashby, *Calling Out to Isis: The Enduring Nubian Presence at Philae* (Piscataway, N.J.: Gorgias Press, 2020).

32. Melissa Dabakis, "Antislavery Sermons in Stone," in *A Sisterhood of Sculptors: American Artists in Nineteenth-Century Rome* (University Park: Pennsylvania State University Press, 2014), pp. 149–80.

33. Thanks to Shawon Kinew, assistant professor in the Department of History of Art and Architecture at Harvard University, for this reference.

34. Kirsten Pai Buick argues for more nuanced readings of Lewis's work in her book *Child of the Fire: Mary Edmonia Lewis and the Problem of Art History's Black and Indian Subject* (Durham, N.C.: Duke University Press, 2010).

35. *Barbara Chase-Riboud: The Monument Drawings*, curated by Lowery Stokes Sims, June 22–September 5, 1999. Chase-Riboud was the recipient of a John Hay Whitney Fellowship.

36. Quoted in Gregory N. Daugherty, "Barbara Chase-Riboud's Multimedia Receptions of Cleopatra," *New Voices in Classical Reception Studies* 8 (2013), p. 49, https://fass.open.ac.uk/sites/fass.open.ac.uk/files/files/new-voices-journal/issue8/daugherty.pdf.

37. Akili Tommasino, "The Cleopatra Sculptures," in *Barbara Chase-Riboud, Monumentale: The Bronzes*, ed. Stephanie Weissberg (St. Louis: Pulitzer Arts Foundation, 2023), pp. 41–46.

38. Dabakis, "Antislavery Sermons in Stone," p. 175.

39. Psalms 68:31.

40. Dabakis, "Antislavery Sermons in Stone," p. 159.

41. In a confluence of politics and religion, Marcus Garvey's promotion of this verse is associated by some with the ascension of Haile Selassie I to the throne of Ethiopia in 1930. See Aswad Walker, *Princes Shall Come out of Egypt: A Comparative Study of the Theologies and Eclessiological Views of Marcus Garvey and Alber B. Cleage Jr.* (Dubuque, Iowa: Kendall Hunt, 2012).

42. Adkins's work made Carver's achievement visible to this author.

43. "Alice Coltrane," *Black Journal*, directed by Stan Latham (New York: National Educational Television, 1970).

44. See, for example, Kenneth Silver, *Esprit de Corps: The Art of the Parisian Avant-Garde and the First World War, 1914–1925* (Princeton, N.J.: Princeton University Press, 1989); and *Chaos and Classicism: Art in France, Italy, and Germany, 1918–1936*, exh. cat., Solomon R. Guggenheim Museum, New York, and Guggenheim Museum, Bilbao, 2010–11 (New York: Guggenheim Museum, 2010).

45. The recurrent engagement of modern and contemporary Black cultural practitioners with ancient Egypt can be read as forming a liberatory retrograde that upends the European art historical paradigm of the interwar return to figuration and its attendant nationalist archaisms.

46. Trimble, "Appropriating Egypt," p. 110. Trimble here summarizes the case made in Robert S. Nelson, "Appropriation," in *Critical Terms for Art History*, ed. Robert S. Nelson and Richard Schiff (Chicago: University of Chicago Press, 1996), pp. 116–28.

47 Douglass, "The Claims of the Negro," pp. 17–22. See also Andrea Myers Achi, "The Problem of the Color Line," in this volume.

48 See Penny M. Von Eschen, *Satchmo Blows Up the World: Jazz Ambassadors Play the Cold War* (Cambridge, Mass.: Harvard University Press, 2004).

49 "John Shabazz & Malcolm Little in L.A.," audio recording, Lectures by the Former Laborers, Nation of Islam Historical Archives Online, https://www.noiwc.info /audio---former-laborers.html.

50 *Richard Pryor: Live on the Sunset Strip*, directed by Joe Latham (Burbank, Calif.: Columbia Pictures, 1982).

51 *Seated Statue of Hatshepsut*, New Kingdom, ca. 1479–1458 BCE. The Metropolitan Museum of Art, New York, Rogers Fund, 1929 (29.3.2).

52 "Abd al-Latif's remarks [in 1200–1202 CE] lead us to think that the Sphinx's nose was still intact, although there are indications that it was cut off as early as the 10th century. The nose was long gone, at any rate, when Napoleon visited the Sphinx in 1798. . . . Already in the early 15th century al-Maqrizi wrote that a Sufi named Sa'im El-Dahr, outraged that the local peasants still made offerings to the Sphinx, destroyed the nose in 1378." Mark Lehner and Zahi Hawass, *Giza and the Pyramids: The Definitive History* (Chicago: University of Chicago Press, 2017), p. 86.

53 Abraham Thomas, *The Roof Garden Commission: Lauren Halsey* (New York: The Metropolitan Museum of Art, 2023), p. 38.

The Problem of the Color Line: Black Americans and the Field of Egyptology Andrea Myers Achi

1 The regions below the Sahara have a deep history with expansive, cosmopolitan kingdoms from antiquity to the early modern period. For a discussion of the modern concept of Africa and a critique of the notion that it lacked a deep history, see Ali A. Mazrui, "The Re-Invention of Africa: Edward Said, V. Y. Mudimbe, and Beyond," *Research in African Literatures* 36, no. 3 (Autumn 2005), pp. 68–82; and particularly V. Y. Mudimbe, *The Invention of Africa: Gnosis, Philosophy, and the Order of Knowledge* (Bloomington: Indiana University Press, 1988). For comprehensive discussions of Black American engagement with the field of Egyptology, see the work of Egyptologist Vanessa Davies, particularly "Egypt and Egyptology in the Pan-African Discourse of Amy Jacques Garvey and Marcus Garvey," *Mare Nostrum* 13, no. 1 (December 2022), pp. 147–78; "Egyptological Conversations on Race and Science," *Rockefeller Archive Center Research Reports* (2018), pp. 1–12; "Pauline Hopkins' Literary Egyptology," *Journal of Egyptian History* 14, no. 2 (December 2021), pp. 127–44; and "Booker T. Washington's Challenge for Egyptology: African-Centered Research in the Nile Valley," *Dotawo: A Journal of Nubian Studies*, Miscellanea (2023), https://doi .org/10.5070/D60060622.

2 Georg Wilhelm Friedrich Hegel, *Lectures on the Philosophy of History* (1861; London: G. Bell and Sons, 1910), p. 103.

3 Race is a malleable concept. For discussions of the term, see James Smalls, "Dressing Up/Stripping Down," in *Fictions of Emancipation: Carpeaux's "Why Born Enslaved!" Reconsidered*, ed. Elyse Nelson and Wendy S. Walters, exh. cat. (New York: The Metropolitan Museum of Art, 2022), pp. 62–63; Geraldine Heng, "The Invention of Race in the European Middle Ages I: Race Studies, Modernity, and the Middle Ages," *Literature Compass* 8, no. 5 (2011), pp. 258–74; Troy Duster, "Buried Alive: The Concept of Race in Science," in *Genetic Nature/Culture: Anthropology and Science beyond the Two-Culture Divide*, ed. Alan H. Goodman, Deborah Heath, and M. Susan Lindee (Berkeley: University of California Press, 2003), pp. 258–77; Michael Omi, "The Changing Meaning of Race," in *America Becoming: Racial Trends and Their Consequences*, ed. Neil J. Smelser, William Julius Wilson, and Faith Mitchell (Washington, D.C.: National Academy Press, 2001), vol. 1, pp. 243–63, https://doi.org/10.17226/9599.

4 For a summary of the development of Egyptology alongside Egyptomania and interests in racial identity of the Egyptians, see, Renée Ater, *Remaking Race and History: The Sculpture of Meta Vaux Warrick Fuller* (Berkeley: University of California Press, 2011), pp. 110–15.

5 W. E. B. Du Bois, *Black Folk Then and Now: An Essay in the History and Sociology of the Negro Race*, vol. 7 of *The Oxford W. E. B. Du Bois*, ed. Henry Louis Gates Jr. (1939; Oxford: Oxford University Press, 2016), p. 18.

6 Hany Rashwan, "Against Eurocentrism: Decolonizing Eurocentric Literary Theories in the Ancient Egyptian and Arabic Poetics," *Howard Journal of Communications* 32, no. 22 (2021), p. 172.

7 For an overview of the one-drop rule see Daniel J. Sharfstein, "Crossing the Color Line: Racial Migration and the One-Drop Rule, 1600–1860," *Minnesota Literary Review* 91 (2007), pp. 592–656. These topics, however, have not expanded to the study of other regional histories in northeastern Africa, for example to what extent the Sudanese or Ethiopians consider themselves to be "Black" in the American sense of the word. It may be that these questions are not asked because the answer is assumed without a critical understanding of the meaning of these color words for those countries in both ancient and modern times.

8 "Pan-African Association. To the nations of the world, ca. 1900," W. E. B. Du Bois Papers (MS 312), Special Collections and University Archives, University of Massachusetts Amherst Libraries, http://credo.library .umass.edu/view/full/mums312-b004-i321.

9 Mabel O. Wilson, "The Cartography of W. E. B. Du Bois's Color Line," in *W. E. B. Du Bois's Data Portraits: Visualizing Black America, The Color Line at the Turn of the Twentieth Century*, ed. Whitney Battle-Baptiste and Britt Rusert (Amherst: The W. E. B. Du Bois Center at the University of Massachusetts Amherst; New York: Princeton Architectural Press, 2018), p. 42.

10 "In July 1926, when Amy Jacques Garvey wanted to talk about African history, she turned to a newly discovered piece of evidence: the gold mask of Tutankhamun that had been unearthed only nine months earlier." Vanessa Davies, "Egypt and Egyptology," p. 148.

11 American Egyptological scholars have considered this topic. For an overview and bibliography of the representation of Black Nubians as prisoners and the differences between Nubians and Egyptians in Egyptian art, see Tara Prakash, "From Saqqara to Brussels: A Head from a Sixth Dynasty Prisoner Statue in the Musées Royaux d'Art et d'Histoire," *Chronique d'Egypte* 95, no. 189 (2020), pp. 5–19. See also Tara Prakash, *Ancient Egyptian Prisoner Statues: Fragments of the Late Old Kingdom* (Columbus, Ga.: Lockwood Press, 2022).

12 Ater, *Remaking Race*, p. 110.

13 Charles S. Finch III, "The Black Roots of Egypt's Glory," Opinion, *Washington Post*, October 10, 1987, https:// www.washingtonpost.com/archive/opinions/1987/10/11 /the-black-roots-of-egypts-glory/1c3faf74-331c-4cc1 -a6a0-3535fa3e098a/.

14 Robert Morkot and Stephen Quirke, "Inventing the 25th Dynasty: Turin Stela 1467 and the Construction of History," in *Begegnungen–Antike Kulturen im Niltal: Festgabe für Erika Endesfelder, Karl-Heinz Priese, Walter Friedrich Reineke, Steffen Wenig*, ed. Caris-Beatrice Arnst, Ingelore Hafemann, and Angelika Lohwasser (Leipzig: Wodtke und Stegbauer, 2001), pp. 349–63.

15 Italics added. George A. Reisner, *Excavations at Kerma, Parts I–III*, Harvard African Studies

(Cambridge, Mass.: Peabody Museum of Harvard
University; Harvard University Press, 1923), vol. 5,
p. 8; see also J. W. Crowfoot, "Excavations at Kerma,
Volumes V and VI, by George A. Reisner," Reviews,
Sudan Notes and Records 7, no. 1 (July 1924), pp. 113–17.

16   Reisner, *Excavations at Kerma*, p. 7.

17   This interpretation of race, which applied to anyone
with African ancestry, even if they were multiracial
or multiethnic, was further complicated by the later
inclusion of North Africans and Middle Easterners in
the "white" category in the U.S. census. Only in the
mid-2020s are "North African" and "Middle Eastern"
gaining traction as potential census categories. See
"Revisions to OMB's Statistical Policy Directive
No. 15: Standards for Maintaining, Collecting, and
Presenting Federal Data on Race and Ethnicity," Office
on Management and Budget, March 29, 2024, https://
www.federalregister.gov/d/2024-06469.

18   Melissa Nobles, *Shades of Citizenship: Race and the
Census in Modern Politics* (Stanford: Stanford University Press, 2000), p. 72, also pp. 44, 58.

19   For example, "Was King Tut a Negro?," *Negro World*,
March 24, 1923.

20   Leila Amos Pendleton, *A Narrative of the Negro* (Washington, D.C.: Press of R. L. Pendleton, 1912), p. 15.

21   John Henrik Clarke, "Pan-Africanism: A Brief History of
an Idea in the African World," *Présence Africaine*, n.s.,
no. 145 (1988), pp. 26–56.

22   See, for example, W. E. B. Du Bois and W. M. Flinders
Petrie, "Self-Righteous Europe and the World: Corre-
spondence with W. M. Flinders Petrie," *The Crisis* 4, no. 1
(May 1912), pp. 34–37.

23   Vanessa Davies, "Egypt and Egyptology," p. 8.

24   Kehinde Andrews, "Beyond Pan-Africanism: Garveyism, Malcolm X and the End of the Colonial Nation
State," *Third World Quarterly* 38, no. 11 (2017), pp. 2501–16.

25   "If we direct our attention after that to the second
circle, the circle of the continent of Africa, I would
say, without exaggeration, that we cannot, even if we
wish to, in any way stand aside from the sanguinary
and dreadful struggle now raging in the heat of Africa
between five million whites and two hundred million
Africans. We cannot do so for one principal and clear
reason, namely that we are in Africa." Gamal Abdel
Nasser, "The Philosophy of the Revolution, 1959," in
*The Political Thought of African Independence: An
Anthology of Sources*, ed. Gregory R. Smulewicz-Zucker
(Indianapolis: Hackett, 2017), p. 74.

26   Ibid.; see also Adeoye A. Akinsanya, "The Afro-Arab
Alliance: Dream or Reality," *African Affairs* 75, no. 301
(October 1976), pp. 511–29.

27   Kwame Wes Alford, "The Early Intellectual Growth and
Development of William Leo Hansberry and the Birth
of African Studies," *Journal of Black Studies* 30, no. 3
(January 2000), pp. 269–93.

28   From the Charles C. Seifert Papers, Arthur C. Schomburg
Collection, New York Public Library. Cited in Maghan
Keita, *Race and the Writing of History: Riddling the
Sphinx* (Oxford: Oxford University Press, 2000), p. 100;

and J. G. Spady, "Dr. William Leo Hansberry: The Legacy
of an African Hunter," *A Current Bibliography on African
Affairs* 3, nos. 11–12 (November 1970), pp. 28–29.

29   For a longer discussion of Hansberry's multi-disciplinary
work on this topic, see Keita, *Race and the Writing of
History*, pp. 95–123.

30   For debates around Snowden's interpretation of race in
antiquity, see Keita's useful overview in *Race and the
Writing of History*, pp. 123–51.

31   See, for example, Diana Craig Patch and Alisa
LaGamma, "The African Origin of Civilization," special
issue, *The Metropolitan Museum of Art Bulletin*, n.s., 79,
no. 4 (Spring 2022); Marc Van De Mieroop, *A History of
Ancient Egypt*, 2nd ed. (Hoboken, N.J.: Wiley, 2021); and
Andrea Manzo, *Ancient Egypt in Its African Context:
Economic Networks, Social and Cultural Interactions*
(Cambridge: Cambridge University Press, 2022).

32   Martin Bernal, *Black Athena: The Afroasiatic Roots of
Classical Civilization*, vol. 1, *The Fabrication of Ancient
Greece 1785–1985* (New Brunswick, N.J.: Rutgers Univer-
sity Press, 1987); Martin Bernal, *Black Athena Writes
Back: Martin Bernal Responds to His Critics*, ed. David
Chioni Moore (Durham, N.C.: Duke University Press,
2001); and Suzanne Marchand and Anthony Grafton,
"Martin Bernal and His Critics," *Arion: A Journal of
Humanities and the Classics*, 3rd ser., 5, no. 2 (Fall
1997), pp. 1–35. Most of the pushback came from clas-
sics scholars such as Mary Lefkowitz. See Ann Mary
Roth, review of *Not Out of Africa: How Afrocentrism
Became an Excuse to Teach Myth as History*, by Mary
Lefkowitz, and *Black Athena Revisited*, ed. Mary R.
Lefkowitz and Rogers Guy Maclean, *American Histori-
cal Review* 102, no. 2 (April 1977), pp. 493–95, https://doi
.org/10.1086/ahr/102.2.493-a.

33   For example, see Molefi Kete Asante, *The History of
Africa: The Quest for Eternal Harmony*, 3rd ed. (New
York: Routledge, 2018).

34   Christel N. Temple, "Ancient Kemet in African American
Literature and Criticism, 1853 to the Present," *Journal of
Pan African Studies* 5, no. 4 (June 2012), pp. 129–48.

35   David O'Connor, "Egypt and Greece: The Bronze Age
Evidence," in *Black Athena Revisited*, ed. Mary R.
Lefkowitz and Guy Maclean Rogers (Chapel Hill:
University of North Carolina Press, 1996), pp. 49–61;
David O'Connor and Andrew Reid, eds., *Ancient
Egypt in Africa* (2003; London: Routledge, 2016). For
O'Connor's early thoughts on the "Black African" influ-
ence on Egypt (or lack thereof) and vice versa, see
David O'Connor, "Ancient Egypt and Black Africa: Early
Contacts," *Expedition Magazine* 14, no. 1 (September
1971), pp. 2–9, https://www.penn.museum/sites
/expedition/ancient-egypt-and-black-africa/.

36   Solange Ashby received her doctorate in Egyptology in
2016 and is likely the first Black woman to receive her
degree in the field. However, to the author's knowledge, the American Research Center in Egypt (ARCE),
whose mission is to "support research on all aspects of
Egyptian history and culture; to protect, preserve and
promote Egyptian cultural heritage; and to strengthen

American-Egyptian cultural collaboration," has not kept
data on the race and ethnicities of Egyptologists. ARCE
has made efforts to diversify its organization, including
creating a travel grant for underrepresented students
to attend its annual meeting. ARCE "Mission, Vision
and Values," accessed April 22, 2024, https://arce.org
/mission-vision-and-values/. Some ARCE Egyptologists
have undertaken to gather this information themselves.
Egyptology State of the Field, accessed June 19, 2024,
https://egyptologystats.wordpress.com/.

37   Programs like the Mellon Mays Undergraduate Fellowship seek to address this deficiency by creating a
pipeline program from undergraduate through PhD
programs. Egyptology is not an eligible field of study
for the MMUF program, whereas classics is.

38   For an overview of the stakes of the topic in a modern
context, see Tessa Solomon, "Egypt Bans Dutch
Archaeologists from Excavations in Response to
Museum's 'Afrocentric' Egyptian Exhibition," *Artnews*,
June 7, 2023, https://www.artnews.com/art-news/news
/egypt-bans-dutch-archaeologists-leiden-museum
-afrocentric-exhibition-1234670731/.

"We Are Both Myths": Ancient Egypt and Opacity

Mia Matthias

1 Edouard Glissant, "For Opacity," in *Poetics of Relation*, trans. Betsy Wing (Ann Arbor: University of Michigan Press, 1997), pp. 189–94. See also Sylvia Wynter, "Beyond the Word of Man: Glissant and the New Discourse of the Antilles," *World Literature Today* 63, no. 4 (Autumn 1989), pp. 637–48; Adlai Murdoch, "Glissant's Opacité and the De-Nationalization of Identity," *CLR James Journal* 18, no. 1 (Fall 2012), pp. 14–33; and H. Adlai Murdoch, "Édouard Glissant's Creolized World Vision: From Resistance and Relation to 'Opacité,'" *Callaloo* 36, no. 4 (Fall 2013), pp. 875–89.

2 "Pan-African Association. To the nations of the world, ca. 1900," W. E. B. Du Bois Papers (MS 312), Special Collections and University Archives, University of Massachusetts Amherst Libraries, http://credo.library .umass.edu/view/full/mums312-b004-i321.

3 "Materials Compiled by W. E. B. Du Bois," Collection: African American Photographs Assembled for 1900 Paris Exposition, Library of Congress, https://www.loc .gov/collections/african-american-photographs-1900 -paris-exposition/articles-and-essays/materials -compiled-by-web-du-bois/. See also Shawn Michelle Smith, "'Looking at One's Self through the Eyes of Others': W. E. B. Du Bois's Photographs for the 1900 Paris Exposition," *African American Review* 34, no. 4 (Winter 2000), pp. 581–99.

4 Alain Locke, "The Legacy of the Ancestral Arts," in *The New Negro: An Interpretation*, ed. Alain Locke (New York: Albert and Charles Boni, 1925), p. 256.

5 Alain Locke, "A Note on African Art," *Opportunity* 2, no. 17 (May 1924), p. 138.

6 Renée Ater, *Remaking Race and History: The Sculpture of Meta Warrick Fuller* (Berkeley: University of California Press, 2011), p. 115.

7 Ater, *Remaking Race*, p. 111.

8 Judith N. Kerr, "God-Given Work: The Life and Times of Sculptor Meta Vaux Warrick Fuller, 1877–1968" (PhD diss., University of Massachusetts Amherst, 1986), p. 128.

9 Kerr, "God-Given Work," p. 134.

10 Kerr, "God-Given Work," p. 92.

11 Kerr, "God-Given Work," p. 128.

12 Broadside advertising *The Star of Ethiopia* (Washington, D.C., 1915), https://www.loc.gov/item/2020781236/.

13 Ibid.

14 W. E. B. Du Bois, "The Drama Among Black People," *The Crisis* 12, no. 4 (August 1916), p. 171.

15 William E. Leuchtenburg, *The Perils of Prosperity, 1914–32* (Chicago: University of Chicago Press, 1958), pp. 77–81.

16 The Looking Glass, *The Crisis* 23, no. 1 (November 1921), p. 29.

17 "Excavations in Ethiopia," *The Crisis* 2, no. 4 (August 1911), p. 169; see also Renée Ater, "Meta Warrick Fuller's *Ethiopia* and the America's Making Exposition of 1921," in *Women Artists of the Harlem Renaissance*, ed. Amy Helene Kirschke (Oxford: University Press of Mississippi, 2014), pp. 59–60.

18 Meta Warrick Fuller to Mrs. W. P. Hedden, October 5, 1921, Meta Warrick Fuller Papers, Manuscripts, Archives, and Rare Books Division, Schomburg Center for Research in Black Culture, New York Public Library, quoted in Ater, "Fuller's *Ethiopia*," p. 59.

19 These include versions at the Danforth Art Museum, the New York Public Library, and the Smithsonian National Museum of African American History and Culture. See also Renée Ater, "Race, Gender, and Nation: Rethinking the Sculpture of Meta Warrick Fuller" (PhD. diss., University of Maryland, 2000).

20 Ater, "Fuller's *Ethiopia*," p. 60.

21 Meta Warrick Fuller to Mrs. W. P. Hedden, October 5, 1921, Meta Warrick Fuller Papers, Manuscript, Archives, and Rare Books Division, Schomburg Center for Research in Black Culture, New York Public Library, quoted in Ater, "Fuller's *Ethiopia*," p. 59.

22 W. E. B. Du Bois, "Criteria of Negro Art," *The Crisis* 32, no. 6 (October 1926), p. 296.

23 W. E. B. Du Bois, "The Star of Ethiopia," and Opinion, "The Slanderous Film," *The Crisis* 11, no. 2 (December 1915), pp. 91, 76.

24 Alex Haley, *Roots: The Saga of an American Family* (Garden City, N.Y.: Doubleday, 1976).

25 Miss Rosen, "Heaven on Earth: FESTAC '77 and the Dream of a Pan African Society," Culture Crush, accessed November 11, 2023, https://www .theculturecrush.com/feature/heaven-on-earth.

26 Saidiya V. Hartman, "The Time of Slavery," *South Atlantic Quarterly* 101, no. 4 (Fall 2002), p. 758.

27 Kellie Jones, *EyeMinded: Living and Writing Contemporary Art* (Durham, N.C.: Duke University Press, 2011), p. 466.

28 Glissant, "For Opacity," p. 190.

29 Glissant, "For Opacity," p. 192.

30 Betye Saar, interview by Karen Anne Mason, August 15, 1990, Tape 3, Side 1, transcript, African American Artists of Los Angeles, Center for Oral History Research, UCLA Library, https://static.library.ucla.edu/oralhistory/text /submasters/21198-zz0008zpzb-4-submaster.html.

31 "Statement of Artist, *Three Women Artists*, Palos Verdes Art Center, 1974," reproduced in Carla Cugini, ed., *Betye Saar: Wolfgang-Hahn-Preis 2020 / 2020 Wolfgang Hahn Prize*, exh. cat., Museum Ludwig, 2021 (Cologne: Verlag der Buchhandlung Walther König, 2020), p. 48.

32 Jane H. Carpenter with Betye Saar, *Betye Saar* (San Francisco: Pomegranate, 2003), p. 28.

33 "Irvine MacManus records related to 'Treasures of Tutankhamun' exhibition, 1975-1979," finding aid prepared by Celia Hartmann, p. 5. The Metropolitan Museum of Art Archives, https://libmma.org/digital _files/archives/MacManus_Tutankhamun_records _b18131165.pdf.

34 Helen Molesworth, with Linda Goode Bryant and Marci Kwon, "Bettye Saar: Working My Mojo," *Radical Women*, Getty podcast, https://www.getty.edu /recordingartists/season-1/saar/.

35 Betye Saar, interview by Karen Anne Mason, August 15, 1990, Tape 3, Side 2, transcript, African American Artists of Los Angeles, Center for Oral History Research, UCLA Library, https://oralhistory .library.ucla.edu/catalog.

36 Ibid.

37 Kellie Jones, *South of Pico: African American Artists in Los Angeles in the 1960s and 1970s* (Durham, N.C.: Duke University Press, 2017), pp. 213, 242.

38 Jones, *South of Pico*, p. 221.

39 Rosalind Robinson Jeffries, "Arthur Carraway and Houston Conwill: Ethnicity and Re-Africanization in American Art" (PhD diss., Yale University, 1992).

40 Kiatezua Lubanzadio Luyaluka, "The Deep Meaning of the Kongo Cosmogram," *Nzil'alowa* (blog), April 19, 2015, https://animic.wordpress.com/the-deep-meaning -of-the-kongo-cosmogram/.

41 *Houston Conwill: Works*, exh. brochure (Washington, D.C.: Hirshhorn Museum, 1989).

42 Eugenio Matibag, *Afro-Cuban Religious Experience: Cultural Reflections in Narrative* (Gainesville: University Press of Florida, 1996), pp. 161–62.

43 Mira Dayal, "Close-Up: Theory of Relativity," *Artforum* 59, no. 5 (March 2021), https://www.artforum .com/features/mira-dayal-on-lorraine-ogradys -miscegenated-family-album-1980-1994-249366/.

44 Lorraine O'Grady, "Some Thoughts on Diaspora and Hybridity: An Unpublished Slide Lecture (1994)," *BOMB*, October 22, 2020, https://bombmagazine.org /author/lorraine-ogrady/.

45 Catherine Damman, "Risk Everything," *Artforum* 59, no. 5 (March 2021), https://www.artforum.com /features/catherine-damman-on-the-art-of-lorraine -ogrady-249359/.

46 O'Grady, "Some Thoughts."

47 This is likely a reference to a similar figure with a mirrored face in filmmaker and choreographer Maya Deren's experimental film *Meshes of the Afternoon* (1943).

48 *Space Is the Place*, directed by John Coney (1974; London: Harte Recordings, 2015).

49 Ibid.

50 Ibid.

51 Glissant, "For Opacity," p. 194.

52 Glissant, "For Opacity," pp. 191–92.

53 "2006.82: *Abu Simbel*," Harvard Art Museums, accessed April 5, 2024, https://harvardartmuseums.org /collections/object/315230.

54 Robin D. G. Kelley, "Confounding Myths," in *Ellen Gallagher: AxME*, exh. cat., Tate Modern, London; Sara Hildén Art Museum, Tampere; and Haus der Kunst, Munich, 2013-14 (London: Tate Publishing, 2013), p. 19.

55 Ibid.

56 Adrienne Edwards, "Vectors and Veneers: The Thickness of Blackness," in *Ellen Gallagher: Accidental Records*, exh. cat., Hauser & Wirth Los Angeles (Zurich: Hauser & Wirth, 2017), pp. 31–32.

57 Cited in Ulrich Wilmes, "Reading Pictures," in *Ellen Gallagher: AxME*, p. 201.

Compressive of Ideas: Black Photography and Ancient Egypt Makeda Best

1   Chester Higgins, *Feeling the Spirit* (New York: Bantam Books, 1994), p. 9; quoted in Carol Squiers, "The Spirit of Africa, the World Over," Photography Review, *New York Time*s, November 24, 1995.

2   Dominique François Arago, "Report," in *Classic Essays on Photography,* ed. Alan Trachtenberg (New Haven: Leete's Island Books, 1980), p. 17.

3   Derek Gregory, "Emperors of the Gaze: Photographic Practices and Productions of Space in Egypt, 1839–1914," in *Picturing Place: Photography and the Geographical Imagination*, ed. Joan M. Schwarz and James R. Ryan (London: I. B. Tauris, 2003), pp. 195–225.

4   Mirjam Brusius, Katrina Dean, and Chitra Ramalingam, eds. *William Henry Fox Talbot: Beyond Photography* (New Haven: Yale University Press, 2013).

5   See, for example. Stephen Sheehi, *The Arab Imago: A Social History of Portrait Photography, 1860–1910* (Princeton, N.J.: Princeton University Press, 2016); and Maria Golia, *Photography in Egypt* (London: Reaktion, 2010).

6   Toni Morrison, foreword to *Black Photographers Annual* 1 (New York: Black Photographers Annual, 1973), p. 5.

7   Maurice O. Wallace and Shawn Michelle Smith, "Introduction: Pictures and Progress," in *Pictures and Progress: Early Photography and the Making of African American Identity* (Durham: Duke UP, 2012), p. 4. See also Deborah Willis, *Reflections in Black: A History of Black Photographers, 1840 to the Present* (New York: W. W. Norton, 2000); and Deborah Willis, ed., *Picturing Us: African American Identity in Photography* (New York: New Press, 1994).

8   Christel N. Temple, "Ancient Kemet in African American Literature and Criticism, 1853 to the Present," *Journal of Pan African Studies* 5, no. 4 (June 2012), p. 130.

9   Evan Lee, "Classical Tradition and Black Nationalism in W. E. B. Du Bois's *The Star of Ethiopia*," *International Journal of the Classical Tradition* 26, no. 1 (2019), p. 55.

10   See David Krasner, "'The Pageant Is the Thing': Black Nationalism and *The Star of Ethiopia*," in *Performing America: Cultural Nationalism in American Theater,* ed. Jeffrey D. Mason and J. Ellen Gainor (Ann Arbor: University of Michigan Press, 1999), pp. 106–22.

11   Louise Siddons, "African Past or American Present? The Visual Eloquence of James VanDerZee's *Identical Twins*," *African American Review* 46, nos. 2–3 (Summer/Fall 2013), p. 452.

12   Sara Marzioli, "Snapshots of the Eternal City: Ralph Ellison in Rome," *Modernism/modernity* 24, no. 4 (November 2017), p. 828.

13   Marzioli, "Snapshots," pp. 827–28.

14   Marzioli, "Snapshots," p. 828.

15   Elliot E. Bratton, "The Sound of Freedom: Jazz and the Cold War," *The New Crisis* 105, no. 1 (February/March 1998), p. 17.

16   On his visit to Ghana in 1956 he is reported to have said, "I came from here, way back. At least my people did. Now I know this is my country too." Robert Raymond, *Black Star in the Wind* (London: MacGibbon and Kee, 1960), p. 241; cited in Penny M. Von Eschen, *Satchmo Blows Up the World: Jazz Ambassadors Play the Cold War* (Cambridge, Mass.: Harvard University Press, 2004), p. 61.

17   Cynthia A. Young, *Soul Power: Culture, Radicalism, and the Making of a U.S. Third World Left* (Durham, N.C.: Duke University Press, 2006), p. 22.

18   Vaughn Rasberry, *Race and the Totalitarian Century: Geopolitics in the Black Literary Imagination* (Cambridge, Mass.: Harvard University Press, 2016), pp. 135–36.

19   Bridget R. Cooks, "Pan-African Politics in African American Visual Art: Where Have We Been? Where Are We Going?" *International Journal of Media and Cultural Politics* 2, no. 2 (2006), p. 193.

20   "Kamoinge" means "a group of people acting together" in the language of the Kikuyu people of Kenya.

21   John A. Williams, "Introduction," *Black Photographers Annual* 4 (New York: Another View, 1980), p. 3.

22   "108 C. Daniel Dawson, Olaifa and Egypt, 1978," transcript of audio tour for *Working Together: The Photographers of the Kamoinge Workshop,* Cinncinnati Art Museum, February 25–May 15, 2022, https://www .cincinnatiartmuseum.org.

23   See Marcel Swiboda, "Re Interpretations: Sun Ra's Egyptian Inscriptions," *Parallax* 13, no. 2 (2007), p. 104.

24   "108 C. Daniel Dawson, Olaifa and Egypt, 1978."

Works in the Exhibition

The works in this checklist appear in alphabetical order by maker. Commercially released films, television episodes, and works by unidentified makers appear alphabetically by title.

Slim Aarons (American, 1916–2006)
Slim and Sphinx, 1964, printed 2024
Digital chromogenic print, 30 x 30 in.
(76.2 x 76.2 cm)
Courtesy Getty Images Gallery
Plate 106

John Henry Adams Jr.
(American, 1880–1944)
Cover of *The Crisis* 3, no. 3, January 1912
Collection of the Smithsonian National
Museum of African American History and
Culture, Washington, D.C. (2015.97.14.2)
Plate 27

John Henry Adams Jr.
(American, 1880–1944)
Cover of *The Crisis* 3, no. 5, March 1912
Collection of the Smithsonian National
Museum of African American History and
Culture, Washington, D.C. (2015.97.14.3)
Plate 25

John Henry Adams Jr.
(American, 1880–1944)
Cover of *The Crisis* 5, no. 1, November 1912
Collection of the Smithsonian National
Museum of African American History and
Culture, Washington, D.C. (2015.97.14.5)
Plate 26

Terry Adkins (American, 1953–2014)
Harlem Encore, 1999
Aluminum panels, located at Metro North
Railroad Harlem–125th Street station
Metropolitan Transportation Authority
Plate 6

Terry Adkins (American, 1953–2014)
Obelisks in Rome, 2010
Video, color, sound, 46 min., 10 sec.
The Estate of Terry Adkins, courtesy Paula
Cooper Gallery, New York
Plate 5

Terry Adkins (American, 1953–2014)
Luxor Solo (*Mystical Score for the Ghost of Bud Powell*), 2011, printed 2024
Commissioned by Clifford Owens for
publication in *Anthology: Clifford Owens*
(Long Island City, N.Y.: MoMA PS1, 2012)
Printer ink on paper, 11 x 8 in. (27.9 x
21.6 cm)
Collection of Clifford Owens, New York
Plate 150

Terry Adkins (American, 1953–2014)
Oxidation Blue 1, 2013
Polychrome wood, H. 36 in. (91.4 cm),
W. 9 in. (22.9 cm), D. 7 in. (17.8 cm)
Collection of Beth Rudin DeWoody,
New York
Plate 4

"Alice Coltrane," *Black Journal*,
episode 26, 1970
Directed by Stan Lathan
Video, color, sound, 17 min.
Courtesy Smithsonian National Museum
of African American History and Culture,
Washington, D.C.
Plate 140

Al Mussawar, no. 1254, October 22, 1948
Special issue, "Nefertiti Speaks"
Cover photography by Armand
University of Washington Libraries,
Seattle
Plate 70

Ra Un Nefer Amen
(Panamanian, born 1944)
*Metu Neter: The Great Oracle of Tehuti
and the Egyptian System of Spiritual
Cultivation*, 1990
Brooklyn, N.Y.: Khamit Media Trans
Visions
Plate 101

Ghada Amer (Egyptian, born 1963)
Homage à Tut in Black and White, 2021
Painted bronze, H. 23⅜ in. (59.4 cm),
W. 17⅜ in. (44.1 cm), D. 1⅛ in. (2.9 cm)
Collection of the artist
Plate 67

*Ancient Egyptian Arabic Order Nobles
Mystic Shrine Red Fez*, 2024
Wool felt and leather with silk tassel and
rhinestones, H. 8 in. (20.3 cm), Diam.
7½ in. (19.1 cm)
Plate 89

Eve Arnold (American, 1912–2012)
*Black Muslim children at the Metropolitan
Museum in New York. They are taught
black history*, 1961, printed 2024
Archival pigment print, 15 x 10 in.
(38.1 x 25.4 cm)
Eve Arnold Estate
Plate 88

Art Ensemble of Chicago
Tutankhamun, 1974
Record cover, Freedom and Black Lion
Records FLP 40122
Design by Hamish Grimes
Plate 114

Muata Ashby
*Egyptian Yoga: The Philosophy of
Enlightenment*, 1995
Miami: Cruzian Mystic Books
Plate 102

Muata Ashby
*Egyptian Yoga Volume 2: Mysteries of
Amun and The Supreme Wisdom of
Enlightenment*, 1998
Miami: Cruzian Mystic Books
Plate 103

Solange Ashby
*Calling Out to Isis: The Enduring Nubian
Presence at Philae*, 2020
Piscataway, N.J.: Gorgias Press
Plate 16

Ayé Aton (American, 1940–2017)
Untitled, ca. 1975
Chromogenic print, 8 x 10 in.
(20.3 x 25.4 cm)
Collection of John Corbett and
Terri Kapsalis
Plate 160

Ayé Aton (American, 1940–2017)
Untitled (wall mural), 1972
Chromogenic print, 10 x 8 in.
(25.4 x 20.3 cm)
Collection of John Corbett and
Terri Kapsalis
Plate 161

Erykah Badu (American, born 1971)
Next Lifetime, 1997
Record cover, Universal Records and
Kedar Entertainment U8P1153
Photography by Perou; design by
Ben Young
Plate 134

Amiri Baraka (American, 1934–2014)
It's Nation Time—African Visionary Music, 1972
Record cover, Motown Records B 457L
Photography by Fundi
Plate 113

The Bar-Kays
As One, 1980
Record cover, Mercury Records SRM-1-3844
Illustration by David Beck; concept by Allen Jones and the Bar-Kays; art direction by Joe Kotleba
Plate 125

Jean-Michel Basquiat (American, 1960–1988)
Kings of Egypt II, 1982
Oil on canvas, 72¼ x 72¼ in. (183.5 x 183.5 cm)
Collection Museum Boijmans Van Beuningen, Rotterdam, Loan Stichting Museum Boijmans Van Beuningen, Gift Hans Sonnenberg
Plate 165

Sidra Bell (American, born 1979)
G R A P H, 2025
Live performance

Yosef A. A. ben-Jochannan (Ethiopian American, 1918–2015)
Black Man of the Nile and His Family, 1972
New York: Alkebu-Lan Books
Plate 13

Martin Bernal (British, 1937–2013)
Black Athena: The Afroasiatic Roots of Classical Civilization, 1987
New Brunswick, N.J.: Rutgers University Press
Plate 15

John Thomas Biggers (American, 1924–2001)
Taharqa King of Nubia (710–664 BC), 1984
Poster, 12½ x 20 in. (31.8 x 50.8 cm)
Plate 93

Barbara Higgins Bond (American, born 1951)
Akhenaten Pharaoh of Egypt (1375–1358 BC), 1984
Poster, 12½ x 20 in. (31.8 x 50.8 cm)
Plate 94

LaKela Brown (American, born 1982)
Triangle Pairs with Pharaoh Heads and Nefertiti Recesses, 2018
Plaster, H. 20 in. (50.8 cm), W. 16 in. (40.6 cm), D. 2 in. (5.1 cm)

Museum of Fine Arts, Boston, James N. Krebs Purchase Fund for 21st Century Paintings (2020.354)
Plate 96

Rashida Bumbray (American, born 1978)
How High the Moon, 2024
Video, color, sound, 12 min., 33 sec.
Collection of the artist
Plate 153

Rashida Bumbray (American, born 1978)
Way Down, 2024
Live performance

René Burri (Swiss, 1933–2014)
Barbara Chase-Riboud at Deir el-Bahri, 1958, printed 2024
Archival pigment print, 12¼ x 8 in. (31.1 x 20.3 cm)
René Burri Estate
Plate 20

Harry Burton (British, 1879–1940)
Deir el-Bahri: Progress of the Work, January 1929, 1929
Gelatin silver print from glass negative, 6¾ x 9 in. (17.1 x 22.9 cm)
The Metropolitan Museum of Art, New York, Department of Egyptian Art Archives (M10C 49)
Plate 7

George Washington Carver (American, ca. 1864–1943)
Dr. Carver's Egyptian Blue 9th Oxidation, 1930s
Glass bottle containing pigment, H. 3¾ (9.5 cm), W. 2¼ in. (5.7 cm), D. 1½ in. (3.8 cm)
Special Collections and University Archives, Iowa State University Library, Ames (2007-349.003)
Plate 3

Cecil Taylor Jazz Unit
Nefertiti, the Beautiful One Has Come, 1969
Record cover, Fontana Records SFJL 926 (U.K. reissue)
Plate 110

Barbara Chase-Riboud (American, born 1939)
Cleopatra's Chair, 1994
Multicolored cast bronzed plaques over oak, H. 39⅜ in. (100 cm), W. 49⅝ in. (126 cm), D. 43¼ in. (109.9 cm)
Private collection
Plate 21

Ed Clark (American, 1926–2019)
Untitled (Egyptian Series), 1997

Acrylic and pencil on papyrus, 17 x 24 in. (43.2 x 61 cm)
Hudgins Family Collection, New York
Plate 157

Irene Clark (American, 1927–1984)
Cleopatra, ca. 1940–50
Gouache on plywood board, 15¼ x 11¼ in. (38.7 x 28.6 cm)
Collection of Leah D. Daughtry, Washington, D.C.
Plate 39

Robert Colescott (American, 1925–2009)
Nubian Queen, 1966
Acrylic on canvas, 78 x 59 in. (198.1 x 150 cm)
Private collection
Plate 44

Alice Coltrane (American, 1937–2007)
Ptah, the El Daoud, 1970
Record cover, Impulse! Records AS-9196
Cover design by Jim Evans
Plate 112

Houston Conwill (American, 1947–2016)
The Open Secret, 1986
Bronze relief, located at New York City Transit 125th Street station
Metropolitan Transportation Authority
Plate 156

Houston Conwill (American, 1947–2016) with Joseph De Pace (American, born 1954) and Estella Conwill Majozo (American, born 1949)
Langston Hughes' Rivers, 1991
Screenprint, 32¾ x 33⅛ in. (83.2 x 84.1 cm)
The Museum of Modern Art, New York, Gift of Agnes Gund, 1994 (143.1994)
Plate 155

Renee Cox (Jamaican American, born 1960)
Rajé to the Rescue, 1998
Cibachrome print, 48 x 60 in. (121.9 x 152.4 cm)
Collection of the artist, New York
Plate 163

Marc Crawford (American, 1929–1996)
"The Scholar Nobody Knows: Unsung Howard U. Professor Is World's Best African Authority," in *Ebony*, February 1961
Robert S. Cox Special Collections and University Archives Research Center, University of Massachusetts Amherst Libraries, Amherst, Massachusetts (MS 312)
Plate 11

Shani Crowe (American, born 1989)
Sun Trust, 2016
Inkjet print, 65¼ x 43½ in.
(165.7 x 110.5 cm)
Museum of Fine Arts, Boston, Museum
purchase with funds donated by the Ford
Foundation (2021.340)
Plate 61

Daughters of Isis Gloves, 2024
Nylon each: 9½ x 3 in. (24.1 x 7.6 cm)
Plate 90

Damien Davis (American, born 1984)
Ancient Still Life, 2015
Digital print on cold-press paper,
20 x 30 in. (50.8 x 76.2 cm)
Collection of the artist, Brooklyn
Plate 95

Karon Davis (American, born 1977)
He Who Floods the Nile, 2019
Plaster cloth, wire, glass eyes, artist's hair
weave, brass beads, gold leaf, black glitter,
raw frankincense, wood, and prayers,
H. 85 in. (215.9 cm), W. 32½ in. (82.6 cm),
D. 32½ in. (82.6 cm)
Private collection, London
Plate 55

Karon Davis (American, born 1977)
The Resurrection of Osiris, 2025
Live performance

Miles Davis (American, 1926–1991)
Nefertiti, 1968
Record cover, Columbia Records CS 9594
Photography by Bob Cato
Plate 111

Noah Davis (American, 1983–2015)
Untitled, 2010
Oil on canvas, 40¼ x 29¾ in.
(102.2 x 75.6 cm)
The Estate of Noah Davis
Plate 17

C. Daniel Dawson (American, born 1943)
Olaifa and Egypt, 1978
Gelatin silver print, sheet: 8⅛ x 9⅞ in.
(20.6 x 25.1 cm)
Collection of Charles Daniel Dawson,
courtesy of Virginia Museum of Fine Arts,
Richmond (L2023.20.8)
Plate 47

Charles Clarence Dawson
(American, 1889–1981)
Cover of *The Negro in Art Week*,
November 16–23, 1927

Chicago: Chicago Woman's Club
The Museum of Modern Art Library,
New York
Plate 28

Charles Clarence Dawson
(American, 1889–1981)
"O, Sing a New Song," 1934
Color lithograph, sheet: 21½ x 13½ in.
(54.6 x 34.3 cm)
The Metropolitan Museum of Art,
New York, Gift of Reba and Dave Williams,
1999 (1999.529.58)
Plate 105

De La Soul
Eye Know, 1989
Record cover, BCM Records 12358
Plate 131

Denim Tears
Tracy's King Tut Vest, 2023
Designed by Tremaine Emory
Leather and embroidery, 28½ x 21½ in.
(72.4 x 54.6 cm)
Collection of Denim Tears
Plate 97

Denim Tears
Tracy's King Tut Belt, 2023
Designed by Tremaine Emory
Leather and brass, 39⅞ x 1½ in.
(101.3 x 3.8 cm)
Collection of Denim Tears
Plate 98

Artin DerBalian (Egyptian, 1934–2015)
Louis and Lucille in Egypt at the Sphinx,
1961
Gelatin silver print, 8 x 10 in.
(20.3 x 25.4 cm)
Louis Armstrong House Museum, Queens,
New York
Plate 73

Cheikh Anta Diop (Senegalese, 1923–1986)
*The African Origin of Civilization: Myth or
Reality*, 1974
New York: Lawrence Hill Books
Plate 14

Jeff Donaldson (American, 1932–2004)
Message from Tehuti, 1988
Acrylic on canvas, 68 x 45 in.
(172.7 x 114.3 cm)
Collection of Beth Rudin DeWoody,
New York
Plate 164

Aaron Douglas (American, 1899–1979)
Cover of *Fire!! A Quarterly Devoted to the
Younger Negro Artists*, November 1926
Collection of Walter O. and Linda Evans
Plate 35

Aaron Douglas (American, 1899–1979)
*Princes shall come out of Egypt; Ethiopia
shall soon stretch out her hands unto God*,
cover of *The Crisis* 34, no. 3, May 1927
Art and Artifacts Division, Schomburg
Center for Research in Black Culture, The
New York Public Library, New York, Astor,
Lenox and Tilden Foundations
Plate 37

Aaron Douglas (American, 1899–1979)
Let My People Go, ca. 1935–39
Oil on Masonite, 48 x 36 in.
(121.9 x 91.4 cm)
The Metropolitan Museum of Art,
New York, Purchase, Lila Acheson Wallace
Gift, 2015 (2015.42)
Plate 36

Aaron Douglas (American, 1899–1979)
Building More Stately Mansions, 1944
Oil on canvas, 20 x 16 in. (50.8 x 40.6 cm)
Museum of Art, Rhode Island School of
Design, Providence, Purchased with the
Frederick Lippitt Bequest (2008.30)
Plate 38

Emory Douglas (American, born 1943)
Mother and Daughter, 1995
Acrylic on board, 8 x 11 in. (20.3 x 27.9 cm)
Collection of the artist, San Francisco
Plate 58

Louis Draper (American, 1935–2002)
Untitled (*Girl with Egyptian Mural*),
ca. 1965
Gelatin silver print, 7 x 8¾ in.
(17.8 x 22.2 cm)
Virginia Museum of Fine Arts, Richmond,
Arthur and Margaret Glasgow Endowment
(2015.302)
Plate 57

Dream The Combine (Jennifer Newsom,
American, born 1979, and Tom
Carruthers, Canadian, born 1978)
Pyramidion, 2024
Aluminized Mylar sailcloth, steel, and
LEDs, H. 16 ft. (487.7 cm), W. 30 in.
(76.2 cm), D. 30 in. (76.2 cm)
Collection of the artists
Fabrication made possible by the Graham
Foundation for Advanced Studies in
the Fine Arts
Plate 170

Dows Dunham (American, 1890–1984)
Letter to William Leo Hansberry,
February 2, 1932
Museum of Fine Arts, Boston
Plate 10

Dusé Mohamed Ali, 1911, printed 2024
From *In the Land of the Pharaohs*
(London: Stanley Paul)
Inkjet print, 12 x 8 in. (30.5 x 20.3 cm)
Manuscripts, Archives and Rare Books
Division, Schomburg Center for Research
in Black Culture, The New York Public
Library, New York
Plate 12

Oasa DuVerney (American, born 1979)
Assata Shakur as Ahmes Nefertari, 2018
Graphite and gold dust on hand-cut paper,
19 x 21½ in. (48.3 x 54.6 cm)
Collection of David Tobey
Plate 60

Earth, Wind & Fire
Spirit, 1976
Record cover, Columbia Records PC 34241
Cover photography by Ethan Russell;
design and illustration by Tom Steele
Plate 118

Earth, Wind & Fire
All 'n All, 1977
Record cover, Columbia Records JC 34905
Lettering design by Jim Wood; illustration
by Shusei Nagaoka; album design by Roger
Carpenter; photography by Jurgen Reisch
Plate 117

Earth, Wind & Fire
Best of Earth, Wind & Fire, Vol. 1, 1978
Record cover, Columbia Records 35647
Art by Shusei Nagaoka
Plate 120

"Egypt 1909," *The Richard Pryor Show*,
season 1, episode 2, 1977
Created by Richard Pryor
Video, color, sound, 2 min., 49 sec.
Courtesy Burt Sugarman Productions
Plate 8

The Egyptian Lover
(American, born 1963)
On the Nile, 1984
Record cover, Egyptian Empire Records
DMSR-0663
Cover photography by Phil Bedel;
art direction by Unicorn
Plate 121

The Egyptian Lover
(American, born 1963)
Freak-A-Holic, 1986
Video, color, sound, 3 min., 8 sec.
Courtesy Egyptian Empire Records
Plate 141

Zekkereya El-magharbel
(Egyptian American, born 1995)
Landscapes of the North East, 2025
Live performance

Awol Erizku
(Ethiopian American, born 1988)
Nefertiti–Miles Davis, 2017
Hand-coated foam and mirrored tile,
H. 30 in. (76.2 cm), W. 15 in. (38.1 cm),
D. 23 in. (58.4 cm)
Private collection
Plate 143

Awol Erizku
(Ethiopian American, born 1988)
Nefertiti (*Black Power*), 2018
Neon light on coated stainless steel,
H. 70⅞ in. (180 cm), W. 51⅜ in. (130.5 cm),
D. 5⅛ in. (13 cm)
Museum of Fine Arts, Boston
Plate 144

Fred Eversley (American, born 1941)
Untitled (*gold layered step pyramid*), 1983
Clear acrylic and gold plated aluminum,
H. 9¾ in. (24.8 cm), W. 21⅝ in. (54.9 cm),
D. 30½ in. (77.5 cm)
Collection of the artist, New York
Plate 167

Fela Kuti and Egypt 80
Perambulator, 1983
Record cover, Lagos International Records
LIR 6
Photography by Afrika 70 Photo Agency;
graphics by Ajao Bello
Plate 130

Derek Fordjour (American, born 1974)
Board Meeting (*Brotherhood Smoke*), 2021
Acrylic, charcoal, cardboard, foil, glitter,
and oil pastel on newspaper mounted
on canvas, 74¾ in. x 9 ft. 7 in. (189.9 x
292.1 cm)
Collection of Robert F. Smith
Plate 92

Meta Vaux Warrick Fuller
(American, 1877–1968)
Ethiopia Awakening, ca. 1914–21
Plaster, H. 69 in. (175.3 cm), W. 20 in.
(50.8 cm), D. 16 in. (40.6 cm)

Art and Artifacts Division, Schomburg
Center for Research in Black Culture, The
New York Public Library, New York, Astor,
Lenox and Tilden Foundations
Plate 22

Genevieve Gaignard
(American, born 1981)
Kings and Queens, 2017
Chromogenic print, 32 x 48 in.
(81.3 x 121.9 cm)
Collection of Thomas Lavin
Plate 63

Ellen Gallagher (American, born 1965)
Abu Simbel, 2005
Photogravure, etching, scraping, aqua-
tint, and drypoint, with watercolor, color
pencil, varnish, pomade, Plasticine,
synthetic fur, gold leaf, and red and white
crystals, 24½ x 35½ in. (62.2 x 90.2 cm)
Whitney Museum of American Art, New
York, Purchase, with funds from the Print
Committee (2007.35a-b)
Plate 162

Sam Gilliam (American, 1933–2022)
Nile, 1972
Lithograph, 24⅞ x 17¾ in. (63.2 x 45.1 cm)
The Museum of Modern Art, New York,
Purchase, 1973 (317.1973)
Plate 177

Sam Gilliam (American, 1933–2022)
Pyramid, 2020
Wood, stain, lacquer, and aluminum,
H. 9 ft. 2 in. (279.4 cm), W. 10 ft. 2 in.
(309.9 cm), D. 10 ft. 2 in. (309.9 cm)
Courtesy Sam Gilliam Foundation, David
Kordansky Gallery, and Pace Gallery
Plate 178

Chet Gold (American, born 1986)
Mirror Malcolm, 2011
Silkscreen on mirror, 12 x 12 in.
(30.5 x 30.5 cm)
Museum of Fine Arts, Boston, Museum
purchase with funds donated by the Ford
Foundation (2021.338)
Plate 74

Lauren Halsey (American, born 1987)
FreedomEx, 2022
Gypsum on wood, H. 94 in. (238.8 cm),
W. 94⅛ in. (239.1 cm), D. ⅝ in. (1.6 cm)
The Metropolitan Museum of Art,
New York, Purchase, Lila Acheson Wallace
Gift, 2022 (2022.359)
Plate 182

Lauren Halsey (American, born 1987)
Untitled, 2024
Gypsum, each: H. 8 ft. (243.8 cm),
W. 24 in. (61 cm), D. 24 in. (61 cm)
Courtesy the artist
Plate 183

David Hammons (American, born 1943)
Unknown, ca. 1977
Paper-pulp and hair works on paper, each:
12 x 8 in. (30.5 x 20.3 cm)
Hudgins Family Collection, New York
Plates 171–73

Maren Hassinger (American, born 1947)
Message from Malcolm, 1998
Mosaic tile, located at New York City
Transit Central Park North–110th Street
station
Metropolitan Transportation Authority
Plate 174

Maren Hassinger (American, born 1947)
Love (Pyramid), 2008/24
Pink plastic bags filled with air, breath,
love notes, and steelhead pushpins
Courtesy the artist and Susan Inglett
Gallery, New York
Plate 175

Maren Hassinger (American, born 1947),
Ulysses Jenkins (American, born 1946),
Senga Nengudi (American, born 1943), and
Franklin Parker (American, 1945–2001)
Flyer for *Flying*, 1982
Xerox print, 11 x 8½ in. (27.9 x 21.6 cm)
Courtesy Susan Inglett Gallery, New York
Plate 145

Maren Hassinger (American, born 1947),
Ulysses Jenkins (American, born 1946),
Senga Nengudi (American, born 1943), and
Franklin Parker (American, 1945–2001)
Flying, July 6, 1982
Performed with Juana Nash, Lofty Amono,
"Nastyee," and N'Dugu Jungles at Los
Angeles Municipal Art Gallery, Barnsdall
Art Park, Los Angeles
Four photographs by Adam Avila, printed
2019
Courtesy Sprüth Magers
Plates 146–49

Chester Higgins (American, born 1946)
*Tomb of Irukaptah, A Libationer. Saqqara
Necropolis, Egypt*, 1979, printed 2024
Archival pigment inkjet print, 26 x 40 in.
(66 x 101.6 cm)
Collection of the artist
Plate 85

Chester Higgins (American, born 1946)
*African American pilgrims dance in honor
of ancient spirits. Lake Nasser, Egypt*,
2006, printed 2024
Archival pigment inkjet print, 26 x 40 in.
(66 x 101.6 cm)
Collection of the artist
Plate 86

EJ Hill (American, born 1985)
A Divine Mother (after Charles Dickson),
2018
Archival inkjet print, 52 x 34½ in.
(132.1 x 87.6 cm)
Private collection
Plate 180

Lonnie Holley (American, born 1950)
Ruling for the Child, 1982
Investment casting materials,
H. 20 in. (50.8 cm), W. 10½ in. (26.7 cm),
D. 15½ in. (39.4 cm)
The Metropolitan Museum of Art,
New York, Gift of Souls Grown Deep
Foundation from the William S. Arnett
Collection, 2014 (2014.548.9)
Plate 54

Homecoming: A Film by Beyoncé, 2019
Directed and produced by Beyoncé
Knowles-Carter
Video, color, sound, 137 min.
Courtesy Parkwood Entertainment
Plate 142

Madeleine Hunt-Ehrlich
(American, born 1987)
Cleopatra at the Mall, 2024
High-definition video, transferred from
16 mm film, color, sound
Courtesy the artist; commissioned by
The Metropolitan Museum of Art, 2024,
This commission is made possible by the
Ford Foundation
Plate 19

Gregston Hurdle (American, born 1987)
*Kamau Amu Patton performing "Amun
(The Unseen Legends)" at An Evening
with Kamau Amu Patton, The Museum of
Modern Art, New York*, 2017, printed 2024
Inkjet print, 9 x 12 in. (22.9 x 30.5 cm)
Courtesy the photographer
Plate 151

Weldon Irvine (American, 1943–2002)
Cosmic Vortex (Justice Divine), 1974
Record cover, RCA Records Victor
APL1-0703

Design by Dennis Pohl; art direction by
Acy Lehman
BMG Special Products
Plate 116

Iman Issa (Egyptian, born 1979)
Heritage Studies #7, 2015
Wood, painted steel, and vinyl text,
H. 71⅝ in. (182 cm), W. 42½ in. (108 cm),
D. 8¾ in. (22.2 cm)
Courtesy the artist and Sylvia Kouvali
Plate 69

Michael Jackson (American, 1958–2009)
Remember the Time, 1991
Video, color, sound, 4 min.
Courtesy of Epic Records and MJJ Produc-
tions Inc., By arrangement with Sony
Music Entertainment

Steffani Jemison (American, born 1981)
Recitatif: Perfect Mind, 2025
Live performance

Steffani Jemison (American, born 1981)
and Jamal Cyrus (American, born 1973)
Alpha's Bet Is Not Over Yet, 2011
Newsstand, chairs, tables, 575 facsimiles of
Black periodicals published between 1900
and 1940
Courtesy the artists and Greene Naftali
Plate 34

Malvin Gray Johnson
(American, 1896–1934)
Negro Pharaoh–Eighteenth Dynasty, 1934
Oil on cardboard, 12 x 16 in.
(30.5 x 40.6 cm)
Art and Artifacts Division, Schomburg
Center for Research in Black Culture, The
New York Public Library, New York, Astor,
Lenox and Tilden Foundations
Plate 40

John Shabazz & Malcolm Little in L.A.,
1962
Audio, 187 min., 23 sec.
Nation of Islam Historical Archives,
used with Permission of X Legacy, LLC

Rashid Johnson (American, born 1977)
Pyramid, 2009
Black soap, wax, vinyl, CB radio,
brass, books, glass, spray paint, plants,
wood, shea butter, and space rocks,
H. 11 ft. 1 in. (337.8 cm), W. 16 ft. 2 in.
(492.8 cm), D. 10 in. (25.4 cm)
The Phelan Art Collection, courtesy David
Kordansky Gallery and Hauser & Wirth
Plate 176

Rashid Johnson (American, born 1977)
with Kahil El'Zabar (American, born 1953)
Pharaoh's Song, 2025
Live performance

Loïs Mailou Jones (American, 1905–1998)
The Ascent of Ethiopia, 1932
Oil on canvas, 23½ x 17¼ in.
(59.7 x 43.8 cm)
Milwaukee Art Museum, Purchase, African
American Art Acquisition Fund, matching
funds from Suzanne and Richard Pieper,
with additional support from Arthur and
Dorothy Nelle Sanders (M1993.191)
Plate 23

Loïs Mailou Jones (American, 1905–1998)
Egyptian Heritage, 1953
Oil on Masonite, 23¾ x 40½ in.
(60.3 x 103 cm)
Clark Atlanta University Art Museum,
Atlanta Art Annuals (1955.004)
Plate 43

The Jones Girls
Nights Over Egypt, 1981
Record cover, Philadelphia International
Records ZS5 02713
Plate 129

Barbara Jones-Hogu
(American, 1938–2017)
Relate to Your Heritage, 1971
Color screenprint, sheet: 34 x 43 in.
(86.4 x 109.2 cm)
Brooklyn Museum, Gift of R.M. Atwater,
Anna Wolfrom Dove, Alice Fiebiger,
Joseph Fiebiger, Belle Campbell Harriss,
and Emma L. Hyde, by exchange, Desig-
nated Purchase Fund, Mary Smith
Dorward Fund, Dick S. Ramsay Fund, and
Carll H. de Silver Fund (2012.80.26)
Plate 45

Armia Malak Khalil (Egyptian, born 1979)
Hope–I Am a Morning Scarab, 2024
Wood, H. 22 in. (55.9 cm), W. 16 in.
(40.6 cm), D. 14 in. (35.6 cm)
Collection of the artist, New Jersey
Plate 72

Jas Knight (American, born 1977)
The African Origin of Civilization, 2023
Oil on linen laid on board and gold leaf,
15 x 26 in. (38.1 x 66 cm)
Collection of the artist, Brooklyn
Plate 9

Solange Knowles (American, born 1986)
Orion's Rise, 2018, printed 2024
Chromogenic print, 30 x 30 in.
(76.2 x 76.2 cm)
Collection of the artist
Plate 78

Kool Moe Dee (American, born 1962)
Funke Funke Wisdom, 1991
Record cover, Jive Records 1388-1-J
Art direction, design, and hand-lettering
by ZombArt NG; photography and illustra-
tion by Sally Boon
Plate 132

Ashra and Merira Kwesi
Kemet Nu "Know Thyself" Tour, ca. 2019
Video, color, sound, 4 min., 29 sec.
Courtesy Ashra Kwesi
Plate 80

M. Lamar (American, born 1972) and
The Living Earth Show
*Machines & Other Intergalactic
Technologies of The Spirit*, 2025
Live performance

Jamal Lance, Menelek III, and
Kiambu Zawadi
Egypt Symbols in Arches, *Olmec Head*, and
Three Pharaohs, Bedford Bowling Center
murals, 1980–94, printed 2024
Photograph by Janet Braun-Reinitz
Inkjet print, 16 x 20 in. (40.6 x 50.8 cm)
Courtesy Artmakers, Inc.
Plate 62

Simone Leigh (American, born 1967)
Sharifa, 2022
Bronze, H. 9 ft. 3½ in. (283.2 cm),
W. 40¾ in. (103.5 cm), D. 40½ in.
(102.9 cm)
Glenstone Museum, Potomac, Maryland
Plate 181

Glenn Ligon (American, born 1960)
Gold Nobody Knew Me #1, 2008
Acrylic and oil stick on canvas, 32 x 32 in.
(81.3 x 81.3 cm)
Rubell Museum, Miami and
Washington, D.C.
Plate 81

Maha Maamoun (Egyptian, born 1972)
Domestic Tourism II, 2009
Video, color, sound, 62 min.
Courtesy the artist and Gypsum Gallery,
Cairo
Plate 68

Eric Mack (American, born 1987)
See, The Sarcophagus Is Moot, Too, 2022
Silk, wool, cotton, polyester, ribbon,
thread, microfiber, velvet, found hand-
kerchief, and denim, 9 ft. 8⅝ in. x 48 in.
(296.3 x 121.9 cm)
Collection of Robert D. Summer
Plate 158

*Mahmoud Mokhtar Supervising the
Installation of "Egypt Awakening"
(Nahdat Misr)*, ca. 1926, printed 2024
Inkjet print, 10 x 8 in. (25.4 x 20.3 cm)
Collection of Emad Abou Ghazi, Cairo
Plate 64

Malcolm X in Cairo, 1964
Video, color, silent, 2 min., 17 sec.
Schomburg Center for Research in Black
Culture, The New York Public Library,
New York, used with Permission of X
Legacy, LLC
Plate 75

Julie Mehretu
(Ethiopian American, born 1970)
Stelae 3 (Bardu), 2016
Ink and acrylic on canvas, 10 x 12 ft.
(304.8 x 365.8 cm)
Collection of Lisa and Steven Tananbaum
Plate 166

Roy Meriwether (American, 1943–2021)
Nubian Lady, 1973
Record cover, Stinger Productions LP 1000
Design by Joan M. Loykovich
Plate 109

Nicki Minaj (Trinidadian, born 1982)
Queen, 2018
Record cover, Young Money Entertain-
ment / Cash Money Records / Republic
Records 00602567817529
Design by Mert and Marcus
Plate 138

The Modern Jazz Quartet
Pyramid, 1960
Record cover, Atlantic Records 1325
Plate 108

Mahmoud Mokhtar (Egyptian, 1891–1934)
Bride of the Nile (Arous El Nil), Bust,
ca. 1930
Bronze and silver, H. 20⅛ in. (51.1 cm),
W. 9⅛ in. (23.2 cm), D. 11¾ in. (30 cm)
Private collection, United Arab Emirates
Plate 65

Ronald Moody (Jamaican, 1900–1984)
Tacet (Head), 1938
Wood, H. 30 in. (76.2 cm), W. 13⅜ in.
(34 cm), D. 14⅛ in. (35.9 cm)
National Gallery of Jamaica Collection,
Kingston (1978.028)
Plate 41

John W. Mosley (American, 1907–1969)
Guests at Pyramid Club Art Exhibition,
1947, printed 2024
Inkjet print, 8 x 10 in. (20.3 x 25.4 cm)
Temple University Libraries, Philadelphia
Plate 84

Mtume Umoja Ensemble
Alkebu-Lan: Land of the Blacks, 1972
Record cover, Strata-East SES-1972-4
Art and design by Wabembe
Plate 115

Muhammad Ali at Giza, 1966, printed 2024
Inkjet print, 8 x 10 in. (20.3 x 25.4 cm)
Courtesy Associated Press
Plate 76

Nas (American, born 1973)
I Am . . . , 1999
Record cover, Columbia Records C2 68773
Photography by Daniel Hastings/Lab
1228; mask casting and sculpting by Dave
Cortés and Nicolas Villella
Plate 135

The Negro World 14, no. 12, May 5, 1923
Charles Evans Inniss Memorial Library
Archives and Special Collections, Medgar
Evers College, The City University of
New York
Plate 24

Kantiba Nerouy
"Tutankh-Amen and Ras Tafari," in
The Crisis 29, no. 2, December 1924
Collection of Walter O. and Linda Evans
Plate 33

Offset (American, born 1991)
Father of 4, 2019
Cover photography by Pep Williams
Record cover, Quality Control Music
B003010501
Plate 139

Lorraine O'Grady (American, born 1934)
*Nefertiti/Devonia Evangeline: Told to
swing an incense censer, she stirs sand
instead*, 1981, printed 2018
Photograph by Freda Leinwand
Cibachrome print, 13¾ x 20¼ in.
(34.9 x 51.4 cm)

Courtesy of the artist and Mariane Ibrahim
(Chicago, Paris, and Mexico City)
Plate 48

Lorraine O'Grady (American, born 1934)
*Nefertiti/Devonia Evangeline: You are
protected, and you shall not die*, 1981,
printed 2018
Photograph by Freda Leinwand
Cibachrome print, 13¾ x 20¼ in.
(34.9 x 51.4 cm)
Courtesy of the artist and Mariane Ibrahim
(Chicago, Paris, and Mexico City)
Plate 49

Lorraine O'Grady (American, born 1934)
Miscegenated Family Album (Sisters I),
*L: Nefernefruaten Nefertiti; R: Devonia
Evangeline O'Grady*, 1980/94
Cibachrome print, 20 x 16 in.
(50.8 x 40.6 cm)
Museum of Fine Arts, Boston, Barbara
Lee Endowment for Contemporary Art by
Women (2018.274.2a-b)
Plate 50

Lorraine O'Grady (American, born 1934)
Miscegenated Family Album (Sisters II),
*L: Nefertiti's daughter Merytaten;
R: Devonia's daughter*, 1980/94
Cibachrome print, 20 x 16 in.
(50.8 x 40.6 cm)
Museum of Fine Arts, Boston, Barbara
Lee Endowment for Contemporary Art by
Women (2018.274.3a-b)
Plate 52

Lorraine O'Grady (American, born 1934)
Miscegenated Family Album (Sisters III),
*L: Nefertiti's daughter, Maketaten;
R: Devonia's daughter, Kimberley*, 1980/94
Cibachrome print, 20 x 16 in.
(50.8 x 40.6 cm)
Museum of Fine Arts, Boston, Barbara
Lee Endowment for Contemporary Art by
Women (2018.274.4a-b)
Plate 51

Lorraine O'Grady (American, born 1934)
Miscegenated Family Album (Sisters IV),
*L: Devonia's sister, Lorraine; R: Nefertiti's
sister, Mutnedjmet*, 1980/94
Cibachrome print, 20 x 16 in.
(50.8 x 40.6 cm)
Museum of Fine Arts, Boston, Barbara
Lee Endowment for Contemporary Art by
Women (2018.274.5a-b)
Plate 53

Osiris
Since Before Our Time, 1979
Record cover, Warner Bros. Records
BSK 3311
Art direction by Peter Whorf; design by
Frank Mulvey and David Fleming/Gribbitt!;
illustration by Jeff Wack
Plate 122

Clifford Owens (American, born 1971)
*Luxor Solo (Mystical Score for the Ghost
of Bud Powell)*, 2010/2024
Live performance

Gordon Parks (American, 1912–2006)
Untitled, Harlem, New York, 1963
Archival pigment print, sheet: 16 x 20 in.
(40.6 x 50.8 cm)
Museum of Fine Arts, Boston, Museum
purchase with funds donated by the Ford
Foundation (2021.339)
Plate 87

Parliament
Trombipulation, 1980
Record cover, Casablanca Records
NBLP 7249
Concept by George Clinton; art direction
by Overton Loyd; artwork and nose sculp-
ture by Tim (Mr. 2 HEP) Bruckner/Art
Hotel; graphics by Art Hotel
Plate 124

Kamau Amu Patton (American, born 1972)
SEKHET HETEPU, 2024
Live performance

Kamau Amu Patton (American, born 1972)
The Past and Other Dreams, 2020
Double audio cassette, Experimental
Sound Studio
Plate 152

The Pharaohs
The Awakening, 1971/1996
Record cover, Scarab Records; reissued
by Luv N'Haight LHLP025
Artwork by Berry Horton
Plate 127

Leontyne Price (American, born 1927)
with Rome Opera House Orchestra and
Chorus, conducted by Georg Solti
Aïda, 1962
Record cover, London Records OSA 1393
Cover photography by Louis Melançon
Plate 107

Robert Pruitt (American, born 1975)
Negra Es Bella, 2015
Two-color lithograph, 37½ x 26 in.
(95.3 x 66 cm)
Worcester Art Museum, Worcester,
Massachusetts, Chapin Riley Fund at
the Greater Worcester Community
Foundation (2019.1)
Plate 59

Baaba Heru Ankh Ra Semahj Se Ptah
(Tortolian American)
The Ankh of Love, ca. 1975
Copper, brass, and silver, 12½ x 6½ in.
(31.8 x 16.5 cm)
Collection of the artist
Plate 100

Pyramid Club
Pictorial Album of the Pyramid Club,
October 1941
James Weldon Johnson Memorial Collection in the Yale Collection of American
Literature, Beinecke Rare Book and Manuscript Library, Yale University, New Haven
Plate 82

Pyramid Club
Pictorial Album of the Pyramid Club,
1947–48
James Weldon Johnson Memorial Collection in the Yale Collection of American
Literature, Beinecke Rare Book and Manuscript Library, Yale University, New Haven
Plate 83

Ras G and The Afrikan Space Program
Back on the Planet, 2013
Record cover, Brainfeeder Records BF039
Design and layout by Stephen Serrato
Plate 137

The Ritchie Family
African Queens, 1977
Record cover, Marlin Records MARLIN
2206
Photography by John Galluzzi; design by
Richard Roth
Plate 128

Roche
Nile Queen For Hair and Skin, back cover
of *The Crisis* 20, no. 4, August 1920
Collection of Walter O. and Linda Evans
Plate 29

Betye Saar (American, born 1926)
Window of Ancient Sirens, 1979
Paper, paint, feathers, and found objects
on wood, 14¾ x 24¾ in. (37.5 x 62.9 cm)

Studio Museum in Harlem, New York, Gift
of Wynn and Sally Kramarsky, New York
(1982.6.1)
Plate 46

Mahmoud Saïd (Egyptian, 1897–1964)
L'invitation au voyage, 1932
Oil on canvas, 31½ x 23⅝ in. (80 x 60 cm)
Collection of Amr Eldib, Cairo
Plate 66

Pharoah Sanders (American, 1940–2022)
Africa, 1987
Record cover, Timeless Records SJP 253
Design by Erik Vos; photography by Frans
Schellenkens and Erik Vos
Plate 126

Kaneza Schaal (American, born 1985)
GO FORTH, 2016/2024
Live performance

Addison N. Scurlock
(American, 1883–1964)
*Collage of Photographs of the Alpha Phi
Alpha "Sphinx Club" Fraternity*, 1923
Ink on paper, 8¼ x 10 in. (21 x 25.4 cm)
Collection of the Smithsonian National
Museum of African American History and
Culture, Washington, D.C. (2010.54.7)
Plate 91

Ahmed Shehaby
Mike and Kiki Tyson at Giza, 2019,
printed 2024
Inkjet print, 8 x 10 in. (20.3 x 25.4 cm)
Courtesy the photographer
Plate 77

Lorna Simpson (American, born 1960)
Older Queen, 2017
Found photograph and collage on paper,
14⅜ x 12⅛ in. (36.5 x 30.8 cm)
Courtesy the artist and Hauser & Wirth
Plate 56

Ming Smith (American, born 1947)
Womb, 1992, printed 2023
Gelatin silver print, 16 x 20 in.
(40.6 x 50.8 cm)
Courtesy the artist and Jenkins Johnson
Gallery
Plate 79

Space Is the Place, 1974
Directed by John Coney, written by Sun Ra
and Joshua Smith
Video, sound, color, 85 min.
Courtesy North American Star System
Production
Plate 159

Steel Pulse
Babylon the Bandit, 1985
Record cover, Elektra Records 60437-1
Concepts, graphics, and illustration by
Neville Garrick
Plate 133

Luke Stewart (American, born 1986)
Blacks' Myths–"Kemetic Hymns," 2024
Live performance

Tavares Strachan
(Bahamian American, born 1979)
ENOCH (display unit), 2015–17
Bronze, 24k gold, steel, radar retroreflectors, and sacred air blessed by Shinto
priest, H. 14⅜ in. (36.5 cm), W. 3½ in.
(8.9 cm), D. 4⅛ in. (10.5 cm)
The Metropolitan Museum of Art,
New York, Gift of Perrotin Gallery, 2021
(2021.385a–c)
Plate 168

Sun Ra (American, 1914–1993)
Horizon, 1972/2020
Record cover, El Saturn Records/Thoth
Intergalactic; reissued by Strut/ArtYard
STRUT 229LP
Plate 119

Henry Ossawa Tanner
(American, 1859–1937)
Interior of a Mosque, Cairo, 1897
Oil on canvas, 20½ x 26 in. (52.1 x 66 cm)
Museum of Fine Arts, Boston, Museum
purchase with funds by exchange from
The Hayden Collection—Charles Henry
Hayden Fund, Bequest of Kathleen Rothe,
Bequest of Barbara Brooks Walker, and
Gift of Mrs. Richard Storey in memory of
Mrs. Bayard Thayer (2005.92)
Plate 1

Henry Ossawa Tanner
(American, 1859–1937)
Flight into Egypt, 1923
Oil on canvas, 29 x 26 in. (73.7 x 66 cm)
The Metropolitan Museum of Art,
New York, Marguerite and Frank A.
Cosgrove Jr. Fund, 2001 (2001.402a)
Plate 2

Henry Taylor (American, born 1958)
Michelle, 2023
Acrylic on canvas, 83¾ x 60 in.
(212.7 x 152.4 cm)
The George Economou Collection,
Athens, Greece
Plate 18

Mildred Thompson
(American, 1936–2003)
Stele, ca. 1963
Acrylic on found wood, H. 38 in. (96.5 cm),
W. 7¾ in. (19.7 cm), D. 8½ in. (21.6 cm)
Glenstone Museum, Potomac, Maryland
Plate 169

Thunder
7th Wonder, 1980
Record cover, Chocolate City CCLP 2012
Concept by Little Boo; graphics by
Leo McIntire/Gribbitt!; illustration by
Jeff Wack
Plate 123

Vogue Arabia, November 2017
Cover featuring Rihanna
Photography by Greg Kadel
Plate 71

Kara Walker (American, born 1969)
*Untitled (Study for A Subtlety, or the
Marvelous Sugar Baby)*, 2013–14
Charcoal on paper, 59 in. x 8 ft. 5 in.
(149.9 x 256.5 cm)
Collection of Richard and Michelle
Jeschelnig
Plate 179

Laura Wheeler Waring
(American, 1887–1948)
Egypt and Spring, cover of *The Crisis* 25,
no. 6, April 1923
Collection of Walter O. and Linda Evans
Plate 30

Laura Wheeler Waring
(American, 1887–1948)
Africa in America, cover of *The Crisis* 28,
no. 2, June 1924
Collection of Walter O. and Linda Evans
Plate 31

Laura Wheeler Waring
(American, 1887–1948)
The Strength of Africa, cover of *The Crisis*
28, no. 5, September 1924
Collection of Walter O. and Linda Evans
Plate 32

Frances Cress Welsing
(American, 1935–2016)
The Isis Papers: The Keys to the Colors,
2004
Washington, D.C.: C. W. Publishing
Plate 104

William T. Williams
(American, born 1942)
Nu Nile, 1973
Acrylic on canvas, 84 x 60 in.
(213.4 x 152.4 cm)
Courtesy the artist and Michael Rosenfeld
Gallery LLC, New York
Plate 154

Fred Wilson (American, born 1954)
Grey Area (Brown version), 1993
Pigment, plaster, and wood, overall: 20 x
84 in. (50.8 x 213.4 cm)
Brooklyn Museum, Bequest of William K.
Jacobs, Jr. and bequest of Richard J.
Kempe, by exchange (2008.6a–j)
Plate 42

Fred Wilson (American, born 1954)
Black Egypt, 2019
Postcard, 4 x 6 in. (10.2 x 15.2 cm)
Tommasino Family Collection
Plate 99

X Clan
Xodus (The New Testament), 1992
Record cover, Polydor Records 513 225-1
Photography and art direction by
George Dubose for Pop Eye Designs;
design by Ron Jaramillo and Dana Shimizu
for Pop Eye Designs
Plate 136

Selected Bibliography

Alford, Kwame Wes. "The Early Intellectual Growth and Development of William Leo Hansberry and the Birth of African Studies." *Journal of Black Studies* 30, no. 3 (January 2000), pp. 269–93.

Andrews, Kehinde. "Beyond Pan-Africanism: Garveyism, Malcolm X and the End of the Colonial Nation State." *Third World Quarterly* 38, no. 11 (2017), pp. 2501–16.

Ashby, Solange. *Calling Out to Isis: The Enduring Nubian Presence at Philae.* Piscataway, N.J.: Gorgias Press, 2020.

Ater, Renée. "Meta Warrick Fuller's *Ethiopia* and the America's Making Exposition of 1921." In *Women Artists of the Harlem Renaissance*, edited by Amy Helene Kirschke, pp. 53–84. Oxford: University Press of Mississippi, 2014.

ben-Jochannan, Yosef A. A. *Black Man of the Nile and His Family.* New York: Alkebu-Lan Books, 1972.

Bernal, Martin. *Black Athena: The Afroasiatic Roots of Classical Civilization.* New Brunswick, N.J.: Rutgers University Press, 1987.

Black Photographers Annual. Vol. 4. New York: Another View, 1980.

Buick, Kirsten Pai. *Child of the Fire: Mary Edmonia Lewis and the Problem of Art History's Black and Indian Subject.* Durham, N.C.: Duke University Press, 2010.

Carpenter, Jane H., with Betye Saar. *Betye Saar.* San Francisco: Pomegranate, 2003.

Chase-Riboud, Barbara. *I Always Knew: A Memoir.* Princeton, N.J.: Princeton University Press, 2022.

Clarke, John Henrik. "Pan-Africanism: A Brief History of an Idea in the African World." *Présence africaine*, n.s., no. 145 (1988), pp. 26–56.

Davies, Vanessa. "Egypt and Egyptology in the Pan-African Discourse of Amy Jacques Garvey and Marcus Garvey." *Mare Nostrum* 13, no. 1 (December 2022), pp. 147–78.

——. "Pauline Hopkins' Literary Egyptology." *Journal of Egyptian History* 14, no. 2 (December 2021), pp. 127–44.

——. "W. E. B. Du Bois, A New Voice in Egyptology's Disciplinary History," *ANKH: Journal of Egyptology and African Civilizations*, no. 28/29 (2019–20), pp. 18–29.

Diop, Cheikh Anta. *The African Origin of Civilization: Myth or Reality.* Chicago: Lawrence Hill Books, 1974.

Douglass, Frederick. "The Claims of the Negro, Ethnologically Considered: An Address before the Literary Societies of Western Reserve College, At Commencement, July 12, 1864." Rochester: Lee, Mann, 1854. https://www.loc.gov/resource/rbaapc.07900.

Douglass, Frederick. Diary, 1886–1894; Tour of Europe and Africa, 1886–1894. Frederick Douglass Papers. Library of Congress. https://www.loc.gov/item/mss1187900001/.

Du Bois, W. E. B. *Black Folk Then and Now: An Essay in the History and Sociology of the Negro Race.* Vol. 7 of *The Oxford W. E. B. Du Bois*, edited by Henry Louis Gates Jr. 1939; Oxford: Oxford University Press, 2016.

Gilroy, Paul. *The Black Atlantic: Modernity and Double Consciousness.* Cambridge, Mass.: Harvard University Press, 1993.

Glissant, Edouard. *Poetics of Relation*, translated by Betsy Wing. Ann Arbor: University of Michigan Press, 1997.

Gregory, Derek. "Emperors of the Gaze: Photographic Practices and Productions of Space in Egypt, 1839–1914." In *Picturing Place: Photography and the Geographical Imagination*, edited by Joan M. Schwarz and James R. Ryan, pp. 195–225. London: I. B. Tauris, 2003.

Hartman, Saidiya V. "The Time of Slavery," *South Atlantic Quarterly* 101, no. 4 (Fall 2002), pp. 757–77.

Higgins, Chester. *Feeling the Spirit.* New York: Bantam Books, 1994.

Jones, Kellie. *South of Pico: African American Artists in Los Angeles in the 1960s and 1970s.* Durham, N.C.: Duke University Press, 2017.

Keita, Maghan. *Race and the Writing of History: Riddling the Sphinx* (Oxford: Oxford University Press, 2000).

Kerr, Judith N. "God-Given Work: The Life and Times of Sculptor Meta Vaux Warrick Fuller, 1877–1968." PhD diss., University of Massachusetts Amherst, 1986. https://scholarworks.umass.edu/dissertations_1/1143.

Lee, Evan. "Classical Tradition and Black Nationalism in W. E. B. Du Bois's *The Star of Ethiopia*." *International Journal of the Classical Tradition* 26, no. 1 (2019), pp. 54–71. https://doi.org/10.1007/s12138-018-0479-5.

Locke, Alain. "The Legacy of the Ancestral Arts." In *The New Negro: An Interpretation*, edited by Alain Locke, pp. 254–67. New York: Albert and Charles Boni, 1925.

Manzo, Andrea. *Ancient Egypt in Its African Context: Economic Networks, Social and Cultural Interactions.* Cambridge: Cambridge University Press, 2022.

Mazrui, Ali A. "The Re-Invention of Africa: Edward Said, VY Mudimbe, and Beyond." *Research in African Literatures* 36, no. 3 (Autumn 2005), pp. 68–82.

Mudimbe, V. Y. *The Invention of Africa: Gnosis, Philosophy, and the Order of Knowledge.* Bloomington: Indiana University Press, 1988.

Nasser, Gamal Abdel. *The Philosophy of the Revolution.* 1952; Buffalo, N.Y.: Smith, Keynes, and Marshall, 1959.

Nerouy, Kantiba. "Tutankh-Amen and Ras Tafari." *The Crisis* 29, no. 2 (December 1924), pp. 64–68.

O'Connor, David. "Ancient Egypt and Black Africa: Early Contacts." *Expedition Magazine* 14, no. 1 (September 1971), pp. 2–9.

O'Connor, David, and Andrew Reid, eds. *Ancient Egypt in Africa.* 2003; London: Routledge, 2016.

O'Grady, Lorraine. "Some Thoughts on Diaspora and Hybridity: An Unpublished Slide Lecture (1994)." *BOMB*, October 22, 2020. https://bombmagazine.org/author/lorraine-ogrady/.

Patch, Diana Craig, and Alisa LaGama. "The African Origin of Civilization." Special issue, *The Metropolitan Museum of Art Bulletin*, n.s., 79, no. 4 (spring 2022).

Rasberry, Vaughn. *Race and the Totalitarian Century: Geopolitics in the Black Literary Imagination.* Cambridge, Mass.: Harvard University Press, 2016.

Rashwan, Hany. "Against Eurocentrism: Decolonizing Eurocentric Literary Theories in the Ancient Egyptian and Arabic Poetics." *Howard Journal of Communications* 32, no. 22 (2021), pp. 171–96. https://doi.org/10.1080/1064 6175.2021.1879695.

Smith, Shawn Michelle. "'Looking at One's Self through the Eyes of Others': W. E. B. Du Bois's Photographs for the 1900 Paris Exposition." *African American Review* 34, no. 4 (Winter 2000), pp. 581–99.

Sorek, Susan. *The Emperor's Needles: Egyptian Obelisks and Rome.* Bristol, U.K.: Phoenix Press, 2010.

Swiboda, Marcel. "Re Interpretations: Sun Ra's Egyptian Inscriptions." *Parallax* 13, no. 2 (2007), pp. 93–106. https://doi .org/10.1080/13534640701267347.

Temple, Christel N. "Ancient Kemet in African American Literature and Criticism, 1853 to the Present." *Journal of Pan African Studies* 5, no. 4 (June 2012), pp. 129–48.

Thomas, Abraham. *The Roof Garden Commission: Lauren Halsey.* Exh. cat. New York: The Metropolitan Museum of Art, 2023.

Tommasino, Akili. "The Cleopatra Sculptures." In *Barbara Chase-Riboud, Monumentale: The Bronzes*, edited by Stephanie Weissberg, pp. 41–46. Exh. cat. St. Louis: Pulitzer Arts Foundation, 2023.

Trimble, Jennifer. "Appropriating Egypt for the Ara Pacis Augustae." In *Rome, Empire of Plunder: The Dynamics of Cultural Appropriation*, edited by Matthew P. Loar, Carolyn MacDonald, and Dan-el Padilla Peralta, pp. 109–36. Cambridge: Cambridge University Press, 2018.

Van De Mieroop, Marc. *A History of Ancient Egypt.* 2nd ed. Hoboken, N.J.: Wiley, 2021.

Wilson, Mabel O. "The Cartography of W. E. B. Du Bois's Color Line." In *W. E. B. Du Bois's Data Portraits: Visualizing Black America, The Color Line at the Turn of the Twentieth Century*, edited by Whitney Battle-Baptiste and Britt Rusert. New York: Princeton Architectural Press, 2018.

Index

Page numbers in *italics* refer to illustrations.

A

Aarons, Slim, *Slim and Sphinx*, 1964 (pl. 106), *167*, 249
abolition or abolitionists, 17, 23, 34, 242
abstraction, 16, 17, 22, 27, 30–31, *32*, 54
Abu Simbel, 21, 26, 31, *51*, *208*, 213
Adams, John Henry, Jr., covers of *The Crisis*, 1912 (pls. 25–27), *88*, *89*, 249
Adkins, Terry
    biography, 240, *240*
    Harlem Encore, 1999 (pl. 6), 23, *68–69*, 249
    Luxor Solo (*Mystical Score for the Ghost of Bud Powell*), 2011 (pl. 150), *198*, 249
    Obelisks in Rome, 2010 (pl. 5), 18, *67*, 240, 249
    Oxidation Blue 1, 2013 (pl. 4), 23, *66*, 240, 249
African diaspora
    ancient Egypt's global resonance in, 16–17, 23, 61
    and Black identity, 25, 27, 30, 44, 49
    defined, 17, 244n6
    musical forms of, 26
    and Pan-African movement, 20
    pilgrimages to Egypt, 28–29
    "roots tourism," 43–44
    spirituality, 29, 52
African Methodist Episcopal (AME) Church, 16, 243
AfriCOBRA (African Commune of Black Relevant Artists), 44, *44*
Afrocentric art, emergence of, 23, 241
Afrofuturism, 30–31, 49–51, *206–9*
Afropastism, 31
Ahmose (Egyptian king), 27
Aïda (Verdi opera; pl. 107), 26, *168*, 255
Akhenaten (Egyptian king), 24, 26, *159*, 215
Alexander the Great, 18
Ali, Dusé Mohamed
    In the Land of the Pharaohs, 1911 (fig. 27), 20, 38, *38*
    portrait of, 1911 (pl. 12), *76*, 252
Ali, Muhammad (pl. 76), 29, 60, *137*, 255

Al Mussawar magazine cover, October 1948 (pl. 70), 28, *132*, 249
Alpha Phi Alpha fraternity (pls. 91, 92), 30, *155–57*, 256
Amen, Ra Un Nefer, *Metu Neter*, 1990 (pl. 101), *165*, 183, 249
Amenhotep III (Egyptian king), 140, 215
Amer, Ghada, *Homage à Tut in Black and White*, 2021 (pl. 67), 28, *127*, 249
American Academy in Rome, 18, 21, 55, 240, 244n16
American Research Center in Egypt (ARCE), 246n36
America's Making Exposition (New York, 1921), 42–43, 241
Ancient Egyptian Arabic Order Nobles Mystic Shrine red fez (pl. 89), 30, *154*, 249
Angelou, Maya, 46, 48
ankh symbol, 27, *164*, 182
Arago, François, 52
Armstrong, Louis (pl. 73), 28, 55, *134–35*, 248n16, 251
Arnold, Eve, *Black Muslim children at the Metropolitan Museum in New York. They are taught black history*, 1961 (pl. 88), 29, *153*, 249
Art Ensemble of Chicago, *Tutankhamun*, 1974 (pl. 114), *172*, 249
Ashby, Muata, *Egyptian Yoga*, vol. 1 (1995) and vol. 2 (1998) (pls. 102, 103), *165*, 249
Ashby, Solange
    Calling Out to Isis, 2020 (pl. 16), 20, *77*, 249
    and diversity in field of Egyptology, 20, 246n36
Askew, Thomas A., 40
Astatke, Mulatu, 213
Aswan Dam, 20–21, 51
Ater, Renée, 41
Aton, Ayé, *Untitled* (*wall mural*), 1972, and *Untitled*, ca. 1975 (pls. 160–61), 31, *207*, 249
Augustus (Roman emperor), 18, 220

B

Badu, Erykah
    artist statement, 181–84
    Next Lifetime, 1997 (pl. 134), *180*, 249
Baldwin, James, 58, *58*
Baraka, Amiri
    dancing with Maya Angelou (fig. 40), 46, *48*
    It's Nation Time–African Visionary Music, 1972 (pl. 113), *172*, 250
The Bar-Kays, *As One*, 1980 (pl. 125), *177*, 250
Barr, Jerry, 30, 31
Basquiat, Jean-Michel, *Kings of Egypt II*, 1982 (pl. 165), 26, *211*, 250
Beatrizet, Nicolas, *Circus Maximus*, after P. Ligorio, 1553 (fig. 3), 18, *18*

Bedford Bowling Center murals, Brooklyn, 1980–94 (pl. 62), 26, *122*, 254
Bell, Sidra, 30, 250
Ben-Jochannan, Yosef A. A., *Black Man of the Nile and His Family*, 1972 (pl. 13), 20, *77*, 250
Bernal, Martin, *Black Athena: The Afroasiatic Roots of Classical Civilization*, 1987 (pl. 15), 20, 39, *77*, 102–3, 246n32, 250
Beyoncé. *See* Knowles-Carter, Beyoncé
biblical themes
    Exodus of the Israelites, 16, 23
    Hagar (Egyptian woman), 242
    Holy Family's flight to Egypt, 16, 18, 140, 243
    psalmic prophecy for Egypt and Ethiopia, 23, 94, 241, 244n41
Biggers, John Thomas, *Taharqa King of Nubia (710–664 BC)*, 1984 (pl. 93), *158*, 250
The Birth of a Nation (1915 film), 43
Black Arts Movement, 53
Black Journal television series, "Alice Coltrane" episode, 1970 (pl. 140), 26, *187*, 240, 249
Black Panther Party, 27
    Black Photographers Annual (1973–80), 53, 60
Black Power, 26–27
Bleiberg, Edward, 35
Bond, Barbara Higgins, *Akhenaten Pharaoh of Egypt (1375–1358 BC)*, 1984 (pl. 94), *159*, 250
Book of the Dead (ancient Egyptian text), 46, 183
Braun-Reinitz, Janet, 122, 254
British Museum, London, 23, 44, 214
Brown, LaKela, *Triangle Pairs with Pharaoh Heads and Nefertiti Recesses*, 2018 (pl. 96), *161*, 250
Brown, Richard, 53, 54
Buick, Kirsten Pai, 21, 244n34
Bumbray, Rashida
    How High the Moon, 2024 (pl. 153), 29, *200–201*, 250
    live performance at The Met, 30, 250
Burri, René, *Barbara Chase-Riboud at Deir el-Bahri*, 1958 (pl. 20), 28, *82*, 250
Burton, Harry
    Arthur Mace and Alfred Lucas working inside the makeshift "laboratory" set up in Sethos II's tomb, 1924 (fig. 11), 24, *24*
    Deir el-Bahri: Progress of the Work, January 1929 (pl. 7), *70*, 250

C

Cagnacci, Guido, *Death of Cleopatra*, 1660–62 (fig. 6), 20, *21*
Cairo
    Egyptian Museum, 44, 214
    Malcolm X's 1964 trip to, 28–29, 55–57, *56*, *136*, 242

Mokhtar's monumental sculpture, 28, 124, 242
music scene, 213–14
Naghi's mural in Egyptian Parliament, *27, 28*
Newsom's trip to, 220–21
Smith's photo of street market, ca. 1973, 60–61, *61*
Tanner's painting of mosque interior, 16, *64*
Wilson's experiences in, 102–3
Calloway, Thomas J., 40, 41
canopic jars, 31, *217*
Carruthers, Tom. *See* Dream The Combine
Carter, Howard, 19, 35
Carver, George Washington, Egyptian Blue pigment formula, 1930s (pl. 3), 20, 23, *66*, 250
Castro, Fidel, 58
Cecil Taylor Jazz Unit, *Nefertiti, The Beautiful One Has Come,* 1969 (pl. 110), *169,* 250
Chase-Riboud, Barbara
    at American Academy in Rome, 21, 244n16
    "Cleopatra II" (poem), 83
    Cleopatra's Cape, 1973 (fig. 7), 21, 22
    Cleopatra's Chair, 1994 (pl. 21), 22, *85,* 250
    at Deir el-Bahri, 1958 (pl. 20), 28, *82,* 250
    on Egyptian architecture, 139
    John Hay Whitney Fellowship., 244n35
civil rights movement, 26–27, 43, 46, 54–60
Clark, Ed
    painting en plein air at Giza, 1990s (fig. 16), *28, 30*
    Untitled (Egyptian Series), 1997 (pl. 157), 30, *204,* 250
Clark, Irene, *Cleopatra,* ca. 1940–50 (pl. 39), 22, *96,* 250
Cleopatra VII (Egyptian queen)
    dressing in costume as, 139, *141*
    film depictions of, 21, 24, *25,* 80–81
    historical details of, 18, 21
    painted depictions of, 20, 21, 22, *96*
    poem inspired by, 83
    sculptural depictions of, 20, 21–22, *21*
    sculptural objects made for, 21, 22, *85*
Clinton, George, 51, 235, 255
Colescott, Robert, *Nubian Queen,* 1966 (pl. 44), *105,* 250
colonialism
    and appropriation of ancient cultures, 27, 28
    Egyptology as informed by, 19, 24, 34
    and extraction of Egyptian antiquities, 18, 44
    Pan-African opposition to, 20, 40
    and photographic technology, 52
    resistance to or independence from, 41, 43, 55, 58–60
Coltrane, Alice
    biography, 240, *240*
    Black Journal episode on (pl. 140), 26, *187,* 240, 249
    Ptah the El Daoud, 1970 (pl. 112), *171,* 240, 250

Coltrane, John, 240
Coney, John, 49, *49,* 256
Conwill, Houston
    artist statement, 1977 (fig. 38), 46, *46*
    diagram of *The Cakewalk Humanifesto,* 1989 (fig. 39), 46, *47*
    Langston Hughes' Rivers, 1991 (with other artists; pl. 155), 23, 46–48, *203,* 250
    The Open Secret, 1986 (pl. 156), *203,* 250
Cooks, Bridget, 60
cosmograms, 23, 46, *47, 203*
Cox, Renee, *Rajé to the Rescue,* 1998 (pl. 163), 31, *209,* 250
Crawford, Marc, "The Scholar Nobody Knows," *Ebony,* February 1961 (pl. 11), 19–20, *75,* 250
The Crisis magazine
    Adams's covers for (pls. 25–27), *88, 89,* 249
    on archaeological excavations, 42
    Douglas's cover for (pl. 37), 23, *94,* 241, 251
    Nile Queen for Hair and Skin advertisement (pl. 29), *91,* 256
    peak circulation of, 54
    pharaonic masthead logo (fig. 10), 23, 24
    on *The Star of Ethiopia* pageant, 42, 43, *52, 53,* 54
    "Tutankh-Amen and Ras Tafari" article (Nerouy; pl. 33), *92,* 255
    Waring's covers for (pls. 30–32), 37, 38, *91, 243,* 257
Crowe, Shani, *Sun Trust,* 2016 (pl. 61), *121,* 251
Cyrus, Jamal, and Steffani Jemison, *Alpha's Bet Is Not Over Yet,* 2011 (pl. 34), 24, *93,* 253

D
Dabakis, Melissa, 23
Daguerre, Louis-Jacques-Mandé, 52
Damman, Catherine, 49
Daughters of Isis gloves, 2024 (pl. 90), 30, *154,* 251
Davis, Damien, *Ancient Still Life,* 2015 (pl. 95), *160,* 251
Davis, Karon
    He Who Floods the Nile, 2019 (pl. 55), *114,* 251
    live performance at The Met, 30, 251
Davis, Miles, *Nefertiti,* 1968 (pl. 111), 26, *170,* 251
Davis, Noah, *Untitled,* 2010 (pl. 17), 21, *78,* 251
Dawson, C. Daniel, *Olaifa and Egypt,* 1978 (pl. 47), 61, *108–9,* 251
Dawson, Charles Clarence
    cover of *The Negro in Art Week* catalogue, 1927 (pl. 28), *90,* 251
    "O, Sing a New Song," 1934 (pl. 105), 26, *166,* 251
Deir el-Bahri, 28, *70,* 82
De La Soul, *Eye Know,* 1989 (pl. 131), *179,* 251
Denim Tears (brand)
    Tracy's King Tut Belt, 2023 (pl. 98), 30, *162,* 251

Tracy's King Tut Vest, 2023 (pl. 97), 30, *162,* 251
De Pace, Joseph, 46, 250
DerBalian, Artin, *Louis and Lucille in Egypt at the Sphinx,* 1961 (pl. 73), 28, *134–35,* 251
Derbew, Sarah F., *Untangling Blackness in Greek Antiquity,* 2022 (fig. 29), 39, *39*
Deren, Maya, 247n47
Diop, Cheikh Anta, *The African Origin of Civilization: Myth or Reality,* 1974 (pl. 14), 19, 20, 39, 77, 191–92, 251
Domino Sugar Refinery, Brooklyn, 32–33, *32*
Donaldson, Jeff
    on Jones as "Grande Dame," 241
    Message from Tehuti, 1988 (pl. 164), 31, *210,* 251
Douglas, Aaron
    as Adkins's mentor, 240
    biography, 241, *241*
    Building More Stately Mansions, 1944 (pl. 38), 23, *95,* 251
    cover of *Fire!!* magazine, November 1926 (pl. 35), 23, *94,* 251
    cover of *The Crisis* magazine, May 1927 (pl. 37), 23, *94,* 241, 251
    Krigwa Players Little Negro Theatre, ca. 1926 (fig. 31), 41, *41,* 43
    Let My People Go, ca. 1935–39 (pl. 36), 23, *94,* 251
Douglas, Emory, *Mother and Daughter,* 1995 (pl. 58), 27, *118,* 251
Douglass, Frederick, 17, 27, 243
Draper, Louis, *Untitled (Girl with Egyptian Mural),* ca. 1965 (pl. 57), 26–27, 60, 61, *116–17,* 251
Dream The Combine (Jennifer Newsom and Tom Carruthers)
    at American Academy in Rome, 244n16
    Pyramidion, 2024 (pl. 170), 31, *219,* 251
Du Bois, David Graham, 60, *60*
Du Bois, Shirley Graham, 60, *60*
Du Bois, W. E. B.
    and America's Making Exposition, 42, 241
    on art as propaganda, 43, 51
    The Georgia Negro, 1900 (figs. 23, 30), 34, *34,* 40, *40*
    Krigwa Players Little Negro Theater founded by, 41, 43
    and Pan-African movement, 20, 34, 38, 40
    second wife, Shirley Graham, 60
    The Star of Ethiopia pageant, 41–43, *42,* 51, *52, 53,* 54
    See also The Crisis magazine
Dunham, Dows, *Letter to William Leo Hansberry,* February 2, 1932 (pl. 10), 19, *74,* 252
DuVerney, Oasa, *Assata Shakur as Ahmes Nefertari,* 2018 (pl. 60), 27, *120,* 252

E

Eakins, Thomas, 16, 243
Earth, Wind & Fire
    All 'n All, 1977 (pl. 117), 26, *174*, 252
    Best of Earth, Wind & Fire, Vol. 1, 1978
        (pl. 120), *175*, 252
    Spirit, 1976 (pl. 118), 141, *175*, 252
Ebony magazine article, 1961 (pl. 11), 75, 250
Edwards, Adrienne, 51, 215
Egypt, ancient
    and Afrofuturism, 30–31, 49–51
    artist statements on, 130–31, 191–93, 213–15
    biblical references to, 16, 18, 23, *94*, 140, 241,
        242, 243
    as Black African civilization, 17, 19, 24–25, 29,
        34–39, 42–43, 61, 242
    and Black racial pride, 25–27
    fashion inspired by, 28, 30, 54, *54*, 132, *154*, *162*
    geographic and historical overview of, 17–18
    and Glissant's concept of opacity, 40, 44, 51
    and Harlem Renaissance (New Negro)
        artists, 22–23, 41, 51, 241, 243
    Nubians enslaved in, 35
    obelisks, 17–19, *18*, 31, 55, *67*, 220, 244n11,
        244n14
    "Opening of the Mouth" ceremony, 48
    See also Egyptology; hieroglyphs; pyramids;
        sphinxes; *and specific deities, rulers,*
        and sites
Egypt, modern
    African American artists' pilgrimages to, 16,
        21, 28–29, 48, 52, 139–40, 220
    Aswan Dam's creation, 20–21, 51
    Douglass's visit to, as statesman, 17
    Egyptian artists' engagement with ancient
        themes, 27–28, *124–29*, 133, 243
    Egyptian photographers' views of, 52–53
    magazine covers, 28, *132*
    Napoleon's conquests of, 19, 31, 34
    Nasser as leader of, 38, 58–60, *59*
    racial identity, 28, 36, 246n17
    See also Cairo; Giza
Egyptian Blue (pigment), 20, 23, 42, *66*
The Egyptian Lover (Greg Broussard)
    Freak-A-Holic, 1986 (pl. 141), 26, *187*, 252
    On the Nile, 1984 (pl. 121), *175*, 252
Egyptology
    Afrocentric perspectives on, 20, 39,
        191–92, 240
    archaeological excavations, 19, 24, 35–36,
        41, 42, 44, 49, *70*
    Black scholars' exclusion from, 19–20
    current lack of diversity in, 20, 39,
        246nn36–37
    Douglass's critique of, 17
    Eurocentrism of mainstream, 17, 19, 24,
        34–35, 38–39, 191
    Nubian studies, 24, 35–36

and photographic technology, 52
and spiritual awakening, 141
Egyptomania, 18, 245n4
Ellison, Ralph
    Invisible Man, 220
    Via della Conciliazione, 1955–57 (fig. 46),
        55, *55*
El-magharbel, Zekkereya, 30, 252
Emancipation Proclamation, fiftieth anniver-
    sary of, 41–42, 54
Emory, Tremaine, 30, 251. *See also* Denim Tears
enslavement
    abolition or abolitionists, 17, 23, 34, 242
    and African heritage, 17, 29, 38
    and America's Making Exposition, 42
    ancient Egypt as a means of sidestepping,
        41, 51
    and Egyptology's development, 34
    Nubians enslaved by Egyptians, 35
    Tanner's mother as formerly enslaved, 243
Erizku, Awol
    artist statement, 191–93
    Nefertiti (Black Power), 2018 (pl. 144),
        195, 252
    Nefertiti–Miles Davis, 2017 (pl. 143), 26,
        190, 252
Ethiopia
    allegorical figures of, 23, 42–43, *86*, *87*
    archaeological excavations, 41, 42
    definitions of, 18
    Du Bois's *Star of Ethiopia* pageant, 41–43, *42*,
        51, *52*, *53*, 54
    Haile Selassie I's rule of, 58, 244n41
    music, 213–14
    psalmic prophecy about, 23, *94*, 241, 244n41
    racial identity, 245n7
Eurocentrism
    Black Arts Movement's challenge of, 53
    of Egyptology, 17, 19, 24, 34–35, 38–39, 191
    of idealizing classical Greece, 27, 54, 193
Eversley, Fred, *Untitled (gold layered step
        pyramid)*, 1983 (pl. 167), 31, *216*, 252
"Exhibit of American Negroes" (Paris, 1900),
    34, 40, 54
Exodus of the Israelites, 16, 23

F

Falda, Giovanni Battista
    *Another View of the Fountain in Piazza
        Navona*, 1691 or after (fig. 2), 17, *18*
    View of the Entire Vatican Basilica, 1665–69
        (fig. 4), 18, *19*
fashion, Egyptian-inspired, 28, 30, 54, *54*, 132,
    154, *162*
Fela Kuti and Egypt 80, *Perambulator*, 1983
    (pl. 130), *178*, 252
fez, Ancient Egyptian Arabic Order Nobles
    Mystic Shrine (pl. 89), 30, *154*, 249

Field Museum of Natural History, Chicago, 44
figuration, 16, 17, 22, 23, 28, 41, 244n45
film depictions of ancient Egypt
    Cleopatra, 21, 24, 25, *80–81*
    music-related, 26, *189*
    Space Is the Place, 1974 (fig. 41, pl. 159),
        30–31, 49–51, *49*, *206*, 256
Fire!! magazine cover, November 1926 (pl. 35),
    23, *94*, 251
Fisk University, 23, 240, 241
Five Percenters, 182
Fordjour, Derek, *Board Meeting (Brotherhood
        Smoke)*, 2021 (pl. 92), 30, *156–57*, 252
fraternities, Black, 30, *155–57*
Freud, Sigmund, 51
Fuller, Meta Vaux Warrick
    biography, 241, *241*
    Emancipation, 1913, 41
    Ethiopia Awakening, ca. 1914–21 (pl. 22), 23,
        28, 42–43, *86*, 241, 252
    maquette for *Ethiopia Awakening*, 1921
        (fig. 34), 42–43, *43*

G

Gaignard, Genevieve, *Kings and Queens*, 2017
    (pl. 63), 26, *123*, 252
Gallagher, Ellen
    Abu Simbel, 2005–6 (pl. 162), 31, 51, *208*, 252
    Pomp-Bang, 2003 (fig. 42), *50*, 51
Garvey, Amy Jacques, 35, 38, 245n10
Garvey, Marcus, 20, 23, 38, 41, 241, 244n41
Getatchew Mekuria, 213
Gilliam, Sam
    Nile, 1972 (pl. 177), *228*, 252
    Pyramid, 2020 (pl. 178), 32, *229*, 252
Giza
    African American artists or activists at,
        28–29, *28*, 30, 55, 60, *60*, *134–37*
    Great Sphinx, 28, 31, 55, *135*, *137*, *209*, 245n52
    pyramids, 28, 30, 57, 60, 139, 142, *214*
Glissant, Edouard, 40, 44, 51
gloves, Daughters of Isis (pl. 90), 30, *154*, 251
Gold, Chet, *Mirror Malcolm*, 2011 (pl. 74), 29,
    136, 252
Golia, Maria, 52
Grambling State University, 182
Great Migration, 16, 41
Greece, ancient
    and Egyptian obelisks, 18
    Egyptian precedents of Greek civilization,
        17, 20, 21, 39, 191
    modern claims to heritage of, 27, 54, 193
    racial perceptions, 39
    Roman art as derivative of, 22
Griffith, Frances Llewellyn, 19
Gutekunst, Frederick, *Henry Ossawa Tanner*,
    ca. 1897, 243

H

Haile Selassie I (emperor of Ethiopia), 58, 244n41
hair
    artworks made of, *31, 32, 222–23*
    braids, 28, *121, 133, 181, 215*
    commercial products for, 30, *91*
    wig of yellow Plasticine, *50*
Haley, Alex, *Roots*, 43–44
Halsey, Lauren
    artist statement, 235
    the eastside of south central los angeles hieroglyph prototype architecture (I), 2022 (fig. 22), *33, 33*
    FreedomEx, 2022 (pl. 182), *33, 234, 252*
    Untitled, 2024 (pl. 183), *33, 236–37, 253*
Hammons, David
    at American Academy in Rome, 18, 244n16
    Delta Spirit, 1985 (with other artists; fig. 18), *30, 31*
    Hair Pyramids, 1976 (fig. 20), *31, 32*
    Unknown, ca. 1977 (pls. 171–73), *32, 222, 223, 253*
Hansberry, William Leo
    Dunham's letter of rejection to, 19, *74*
    and Reisner's Eurocentrism, 38–39
    as renowned professor at Howard, 19–20, *75*
    William Leo Hansberry Society, 39
Harlem, New York
    Black Power movement, 26–27
    Krigwa Players Little Negro Theater, 41, *41, 43*
    Metro North Railroad art installation, Harlem–125th Street station, 23, *68–69, 249*
    Michaux's National Memorial African Bookstore, 57–60, *57, 58*
    performance art, 18
    photographer Van Der Zee, 54
    rallies, 57–60, *59, 152*
    Schomburg Center for Research in Black Culture, 23, *46, 48*
Harlem Renaissance (New Negro movement), 19, 22–23, 40–41, 51, 241, 243
Harvard University, 19, 38–39, 243
Hassinger, Maren
    Flying, 1982 (with other artists; pls. 145–49), *30, 196, 197, 253*
    Love (Pyramid), 2008/24 (pl. 175), *32, 225, 253*
    Message from Malcolm, 1998 (pl. 174), *29, 224, 253*
Hastings, Danny, 26, 255
Hatshepsut (Egyptian queen), 28, 29, *140, 215*
Heathcote, Reginald St. Alban, *Workmen transporting wooden crates containing blocks from Shrine of Taharqa*, 1922–33 (fig. 25), *36, 36*

Hegel, Georg Wilhelm Friedrich, 34, 38
hieroglyphs
    as "decoding life," 139
    and Egyptian worldview, 192
    paintings inspired by, 31
    photographic documentation of, 52
    record cover designs with, 26
    sculptural depictions of, 21, 22, 33
    on stage set of pageant, 54
Higgins, Chester
    African American pilgrims dance in honor of ancient spirits. Lake Nasser, Egypt, 2006 (pl. 86), *29, 52, 151, 253*
    Maya Angelou dancing with Amiri Baraka at the Schomburg Center, 2014 (fig. 40), *46, 48*
    Tomb of Irukaptah, A Libationer. Saqqara Necropolis, Egypt, 1979 (pl. 85), *150, 253*
Hill, EJ, *A Divine Mother (after Charles Dickson)*, 2018 (pl. 180), *232, 253*
Holley, Lonnie, *Ruling for the Child*, 1982 (pl. 54), *114, 253*
Homecoming: A Film by Beyoncé, 2019 (pl. 142), *26, 189, 253*
Horus, Eye of, 44
Howard University, 19–20, *75*
Hughes, Langston, 23, 46, 48
Hunt-Ehrlich, Madeleine, *Cleopatra at the Mall*, 2024 (pl. 19), *21, 80–81, 253*
Hurdle, Gregston, *Kamau Amu Patton performing "Amun (The Unseen Legends),"* 2017 (pl. 151), *199, 253*

I

Iman (model), 26
Irvine, Weldon, *Cosmic Vortex (Justice Divine)*, 1974 (pl. 116), *173, 253*
Isis (goddess), 27, 28, 30, *154*
Islam
    and birth of modern Egyptology, 19
    Black Muslim children at The Met, 29, *153*
    Coltrane's encounters with, 240
    Malcolm X at Islamic holy sites, 28–29, *56, 57*, 242
    Nation of Islam, 29, 57, *182*, 242
    and Pan-Africanism, 38
    Tanner's painting of mosque interior, 16, *64*
Issa, Iman
    artist statement, 130–31
    Heritage Studies #7, 2015 (pl. 69), *27, 129, 253*
Itasse-Broquet, Jeanne, *Egyptian Harpist*, 1891 (fig. 32), *41, 42*

J

Jackson, Michael, 26, 253
Jemison, Steffani
    Alpha's Bet Is Not Over Yet, 2011 (with Jamal Cyrus; pl. 34), *24, 93, 253*

live performance at The Met, 30, 253
Jenkins, Ulysses, *Flying*, 1982 (with other artists; pls. 145–49), *30, 196, 197*, 253
Johnson, Charles S., 241
Johnson, Earvin "Magic," 26
Johnson, Malvin Gray, *Negro Pharaoh–Eighteenth Dynasty*, 1934 (pl. 40), *23, 97, 253*
Johnson, Rashid
    live performance at The Met, 30, 254
    Pyramid, 2009 (pl. 176), *32, 226–27, 253*
Jones, Kellie, 44
Jones, Loïs Mailou
    The Ascent of Ethiopia, 1932 (pl. 23), *23, 87*, 241, 254
    biography, 241–42, *241*
    Egyptian Heritage, 1953 (pl. 43), *25–26, 104, 254*
    sphinx and pyramid symbols used by, 41
The Jones Girls, *Nights Over Egypt*, 1981 (pl. 129), *178, 254*
Jones-Hogu, Barbara, *Relate to Your Heritage*, 1971 (pl. 45), *106, 254*

K

Kamoinge (photography collective), 44, 60, 248n20
Kelley, Robin D. G., 51
Kemet (*kmt*), 17, 39
Kemetic spirituality, 29, 30, 52, *151, 165, 182–83*
Kemet Nu Tours (pl. 80), *29, 146, 254*
Khalil, Armia Malak, *Hope–I Am a Morning Scarab*, 2024 (pl. 72), *28, 133, 254*
Khorshid, Omar, 213
Knight, Jas, *The African Origin of Civilization*, 2023 (pl. 9), *19, 72–73, 254*
Knowles, Solange
    artist statement, 139–42
    family photos, *138, 141*
    Orion's Rise, 2018 (pl. 78), *30, 141–42, 143, 254*
Knowles-Carter, Beyoncé, *Homecoming* film, 2019 (pl. 142), *26, 189, 253*
Kongo cosmogram, 46
Kool Moe Dee, *Funke Funke Wisdom*, 1991 (pl. 132), *179, 254*
Krigwa Players Little Negro Theater (fig. 31), *41, 41, 43*
Kriyananda, Swami, 139
Kulthum, Umm, 213
Kuti, Fela. *See* Fela Kuti and Egypt 80
Kwesi, Ashra and Merira, *Kemet Nu "Know Thyself" Tour*, ca. 2019 (pl. 80), *29, 146, 254*
Kwon, Miwon, 45

L

Lamar, M., 30, 254

Lance, Jamal, Bedford Bowling Center murals, 1980–94 (with other artists; pl. 62), 26, 122, 254

Launois, John, *Malcolm X prays in the great Mosque of Mohammed Ali in Cairo*, 1964 (fig. 47), 56, 57

Lawrence, Jacob, panel 24 from The Migration Series, 1940–41 (fig. 9), 22, 23

Lawrence, Robert Henry, Jr., 31

Lee, Evan, 54

Leigh, Simone, *Sharifa*, 2022 (pl. 181), 33, 233, 254

Leinwand, Freda, 30, 255

Lewis, Edmonia

    biography, 242, 242

    The Death of Cleopatra, 1876 (fig. 5), 20, 21–22, 242

Life magazine, 57

Ligon, Glenn, *Gold Nobody Knew Me #1*, 2008 (pl. 81), 29, 147, 254

Little Rock Nine, 55

live performance, 18, 30, 250, 251, 252, 253, 254, 255, 256

Locke, Alain, 19–20, 40–41, 53, 241

Lone Wolf Recital Corps, 18, 240

Los Angeles, South Central, 33, 235

Loving v. Virginia (1967 Supreme Court case), 48

lynchings, 42

M

Maamoun, Maha, *Domestic Tourism II*, 2009 (pl. 68), 28, 128, 254

Mack, Eric

    at American Academy in Rome, 244n16

    See, The Sarcophagus Is Moot, Too, 2022 (pl. 158), 205, 254

Majozo, Estella Conwill, 46, 250

Malcolm X (El-Hajj Malik El-Shabazz)

    artworks inspired by, 29, 136, 224

    biography, 242, 242

    in Cairo, 1964 (fig. 47, pl. 75), 28–29, 55–57, 56, 136, 242, 254

    at Michaux's bookstore in Harlem, 1964 (fig. 48), 57–58, 57

Mankiewicz, Joseph L., *Cleopatra* film, 1963 (fig. 13), 24, 25

Marzioli, Sara, 55

Mehretu, Julie

    artist statement, 213–15

    Stelae 3 (Bardu), 2016 (pl. 166), 31, 212, 254

Mellon Mays Undergraduate Fellowship, 246n37

Mendieta, Ana, *Nile Born*, 1984 (fig. 17), 29, 30

Menelek III, Bedford Bowling Center murals, 1980–94 (with other artists; pl. 62), 26, 122, 254

Meriweather, Roy, *Nubian Lady*, 1973 (pl. 109), 169, 254

The Metropolitan Museum of Art, New York

    Arnold's photo of Black Muslim children at, 29, 153

    Bumbray's video recorded at, 29, 200–201

    and Carver's Egyptian Blue pigment, 20

    Chase-Riboud solo exhibition, 21, 244n35

    Eurocentric treatment of Egyptian art, 19

    Halsey's Roof Garden installation, 33, 33

    Khalil as security officer at, 28

    live performance at, 30

    Tanner's works in, 16

    Temple of Dendur, 21

Michaux, Lewis H., 57–60, 57, 58

Minaj, Nicki, *Queen*, 2018 (pl. 138), 186, 254

The Modern Jazz Quartet, *Pyramid*, 1960 (pl. 108), 169, 254

Mokhtar, Mahmoud

    biography, 242–43, 242

    Bride of the Nile (Arous El Nil), Bust, ca. 1930 (pl. 65), 28, 125, 243, 254

    as father of modern Egyptian sculpture, 27–28, 242

    supervising installation of *Egypt Awakening*, ca. 1930 (pl. 64), 28, 124, 242, 254

Moody, Ronald, *Tacet (Head)*, 1938 (pl. 41), 23, 99, 255

Morris, Lenwood, 53, 54

Morrison, Toni, 53

Mosley, John W., *Guests at Pyramid Club Art Exhibition*, 1947 (pl. 84), 30, 149, 255

Mtume Umoja Ensemble, *Alkebu-Lan: Land of the Blacks*, 1972 (pl. 115), 172, 255

Muhammad, Akbar, 57

mummification, 23, 30, 31, 43, 49

Murphy, Eddie, 26

Murray, Daniel, 40, 41

Murray's Nu Nile Hair Slick Dressing Pomade, 30

Museum of Fine Arts, Boston, 19, 24

music

    Coltrane as jazz harpist, 26, 187, 240

    DJ Slim with sphinxes, 167

    Egyptian Harpist (Itasse-Broquet; fig. 32), 41, 42

    films or videos, 26, 187, 189

    record covers, 26, 141, 169–80, 185–86

    stage productions, 26, 42, 143, 166, 168

N

Nagaoka, Shusei, 26, 252

Naghi, Mohamed, *The Egyptian Renaissance, or The Cavalcade of Isis*, 1919 (fig. 15), 27, 28

Napoleon I (French emperor), 19, 31, 34, 245n52

Nas, *I Am . . .* , 1999 (pl. 135), 26, 185, 255

Nasser, Gamal Abdel, 38, 58–60, 59, 246n25

Nasser, Lake (Egypt), 29, 52, 151

National Association for the Advancement of Colored People (NAACP), 23, 54. *See also The Crisis* magazine

National Geographic magazine cover, February 2008 (fig. 12), 24, 24

National Memorial African Bookstore, Harlem, 57–60, 57, 58

Nation of Islam, 29, 57, 182, 242

Nefertiti (Egyptian queen)

    L. Brown's recessed images of, 161

    as distinct individual, 215

    Erizku's mirrored or lighted images of, 26, 190, 195

    fashion inspired by, 28, 132

    in music productions or on record covers, 26, 169, 170

    O'Grady's pairings of family photos with, 26, 30, 48–49, 110–13

    painted images of, 25–26, 104

    Wilson's replicas of bust of, 24–25, 100–101

The Negro in Art Week exhibition (Chicago, 1927), 90, 251

The Negro World newspaper (pl. 24), 23, 38, 88, 255

Nengudi, Senga, *Flying*, 1982 (with other artists; pls. 145–49), 30, 196, 197, 253

Nerouy, Kantiba, "Tutankh-Amen and Ras Tafari" in *The Crisis*, December 1924 (pl. 33), 92, 255

Neues Museum, Berlin, 24–25, 214

New Negro movement (Harlem Renaissance), 19, 22–23, 40–41, 51, 241, 243

Newsom, Jennifer

    artist statement, 220–21

    See also Dream The Combine

New York City Metropolitan Transportation Authority (MTA)

    Adkins's installation for Harlem-125th St. Station (pl. 6), 23, 68–69, 249

    Conwill's bronze relief for 125th St. Station (pl. 156), 203, 250

    Hassinger's mosaic tile for Central Park North station (pl. 174), 29, 224, 253

    and relevance of Egyptian-themed art, 17

New York Times, 48, 52

Nile River

    artworks inspired by, 29, 30, 31, 114, 125, 175, 202, 228

    Aswan Dam's creation, 20–21, 51

    cosmetic products named after, 30, 91

    Hughes's reference to, in poem, 23, 46

    and lands of ancient Egypt, 17, 213

    and Nubians, 24, 36

    riverboat cruise, 138, 139

Nubia

    artworks inspired by, 105, 158, 169

    Ashby's study of Nubian religion, 20, 77

    as Black African civilization, 24, 35–36, 39

and lands of ancient Egypt, 17, 23, 35–36, 213
relocation of monuments, 20–21

O

obelisks, *17–19*, 18, 31, 55, *67*, 220, 244n11, 244n14
O'Connor, David, 39, 246n35
Offset, *Father of 4*, 2019 (pl. 139), *186*, 255
O'Grady, Lorraine
    Miscegenated Family Album, 1980/1994
      (pls. 50–53), 26, 30, 48–49, *112*, *113*, 255
    Nefertiti/Devonia Evangeline, 1980 (pls. 48,
      49), 30, 48, *110*, *111*, 255
"one-drop rule" (racial classification), 34, 36
opacity, Glissant's concept of, 40, 44, 51
"Opening of the Mouth" ceremony, 48
Opportunity: A Journal of Negro Life, 24, 241
Organization of Afro-American Unity, 55
orphism, 23
Osiris (god), 18, 240
Osiris (musical group), *Since Before Our Time*,
    1979 (pl. 122), *176*, 255
Owens, Clifford, 30, 249, 255

P

Palmer Raids, 42
Pan-African movement
    first Pan-African Conference (London,
      1900), 34, 40
    Garvey's championing of, 23, 38, 41
    Malcolm X's dedication to, 242
    and Michaux's bookstore in Harlem, 57–60
    objectives of, 20, 38, 40
Paris Exposition Universelle (1900), 34, 40, 41, 54
Parker, Franklin, *Flying*, 1982 (with other
    artists; pls. 145–49), 30, *196*, *197*, 253
Parker, Grant, 18
Parks, Gordon, *Untitled, Harlem, New York*,
    1963 (pl. 87), 57, *152*, 255
Parliament, *Trombipulation*, 1980 (pl. 124),
    176, 255
Patton, Kamau Amu
    Amun (The Unseen Legends), 2017 (pl. 151),
      199, 253
    live performance at The Met, 30, 255
    The Past and Other Dreams, 2020 (pl. 152),
      31, *199*, 255
Pendleton, Leila Amos, 36
Pennsylvania Academy of Fine Arts,
    Philadelphia, 16, 241, 243
performance art, 18, 30–31, 48, *110*, *111*,
    196–99, 240
The Pharaohs, *The Awakening*, 1971/1996
    (pl. 127), *177*, 255
pharaonic imagery and Black racial pride, 25–27
Philadelphia Centennial Exhibition (1876), 242
photography, Black, 40, 44, 52–61. *See also*
    specific photographers
phrenology, 49

Powell, Adam Clayton, Jr., 57
Powell, Bud, *198*
Price, Leontyne, *Aïda*, 1962 (pl. 107), 26,
    168, 255
Pruitt, Robert, *Negra Es Bella*, 2015 (pl. 59),
    119, 256
Pryor, Richard
    "Egypt 1909" skit, *The Richard Pryor Show*,
      1977 (pl. 8), *19*, 30, *70*, 252
    Ligon's reference to joke by, 29
Psalm 68:31 ("Princes shall come out of
    Egypt"), 23, 94, 241, 244n41
Ptah, Baaba Heru Ankh Ra Semahj Se
    (Baaba Heru)
    The Ankh of Love, ca. 1975 (pl. 100), 30,
      164, 256
    and Erykah Badu, 183
Ptolemaic Dynasty, 18, 21
Pyramid Club (social organization)
    art exhibition, 1947 (pl. 84), 30, *149*, 255
    pictorial albums, 1941 and 1947–48 (pls. 82,
      83), 30, *148*, 256
pyramids
    in Douglas's art, 23, 41
    at Giza, 28, 30, 57, 60, 139, 142, 214
    Hughes's reference to, in poem, 23, 46
    in performance art, 30, 31
    on record covers, *141*, *169*, *174–76*
    sculptures or installations in shape of, *31*, *31*,
      32, 216, 225–27, 229
    as symbol of innovation, 192

R

Ra (sun deity), 49, 139–40
race, conceptualizations of, 24–25, 34–39, 245n7,
    246n17
Ramesses II (Egyptian king), 21, 26, 51, 215
Ras G and The Afrikan Space Program, *Back on
    the Planet*, 2013 (pl. 137), *186*, 256
Rashwan, Hany, 34
Ra Un Nefer Amen. *See* Amen, Ra Un Nefer
Reisner, George, 36, 38–39
Reiss, Winold, 241
Rhodes-Pitts, Sharifa, 33, 233
The Richard Pryor Show, "Egypt 1909" skit,
    1977 (pl. 8), *19*, 30, *70*, 252
Rihanna (pl. 71), 28, *132*, 257
The Ritchie Family, *African Queens*, 1977
    (pl. 128), *178*, 256
Roche, *Nile Queen for Hair and Skin* (pl. 29),
    91, 256
Rocher, Henry, *Edmonia Lewis*, ca. 1870, 242
Rodin, Auguste, 41
Rome, American Academy in, 18, 21, 55, 240,
    244n16
Rome, ancient
    Egyptian obelisks in, *17–19*, 18, 55, *67*, 220,
      244n11, 244n14

Egyptian precedents of Roman civilization,
    17, 21, 191
Italian Renaissance as inspired by, 22
modern claims to heritage of, 27, 54
racial perceptions, 39

S

Saar, Betye
    and Conwill's art, 46
    Essence of Egypt, 1972 (fig. 37), 44–45, *45*
    mojo series, 44
    Window of Ancient Sirens, 1979 (pl. 46), 45,
      107, 256
Saïd, Mahmoud
    as father of modern Egyptian painting, 27
    L'invitation au voyage, 1932 (pl. 66), 28,
      126, 256
sandals of Tutankhamun (fig. 24), 35, *35*
Sanders, Pharoah, *Africa*, 1987 (pl. 126), *177*, 256
Saqqara, 150, 221
Saturday Evening Post, 55–57, *56*
scarabs, 28, 44, 133
Schaal, Kaneza, 30, 256
Schapiro, Steve, *James Baldwin with his
    Nephew and Namesake outside Lewis H.
    Michaux's National Memorial African
    Bookstore, Harlem*, 1963 (fig. 49), 58, *58*
Schomburg, Arturo A., 46
Schomburg Center for Research in Black
    Culture, New York Public Library, 23,
    46, 48
Scurlock, Addison N.
    *Collage of Photographs of the Alpha Phi
    Alpha "Sphinx Club" Fraternity*, 1923
    (pl. 91), 30, *155*, 256
    *The Pageant, "Star of Ethiopia," in
    Philadelphia*, 1916 (figs. 43, 44), *52*, *53*, 54
Scurlock, Robert S., *Loïs Mailou Jones*,
    1950, 241
Semahj, Baaba Heru. *See* Ptah, Baaba Heru
    Ankh Ra Semahj Se (Baaba Heru)
Serotta, Anna, 20
Sethos II (Egyptian king), 24
Seti I (Egyptian king), 43
Shabti of Seti I (fig. 35), 42, *43*
Shakur, Assata (pl. 60), 27, *120*, 252
Sheehi, Stephen, 52
Shehaby, Ahmed, *Mike and Kiki Tyson at Giza*,
    2019 (pl. 77), 29, *137*, 256
Shenoda, Matthew, "Theft at the Tomb II"
    (poem), 71
Simpson, Lorna, *Older Queen*, 2017 (pl. 56), 26,
    115, 256
Sixtus V (pope), 18, 220
slavery. *See* enslavement
Smith, Beuford, *Malcolm X in front of Mr. Lewis
    Michaux's Bookstore*, 1964 (fig. 48),
    57–58, *57*

Smith, Joshua, 49, *49*, 256
Smith, Ming
    Street Market, Cairo, Egypt, ca. 1973 (fig. 52), 60–61, *61*
    Womb, 1992 (pl. 79), 29, 144–45, 256
Smith, Shawn Michelle, 53
Snowden, Frank M., Jr., *Blacks in Antiquity*, 1970 (fig. 28), 38, *39*
social organizations, 30, 148, *149*, 154–57
Sorek, Susan, 18, 244n14
Space Is the Place film, 1974 (fig. 41, pl. 159), 30–31, 49–51, *49*, *206*, 256
spaceships or outer space, 19, 30–31, 49–51, *206–8*, 219
sphinxes
    DJ Slim with, *167*
    in Douglas's art, 23, 41
    as fraternity logos, 30, *155*
    Great Sphinx at Giza, 28, 31, 55, *135*, *137*, *209*, 245n52
    of Khartoum, *139*
    in modern sculpture, 32–33, *32*, *33*, *124*, *235*
The Star of Ethiopia pageant, 41–43, *42*, 51, *52*, *53*, 54
Steel Pulse, *Babylon the Bandit*, 1985 (pl. 133), *179*, 256
stelae (commemorative markers), 31–32, *218*
Stewart, Luke, 30, 256
Story, William Wetmore, *Cleopatra*, 1858, carved 1869 (fig. 8), 21, *22*
Strachan, Tavares, *ENOCH (display unit)*, 2015–17 (fig. 19, pl. 168), 31, *31*, *217*, 256
Studio Museum, Harlem, 18
Sudan
    D. M. Ali's Sudanese heritage, 20, 38
    archaeological excavations, 19, 41, 42
    and Conwill's sources of inspiration, 46
    Khartoum, *139*, *213*, *214*
    and lands of ancient Egypt, 17, 23, 35–36
    racial identity, 36, 39, 245n7
Sun Ra
    Arkestra, 31, 142
    artists inspired by, 31, 51, 61
    Horizon, 1972/2020 (pl. 119), *175*, 256
    mystical experience in pyramid, 139–40
    performing in front of *Delta Spirit*, 1985 (fig. 18), 30, *31*
    Space Is the Place, 1974 (fig. 41, pl. 159), 30–31, 49–51, *49*, *206*, 256

T

Taharqa (Nubian king), *36*, *158*
Talbot, William Henry Fox, 52
Tanner, Benjamin, 16
Tanner, Henry Ossawa
    biography, 243, *243*
    in Egypt, 16, 243, 244n5

Flight into Egypt, 1923 (pl. 2), 16–17, *65*, 243, 244n5, 256
Interior of a Mosque, Cairo, 1897 (pl. 1), 16, *64*, 243, 256
and Paris art scene, 16, 41, 241, 243
Untitled (Flight into Egypt), ca. 1923 (fig. 1), 16, *16*
Taylor, Cecil. *See* Cecil Taylor Jazz Unit
Taylor, Elizabeth, 24, *25*
Taylor, Henry, *Michelle*, 2023 (pl. 18), *79*, 256
Temple, Christel N., 54
Thompson, Mildred
    interview with Jones, 242
    Stele, ca. 1963 (pl. 169), 31–32, *218*, 257
Thunder, *7th Wonder*, 1980 (pl. 123), *176*, 257
Tiye (Egyptian queen), 26, *115*
Treasures of Tutankhamun exhibition (U.S. tour, 1976–79), 44
Trimble, Jennifer, 27
Turner, Tina, 140
Tuskegee syphilis experiment, 51
Tutankhamun (Egyptian king)
    fashion inspired by, 30, *162*
    funerary mask, 28, 35, 45, 245n10
    magazine article on, *92*
    in music productions or on record covers, 26, *172*
    painted depictions of, 26
    sandals, 35, *35*
    tomb's discovery and excavation, 19, 20, 35, 44, 49, 54, 243
    Treasures of Tutankhamun exhibition (U.S. tour, 1976–79), 44
Tyson, Mike (pl. 77), 29, 137, 256

U

Universal Negro Improvement Association (UNIA), 23, 38
Upper Part of the Seated Statue of a Queen, ca. 1580–1550 BCE (fig. 14), 26, *27*

V

Valerio, Angela, *30*, *31*
Valley of the Kings, 35, 139, 214
Van Der Zee, James, *Identical Twins*, 1924 (fig. 45), 54, *54*
Vatican obelisk, Rome, 18, *19*, 55
Vechten, Carl Van, *Aaron Douglas*, 1933, 241
video
    music videos, 26, *187*, *189*
    television episodes, 19, 26, *70*, 187
    video art, 18, 28, 29, *67*, *128*, *200–201*
    See also film depictions of ancient Egypt
Vogue Arabia magazine cover, November 2017 (pl. 71), 28, *132*, 257

W

Walker, Kara
    A Subtlety, or the Marvelous Sugar Baby, 2014 (fig. 21), 32–33, *32*
    Untitled (Study for A Subtlety, or the Marvelous Sugar Baby), 2013–14 (pl. 179), 230–31, 257
Wallace, Maurice O., 53
Waring, Laura Wheeler
    Africa in America, cover of *The Crisis*, June 1924 (pl. 31), *91*, 243, 257
    biography, 243, *243*
    Egypt and Spring, cover of *The Crisis*, April 1923 (pl. 30), *91*, 243, 257
    The Strength of Africa, cover of *The Crisis*, September 1924 (pl. 32), 37, 38, *91*, 243, 257
Welsing, Frances Cress, *The Isis Papers*, 2004 (pl. 104), *165*, 257
White, Verdine, 142
Whitney Biennial, 25, 103
Williams, John A., 60
Williams, William T., *Nu Nile*, 1973 (pl. 154), 30, *202*, 257
Willis, Deborah, 53
Wilson, Fred
    at American Academy in Rome, 244n16
    artist statement, 102–3
    Black Egypt, 2019 (pl. 99), *163*, 257
    Grey Area (Brown version), 1993 (pl. 42), 24–25, *100–101*, 103, 257
World War I, 16, 41, 42, 54

X

X, Malcolm. *See* Malcolm X
X Clan, *Xodus (The New Testament)*, 1992 (pl. 136), *186*, 257

Z

Zawadi, Kiambu, Bedford Bowling Center murals, 1980–94 (with other artists; pl. 62), 26, *122*, 254

Photography Credits

Private collection of Emad Abou Ghazi: pl. 64, p. 242; © Terry Adkins, Metro-North Harlem–125 St. Commissioned by MTA Arts & Design. Photo: Trent Reeves: pl. 6; © 2024 The Estate of Terry Adkins / Artists Rights Society (ARS), New York. Courtesy Paula Cooper Gallery, New York and Salon 94, New York: pl. 4; © 2024 The Estate of Terry Adkins / Artists Rights Society (ARS), New York. Courtesy Paula Cooper Gallery, New York: pl. 5; AP Photo: pl. 76; Courtesy of the Louis Armstrong House Museum. The Louis Armstrong Educational Foundation, www.louisarmstrongfoundation.org: pl. 73; Eve Arnold / Magnum Photos: pl. 88; © Archives Center, National Museum of American History. National Portrait Gallery, Smithsonian Institution: p. 241; Art & Artifacts Division, Schomburg Center for Research in Black Culture, New York Public Library: pls. 37, 40; Photo courtesy of Artmakers Inc.: pl. 62; © Estate of Jean-Michel Basquiat. Licensed by Artestar, New York. Collection Museum Boijmans Van Beuningen, Rotterdam, photo by Studio Tromp: pl. 165; Beinecke Rare Book and Manuscript Library: pls. 82, 83; Jean Blackwell Hutson Research and Reference Division, Schomburg Center for Research in Black Culture, The New York Public Library: fig. 43; Brooklyn Museum: pl. 45; Brooklyn Museum Libraries & Archives: pl. 32; René Burri / Magnum Photos: pl. 20; © Barbara Chase-Riboud. Courtesy of the artist and Hauser & Wirth: fig. 7; © Barbara Chase-Riboud. Courtesy of the artist and Hauser & Wirth, photo by Alise O'Brien: pl. 21; Allen Chen/SLH Studio. Courtesy of Lauren Halsey and Gagosian: pl. 183; © The Estate of Ed Clark. Courtesy the Estate and Hauser & Wirth: fig. 16; © The Estate of Ed Clark. Courtesy the Estate and Hauser & Wirth, photo by Eileen Travell: pl. 157; © 2024 The Robert H. Colescott Separate Property Trust / Artists Rights Society (ARS), New York. Private collection, photo by Adam Reich: pl. 44; © Houston Conwill, NYCT 125 St. Commissioned by MTA Arts & Design, photo by Trent Reeves: pl. 156; Courtesy of Creative Time, photo by Lawrence Lesman: fig. 18; Courtesy of artist: pls. 9, 153; Image courtesy of artist and Jenkins Johnson Gallery, San Francisco and New York: pl. 79; Image courtesy of artist and Tina Kim Gallery, photo by Hyunjung Rhee: pl. 67; Copyright of artist, courtesy David Kordansky Gallery: pl. 176; Courtesy of artist and Greene Naftali, New York: pl. 34; Courtesy of artist and Gypsum Gallery: pl. 68; Courtesy of artist and Morán Morán, photo by WhiteBalanceMX: pl. 158; Courtesy of artist and Perrotin Gallery: fig. 19; Courtesy of artist and Vielmetter Los Angeles: pl. 63; Courtesy of artist and Wilding Cran Gallery: pl. 55; Renee Cox: pl. 163; © CULTNAT, Dist. RMN-GP / Art Resource, NY: fig. 24; Courtesy of the Danforth Art Museum at Framingham State University, photo by Will Howcroft: fig. 34; © Damien Davis, 2024: pl. 95; © Estate of Noah Davis. Courtesy Estate of Noah Davis and David Zwirner: pl. 17; Courtesy the Estate of Jeff Donaldson and Kravets Wehby Gallery: pl. 164; © 2024 Emory Douglas / Artists Rights Society (ARS), New York: pl. 58; © 2024 Heirs of Aaron Douglas / Licensed by VAGA at Artists Rights Society (ARS), NY. Image © The Metropolitan Museum of Art: pl. 36; © 2024 Heirs of Aaron Douglas / Licensed by VAGA at Artists Rights Society (ARS), NY. Courtesy of the Rhode Island School of Design Museum, Providence, RI: pl. 38; © 2024 Heirs of Aaron Douglas / Licensed by VAGA at Artists Rights Society (ARS), NY. Image courtesy Walter O. Evans Foundation for Art and Literature: pl. 35; Dream The Combine: pl. 170; Photo courtesy of Oasa DuVerney: pl. 60; © Awol Erizku. Courtesy of the artist and Sean Kelly, New York/Los Angeles, photo by Joshua White: pl. 143; Charles Evans Inniss Memorial Library Archives & Special Collections, Medgar Evers College, City University of New York: pl. 24; Image courtesy Walter O. Evans Foundation for Art and Literature: fig. 35; © Fred Eversley. Courtesy the artist and David Kordansky Gallery, photo by Tom Powel Imaging: pl. 167; © Derek Fordjour, courtesy David Kordansky Gallery, photo by Mark Blower, Daneil Greer: pl. 92; © Ellen Gallagher. Courtesy the Estate and Hauser & Wirth, photo by Mike Bruce Digital image © Whitney Museum of American Art / Licensed by Scala / Art Resource, NY: pl. 162; Getty Images, photo by Slim Aarons: pl. 106; Courtesy of Sam Gilliam Foundation, David Kordansky Gallery, and Pace Gallery © 2024 Estate of Sam Gilliam / Artists Rights Society (ARS), New York. Digital Image © The Museum of Modern Art/Licensed by SCALA / Art Resource, NY: pl. 177; Courtesy of Sam Gilliam Foundation, David Kordansky Gallery, and Pace Gallery © Sam Gilliam / Artists Rights Society (ARS), New York, photo by Melissa Goodwin: pl. 178; © Griffith Institute, University of Oxford: figs. 11, 25; Courtesy of Lauren Halsey, archive images: p. 235; © Lauren Halsey. Image © The Metropolitan Museum of Art. Allen Chen / SLH Studio. Courtesy of David Kordansky Gallery: pl. 182; © 2024 David Hammons / Artists Rights Society (ARS), New York. From Kobena Mercer, Pop Art and Vernacular Culturest, Cambridge, 2007. Image © The Metropolitan Museum of Art, photo by Teri Aderman: fig. 20; © 2024 David Hammons / Artists Rights Society (ARS), New York, photo by Eileen Travell: pls. 171–73; © Maren Hassinger, NYCT Central Park North (110 St). Commissioned by MTA Arts & Design, photo by Rob Wilson: pl. 174; Harvard University Press: fig. 28; Chester Higgins Jr./The New York Times: fig. 40; © Chester Higgins, All rights reserved. Courtesy Bruce Silverstein Gallery, New York: pls. 85, 86; © Lonnie Holley. Image © The Metropolitan Museum of Art: pl. 54; Photo by Gregston Hurdle: pl. 100; © Gregston Hurdle: pl. 151; Courtesy of Susan Inglett Gallery, NYC: pls. 145–49, 175; Iowa State University Library: pl. 3; Bernard Jaffe Papers, Robert S. Cox Special Collections and University Archives Research Center, University of Massachusetts Amherst Libraries: fig. 51; Knowles Family Archives, 1985: pp. 138, 141; Solange Knowles, 2018: pl. 78; Ashra and Merira Kwesi, Kemet Nu Tours: pl. 80; © 2024 The Jacob and Gwendolyn Lawrence Foundation, Seattle / Artists Rights Society (ARS), New York. Digital Image © The Museum of Modern Art/Licensed by SCALA / Art Resource, NY: fig. 9; Courtesy of Library of Congress: figs. 23, 30, 46; © Simone Leigh. Courtesy Matthew Marks Gallery, photo by Timothy Schenck: pl. 181; © 1977 Long Beach Museum of Art. From Studio Z: Individual Collective (December 11, 1977–January 15, 1978), Long Beach, 1977, Image © The Metropolitan Museum of Art, photo by Teri Aderman: fig. 20; Malcolm X photos © SEPS licensed by Curtis Licensing Indianapolis, Indiana: fig. 47; © Julie Mehretu. Courtesy of the artist and Marian Goodman Gallery, photo by Tom Powel Imaging: pl. 166; © 2024 The Estate of Ana Mendieta Collection, LLC / Licensed by Artists Rights Society (ARS), New York. Courtesy Galerie Lelong & Co. Digital Image © The Museum of Modern Art/Licensed by SCALA / Art Resource, NY: fig. 17; Image © The Metropolitan Museum of Art: figs. 2–4, 8, 14, 22, 35, pls. 7, 105; Image © The Metropolitan Museum of Art, photo by Teri Aderman: fig. 12; Image © The Metropolitan Museum of Art, photo by Eugenia Burnett Tinsley: pl. 72; Image © The Metropolitan Museum of Art, photo by Anna-Marie Kellen: pls. 89–90; Image © The Metropolitan Museum of Art, photo by Mark Morosse: pls. 93–94; Image © The Metropolitan Museum of Art, photo by Juan Trujillo: fig. 1, pls. 2, 13–16, 70–71, 101–04, 107–39, 152; Image Courtesy of the Milwaukee Art Museum, photo by John R. Glembin: pl. 23; Ronald Moody Trust. National Gallery of Jamaica: pl. 41; Private collection of Sophie Mörner: pl. 180; John W. Mosley Photograph Collection, Charles L. Blockson Afro-American Collection, Temple University Libraries, Philadelphia, PA: pl. 84; © Museum Associates/ LACMA. Image © The Metropolitan Museum of Art, photo by Katherine Dahab: pl. 168; Photograph © 2024 Museum of Fine Arts, Boston: pls. 1, 10, 61, 74, 96, 144; Digital Image © The Museum of Modern Art/Licensed by SCALA / Art Resource, NY: pl. 155; National Portrait Gallery, Smithsonian Institution: pp. 242-43; New York Public Library, Schomburg Center for Research in Black Culture, Jean Blackwell Hutson Research and Reference Division: figs. 33, 44; Courtesy of New York Public Library: pl. 12; Courtesy of New York Public Library, photo by Gregston Hurdle: pl. 22; Photo by Luca Nostri: p. 240; Michael Ochs Archives / Stringer: p. 240; © 2024 Lorraine O'Grady / Artists Rights Society (ARS), New York: pls. 48–49; © 2024 Lorraine O'Grady / Artists Rights Society (ARS), New York. Photograph © 2024 Museum of Fine Arts, Boston: pls. 50–53; Courtesy of and copyright Gordon Parks Foundation. Photograph © 2024 Museum of Fine Arts, Boston: pl. 87; Courtesy of Parkwood Entertainment: pl. 142; PictureLux / The Hollywood Archive / Alamy Stock Photo: fig. 13; Courtesy of Nadia Radwan: fig. 15; Reproduced with permission of The Licensor through PLSclear: fig. 29; Courtesy of Rubell Museum, Miami and Washington, DC: pl. 81; © Betye Saar: pl. 46; © Betye Saar. Courtesy of the artist and Roberts Projects, Los Angeles CA, photo by Robert Wedemeyer: fig. 37; Andrew Saint-George / Magnum Photos: fig. 50; Scala / Art Resource, NY: fig. 6; Photographs and Prints Division, Schomburg Center for Research in Black Culture, New York Public Library: pp. 241, 243; © Lorna Simpson. Courtesy the artist and Hauser & Wirth, photo by James Wang: pl. 56; © Beuford Smith. Digital image © Whitney Museum of American Art / Licensed by Scala / Art Resource, NY: fig. 48; Smithsonian American Art Museum: fig. 5; Collection of the Smithsonian National Museum of African American History and Culture: fig. 10, pls. 25-27, 91; © Photo courtesy of Sotheby's, 2024: pl. 65; Steve Schapiro / Contributor: fig. 49; Image courtesy of Special Collections and University Archives Research Center, University of Massachusetts Amherst Libraries: fig. 31; Courtesy of Swann Auction Galleries: fig. 36; © Henry Taylor. Courtesy the artist and Hauser & Wirth, photo by Nicolas Brasseur: pl. 18; Team-Cairo.com, photo by Ahmed Shehaby: pl. 77; Photo © Galerie Elisabeth & Klaus Thoman / kunstdokumentation.com: pl. 69; © The Mildred Thompson Estate. Courtesy Galerie Lelong & Co., New York, photo by Chris Burke: pl. 169; Used with Permission of X Legacy, LLC: pl. 75; © James Van Der Zee Archive, The Metropolitan Museum of Art: fig. 45; © Van Vechten Trust, Carl Van Vechten Papers Relating to African American Arts and Letters. James Weldon Johnson Collection in the Yale Collection of American Literature, Beinecke Rare Book and Manuscript Library: p. 241; Virginia Museum of Fine Arts, Richmond: pls. 47, 57; Artwork © Kara Walker, courtesy of Sikkema Jenkins & Co. and Sprüth Magers: pl. 179; Artwork © Kara Walker, courtesy of Sikkema Jenkins & Co. and Sprüth Magers, photo by Jason Wyche: fig. 21; Image courtesy of W. E. B. Du Bois Papers, Robert S. Cox Special Collections and University Archives Research Center, University of Massachusetts Amherst Libraries: fig. 31; © Laura Wheeler Waring. Image courtesy Walter O. Evans Foundation for Art and Literature: fig. 26, pls. 30–32; © William T. Williams, courtesy of Michael Rosenfeld Gallery LLC, New York, NY: pl. 154; © Fred Wilson, courtesy Pace Gallery. Brooklyn Museum: pl. 42; © Fred Wilson, courtesy Pace Gallery. Studio Museum in Harlem, Harlem Postcards Collection: pl. 99; © Worcester Art Museum, Massachusetts, USA / Bridgeman Images: pl. 59

This catalogue is published in conjunction with *Flight into Egypt: Black Artists and Ancient Egypt, 1876–Now*, on view at The Metropolitan Museum of Art, New York, from November 17, 2024, through February 17, 2025.

The exhibition is made possible by the Gail and Parker Gilbert Fund, the Jane and Robert Carroll Fund, the Ford Foundation, and the Hobson/Lucas Family Foundation.

Ford Foundation

Additional support is provided by The Hayden Family Foundation, Allison and Larry Berg, The Holly Peterson Foundation, The Andy Warhol Foundation for the Visual Arts, and the National Endowment for the Arts.

This publication is made possible by Mellon Foundation and Denise Littlefield Sobel.

Additional support is provided by The Witten Family Foundation, Lonti Ebers, the Jeffrey and Leslie Fischer Family Foundation, and Kent Kelley.

Published by The Metropolitan Museum of Art, New York
Mark Polizzotti, Publisher and Editor in Chief
Peter Antony, Associate Publisher for Production
Michael Sittenfeld, Associate Publisher for Editorial

Edited by Eleanor Hughes and Kayla Elam
Production by Christina Grillo
Designed by Polymode: Edgar Casarin, Brian Johnson, and Silas Munro
Additional typesetting by Tina Henderson, Miko McGinty Inc.
Bibliographic editing by Eleanor Hughes
Image acquisitions and permissions by Josephine Rodriguez

Photographs of works in The Met collection are by the Imaging Department, The Metropolitan Museum of Art, unless otherwise noted.

Additional photography credits appear on page 267.

Typeset in Gza and Freight
Printed on 150 gsm Garda Ultra Matte
Separations by Verona Libri, Verona, Italy
Printed and bound by Verona Libri, Verona, Italy

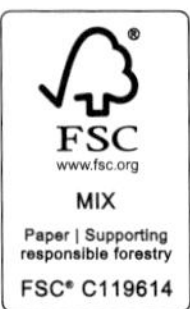

Jacket illustrations: front, Awol Erizku, *Nefertiti (Black Power)*, 2018 (plate 144, detail); back, Loïs Mailou Jones, *The Ascent of Ethiopia*, 1932 (plate 23, detail)
Cover illustration: Fred Wilson, *Grey Area (Brown version)*, 1993 (plate 42, detail); artist's statement: "It is my belief that, as the science of DNA has now revealed, the ancient Egyptians were unique: their DNA was like that of no other group of humans, then or now." Additional illustrations: p. 2: Henry Ossawa Tanner, *Flight into Egypt*, 1923 (plate 2, detail); p. 6: Eve Arnold, *Black Muslim children at the Metropolitan Museum in New York. They are taught black history*, 1961 (plate 88, detail)

The Metropolitan Museum of Art
1000 Fifth Avenue
New York, New York 10028
metmuseum.org

Distributed by
Yale University Press, New Haven and London
yalebooks.com/art
yalebooks.co.uk

Cataloguing-in-Publication Data is available from the Library of Congress.
ISBN 978-1-58839-785-0